D1871894

CENSUS OF INDIA 1931

Census of India 1871-1951, 9 Sets In 384 Bindings (9788121258876) Rs. 700000

Census of India 1931, 28 Vols. In 52 Bindings (9788121271233) Rs. 102000

1. India - Report (9788121276153) Rs. 2820 (Vol. I, Pt. 1)
2. India - Imperial Tables (9788121276139) Rs. 3210 (Vol. I, Pt. 2)
3. India - Ethnographical and Administration Report (9788121276115) Rs. 2900 (Vol. I, Pt. 3 & 5)
4. The Andaman And Nicobar Islands - Report, Tables (9788121276078) Rs. 720 (Vol. II, Pt. 1, Pt. 2)
5. Assam - Report (9788121276054) Rs. 1340 (Vol. III, Pt. 1)
6. Assam - Tables and Administrative Report (9788121276030) Rs. 1830 (Vol. III, Pt. 2 & 3)
7. Baluchistan - Report, Imeprial and Provincial Tables and Administrative Report (9788121276016) Rs. 2320 (Vol. IV, Pt. 1 & 2 & 3)
8. Bengal & Sikkim - Report (9788121275972) Rs. 2860 (Vol. V, Pt. 1)
9. Bengal & Sikkim - Tables (9788121275958) Rs. 1660 (Vol. V, Pt. 2)
10. Calcutta (9788121275910) Rs. 960 (Vol. VI, Pt. 1 & 2)
11. Bengal, Sikkim And Calcutta - Administrative Report (9788121275934) Rs. 580 (Vol. V & VI, Pt. 3)
12. Bihar And Orissa - Report (9788121275897) Rs. 1780 (Vol. VII, Pt. 1)
13. Bihar And Orissa - Tables and Administrative Report (9788121275873) Rs. 1190 (Vol. VII, Pt. 2 & 3)
14. Bombay Presidency - General Report (9788121275835) Rs. 3620 (Vol. VIII, Pt. 1)
15. Bombay - Statistical tables (9788121275811) Rs. 3060 (Vol. VIII, Pt. 2)
16. Bombay Presidency Aden - report and tables and Administrative report (9788121275798) Rs. 520 (Vol. VIII, Pt. 3 & 4)
17. Cities of the Bombay Presidency Report & Statistical tables (9788121275750) Rs. 2020 (Vol. IX, Pt. 1 & 2)
18. The Western India States Agency, In Two Parts - The Report & The Statistical Tables (9788121275736) Rs. 2560 (Vol. X, Pt. 1 & 2)
19. Burma - Report (9788121275712) Rs. 1860 (Vol. XI, Pt. 1)
20. Burma - Tables and Administrative Report (9788121275699) Rs. 1690 (Vol. XI, Pt. 2 & 3)
21. Central Provinces & Berar - Report (9788121275651) Rs. 2340 (Vol. XII, Pt. 1)
22. Central Provinces & Berar - Tables and Administrative Report (9788121275637) Rs. 3120 (Vol. XII, Pt. 2 & 3)
23. Coorg - Report And Tables and Madras - Report (9788121275613) Rs. 2680 (Vol. XIV, Pt. 1)
24. Madras - Imperial And Provincial Tables and The Administration Report (9788121275576) Rs. 1950 (Vol. XIV, Pt. 2 & 4)
25. North - West Frontier Province - Report & Tables (9788121275538) Rs. 2300 (Vol. XV, Pt. 1 & 2)
26. Delhi - Report & Tables (9788121275514) Rs. 1180 (Vol. XVI, Pt. 1 & 2)
27. Punjab - Report (9788121275491) Rs. 2070 (Vol. XVII, Pt. 1)
28. Punjab - Tables (9788121275477) Rs. 1690 (Vol. XVII, Pt. 2)
29. United Provinces of Agra And Oudh - Report (9788121275453) Rs. 3380 (Vol. XVIII, Pt. 1)
30. United Provinces of Agra And Oudh - Imperial And Provincial Tables and Administrative (9788121275439) Rs. 3600 (Vol. XVIII, Pt. 2 & 3)
31. Baroda - Report (9788121275415) Rs. 2800 (Vol. XIX, Pt. 1)
32. Baroda - Tables (9788121275392) Rs. 730 (Vol. XIX, Pt. 2)
33. Baroda - Administrative (9788121275378) Rs. 780 (Vol. XIX, Pt. 3)
34. Central India Agency - Report (9788121275354) Rs. 1690 (Vol. XX, Pt. 1)
35. Central India Agency - Tables and Administrative Volume (9788121275330) Rs. 2260 (Vol. XX, Pt. 2 & 3)
36. Cochin - Report & Tables (9788121275293) Rs. 2460 (Vol. XXI, Pt. 1 & 2 - A & B.)
37. Gwalior - Report (9788121275279) Rs. 1470 (Vol. XXII, Pt. 1)
38. Gwalior - Tables (9788121275255) Rs. 980 (Vol. XXII, Pt. 2)
39. H. E. H. The Nizam's Dominions (Hyderabad State) - Report (9788121275231) Rs. 1540 (Vol. XXIII, Pt. 1)
40. H. E. H. The Nizam's Dominions (Hyderabad State) - Tables (9788121275217) Rs. 1510 (Vol. XXIII, Pt. 2)
41. Jammu & Kashmir State - Report (9788121275194) Rs. 2060 (Vol. XXIV, Pt. 1)
42. Jammu & Kashmir State - Imperial & State Tables (9788121275170) Rs. 1940 (Vol. XXIV, Pt. 2 & 3)
43. Mysore - Report (9788121275156) Rs. 1950 (Vol. XXV, Pt. 1)
44. Mysore - Tables (9788121275132) Rs. 1380 (Vol. XXV, Pt. 2)
45. Ajmer-Merwara - Report And Tables (9788121275118) Rs. 780 (Vol. XXVI)
46. Rajputana Agency And Ajmer-Merwara - Report and Tables and Administrative (9788121275095) Rs. 2380 (Vol. XXVII, Pt. 1 & 2)
47. Travancore - Report (9788121276092) Rs. 2960 (Vol. XXVIII, Pt. 1)
48. Travancore - Tables & Administrative (9788121275996) Rs. 1360 (Vol. XXVIII, Pt. 2 & 4)
49. Jaipur State- Report (9788121275859) Rs. 1280 (Pt. 1)
50. Jaipur State- Tables (9788121275774) Rs. 2030 (Pt. 2)
51. Mayurbhanj state- Report (9788121275675) Rs. 3180 (Pt. 1)
52. Mayurbhanj state- Tables (9788121275552) Rs. 3070 (Pt. 2)

Owing to the antiquity and rarity of this book, certain pages are regrettably absent, and readability is compromised due to the blurring of the original text. If you possess any insights regarding the availability of these missing sections, kindly inform us. Your assistance is crucial in ensuring the completion of this significant work for the benefit of future generations.

CENSUS OF INDIA, 1931

BOOK - 36: VOLUME - XXI

COCHIN

PART I - REPORT
PART II - A & B. - TABLES

T. K. SANKARA MENON

GYAN

Published by

Gyan Publishing House
5, Ansari Road
Daryaganj, New Delhi-110002
Phone: 011-47034999, 9811692060
E-mail: books@gyanbooks.com

Distribution Network
gyanbooks.com
India, USA, Canada, UK, Australia

© Publisher
All rights reserved. No part of this work may be reproduced, stored, adapted, or transmitted in any form or by any means, electronic, mechanical, photocopying, micro-filming, recording or othrwise, or translated in any language, without the prior written permission of the copyright owner and the publisher.

ISBN: 978-81-212-7123-3 (Set) 28 Vols. In 52 Bindings

ISBN: 978-81-212-7529-3 (PB) Vol. XXI, Pt. I, II - A & B

First Published, 1933

2nd Impression 2024

Printed at: Gyan Press, Delhi.

The book is sold subject to the condition that it shall not, by way of trade or otherwise, be lent, resold, hired out, or otherwise circulated without the prior publisher's written consent.

CENSUS OF INDIA 1931

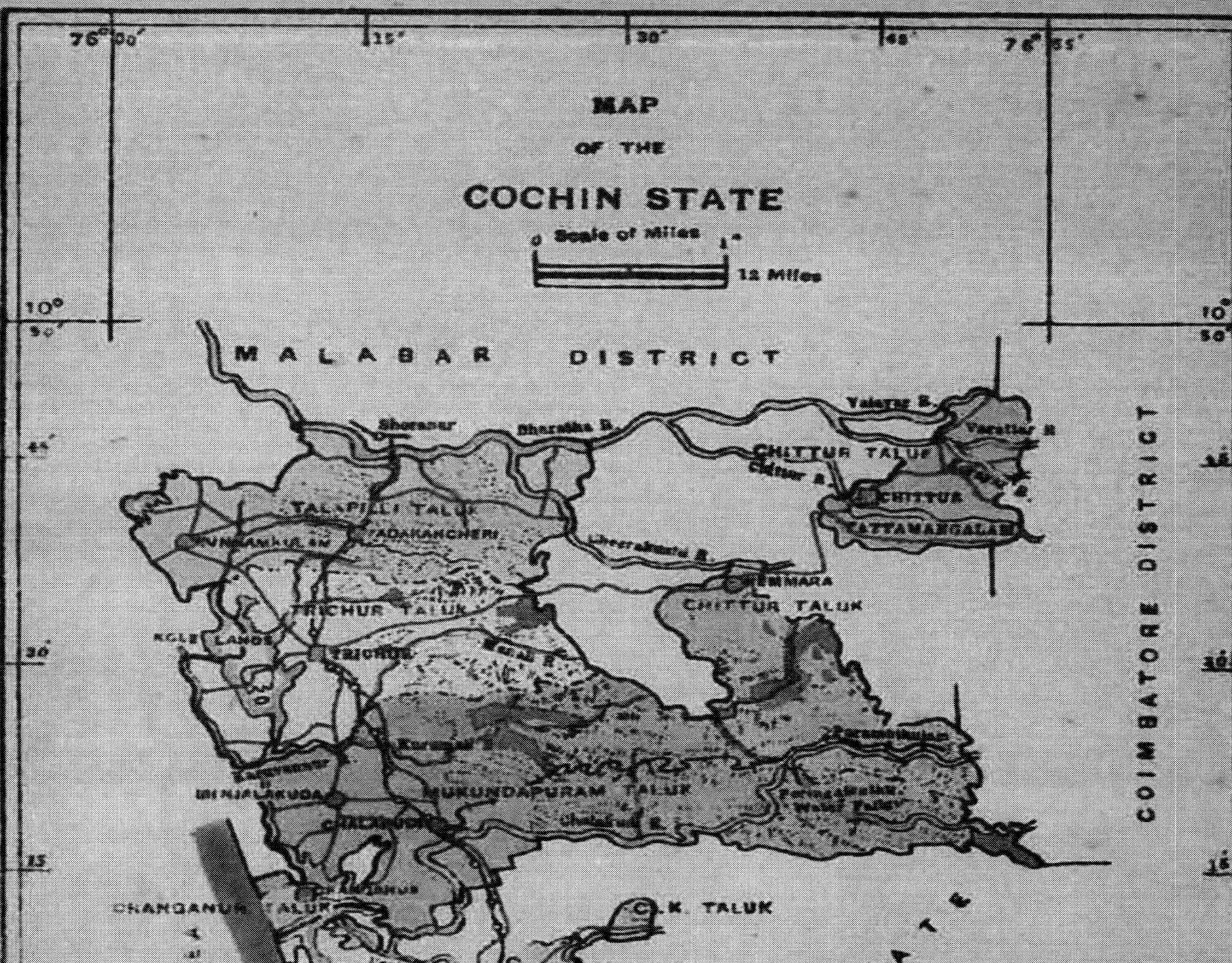

Register No. 126
Copies 850

Litho print - Survey & Land Records Office, Trichur.
1107

Census of India, 1931

VOLUME XXI

COCHIN

31131

PART I.—REPORT

PART II.—A & B.—TABLES

By

T. K. SANKARA MENON, M. A.,

Superintendent of Census Operations,

Cochin State.

1933

PRINTED BY THE SUPERINTENDENT, COCHIN GOVT. PRESS

ERNAKULAM

TABLE OF CONTENTS.

VOLUME XXI.—PART I.

THE REPORT.

LIST OF MAPS AND DIAGRAMS.

Maps.

Diagrams.

PART II—A.

IMPERIAL TABLES.

PART II—B.

STATE TABLES.

REPORT

ON THE

CENSUS OF COCHIN.

1931.

INTRODUCTION.

Previous censuses

The first attempt to number the people of Cochin appears to have been made in 1820, when a rough estimate of the population was prepared through the agency of the ordinary village staff. Similar attempts were made in 1836, 1849 and 1858, but the estimates being rough, the results of these attempts were but of little value from an administrative or scientific point of view.

A regular census of the modern type was taken in Cochin for the first time in 1875, three years after the general Indian census of 1871. From 1881 onwards the census of the State has been taken synchronously with the rest of India, the procedure laid down by the Census Commissioner for India for the decennial Indian census being followed here also; and the Census Reports of Cochin have, since 1901, regularly formed one of the volumes of the Census of India series, issued under the general editorship of the all-India Commissioner. The Report of 1931 forms Volume XXI of the series.

Census of 1931

2. The census of 1931, the results of which are embodied in this Report, was taken on the morning of the 27th February, 1931. A full account of the procedure adopted in connection with the taking of the census and the compilation of its results is given separately in the Administrative Volume which, being intended chiefly, if not solely, for the use of future Census Superintendents, is not likely to come within the ken of the general reader. It is therefore usual to give in this introduction a brief account of the more important stages of the census operations, under the fond assumption that the following pages will find a general reader and that he may want "to know how the thing is done, if only to rid his mind of a lingering doubt as to whether the Census Superintendent is not indebted to his imagination for many of the facts which he sets forth".

Census divisions and agency

3. As in 1921, the State was, for census purposes, divided into ten *charges*, each of the six taluks and the four municipal towns being treated as a separate charge. The Tahsildars of the taluks and the Chairmen of the municipalities were appointed Superintendents of the several charges. The ten charges in their turn were divided into 599 *circles*, which were sub-divided into 5,813 *blocks*. The average number of blocks in a circle was 10, and the average number of houses in a block 42. A Supervisor was appointed

Charge Superintendents	..	10
Assistant Charge Superintendents	..	5
Supervisors	..	602
Enumerators	..	5,823
Special Enumerators (for floating population etc.)	..	482
Total	..	6,922

for each circle and an Enumerator for each block. All the Supervisors and a majority of the Enumerators were English-educated persons. They were recruited chiefly from the ranks of Government servants and teachers of aided schools, but considerable numbers of private gentlemen also had to be enrolled for the work. No remuneration was given to census officers, but the non-official Supervisors and Enumerators were paid their actual travelling expenses. The marginal statement gives the details of the agency employed.

House-numbering

4. The first step towards the taking of the census was the numbering of houses and the preparation of House Lists. This work was carried out by Sanitary Inspectors and Maistries in municipal towns and by village officers elsewhere, and it was completed by the end of May, 1930. When all the houses had been numbered, statements showing the number of houses in each village and the number of Supervisors and Enumerators required for each charge were prepared. The division of the charges into circles and blocks was then effected, and Supervisors and Enumerators were appointed for all circles and blocks.

Preliminary record

5. The preparation of the preliminary record followed; and the prescribed particulars regarding all persons ordinarily resident in each house were entered in the respective columns of the enumeration schedule. For this the census officers had to be trained properly. Classes were accordingly held in different centres in each taluk for the instruction of Supervisors and Enumerators, and no pains were spared to give these officers a thorough and accurate knowledge of their duties. Thus wrong or misleading returns in the schedules were reduced to a minimum. The preliminary enumeration commenced on the 5th January, 1931, in rural areas, and on the 15th January in towns, and was completed by the end of the month. The entries were first made in rough schedule books and they were scrutinized by the Supervisors, and corrected where necessary, before they were copied in the standard schedule books. These were then carefully compared with the originals and all mistakes rectified.

Actual census

6. The final enumeration (the actual census) was carried out on the 27th February between day-break and noon. Each Enumerator visited all the houses of his block in turn and brought the record up-to-date by striking out the entries relating to persons who were no longer present and entering the necessary particulars for new arrivals. Special arrangements were made for the enumeration of travellers by rail, road and canal, the sea-going population and the houseless poor. There were as many as 8 festivals connected with temples on the final census day, and special Enumerators were appointed to census the persons assembled at these festivals. The Charge Superintendents and their assistants supervised the work in person and no difficulty was experienced in this connection.

The census of the Forest tracts, which could not be taken synchronously because of the wandering habits of the hill tribes and of the vast extent of the area to be traversed by the census officers, was conducted leisurely between the 15th and 24th of February.

Attitude of people

7. The attitude of the public was, as usual, friendly and there was no difficulty in securing the information required for filling up the columns of the schedules. The difficulty experienced in enlisting unpaid non-official workers for the census is explained in detail in the Administrative Volume.

Provisional totals

8. As soon as the final enumeration was over, the Supervisor of each circle met his Enumerators at a place previously agreed upon, and the abstract for each block, showing the number of houses and of persons, male and female,

in it, was prepared with the utmost despatch and care. The abstract for the whole circle was then compiled from the block abstracts with the same degree of care, and despatched along with the schedule books to the Charge Superintendent by the quickest possible route. The circle abstracts were carefully checked under the personal supervision of the Charge Superintendent and the summary for the whole charge was prepared and forwarded to the Central (Census) Office with the least possible delay. The first charge summary to arrive was that of Trichur municipality and the last that of the Cochin-Kanayannur taluk. The latter was received on the afternoon of the 28th February. The compilation of the provisional totals for the State from the charge summaries, which had progressed step by step as the summary from each charge was received, was immediately completed and these totals were wired to the Census Commissioner that very evening (28th February, the very next day after the census). It may be noted here that the provisional totals of 1921 were ready only on the 4th day, and of 1911 on the 3rd day, after the final census. The total population according to the provisional figures was 1,205,434, or 418 more than the number actually arrived at after detailed tabulation in the Central Office. The difference between the two totals was thus only ·035 per cent or 35 persons in 100,000, as against 6 and 57 in the same number in 1921 and 1911 respectively.

9. The work of abstracting the information contained in the schedules was immediately taken in hand. A staff of 60 Copyists, 6 Assistant Supervisors and 6 Supervisors was appointed for the purpose. The work fell into 3 clear stages. The first was the abstraction or copying of details from the enumeration schedules on to the slips. Tabulation or successive sortings of the slips in order to obtain materials for the various Imperial and State Tables followed. Compilation or the posting and addition of the results of the several sortings was the third and last stage of the work. Slip-copying together with checking occupied 45 working days and was completed towards the end of May. The tabulation staff was slightly reduced in strength when sorting commenced; and the sorters' tickets containing the figures for the Imperial Tables were ready in 3 months (by the beginning of September). The work of compiling the figures from the sorters' tickets was taken up soon after sorting had begun, and it was entrusted to well qualified Supervisors and Assistant Supervisors of proved ability. The compilation of the Imperial Tables was over by the end of September. **Abstraction and tabulation**

10. Unemployment among English-educated persons, the size and sex constitution of families and the fertility of married life, emigration from the State and agricultural stock formed the subjects of special enquiries undertaken along with the general census. Statistics were collected also of the children of school-going age, who were attending schools, and of vaccinated persons. The special enquiries were conducted along with the preliminary enumeration. **Special enquiries**

The schedules relating to the special enquiries were taken up for slip-copying and sorting only after the work of abstraction and tabulation in connection with the general census was completed. The compilation of the results of the special enquiries was finished by the end of October.

11. The Subsidiary Tables for the 12 chapters of the Report, which present the statistics contained in the Imperial Tables in proportional and condensed forms, were prepared by the office staff. This work was over by the end of January, 1932. **Subsidiary Tables**

Report drafting

12. The drafting of the Report—the least congenial part of the whole work—was taken in hand in December, 1931, and was completed by the end of October, 1932. For more than a month during the period I had to attend to other duties of an urgent nature which occupied all my time, so much so that the actual time taken for writing the Report was a little less than 10 months.

Cost of census

13. The cost of the census from the date of my appointment as Census Superintendent in January, 1930, up to the 15th November, 1932, amounted to Rs. 37,800 in round figures, and an expenditure of about Rs. 700 more may have to be incurred before the work is finally completed. The total cost will thus amount approximately to Rs. 38,500 or Rs. 32 per 1,000 of the population. This is considerably in excess of the expenditure incurred at previous censuses, the corresponding figures for 1921 and 1911 being Rs. 24 and Rs. 26 respectively per 1,000 of the population. Various reasons contributed to this increase in expenditure. The Superintendent's pay was higher than in 1921. The volume of statistical work done at the present census was much greater than on previous occasions, and accordingly the work occupied a longer period of time. The office staff also had to be strengthened for the same reason. The travelling expenses paid to non-official census officers in 1931 amounted to a bigger sum than in 1921. The census office was held in hired buildings and the expenditure under rent alone exceeded Rs. 1,000. In 1921 no expenditure was incurred under this head as Government buildings were available for the location of the office. A detailed explanation for the higher cost of the census under Report is given in the Administrative Volume.

In spite of this increase in expenditure, it is noteworthy that our figures compare not unfavourably with those of some other Indian States. The cost of the Baroda Census, for instance, has amounted to Rs. 43·7 per 1,000 of the population, even though Baroda effected a saving of Rs. 11,300 (Rs. 5 per 1,000 of the population) by introducing the Bulletin Individuals system according to which enumeration was carried out not in schedule books but in enumeration cards, so that the process of slip-copying was done away with, the enumeration cards taking the place of the slips for sorting purposes.

Acknowledgments

14. Acknowledgments are due to many whose co-operation is chiefly responsible for the successful termination of the census operations. In the first place I must express my sincere thanks to the large staff of honorary census officers. The accuracy of the enumeration and the promptitude with which it was carried out were in no small measure due to the enthusiasm and devotion to duty of the Enumerators and Supervisors on whom fell the heaviest part of the work. To the Tahsildars and Municipal Chairmen, census work comes as a troublesome addition to their ordinary duties that are in themselves heavy enough to occupy their whole time. Yet it is no exaggeration to state that census matters received prompt and careful attention at their hands, and any success which attended the enumeration is to be attributed to the admirable arrangements made by them. In acknowledging my deep obligations to these officers, I should not forget the Assistant Charge Superintendents of the five big charges *, who relieved the Charge Superintendents of the heaviest part of their duties, and personally attended to the arrangements with much zeal and energy. I am particularly

---

* The Assistant Charge Superintendents were
Messrs. P. Sivaramakrishna Ayyar, B. A., L. T., (Cochin Kanayannur taluk),
K. A. Dharmaraja Ayyar, B. A., L. T., (Mukundapuram taluk),
P. M. Sankaran Nambiyar, M. A., L. T., (Trichur taluk),
R. Kalyanakrishna Ayyar, B. A., L. T., (Talapilli taluk),
and C. S. Narayana Ayyar, B. A., L. T., (Chittur taluk)—all senior teachers of the State Educational Service.

indebted to the Assistant Charge Superintendent of Trichur, Mr. P. M. Sankaran Nambiyar, for the valuable help received from him in the translation of circular letters and notes of instructions, in the holding of classes for the training of census officers and in many other ways.

In the Central Office, where abstraction and tabulation were carried out, the strain was particularly heavy, especially for the Supervisors and their assistants; but they all did their work cheerfully and satisfactorily. Where all did well it would be invidious to particularise; but the services of Messrs. M. Kochunni Menon, B. A., and C. V. Sethu Ayyar deserve special mention. The former was my Personal Assistant and was in direct charge of the abstraction and tabulation staff. That the work, whose volume was almost double that of 1921, was done by the same number of hands, and within the same period of time as at the last census, was chiefly due to the energy, enthusiasm and devotion to duty of Mr. Kochunni Menon. Mr. Sethu Ayyar, the Head Clerk of the Census Office, was the Head Clerk of the Census Office of 1921 also, and his experience was of much service in the compilation of the Imperial and State Tables. Most of the Subsidiary Tables also, appended to the various chapters of this Report, were prepared by him.

Mr. C. Achyuta Menon, the veteran Census Reporter of 1891 and 1911, and retired Secretary to the Diwan, has laid me under very deep obligations to him. His knowledge of the State and his experience of men and things in Cochin being unrivalled, the advice and suggestions with which he was kind enough to help me from the very commencement of the census operations were invaluable, and I take this opportunity to express my warmest thanks to him.

My thanks are also due to Messrs. K. Govinda Menon, retired Conservator of Forests, C. Matthai, retired Director of Public Instruction, I. Raman Menon, retired Superintendent of Agriculture, and V. K. Achyuta Menon, Superintendent of the Government Trades School, Trichur, for their valuable contributions to this Report.

The maps and diagrams which illustrate this Report were all printed at the Survey and Land Records Office, Trichur, and I am obliged to Messrs. I. Achyuta Menon, Superintendent of Survey and Land Records, and V. K. Gopala Menon, B. A., the Manager of the Survey Office, for the readiness and promptitude with which they complied with all my requests.

A heavier debt is due to the Superintendent of the Government Press, Ernakulam, and his over-worked assistants, from whom I have received all possible consideration and help at every stage of the work. The census involves much additional work for the Press. The printing of the Tables and this Report demands the utmost care and accuracy. But the Superintendent, Mr. N. M. Parameswara Ayyar, an officer of experience and resource, answered every demand with unfailing courtesy and promptitude. All census printing was done under his direct personal supervision. And it is much to his credit that, with the equipment at his disposal which is certainly inadequate for printing a Census Report, he has managed to produce fairly satisfactory results.

To Dr. J. H. Hutton, the Census Commissioner for India, my personal indebtedness is great. Apart from the guidance which I received from him at all stages of the work, the many suggestions which he was good enough to offer in the course of his careful review of the various chapters of this Report were of the utmost value to me.

I must also gratefully acknowledge the kind and cordial support I have throughout received from the successive Diwans who presided over the administration while my work was in progress.

Report

15. The following Report does not profess to do anything more than to deal with the statistics in the various Tables in conformity with the instructions issued by the Census Commissioner, and to draw the more obvious inferences deducible from them. The general plan and methods of statistical analysis followed at the present census being much the same as those of previous censuses, one naturally finds very useful guidance in the Reports of these censuses. I have therefore freely consulted the India, Baroda and Madras Reports of 1921, the Madras and Cochin Reports of 1911 and the Cochin Report of 1901, borrowed many hints and suggestions from them and generally followed their methods. And it is but fitting that I should gratefully record my heavy indebtedness to them before I conclude this introduction.

CHAPTER I.—DISTRIBUTION AND MOVEMENT OF THE POPULATION.

THIS report deals with the small Indian State of Cochin which, together with its sister State of Travancore, occupies the southernmost portion of "Malabar and Konkan" in the Imperial scheme of Natural Divisions into which the different parts of India were grouped for census purposes in 1911. Though situated on the sea-board, more than a third of its area of 1,480 square miles is mountainous and covered with the dense forests of the Western Ghats sheltering but a few scores of the Kadar hill tribe in addition to large herds of wild animals. With such diversity in its physical features, it is no doubt possible to divide the State for statistical purposes into distinct areas or Natural Divisions in which the natural features are more or less homogeneous, but the small area of Cochin will neither warrant such divisions nor justify the time and labour involved in the preparation of separate statistics for each of them. **The State and its Divisions**

2. For administrative purposes the State is divided into six taluks: Cochin-Kanayannur, Cranganur, Mukundapuram, Trichur, Talapilli and Chittur. The taluks are of unequal extent, Mukundapuram being the largest with an area of 510 square miles and Cranganur the smallest having an area of only 17 square miles. During the past decade there have been no changes through territorial re-distribution in the area of these administrative divisions and, as at previous censuses, they form the units for which separate statistics are given in the Imperial Tables.

3. There are two kinds of population for statistical purposes—the *de jure* and the *de facto*. The *de jure* population comprises all persons normally resident in any locality including temporary absentees and excluding temporary arrivals or visitors, while the *de facto* population consists of all persons enumerated as being alive and present in that locality at a particular point of time. The Indian census aims at being a *de facto* census, and though the result of a general enumeration of the *de facto* population of an area at any given point of time may not be exactly representative of the normal resident population of that area on account of the small tidal migrations that must be continuously occurring in most localities, still this result has been regarded as sufficiently representative of the *de jure* population to justify foregoing the costly and laborious processes of a *de jure* census involving the identification of the normal residence of each unit of the population. **Definition of 'Population'**

4. The statistics of birth-place given in Imperial Table VI will be of no help to us in finding out the difference between the *de facto* and the *de jure* population of the State. The table shows that out of a total population of 1,205,016 enumerated on the census day, 87,417 persons were born outside Cochin. But a large majority of this number must certainly be permanent residents and not temporary migrants. The last column of Imperial Table III gives 12,485 as the number of travellers enumerated in Cochin. Even here it may be safely assumed that most of these travellers are permanent residents of some locality or other within the State. The difference between the *de facto* and the *de jure* population must therefore be regarded as negligible, and the figures may be taken as truly representative of the State's normal population for all practical purposes. **De facto and de jure population**

The forest tracts in Cochin form a non-synchronous area where it is not possible to take a final count on any given date, and so the returns from this area record its *de jure* population which may be taken for all practical purposes as identical with its *de facto* population.

Accuracy of enumeration

5. Before dealing with the statistics presented in the various tables, it will be only in the fitness of things to examine the degree of accuracy that can be attributed to the census figures. Human nature being what it is, these figures collected from returns prepared by an army of enumerators can never lay claim to mathematical accuracy; and, so far as absolute numbers are concerned, there is no doubt whatever that a considerable number of persons must have escaped enumeration, while quite a small number might have been enumerated twice. In crowded and busy centres like towns, owing to the rapidly changing population, omissions are more likely to occur than in rural areas. All the same these errors must certainly be so small as to be utterly negligible and they can never detract from the value of the statistics collected at the census.

6. There is, however, an important factor in favour of Cochin, which cannot but make the results of its census more accurate than in most other States and Provinces in India. Cochin occupies one of the foremost places in all India in literacy and education. The census officers including enumerators were well-educated persons, most of them being recruited from the ranks of teachers in Anglo-vernacular schools. Their work was conscientious and satisfactory. Timely and careful arrangements were also made for the preliminary and final enumeration. And I venture to hope that the result, as revealed in the census figures of 1931, has been the attainment of the highest degree of accuracy possible in the circumstances.

Area and population

7. Imperial Table I gives the area and population of the State and of its divisions while the Subsidiary Tables at the end of this Chapter contain the salient features of the statistics relating to the density and movement of the population. The area of Cochin including its lagoons or backwaters and its extensive forest tracts is 1,480 square miles, and its total population enumerated on the morning of the 27th February, 1931, numbered 1,205,016 persons of whom 589,813 were males and 615,203 females. This shows an increase of 225,936 over the numbers returned at the census of 1921, corresponding to a decennial rate of increase of 23·1 per cent against an increase of only 6·6 per cent recorded in 1921. But before we proceed to investigate and discuss what must appear to be an abnormal increase in the population and account for the wide difference between the rates of increase of the two intercensal periods, it is necessary to survey the conditions that have influenced the movement of population during the decade under review.

Factors determining growth of population

8. The movement of population in any area is ultimately determined by the result of the 'gain by births and immigration minus the loss by deaths and emigration' during the intercensal period. When the gain is greater than the loss the population increases, but when it is smaller the population must show a corresponding decrease in numbers. Were the conditions of the decade prosperous on the whole? Did they react favourably on the birth-rate and promote immigration? Or were these conditions adverse, leading to scarcity, distress and a high death-rate and forcing the people to emigrate to more favoured and congenial tracts? These are some of the questions to be considered in this connection.

9. The decade under review was prosperous on the whole and conducive to a normal increase in population. The worst calamities that overtook the people during the period were the floods of 1924 and 1929. The ravages wrought by the devastating floods of 1924 were wide-spread and unequalled in severity. Travancore, Cochin and Malabar were all stricken alike and experienced the most acute distress. The 1929 floods were less disastrous and caused but less damage. On both occasions, however, a rapid recovery was made from the ill-effects of these floods which therefore do not appear to have operated as a serious check on the growth of population. **Conditions of the past decade: floods**

10. But for these floods the seasons were mostly normal, the monsoon rains timely and regular on the whole and the harvests generally favourable. There was considerable expansion in agriculture. And the prosperity of a State like Cochin, where more than 80 per cent of the population live in rural areas, must to a great extent, depend on the development of agriculture. The Durbar offered facilities which the people were not slow to take advantage of. Uncultivated wastes, disafforested areas from the forest tracts and reclaimed areas from the backwaters were all assigned for cultivation. Irrigation projects were successfully undertaken and, as seen from Subsidiary Table I, 67·2 per cent of the cultivated area came to be irrigated against 36·4 per cent in 1921. As a further measure of encouragement agricultural loans on easy terms were granted to the ryots by the Durbar. It is also noteworthy in this connection that the major portion of the loans disbursed by co-operative credit societies, whose number rose from 77 to 214 during the decade, was for agricultural and productive purposes. **Seasons and agricultural conditions**

11. Nor did commercial and industrial development lag behind. The improvement of the Cochin harbour progressed apace and by 1929 it was possible for ocean-going steamers to enter the sheltered waters of the inner harbour through the newly dredged channel. Rice and oil mills, and brick and tile factories flourished in increasing numbers, and the spinning and weaving mill at Trichur grew into a big concern. Facilities for transport and communication improved, many additional miles of metalled roads being built by the Public Works Department. The Nelliampathi Ghat Road, that has just been completed, deserves special mention here since it will serve as a cheap and easy outlet for the rich produce of the tea and coffee estates of the Nelliampathy Hills. Similar facilities were extended in rural areas also, thanks chiefly to the endeavours of the steadily growing Village Panchayats with their widening sphere of activities. In 1921 there were but 9 Sirkar and 45 private (licensed) markets. Their numbers in 1931 were 17 and 67 respectively. Trade was flourishing and the economic conditions were on the whole favourable, the cultivator getting a fair price for his produce and the labourer receiving good wages for his work. And though the storm of the world-wide economic crisis burst towards the end of the decade, and the unparalleled and universal economic depression enveloped the State in its gloom, the decade closed before the chilling effects of these adverse conditions had time to manifest themselves except in centres like Mattancheri which, perhaps on account of its importance as the commercial capital of Cochin and one of the most important marts on the Malabar coast for centuries, is seen to have been more immediately sensitive to the effects of the depression in that many mills and business concerns were closed down and a large number of families migrated to Alleppey, Quilon and other places. **Commercial and industrial development**

12. The prosperous conditions of the decade were reflected in the public health of the period which was generally satisfactory. There were no ravages **Public health**

from epidemic diseases. A threatened out-break of plague in 1928 was stamped out before it could claim a dozen victims. It was only during the closing years of the decade (1930 and 1931) that small-pox appeared in an epidemic form* and, except for this, the mortality from the scourges of small-pox and cholera never assumed serious proportions. Questions relating to water supply, drainage, general sanitation and medical relief received careful attention. The sinking of wells in rural areas and the supply of pure drinking water by the pipe system in towns like Mattancheri, Trichur and Nemmara, were successfully undertaken to the great relief of their population. And the number of hospitals and dispensaries in the State rose from 30 to 50 in the course of the decade.

Vital statistics

13. A high birth-rate and a low death-rate leading to a steady growth of population was the natural outcome of these favourable conditions, and an analysis of the vital statistics of the period, if such statistics of a reliable nature were available, would have supported the above conclusion. Unfortunately, however, the registration of births and deaths is still wholly unsatisfactory except in municipal areas. How barren the results of this registration have been will be seen from Subsidiary Table V. The births registered in the decade number in all 142, 516, but the census returns show 354, 399 children under 10 years, born during the intercensal period. These figures lead us to the happy and flattering inference that our State is a veritable children's Paradise and that an army of children numbering 211, 883 (17·6 per cent of the total population) immigrated into it during the last 10 years. The death-rate according to these statistics is no less flattering, there being but 91,233 deaths in a population of 979,080 registered between 1921 and 1931, corresponding to an annual rate of 9·3 per mille. The excess of births over deaths according to the vital statistics numbered 51,283 whereas the natural increase in population to be accounted for by this excess is 202,934 as shown in Subsidiary Tables IV and V.

The vital statistics of Municipal towns are far more reliable and furnish another proof, if such proof were required, of the worthless character of the vital statistics of the State as a whole. In the four Municipal towns the average annual birth-rate per mille of the population during the intercensal period was 31·73 against 12·73 in rural areas—a very unnatural state of affairs. The death-rate in Municipal towns was 18·34, but only 8·36 elsewhere. Be it remembered at the same time that our Municipal towns with the exception of Mattancheri are not after all overcrowded or unhealthy and there is therefore no reason why the death-rate in towns should be more than double the rate in villages. The only explanation for this wide difference is to be found in the utterly unreliable character of these rural statistics. Thirty-six years have passed since the registration of vital statistics was initiated in the State. Many new rules designed to improve the system of registration and secure more accurate results were framed from time to time during this period. And yet there is hardly any improvement seen in the value of the statistics thus collected.

Statistics of migration

14. If we now turn to the second factor affecting the movement of population and analyse the results of migration, here too the absence of statistics on the subject renders our task difficult and we have to depend wholly on the returns of birth-place recorded at the census. Chapter III deals with this subject in detail and Imperial Table VI gives the statistics of birth-place. From the migration statistics contained in Subsidiary Table IV it will be seen that

* Reported deaths from small-pox numbered 1,130 212, and 16 in 1930, 1929 and 1928 respectively.

DIAGRAM A

Population of Cochin at each Census

since 1881

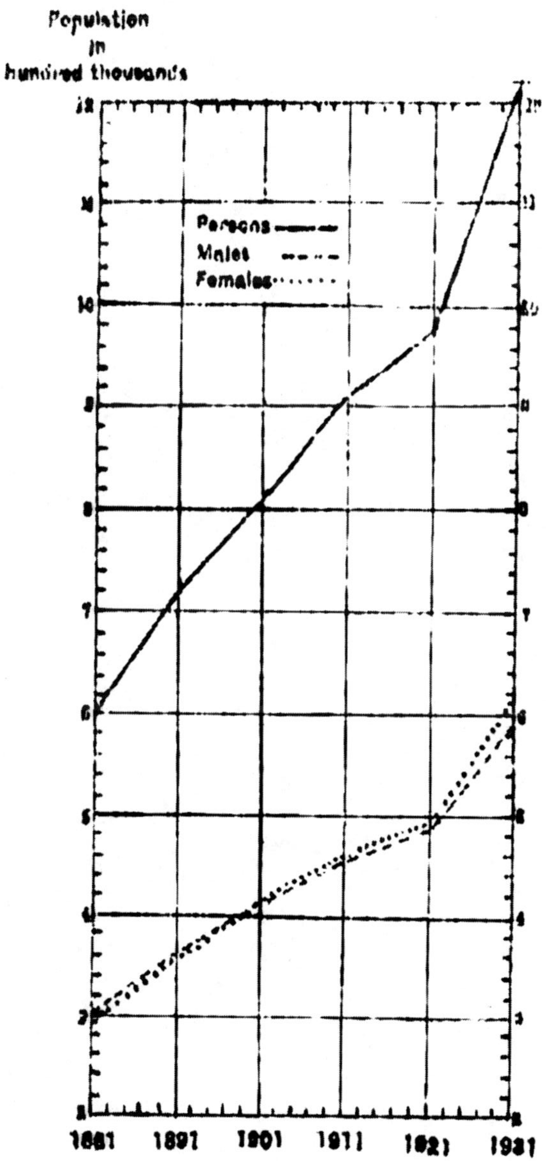

DIAGRAM B

Specific Increase of Population in Cochin

since 1881

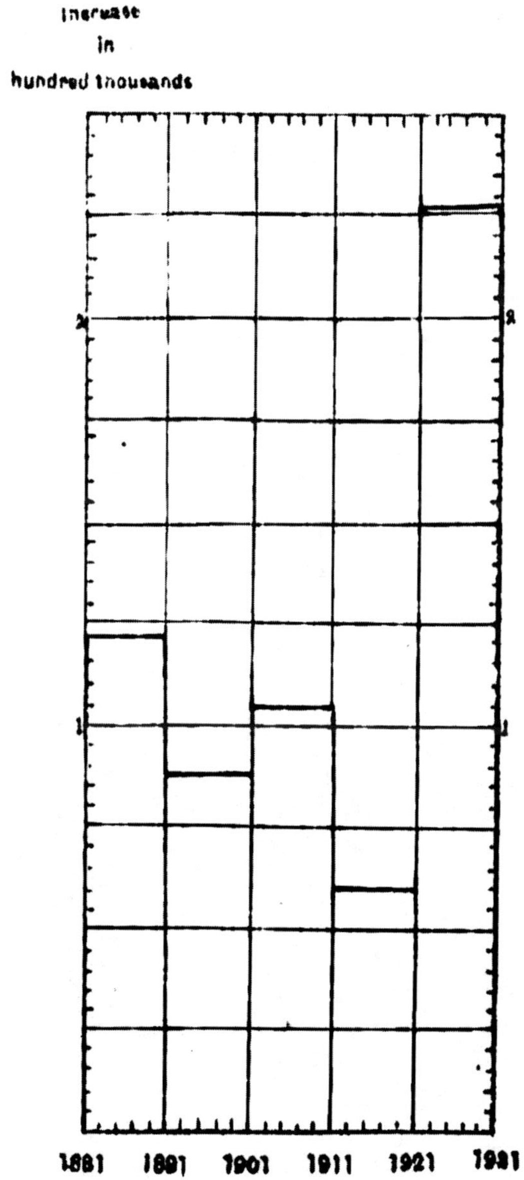

DIAGRAM C

Rate of Increase of Population in Cochin

in each intercensal period

since 1881

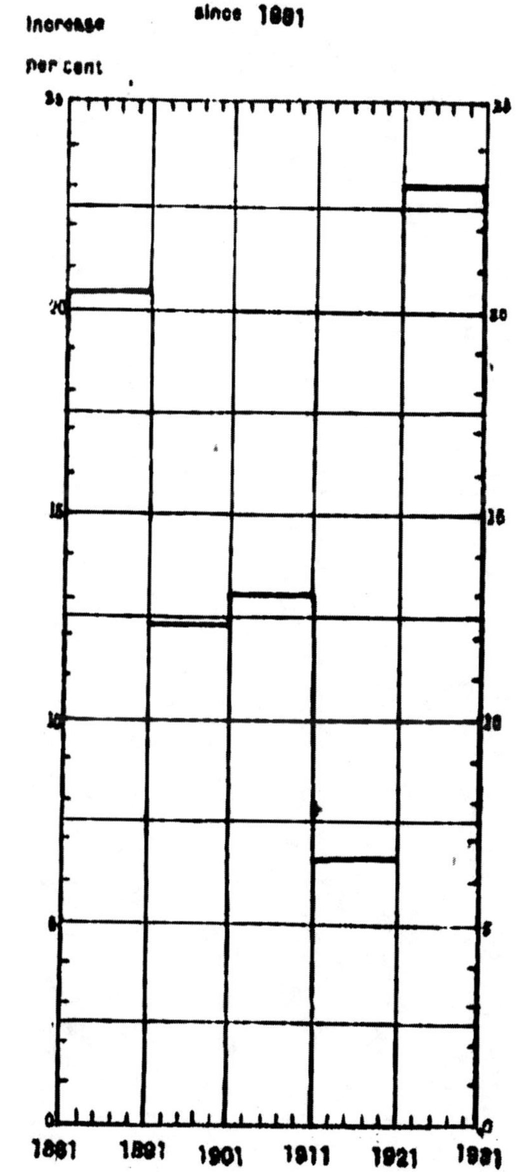

87,417 persons or 7·3 per cent of the population enumerated in Cochin were born outside the State, whereas the number of persons born in Cochin and enumerated elsewhere is only 48,168 according to the figures hitherto available. The State will thus appear to have gained 39,249 persons from the balance of migration during the past decade. The corresponding figures for 1921 were 39,759 immigrants and 23,512 emigrants and the apparent gain to the State's population on account of the excess of immigrants over emigrants was 16,247.

I use the words *appear* and *apparent* advisedly. For these figures taken from birth-place statistics can at best be regarded only as an approximate representation of the results of actual migration inasmuch as many of these migrants might have been but travellers or temporary sojourners. Moreover it will be seen from Chapter III that the figures for emigrants given above are incomplete and inaccurate. And for this reason the actual gain resulting from migration must probably be less than 39,249.

Variation in population at previous censuses

15. A statement containing the details of variation in the State's population between successive censuses is given below and it will be seen therefrom that the rate of increase of 23·1 per cent recorded in 1931 is by far the highest for any decade since 1875 when the first systematic enumeration of the population was undertaken.

Census year	Interval between successive censuses	Population	Percentage of increase (+) or decrease (—)
1875	..	601,114	..
1881	6 years	600,278	—·14
1891	10 ,,	722,906	+20·4
1901	10 ,,	812,025	+12·3
1911	10 ,,	918,110	+13·1
1921	10 ,,	979,080	+ 6·6
1931	10 ,,	1,205,016	+23·1

Each intercensal period here marks a steady growth in the population, the only exception being the period of six years preceding the census of 1881. But even this exception disappears in the light of the explanation given in the Report on the census of 1891 where it is proved that the decrease in numbers recorded in 1881 was the outcome of careless enumeration leading to short-counting. If we go further back, we find rough estimates of the population recorded in 1820, 1836, 1849 and 1858; and, incomplete as these estimates are bound to be, they all show a gradual rise in numbers so much so that the population of 223,003 returned in 1820 has increased by no less than 440 per cent during the space of eleven decades. The figures and percentages of increase for the last 50 years are given in Imperial Table II and Subsidiary Table III. These reveal the fact that the population has grown by 100·7 per cent during the period, the State's area undergoing no change all the time. This enormous increase is illustrated in diagrams A to C.

Low increase in population registered in 1921

16. The rate of increase recorded for the period between 1911 and 1921 was, as we have already seen, only 6·6 per cent against 13·06 and 12·33 per cent for the two previous decades. The low rate was attributed to the unfavourable conditions of the closing years of the period, conditions resulting from the post-war economic depression and the scarcity consequent on it, the partial failure of the monsoon rains for more than one season and the poor harvests and distress caused thereby, and the ravages of small-pox, cholera and influenza epidemics. While admitting the force of these arguments and while

conceding that the circumstances explained above might have operated to a certain extent as a check on the normal growth of population, we have reasons to think that the fall in the rate of increase is partly if not mainly to be accounted for by short-counting in 1921.

not in entire consonance with the conditions of the decade

17. The general conditions of the period between 1911 and 1921 were not unlike the conditions of the closing decade of the 19th century. The high mortality of the later period arising from small-pox, cholera and influenza epidemics had a parallel in the heavy toll levied by the many and severe outbreaks of small-pox and cholera in the earlier period. Partial failure of the monsoons leading to agricultural depression, scarcity and distress of a temporary character, was common to both decades. And yet an increase of 12·33 per cent was recorded at the census of 1901 against 6·6 per cent in 1921. It is hard to believe that the economic depression that followed in the wake of the great war was acute enough to be solely responsible for this heavy fall in the rate of increase.

nor with the corresponding variation in Travancore

18. Travancore and Cochin share the same physical and political features and possess the same ethnical characteristics. The conditions prevailing in both the States are therefore almost always identical and naturally a certain proportion is to be observed between the rates of increase recorded at successive censuses in the two States, as illustrated in the marginal statement. The adverse influences of the period between 1911 and 1921 were as much at work in Travancore as here. And yet Travancore instead of showing any fall registered a slight rise in the normal rate of growth as seen from the statement. There appears no reason why Cochin should have fared differently from Travancore in this respect.

Census year	Percentage of decennial increase in	
	Travancore	Cochin
1901	15·4	12·33
1911	16·2	13·6
1921	16·8	6·6
1931	27·2	23·1

Proof of omissions in 1921 furnished (i) by age statistics

19. An analysis of the figures of the present census will afford further proof of omissions at the census of 1921. The number of children aged 0—5 returned in 1921 was 132,758. At the census of 1931 these children will be aged 10—15 and their numbers must show a fall in proportion to the death-rate among children. But it is seen from Imperial Table VII that there are 148,115 children in the age group 10—15 according to the returns of 1931. Instead of any decrease in numbers, here we have an actual increase of 15,357 and when due allowance is made for the loss from death, the difference will be much greater. Gain from immigration alone cannot account for this big difference, for the ranks of migrants generally contain but a small percentage of children. Nor can it be attributed to wrong age returns, for, if one age-group gains in numbers in this way, other groups must show a corresponding loss, and then the proportion between one group and another will suffer. But the age-groups are all proportionate as seen from Imperial Table VII. Besides, several of the other groups also, though they do not show an actual excess in numbers over the corresponding age-groups of 1921, reveal but a very low rate of decrease from death. In the circumstances it is but reasonable to conclude that there were omissions in 1921 and that the population was therefore under-estimated.

20. Likewise the percentage of increase between 1921 and 1931 noticed in the population of several castes and tribes is so high that it cannot be satisfactorily explained on any ground other than that of short-counting in 1921. A

(ii) by variation in numbers of selected castes or tribes

new outstanding instances are given in the margin. Misleading or wrong returns of caste names leading to members of one caste being included in another cannot account for the low figures of 1921, for the castes shown in the marginal list are too well known to be mistaken for, or confused with, others. It is also significant that the most serious omissions are seen among the lower classes. The Malayans are a wandering hill tribe living partly on the hills and partly in the plains on the outskirts of forests. The Eravalans also are another primitive tribe. The Kanakkans and Velans are two of the many 'unapproachable' communities and the Kudumi Chetties are labourers. An irresponsible or negligent enumerator can safely ignore such lowly and humble folk and naturally they stand to lose more by short-counting than others. The figures in the margin show for example that not more than a fourth of the Malayan tribe could have been returned at the census of 1921.

Caste or tribe	Population			Increase per cent between 1921 and 1931.
	1911	1921	1931	
Kanakkan ..	7,527	8,424	13,192	57
Kudumi Chetty..	12,371	10,328	16,104	56
Velan ..	9,322	6,232	10,895	75
Eravalan ..	503	Nil.	541	..
Malayan ..	2,461	594	3,185	436

and (iii) by statistics of occupied houses

21. The increase in the number of occupied houses recorded in 1921 furnishes another proof in the same direction. The marginal statement gives the percentage of increase in occupied houses side by side with the percentage of increase in population at 5 censuses in Travancore and Cochin, and we see that the increase in population is uniformly higher than the increase in occupied houses, the only exception being the percentage recorded for Cochin in 1921. It must therefore follow that, if the 1921 figures are reliable, the economic conditions of the decade preceding 1921 were not unfavourable, that the standard of living had improved much and that the people had more house-room and enjoyed a greater degree of comfort than in other decades. As the economic conditions of the period do not warrant this conclusion, the only possible inference is that the low rate of increase in population recorded in 1921 is chiefly to be attributed to short-counting.

Census year		Percentage of increase in Occupied houses	Percentage of increase in Population
1891	Cochin ..	6·3	20·4*
	Travancore ..	4·7	6·5
1901	Cochin ..	9·5	12·3
	Travancore ..	12·4	15·4
1911	Cochin ..	12·0	13·1
	Travancore ..	14·0	16·2
1921	Cochin ..	9·1	6·6
	Travancore ..	14·9	16·8
1931	Cochin ..	16·5	23·1
	Travancore ..	22·1	27·2

Probable extent of short counting in 1921

22. Obviously it is not possible to gauge with accuracy the extent of the omissions of 1921. But the statistics of the two previous decades must be of some help to us in this connection and we may perhaps be erring only on the safe side if we assume that, as against the increase of 12·3 per cent in 1901 and 13·1 per cent in 1911, there was an increase of not less than 10 per cent in 1921, due allowance being made for the economic depression and epidemic diseases of the period. The corresponding increase of 16·8 per cent in Travancore will strongly support this assumption. According to this calculation the population of Cochin in 1921 would have exceeded a million. The increase of 225,936 in

* In the Census Report of 1891 it is shown that the high rate of increase was only apparent and not real as there was short-counting in 1881. The actual rate of increase was much lower.

the State's population recorded in 1931 will then be reduced to less than 200,000 and the percentage of increase for the past decade will fall from 23·1 to 19 or thereabouts.

Movement of population during the last decade.

23. It is now necessary to discuss the subject of the actual growth in population during the past decade and explain the phenomenal increase of 23·1 per cent. As seen from the last paragraph the theory of short-counting in 1921 may account for a difference of about 4 per cent. But does this difference take us to what has hitherto been considered as a normal rate of increase for Cochin? Commenting on the movement of population in the State, the Census Reports of 1901 and 1911 both refer to an average decennial increase of about 12 to 13 per cent as normal for the State under normal conditions and contentedly quote the opinion of eminent statisticians that the above rate "is the best from a national point of view at once stimulating activity and yet not overrunning or even pressing upon the means of subsistence". A higher percentage was regarded as improbable if not impossible. Indeed, in densely peopled areas like Cochin, as the population rises in numbers the rate of growth must tend to fall on account of over-crowding and the pressure of population on the means of subsistence. And yet during the past decade we see an apparent increase of 23·1 and an actual rise of about 19 per cent. Subsidiary Table IV further shows that, if the increase in the actual population be taken as 23·1 per cent, the increase in the natural population alone from excess of births over deaths will be 21·1 per cent, while the explanation given in paragraph 14 above points to a still higher rate of growth in the natural population. If in 1901, when there were but 549 persons to the square mile, an increase of 12 to 13 per cent was considered to be normal, safe and healthy for the State, certainly an increase of 19 per cent must be looked upon as positively abnormal, if not dangerous, in 1931 when there are as many as 814 persons to the square mile. All the same the present increase has to be accepted as normal under the circumstances in as much as it is the outcome of the normally favourable conditions that prevailed during most years of the decade, of agricultural expansion and industrial development, of prosperous trade and steady progress. And we have to infer that the material resources of the State have not yet been taxed to their utmost capacity, that they are at least for the present elastic enough to bear the strain of this high rate of increase and support the rising numbers in tolerable comfort, and that the adverse effects of over-crowding and of the pressure of population on the means of subsistence have not hitherto been felt to any appreciable extent.

24. In this connection it has to be remembered that, everywhere in India, the increase in population recorded at the Census of 1931 is much higher than the increase registered in 1921, as seen from the inset table.

Province or State	Percentage of increase (+) or decrease (—) at the Census of	
	1921	1931
India	+ 1·2	+10·6
Bengal	+ 2·7	+ 7·3
Bombay Presidency	— 1·2	+13·3
Baroda	+ 4·6	+14·9
Madras	+ 2·2	+10·4
Gwalior	— 1·3	+10·3
Hyderabad	— 6·8	+15·8
Jammu and Kashmir	+ 5·1	+ 9·8
Mysore	+ 3·0	+ 9·7

It has already been noted that Travancore has an increase of 27·2 per cent at the present census against 16·8 in 1921. The corresponding figures for Malabar and South Canara are 14·0 and 10·0 against 2·8 and 4·4 in 1921. However, if the alarming increase in numbers in our State is to be regarded as a positive evil from an agricultural or economic point of view, it is not much of a consolation to us to find that the evil is more or less wide-spread.

DIAGRAM. D

Cochin State – Density of Population

1881 – 1931

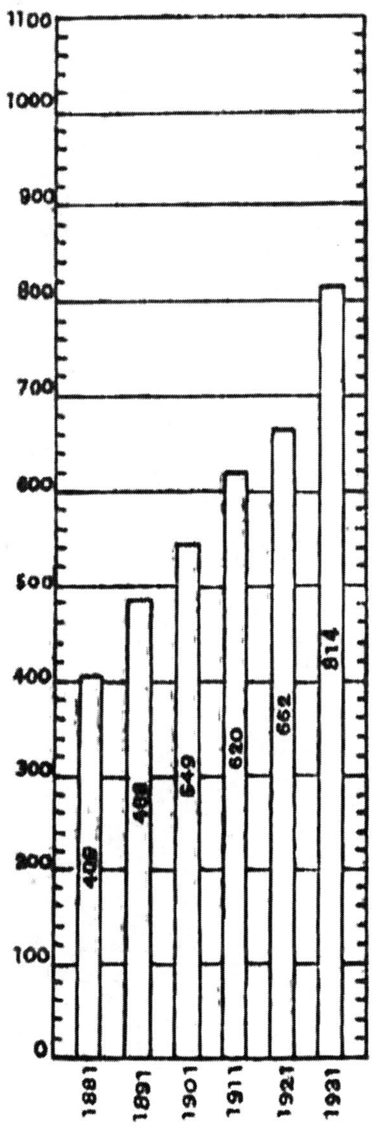

DIAGRAM. E

Showing the Density of Population in

Cochin as compared with other States, Provinces etc.

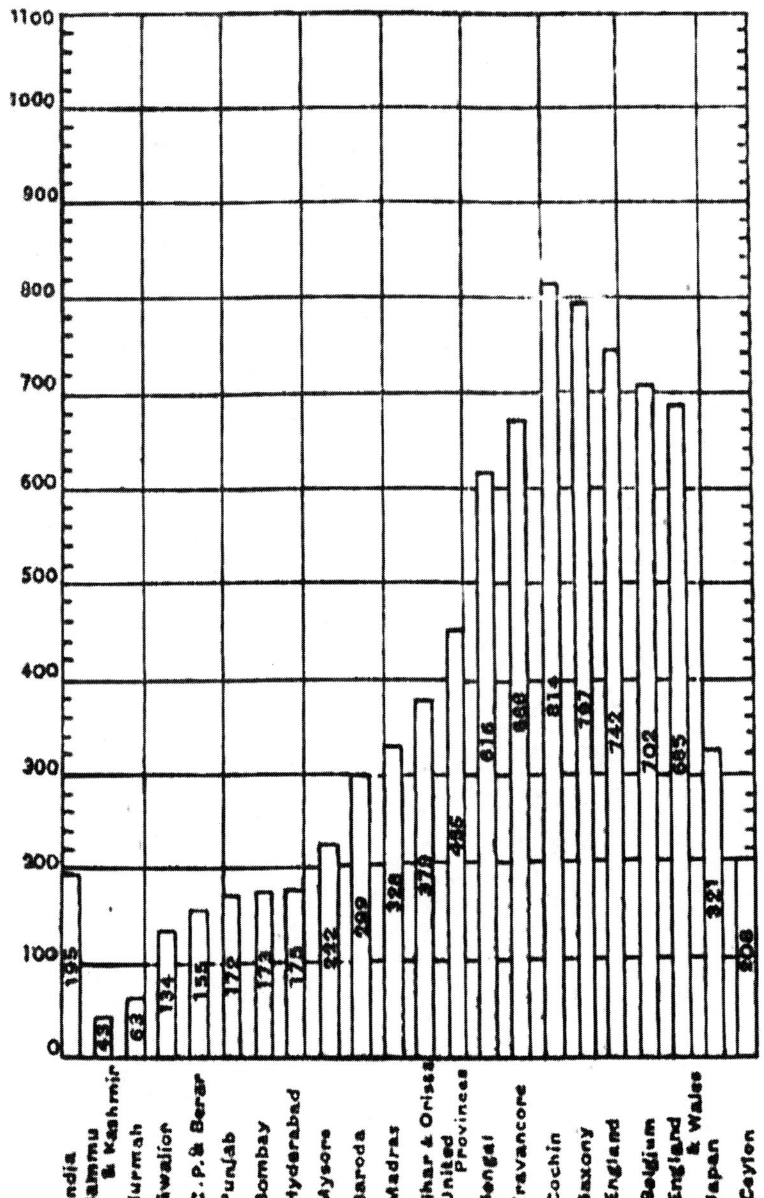

DIAGRAM. F

Showing the Density of Population in

Cochin as compared with certain Districts

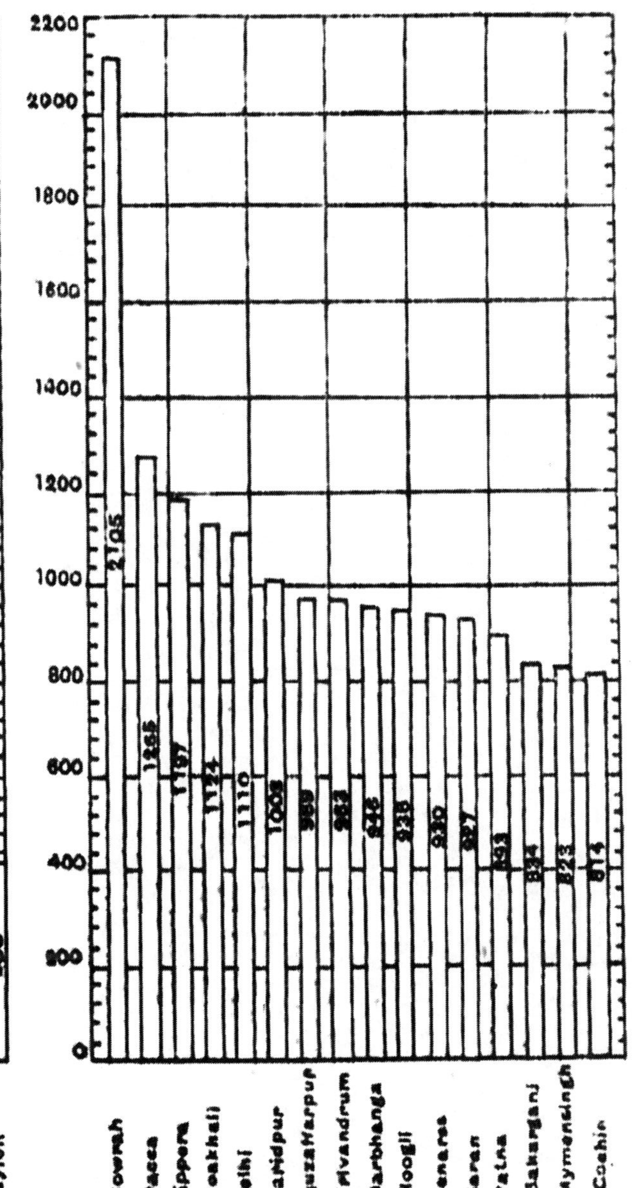

With an already over-crowded population, the position of Cochin will be much more precarious than that of others.

Density of population: reference to Statistics

25. Subsidiary Table I at the end of the Chapter compares the density of the State and of its divisions with the water supply and crops. Subsidiary Table II shows the distribution of the population classified according to density. The variation of population in relation to density since 1881 is given in Subsidiary Table III, while Subsidiary Tables VI and VII deal with variation by taluks classified according to density. Two maps have also been inserted in this chapter to illustrate the present density of the population per square mile and the variation in density between 1921 and 1931 in each taluk.

The area of the State being 1,480 square miles and the population 1,205,016, there are as many as 814 persons to each square mile if we assume an even distribution of this population over the whole area. Each unit of the population will thus get but ·79 of an acre. The marginal statement gives the figures of density and areality for seven successive censuses in Cochin together with the corresponding figures for Travancore and England and Wales. The density of 406 per square mile in 1875 is seen to have doubled itself in the course of five and a half decades. This phenomenal increase is illustrated in diagram D.

Census date		Persons per square mile	Acres per person
1875 (1871)	Cochin ..	406	1·58
	Travancore ..	303	2·1
	England & Wales ..	389	1·64
1881	Cochin ..	406	1·58
	Travancore ..	314	2·0
	England & Wales ..	445	1·44
1891	Cochin ..	488	1·31
	Travancore ..	335	1·9
	England & Wales ..	497	1·29
1901	Cochin ..	549	1·17
	Travancore ..	387	1·7
	England & Wales ..	558	1·15
1911	Cochin ..	620	1·03
	Travancore ..	449	1·4
	England & Wales ..	618	1·04
1921	Cochin ..	662	0·97
	Travancore ..	525	1·2
	England & Wales ..	649	0·99
1931	Cochin ..	814	0·79
	Travancore ..	668	0·96
	England & Wales ..	685	0·93

Comparison with other States and Provinces

26. Among the tracts comprised in the Natural Division "Malabar and Konkan" Cochin has the highest density. For, Travancore, Malabar and South Canara have a density of only 668, 610 and 341 respectively to the square mile, while the Bombay States and Districts come far below. If small things may be compared with great ones, the density of our small State may be compared with that of other States, Provinces or Countries. It will then be seen that there is not a single State or Province in the Indian Empire the density of which exceeds or at least equals that of Cochin, Delhi alone which, with an area of only 593 square miles, is treated as a separate Province on administrative grounds, being excluded. And even the most densely peopled countries in Europe stand below our State in this respect. The following statement together with diagram E will illustrate our point.

Province, State or Country	Density per sq. mile	Province, State or Country	Density per sq. mile
Jammu and Kashmir ..	43	Behar and Orissa ..	379
Burma ..	63	United Provinces of Agra and Oudh ..	455
Gwalior ..	134	Bengal ..	616
Central Provinces and Berar ..	155	Travancore ..	668
Punjab ..	172	COCHIN ..	**814**
Bombay ..	173	Saxony ..	797
Hyderabad ..	175	England (excluding Wales) ..	742
INDIA ..	**195**	Belgium ..	702
Mysore ..	222	England and Wales ..	685
Baroda ..	299	Japan ..	321
Madras ..	328	Ceylon ..	208

Travancore and Bengal that stand second and third lag far behind Cochin, having a density of only 668 and 616 respectively to the square mile. Saxony, the most densely peopled tract in Europe, had 177 persons more to the square mile than Cochin in 1901, but now it has only 17 persons less. Thirty years ago Belgium and England and Wales were more densely peopled than our State whereas now the density of Cochin is far higher than that of these countries.

27. The difference between Cochin and other Indian States in respect of the density of population will be seen more clearly from a comparative study of the statistics of the area and population of these States. Next to Cochin Travancore is the most densely peopled State in India and yet Travancore with more than five times the area of Cochin has but little more than four times our population. Baroda has five and a half times the area but only twice the population of our State. Gwalior is eighteen times and Mysore twenty times as big as Cochin, but Gwalior contains less than thrice and Mysore less than six times Cochin's population. Hyderabad has less than twelve times our population though its area is fifty-six times that of Cochin, while Jammu and Kashmir with fifty-seven times our area contain but three times the population of our pigmy State.

Comparison with selected districts

28. Considering the wide disparity in area between Cochin and these Provinces and Countries there is but little sense of proportion in this comparison and units of smaller area must be selected if the comparison is to be just. A list of those districts in India whose density exceeds 814 per square mile is given in the margin together with the figures of their areas and density. According to this there are but 15 districts* in India at present with a density higher than that of Cochin, whereas in 1901 there were more than 50 and in 1911 about 30 districts that were more densely peopled than our State.

District.	Area in square miles	Density per square mile.
Howrah ..	530	2,105
Dacca ..	2,723	1,265
Tippera ..	2,560	1,197
Noakhali ..	1,515	1,124
Delhi ..	593	1,110
Faridpur ..	2,371	1,003
Muzaffarpur ..	3,036	969
Southern (Trivandrum) Division in Travancore ..	1,490	963
Darbhanga ..	3,348	946
Hoogli ..	1,188	938
Benares ..	1,093	930
Saran ..	2,683	927
Patna ..	2,068	893
Bakarganj ..	3,490	834
Mymensingh ..	6,238	823
Cochin ..	1,480	814

Density of the State excluding uninhabitable area

29. In calculating the density of population, it must not be forgotten that more than a third of the State's area comprising the forest tracts and lagoons is uninhabited and uninhabitable. If these tracts are excluded and only the habitable area of about 865 square miles is taken into consideration for purposes of our calculation, the density will rise almost to 1,400 per square mile, each unit of the population having only ·46 of an acre.

Density by divisions: sea-board taluks

30. High as this density is, we find but little uniformity in the distribution of this crowded population in the different parts of the State, and the diversity in its physical features is responsible for one taluk returning a density of 2,429 while another has but 365 persons to the square mile. The sea-board taluks of Cranganur and Cochin-Kanayannur are very much more densely peopled than the interior or forest taluks of Mukundapuram, Trichur, Talapilli and Chittur. The mean density of the coastal taluks is 2,232 per square mile, Cranganur leading with 2,429 and Cochin-Kanayannur following with 2,210. The specific population of these two taluks is 392,799 while their area is only 176 square miles. In other words almost a third of the State's population is

* Of the 15 districts, Howrah and Delhi may be excluded from the list as their density is urban rather than rural in character.

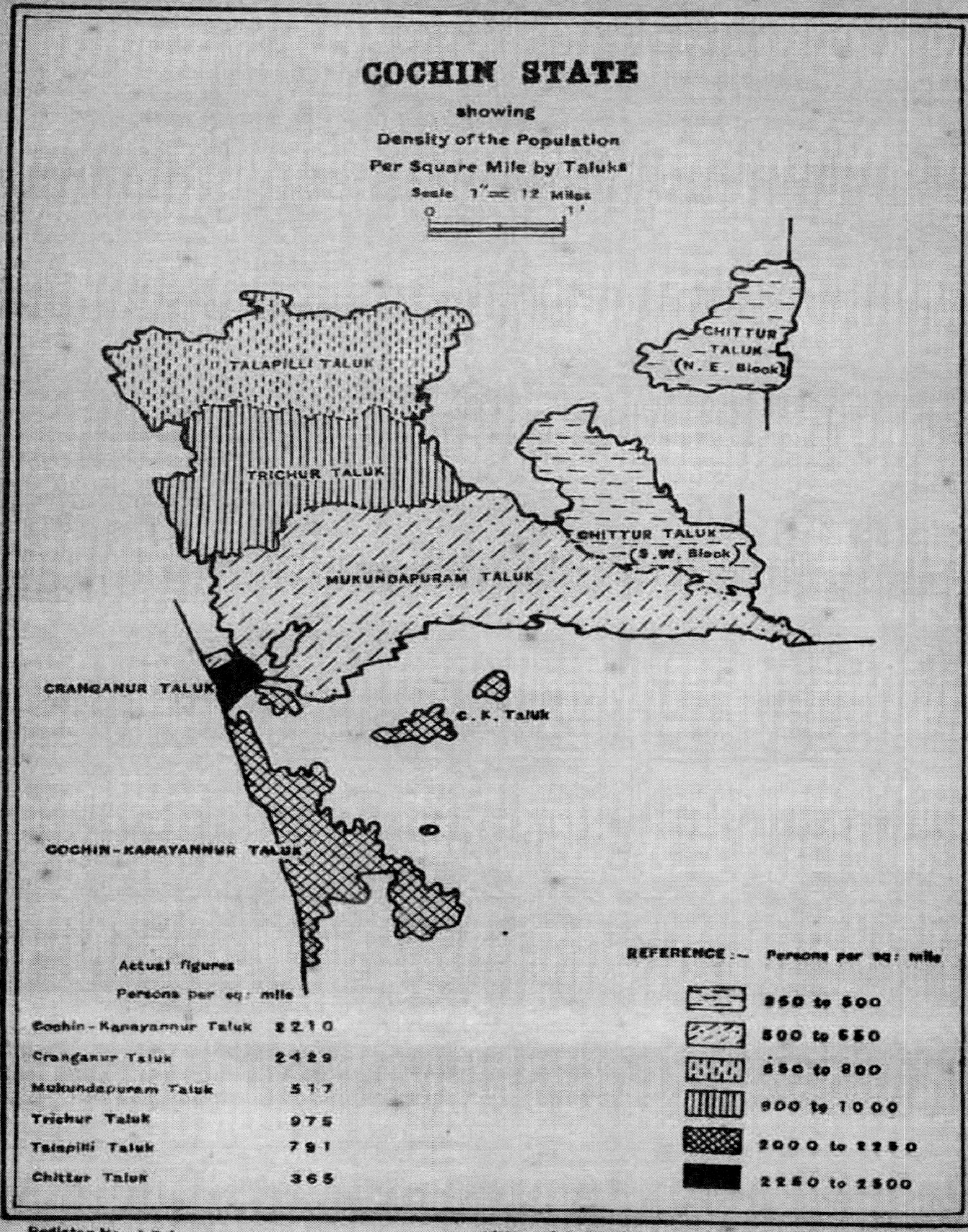

Register No. 124
Copies 850

Litho print Survey & Land Records Office, Trichur
1107

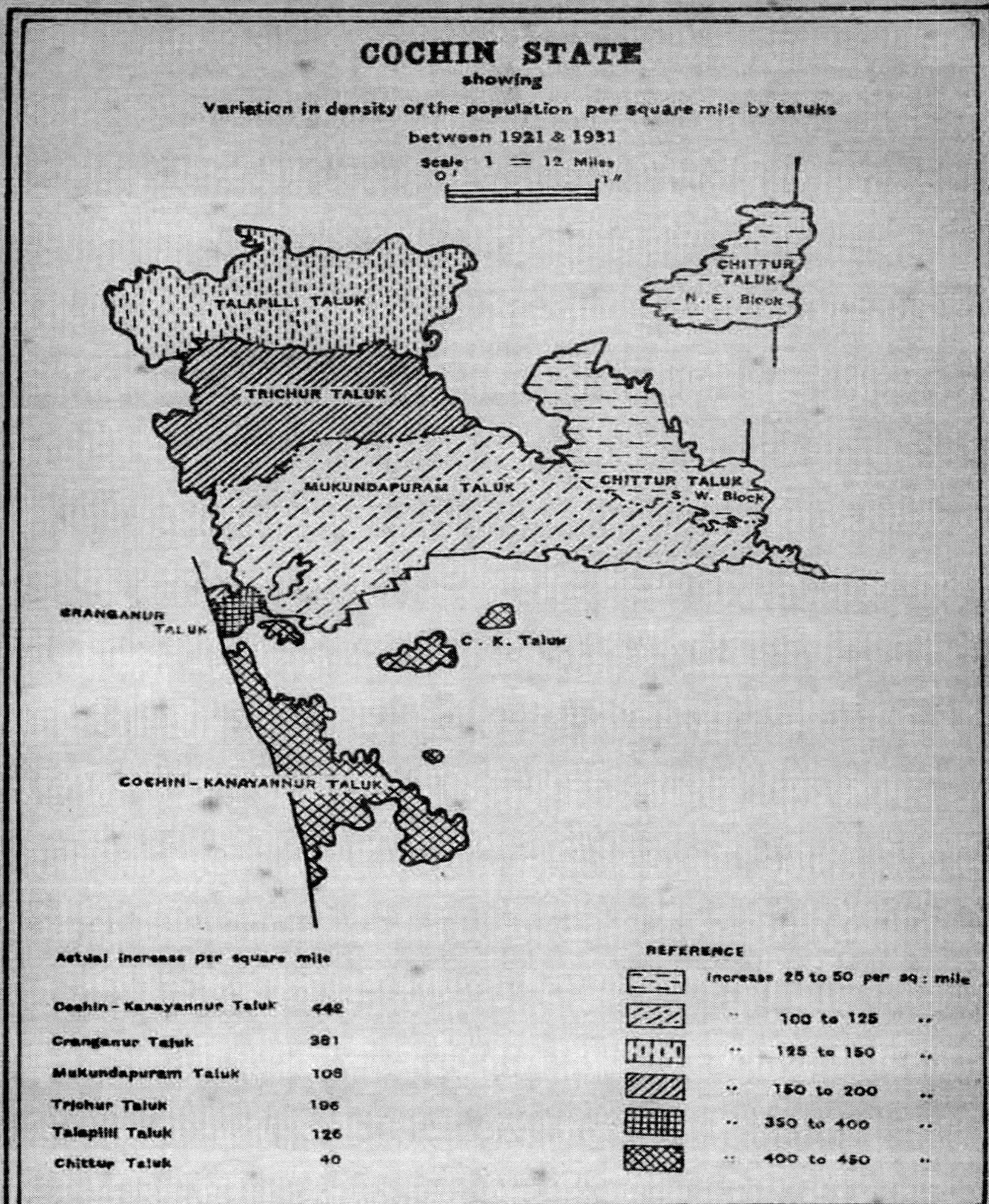

Register No. 127
Copies 850

Litho Print Survey & Land Records Office, Trichur.
1107.

massed in a division which covers but less than one-eighth of the total area of the State. If we revert to the administrative divisions of 1901 when Cochin and Kanayannur were separate taluks, we shall find that Cochin, lying wholly on the sea-board like Cranganur and having an area of 66 square miles, takes the first place with a phenomenal density of 2,723, Cranganur receding to the second place. And the old Kanayannur taluk with an area of 92 square miles will, in spite of its sparsely peopled upland tracts, still have 1,840 persons to the square mile and occupy the third place in the scale of density.

The most densely peopled taluk in Travancore is the taluk of Trivandrum in the Southern Division. It has an area of 92 square miles and its density of 2,336 places it below Cochin and Cranganur.

and villages

31. If a whole taluk has a mean density of over 2,700 per square mile, the density of some of the villages in that taluk must naturally be still higher. And this is what we actually find in the sea-board tract. The narrow strip of land lying between the Arabian Sea on the west and the backwaters on the east is most densely packed. The village of Elankunnapuzha in Cochin taluk with an area of 3·8 square miles has no less than 4,090 persons to the square mile. Other villages of about the same or even larger area follow close behind with densities ranging between 3,500 and 4,000. The villages on the mainland in Kanayannur taluk washed by the backwaters on the west are also very densely peopled, some of them having a density of about 2,500.

Density of the sea board tract excluding uninhabitable area

32. If the uninhabitable area occupied by the lagoons is deducted from the coastal tract and the density calculated on the basis of the inhabitable area only, Cochin will have 3,472, Cranganur 2,700, and Kanayannur 2,233 persons per square mile, with an average density of 2,733 for the three taluks together. The figures will speak for themselves and give us an idea of the overcrowding in this tract.

Density of forest taluks

33. Compared with the sea-board area, the forest taluks are to be regarded as sparsely peopled. These taluks comprise more than seven-eighths of the State's area, and yet they contain but two-thirds of the total population. Their mean density is only 623 against 2,232 in the coastal taluks. The specific population of Mukundapuram, the biggest of the taluks, is 263,722. Trichur has a population of 239,257, Talapilli 202,424 and Chittur 106,814. Of these Trichur, which has the smallest forest area, has the highest density with 975 persons to the square mile. Talapilli stands next with 791, Mukundapuram with the largest forest area follows with 517, while Chittur comes last with only 365 per square mile. If due allowance is made for the forest areas in each taluk, it will be seen that, the conditions in Mukundapuram, Trichur and Talapilli being mostly similar, the distribution of population and density in these three taluks are more or less uniform. But even when the uninhabitable forest tracts are excluded for purposes of calculation, the mean density per square mile of the four forest taluks is seen to be only 1,126 while the density of the coastal taluks calculated in the same manner is 2,733 as we have seen from the preceding paragraph.

Difference in density between the sea-board and the interior explained

34. The reasons for this marked disparity in the distribution of population between the sea-board and forest taluks have been fully explained in the Census Reports of 1901 and 1911. But for the small area occupied by the lagoons, the former taluks comprise extensive cocoanut gardens thickly dotted with houses, the cultivation of cocoanut trees not interfering with the rearing of homesteads in their midst. " The various industries in connection with the

cultivation of the cocoanut palm, the rich fisheries of the sea and the lagoons, the fertile rice fields on the margin of the latter, and the multifarious occupations of a commercial and maritime tract" can afford to maintain in a fair degree of comfort a population so densely packed that it must inevitably starve in less favoured regions. In the forest taluks the inhabitable area is only less than two-fifths of their total area. These taluks depend mainly on rice cultivation for the support of their population and they contain extensive rice fields in which no houses can be reared. The cultivation of rice in a given area, involving as it does more capital and labour than the cultivation of the cocoanut palm, cannot find occupation for, or supply means of livelihood to, as many people as may be maintained in an equal area on the sea-board with its cocoanut plantations, fisheries and other facilities. The rise in density in the several taluks from decade to decade has been influenced by the same considerations and Subsidiary Table III shows, and diagram G illustrates, that the variation in density for the last 50 years has been an increase per square mile of 1,083 in Cochin-Kanayannur (1,369 in Cochin and 877 in Kanayannur,) 1,233 in Cranganur, 291 in Mukundapuram, 549 in Trichur, 349 in Talapilli and 134 in Chittur, the increase in the coastal taluks being much higher than in the forest taluks. The relative position of the taluks in the scale of density has also been maintained almost intact throughout the period.

Variation in population by taluks

35. If we now examine the variation in population in relation to density as illustrated in Subsidiary Table III, it will be seen that no correspondence or relation exists between the density of population and the variation in population in most of the taluks. Thus while Chittur with the lowest density has the lowest rate of increase (12·2 per cent) for the intercensal period, Mukundapuram, which is the last but one in respect of density, shows the highest percentage of increase (26·4 per cent) for the same period. The coastal taluk of Cochin-Kanayannur and the forest taluk of Trichur both register an increase of 25·4 per cent. Cranganur takes the fourth place, with an increase of 22·2 per cent though it stands first in the scale of density. And Talapilli follows Cranganur, its rate of increase being 19 per cent. The marginal statement gives the relative position of these taluks in respect of the increase in population as compared with their relative position in respect of density. And the map facing this page shows for each taluk the variation in population between 1921 and 1931.

Taluk	Rank according to	
	Density of population	Increase in population
Cochin-Kanayannur ..	2	2
Cranganur ..	1	4
Mukundapuram ..	5	1
Trichur ..	3	2
Talapilli ..	4	5
Chittur ..	6	6

Reasons for the varying rate of increase

36. An explanation for this varying rate of increase in the several taluks is not hard to find. We have seen that the increase in Mukundapuram, Cochin-Kanayannur and Trichur is higher than the average increase of 23·1 per cent for the State as a whole. And though Cranganur stands below the average, still its increase of 22·2 per cent is very high. The exceptional facilities enjoyed by the coastal taluks of Cochin-Kanayannur and Cranganur have already been explained in paragraph 33 above.' Besides, the improvement in agricultural conditions in Cochin-Kanayannur during the past decade is noteworthy in that 68·4 per cent of the area under cultivation came to be irrigated against 18·5 per cent in the previous decade. The presence of a fine natural harbour at Cochin is a valuable asset to Cochin-Kanayannur and the commercial importance of Cochin is growing fast with the development of this harbour. The numerous rice and oil mills

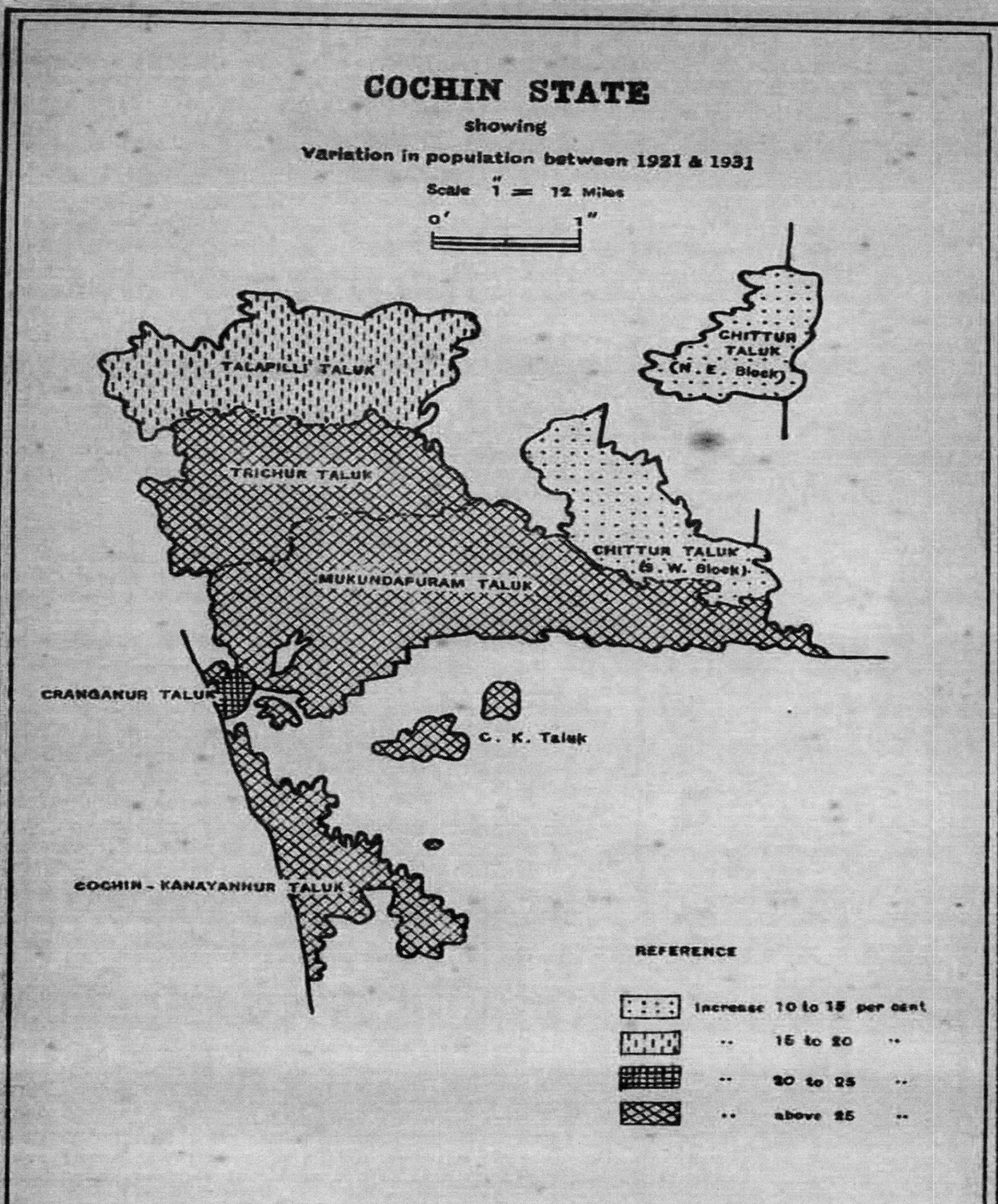

Register No. 126
Copies 850

Litho Print Survey & Land Records Office, Trichur.
1107.

DIAGRAM. G

Density of Population by Taluks 1881 - 1931

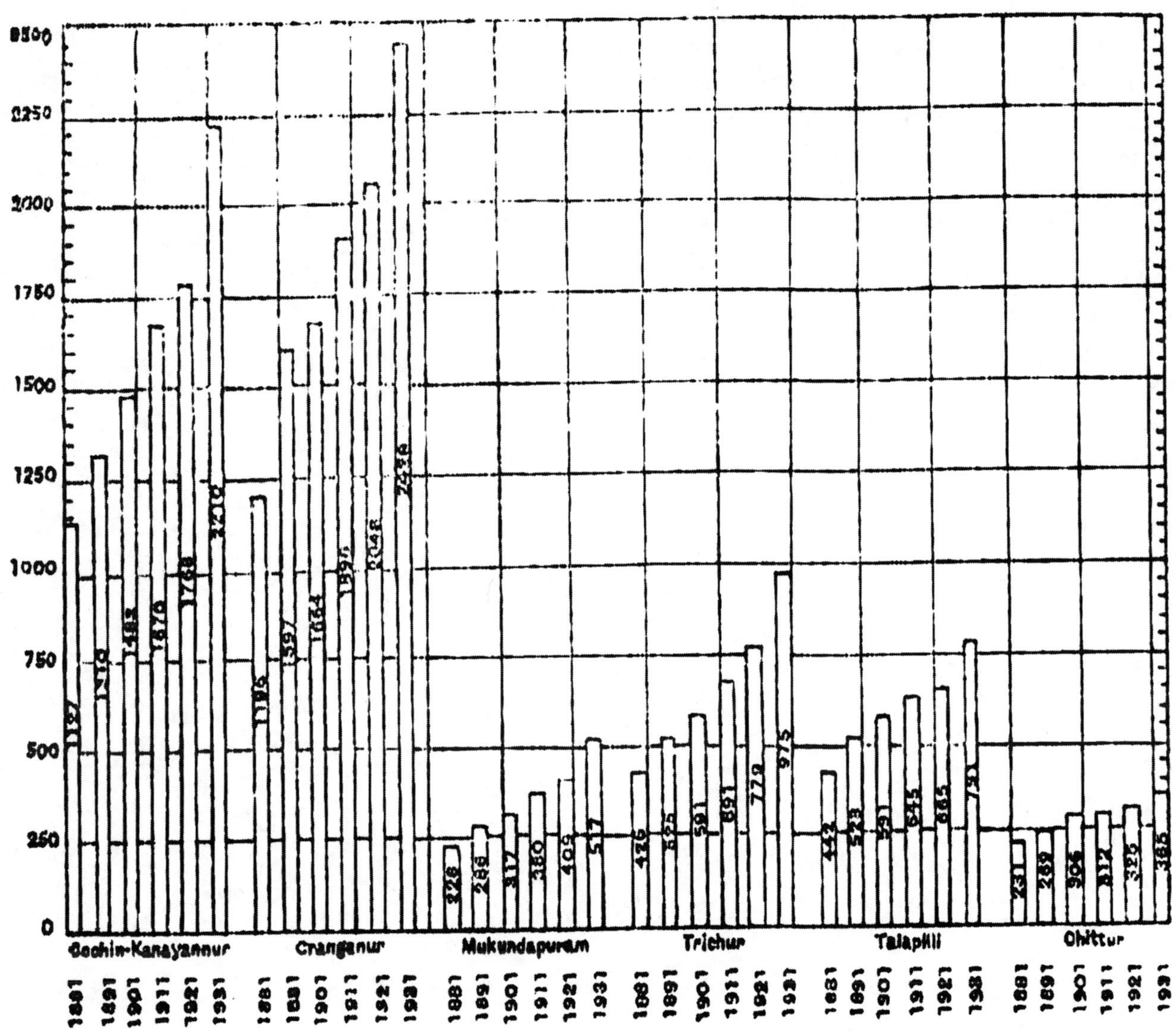

DIAGRAM. H

Density of Population by Taluks 1931

(Cochin & Kanayannur shown separately)

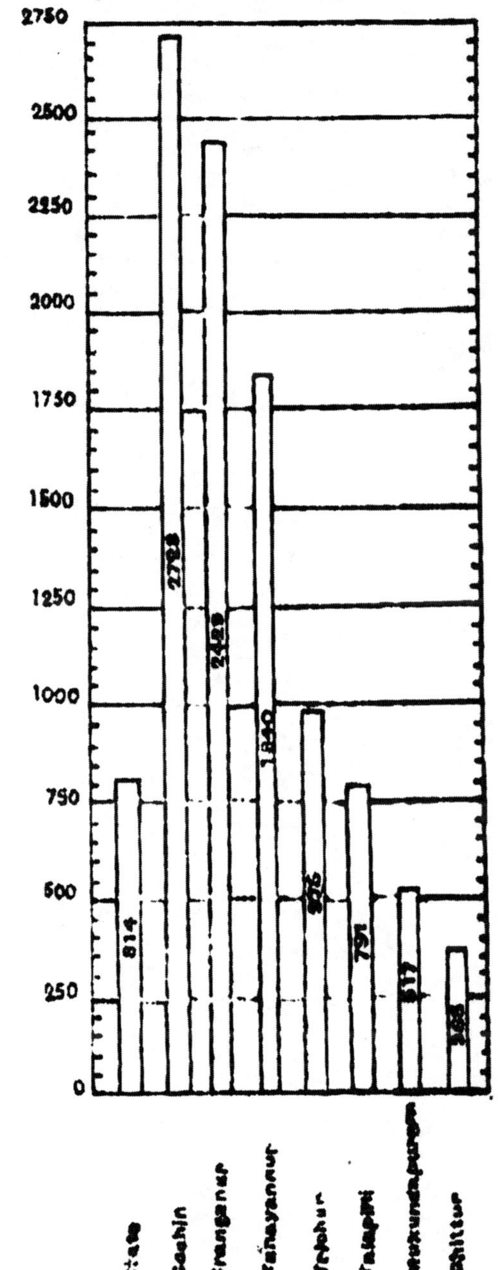

of Mattancheri and Ernakulam are indications of the industrial progress of this taluk. As additional attractions to the taluk, the capital of the State and the residence of His Highness the Maharaja are both here. It is therefore no wonder that the population of the taluk has been growing at an almost appalling rate in spite of its already enormous density. Trichur, the head-quarters of Trichur Taluk, is an important centre of trade. There are many brick and tile factories and rice mills in the taluk. The spinning and weaving mill at Trichur is a growing industrial concern. As in Cochin-Kanayannur, here too we have indications of industrial progress and the taluk is developing both agricultural and non-agricultural resources for the support of its rapidly increasing population. Mukundapuram too has its rice mills and tile factories. Besides, planting industry is carried on in its forest tracts on a large scale, as a result of which there are many estates and plantations in this taluk. And it is most significant that, while only 24·2 per cent of the cultivated area in the taluk was irrigated in 1921, the whole area under cultivation came to be irrigated in the course of the last 10 years. The very high rate of increase in Mukundapuram is not therefore unaccountable. Talapilli taluk being mainly agricultural, the developments characteristic of Mukundapuram and Trichur are absent in it, and naturally the increase in the population of this taluk is lower than the average increase for the State.

The half-detached and scattered taluk of Chittur does not conform to the standards of the other five taluks of the State. The scanty rainfall, the extensive forest area and the scourge of malaria characteristic of Chittur have turned it into an unhealthy and uncongenial tract where the density of population and the rate of increase in population are both very low. The unfavourable conditions are perhaps more marked in the north-east block of the taluk in the Tamil-Malayalam cultural border zone, lying detached from the rest of the State.

Net variation in population for the last 50 years

37. The net increase in population in the several taluks for the last 50 years is not at variance with these conclusions. The increase for the State as a whole during this period is 100·7 per cent. Mukundapuram and Trichur stand above this average with an increase of over 128 per cent. Cranganur and Cochin-Kanayannur come next with variations approximating to the State average. In view of the very high density of population in these two taluks it is not surprising that they have not kept pace with Mukundapuram and Trichur. The increase in Talapilli is only 79 per cent and, as may be expected, Chittur comes last with an increase of only 57·8 per cent.

Distribution of population by taluks according to density

38. Subsidiary Table II shows that 8·9 per cent of the population now live in taluks where the density is between 300 and 450 per square mile and 21·9 per cent in taluks having 450 to 600 persons to the square mile whereas, in 1921, 31 per cent of the population lived in taluks with a density of 300 to 450. At the last census 17·4 per cent of the population lived in taluks which had 600 to 750 persons per square mile, and 19·5 per cent in taluks where there were 750 to 900 persons to the square mile. But now we have 16·8 per cent living in taluks with a density of 750 to 900 and 19·8 per cent living in taluks where the density is 900 to 1,050. The percentage of population living in the most densely peopled taluks is seen to have remained constant at about 33 ever since 1875 when the first systematic census of the people was taken. The sum total of the changes in distribution noted above is that the percentage living in sparsely populated taluks has decreased during the last ten years.

Factors determining future variations:

39. The factors that are to determine the probable future trend of population in this State may now be examined so that we may form some rough

present economic depression

estimate of our population as it will stand at the close of the current decade. In the first place there are certain considerations of a temporary character to be dealt with in this connection. The new decade has opened inauspiciously (or shall we say auspiciously in view of the fact that any further increase in the State's population is not likely to prove an unmixed blessing?) with an economic depression the depth of which has not yet been fathomed. We have been living through the dark night of acute distress. And though a stricken and paralysed world has been anxiously watching for the dawn of the era of economic recovery, there is as yet hardly any streak of light visible on the horizon. In the absence of an early improvement in economic conditions, this distress cannot but react on the normal rate of growth in population.

and epidemics

It has already been remarked that small-pox appeared in an epidemic form during the closing years of the last decade. This epidemic has been wide-spread and fatal in 1931 and 1932 and the mortality from small-pox has already led to a perceptible rise in the death-rate.

Pressure of population

40. There is then the important question of pressure of population and the room for further expansion to be considered. It was remarked in paragraph 23 above that the adverse effects of over-crowding and of the pressure of population on the means of subsistence have not hitherto been felt to any considerable extent. The abstract figures of density and particularly the figures for the coastal tract may, in themselves, be frightening. But the material resources of the area have been sufficient for the support of its population till now. And there is apparently no reason why further development of these resources should not maintain larger numbers. At the same time it must not be forgotten that the statistics of migration discussed in Chapter III are not without signs to show that the stream of emigration is gradually swelling and that its sluggish current may, at no distant date, pass the limits of the level and stagnant plains of economic comfort and independence and enter uneven ground to gather force and velocity in its attempts to find a suitable outlet for the increasing volume of waters.

Possibilities of industrial and commercial development and likely increase in population

41. Lastly there are the unlimited possibilities of industrial and commercial development connected with the improvement of the Cochin harbour. In view of the size of its inner harbour, its geographical situation and the rich hinterland it will serve, Cochin must rank as one of the most important and flourishing sea ports in all India when the work of developing the harbour is completed. The proposed conversion of the present metre gauge railway in the State into the broad gauge will connect Ernakulam and Cochin with the broad gauge lines of South India and very much facilitate transport and communication. The towns of Mattancheri and Ernakulam are certain to grow in importance. The rate of increase in population in the sea-board taluks is therefore likely to rise above the normal. Nor can the developments connected with the harbour and the railway fail to influence, at least to a certain extent, the taluks of Mukundapuram, Trichur and Talapilli. It is therefore not improbable that, in the absence of any unforeseen circumstances of an exceptional character, the next census may record a further increase in population despite the present adverse conditions and the already high density, particularly in view of the fact that artificial methods of keeping down the population like abortion, neglect of infant life or the adoption of modern devices of 'birth-control', are almost unknown in this land.

Houses and families: house defined

42. As at previous censuses a house was defined to be "the dwelling place of one or more families with their resident servants, having a separate

principal entrance from the common way." The definition has been elastic enough to be extended to the princely mansions of the richest classes and the flimsy, thatched huts of the humble, labouring classes. And, as the single homestead in separate premises occupied by a joint family is the general rule on the Malabar coast, the application of this definition does not present any great difficulty except in crowded places where houses are built on the street system. The orthodox type of Malayali house, the quadrangular building with an open yard in the centre and a clean court-yard all around, surrounded by a compound in which fruit trees and vegetables are grown, is fully described in the Census Reports of 1901 and 1911. The improvement in the planning and construction of buildings noticed in 1921 has been steadily maintained and many new and better types of buildings have accordingly come into existence.

Increase in houses during the decade

43. Imperial Table I shows the number of occupied houses in the State and in each of its divisions and Subsidiary Table VII gives the average number of persons per occupied house and the average number of houses per square mile since 1881. The total number of houses returned in 1931 is 242,267 of which 207,563 were occupied and 34,704 unoccupied houses, the latter consisting chiefly of shops, public buildings and places of worship. The corresponding figures for 1921 were 178,211 occupied and 30,707 unoccupied houses. Occupied houses thus show an increase of 29,352 or 16·47 per cent for the decade whereas the increase in unoccupied houses is 3,997 or only 13 per cent for the same period. Of the unoccupied buildings 3,119 are places of worship.

lower than usual

The proportion between the rate of increase in occupied houses and the rate of increase in population at successive censuses (given in the marginal statement to paragraph 20 above) has been slightly upset during the decade under review, the increase in occupied houses being lower than usual when compared with the increase in population. This is in all probability to be attributed to the short-counting of population at the last census. From the operation of the new Nayar Regulation of 1921 which facilitated the partition of joint Nayar families, a large increase in occupied houses was anticipated in the Census Report of 1921. Hundreds of families have been partitioned during the last ten years but the anticipated increase in occupied houses is not seen apparently because the divided branches, each setting up for itself, found their resources too slender to afford the luxury of new houses and had perforce to be satisfied with such buildings as they might have received for their share at the partition.

House-room

44. As the rate of increase in occupied houses is lower than the rate of increase in population, there is a rise in the average number of persons per occupied house in the State. The 1931 average for the State is 5·8 against 5·5, 5·6 and 5·6 in 1921, 1911 and 1901 respectively. All taluks share in this rise in the average, as seen from Subsidiary Table VII.

Comparison with Travancore, Malabar, &c.

45. As against the increase in occupied houses of 16·47 per cent in Cochin, Travancore has 22·1 per cent, Malabar 9 per cent and the Madras Presidency 11 per cent. The average number of persons per occupied house is 5·5 in Travancore, 5·7 in Malabar and 5 in the Presidency as a whole. The low average in the Presidency does not necessarily indicate a higher standard of living or greater degree of comfort enjoyed by the people. For the Malayali system of each house being built in separate premises with its court-yard and compound relieves congestion and gives more house-room and comfort than the street system of houses on the other side of the Ghats.

House-room in towns and in villages

46. Of the occupied houses, 32,506 or 15·7 per cent are in towns and the rest in villages. The number of persons per occupied house in towns is 6·3 and in villages 5·7. The corresponding figures for Travancore are 5·9 and 5·4 and for Malabar 6·8 and 5·6 respectively. Among the towns, Ernakulam has the highest average of 7 persons per house while certain wards in Ernakulam and Mattancheri are very much crowded and have as many as 8 persons to a house. At the same time there are some villages in Mukundapuram and Trichur where the average rises almost to 7.

Size of families

47. The average number of persons per occupied house cannot be taken as an indication of the size of families. For according to the joint family system obtaining in Malabar, the average strength of a family is much higher.

Houses per square mile

48. Subsidiary Table VII reveals a steady increase from decade to decade in the number of houses per square mile in most taluks of the State. In 1881 the average number per square mile was 84·7 for the whole State while, in 1931, it is 140·2, the increase for 50 years being 55·5. Travancore has 122, Malabar 107·7 and the Presidency as a whole 64·9 houses to the square mile according to the 1931 census. The average per square mile in the several taluks varies according to density, Cranganur leading with 431·4 and Chittur bringing up the rear with 70·4.

SUBSIDIARY TABLES.

I.—Density, Water supply and crops.

Natural Division "Malabar and Konkan"	Mean density per square mile in 1931.	Percentage of total area		Percentage of cultivated area which is irrigated.	Normal rainfall.	Percentage of cultivated area under			
		Cultivable	Cultivated			Rice	Wheat	Pulses	Other crops.
1	2	3	4	5	6	7	8	9	10
COCHIN STATE ..	814	54.2	51.7	63.2	117.8	64.2	..	1.8	34.0
Cochin-Kanayannur ..	2,210	74.6	74.4	68.4	121.6	42.5	..	..	57.5
Cranganur ..	2,429	85.4	85.4	0.1	124.8	29.5	..	..	70.5
Mukundapuram ..	517	41.3	41.0	100.0	143.5	54.3	..	2.6	43.1
Trichur ..	975	65.4	60.7	50.2	119.3	95.1	..	0.7	1.2
Talapilli ..	791	68.8	63.1	44.2	126.0	60.9	..	1.0	38.1
Chittur ..	365	41.3	38.6	42.2	71.8	70.8	..	5.1	24.1

II.—Distribution of the population classified according to Density.

Natural Division "Malabar and Konkan"	Taluks with a population per square mile of													
	Under 300		300—450		450—600		600—750		750—900		900—1,050		2,200 and over	
	Area	Population 000's omitted	Area	Population 000's omitted	Area	Population 000's omitted	Area	Population 000's omitted	Area	Population 000's omitted	Area	Population 000's omitted	Area	Population 000's omitted
1	2	3	4	5	6	7	8	9	10	11	12	13	14	15
COCHIN STATE ..	.. ..	.. ..	292.75 19.8	107 8.9	510.00 34.4	264 21.9	.. ..	.. ..	256.00 17.3	202 16.8	245.50 16.6	239 19.8	176.03 11.9	393 32.6
Cochin-Kanayannur ..	.. ..	.. ..	.. ..	.. ..	.. ..	.. ..	.. ..	.. ..	.. ..	.. ..	.. ..	.. ..	158.52 10.7	350 29.1
Cranganur ..	.. ..	.. ..	.. ..	.. ..	.. ..	.. ..	.. ..	.. ..	.. ..	.. ..	.. ..	.. ..	17.51 1.2	43 3.5
Mukundapuram ..	.. ..	.. ..	.. ..	.. ..	510.00 34.4	264 21.9	.. ..	.. ..	.. ..	.. ..	.. ..	.. ..	.. ..	.. ..
Trichur ..	.. ..	.. ..	.. ..	.. ..	.. ..	.. ..	.. ..	.. ..	.. ..	.. ..	245.50 16.6	239 19.8	.. ..	.. ..
Talapilli ..	.. ..	.. ..	.. ..	.. ..	.. ..	.. ..	.. ..	.. ..	256.00 17.3	202 16.8	.. ..	.. ..	.. ..	.. ..
Chittur ..	.. ..	.. ..	292.75 19.8	107 8.9	.. ..	.. ..	.. ..	.. ..	.. ..	.. ..	.. ..	.. ..	.. ..	.. ..

III.—Variation in relation to Density since 1881.

Natural Division "Malabar and Konkan"	Percentage of variation Increase (+) Decrease (—)					Net variation 1881 to 1931	Mean density per square mile						Variation of mean density per square mile from 1881 to 1931
	1921 to 1931	1911 to 1921	1901 to 1911	1891 to 1901	1881 to 1891		1931	1921	1911	1921	1891	1881	
1	2	3	4	5	6	7	8	9	10	11	12	13	14
COCHIN STATE ..	+23.1	+0.6	+13.1	+12.3	+20.4	+100.7	814	662	620	549	488	406	408
Cochin-Kanayannur ..	+25.4	+5.5	+12.6	+13.2	+16.2	+96.1	2,210	1,768	1,670	1,483	1,310	1,127	1,083
Cranganur ..	+22.2	+4.9	+13.9	+4.2	+33.5	+193.0	2,429	2,048	1,896	1,664	1,597	1,196	1,233
Mukundapuram ..	+26.4	+7.6	+10.8	+11.1	+26.4	+128.9	517	400	350	317	286	226	291
Trichur ..	+25.4	+12.4	+17.0	+12.5	+23.2	+128.5	975	779	691	591	535	426	549
Talapilli ..	+19.0	+3.1	+9.1	+13.0	+18.4	+79.0	791	665	645	591	523	442	349
Chittur ..	+12.2	+4.3	+1.9	+13.7	+16.4	+57.8	365	325	312	306	269	231	134

The figures for 1911, 1901, 1891 and 1881 have been revised. They are based on the revised area of 1,480 square miles.

IV.—Variation in Natural Population.

Natural Division "Malabar and Konkan"	Population in 1931				Population in 1921				Variation per cent (1921-1931) in Natural Population Increase(+) Decrease(—)
	Actual Population	Immigrants	Emigrants	Natural Population	Actual Population	Immigrants	Emigrants	Natural Population	
1	2	3	4	5	6	7	8	9	10
Cochin State ..	1,205,016	87,417	48,168	1,165,767	979,080	39,759	23,512	962,833	+ 21.1

V.—Comparison with Vital Statistics.

Natural Division "Malabar and Konkan"	In 1921–1930. Total number of					
	Births			Deaths		
	Total	Male	Female	Total	Male	Female
1	2	3	4	5	6	7
Cochin State ..	142,516	73,361	69,155	91,233	48,097	43,136

Number per cent of population of 1921 of						Excess (+) or Deficiency (—) of births over deaths			Increase (+) or Decrease (—) of population of 1931 compared with 1921	
Births			Deaths							
Total	Male	Female	Total	Male	Female	Total	Male	Female	Natural Population	Actual Population
8	9	10	11	12	13	14	15	16	17	18
14·6	15·2	13·9	9·3	10·0	8·7	+ 51,283	+ 25,264	+ 26,019	+ 202,934	+ 225,936

VI.—Variation by Taluks classified according to Density.

(A) Actual Figures.

Natural Division "Malabar and Konkan"	Decade	Variation in Taluks with a population per square mile at commencement of decade of						
		Under 300	300 to 450	450 to 600	600 to 750	750 to 900	900 to 1050	1050 and over
1	2	3	4	5	6	7	8	9
COCHIN STATE ..	1921—1931	..	+11,606	+55,009	..	+32,270	+48,444	+78,607
	1911—1921	..	+3,919	+14,783	+5,040	+21,057	..	+16,171
Cochin-Kanayannur ..	1921—1931	..	..	..	..	..	..	+70,884
	1911—1921	..	..	..	..	..	..	+14,556
Cranganur ..	1921—1931	..	..	..	..	..	..	+7,723
	1911—1921	..	..	..	..	..	..	+1,615
Mukundapuram ..	1921—1931	..	..	+55,009	..	..	..	..
	1911—1921	..	..	+14,783	..	..	..	..
Trichur ..	1921—1931	..	..	..	..	..	+48,444	..
	1911—1921	..	..	..	..	+21,057	..	..
Talapilli ..	1921—1931	..	..	..	..	+32,270	..	..
	1911—1921	..	..	..	+5,040	..	..	..
Chittur ..	1921—1931	..	+11,606	..	..	..	..	..
	1911—1921	..	+3,919	..	..	..	..	..

VI.—Variation by Taluks classified according to Density.

(B) Proportional Figures.

Natural Division "Malabar and Konkan"	Decade	Variation per cent in Taluks with a population per square mile at commencement of decade of						
		Under 300	300 to 450	450 to 600	600 to 750	750 to 900	900 to 1050	1050 and over
1	2	3	4	5	6	7	8	9
COCHIN STATE ..	1921—1931	..	+12·2	+26·4	..	+19·0	+25·4	+25·0
	1911—1921	..	+4·3	+7·6	+3·1	+12·4	..	+5·4
Cochin-Kanayannur ..	1921—1931	..	..	..	..	..	..	+25·4
	1911—1921	..	..	..	..	..	..	+5·5
Cranganur ..	1921—1931	..	..	..	..	..	..	+22·2
	1911—1921	..	..	..	..	..	..	+4·9
Mukundapuram ..	1921—1931	..	..	+26·4	..	..	..	..
	1911—1921	..	..	+7·6	..	..	..	..
Trichur ..	1921—1931	..	..	..	..	..	+25·4	..
	1911—1921	..	..	..	..	+12·4	..	..
Talapilli ..	1921—1931	..	..	..	..	+19·0	..	..
	1911—1921	..	..	..	+3·1	..	..	..
Chittur ..	1921—1931	..	+12·2	..	..	..	..	..
	1911—1921	..	+4·3	..	..	..	..	..

VII.—Persons per house and houses per square mile.

Natural Division "Malabar and Konkan"	Average number of persons per house						Average number of houses per square mile					
	1931	1921	1911	1901	1891	1881	1931	1921	1911	1901	1891	1881
1	2	3	4	5	6	7	8	9	10	11	12	13
COCHIN STATE ..	5·8	5·5	5·6	5·6	5·4	4·8	140·2	120·5	110·3	98·6	90·0	84·7
Cochin-Kanayannur ..	5·8	5·4	5·5	5·5	5·2	4·5	378·2	326·7	303·3	269·3	252·3	248·5
Cranganur ..	5·6	5·3	5·4	5·2	5·5	4·6	431·4	372·9	349·0	317·3	288·7	258·0
Mukundapuram ..	5·9	5·5	5·7	5·6	5·5	4·7	88·0	74·1	66·9	57·1	51·7	47·5
Trichur ..	6·1	5·8	5·9	5·8	6·0	5·3	159·9	134·1	116·1	101·3	87·2	80·8
Talapilli ..	5·7	5·6	5·8	5·7	5·8	5·1	137·9	119·3	111·0	102·7	90·5	85·8
Chittur ..	5·2	5·0	5·0	5·1	4·6	4·1	70·4	64·5	61·7	59·4	58·7	52·4

CHAPTER II.—THE POPULATION OF CITIES, TOWNS AND VILLAGES.

Reference to Statistics

THE urban population of the State is distinguished from its rural population in Imperial Table I. Imperial Table III contains the figures of the population living in towns and villages of different sizes. A list of towns classified by population with variations since 1881 is given in Imperial Table IV, and another list of these towns arranged territorially with the population classified by religion is contained in Imperial Table V. Three Subsidiary Tables are to be found at the end of this Chapter, the first showing the distribution of the population between towns and villages, the second giving the number per mille of the population and of each religion living in towns, and the third classifying towns by population.

Definitions & their application

2. The Imperial Code of Census Procedure defines a city as "every town containing not less than 100,000 inhabitants and any other town which the Provincial Superintendent, with the sanction of the Local Government, may decide to treat as a city for census purposes ; " and a town itself is to include "every municipality, all Civil lines not included within municipal limits, every cantonment and every other continuous collection of houses, inhabited by not less than 5,000 persons, which the Provincial Superintendent may decide to treat as a town for census purposes, having regard to the character of the population, the relative density of the dwellings, the importance of the place as a centre of trade, and its historic associations." According to this definition, nine places were treated as towns at the census of 1921, four municipalities and five non-municipal areas. At the present census three new places were added to this list—Narakkal, Chalakkudi and Vadakkancheri. In each case the area selected to be treated as a town is only about a square mile in extent, and the population of this area exceeds 5,000 in all the three places. Besides, Vadakkancheri, the head-quarters of Talapilli Taluk, has its public offices and courts, a Government Dispensary and a Government High School. And Ottupara suburb (included in the town) is a trading centre on a small scale. Chalakkudi is the junction of the State Railway and the Forest Tramway. The Office of the Conservator of Forests, the Tramway Engineer's Office, the Tramway Workshop and the Government Pottery works are at Chalakkudi which has its Government High School and Government Hospital also. Narakkal stands midway between Cranganur and Cochin on the coastal strip lying between the backwaters and the Arabian Sea. Instead of metalled roads it has only canals for purposes of communication and transport. But it is an important Christian centre with a Government High School, and a Government Dispensary for medical relief. And in addition to the cottage industries connected with the cocoanut palm, Narakkal has its fish-curing yards. It may be that the non-municipal towns of the State have fewer urban characteristics than the municipal towns, but they too have their own importance in that they primarily exist as the necessary market centres for the service of adjacent rural areas.

3. The marginal statement gives the percentages for five censuses of the population living in urban areas in Cochin, Travancore, Malabar and

Urban population compared with that of other States or Provinces

the Madras Presidency as a whole. It will be seen from the statement and from diagram A that the proportion of urban population in our State has been steadily growing and that it has risen from 7 per cent in 1891 to 17·1 per cent in 1931. And though Cochin cannot approach anywhere near the proportion of urban population in the industrial countries of Europe where more than three-fourths of the population live in towns, and though there are certain advanced States and Provinces in North India like Baroda and Ajmer-Merwara that show a higher proportion of urban population than Cochin, still it is ahead of its neighbours in Southern India.

Census year	Percentage of urban population in			
	Cochin	Travancore	Malabar	Madras Presidency
1891	7·0	4·2	7·3	9·5
1901	10·8	6·2	7·8	11·2
1911	12·0	6·2	8·0	11·8
1921	13·0	10·0	7·6	12·4
1931	17·1	10·8	7·7	13·6

Growth of population in towns

4. The urban population in the State numbered 127,141 in 1921 whereas it is 206,340 at present. This marks an increase of 62·3 per cent during the past decade. The percentage of increase in municipal towns alone is 50 and in non-municipal towns 97. Part of this large increase is due to the normal growth of the population of the old towns, but the major portion of it is to be attributed to the new areas treated as urban at the present census. In addition to the formation of three non-municipal towns referred to in paragraph 2 above, Trichur, Mattancheri and Ernakulam among the municipal towns and Trippunithura and Kunnamkulam among the non-municipal towns have extended their limits by the absorption of outlying suburbs. If the area newly treated as urban is deducted from the total urban area and the calculation confined to the urban area of 1921, the municipal towns will show an increase of about 21 per cent and the non-municipal towns about 25 per cent for the decade, and the average increase for both classes of towns together will be below 22 per cent while the State as a whole records an increase of 23·1 per cent. It will thus appear that the growth of population in municipal towns has not kept pace with the growth in rural tracts. But Ernakulam and Mattancheri have registered an increase of 33·5 and 27·8 per cent respectively on their 1921 area. The corresponding increase in Trichur is only 14·4 per cent against an average increase of 25·4 per cent for the whole taluk. The facts that the northern suburbs of Trichur town show a very high rate of growth (ranging from 30 to 35 per cent) and that most of the mill hands working within the town live outside the municipal limits are significant in this connection, and the wide prevalence of small-pox within the town at the time of the final census will further explain the low rate of increase. The municipal town of Chittur-Tattamangalam comes last with an increase of only 4·2 per cent against the average increase of 12 per cent for the taluk of Chittur. The adjoining villages have not fared better in this respect, the highest rate of growth recorded by them being only 6 per cent. Some of them even show an actual decrease in population. Malarial fever which has infected the whole area accounts for this state of affairs. Year after year it has been claiming its victims in increasing numbers. But for these exceptional circumstances the growth of population in towns would have been higher than in rural areas. And it will not be wrong to conclude that the facilities for higher education and medical relief and other amenities associated with urban life as also the higher wages available for labour have been attracting to the urban areas people of all grades in steadily increasing numbers.

B
Proportion per Mille of the Population of each Taluk living in

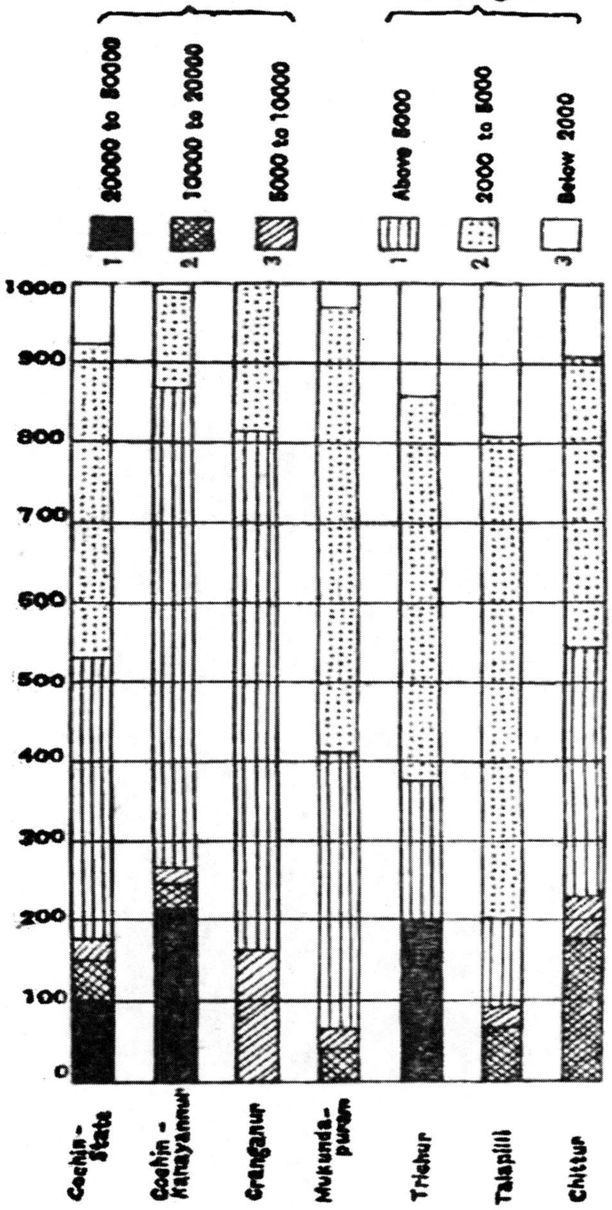

A
Proportion per cent of Rural & Urban Population to total Population at each census since 1891.

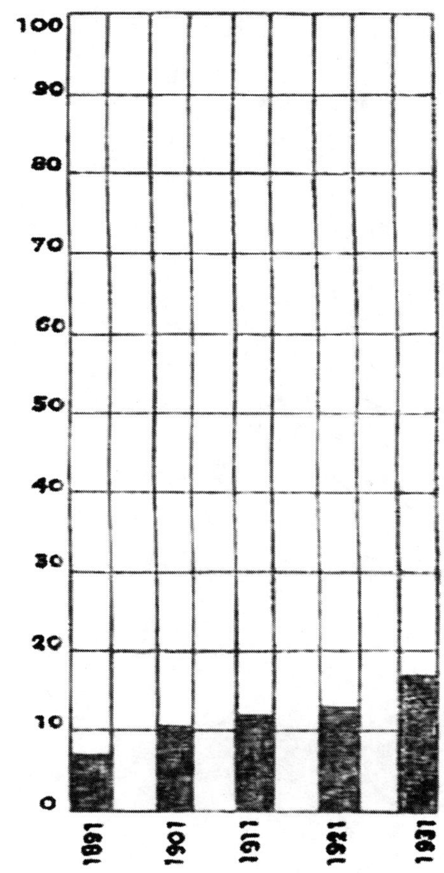

Urban population coloured black

	A			B		
	1.	2.	3.	1.	2.	3.
State	101.	45.	25	358	392.	79
Cochin Kanayannur	218.	31.	18.	605	117.	11
Cranganur	..	..	161.	652.	187.	..
Mukundapuram	..	42.	22.	348.	556.	32.
Trichur	191.	..	..	187	481.	141
Talapilli	..	68	26.	107.	608.	191
Chittur	..	177.	52.	318	361.	92

5. The appended statement gives the area, population and density of the towns. It will be seen therefrom that Mattancheri and Ernakulam, the commercial and political capitals of the State, which have recorded the highest increase in population among municipal towns, are the most congested. These towns are so situated that they have little scope for expansion and therefore they are likely to become more congested as they grow further in importance with the completion of the Cochin harbour works. The situation of Trichur on the other hand affords it exceptional facilities for extension, and it is likely to grow in future also as it has done in the past in view of its many-sided importance. The town has its historic associations. It is also the industrial, commercial and educational centre of the northern division of the State. And many departments of the Government have their head-quarters at Trichur. Among non-municipal towns Trippunittura, the seat of the Ruling Family, and Kunnamkulam, the most important town in Talapilli taluk and a flourishing Christian centre, are not only congested but have also recorded the highest growth. Area, population and density of towns

Town	Area in square miles	Population	Persons per square mile	Persons per acre
Trichur	4·87	45,658	9,375	14·7
Mattancheri	2·69	39,645	14,738	23·0
Ernakulam	3·12	36,638	11,743	18·3
Chittur-Tattamangalam	2·14	18,915	8,839	13·8
Kunnamkulam	1·89	13,822	7,313	11·5
Irinjalakkuda	2·02	11,047	5,442	8·6
Trippunithura	1·27	10,717	8,373	13·1
Cranganur	1·26	6,866	5,449	8·5
Narakkal	0·97	6,475	6,675	10·5
Chalakkudi	1·72	5,886	3,402	5·3
Nemmara	0·69	5,513	7,990	12·6
Vadakkancheri	1·25	5,158	4,126	6·4
Average ..	1·99	17,195	8 637	13·5

It will be instructive to compare the figures in the foregoing paragraph with similar figures for Travancore. There are 19 municipal and 27 non-municipal towns in Travancore against the 4 municipal and 8 non-municipal towns of our State. The total urban area in Cochin is 23·89 square miles while the corresponding area in Travancore is 171·76 square miles. The average population of a town here is 17,195 and the mean density 8,637, the corresponding figures for Travancore being only 11,995 and 3,213 respectively. Alleppy, the commercial capital of Travancore, has the highest density among the more important towns of that State. But even Alleppy is much less crowded than Mattancheri and Ernakulam, having only 15 persons per acre against 23 and 18·3 in Mattancheri and Ernakulam respectively.

6. From Imperial Table I it will be seen that Cochin-Kanayannur taluk with its four towns has the largest urban population in the State. Trichur with its only town comes next, Chittur, Talapilli and Mukundapuram with two towns each follow in due order, and Cranganur with its one town comes last. Subsidiary Table I and diagram B will show the proportion of the population of each taluk living in towns and villages of different sizes. Here too Cochin-Kanayannur is seen to have proportionately the largest urban population with 267 persons in every 1,000 living in towns, no doubt because Ernakulam and Mattancheri are both in this taluk. Next in order comes Chittur with 229 per mille of the population living in towns. The largest percentage of non-Malayali communities is to be found in Chittur and the presence of these people who like to congregate in towns gives the taluk its high proportion of urban population. Proportion of urban population in different taluks

After Chittur comes Trichur, and Cranganur, Talapilli and Mukundapuram follow with still lower proportions. The natural aversion of the purely Malayali Hindu castes for the congested life in towns, which has always stood against the growth of big towns in the State, is responsible for the low proportion of urban population in these taluks.

Distribution of urban population in towns according to their size

7. In 1921, 18·7 per cent of the urban population lived in towns containing a population of 5,000 to 10,000, 14·3 per cent in towns with a population of 10,000 to 20,000 and 59·6 per cent in towns having a population of over 20,000. The corresponding figures for 1931 are 14·5 per cent, 26·4 per cent and 59·1 per cent. The percentage of urban population living in small towns is thus seen to be lower than in 1921, because the towns have been growing rapidly.

Distribution of urban population by religion

8. The Census Report of 1911 refers to the growth of towns on the west coast as "mainly due to the habits of living and enterprise of native Christians, Muslims and non-indigenous Hindus, chiefly Tamil Brahmans, so that they preponderate over the indigenous Hindus in towns, specially in the more important ones." In the three most important towns of Mattancheri, Ernakulam and Trichur, the Hindus form but less than 50 per cent of the population though their proportion in the total population of the State is 64·8 per cent. If the Tamil and Konkani Brahmans and other non-Malayali Hindus are excluded, the proportion of the Hindu population in these towns will be seen to be very low indeed. And while 17·1 per cent of the total population of the State live in towns, it is noteworthy that 22 per cent of the Christians and 21 per cent of the Muslims but only 14·5 per cent of the Hindus of the State are residents of towns.

The census village

9. The census villages in the State are not residential units but only units of revenue administration. The villages on the Malabar coast form a class by themselves and are entirely different from the villages in other parts of South India. Except for a few bazaars, the street system of houses is not to be found on this coast where "the huddled squalor of the eastern villages gives place to the solid comfort and freedom of substantial homesteads, scattered over the country side," and where "each house, even the humblest, stands in its own little compound or garden, which is usually thickly planted with areca and cocoanut palms, jack trees, plantains, betel and pepper vines and the like."

Distribution of rural population in villages according to size

10. The State, exclusive of the unsurveyed forests, is divided into 273 revenue villages that are more or less uniform in size. The average area of a village will thus be 3·29 square miles. Each town, municipal or non-municipal, has been formed from areas selected out of two or three adjoining villages and as a result several of them have become very much attenuated. The village of Mattancheri in Cochin-Kanayannur taluk has been wholly absorbed in the municipal town of Mattancheri while Punkunnam village in Trichur taluk has all but disappeared, there being only a few uninhabited acres remaining in it after the extension of the limits of Trichur municipality. Of the remaining 271 villages, there are only seven with a population below 500 (three of these being only remnants left after the formation of towns,) and but 0·17 per cent of the State's rural population live in them. Fourteen villages out of which two are but scraps left by towns have between 500 and 1,000 inhabitants each and they contain 1·1 per cent of the rural population. There are 54 villages with a population ranging between 1,000 and 2,000 and 8·2 per cent of the rural population are to be found in them. 143 villages, thirteen of which have surrendered large areas to form towns, have two to five thousand inhabitants each and 46·34 per

cent of the State's rural population are grouped in these villages. Forty-three villages of which thirteen are in Cochin-Kanayannur and three in Cranganur contain between five and ten thousand inhabitants. Five of them have been reduced in size as a result of the formation of towns. The villages of this class account for 29·93 per cent of the rural population. Nine villages in Cochin-Kanayannur and one in Cranganur have a population of ten to twenty thousand and 13·23 per cent of the rural population live in them. It is villages of this class lying on the sea-board that are almost as much crowded as urban areas. And it is here that we find instances of rural tracts having a density of over 4,000 persons to the square mile.

SUBSIDIARY TABLES.

I.—*Distribution of the population between Towns and Villages.*

Natural Division "Malabar and Konkan"	Average population per		Number per mille residing in		Number per mille of urban population residing in towns with a population of				Number per mille of rural population residing in villages with a population of			
	Town	Village	Towns	Villages	20,000 and over	10,000 to 20,000	5,000 to 10,000	Under 5,000	5,000 and over	2,000 to 5,000	500 to 2,000	Under 500
1	2	3	4	5	6	7	8	9	10	11	12	13
COCHIN STATE.	17,195	3,685	171	829	591	264	145	..	441	462	95	2
Cochin-Kanayannur ..	23,369	7,133	267	733	816	115	69	..	829	156	15	..
Cranganur ..	6,866	7,133	161	839	..	..	1,000	..	783	217	..	..
Mukundapuram ..	8,467	4,113	64	936	..	652	348	..	397	568	35	..
Trichur ..	45,658	2,727	191	809	1,000	..	..	..	233	592	169	6
Talapilli ..	9,490	2,479	94	906	..	728	272	..	119	669	212	..
Chittur ..	12,214	3,295	229	771	..	774	226	..	426	451	115	8

II.—*Number per mille of the total population and of each main religion who live in towns.*

Natural Division "Malabar and Konkan"	Number per mille who live in towns							
	Total population	Hindu	Muslim	Christian	Jain	Jew	Buddhist	Zoroastrian
1	2	3	4	5	6	7	8	9
COCHIN STATE.	171	145	210	220	995	734	354	1,000
Cochin-Kanayannur ..	267	245	501	253	1,000	822	1,000	1,000
Cranganur ..	161	209	58	79	..	..	..	..
Mukundapuram ..	64	52	64	87	..	6	..	..
Trichur ..	191	138	226	310	..	..	326	..
Talapilli ..	94	63	58	285	..	..	..	..
Chittur ..	229	238	253	60	..	..	..	..

III.—Towns classified by population.

Class of Town	Number of towns of each class in 1931	Proportion (per mille) to total urban population	Number of females per 1,000 males	Increase per cent in the population of towns as classed at previous censuses: 1921 to 1931	1911 to 1921	1901 to 1911	1891 to 1901	1881 to 1891	Increase per cent in urban population of each class from 1881 to 1931: (a) in towns as classed in 1881	(b) in the total of each class in 1931 as compared with the corresponding total in 1881
1	2	3	4	5	6	7	8	9	10	11
Total ..	**12**	**1,000**	**980**	**48·5**	**10·4**	**25·7**	**18·8**	**15·7**	**+108·2**	**+224·0**
I. 100,000 and over ..	..	..	..	..	..	..	..	..	..	..
II. 50,000 to 100,000 ..	..	..	..	..	..	..	..	..	..	..
III. 20,000 to 50,000 ..	3	591	932	66·0	10·9	6·5	..	..	..	..
IV. 10,000 to 20,000 ..	4	264	1,061	4·2	..	51·3	19·7	17·5	+170·4	+4·6
V. 5,000 to 10,000 ..	5	145	1,040	33·5	5·5	6·0	16·9	11·5	+67·2	+352·6
VI. Under 5,000 ..	..	..	..	71·6	—4·8	..	..	13·9	+177·1	..

Note.—Subsidiary Table IV has not been prepared as there are no cities in the State.

CHAPTER III—BIRTH-PLACE AND MIGRATION.

Reference to statistics

THE statistics of birth-place are given in Imperial Table VI while the Subsidiary Tables at the end of this chapter summarise the salient features of these statistics thus:

Subsidiary Table I presents the actual figures of immigration into the State.

Subsidiary Table II is the complement of Table I and gives the actual figures of emigration from the State.

Subsidiary Table III shows the migration between Cochin and other parts of India and other countries.

A special enquiry was undertaken regarding emigration from the State and the results have been embodied in seven Special Tables reviewed at the end of this chapter.

Summary of Immigration statistics

2. According to these statistics, of the 1,205,016 persons enumerated in Cochin on the day of the final census as many as 1,117,599 or 927 per mille of the total population were born in the State. The remaining 87,417 persons (73 per mille of the total population) were immigrants from outside. The number of immigrants in 1921 was but 39,759 and there is therefore an increase of 119·9 per cent in immigrants during the decade. The proportion of outside-born persons in the State's population for four censuses is shown in the margin and it is seen that the figure for 1931 is by far the highest of the four.

Census year	1931	1921	1911	1901
Number of immigrants in every 1,000 of the total population.	73	41	50	62

Immigrants classified: the casual, temporary and periodic types

3. The large increase in the number of immigrants should not, however, lead us to the conclusion that Cochin had any superior or new attractions to tempt outsiders more than in the past. For, a classification of the immigrants according to their birth-place reveals the fact that 94·4 per cent of their total number corresponding to more than 68 per mille of the State's population are our next-door neighbours from Travancore (31,167), Coimbatore (4,909) and Malabar (46,415). They have therefore just stepped over the border. The fact that females preponderate in this class proves the *casual type* of this migration, which "arises largely from the very common practice amongst Hindus of taking a wife from another village, and from the fact that young married women often go to their parents' home for their first confinement." The majority of the immigrants from Coimbatore are labourers working in the tea, coffee or rubber estates of the Nelliampathi and other hills, and they therefore belong either to the *temporary* or the *periodic* type of migrants whose movements will be regulated by the temporary or periodic demands for labour. The immigrants from Travancore show an increase of 151·7 per cent during the intercensal period, those from Malabar an increase of 114·3 per cent and those from Coimbatore 110 per cent.

Immigrants from		No. of females to 100 males.
Travancore	..	154
Coimbatore	..	116
Malabar	..	115

The semi-permanent type

4. Of the total number of immigrants only 4,926 or 5·6 per cent remain to be accounted for. The adjacent districts of Madura, Salem, South Canara,

Tinnevelly and Trichinopoly claim more than half this number. The marginal table gives the specific figures and the sex proportion of the immigrants from these districts. The bulk of these people being men, it is clear that most of them belong to the *semi-permanent* class of migrants "who reside and earn their living in this State, but retain their connection with their own homes, where they leave their families and to which they return in their old age. and at more or less regular intervals in the meantime." The immigrants from South Canara and Tinnevelly are mostly Brahmans. The services of the Canarese Brahman or Embran have always been in demand in the Hindu temples of the State where they officiate as priests. As dealers in cotton fabrics and bankers the Tinnevelly Brahmans were connected with Cochin as with other parts of Malabar from early times; and, though they have been superseded to a great extent by others in their trade, there are still many interests binding them to the State. There is a certain amount of periodic immigration of labour from Salem and Madura, many of the coolies working in the Malakipara estate (adjoining the estates of the Anamalai hills in Coimbatore district,) having returned either of these districts as their birth-place. The immigrants from these five districts together form but little more than 2 per mille of the State's population.

District	No. of Immigrants	No. of females to 100 males.
Madura ..	353	87
Salem ..	470	80
South Canara ..	994	60
Tinnevelly ..	687	72
Trichinopoly ..	151	80

5. All other parts of India and foreign countries together claim but 2,271 immigrants (2·6 per cent of the total number). Of these 839 are from other parts of South India and 991 from the Bombay Presidency, Bombay States (Kathiawar) and Western India Agency (Cutch). The sex proportion among them shows that many of them are of the *semi-permanent* class of migrants though there are *permanent* settlers also among them. The most prominent merchants of Mattancheri are Baniyas and Muslims hailing from Bombay, Kathiawar and Cutch and most of them belong to the latter group. They have long been connected with the place and Mattancheri owes its commercial prosperity and importance almost entirely to these people. Permanent immigrants

District	No. of immigrants	No. of females to 100 males
Bombay Presidency ..	291	62
Bombay States (Kathiawar) ..	491	57
Western India Agency (Cutch) ..	209	87

6. Of the handful of foreign-born persons (203 in number) enumerated in Cochin, perhaps those from Ceylon and the Straits Settlements (62 and 48 respectively) are mostly the children of emigrants from the State, born to them during their sojourn in these foreign countries. Most of those from the United Kingdom and Ireland (38) are planters. Other European countries (30) have sent several Christian missionaries to Cochin. Immigrants from foreign countries

7. The statistics of persons born in Cochin and enumerated in other States or Provinces of India have been received from the Provincial Superintendents concerned. Ceylon, Borneo and Seychelles also have furnished statistics on the subject. But the figures for other countries are not available though it is well known that hundreds have emigrated to the Straits Settlements and Malaya and that at least a few scores of Cochin-born persons are to be found in other Asiatic countries, Africa and Europe. The results of the special enquiry regarding emigration throw some light on the subject and, as we shall presently Emigration statistics

see, they give rise to doubts about the accuracy of many of the figures furnished from other States and Provinces.

Summary of these statistics. emigrants to contiguous districts

8. Subsidiary Table II compiled from the figures obtained from outside gives 48,168 as the number of emigrants from Cochin. The corresponding figure for 1921 was 23,512 so that the emigrants have increased by 24,656 or 104·9 per cent. The figures of previous censuses also point to the fact that emigration has been gradually increasing in volume. Like the immigrants into the State, most of the emigrants also belong to the *casual* type and as many as 37,441 of them (77·7 per cent of the total number) have but stepped over the border and are to be found in Travancore (26,964), Coimbatore (2,364) and Malabar (8,113), Coimbatore alone showing a low proportion of females. The net result of the migration between Cochin and these three neighbours has been a gain of 45,050 persons to the State's population (4,203 from Travancore, 2,545 from Coimbatore and 38,302 from Malabar).

Census year ..	1931	1921	1911	1901
No. of emigrants ..	48,168	*23,512	25,047	*14,790

*Does not include the emigrants to Ceylon who numbered 4,056 in 1911.

Emigrants to	No. of females to 100 males
Travancore ..	151
Malabar ..	110
Coimbatore ..	46

and to other parts of South India

9. 4,886 emigrants (10·2 per cent of the total number) are distributed in other parts of the Madras Presidency including Mysore, Pudukkottai and the French Settlements in South India. The city of Madras alone claims 1,010 of this number, facilities for higher education, professional careers and prospects of employment in the public service being the main attractions that take people to the capital of the Presidency. Tanjore and Trichinopoly too have, like Madras, a considerable number of students among the Cochin-born population enumerated in those districts.

Emigrants to other parts of India and their sex proportion

10. Other States and Provinces in India together claim only 3,391 or 7 per cent of the total number of emigrants; and of these the Presidency of Bombay including the Bombay States and Agencies accounts for 3,035. The sex proportion in this number is perplexing. The figures furnished by the Provincial Superintendent of Bombay show that Bombay city contains 2,304 females against 642 males born in Cochin. We have already seen that the merchant magnates of Mattancheri are immigrants from Bombay. Of the Cutch Memons, Havais and Baniyas—the three prominent classes among them—, the last two have not lost touch with their native Province. Mattancheri has commercial dealings with Bombay and several of the cargo boats plying between the two places are manned by Muslims (Mappillas) from Cochin. It is also understood that many Mappillas have settled in Bombay as petty traders. But these facts throw no light on the abnormal proportion of females in the emigrant population from Cochin found in Bombay city. The Census Report of Cochin for 1911 explains the presence of Cochin-born persons in Bombay thus: "Of the 1,032 (Cochin-born persons) found in the Bombay Presidency, probably the majority are persons born in Cochin during the temporary sojourn of their parents here." But then there were only about 100 females in this number so that the proportion of males was very high in 1911. For this reason, if we adopt the above explanation, it must follow that Mattancheri, which had a predilection for male children in the past, developed a partiality for the fair sex later on, so much so that seven

out of every nine children born in the town during the last two decades were females! The Cutch Memons have for long lost all touch with their original home. The Havais do not bring their families to Mattancheri, but return to their homes periodically. There can therefore be no Cochin-born Havais in Bombay or elsewhere. Very few Baniya girls born in Cochin are given in marriage to men in distant Bombay. In the circumstances I can offer no satisfactory explanation for the abnormal proportion of females in the figures of emigrants furnished by the Bombay Superintendent.*

Emigrants to foreign countries

11. Of 2,450 emigrants enumerated outside India, 2,446 are to be found in Ceylon, 3 in Borneo and 1 in Seychelles. Almost all the emigrants to Ceylon are labourers working in estates.

Gain to State's population by migration

12. From the statistics of emigration given in Subsidiary Table II it will appear that the net result of migration has been a gain to the State's population of 39,249 persons, this number being the excess of immigrants over emigrants during the decade. The corresponding gains for 1921, 1911 and 1901 were 16,247, 22,219 and 35,264 persons respectively. The figures for 1921 and 1901 would have been reduced further if the statistics of the emigrants to Ceylon for those years had been available.

Scope of special enquiry and accuracy of its results

13. In paragraph 14 of Chapter I it was remarked that the gain resulting from migration calculated on the basis of these satistics was only apparent and that the actual gain must probably be less. The figures presented in the Special Emigration Tables at the end of this chapter will support this contention. From its very nature the special enquiry regarding emigration from the State was bound to be incomplete and imperfect in its results. A separate schedule was issued for the purpose, and enumerators were instructed to ask each householder whether any member or members of his family born in the State had left it for places outside Cochin. In the event of an affirmative answer being received to this question, the particulars required for the several columns of the schedule regarding the person or persons who had thus emigrated were to be ascertained and entered in the schedule. Where whole families had emigrated, it is obvious that no returns could be secured through this procedure. Nor was this the only difficulty. For, the information obtained from the lower, ignorant classes of people was but meagre. It was further observed that grown up sons who had emigrated with their families were not generally returned because they were no longer regarded as members of their parents' families. Likewise grown up daughters, who were married to persons from outside the State and who had left for their husbands' homes, were also frequently omitted, because they too had ceased to be members of their parents' families. In the circumstances, the statistics collected by means of the special enquiry are far from complete as seen from the marginal table in which a few of the figures returned at the special enquiry are given side by side with the corresponding figures furnished by Provincial Superintendents.

District, State or Province		No. of emigrants according to the returns received from Provincial Superintendents	No. of emigrants returned at the special enquiry
Coimbatore	..	2,364	1,729
Nilgiris	..	578	283
Salem	..	250	124
Travancore	..	26,964	6,974
Bombay	..	3,013	822

* It is suggested that a considerable proportion of the Cochin-born women enumerated in the city of Bombay may be the wives of emigrants from Travancore or British Malabar, who have married from Cochin.

Statistics of emigrants and their sex proportion according to special enquiry

14. The Special Emigration Tables give 39,742 as the total number of emigrants from the State. The figure includes 2,576 persons who have emigrated to the Straits Settlements and Malaya and other foreign countries, from which statistics of emigrants have not been received. Excluding this number from the total, we have 37,166 persons returned at the special enquiry against 48,168 according to the returns of the Provincial Superintendents. If we now turn to the sex proportion in the two sets of statistics and study the marginal figures, it will be seen that the number of male emigrants according to the special enquiry is considerably in excess of the number furnished by Provincial Superintendents, whereas the number of female emigrants is but a third of that returned from outside. Obviously, the omissions referred to in the last paragraph have chiefly affected the returns of female emigrants, and it is not unlikely that the reticence of most people on matters connected with their women is partly responsible for such wholesale omissions.

	Males	Females
Number of emigrants according to the returns from Provincial Superintendents ..	22,878	25,290
* Number returned at the special enquiry ..	28,484	8,682

* Does not include the emigrants to the Straits Settlements, Malaya, &c.

These statistics compared with statistics of emigrants received from other States and Provinces

15. A comparison of the statistics given in Subsidiary Table III with the statistics in Special Emigration Table VII will show that the numbers of emigrants from Cochin enumerated in the various districts or Provinces are as a rule higher than the numbers returned at the special enquiry. The difference is striking in regard to Travancore and Bombay as seen from the margin of paragraph 13 above. There are, however, certain exceptions worth noting, and Madras, Malabar, Burma and Ceylon are seen to claim larger numbers of emigrants from Cochin than are accounted for by the Provincial Superintendents. It may be argued that the information elicited at the special enquiry regarding the place to which a person has emigrated might be inaccurate, the house-holder in his ignorance giving the name of one place instead of another. A large allowance may be made for such errors. But the difference is too wide to be covered by these errors alone particularly in view of the well known fact that large numbers of labourers flocked to Ceylon, the Straits Settlements and Malaya before the present economic depression had paralysed those countries*. These statistics and particularly the statistics of emigrants to countries outside India lead us to the conclusion that more people have emigrated from Cochin than are accounted for in the figures supplied from other States and Provinces and embodied in Subsidiary Table II.

District, State or Province	No. of emigrants according to the returns received from Provincial Superintendents	No. of emigrants returned at the special enquiry
Madras ..	1,010	2,803
Malabar ..	8,113	10,558
Burma ..	239	642
Ceylon ..	2,446	9,618

16. If the results of the special enquiry have been disappointing in that the figures of emigrants collected by this means are not reliable, still these results are interesting and important in other ways. The seven Special Emigration Tables at the end of the chapter are so compiled as to exhibit all salient features

* The repatriation of labour from these countries on account of economic depression had not started on any large scale at the time of the final census.

connected with emigration from the State. Table I containing the actual figures of emigrants by locality, religion and caste shows that 73·8 per cent of the emigrants are Hindus, 5·2 per cent are Muslims and 21 per cent Christians. These figures are not without their significance in view of the fact that the Muslims and Christians in the State's population have recorded a higher rate of increase than the Hindus. The marginal table gives the specific numbers of the emigrants from selected communities side by side with the strength of these communities in the State's population. The very high proportion of Brahman emigrants—almost all of them are Tamil Brahmans—is specially noteworthy. That the number of Tamil Brahmans in the State has actually decreased by 0·04 per cent during a decade of abnormal increase in population may be explained in the light of these useful figures. 24·2 per cent of the emigrants are from Talapilli taluk, 20·9 per cent from Trichur and 20·3 per cent from Mukundapuram. Emigration of labour to Ceylon and other places is mostly from these taluks and they naturally show a very low proportion of female emigrants. Cochin-Kanayannur in spite of its overcrowding accounts for but 18·6 per cent of the emigrants, Chittur claims 13·5 per cent and Cranganur 2·5 per cent.

Results of special enquiry reviewed: emigrants by locality, religion and caste

Caste or community	Strength of the community in the State's population	Number of emigrants from the community
Brahman ..	41,324	3,501
Nayar ..	142,637	8,644
Iluvan ..	276,649	10,265
Muslim ..	87,902	2,067
Christian ..	334,870	8,338

Emigrants from	Number of females to 100 males
Cochin-Kanayannur ..	70
Cranganur ..	14
Mukundapuram ..	13
Trichur ..	7
Talapilli ..	22
Chittur ..	99

Emigrants by age-periods

17. Table II gives the actual figures of emigrants by age, sex and locality. As may be expected, the proportion of children and aged people is but small. 78·6 per cent of the emigrants are between 15 and 40 years of age, 7·5 per cent below 15 years and 13·9 per cent above 40 years.

Educational qualifications, occupation and monthly income of emigrants

18. Tables III, IV, V and VI are perhaps more interesting and important than the others in that they classify the emigrants into earners and dependants by age, sex and locality, and show their occupation, monthly income and educational qualifications. As many as 67·5 per cent of the emigrants are seen to be earners and they include a considerable number of women also (16·1 per cent of the female emigrants). The dependants are mostly children under 15 years and women. Agriculture supports 3·9 per cent of the emigrants, industries maintain 9·7 per cent and transport and commerce 10·3 per cent. No less than 18·9 per cent depend on domestic service. Liberal professions and public service support a fair number (10·0 per cent), and other occupations 19·8 per cent. While most of the emigrants belong to the lower orders and are uneducated, it is seen that quite an appreciable number (2,162 or more than 5 per cent of the total,) is from the educated classes, scores of them being graduates of universities with high professional or literary qualifications. The adverse effects of overcrowding and the pressure of population on the means of subsistence account for the former type of emigrants, while educated unemployment is responsible for the latter. Young men who have received English education find no suitable employment in the State. They are therefore forced to emigrate

and are willing to go anywhere if only they have a chance of getting employed. The days when love of home and restrictions of caste checked emigration seem to have departed for ever.

Where emigrants go to

19. Table VII classifies the emigrants according to the places to which they have emigrated. The figures show that the contiguous districts of Travancore, Coimbatore and Malabar claim but 48·5 per cent of the total number. The rest are to be found in more or less distant places. The fact that emigrants from the State have gone to Mesopotamia (5), Arabia (7), Persia (12), Africa (21), and Australasia (11) is specially noteworthy. Most of those found in England and Wales (26) and Continental Europe (8) are students.

SUBSIDIARY TABLES.

I.—Immigration.

Natural Division where enumerated 'Malabar and Konkan'	Born in														
	Cochin State			Contiguous Districts and States in the Madras Presidency (Malabar, Coimbatore and Travancore)			Other parts of the Madras Presidency including Indian States of Mysore and Pudukkottai and the French Settlements			Provinces and States outside the Madras Presidency including the Portuguese Settlements			Outside India		
	Total	Males	Females	Total	Males	Females	Total	Males	Females	Total	Males	Females	Total	Males	Females
1	2	3	4	5	6	7	8	9	10	11	12	13	14	15	16
Cochin State	1,117,599	553,453	564,146	82,491	33,497	48,994	3,451	1,967	1,484	1,272	790	482	203	106	97

II.—Emigration.

Natural Division of Birth 'Malabar and Konkan'	Enumerated in														
	Cochin State			Contiguous Districts and States in the Madras Presidency (Malabar, Coimbatore and Travancore)			Other parts of the Madras Presidency including the States of Mysore and Pudukkottai and the French Settlements			Provinces and States outside the Madras Presidency including the Portuguese Settlements			Outside India		
	Total	Males	Females	Total	Males	Females	Total	Males	Females	Total	Males	Females	Total	Males	Females
1	2	3	4	5	6	7	8	9	10	11	12	13	14	15	16
Cochin State	1,117,599	553,453	564,146	37,441	16,213	21,228	4,886	3,315	1,571	3,391	968	2,423	2,450	2,382	68

Note.—For census purposes the State has not been sub-divided into Districts or Natural Divisions, and Subsidiary Table III has not therefore been prepared and Subsidiary Table IV has been re-numbered as III.

III.—Migration between Cochin State and the other parts of India.

Province or State	Immigrants to Cochin			Emigrants from Cochin			Excess (+) or deficiency (—) of Immigration over Emigration	
	1931	1921	Variation	1931	1921	Variation	1931	1921
1	2	3	4	5	6	7	8	9
GRAND TOTAL	87,417	39,759	+ 47,658	48,168	23,512	+ 24,656	+ 39,249	+ 16,247
A. INDIA	87,214	39,689	+ 47,525	45,718	23,479	+ 22,239	+ 41,496	+ 16,210
i. Madras Presidency	85,790	38,769	+ 47,021	41,784	22,490	+ 19,294	+ 44,006	+ 16,279
(a) British territory ..	54,614	26,380	+ 28,234	14,743	10,103	+ 4,640	+ 39,871	+ 16,277
Agency ..	..	..	..	..	5	— 5	..	— 5
Anantapur ..	6	..	+ 6	46	16	+ 30	— 40	— 16
Bellary ..	5	3	+ 2	33	26	+ 7	— 28	— 23
Chingleput ..	15	..	+ 15	180	111	+ 69	— 165	— 111
Chittur ..	2	..	+ 2	131	9	+ 122	— 129	— 9
Coimbatore ..	4,909	2,338	+ 2,571	2,364	1,544	+ 820	+ 2,545	+ 794
Cuddapah ..	..	..	..	12	..	+ 12	— 12	..
Ganjam ..	3	1	+ 2	24	..	+ 24	— 21	+ 1
Godavary ..	7	2	+ 5	38	53	— 15	— 31	— 51
Guntur ..	1	..	+ 1	17	2	+ 15	— 16	— 2
Kistna ..	3	..	+ 3	45	..	+ 45	— 42	..
Karnool ..	3	1	+ 2	25	25	..	— 22	— 24
Madras ..	285	228	+ 57	1,010	867	+ 143	— 725	— 639
Madura ..	353	216	+ 137	205	101	+ 104	+ 148	+ 115
Malabar ..	46,415	21,656	+ 24,759	8,113	6,341	+ 1,772	+ 38,302	+ 15,315
Nellore ..	2	5	— 3	20	..	+ 20	— 18	+ 5
Nilgiris ..	82	29	+ 53	578	218	+ 360	— 496	— 189
North Arcot ..	31	16	+ 15	154	62	+ 92	— 123	— 46
Ramnad ..	15	..	+ 15	231	53	+ 178	— 216	— 53
Salem ..	470	181	+ 289	250	79	+ 171	+ 220	+ 102
South Arcot ..	10	3	+ 7	103	42	+ 61	— 93	— 39
South Canara ..	994	853	+ 141	177	73	+ 104	+ 817	+ 780
Tanjore ..	161	117	+ 44	432	196	+ 236	— 271	— 79
Tinnevelly ..	687	607	+ 80	128	103	+ 25	+ 559	+ 504
Trichinopoly ..	151	121	+ 30	373	141	+ 232	— 222	— 20
Vizagapatam ..	4	3	+ 1	54	36	+ 18	— 50	— 33
(b) Indian States ..	31,176	12,389	+ 18,787	27,041	12,387	+ 14,654	+ 4,135	+ 2
Banganapalle ..	..	..	..	..	1	— 1	..	— 1
Travancore ..	31,167	12,381	+ 18,786	26,964	12,366	+ 14,598	+ 4,203	+ 15
Pudukkottai ..	9	8	+ 1	76	20	+ 56	— 67	— 12
Sandur ..	..	..	..	1	..	+ 1	— 1	..
ii. Other Provinces and States in India..	1,293	848	+ 445	3,934	997	+ 2,937	— 2,641	— 149
(a) British territory ..	434	264	+ 170	3,321	573	+ 2,748	— 2,887	— 309
Andamans and Nicobars ..	..	..	..	15	..	+ 15	— 15	..
Assam ..	3	..	+ 3	1	4	— 3	+ 2	— 4
Baluchistan ..	8	..	+ 8	3	8	— 5	+ 5	— 8
Bengal ..	33	9	+ 24	23	..	+ 23	+ 10	+ 9
Bihar and Orissa..	..	..	..	10	29	— 19	— 10	— 29
Bombay ..	291	177	+ 114	3,013	469	+ 2,544	— 2,722	— 292
Burma ..	31	8	+ 23	239	..	+ 239	— 208	+ 8
Central Provinces and Berar ..	11	55	— 44	..	..	..	+ 11	+ 55
Coorg ..	2	1	+ 1	..	27	— 27	+ 2	— 26
Delhi ..	1	..	+ 1	17	..	+ 17	— 16	..
North West Frontier Province	2	..	+ 2	..	..	..	+ 2	..
The Punjab ..	19	7	+ 12	..	36	— 36	+ 19	— 29
United Provinces of Agra and Oudh	33	7	+ 26	..	..	..	+ 33	+ 7
(b) Indian States ..	859	584	+ 275	613	424	+ 189	+ 246	+ 160
Ajmer-Merwara ..	..	..	..	1	..	+ 1	— 1	..
Baroda State ..	3	9	— 6	14	..	+ 14	— 11	+ 9
Bombay States (Kathiawar) ..	491	462	+ 29	10	10	..	+ 481	+ 452
Central India Agency (Bhopal).	1	..	+ 1	..	25	— 25	+ 11	— 25
Central Provinces (Udaipur) ..	2	..	+ 2	..	..	..	+ 2	..
Hyderabad ..	13	9	+ 4	31	14	+ 17	— 18	— 5
Kashmir ..	1	1	..	..	..	..	+ 1	+ 1
Mysore ..	127	77	+ 50	543	367	+ 176	— 416	— 290

III.—*Migration between Cochin State and the other parts of India.—(cont.)*

Province or State	Immigrants to Cochin			Emigrants from Cochin			Excess (+) or deficiency (—) of Immigration over Emigration	
	1931	1921	Variation	1931	1921	Variation	1931	1921
1	2	3	4	5	6	7	8	9
Rajputana ..	12	11	+ 1	2	8	— 6	+ 10	+ 3
Western India States Agency (Cutch) ..	209	15	+ 194	12	..	+ 12	+ 197	+ 15
(c) French and Portuguese Settlements.	66	72	— 6	..	..	..	+ 66	+ 72
1. French Settlements ..	25	18	+ 7	..	..	..	+ 25	+ 18
2. Portuguese Settlements ..	41	54	— 13	..	..	..	+ 41	+ 54
(d) Unspecified (India)	65	..	+ 65	..	..	..	+ 65	..
B. OTHER ASIATIC COUNTRIES ..	122	18	+ 104	2,450	25	+ 2,425	— 2,328	— 7
i. Within British Dominions ..	110	9	+ 101	2,450	25	+ 2,425	— 2,340	— 16
Ceylon (Colombo)	62	9	+ 53	2,446	..	+ 2,446	— 2,384	+ 9
Straits Settlements and Malaya ..	48	..	+ 48	..	25	— 25	+ 48	— 25
Borneo ..	..	..	..	3	..	+ 3	— 3	..
Seychelles ..	..	..	..	1	..	+ 1	— 1	..
ii. Outside British Dominions ..	12	9	+ 3	..	..	..	+ 12	+ 9
Afghanistan ..	3	..	+ 3	..	..	..	+ 3	..
Arabia ..	2	1	+ 1	..	..	..	+ 2	+ 1
China ..	2	..	+ 2	..	..	..	+ 2	..
Japan ..	1	..	+ 1	..	..	..	+ 1	..
Nepal ..	2	..	+ 2	..	..	..	+ 2	..
Persia ..	2	1	+ 1	..	..	..	+ 2	+ 1
Turkey in Asia ..	..	7	— 7	..	..	..	..	+ 7
C. BORN IN EUROPE	68	45	+ 23	..	..	..	+ 68	+ 45
i. United Kingdom and Ireland ..	38	27	+ 11	..	..	..	+ 38	+ 27
ii. Other European Countries (Continental Europe)	30	18	+ 12	..	..	..	+ 30	+ 18
D. BORN IN AFRICA (British Dominions)	5	..	+ 5	..	..	..	+ 5	..
E. BORN IN AMERICA (Outside British Dominion).	3	3	..	..	..	..	+ 3	+ 3
F. BORN IN AUSTRALASIA (British Dominions)	4	4	..	..	..	..	+ 4	+ 4
G. BORN AT SEA ..	1	..	+ 1	..	..	..	+ 1	..

SPECIAL EMIGRATION TABLES.

I.—Emigrants by locality, religion and caste or tribe.

TALUK	Total Emigrants			Hindu											
				Brahman			Nayar			Iluvan			Pulayan		
	Persons	Males	Females	Persons	Males	Females	Persons	Males	Females	Persons	Males	Females	Persons	Males	Females
1	2	3	4	5	6	7	8	9	10	11	12	13	14	15	16
COCHIN STATE ..	39,742	30,707	9,035	3,501	2,442	1,059	8,644	7,270	1,374	10,265	8,995	1,270	554	307	247
Cochin-Kanayannur ..	7,401	4,345	3,056	453	320	133	1,123	932	191	792	406	386	179	66	113
Cranganur ..	996	871	125	62	58	4	367	290	77	310	300	10	3	3	..
Mukundapuram ..	8,069	7,169	900	424	295	129	1,483	1,345	138	2,971	2,898	73	54	42	12
Trichur ..	8,313	7,763	550	518	412	106	1,776	1,584	192	3,159	3,107	52	18	13	5
Talapilli ..	9,609	7,872	1,737	1,098	752	346	2,522	2,170	352	2,264	2,034	230	178	154	24
Chittur ..	5,354	2,687	2,667	946	605	341	1,373	949	424	769	250	519	122	29	93

TALUK	Hindu						Muslim			Christian			Jew		
	Others			Total Hindu											
	Persons	Males	Females	Persons	Males	Females	Persons	Males	Females	Persons	Males	Females	Persons	Males	Females
	17	18	19	20	21	22	23	24	25	26	27	28	29	30	31
COCHIN STATE ..	6,353	4,124	2,229	29,317	23,138	6,179	2,067	1,578	489	8,338	5,972	2,366	20	19	1
Cochin-Kanayannur ..	911	393	518	3,458	2,117	1,341	271	132	139	3,657	2,081	1,576	15	15	..
Cranganur ..	104	81	23	846	732	114	138	129	9	12	10	2	..	..	..
Mukundapuram ..	886	763	123	5,818	5,343	475	312	287	25	1,934	1,535	399	5	4	1
Trichur ..	1,106	1,026	80	6,577	6,142	435	349	342	7	1,387	1,279	108	..	..	..
Talapilli ..	1,592	1,157	435	7,654	6,267	1,387	684	571	113	1,271	1,034	237	..	..	..
Chittur ..	1,754	704	1,050	4,964	2,537	2,427	313	117	196	77	33	44	..	..	..

II.—*Emigrants by age, sex and locality.*

TALUK	Total Emigrants			Below 15 years of age			Aged 15—40			Aged 40 and over		
	Persons	Males	Females	Persons	Males	Females	Persons	Males	Females	Persons	Males	Females
1	2	3	4	5	6	7	8	9	10	11	12	13
COCHIN STATE.	39,742	30,707	9,035	2,978	1,687	1,291	31,228	24,443	6,785	5,536	4,577	959
Cochin-Kanayannur ..	7,401	4,345	3,056	562	301	261	5,841	3,411	2,430	998	633	365
Cranganur ..	996	871	125	78	45	33	782	701	81	136	125	11
Mukundapuram ..	8,069	7,169	900	396	271	125	6,487	5,824	663	1,186	1,074	112
Trichur ..	8,313	7,763	550	445	275	170	6,670	6,333	337	1,198	1,155	43
Talapilli ..	9,609	7,872	1,737	729	430	299	7,507	6,273	1,234	1,373	1,169	204
Chittur ..	5,354	2,687	2,667	768	365	403	3,941	1,901	2,040	645	421	224

III.—*Classification of Emigrants into Earners and Dependents by age, sex and locality.*

TALUK	Total emigrants			Below 15 years of age						Aged 15—40						Aged 40 and over					
				Earners			Dependents			Earners			Dependents			Earners			Dependents		
	Persons	Males	Females	Persons	Males	Females	Persons	Males	Females	Persons	Males	Females	Persons	Males	Females	Persons	Males	Females	Persons	Males	Females
1	2	3	4	5	6	7	8	9	10	11	12	13	14	15	16	17	18	19	20	21	22
COCHIN STATE ..	39,742	30,707	9,035	421	330	91	2,557	1,357	1,200	22,196	21,062	1,134	9,032	3,381	5,651	4,214	3,986	228	1,322	591	731
Cochin-Kanayannur ..	7,401	4,345	3,056	60	44	16	502	257	245	3,177	2,813	364	2,664	598	2,066	641	577	64	357	56	301
Cranganur ..	996	871	125	7	7	..	71	38	33	626	613	13	156	88	68	112	112	..	24	13	11
Mukundapuram ..	8,069	7,169	900	103	88	15	293	183	110	5,058	4,968	90	1,429	856	573	924	901	23	262	173	89
Trichur ..	8,313	7,763	550	61	56	5	384	219	165	5,657	5,588	69	1,013	745	268	1,016	1,003	13	182	152	30
Talapilli ..	9,609	7,872	1,737	95	88	7	634	342	292	5,674	5,440	234	1,833	833	1,000	1,055	1,002	53	318	167	151
Chittur ..	5,354	2,687	2,667	95	47	48	673	318	355	2,004	1,640	364	1,937	261	1,676	466	391	75	179	30	149

IV.—Occupation of Emigrants by age, sex and locality.

TALUK	Total number of Emigrants			Number of persons (Earners and Dependents) supported by — Agriculture: Below 15 years of age		Aged 15—40		Aged 40 and over		Industry: Below 15 years of age		Aged 15—40		Aged 40 and over	
	Persons	Males	Females	Males	Females	Males	Females	Males	Females	Males	Females	Males	Females	Males	Females
1	2	3	4	5	6	7	8	9	10	11	12	13	14	15	16
COCHIN STATE ..	39,742	30,707	9,035	21	7	840	424	213	61	42	11	3,065	218	478	27
Cochin-Kanayannur ..	7,401	4,345	3,056	6	2	158	99	30	18	5	6	525	120	57	16
Cranganur ..	996	871	125	..	..	1	1	4	..	2	..	79	..	25	..
Mukundapuram ..	8,069	7,169	900	1	..	103	30	21	6	9	2	572	16	88	1
Trichur ..	8,313	7,763	550	6	..	372	..	79	..	11	..	560	..	120	..
Talapilli ..	9,609	7,872	1,737	4	..	132	44	45	11	15	..	1,180	30	120	4
Chittur ..	5,354	2,687	2,667	4	5	71	250	34	26	..	3	189	52	56	6

TALUK	Number of persons (Earners and Dependents) supported by — Transport and Commerce: Below 15 years of age		Aged 15—40		Aged 40 and over		Domestic Service: Below 15 years of age		Aged 15—40		Aged 40 and over		Liberal professions and Public service: Below 15 years of age	
	Males	Females	Males	Females	Males	Females	Males	Females	Males	Females	Males	Females	Males	Females
	17	18	19	20	21	22	23	24	25	26	27	28	29	30
COCHIN STATE ..	54	..	3,222	91	720	13	132	50	4,751	1,475	860	232	14	4
Cochin-Kanayanur ..	6	..	223	32	60	2	17	9	15	565	16	95	2	3
Cranganur ..	4	..	185	1	24	..	1	..	15	19	5	2	..	..
Mukundapuram ..	14	..	616	5	98	3	47	[illegible]	2,330	187	342	29	3	1
Trichur ..	10	..	698	3	197	..	13	8	1,056	57	176	12	4	..
Talapilli ..	9	..	907	24	236	3	33	10	1,210	342	295	63	3	..
Chittur ..	11	..	493	26	105	5	21	11	116	305	26	32	2	..

IV.—Occupation of Emigrants by age, sex and locality.—(cont.)

TALUK	Number of persons (Earners and Dependents) supported by															
	Liberal professions and Public service				Other occupations						No occupation					
	Aged 15—40		Aged 40 and over		Below 15 years of age		Aged 15—40		Aged 40 and over		Below 15 years of age		Aged 15—40		Aged 40 and over	
	Males	Females	Males	Females	Males	Females	Males	Females	Males	Females	Males	Females	Males	Females	Males	Females
	31	32	33	34	35	36	37	38	39	40	41	42	43	44	45	46
COCHIN STATE ..	3,255	132	548	14	192	55	6,224	273	1,089	38	1,232	1,164	3,086	4,172	669	574
Cochin-Kanayannur ..	549	36	112	9	29	22	1,730	107	306	14	236	219	111	1,471	52	211
Cranganur ..	146	2	27	..	1	..	205	8	24	..	37	33	70	50	13	9
Mukundapuram ..	410	11	53	..	29	6	1,041	22	304	3	168	104	783	392	168	70
Trichur ..	978	30	164	..	36	16	1,973	24	281	6	195	146	696	213	138	25
Talapilli ..	617	39	102	3	74	5	1,004	59	112	5	292	284	1,223	696	250	116
Chittur ..	555	14	90	2	23	6	271	43	62	10	304	378	203	1,350	48	143

V.—Emigrants by taluks (earners only) classified according to their monthly income.

TALUK	Number of Emigrants who are earners			No. of persons whose monthly income amounts to													
				Below Rs. 15		Rs. 15—25		Rs. 25—50		Rs 50—100		Rs. 100—500		Rs. 500 & over		Unspecified	
	Persons	Males	Females	Males	Females	Males	Females	Males	Females	Males	Females	Males	Females	Males	Females	Males	Females
1	2	3	4	5	6	7	8	9	10	11	12	13	14	15	16	17	18
COCHIN STATE ..	26,831	25,378	1,453	3,816	842	7,064	170	8,042	166	1,832	50	1,183	28	66	..	3,375	257
Cochin-Kanayannur ..	3,878	3,434	444	627	296	929	41	972	80	278	17	251	8	22	..	355	62
Cranganur ..	745	732	13	106	3	204	2	207	3	71	1	47	1	2	..	95	3
Mukundapuram ..	6,085	5,957	128	948	65	1,885	22	1,816	11	236	5	108	2	5	..	959	23
Trichur ..	6,734	6,647	87	663	32	1,859	12	2,341	16	442	7	272	5	15	..	1,055	15
Talapilli ..	6,824	6,530	294	1,297	124	1,837	38	2,071	22	402	9	231	2	7	..	685	99
Chittur ..	2,165	2,078	487	175	322	350	55	635	34	403	11	274	10	15	..	226	55

VI.—Emigrants by locality and educational qualifications.

Qualifications	Total number of Emigrants			Cochin-Kanayannur		Cranganur		Mukundapuram		Trichur		Talapilli		Chittur	
	Persons	Males	Females	Males	Females	Males	Females	Males	Females	Males	Females	Males	Females	Males	Females
1	2	3	4	5	6	7	8	9	10	11	12	13	14	15	16
Imperial Services															
I. C. S. ..	4	4	..	..	..	..	..	..	..	1	..	..	..	3	..
F. C. S. ..	2	2	..	1	..	..	..	..	..	..	..	1	..	..	..
British Degrees															
Medical ..	4	3	1	2	..	..	..	..	1	1	..	..	..	..	..
Legal ..	1	1	..	1	..	..	..	..	..	..	..	..	..	..	..
Arts and Sciences (M. A., Ph. D.) ..	2	2	..	..	..	..	..	1	..	1	..	..	..	..	..
Indian Degrees and diplomas															
Medical ..	96	89	7	47	3	10	..	6	1	9	1	7	2	10	..
Veterinary ..	11	11	..	..	..	..	..	3	..	..	..	6	..	2	..
Sanitation ..	26	26	..	..	..	..	..	4	..	7	..	..	..	15	..
Legal (B. L. or L.L. B.) ..	76	76	..	11	..	10	..	7	..	8	..	10	..	30	..
Agricultural ..	1	1	..	..	..	..	..	1	..	..	..	..	..	..	..
Commerce (B. Com.) ..	9	9	..	8	..	..	..	1	..	..	..	..	..	..	..
Engineering															
B. E. ..	6	6	..	3	..	..	..	..	..	..	..	3	..	..	..
L. M. E. ..	54	54	..	..	..	3	..	51	..	..	..	..	..	..	..
Electrical Engineering ..	88	88	..	38	..	..	..	6	..	32	..	..	..	11	..
Overseer's Test ..	9	9	..	..	..	..	..	1	..	5	..	..	..	3	..
Arts and Sciences															
M. A. ..	43	40	3	16	1	3	..	11	..	6	2	2	..	2	..
B. A. ..	195	181	14	57	4	8	1	11	2	24	4	25	..	56	3
B. Sc. ..	6	6	..	5	..	..	..	..	..	1	..	..	..	..	..
L. T. ..	30	22	8	5	2	..	..	3	1	6	3	3	1	5	1
Intermediate ..	238	222	16	28	3	8	..	15	2	22	8	99	2	40	1
School Final ..	1,157	1,112	45	164	13	78	1	86	6	230	13	297	10	257	2
Miscellaneous															
Account Test ..	2	2	..	..	..	..	..	2	..	..	..	..	..	..	..
Shorthand and Typewriting ..	72	71	1	5	1	..	..	16	..	22	..	..	..	28	..
Co-operative Test ..	1	1	..	..	..	..	..	1	..	..	..	..	..	..	..
Compounding ..	7	6	1	..	..	..	..	6	1	..	..	..	..	..	..
Telegraphic ..	11	11	..	..	..	..	..	..	..	11	..	..	..	..	..
Railway Test ..	8	8	..	..	..	..	..	1	..	..	..	..	..	7	..
Survey Test ..	2	2	..	..	..	..	..	2	..	..	..	..	..	..	..
Gymnastics ..	1	1	..	..	..	..	..	1	..	..	..	..	..	..	..
Below S. F. or Unspecified ..	37,580	28,641	8,939	3,944	3,029	751	123	6,933	886	7,377	519	7,415	1,722	2,217	2,660
Total ..	39,742	30,707	9,035	4,345	3,056	871	125	7,169	900	7,763	550	7,872	1,737	2,687	2,667

VII.—Place of Emigration.

Place to which emigrated	Total number of Emigrants			Emigrants from: Cochin-Kanayannur		Cranganur		Mukundapuram		Trichur		Talapilli		Chittur	
	Persons	Males	Females	Males	Females	Males	Females	Males	Females	Males	Females	Males	Females	Males	Females
1	2	3	4	5	6	7	8	9	10	11	12	13	14	15	16
GRAND TOTAL ..	39,742	30,707	9,035	4,345	3,056	871	125	7,169	900	7,763	550	7,872	1,737	2,687	2,667
I. Provinces and States in India beyond Cochin State ..	26,445	18,122	8,323	3,671	2,668	421	103	1,899	859	4,011	505	5,598	1,633	2,522	2,555
a. Provinces and States adjacent to Cochin State ..	24,106	16,342	7,764	3,140	2,402	366	100	1,672	841	3,378	454	5,444	1,571	2,342	2,396
i. British Territory (Madras Presidency) ..	17,056	11,970	5,086	1,298	689	231	56	1,173	298	2,819	343	4,192	1,386	2,257	2,314
Anantapur ..	2	2	..	..	..	..	..	..	..	..	..	..	..	2	..
Bellary ..	20	15	5	..	..	..	..	..	..	..	..	14	4	1	1
Chingleput ..	18	9	9	..	..	..	..	1	..	..	..	..	..	8	9
Coimbatore ..	1,729	1,120	609	205	75	20	9	110	20	107	35	128	47	550	437
Cuddapah ..	8	5	3	3	..	..	..	2	3	..	..	..	..	..	..
Ganjam ..	8	8	..	2	..	..	..	..	..	6	..	..	..	..	..
Godavari ..	22	18	4	..	..	..	..	4	2	3	..	8	..	3	2
Guntur ..	10	6	4	2	..	..	..	..	..	..	..	4	4	..	..
Kistna ..	7	7	..	2	..	..	..	..	..	..	..	..	..	5	..
Madras ..	2,803	2,337	466	357	209	135	13	260	36	207	57	1,115	76	233	75
Madura ..	587	389	198	112	89	..	1	49	8	146	53	42	25	40	22
Malabar ..	10,558	7,183	3,375	435	249	76	33	482	174	2,163	133	2,690	1,160	1,337	1,626
Nellore ..	39	31	8	..	..	..	..	13	3	2	..	13	5	3	..
Nilgiris ..	283	217	66	89	27	..	..	41	3	28	7	85	18	4	11
North Arcot ..	85	57	28	7	1	..	..	22	4	2	..	19	6	7	17
Ramnad ..	103	72	31	6	1	..	..	10	3	18	11	29	9	9	7
Salem ..	124	60	64	12	6	..	..	24	9	9	1	5	5	10	43
South Arcot ..	34	20	14	17	7	..	..	3	7	..	..	..	..	..	..
South Canara ..	60	44	16	..	..	..	..	24	3	16	3	..	..	4	10
Tanjore ..	231	143	88	37	24	..	..	63	19	25	1	6	17	12	27
Tinnevelly ..	70	39	31	6	1	..	..	..	..	36	23	..	..	3	7
Trichinopoly ..	211	158	53	..	..	..	..	58	4	44	16	33	8	21	25
Vizagapatam ..	44	30	14	6	..	..	..	7	..	13	3	1	6	3	5
ii. Indian States ..	7,050	4,372	2,678	1,842	1,713	135	41	499	543	559	111	1,252	185	85	82
Travancore ..	6,974	4,316	2,658	1,838	1,713	133	44	484	543	550	111	1,237	177	74	70
Pudukkottai ..	76	56	20	4	..	2	..	15	..	9	..	15	8	11	12
b. Other Provinces and States in India ..	2,333	1,776	557	527	266	55	3	227	18	633	51	154	62	180	157

VII.—Place of Emigration—(cont.)

Place to which emigrated	Total number of Emigrants			Emigrants from											
				Cochin-Kanayannur		Cranganur		Mukundapuram		Trichur		Talapilli		Chittur	
	Persons	Males	Females	Males	Females	Males	Females	Males	Females	Males	Females	Males	Females	Males	Females
1	2	3	4	5	6	7	8	9	10	11	12	13	14	15	16
i. British Territory ..	1,849	1,446	403	385	195	52	3	173	10	592	45	106	36	138	114
Assam ..	3	3	..	1	..	..	..	1	..	..	..	..	..	1	..
Bengal ..	208	149	59	53	31	8	1	16	..	43	1	16	5	13	21
Bihar and Orissa ..	6	6	..	3	..	..	..	..	..	..	..	..	..	3	..
Bombay ..	822	595	227	191	118	16	..	112	9	153	11	37	17	86	72
Burma ..	642	552	90	96	26	28	2	29	..	362	30	7	14	30	18
Central Provinces and Berar ..	11	11	..	..	..	..	..	8	..	3	..	..	..	..	..
Coorg ..	49	45	4	4	2	..	..	..	..	5	2	36	..	..	..
The Punjab ..	18	17	1	4	1	..	..	1	..	..	..	9	..	3	..
United Provinces of Agra and Oudh ..	90	68	22	33	17	..	..	6	1	26	1	1	..	2	3
ii. Indian States ..	484	330	154	142	71	3	..	54	8	41	6	48	26	42	43
Baroda ..	21	16	5	4	3	..	..	1	..	11	2	..	..	..	..
Hyderabad ..	46	28	18	2	..	2	..	9	1	..	..	7	6	8	12
Mysore ..	417	286	131	136	68	1	..	44	7	30	4	41	20	34	32
c. French and Portuguese Settlements ..	6	4	2	4	..	..	..	..	..	..	..	..	..	..	2
i. French Settlements ..	3	1	2	1	..	..	..	..	..	..	..	..	..	..	2
Pondicherry ..	1	1	..	1	..	..	..	..	..	..	..	..	..	..	..
Karikal ..	2	..	2	..	..	..	..	..	..	..	..	..	..	..	2
ii. Portuguese Settlements ..	3	3	..	3	..	..	..	..	..	..	..	..	..	..	..
Goa ..	3	3	..	3	..	..	..	..	..	..	..	..	..	..	..
II. Other Asiatic countries ..	12,127	11,603	524	100	230	408	18	4,676	22	3,685	39	2,271	103	154	112
i. Within British Dominions ..	12,108	11,587	521	401	230	408	18	4,671	19	3,684	39	2,267	103	153	112
Ceylon ..	9,618	9,439	179	162	99	361	1	4,310	10	3,178	28	1,377	21	21	20
Mesopotamia ..	5	4	1	..	..	..	..	1	..	..	..	1	1	..	..
Straits Settlements and Malaya ..	2,485	2,144	341	239	131	47	17	331	9	506	11	889	81	132	92
Outside British Dominions ..	19	16	3	8	..	..	..	2	3	1	..	4	..	1	..
Arabia ..	7	4	3	1	..	..	..	1	3	..	..	..	..	..	..
Persia ..	12	12	..	5	..	..	..	1	..	1	..	4	..	1	..
III. Europe ..	31	32	2	19	2	3	..	3	..	4	..	..	..	4	..
i. United Kingdom	26	24	2	13	2	2	..	1	..	3	..	..	..	4	..
England and Wales ..	26	24	2	13	2	3	..	1	..	3	..	..	..	4	..

VII.—Place of Emigration—(cont.)

Place to which emigrated	Total number of Emigrants			Emigrants from: Cochin-Kanayannur		Cranganur		Mukundapuram		Trichur		Talapilli		Chittur	
	Persons	Males	Females	Males	Females	Males	Females	Males	Females	Males	Females	Males	Females	Males	Females
1	2	3	4	5	6	7	8	9	10	11	12	13	14	15	16
ii. Other European countries (Continental Europe)	8	8	..	6	..	..	..	1	..	1	..	..	..	..	..
Belgium ..	3	3	..	2	..	..	..	..	..	1	..	..	..	..	..
Germany ..	1	1	..	..	..	..	..	1	..	..	..	..	..	..	..
Italy ..	4	4	..	4	..	..	..	..	..	..	..	..	..	..	..
IV. Africa ..	21	15	6	3	..	..	..	5	5	1	..	2	1	4	..
V. America ..	1	1	..	..	..	..	..	..	..	1	..	..	..	..	..
VI. Australasia ..	11	11	..	..	..	..	..	7	..	..	..	1	..	3	..
VII. Unspecified ..	1,103	923	180	243	156	39	4	580	14	61	6	..	..	..	..

CHAPTER IV.—AGE.

Reference to statistics

THE statistics regarding age are contained in Imperial Table VII. This Table deals also with the statistics of sex and civil condition, which are to be treated in separate chapters. Other Tables too are concerned with age. Thus Imperial Table VIII shows the civil condition *by age* of selected castes. In Part A of Imperial Table IX the distribution of infirmities *by age-periods* is given, while Imperial Table XIII presents the statistics of literacy *by age*.

There are ten Subsidiary Tables appended to this Chapter, the first seven of which contain the salient features of the age statistics in proportional forms. The remaining three deal with the vital statistics of the decade under review.

Inaccuracies of age returns

2. The statistics of age are justly considered to be one of the most interesting and important features of a census, but unfortunately their value is considerably impaired by the errors in the returns of age recorded in the schedules. The various forms of misstatement of age common at an Indian census have been fully discussed in previous Census Reports. Ignorance plays the most important part in this connection, and because the average Indian knows little or nothing about his age he often states it in a round figure. Thus rises the preference for numbers ending in 0. Figures ending in 5 are also much in favour. Even numbers are otherwise preferred to odd, and a partiality for numbers like 2, 8, 12, 18, 28 and 32 is noticeable. It will not, however, be wrong to assume that the proportion of errors rising from ignorance is likely to be smaller in Cochin than in most other States and Provinces in view of the fact that at least 50 per cent of our children of school-going age are attending schools, that literacy has been spreading more rapidly in Cochin than elsewhere and that the level of ignorance among the masses is lower in this State than in most other parts of India. The common tendency of old people to exaggerate, and of elderly men and adult women to understate, their respective ages also leads to false returns. The Hindu's superstition that his allotted span of life will be shortened if he gave his correct age is gradually dying out and is therefore less responsible than of old for deliberate falsification. The communities in which pre-puberty marriage is compulsory form but a very small section of the population of Cochin and hence errors from understating the age of unmarried girls have always been relatively few in number. On the whole, the age returns of the State may justly be regarded as less inaccurate than those of the greater part of India.

As a result of the errors in the age returns, they have to be carefully corrected and graduated by actuarial calculations before they are used for the construction of Life Tables or the deduction of birth and death rates. This part of the work is undertaken for all India by the Government Actuary. But the Age Tables compiled from the crude figures returned at the census are not without their interest and importance. The large errors in the age returns are no doubt more or less constant at each census. Further the figures are combined into groups so that the defects may be reduced to a minimum. We may therefore use these groups with a certain degree of confidence for gaining some idea of the age-constitution of the people and its periodic variations.

Change in the nature of age returns and their grouping

3. On previous occasions, only completed years of age were to be asked for and entered in the enumeration schedule. A change calculated to secure more accurate results was introduced at the present census. The schedule of 1931 contained these directions: "*Column 7 (Age on 26th February)*.—Enter

Age pyramid 1931

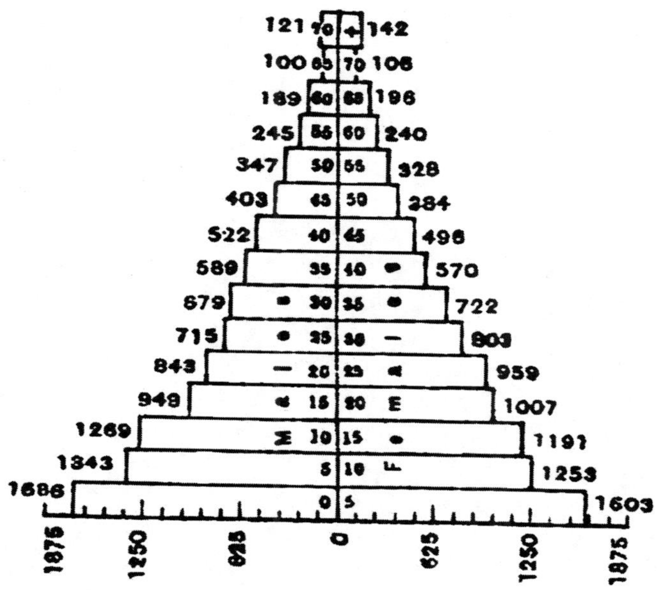

Age pyramid 1921

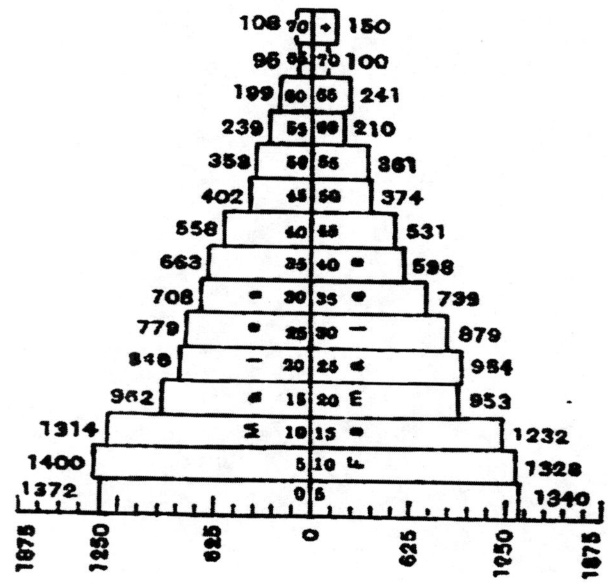

The age distribution of the population of cochin at the census of 1931 compared with that at the previous censuses

1931 & 1921
Males

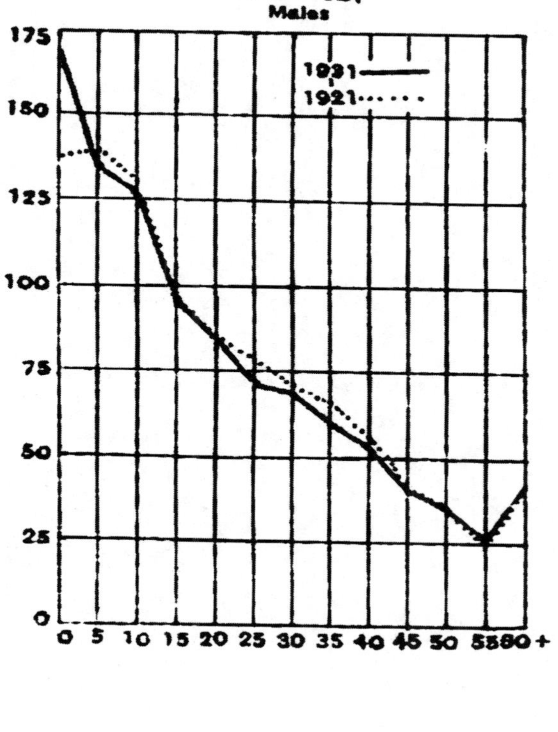

1931 & 1921
Females

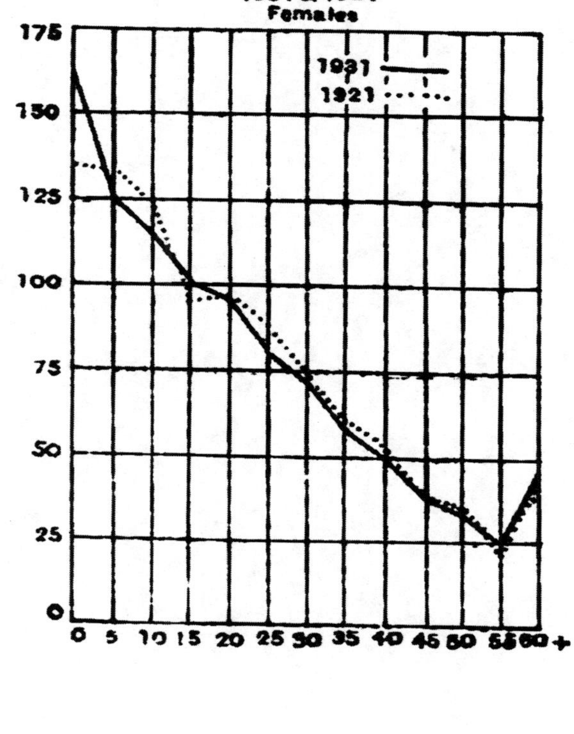

the number of years to the nearest birth-day or the nearest age (in years) known. For infants less than *six* months old enter 0 and for infants of and over *six* months enter 1." According to the instructions issued in 1921, a person who completed his 20th year on the very day of the final census and another who was 20 years and 10 months old on that date would both be returned as 20, whereas the age of the former would be entered as 20 and that of the latter as 21 in the age column of the latest schedule. The age-periods actually returned in 1931 were 0—½ (0), ½—1½ (1), 1½—2½ (2), 2½—3½ (3) and so on. The crude figures were first combined into alternate ternary and septenary groups, namely, 0—3, 4—6, 7—13, 14—16, 17—23, etc. The quinary age-groups of Imperial Table VII were compiled from these ternary and septenary groups.* The quinary groups thus obtained must naturally be more accurate and satisfactory than those of previous censuses.

4. The age pyramid for 1931 shows graphically the proportion which each quinary group bears to the next one. The regular grading of the pyramid indicates that the groups are, without a single exception, proportional and that the numbers decrease as the age rises. That some of the age-groups of 1921 were irregular in this respect will be seen from the grading of the age pyramid for 1921. **Age Pyramid, 1931 and 1921**

5. The following table and the six diagrams inserted in this chapter compare the age distribution of the population of 1931 with that of the three previous censuses. **Variation in age distribution**

Age-period	Number per mille of total population enumerated at each age-period							
	1931		1921		1911		1901	
	Males	Females	Males	Females	Males	Females	Males	Females
1	2	3	4	5	6	7	8	9
0—5	169	161	137	134	147	146	137	140
5—10	134	125	140	133	130	125	139	134
10—15	127	119	131	123	126	118	132	123
15—20	95	100	96	95	99	100	97	98
20—25	84	96	85	97	90	100	89	98
25—30	71	80	78	88	83	90	86	91
30—35	68	72	71	74	74	73	75	72
35—40	59	57	66	60	67	58	64	56
40—45	52	50	56	53	53	51	55	51
45—50	40	38	40	37	39	35	36	34
50—55	35	33	35	36	33	36	34	37
55—60	25	24	24	21	21	21	19	18
60—65	19	20	20	24	19	24	37 (60 and over)	46 (60 and over)
65—70	10	11	10	10	9	9		
70 and over	13	14	11	15	10	14		
	1,000	1,000	1,000	1,000	1,000	1,000	1,000	1,000

* This was done in the following manner: 0—3+½ (4—6) = 0—5; ½ (4—6)+½ (7—13) = 5—10; ½ (7—13) + ½ (14—16) = 10—15, etc.

The remarks made in paragraph 19 of Chapter I regarding the proofs of short-counting in 1921 furnished by age statistics have to be recalled in this connection, and due allowance should be made for the short-counting when the age-groups of 1931 are compared with those of 1921. The most significant feature revealed by the figures in the above table and illustrated by the curves in the diagrams is the remarkable rise in the proportion of children aged 0—5 during the past decade. The figures for the three previous censuses are far below those of 1931. A variety of fluctuations, now significant and now negligible, is seen at the subsequent age-periods. The sum total of all these variations is (1) that the proportion of children (0—10) in 1931 is much higher than at any of the three previous censuses; and (2) that the excess in the earlier groups is balanced by a slight decrease in the proportion of adolescent males (10—20) and by a much more pronounced fall in the ratio of the adult population (20—45). The figures for these combined groups are given below.

Age-period	1931		1921		1911		1901	
	Males	Females	Males	Females	Males	Females	Males	Females
1	2	3	4	5	6	7	8	9
0—10	303	286	277	267	277	271	276	274
10—20	222	219	227	218	225	218	229	221
20—45	334	355	356	372	367	372	369	370
45 and above	141	140	140	143	131	139	126	135
	1,000	1,000	1,000	1,000	1,000	1,000	1,000	1,000

It is observed that 1921, 1911 and 1901 differ among themselves so far as the proportion of the adult population is concerned, though they are in general agreement in respect of the adolescent ages. Both 1931 and 1921 fare alike in the proportion of the elderly and aged population (45 and over), which is higher than that of 1911 and 1901.

Probable causes

6. Here in Cochin we have no legacy left by past famines to determine the age-constitution of our population. Nor was the mortality from the influenza epidemics of the decade 1911—1921 severe enough in this State to affect its age distribution then or afterwards. Other factors must, therefore, explain the variations noticed above. A rise in the birth-rate, or a fall in the death-rate among infants, or the depletion of the adult categories through heavy mortality or emigration may account for the higher proportion of children and the lower proportion of adults. The prosperous conditions of the decade examined in paragraphs 9—12 of Chapter I point to a high birth-rate; but in the absence of reliable statistics on the subject one cannot say whether this birth-rate was higher* than that of previous decades. In all probability the

*The recorded vital statistics, examined in paragraph 12 of this chapter, show a decennial rate of 146 births and 93 deaths per mille of the population for the past decade. The corresponding figures for the previous decade (1911—1920) were *higher*, the birth-rate being 169 and the death rate 145. The higher birth-rate recorded for the period 1911—1920 proves nothing but the unreliable character of the vital statistics.

The age distribution of the population of cochin at the census of 1931 compared with that at the previous censuses

1931 & 1911
Males

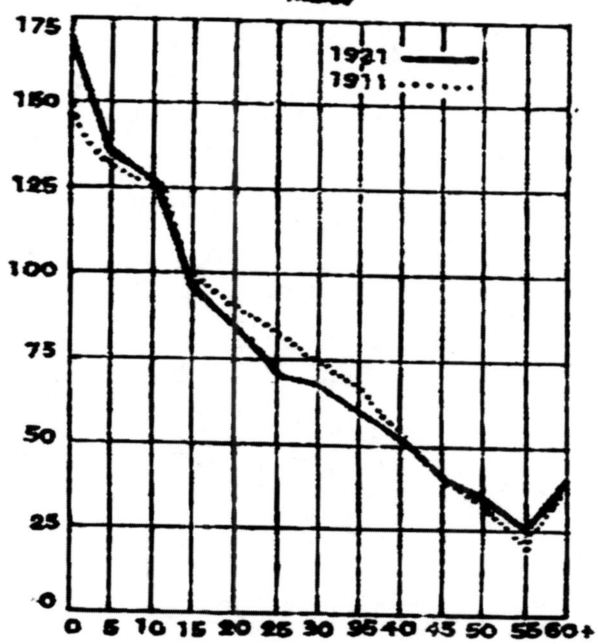

1931 & 1911
Females

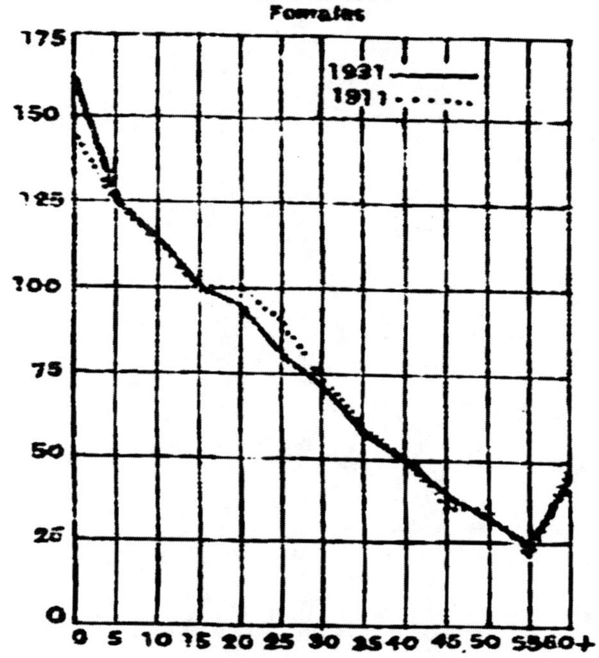

1931 & 1901
Males

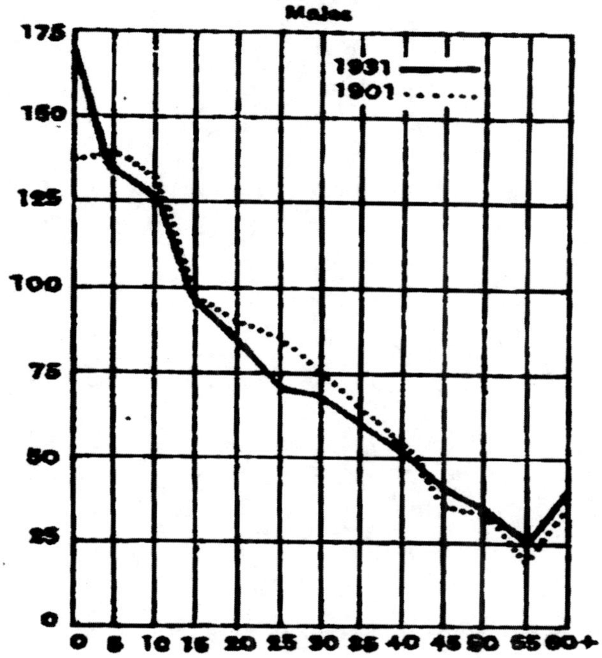

1931 & 1901
Females

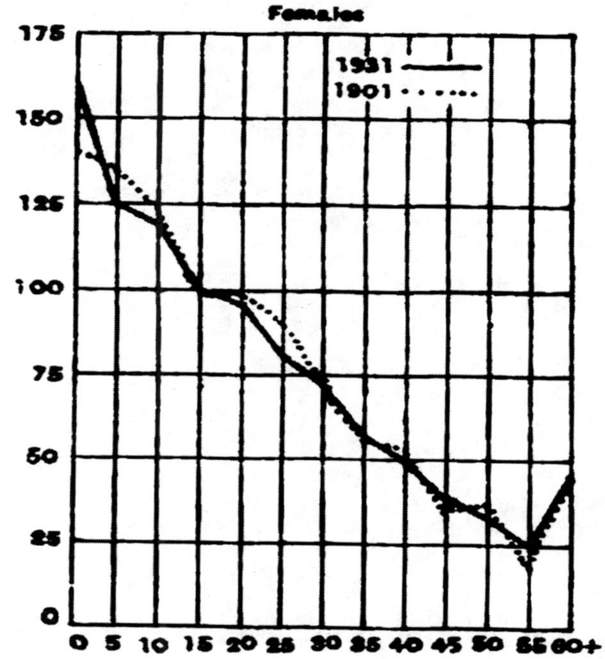

larger proportion of children is to be attributed not so much to an actual rise in the birth-rate as to a fall in the rate of infant mortality. The Malayali castes have no child marriages, and cohabitation and child-birth in these castes generally take place only after the woman is physically mature. The rapid progress of female education has raised the age of marriage and child-birth still further. With the advance of civilization and the spread of enlightenment, primitive and insanitary methods of midwifery are being replaced by civilized and scientific methods. Conditions of living are healthier and facilities of rural medical relief greater than of old. In the circumstances the survival rate of children must be rising steadily.

That the increase in the earliest age-groups, instead of being balanced by a more or less uniform decrease shared by all the subsequent groups, should have affected the adult categories in particular calls for an explanation. The death-rate among adults is relatively low, and the conditions of the decade were favourable to all sections of the population. In the circumstances the fall in the proportion of the adult groups is probably to be attributed to an increasing volume of emigration, emigrants being drawn chiefly from the ranks of adults. The proportion of persons in the effective age-periods reflects the degree of energy and vigour in a population. Any loss in the strength of the adult groups must therefore indicate a corresponding loss of energy. From this point of view the depletion of the adult categories cannot be viewed as a happy sign.

Proportion of children to adults

7. Subsidiary Table V gives the proportion of children aged 0—10 per 100 of adults in the age-groups 15—40 and per 100 of married women in the same age-groups. It is from this proportion that the character of the population in respect of its progressiveness is usually gauged. That the figures for 1931 are by far the highest since 1891 will be seen from the margin. A rise in the proportion of children, which does not result from any heavy mortality in the ranks of their parents, is to be taken as an indication of an increase in the fertility of marriage. In view of the conclusions arrived at in the foregoing paragraph, it is clear that the high proportion of children is the result of favourable conditions and that the population is progressive in character.

	1931	1921	1911	1901	1891
Proportion of children under 10 per 100 persons aged 15—40	75·0	67·2	65·7	66·6	66·5
Do per 100 married women aged 15—40	195·0	177·9	170·2	179·1	157·2

Variation in population at different age-periods.

8. This healthy position is further revealed in Subsidiary Table VI which gives the variation in the population at certain age-periods. The main increase during the past decade is in the period 0—10. At the census of 1921 the position was less favourable, the highest increase being in the age-groups 10—15, 40—60 and 60 and over; while the decade 1901 to 1910 showed the least favourable conditions in that the greatest increase was at ages 60 and above.

Age distribution by religion

9. The age distribution in each of the main religious communities in the State is given in Subsidiary Table II. The appended table shows the principal features of this distribution for the last two censuses.

Religion		Proportion of males and females in certain age-groups in every 1,000 of the population of each sex										Mean age
		0—5		5—15		15—40		40—60		60 and over		
		Males	Females	Males	Females	Males	Females	Males	Females	Males	Females	
1		2	3	4	5	6	7	8	9	10	11	12
Hindus	1931	165	156	259	236	378	410	156	151	41	47	24·3
	1921	135	130	265	245	400	419	159	154	41	52	24·5
Muslims	1931	168	167	265	260	394	421	140	121	33	31	22·7
	1921	137	139	282	274	396	421	148	128	37	38	23·06
Christians	1931	173	168	267	261	372	393	146	136	42	42	23·3
	1921	143	143	284	278	387	398	147	137	39	44	22·4
Jews	1931	154	127	240	230	341	414	200	173	65	56	26·4
	1921	135	131	208	260	371	426	232	126	54	57	25·8

Of the three most populous communities, the Christians are seen to have the highest proportion of children (0—15). The Muslims follow them closely, while the Hindus take the last place. In the oldest group (60 and over) there is little difference between the Hindus and the Christians, but the ratio of the Muslims in this group is the lowest. In the adult group (15—40), which shows the degree of energy and vigour in the community, the Muslims have the highest proportion and the Christians the lowest; while the Hindus far out-number the other two communities in the elderly group (40—60). The distribution is in general conformity with the experience of previous censuses, the younger communities showing a larger proportion of children and a smaller proportion of aged people.

The age distribution of the small community of Jews is significant. The Jews have the lowest proportion in the earlier groups and the highest in the later ones. In spite of the slight improvement in their position noticed during the past decade, their age-constitution* is far less favourable than that of the other communities.

Age distribution by caste

10. The general conclusions regarding age-constitution drawn from the experience of previous censuses are that the lower strata of the community have a larger proportion in the younger age-periods, whereas the higher castes enjoy greater longevity. The age distribution of selected castes given in Subsidiary Table III, taken as a whole, will appear to support these conclusions, though individual figures reveal strange inconsistencies. The proportions for some of the castes are given below.

*According to Sundburg's classification of populations shown in the last paragraph of this chapter, the Jews approximate to the *stationary* type, their proportion in the three age-groups 0—15, 15—50 and 50 and over being 37·6, 49·0 and 13·4 respectively.

Age distribution of 1,000 of each sex in certain castes.

CASTE	Number per mille aged											
	0—6		7—13		14—16		17—23		24—43		44 and over	
	Males	Females	Males	Females	Males	Females	Males	Females	Males	Females	Males	Females
1	2	3	4	5	6	7	8	9	10	11	12	13
Ambalavasi ..	194	180	166	146	66	65	116	121	276	277	182	211
Brahman—Konkani ..	182	188	167	164	69	55	114	124	254	270	214	199
Do Malayali ..	144	145	131	132	70	57	117	113	294	291	244	262
Do Tamil ..	213	212	200	177	71	56	100	113	216	252	200	190
Malayali Kshatriya ..	247	185	156	164	55	63	101	130	241	272	200	186
Iluvan ..	216	199	186	168	76	73	117	133	254	278	151	149
Pulayan ..	217	212	181	164	71	67	100	128	283	288	148	141
Sambavan (Parayan) ..	214	223	171	161	75	64	96	139	286	270	158	131
Vettuvan ..	225	231	186	168	69	70	108	133	273	276	139	122
Muslim—Jonakan ..	216	213	182	174	75	76	118	141	273	280	136	116
Indian Christian ..	219	212	184	180	74	74	120	110	250	258	153	146
Jew ..	200	160	165	163	57	66	109	144	243	284	226	183

The age-constitution of the Malayali Brahmans (Nambudiris) is specially noteworthy. Their community has by far the smallest proportion of children and the largest proportion of aged people. Two factors will account for this position. In the first place the Nambudiris occupy the topmost rung of the caste ladder in Malabar. There is then the peculiar Nambudiri custom according to which only the eldest son of the family marries in his own caste. The result is seen not only in the extremely low proportion of children in this community but also in the very high survival value of Nambudiri women, among whom there are many old spinsters, and whose proportion in the age-group 44 and over is as high as 262 in every 1,000 women. The Konkani Brahmans and the Ambalavasis conform to the standard. But the Tamil Brahmans and the Malayali Kshatriyas both show a very high proportion of children. At the same time there is no shortage in the oldest age-groups of these communities which, therefore, appear to be prolific as well as long-lived.

Age distribution in selected towns

11. Part B of Imperial Table VII contains the statistics of age, sex and civil condition for the municipal towns of the State. The age distribution of 1,000 persons of each sex in the population of these towns is given in the inset table side by side with the figures for the whole State. Naturally the two sets of figures differ even as the population of urban areas differs from the rest. The proportion of children (0—15) of both sexes is lower in the urban population. The shortage is balanced by an increase in the age-groups 15—50, which is to be attributed to the immigration of adults into these towns for reasons already explained in the concluding portion of paragraph 4 in Chapter II.

Age-group	Age distribution of 1,000 persons of each sex in the population of			
	(1) Municipal towns		(2) the State	
	Males	Females	Males	Females
0—5 ..	143	150	169	161
5—10 ..	122	124	134	125
10—15 ..	119	117	127	119
15—20 ..	108	103	95	100
20—25 ..	100	100	84	96
25—30 ..	79	82	71	80
30—35 ..	73	74	68	72
35—40 ..	62	59	59	57
40—45 ..	56	51	52	50
45—50 ..	42	39	40	38
50—55 ..	34	33	35	33
55—60 ..	23	24	25	24
60—65 ..	15	20	19	20
65—70 ..	9	10	10	11
70 and over ..	13	14	12	14
	1,000	1,000	1,000	1,000

Vital Statistics

12. The following table contains the specific numbers of persons at certain age-periods returned at the last four censuses.

Age-period	Year	Age-period	Year	Percentage of decrease 1901—1911	Age-period	Year	Percentage of decrease 1911—1921	Age-period	Year	Percentage of decrease 1921—1931
	1901		1911			1921			1931	
					0—10	266,278		10—20	266,020	0·1
		0—10	251,643		10—20	218,305	13·25	20—30	200,250	8·27
0—10	223,102	10—20	202,936	9·04	20—30	169,999	16·23	30—40	151,256	9·24
10—20	182,573	20—30	166,884	8·59	30—40	132,589	20·55	40—50	108,649	18·06
20—30	147,614	30—40	124,659	15·55	40—50	91,260	26·79	50—60	69,844	23·47
30—40	108,018	40—50	82,135	23·96	50—60	56,895	30·73	60—70	35,666	37·31
40—50	72,708	50—60	50,622	30·37	60—70	31,103	38·56	70 & over	15,902	48·87

To trace the fortunes of each group of the population in its onward march from infancy to old age through successive decades, and to gauge the influences of mortality and migration on it at different stages in its progress reflected in the rate of decrease noted against it in the table after every ten years, will no doubt be highly interesting and instructive. But the available statistics do not enable us to pursue this enquiry with any degree of confidence or success. The inaccuracies in age returns that form a characteristic feature of our censuses; the anomalies noticed in the figures of certain age-groups of 1921 as compared with the related groups of 1931, and commented on in paragraph 19 of Chapter I; the utterly unreliable character of our vital statistics and the absence of accurate statistics on migration mentioned in paragraphs 13 and 14 of the same chapter, are the main difficulties that confront us in the task.

Subsidiary Tables VII and VIII give the birth and death-rates by sex for the past decade. As pointed out in paragraph 13 of Chapter I, these rates bear no proportion to the actual numbers of births or of deaths during the intercensal period. The number of children in the age-group 0—10, returned at the census of 1931, is 354,399 and the proportion of persons born outside Cochin in the State's population is 7·3 per cent. Even though the ranks of children generally hold but few immigrants, let us concede that the age-group 0-10 also contains the average proportion (7·3 per cent) of persons born outside the State. When due allowance is made for this immigrant element in the group, it will be seen that 328,528 children under 10 years, born in the State during the decade, were alive on the date of the final census in 1931. Assuming that the rate of infant mortality was 200 in every 1,000 infants born alive—the rate for all India during the normal years of the decade 1911—1920 was only 211 for males and 199 for females—, the number of children born alive during the past ten years must have been no less than 410,660. This figure represents a decennial rate of 42 births for every 100 of the State's population as it stood in 1921, while the recorded birth-rate is but 14·6 per cent for the whole State and 32·4 per cent for the municipal towns. If there were no deaths during the past 10 years, the population of 1921 (979,080) would have received an addition of 410,660 children born alive during the decade and 39,249 persons representing the excess of immigrants over emigrants. The population of 1931 would then have been 1,428,989 whereas the actual population recorded at the census is only 1,205,016. The difference of 223,973 represents the deaths of the intercensal period. The decennial death-rate according to this calculation must be 22·9 per cent for the whole State. But, according to the vital statistics, it is only 9·3 per cent for the State and 18·8 per cent for the municipal towns. The difference between the birth and death-rates calculated from the census figures and the rates furnished by the vital statistics is disconcertingly wide.

Subsidiary Table X gives the actual and proportional figures of reported deaths from certain diseases. The rise in mortality from small-pox in 1930 is noteworthy.

Mean age

13. The mean age of the Hindus, Muslims, Christians and Jews is shown in the margin. The mean age refers to the average age of the persons who were alive on the date of the census, and does not coincide with the mean duration of life, except where the births and deaths exactly balance one another. A growing population with a large number of children will show a lower mean age than a decadent population in which the children are relatively few in number. Judged from this standard, the figures in the margin lead us to the same conclusions as were arrived at in paragraph 9 above. The Muslims and the Christians with the largest proportion of children have the lowest mean age, and the unfavourable age-constitution of the Jews is revealed by their high figure.

Religion	Mean age			
	1931			1921
	Population	Males	Females	Population
Hindu ..	24·3	23·9	24·6	24·5
Muslim ..	22·7	23·0	22·5	23·1
Christian ..	23·3	23·3	23·3	22·4
Jew ..	26·4	26·5	26·3	25·8

Sundburg's types of population

14. According to the Swedish statistician Sundburg, about half the population in European countries is contained in the age-categories ranging from 15—50, and the proportion observed in the distribution of the remaining half between the two age-groups 0—15 and 50 and over will determine whether the population is of the *progressive, stationary* or *regressive* type. Sundburg's theory is that a progressive population will have about 40 per cent of its total strength in the first age-group and about 10 per cent in the last. In the stationary type the first age-group will contain only about a third of the population, while in the regressive type the proportion in the last group will be higher than that of the first. These proportions are given in the margin. It has been shown at previous censuses that the population of India conforms generally to Sundburg's standards. The age distribution, of the population of Cochin for four censuses based on the above classification, is given in the inset table on the next page. The distributions all appear to be of the progressive type as measured by western standards, but the population of 1901 and 1921 conforms to the types more closely than the population of 1911 and 1931. Indeed,

Type	Number of persons per mille aged		
	0—15	15—50	50 and over
TYPICAL			
Progressive ..	400	500	100
Stationary ..	330	500	170
Regressive ..	200	500	300

the balance of the middle group has been very much upset in favour of the first group during the past decade. The probable reasons for this have already been explained in paragraph 6 above. It is doubtful whether the European proportions will always hold good for the population of an Indian State in view of the fact that "the Indian figures are the result of factors which differ essentially from those in western countries, *viz.*, a higher birth-rate tempered by a high infant death-rate, a lower expectation of life and greater fluctuation in the adult age-categories."

Census year	Number of persons per mille aged		
	0—15	15—50	50 and over
1931	417	482	101
1921	399	498	103
1911	396	506	98
1901	402	502	96

SUBSIDIARY TABLES.

I.—Age distribution of 10,000 of each sex in 1931 and 1921.

Age period	1931		1921	
	Males	Females	Males	Females
1	2	3	4	5
0— 1	341	324	292	286
1— 2	381	365	199	184
2— 3	355	339	283	277
3— 4	316	300	308	313
4— 5	293	275	290	280
5—10	1,343	1,253	1,400	1,328
10—15	1,269	1,191	1,314	1,233
15—20	949	1,007	962	953
20—25	843	959	848	964
25—30	715	803	779	879
30—35	679	722	708	739
35—40	589	570	661	598
40—45	522	496	558	538
45—50	403	384	402	374
50—55	347	328	353	361
55—60	245	240	239	210
60—65	189	196	199	241
65—70	100	106	95	100
70 and over	121	142	108	150
Total	10,000	10,000	10,000	10,000
Mean age	23.7	24.1	23.75	24.23

II.—Age distribution of 10,000 of each sex in each main religion.

Age	Hindu		Muslim		Christian		Jew	
	Males	Females	Males	Females	Males	Females	Males	Females
1	2	3	4	5	6	7	8	9
0— 1	335	317	326	315	358	344	277	288
1 — 2	378	359	370	374	392	378	333	247
2— 3	352	334	356	355	361	349	333	288
3— 4	312	290	321	319	284	318	277	219
4— 5	289	265	304	303	300	292	319	233
5—10	1,333	1,207	1,364	1,344	1,373	1,339	1,290	1,151
10—15	1,257	1,151	1,287	1,258	1,293	1,268	1,110	1,151
15—20	936	997	979	1,058	971	1 018	846	1,041
20—25	824	961	882	1,025	853	936	804	1,055
25—30	721	816	752	846	689	760	652	657
30—35	687	737	720	738	650	685	555	630
35—40	601	588	604	542	558	532	555	753
40—45	534	513	519	448	495	467	610	644
45—50	412	400	376	319	385	362	555	452
50—55	356	342	305	258	338	309	458	342
55—60	250	253	206	186	243	222	374	288
60—65	194	209	152	145	188	179	333	237
65—70	102	112	81	68	100	102	130	164
70 and over	121	148	96	99	129	140	180	164
Total	10,000	10,000	10,000	10,000	10,000	10,000	10,000	10,000

III.—*Age distribution of 1,000 of each sex in certain castes.*

Caste	Males—number per mille aged						Females—number per mille aged					
	0—6	7—13	14—16	17—23	24—43	44 and over	0—6	7—13	14—16	17—23	24—43	44 and over
1	2	3	4	5	6	7	8	9	10	11	12	13
HINDU												
Ambalavasi ..	194	166	66	116	276	182	180	146	65	121	277	211
Ambattan ..	222	165	66	139	254	154	188	167	73	132	310	130
Arayan ..	188	172	72	132	273	163	214	168	69	128	274	147
Brahman—Konkani ..	182	167	69	114	254	214	188	164	55	124	270	199
Do Malayali ..	141	131	70	117	294	244	145	132	57	113	291	262
Do Tamil ..	213	200	71	160	216	200	212	177	56	113	252	190
Chakkan ..	166	159	68	125	314	168	195	150	63	134	285	173
Chaliyan { Chaliyan ..	176	200	49	151	239	185	229	104	78	151	240	198
Chaliyan { Pattariyan ..	218	170	57	113	275	167	206	156	66	135	277	160
Eluthassan ..	207	171	72	120	266	164	193	163	70	127	278	169
Iluvan ..	216	186	76	117	254	151	199	168	73	133	278	149
Kaikolan ..	168	171	54	126	307	174	148	163	77	132	282	198
Kammalan .	208	176	78	121	262	155	206	161	69	138	272	154
Kanakkan ..	222	173	76	110	272	147	219	172	67	130	284	128
Kaniyan ..	197	165	80	136	236	186	165	151	74	145	280	182
Kshatriya—Malayali ..	247	156	55	101	241	200	185	164	63	130	272	186
Kudumi Chetti ..	197	158	60	126	298	161	212	133	67	147	287	154
Kusavan ..	202	185	54	127	263	169	224	144	78	130	286	138
Nayar ..	213	177	73	116	258	163	180	151	66	128	285	190
Pandaran ..	197	165	69	120	283	166	188	166	76	126	278	166
Panditattan ..	209	154	65	130	278	164	193	140	53	148	282	184
Pulayan ..	217	181	71	100	283	148	212	164	67	128	288	141
Sambavan (Parayan) ..	214	171	75	96	286	158	223	161	64	139	279	134
Valan ..	222	182	66	123	252	155	232	177	63	126	262	140
Velakkattalavan ..	219	181	74	103	272	151	185	155	62	133	274	191
Velan ..	200	179	72	121	260	168	194	154	73	137	291	151
Vellalan ..	164	167	64	121	314	170	168	167	54	125	300	186
Veluttedan ..	212	171	80	107	254	176	166	147	66	138	295	188
Vettuvan ..	225	186	69	108	273	139	231	168	70	133	276	122
MUSLIM												
Jonakan ..	216	182	75	118	273	136	213	174	76	141	280	116
Ravuttan ..	205	193	72	128	280	122	206	187	65	137	273	132
Others ..	210	175	77	123	262	153	211	186	72	130	272	129
CHRISTIAN												
Anglo-Indian ..	210	192	82	116	194	206	180	173	76	127	[illegible]	178
European ..	52	69	..	103	483	293	93	55	37	148	537	130
Indian Christian ..	219	184	74	120	250	153	212	180	74	130	253	146
JAIN ..	170	161	42	76	432	119	206	174	32	185	273	141
JEW ..	200	165	57	109	243	226	160	163	66	144	[illegible]	183

IV.—Proportion of children under 14 and of persons over 43 to those aged 14—43 in certain castes; also of married females aged 14—43 per 100 females.

CASTES	Proportion of children, both sexes, per 100		Proportion of persons over 43 per 100 aged 14—43		Number of married females aged 14—43 per 100 females of all ages
	Persons aged 14—43	Married females aged 14—43	Male	Female	
	2	3	4	5	6
HINDU					
Ambalavasi	75	228	40	46	30
Ambattan	76	189	34	25	39
Arayan	78	222	34	31	35
Brahman—Konkani.	79	185	49	44	38
Do Malayali	59	182	51	57	31
Do Tamil	99	220	52	45	36
Chakkan	68	180	33	36	37
Chaliyan { Chaliyan	78	243	42	42	30
Chaliyan { Pattariyan	81	224	38	34	32
Elathassan	79	213	36	35	34
Ilavan	82	232	34	31	32
Kaikolan	67	177	36	40	36
Kammàlan	80	224	34	32	33
Kanakkan	84	229	32	27	34
Kaniyan	72	235	41	36	29
Kshatriya—Malayali	86	212	51	40	33
Kudumi Chetti	71	176	33	31	41
Kusavan	81	192	38	28	40
Nayar	77	237	36	40	28
Pandaran	75	194	35	35	36
Panditattan	73	194	35	38	38
Pulayan	83	215	31	29	36
Sambavan (Parayan)	82	207	35	28	37
Valan	91	250	35	31	33
Velakkattalavan	80	232	34	41	31
Velan	76	201	37	30	35
Vellalan	68	195	34	39	34
Veluttedan	73	210	40	38	31
Vettuvan	87	228	31	26	36
MUSLIM					
Jonakan	82	224	29	23	36
Ravuttan	83	224	25	28	36
Others	83	241	37	27	31
CHRISTIAN					
Anglo-Indian	87	204	53	38	25
European	21	115	50	18	24
Indian Christian	88	248	34	32	32
JAIN	68	190	22	30	42
JEW	76	200	55	37	34

V.—Proportion of children under 10 and of persons over 60 to those aged 15—40; also of married females aged 15—40 per 100 females.

Natural Division "Malabar and Konkan"	Proportion of children, both sexes, per 100						Proportion of persons over 60 per 100 aged 15—40						Number of married females aged 15—40 per 100 females of all ages		
	Persons aged 15—40			Married females aged 15—40			1931		1921		1911				
	1931	1921	1911	1931	1921	1911	Males	Females	Males	Females	Males	Females	1931	1921	1911
1	2	3	4	5	6	7	8	9	10	11	12	13	14	15	16
COCHIN STATE	75·0	67·2	65·7	195·0	177·0	170·2	10·9	11·0	10·1	11·9	9	11	29·5	30·2	32·1

V A.—Proportion of children under 10 and of persons over 60 to those aged 15—40 in certain religions; also of married females aged 15—40 per 100 females.

RELIGIONS	Proportion of children, both sexes, per 100						Proportion of persons over 60 per 100 aged 15—40						Number of married females aged 15—40 per 100 females of all ages		
	Persons aged 15—40			Married females aged 15—40			1931		1921		1911				
	1931	1921	1911	1931	1921	1911	Males	Females	Males	Females	Males	Females	1931	1921	1911
1	2	3	4	5	6	7	8	9	10	11	12	13	14	15	16
Hindu ..	73	65	63	189	173	166	11	12	10	12	9	12	32	30	32
Muslim ..	74	69	68	193	179	179	8	7	9	9	8	8	32	32	33
Christian ..	80	73	73	210	189	180	11	11	10	11	9	11	29	31	33
Jain ..	58	45	18	154	115	52	5	7	3	5	4	3	40	47	59
Jew ..	70	63	59	173	156	155	19	14	15	13	17	15	30	33	30
ALL RELIGIONS..	75·0	67·2	65·7	195·0	177·9	170·2	10·9	11·0	10·1	11·9	9	11	29·5	30·2	32·1

VI.—Variation in population at certain age-periods.

Natural Division "Malabar and Konkan"	Decade	Variation per cent in population (Increase+ Decrease—)					
		All ages	0—10	10—15	15—40	40—60	60 and over
1	2	3	4	5	6	7	8
Cochin State	**1921—1930**	**+ 23·1**	**+ 33·1**	**+ 18·9**	**+ 19·2**	**+20·5**	**+ 17·9**
	1911—1920	+ 6·6	+ 5·8	+ 11·6	+ 2·6	+ 11·6	+ 11·5
	1901—1910	+ 13·1	+ 12·8	+ 7·9	+ 14·4	+ 13·7	+ 15·8

VII.—Reported birth-rate by sex.

Year	Number of births per 1,000 of total population		
	COCHIN STATE		
	Persons	Males	Females
1	2	3	4
1921	15·5	16·4	14·7
1922	14·6	15·4	13·8
1923	13·4	14·0	12·8
1924	12·8	13·3	12·3
1925	12·2	12·8	11·7
1926	14·4	15·0	13·8
1927	14·7	15·3	14·1
1928	14·9	15·3	14·5
1929	16·5	17·2	15·9
1930	16·5	17·3	15·6
Average of the decade	14·6	15·2	13·9

VIII.—Reported death-rate by sex.

Year	Number of deaths per 1,000 of total population		
	COCHIN STATE		
	Persons	Males	Females
1	2	3	4
1921	10·2	10·9	9·5
1922	9·4	10·2	8·6
1923	10·2	11·0	9·4
1924	8·1	8·6	7·6
1925	8·5	8·8	8·1
1926	8·3	8·9	7·8
1927	10·0	10·7	9·3
1928	9·0	9·9	8·2
1929	8·8	9·3	8·3
1930	10·7	11·3	10·1
Average of the decade	9·3	10·0	8·7

Note:—Subsidiary Table IX has not been prepared as the required information by age is not available.

X.—Reported deaths from certain diseases per mille of the population.

COCHIN STATE

Year	Actual number of deaths	Ratio per mille
1	2	3
CHOLERA.		
1921	62	0·1
1922	79	0·1
1923	..	..
1924	97	0·1
1925	179	0·2
1926	44	..
1927	106	0·1
1928	6	..
1929	..	..
1930	32	..
SMALL-POX.		
1921	31	..
1922	81	0·1
1923	630	0·7
1924	165	0·2
1925	114	0·1
1926	16	..
1927	73	0·1
1928	16	..
1929	212	0·2
1930	1,139	1·2
OTHER CAUSES.		
1921	9,884	10·1
1922	9,061	9·2
1923	9,339	9·5
1924	7,677	7·8
1925	7,987	8·2
1926	8,103	8·3
1927	9,589	9·8
1928	8,828	9·0
1929	8,393	8·6
1930	9,290	9·5

Note.—(1). Figures by sex are not available.

(2). In 1928 and 1929 respectively there were 4 and 13 deaths from plague, and they have been included in the numbers under "Other Causes".

CHAPTER V.—PART I—SEX.

Introductory remarks

THE western critics, who impugned the accuracy of the returns of females recorded at Indian censuses on the ground that the Indian sex proportions did not conform to those of Western Europe, have been silenced since the census of 1911, when it was conclusively shown that the excess of females in the population of Western Europe should not necessarily be taken as the standard for the population of India, that there are certain general reasons for the excess of males over females in this country, and that imperfect enumeration of women could have little or nothing to do with the low sex ratio* characteristic of the Indian population.

Sex ratio in Cochin

2. So far as Cochin is concerned, the sex ratio of its population has been approximating to the standard of Western Europe for several decades, and since 1901 the proportion of females has shown a steadily increasing excess over that of males. This was always attributed to the greater accuracy of enumeration in the State. Thus the Census Report of 1891 states: "Successive censuses have enhanced the proportion of females, as, while in 1881 there were only 98·9 females in Cochin for every 100 males, the proportion rose to 99·8 at the census under review. Again, in the four northern taluks of the State the ratio is in favour of females, but it is inverted in the case of the three **Southern Taluks. The preponderance of males in the latter may be real, but there are several indications to show that the census operations were carried out more satisfactorily in the northern taluks. It seems to me, therefore, more than probable that a completely correct enumeration will show a preponderance, however slight, of females over males in Cochin as well." This surmise was regarded as fully justified by the Census Superintendent of 1901 in view of the slight preponderance of females over males disclosed at the census of that year, a preponderance which, in his opinion, afforded "collateral testimony to the comparative accuracy of the enumeration" of 1901. Thus too the Report on the Census of 1911 says: "In view of the preponderance of females over males in most European countries, continental critics of the Census of India are inclined to attribute the deficiency of females to omissions in the Census records. Whether this view is correct or not in regard to other Provinces and States, there can be no doubt of its correctness as regards Cochin and Southern India generally. * * * * * * * * With the gradually increasing accuracy of the returns, successive censuses have enhanced the proportion of females, till in 1901 they outnumbered the males and still more so in 1911. This result, which in its way affords collateral testimony to the comparative accuracy of the enumeration, was anticipated in the last two Census Reports of this State." The Census Superintendent of 1921 also was of opinion that the excess of females in the population returned at the Census of that year gave "collateral testimony to the accuracy of the recent census returns."

Comparison with other States and Provinces

3. It has already been observed that the theory according to which a rise or fall in the masculinity of the population of any tract in India depended on the degree of accuracy in enumeration, was exploded at the Indian Census of 1911. If it is argued that conditions in South India are different and that any rise in the sex ratio here should be attributed to a greater degree of

---

*The term *sex ratio* is used, as in the Census Report of India, 1931, to indicate the number of females per 100 or per 1,000 males.

**Cochin, Kanayannur and Cranganur.

accuracy in the enumeration of females, the appended table will prove the weakness of the argument.

	Number of females per 1,000 males (actual population)					
	1931	1921	1911	1901	1891	1881
India ..	940	945	954	963	958	954
Madras ..	1,025	1,028	1,032	1,029	1,023	1,021
Mysore ..	955	962	979	980	991	1,007
Travancore ..	987	971	981	981	982	1,006
Malabar ..	1,059	1,051	1,034	1,024	1,018	1,014
Cochin ..	1,043	1,027	1,007	1,004	998	989

The figures indicate that the sex ratio in the population of India showed a tendency to rise during the closing decades of the last century. This movement seems to have culminated at the census of 1901 when the proportion of females rose to 963 per 1,000 of the male population.* Since then it has been falling steadily until, at the present census, it has reached 940, the lowest figure recorded at any census. Conditions in South India were different from the very beginning. Recorded statistics show that in regions where the Dravidian-speaking race element predominates the proportion of female births is higher than where the Indo-Aryan-speaking element prevails. In any case the population of the Madras Presidency contained more women than men and this sex proportion has been maintained throughout, though the strength of the female element has been declining since 1911. Mysore and Travancore returned more women than men at the census of 1881, but the position was reversed at the next census. Ever since the proportion of females has continued to fall lower and lower in both these States, though Travancore seems to have recovered a good deal of the lost ground at the present census. It is interesting to note that Cochin and Malabar have progressed on parallel lines in respect of the sex ratio in their population, which has been rising steadily from decade to decade and which conforms to the standard of Western Europe.

Reasons for high sex ratio in Cochin

4. The variations in the proportion of sexes in different Provinces and States noticed above will make it clear that there are factors other than accuracy in enumeration which must account for the steady fall in masculinity in the State of Cochin as also in the district of Malabar. The low sex ratio in the population of India has generally been attributed by those who have studied the question well to infanticide and the neglect of female children, the evil effects of early marriage and premature child bearing, a high birth-rate and primitive methods of midwifery, and the hard treatment accorded to women, especially widows, and the hard work done by women. Most of these factors have never been operative in Cochin. In a land where the law of inheritance is through females among a large section of the population, female infanticide, the neglect of female children and hard treatment of women can have no place. The Malayali communities being free from child marriages, early marriages and premature child bearing will have but little, if any, influence on the sex proportion in the State's population. The conditions in Cochin

*It has been suggested that the rise in the sex ratio till 1901 was due to an increasing accuracy of record and that the true figures, if available, would show a steadily decreasing proportion for India as a whole, though the Malabar Coast, with its peculiar marriage system, must have escaped this tendency.

therefore favoured a high sex ratio in its population from the very beginning and, as we shall presently see, these conditions have been rendered more favourable by the developments of modern times. It is but natural that the district of Malabar, which has almost the same features as Cochin, should reveal like tendencies in respect of its sex proportion; but that Travancore, where conditions are not dissimilar, should differ widely from Cochin and Malabar requires an explanation. This will be attempted in paragraph 10 below dealing with the sex proportion of the various taluks.

Reference to statistics

5. The distribution of the population by sex is shown in all the Census Tables. But Imperial Table VII, in which the statistics of sex are combined with those for age, religion and civil condition, and Imperial Table VIII, in which they are combined with caste, tribe or race, are the most important for the purposes of this chapter. Of the five Subsidiary Tables, which are appended to this chapter, and which contain comparative and proportionate figures drawn from the Imperial Tables and from the records of vital statistics, the first gives the general proportion of the sexes for five censuses, while the second and the third compare the sex proportions at different age-periods by religion. The fourth Subsidiary Table shows the sex distribution in certain selected castes and the fifth presents the actual number of births and deaths reported for each sex during the last thirty years.

Sex proportion at successive censuses

6. Of the 1,205,016 persons enumerated in the State in 1931, 589,813 were males and 615,203 were females. There was thus an excess of 25,390 females over males. The inset table in paragraph 3 above shows, and diagram I illustrates, the steady rise in the sex ratio since 1891.

Birth, death and migration being the factors that determine the numbers of each sex in any population, the vital statistics and statistics of migration have to account for the variations in sex proportion in this State as well. The recorded vital statistics given in Subsidiary Table V are, as usual, useless for our purposes for, according to them, the sex ratio should show an actual decline during the decade at least so far as the natural population is concerned. However, most of the reasons assigned for the low proportion of females in the Indian population as a whole are, as explained in paragraph 4 above, absent in Cochin. Further a steady rise in the age of marriage consequent on the rapid progress of female education in the State and the gradual displacement of primitive methods of midwifery by modern and scientific methods have considerably reduced the dangers which almost all women have to face, and lowered the death-rate among young mothers to an appreciable extent. The gradual rise in the sex ratio is but the natural outcome of these improved conditions. The balance of migration too has been favourable to the high proportion of females in the State's population. We have already seen from paragraph 3 of Chapter III that 94·4 per cent of the immigrants are of the casual type in which females preponderate. At the same time the proportion of women among the emigrants is lower than among immigrants. The result is seen in the difference between the actual and the natural population in respect of the sex ratio, and the figures in Subsidiary Table I are significant in that they show that the proportion of females has always been higher in the actual than in the natural population.

	Males	Females
Immigrants	36,360	51,057
Emigrants	22,878	25,290
Excess of Immigrants over emigrants	13,482	25,767
Excess of females over males	12,285	

No. of females per 1000 males in each main religion for five censuses

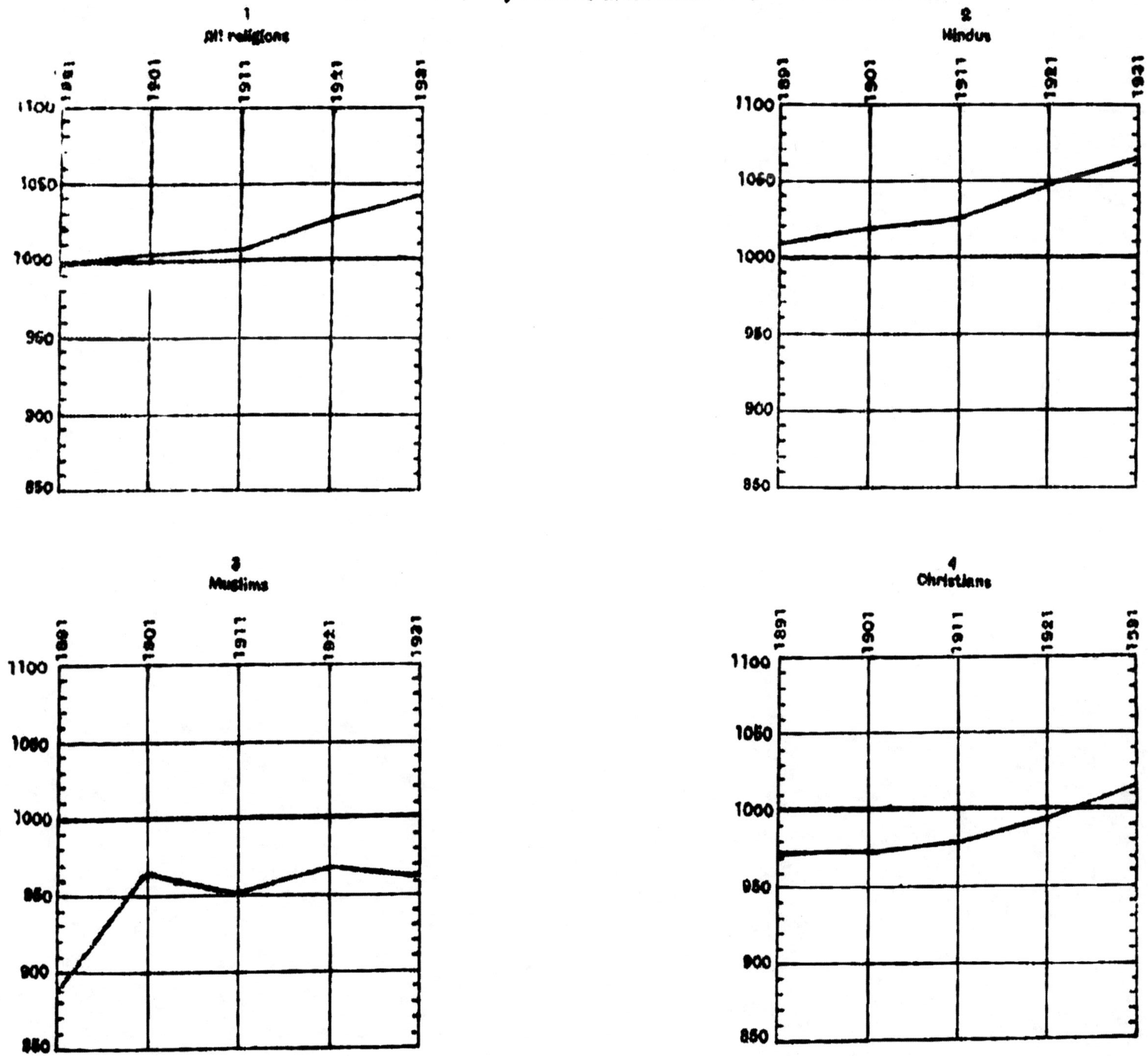

11
Sex proportions per 1,000 of the population by Taluks

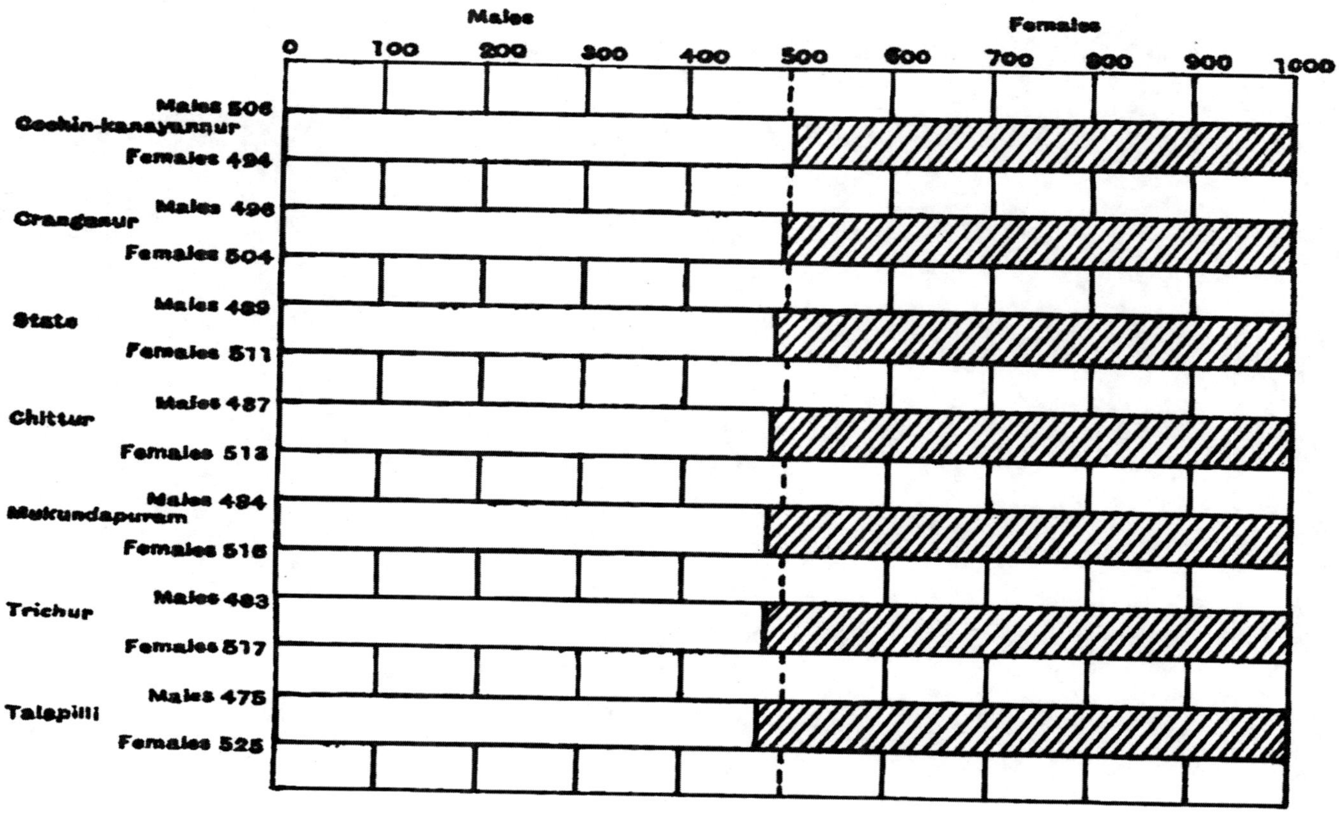

12
No. of Females per 1,000 Males by age periods for 3 Censuses

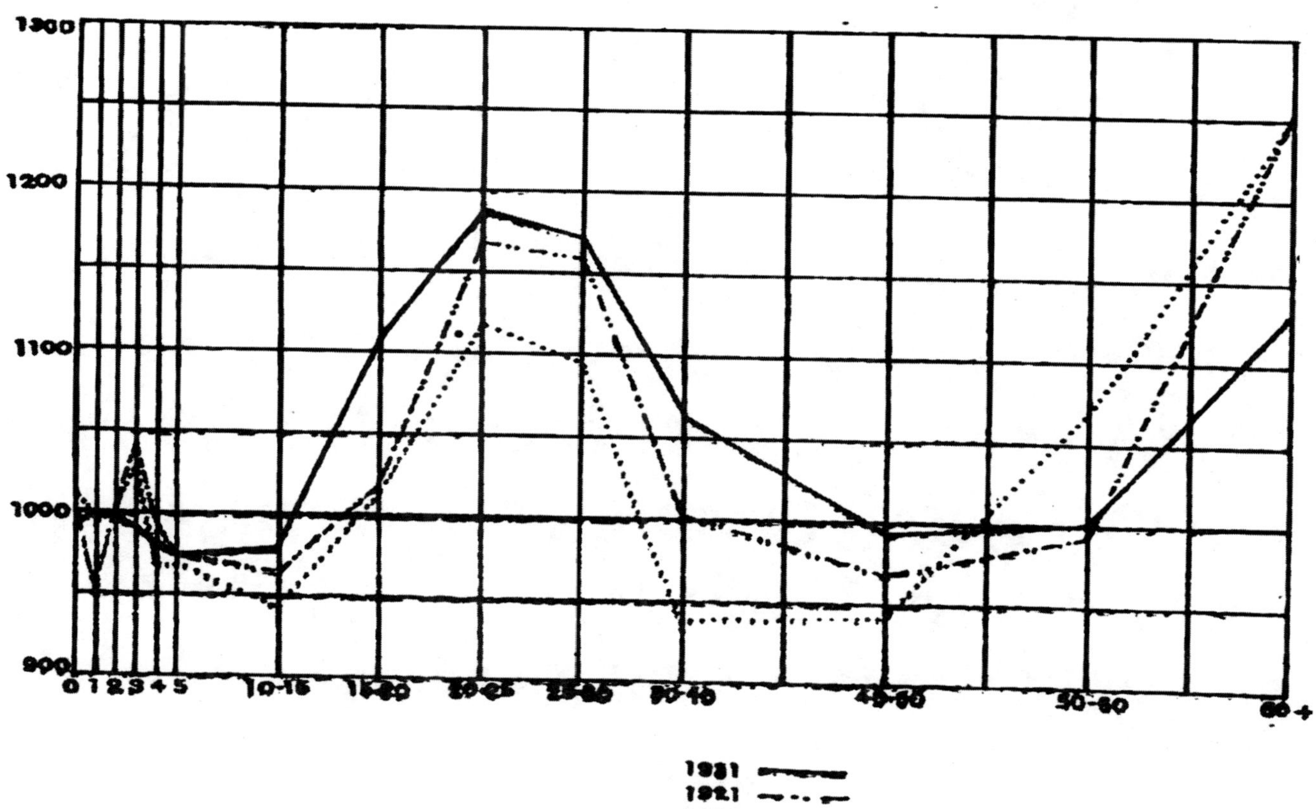

Sex proportion at different ages

7. Population statistics show that, in all countries of the world for which statistics are available, there are more males born than females, the proportions varying for different countries. Diagram 12 shows graphically the number of females per 1,000 males by main age-periods for, the last three censuses in Cochin and Subsidiary Table II gives the proportionate figures. The curves in the diagram indicate that the sex ratio in the age period 0—1 is relatively very high in this State. In 1911 and 1921 the proportion of females in this age-period seems to have exceeded that of males, but the 1931 curve starts below 1,000. If the returns are correct, we have to conclude that the mortality among male infants aged 0—1 was so high during the two previous decades that the relative position of the sexes in respect of their numbers was reversed before the first year of their existence terminated. In any case the 1931 curve appears to behave more reasonably, starting below 1,000 and avoiding the sudden fall at the age-period 1—2, the steep ascent at 3—4 and the sharp decline at 4—5 seen in the curves of 1911 and 1921.

High male infant mortality soon equalises the proportions of males and females in the population. The point at which the curves cross is 10—15 for all three decades. The factors determining sex proportion in the subsequent age-periods are, among females, the dangers of child birth and, among males, the various risks to which men are exposed in their daily avocations. But hard work, exposure in all weathers and accidents of various kinds combine to make the mean duration of life of men less than that of women who are for the most part engaged in domestic duties or occupations of a lighter nature. The curve accordingly rises above 1,000 after the fifteenth year and the proportion of females reaches the maximum (1,186 per 1,000 males) at 20-25. Thereafter it falls, passes below 1,000 at 40—50 and then rises again above the proportion of males, thereby showing a distinct general tendency on the part of women to live longer than men. It is interesting to note that the curves for the three censuses are almost parallel from 10—15 to 40—50.

Sex proportion by religions

8. If we now turn to the sex proportion in different religions, we find from Subsidiary Tables II and III that the Hindus have the highest and the Muslims the lowest sex ratio. The curves in diagrams 2, 3 and 4 illustrate the variations in sex proportion among the Hindus, Muslims and Christians since 1891. While the excess of females in the Hindu population has been growing steadily from decade to decade, the Muslims, who have fewer women than men in their community, show fluctuations in their sex ratio which has never risen above 967. The Christians have returned more females than males for the first time at the census of 1931, but the steady rise in their curve shows that the sex ratio in the community was increasing gradually all the time. The influence of racial factors may perhaps account to a certain extent for the difference in the sex ratio of the three communities, and the fact that migration chiefly affects the Hindus may further explain the relatively high proportion of females among them.

Religion	Number of females per 1,000 males (actual population)				
	1931	1921	1911	1901	1891
All Religions ..	1,043	1,027	1,007	1,004	998
Hindus ..	1,065	1,048	1,025	1,019	1,009
Muslims ..	962	967	951	965	885
Christians ..	1,015	993	978	974	972

by castes

9. The sex distribution of certain selected castes is given in Subsidiary Table IV, and the marginal table shows the sex ratio for most of them. The figures do not help us to arrive at any consistent principle reguiating the proportion of females to males in the various castes. Most of the indigenous Malayali castes, and particularly the *Marumakkathayam* communities, are seen to have a high sex ratio, the Malayali-Kshatriyas leading with 1,180 and the Nayars following with 1,154 females per 1,000 males. The depressed Pulayan has 1,052 women for every 1,000 men. A few of these Malayali castes have, however, an excess of males and the high caste Nambudiri Brahman and the depressed and unapproachable Vettuvan are both in this group. Similar variations are seen in the non-Malayali castes also. It may, however, be observed that the sex ratio of the Malayali castes taken as a whole is higher than that of the alien castes.

Caste.	Sex ratio.	Caste.	Sex ratio.
NON-MALAYALI (MAKKATHAYAM) CASTES			
Panditattan	913	Vellalan	1,016
Kusavan	950	Ambattan	1,023
Kudumi Chetti	960	Chakkan	1,030
Brahman (Tamil)	990	Pandaran	1,039
Do (Konkani)	1,001	Kaikolan	1,041
MALAYALI (MAKKATHAYAM) CASTES			
Arayan	902	Sambavan (Parayan)	1,016
Valan	954	Pulayan	1,052
Brahman (Malayali)	956	Eluthassan	1,054
Kaniyan	970	Kammalan	1,062
Vettuvan	985	Velan	1,093
Kanakkan	1,009		
MALAYALI (MAKKATHAYAM AND MARUMAKKATHAYAM) CASTES			
Chaliyan (Pattariyan)	1,072	Iluvan	1,082
MALAYALI (MARUMAKKATHAYAM) CASTES			
Ambalavasi	1,030	Veluttedan	1,160
Velakkathalavan	1,038	Kshatriya (Malayali)	1,180
Nayar	1,154		

and by taluks

10. The sex ratio of each taluk for five censuses is given in the following table and diagrams 5—10 illustrate the variations in sex proportion in these taluks for four decades.

TALUKS	Number of females per 1,000 males (actual population)				
	1931	1921	1911	1901	1891
Cochin-Kanayannur ..	976	960	932	943	943
Cranganur ..	1,016	982	969	981	982
Mukundapuram ..	1,065	1,036	1,017	1,014	1,001
Trichur ..	1,071	1,061	1,013	1,005	1,016
Talapilli ..	1,105	1,082	1,061	1,048	1,037
Chittur ..	1,053	1,068	1,071	1,054	1,090

The population of Mukundapuram, Trichur, Talapilli and Chittur is seen to have contained an excess of females over males since 1891, and the curves in the diagrams reveal a uniform tendency for a rise in the sex ratio in the first three taluks. In Chittur the proportion of females has fallen from 1,071 in 1911 to 1,053 in 1931. The fact that the north-east block of the taluk is highly malarial and that malarial fever selects adversely to females may perhaps account for the fluctuations and fall in the sex ratio in Chittur. Cranganur had fewer women than men till 1921, but at the present census the population of the taluk shows an excess of females; while Cochin-Kanayannur where males have always been predominant still contains more men than women. From paragraph 2 above we have already seen that the low sex ratio in Cranganur and Cochin-Kanayannur was wrongly attributed to inaccuracy in enumeration. The presence of immigrants in Mattancheri and Ernakulam from distant Provinces or districts may influence the sex ratio in Cochin-Kanayannur to a slight extent, but it is still very doubtful whether immigration

No. of females per 1,000 males in each taluk for five censuses

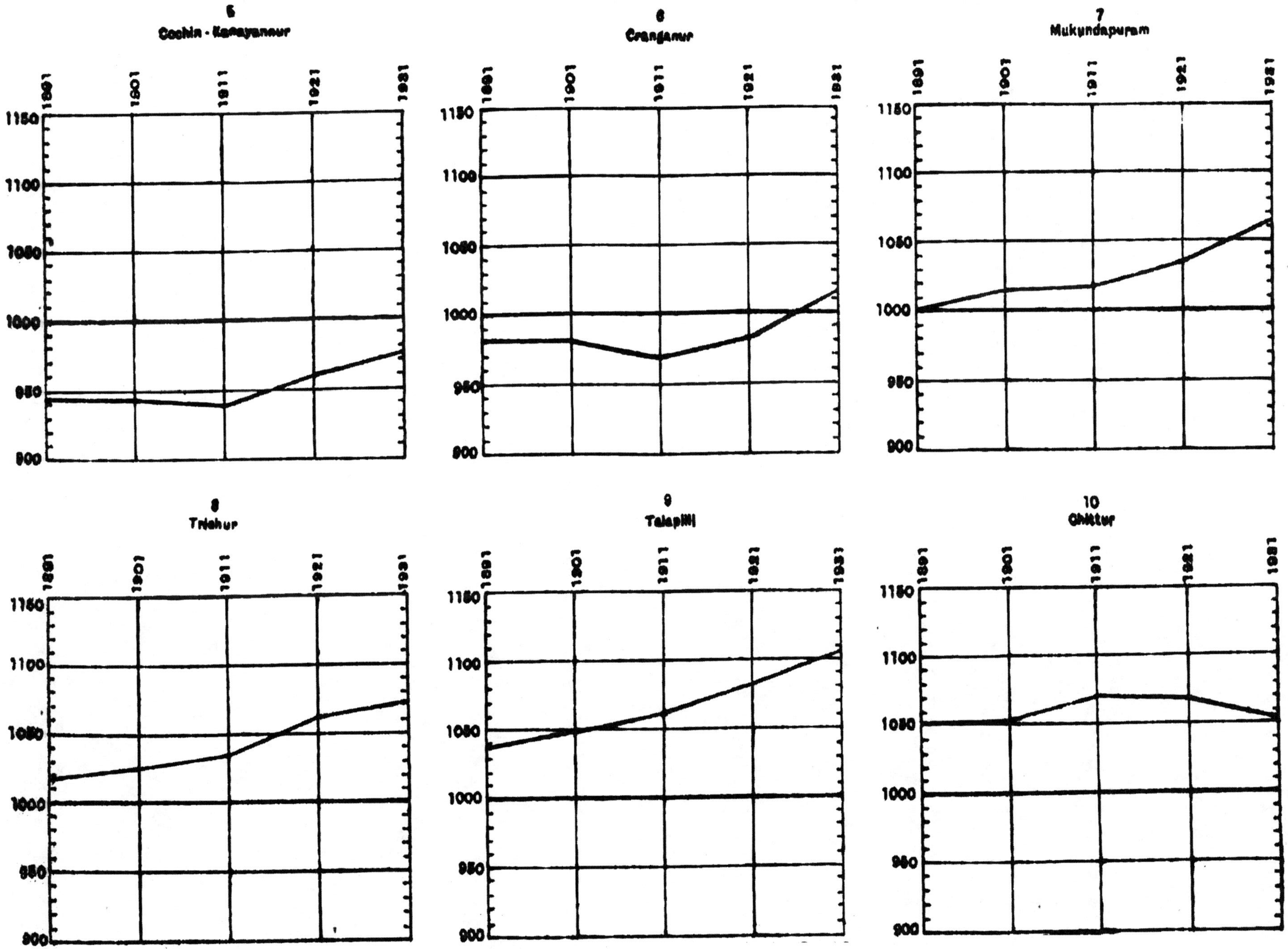

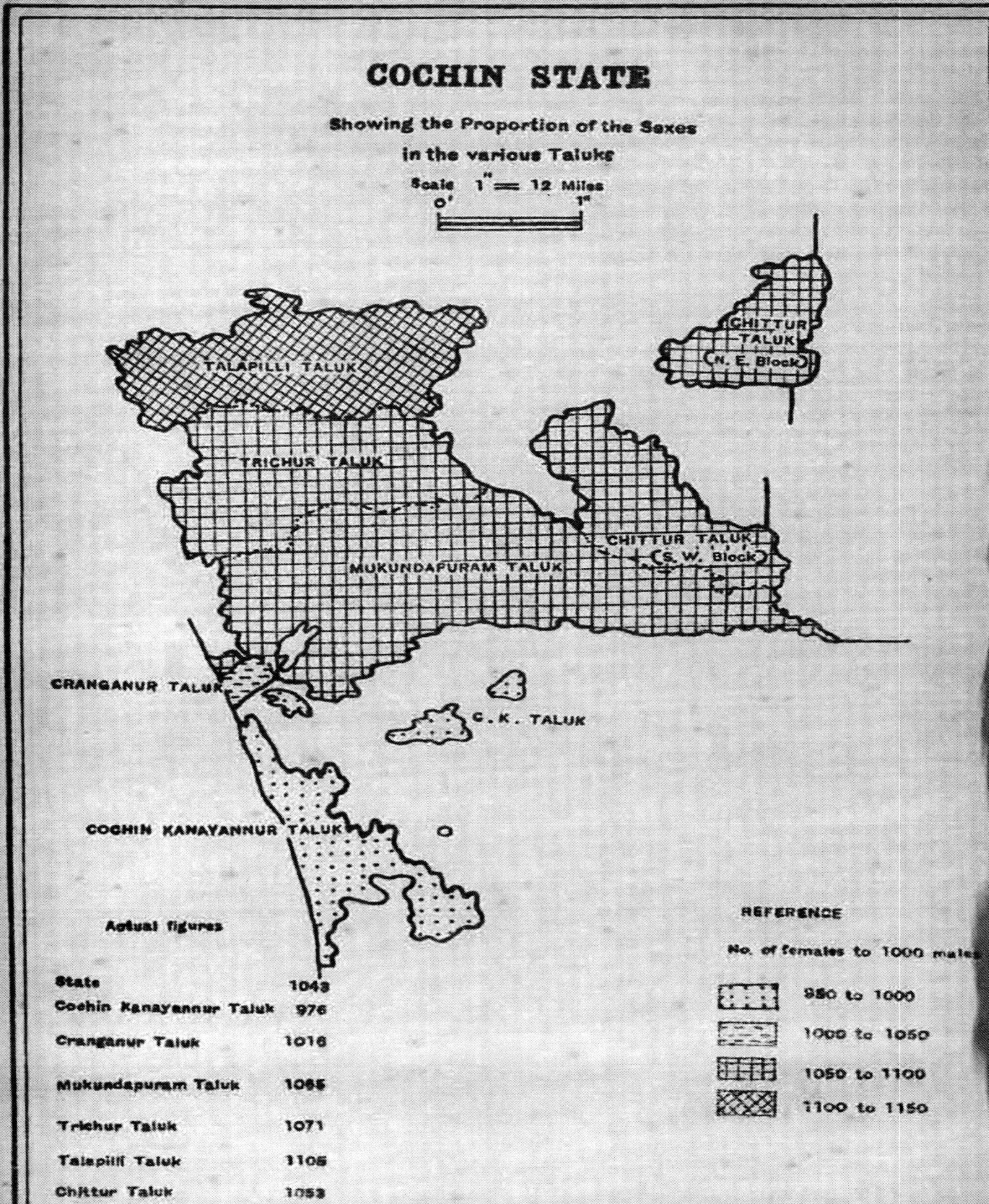

Register No. 129
Copies 850

Litho print Survey & Land Records Office, Trichur.
1107.

alone can account for the wide difference between this taluk and the northern ones. It seems to me that regional factors play an important part in this connection. Cochin-Kanayannur and Cranganur are the two coastal taluks, which differ in their physical features from the four interior taluks. At the same time the conditions in the two coastal taluks are almost identical with those of the populous taluks of north Travancore. It is significant that the population of Cochin-Kanayannur (and of Cranganur also till 1921) should contain more males than females even as the population of several sister taluks in Travancore does. Whether regional factors influence the sex proportion or not, we actually find that, if the coastal tract of Malabar is divided into a northern and a southern half by means of a line running across, or along the southern boundary of, Mukundapuram taluk, the northern division, including the district of Malabar and the four interior taluks of Cochin, contains a population in which females preponderate, while the southern division, comprising the State of Travancore and the two coastal taluks of Cochin, intersected by lagoons and back-waters, has more men than women in its population.

	Number of females per 1,000 males	
	Urban	Rural
Cochin State ..	980	1,057
Ernakulam ..	892	
Mattancheri ..	895	
Trippunittura ..	983	
Trichur ..	999	
Chalakudi ..	1,003	
Narakkal ..	1,022	
Vadakkancheri ..	1,028	
Cranganur ..	1,031	
Irinjalakkuda ..	1,049	
Chittur-Tattamangalam ..	1,074	
Kunnamkulam ..	1,116	
Nemmara ..	1,128	

Sex proportion in urban population

11. The marginal table shows the sex proportion in the population of towns. It will be seen from the figures that the sex ratio in towns is only 980 whereas it is 1,057 in rural areas. The political and commercial capitals of the State will naturally have a large number of immigrants, mostly males, and Ernakulam and Mattancheri accordingly show the lowest proportion of women. Trippunittura and Trichur also show the influence of immigration, but to a much smaller extent. The other towns do not differ from villages so far as the sex ratio in their population is concerned.

CHAPTER V.—PART II.—SIZE AND SEX CONSTITUTION OF FAMILIES.

Introductory

At the census of 1921 an attempt was made by certain Provinces and States in India to collect information bearing on the size and sex constitution of the average family and the fertility of married life. The results of the enquiry were recorded in the Census Reports of 1921. Bengal, Behar and Orissa, Bombay, the Central Provinces, the Punjab, Baroda and Travancore took part in the investigation. The work was, however, carried out more systematically and thoroughly in Baroda than elsewhere.

Agency employed for the enquiry

2. It was suggested by the Census Commissioner for India that enquiries on similar lines might be undertaken at the present census also and that the services of women teachers, wherever they were available, might be made use of in this connection. A special form was issued for the collection of information regarding the rates of fertility and mortality and, as the work could not be done by the agency of ordinary enumeration because of the intimate nature of the questions to be asked of, and answered by, women, the co-operation of the Medical and Education departments was invited. The women teachers were at first reluctant to do the work and, strangely enough, even such among them as had received high English education were inclined to protest against their services being requisitioned for the purpose. They were however persuaded in the end to undertake the work on a small scale. The hospitals and dispensaries in the State extended their hearty co-operation from the very outset. 33,471 returns were received as a result of the joint labours of these two agencies and I take this opportunity to thank those women teachers and medical officers, who did the work, and without whose help the enquiry could not have been undertaken at all.

Sex of the first-born

3. The results of this special enquiry are embodied in the five Sex Tables given at the end of this chapter, but a study of the statistics leads one to entertain considerable doubts about the accuracy of many of the returns. Table I shows the sex of the first-born and from it we find that there are 924 first-born females to 1,000 first-born males. The proportion of females must be regarded as very high, the corresponding figures for Travancore and Baroda in 1921 being only 830 and 718 respectively. The marginal table reveals the interesting fact that the three States maintain the same order of precedence in respect of their sex ratio also.

	No. of females per 1,000 males	No. of first-born females per 1,000 first-born males	
Baroda ..	942	718	1921
Travancore ..	987	830	1921
Cochin ..	1,043	924	

Size of family by occupation of husband

4. Sex Table III gives 'the size of families by occupation of husband'. The subject is of great interest and importance, but the results of the enquiry are unfortunately disappointing in that they serve to throw but very little light on the problem of the influence of occupation on fertility. The average number of children born alive to each married couple is only 3·8, a figure too low to be taken as correct in the light of one's personal knowledge of local conditions. In Baroda where the rate of increase in population is much lower than in Cochin, the average recorded at the census of 1921

---

* The special form wanted the following particulars for each married woman:
Age, husband's age, husband's occupation and caste or religion, duration of married life, sex of first child (whether quick or still born), number of children born alive, number of children still living, age of children still living.

Occupation of husband	No. of families examined	Average No. of children per family	Proportion of surviving children to 1,000 born alive
Landlords	637	4·07	763
Cultivating owners	3,708	3·86	766
Cultivating tenants	702	4·00	756
Agricultural labourers	567	3·83	697
Agriculture (unspecified)	1,511	3·90	752
Toddy drawers	705	4·47	725
Lime burners, etc.	488	3·94	709
Shop-keepers, etc.	1,806	4·09	724
General merchants (trade unspecified)	2,629	3·98	809
Service of the State	1,073	3·59	780
Medical practitioners	70	3·31	905
Healing arts	742	4·26	752
Teaching	923	3·11	832
Clerks (education)	668	3·04	808
Other domestic service	1,085	3·82	723
Labourers (unspecified)	6,692	3·59	668

was 5·3. The figures for the various occupations do not enable us to draw any definite conclusions regarding the effect of occupation on fertility. Samples have not been secured in sufficient numbers from many classes, but the figures for those classes, from which a few hundred samples each were obtained, reveal little or no difference between one occupation and another. The labouring classes show an average ranging from 3 to 4. Those that are engaged in intellectual pursuits or follow learned professions and those that live in retired leisure also show the same average. The survival rate of children, however, differs perceptibly in different classes. The average rate of survival is 735 per 1,000 children born alive, but the ratio generally falls below 700 in the labouring classes, while it rises as a rule to 800 or even higher among merchants and those that follow learned professions. In the margin are given the proportions for certain selected occupations to illustrate this point.

5. The caste statistics also are disappointing and it is not safe to draw any inferences of a general character from them. The average number of children born alive to each married couple in most of the castes, from which a few hundred returns each have been secured, ranges from 3 to 4. If the high caste Nambudiri Brahman shows an average of only 2·7, his Tamil brother has 3·8. The average among the Nayars is only 3·5, while among the Iluvans it is 3·8. The Pulayans and Sambavans (both depressed) stand slightly higher, their figures being 4·1 and 4·3 respectively. The Muslims have an average of 4·2, the Indian Christians 3·9 and the Jews 3·6. Travancore showed a much higher average (ranging from 5 to 6) for these communities in 1921. In any case the statistics do not appear to establish any connection between the degree of fertility on the one hand and castes or communities on the other. And all that can be safely inferred about the survival rate of children is that it falls much below 700 only among the lowest classes.

and by caste

Caste or community	Number of families examined	Average number of children per family	Proportion of surviving children to 1,000 born alive
Ambalavasi	353	2·95	760
Brahman—Nambudiri	88	2·70	761
Tamil	559	3·79	778
Eluthassan	339	3·52	734
Iluvan	6,916	3·77	736
Kammalan	1,244	3·67	718
Kanakkan	458	4·01	705
Nayar	5,474	3·48	727
Pulayan	1,009	4·13	654
Sambavan (Parayan)	124	4·33	642
Valan	256	4·23	693
Vettuvan	243	3·73	700
Muslim	1,902	4·17	705
Anglo India[n]	76	4·45	776
Indian Christian	10,786	3·93	753
Jew	62	3·60	722

Correlation between size of family and age at marriage.

6. In Sex Table V the average size of the family is correlated with the age of the wife at marriage. The figures are puzzling. At the census of 1921 it was shown by Baroda that the rates both of fertility and of survival tended to rise when the age of marriage was raised by a few years to 17 or 20. But according to the statistics in Table V the highest rates are seen where the age of the wife at marriage does not exceed 12 years. The number of children born alive and the number of surviving children both decrease with steady regularity as the age of marriage rises! Surely there must be something seriously wrong with the returns.

Age of wife at marriage	Average number of children per family	Average number of surviving children per family
All ages	3·76	2·76
0—12	4·44	3·31
13—14	4·03	3·03
15—19	3·60	2·67
20—29	3·59	2·48
30 and over	3·13	2·02

Proportion of fertile and sterile marriages.

7. The proportion of fertile and sterile marriages is given in Sex Table VI, and the statement in the margin prepared from it shows the percentage of fertile and sterile marriages in each age-group according to the duration of the marriage. If the enquiry be regarded as sufficiently representative, 2 out of every 100 marriages will appear to be sterile even when the union has lasted for 15 years or more. Where the age of the wife at marriage is not above 12 and the duration of marriage is below 5 years, the proportion of the sterile is seen to be only 78 per cent. In other words 22 out of every 100 married girls of this tender age-group are mothers by the time they attain their 16th year. As the period of the duration of marriage increases, the proportion of sterility declines until it reaches the average of 2 per cent. Thus too, when the age of the wife at marriage is higher, the ratio of the sterile is correspondingly lower until we come to those women that are married after their 20th year. From the fifth year of the duration of marriages, the two groups, 20 to 29 and 30 and over, show a higher proportion of sterility than the other groups.

Proportion of Fertile and Sterile marriages.

Age of wife at marriage	Duration of marriage years: 0—4		5—9		10—14		15 and over	
	Fertile	Sterile	Fertile	Sterile	Fertile	Sterile	Fertile	Sterile
All ages	57	43	92	8	96	4	98	2
0—12	22	78	82	18	95	5	98	2
13—14	45	55	87	13	98	2	98	2
15—19	57	43	95	5	97	3	98	2
20—29	69	31	94	6	94	6	96	4
30 and over	64	36	78	22	89	11	93	7

SUBSIDIARY TABLES.

I.—General proportions of the sexes by Natural Divisions and Districts.

Natural Division "Malabar and Konkan"	Number of females to 1,000 males									
	1931		1921		1911		1901		1891	
	Actual population	Natural population	Actual population	Natural population	Actual population	Natural population	Actual population	Natural population	Actual population	Natural population
1	2	3	4	5	6	7	8	9	10	11
COCHIN STATE ..	1,043	1,033	1,027	1,018	1,007	997	1,004	996	998	992

II.—Number of Females per 1,000 Males at different age-periods by religions at each of the last three censuses.

Age	All religions			Hindu			Muslim			Christian			Jain			Jew		
	1931	1921	1911	1931	1921	1911	1931	1921	1911	1931	1921	1911	1931	1921	1911	1931	1921	1911
1	2	3	4	5	6	7	8	9	10	11	12	13	14	15	16	17	18	19
0—1	994	1,009	1,011	1,009	1,024	1,013	930	937	1,009	977	997	1,009	1,500	500	..	1,050	864	1,000
1—2	999	949	996	1,012	958	997	973	901	945	979	944	1,004	250	1,000	..	750	545	818
2—3	997	1,006	1,001	1,009	1,008	998	959	981	987	980	1,009	1,013	500	2,000	..	875	818	545
3—4	990	1,042	1,030	993	1,047	1,042	957	1,070	1,045	994	1,022	994	1,000	1,000	..	800	1,471	1,143
4—5	979	993	966	978	1,008	969	959	967	914	987	968	977	1,333	..	..	739	944	800
Total 0—5 ..	**992**	**1,004**	**1,001**	**1,001**	**1,013**	**1,004**	**956**	**978**	**981**	**983**	**991**	**1,000**	**813**	**750**	**2,500**	**838**	**962**	**845**
5—10	973	974	969	968	979	964	948	960	967	990	966	992	1,000	500	1,333	903	1,206	1,048
10—15	978	963	942	975	961	951	941	916	899	995	981	931	833	1,400	357	1,050	1,271	1,101
15—20	1,107	1,017	1,011	1,135	1,038	1,077	1,079	1,023	989	1,064	966	949	1,286	1,000	800	1,246	759	1,154
20—25	1,186	1,167	1,116	1,227	1,193	1,128	1,119	1,101	1,079	1,113	1,124	1,089	1,444	2,667	545	1,328	1,140	1,837
25—30	1,172	1,158	1,093	1,205	1,184	1,106	1,082	1,179	1,053	1,130	1,088	1,066	714	300	643	1,021	1,389	1,556
Total 0—30..	**1,045**	**1,030**	**1,012**	**1,058**	**1,043**	**1,021**	**998**	**1,005**	**985**	**1,028**	**1,007**	**995**	**958**	**872**	**673**	**1,027**	**1,096**	**1,179**
30—40	1,063	1,002	939	1,096	1,013	969	931	909	850	1,023	950	882	333	300	778	1,261	1,297	855
40—50	992	967	942	1,026	1,013	970	826	815	841	956	897	898	571	600	59	952	623	890
50—60	1,000	992	1,069	1,047	1,009	1,111	837	870	931	927	987	995	1,500	667	..	767	440	744
60 and over	1,131	1,256	1,252	1,199	1,331	1,305	908	1,003	996	1,025	1,132	1,178	1,000	1,000	1,000	873	1,031	1,111
Total 30 and over..	**1,039**	**1,021**	**998**	**1,080**	**1,059**	**1,033**	**882**	**885**	**876**	**986**	**962**	**939**	**500**	**474**	**436**	**989**	**835**	**885**
Total all ages:																		
Actual population ..	**1,043**	**1,027**	**1,007**	**1,065**	**1,048**	**1,025**	**962**	**967**	**951**	**1,015**	**993**	**978**	**780**	**741**	**563**	**1,012**	**988**	**1,05.**
Natural population..	**1,023**	**1,018**	**997**	..	..	..	..	..	..	..	..	..	..	..	..	..	..	..

III.—Number of Females per 1,000 Males at different age-periods by religions and Natural Divisions.

Cochin State—Natural Division: "Malabar and Konkan."

Age	All religions	Hindu	Muslim	Christian	Jain	Jew
1	2	3	4	5	6	7
0—1	994	1,009	930	977	1,500	1,050
1—2	999	1,013	973	979	250	750
2—3	997	1,009	959	980	500	875
3—4	990	993	957	974	1,000	800
4—5	979	978	959	987	1,333	739
Total 0—5 ..	**992**	**1,001**	**956**	**983**	**813**	**838**
5—10	973	968	948	990	1,000	903
10—15	978	975	941	995	833	1,050
15—20	1,107	1,135	1,039	1,064	1,285	1,246
20—25	1,186	1,227	1,119	1,113	1,444	1,238
25—30	1,172	1,205	1,082	1,120	714	1,021
Total 0—30 ..	**1,045**	**1,058**	**998**	**1,028**	**958**	**1,027**
30—40	1,063	1,096	931	1,023	333	1,263
40—50	992	1,026	826	956	571	952
50—60	1,020	1,047	837	927	1,500	767
60 and over	1,131	1,199	908	1,025	1,000	872
Total 30 and over	**1,039**	**1,080**	**882**	**986**	**500**	**989**
Total all ages:						
Actual population ..	**1,043**	**1,068**	**962**	**1,015**	**718**	**1,012**

IV.—*Number of Females per 1,000 Males for certain selected castes.*

CASTE	Number of females per 1,000 males						
	All ages	0—6	7—13	14—16	17—23	24—43	44 and over
1	2	3	4	5	6	7	8
HINDU							
Ambalavasi	1,030	955	906	1,017	1,070	1,034	1,195
Ambattan	1,023	866	1,039	1,137	972	1,249	858
Arayan	902	1,023	882	866	871	906	816
Brahman { Konkani	1,001	1,033	985	798	1,093	1,060	932
Brahman { Malayali	956	968	963	785	923	943	1,025
Brahman { Tamil	999	991	885	785	1,130	1,165	951
Chakkan	1,030	1,209	970	945	1,105	937	1,061
Chaliyan { Chaliyan	937	1,222	488	1,500	935	939	1,000
Chaliyan { Pattariyan	1,072	1,015	987	1,245	1,276	1,078	1,026
Eluthassan	1,054	987	1,008	1,012	1,115	1,101	1,082
Iluvan	1,082	999	980	1,040	1,222	1,181	1,064
Kaikolan	1,041	915	990	1,480	1,092	959	1,183
Kammalan	1,062	1,050	973	944	1,210	1,104	1,053
Kanakkan	1,009	992	1,004	895	1,193	1,052	881
Kaniyan	970	828	888	898	1,034	1,148	950
Kshatriya-Malayali	1,180	886	1,238	1,351	1,515	1,333	1,096
Kudumi Chetti	960	1,035	810	1,073	1,118	923	918
Kusavan	950	1,050	744	1,359	977	1,034	773
Nayar	1,154	972	986	1,034	1,279	1,273	1,350
Pandaran	1,039	989	1,046	1,146	1,091	1,019	1,041
Panditattan	913	845	833	743	1,035	928	1,024
Pulayan	1,052	1,028	948	986	1,349	1,073	1,026
Sambavan (Parayan)	1,016	1,057	956	876	1,470	993	859
Valan	954	999	1,005	902	978	991	860
Velakkattalavan .. .	1,038	877	892	881	1,330	1,045	1,607
Velan	1,093	1,061	942	1,109	1,237	1,221	984
Vellalan	1,016	1,042	1,016	858	1,050	969	1,112
Veluttedan	1,160	904	997	966	1,495	1,323	1,245
Vettuvan	985	1,009	889	998	1,218	996	867
MUSLIM							
Jonakan	968	958	925	967	1,161	945	822
Ravuttan	940	944	908	838	1,012	917	1,022
Others	958	960	1,020	900	1,004	997	811
CHRISTIAN							
Anglo-Indian	1,094	936	981	1,015	1,200	1,503	947
European	931	1,667	750	..	1,333	1,036	413
Indian Christian	1,015	984	991	1,005	1,099	1,050	966
JAIN	780	950	842	400	1,889	490	929
JEW	1,012	813	1,000	1,659	1,329	1,183	822

V.—Actual number of Births and Deaths reported for each Sex during the decades 1901—1910, 1911—1920, and 1921—1930.

Year	Number of births			Number of deaths			Difference between columns 3 and 4. Excess of latter over former +, deficit —	Difference between columns 6 and 7. Excess of latter over former +, deficit —	Difference between columns 2 and 5. Excess of former over latter +, deficit —	Number of female births per 1,000 births	Number of female deaths per 1,000 deaths
	Total	Males	Females	Total	Males	Females					
1	2	3	4	5	6	7	8	9	10	11	12
1901	5,267	2,693	2,574	6,446	3,671	2,775	— 119	— 896	— 1,179	956	756
1902	5,787	2,846	2,941	7,354	4,191	3,163	+ 95	— 1,028	— 1,567	1,033	755
1903	6,932	3,440	3,492	7,807	4,286	3,521	+ 52	— 765	— 875	1,015	821
1904	7,419	3,787	3,632	7,193	3,965	3,228	— 155	— 737	+ 226	959	814
1905	7,975	..	..	8,455	..	..	..	..	— 480	..	..
1906	8,345	..	..	8,020	.	..	..	..	+ 325	..	..
1907	8,885	..	..	12,960	..	..	..	..	— 4,075	..	..
1908	7,879	3,998	3,881	12,005	..	..	— 117	..	— 4,126	971	..
1909	15,513	7,846	7,667	10,738	..	..	— 179	..	+ 4,775	977	..
1910	15,784	8,210	7,574	10,946	..	..	— 636	..	+ 4,838	923	..
Total 1901—1910 ..	**89,786**	..	..	**91,924**	..	..	..	..	**— 2,138**	..	..
1911	16,602	8,556	8,046	11,876	6,350	5,526	— 510	— 824	+ 4,726	944	870
1912	16,331	8,391	7,940	13,799	7,286	6,513	— 451	— 773	+ 2,532	946	894
1913	14,821	7,581	7,240	16,363	8,575	7,794	— 341	— 781	— 1,548	955	909
1914	16,839	8,647	8,192	12,984	6,746	6,238	— 455	— 508	+ 3,855	947	925
1915	16,529	8,450	8,079	10,486	5,560	4,926	— 371	— 634	+ 6,043	956	886
1916	15,416	7,808	7,608	10,037	5,254	4,783	— 200	— 471	+ 5,379	974	910
1917	15,401	7,769	7,632	10,297	5,388	4,909	— 137	— 479	+ 5,104	982	919
1918	15,328	7,848	7,480	13,850	7,388	6,462	— 368	— 926	+ 1,478	953	875
1919	13,732	6,956	6,776	20,112	10,299	9,813	— 180	— 486	— 6,380	974	955
1920	14,216	7,289	6,937	13,478	7,134	6,344	— 362	— 790	+ 738	950	889
Total 1911—1920 ..	**155,215**	**79,295**	**75,920**	**133,288**	**69,980**	**63,308**	**— 3,375**	**— 6,672**	**+21,927**	**957**	**905**
1921	15,205	7,899	7,306	9,977	5,271	4,706	— 593	— 565	+ 5,228	925	893
1922	14,290	7,445	6,845	9,221	4,935	4,286	— 600	— 649	+ 5,069	919	868
1923	13,122	6,774	6,348	9,969	5,320	4,649	— 426	— 671	+ 3,153	937	874
1924	12,524	6,410	6,114	7,939	4,168	3,771	— 296	— 397	+ 4,585	954	905
1925	11,982	6,168	5,814	8,280	4,261	4,019	— 354	— 242	+ 3,702	943	943
1926	14,103	7,246	6,857	8,163	4,275	3,888	— 389	— 387	+ 5,940	946	909
1927	14,383	7,372	7,011	9,768	5,172	4,596	— 361	— 576	+ 4,615	951	889
1928	14,595	7,385	7,210	8,850	4,775	4,075	— 175	— 700	+ 5,745	976	853
1929	16,203	8,303	7,900	8,605	4,470	4,135	— 403	— 335	+ 7,598	951	925
1930	16,109	8,359	7,750	10,461	5,450	5,011	— 609	— 439	+ 5,648	927	919
Total 1921—1930 ..	**142,516**	**73,361**	**69,155**	**91,233**	**48,097**	**43,136**	**— 4,206**	**— 4,961**	**+51,283**	**943**	**897**

Note:—1. Figures for the columns left blank are not available.

2. Subsidiary Table VI has not been prepared for want of required information by age periods.

SEX TABLES.

I.—Sex of First-born.

TALUKS		Number of females first-born	Number of males first-born	Number of females first-born per 1,000 males first-born	Number of slips examined
1		2	3	4	5
COCHIN STATE	..	**14,275**	**15,451**	**924**	**33,471**
Cochin-Kanayannur	..	3,904	4,076	958	8,906
Cranganur	..	1,763	1,930	913	4,199
Mukundapuram	..	2,439	2,638	925	5,688
Trichur	..	3,489	4,033	865	8,475
Talapilli	..	2,024	2,092	967	4,549
Chittur	..	656	682	962	1,654

Note—Sex Table II has not been prepared.

III.—Size of Families by Occupation of Husband.

Occupation of Husband	Number of families examined	Total number of children born alive	Average per family	Number of children surviving	Proportion of surviving to 1,000 born alive
1	2	3	4	5	6
ALL OCCUPATIONS	33,471	125,878	3·76	92,458	735
EXPLOITATION OF ANIMALS AND VEGETATION.					
Pasture and Agriculture.					
Landlords ..	637	2,595	4·07	1,980	763
Cultivating owners ..	3,708	14,320	3·86	10,982	766
Cultivating tenants ..	702	2,805	4·00	2,120	756
Non-cultivating tenants ..	1	2	2·00	1	500
Agents, managers, etc., of landed estates ..	194	772	3·98	602	780
Agricultural labourers ..	567	2,173	3·83	1,515	697
Rent collectors ..	12	44	3·67	34	773
Stock raising ..	7	18	2·57	12	667
Tea and rubber plantation ..	4	14	3·50	11	786
Cocoanut cultivation ..	83	316	3·81	231	731
Pan-vine cultivation ..	8	17	2·13	14	824
Fruit growers ..	7	25	3·57	17	680
Forest officers and guards ..	12	42	3·50	27	643
Wood cutters ..	49	180	3·67	110	611
Herdsmen ..	3	9	3·00	7	778
Agriculture (unspecified) ..	1,511	5,888	3·90	4,421	752
Fishing and Hunting ..	581	2,374	4·09	1,692	713
INDUSTRY.					
Textiles					
Spinning and weaving ..	225	722	3·21	547	758
Rope, twine, string, etc. ..	322	1,004	3·12		728
Insufficiently described textile industries ..	1	5	5·00	3	600
Hides, skins and hard materials from the animal kingdom					
Working in leather ..	38	157	4·13	100	656
Wood.					
Sawyers ..	254	970	3·82	655	675
Carpenters ..	801	2,928	3·66	2,158	737
Basket makers ..	141	612	4·34	384	611
Metals.					
Blacksmiths ..	244	906	3·71	622	687
Workers in brass, copper and bell metal ..	79	278	3·52	209	751
Workers in other metals ..	21	66	3·14	45	682
Electro-plating ..	6	31	5·17	25	806
Ceramics					
Potters and makers of earthenware ..	145	551	3·80	380	690
Chemical products properly so called and analogous					
Manufacture of matches, fire-works and other explosives ..	9	10	1·11	10	1,000

III.—Size of Families by Occupation of Husband—(cont.)

Occupation of Husband	Number of families examined	Total no. of children born alive	Average per family	Number of children surviving	Proportion of surviving to 1,000 born alive
1	2	3	4	5	6
Chemical products properly so called and analogous—(cont.)					
Manufacture of aerated and mineral waters and ice ..	3	10	3·33	9	900
Manufacture and refining of vegetable oils ..	122	491	4·02	360	733
Food Industries					
Rice pounders and huskers and flour grinders ..	1	1	1·00	..	..
Butchers ..	8	23	2·88	17	739
Sweetmeat and condiment makers ..	79	311	3·94	243	781
Toddy drawers ..	705	3,148	4·47	2,283	725
Manufacturers of tobacco ..	18	57	3·17	41	719
Industries of dress and the toilet					
Tailors, milliners, dress-makers and darners ..	197	582	2·95	450	773
Washing and cleaning ..	189	688	3·64	461	670
Barbers, hair-dressers and wig-makers ..	171	635	3·71	397	625
Building Industries					
Lime burners, stone-cutters, and masons ..	488	1,922	3·94	1,364	709
Miscellaneous and undefined Industries					
Printers, engravers, book-binders, etc. ..	32	130	4·06	95	731
Makers of musical instruments ..	1	3	3·00	[illegible]	667
Makers of jewellery and ornaments ..	354	1,381	3·90	947	686
Other miscellaneous and undefined industries ..	77	251	3·26	191	761
Scavenging ..	23	94	4·09	66	702
TRANSPORT.					
Transport by water					
Ship owners, boat-owners, and their employees, officers, mariners, etc., ships brokers, boatmen and towmen ..	137	526	3·84	391	743
Transport by road					
Owners, managers and employees connected with mechanically driven vehicles ..	236	548	2·32	439	801
Owners, managers and employees connected with other vehicles ..	145	517	3·54	394	762
Bullock owners and drivers ..	88	286	3·25	225	787
Porters and messengers ..	123	419	3·41	318	759
Unspecified ..	146	778	5·33	395	508
Transport by rail					
Railway employees of all kinds other than coolies ..	47	139	2·96	102	734
Post Office, Telegraph and Telephone Services					
Post Office, Telegraph and Telephone services	39	147	3·77	108	734
TRADE					
Banks, establishments of credit, exchange and insurance					
Bank managers, money lenders, etc. ..	38	155	4·08	115	742

III.—Size of Families by Occupation of Husband—(cont.)

Occupation of Husband	Number of families examined	Total no. of children born alive	Average per family	Number of children surviving	Proportion of surviving to 1,000 born alive
1	2	3	4	5	6
TRADE—(*cont.*)					
Brokerage, Commission and Export					
Brokers, commission agents, commercial travellers, warehouse owners and employees ..	15	56	3·73	44	786
Trade in textiles					
Trade in piece goods, wool, cotton, silk, hair and other textiles ..	30	107	3·57	73	682
Trade in skins, leather and furs					
Trade in leather ..	6	34	5·67	29	853
Trade in wood					
Trade in wood ..	20	113	5·65	91	805
Trade in thatches and other forest produce ..	7	14	2·00	12	857
Trade in chemical products					
Trade in drugs ..	12	42	3·50	28	667
Hotels, cafes, restaurants, &c.					
Owners and Managers of hotels, cook shops, sarais, etc. ..	234	723	3·09	517	715
Hawkers of drink and food stuffs ..	22	100	4·55	66	660
Other trade in food stuffs					
Grain and pulse dealers ..	55	49	0·89	35	714
Dealers in sweetmeats, sugar and spices ..	78	281	3·60	211	751
Dealers in dairy products, eggs and poultry ..	13	47	3·62	38	809
Dealers in animal for food ..	21	89	4·24	66	743
Dealers in fodder for animals ..	2	8	4·00	7	875
Dealers in other foodstuffs ..	87	299	3·44	238	796
Dealers in tobacco ..	12	46	3·83	33	717
Dealers in opium ..	1	2	2·00	2	1,000
Trade in furniture					
Hardware, cooking utensils, etc., porcelain, crockery, glassware, bottles, articles for gardening, etc. ..	6	24	4·00	18	750
Trade in building materials					
Trade in building materials ..	2	13	6·50	10	769
Trade in means of transport					
Dealers and hirers of elephants, camels, horses, cattle, asses, mules, etc. ..	6	31	5·17	20	645
Trade in fuel					
Dealers in firewood, charcoal, coal, cow-dung, etc. ..	6	20	3·33	14	700
Trade in articles of luxury, and those pertaining to letters and the arts and sciences					
Dealers in precious stones, jewellery, clocks, optical instruments, etc. ..	11	54	4·91	38	704
Dealers in common bangles, bead necklaces, fans, small articles, toys, hunting and fishing tackle, flowers, etc. ..	5	17	3·40	13	765

III.—Size of Families by Occupation of Husband—(cont.)

Occupation of Husband	Number of families examined	Total no. of children born alive	Average per family	Number of children surviving	Proportion of surviving to 1,000 born alive
1	2	3	4	5	6
Trade in articles of luxury, etc.—(cont.)					
Publishers, booksellers, stationers, dealers in music, pictures, musical instruments and curiosities ..	8	23	2·88	22	957
Trade of other sorts					
General store-keepers, and shop-keepers, otherwise unspecified ..	1,806	7,378	4·09	5,344	724
Other trades ..	18	54	3·00	35	648
General merchants (trade unspecified) ..	2,629	10,465	3·98	8,461	809
PUBLIC FORCE					
Army					
Army (Indian States) ..	1	2	2·00	2	1,000
Police					
Police ..	232	779	3·36	537	689
Village watchmen ..	4	7	1·75	7	1,000
PUBLIC ADMINISTRATION					
Public Administration					
Service of the State ..	1,073	3,850	3·59	3,003	780
Municipal and other local service ..	79	278	3·52	177	637
Village officials and servants other than watchmen ..	113	402	3·56	326	811
PROFESSIONS AND LIBERAL ARTS					
Religion					
Priests, ministers, etc. ..	406	1,915	[illegible]	1,388	725
Servants in religious edifices, burial and burning grounds, pilgrim conductors, circumcisers, etc. ..	7	24	3·43	20	833
Law					
Lawyers' clerks, petition writers, etc. ..	142	558	3·93	468	839
Medicine					
Registered medical practitioners including occulists ..	70	232	3·31	210	905
Other persons practising the healing arts without being registered ..	342	1,457	4·26	1,096	752
Dentists ..	1	11	11·00	11	1,000
Midwives, vaccinators, compounders, nurses, masseurs, etc. ..	32	99	3·09	84	848
Instruction					
Professors and teachers of all kinds ..	923	2,866	3·11	2,385	832
Clerks and servants connected with education..	668	2,012	3·01	1,641	808
Letters, Arts and Sciences					
Public scribes, stenographers, etc. ..	14	24	1·71	19	792
Architects, surveyors, engineers, and their employees ..	13	56	4·31	40	714
Authors, editors, journalists and photographers ..	31	126	4·06	103	817

III.—Size of Families by Occupation of Husband—(cont.)

Occupation of Husband	Number of families examined	Total no. of children born alive	Average per family	Number of children surviving	Proportion of surviving to 1,000 born alive
1	2	3	4	5	6
Letters Arts and Sciences—(*cont.*)					
Artists, sculptors and image makers ..	24	89	3·71	71	798
Horoscope casters, astrologers, fortune tellers, wizards, witches and mediums ..	39	157	4·03	112	713
Musicians, actors, dancers, etc. ..	78	311	3·99	224	720
Managers and employees of places of public entertainments, race courses, societies, clubs ..	8	38	4·75	30	789
PERSONS LIVING ON THEIR INCOME					
Persons living principally on their income					
Proprietors (other than agricultural land) fund and scholarship holders and pensioners ..	504	2,003	3·97	1,539	
DOMESTIC SERVICE					
Domestic Service					
Other domestic service ..	1,085	4,143	3·82	2,995	723
INSUFFICIENTLY DESCRIBED OCCUPATIONS					
General terms which do not indicate a definite occupation					
Manufacturers, businessmen and contractors otherwise unspecified ..	157	694	4·42	480	5
Mechanics otherwise unspecified ..	79	232	2·94	184	793
Labourers and workmen otherwise unspecified ..	6,992	25,129	3·59	16,774	668
UNPRODUCTIVE					
Inmates of Jails, asylums and alms houses					
Inmates of jails, asylums and alms houses ..	4	11	2·75	6	545
Beggars and Vagrants					
Beggars and vagrants ..	15	50	3·33	34	680
No occupation ..	1,274	5,086	3·99	3,930	773
Unspecified ..	19	52	2·74	37	712

IV.—Size of Families by Caste or Religion.

CASTE OR RELIGION	Number of families examined	Total number of children born alive	Average per family	Number of children surviving	Proportion of surviving to 1,000 born alive	Number of families with wife married at 0—12	13—14	15—19	20—29	30 and over
1	2	3	4	5	6	7	8	9	10	11
Total	**33,471**	**125,878**	**3·76**	**92,458**	**735**	**3,854**	**5,502**	**18,177**	**5,528**	**410**
HINDU	**20,626**	**74,957**	**3·63**	**54,526**	**727**	**2,292**	**3,316**	**10,805**	**3,823**	**290**
Ambalavasi	353	1,042	2·95	792	760	22	55	183	85	8
Chakkiyar	3	11	3·67	10	909	..	..	2	1	..
Marar	74	247	3·34	177	717	..	11	11	21	1
Nambiyassan	15	47	3·13	37	872	1	2	10	2	..
Pisharodi	48	146	3·04	120	822	3	7	27	11	..
Pushpakan Nambiyar	11	18	1·64	12	667	2	..	9	..	..
Putuval	23	54	2·35	36	667	1	5	13	3	1
Tiyyattunni	2	4	2·00	4	1,000	..	..	2	..	..
Unni	4	11	2·75	7	636	..	1	3	..	..
Variyar	109	333	3·06	269	808	10	15	55	27	2
Unspecified	64	171	2·67	120	702	5	14	21	20	4
Ambattan	24	69	2·88	46	667	2	6	10	6	..
Arayan	192	744	3·88	513	690	28	40	97	25	2
Brahman	1,724	6,222	3·61	4,888	786	369	542	729	73	11
Embran	24	86	3·58	74	860	5	9	9	1	..
Gauda	208	809	3·89	592	732	43	79	83	3	..
Gujaratti	1	..	..	..	..	..	..	1	..	..
Konkani	120	352	2·93	290	824	43	38	35	3	1
Malayali — Elayad	32	125	3·91	77	616	2	10	16	4	..
Malayali — Muttad	5	22	4·40	19	864	1	..	2	2	..
Malayali — Nambudiri	85	238	2·70	181	761	5	12	44	25	2
Tamil	559	2,116	3·79	1,647	778	141	158	238	17	5
Others	687	2,474	3·60	2,008	812	129	236	301	18	3
Chakkan	24	85	3·54	68	800	3	5	11	4	1
Chakkiliyan	1	2	2·00	1	500	..	..	..	1	..
Chaliyan — Chaliyan	89	307	3·45	220	717	8	17	46	18	..
Chaliyan — Pattariyan	35	157	4·49	109	694	..	9	21	5	..
Chetti	82	239	2·91	187	782	27	14	34	11	1
Dasi	23	66	2·87	51	773	4	5	10	4	..
Devangan	41	82	2·00	59	720	5	9	22	5	..
Eluthassan	339	1,193	3·52	875	734	43	40	202	52	2
Idaiyan	15	44	2·93	30	682	1	..	1	13	..
Iluvan	6,916	26,105	3·77	19,216	736	619	937	3,883	1,384	93
Kaikolan	7	27	3·86	23	852	..	..	5	2	..
Kakkalan	21	63	3·00	29	460	3	7	6	5	1
Kallan	31	94	3·03	77	819	4	8	15	4	..
Kammalan	1,244	4,565	3·67	3,279	718	130	214	686	197	17
Kallasari	66	251	3·80	179	713	2	18	34	10	2
Kollan	223	829	3·72	561	677	16	44	130	29	4
Marasari	591	2,160	3·65	1,595	728	28	90	313	103	7
Moosari	51	179	3·51	123	687	8	6	28	8	1
Tattan	298	1,080	3·62	784	726	25	53	172	46	2
Tolkollan	15	66	4·40	37	561	1	3	9	1	1

IV.—Size of Families by Caste or Religion—(cont.)

CASTE OR RELIGION	Number of families examined	Total number of children born alive	Average per family	Number of children surviving	Proportion of surviving to 1,000 born alive	Number of families with wife married at 0—12	13—14	15—19	20—29	30 and over
1	2	3	4	5	6	7	8	9	10	11
HINDU—(cont.)										
Kanakkan ..	458	1,840	4·01	1,297	705	37	81	247	84	9
Kaniyan ..	56	229	4·09	168	734	..	8	30	18	..
Kavara ..	4	10	2·50	4	400	..	..	3	1	..
Kavundan ..	6	6	1·00	5	833	..	2	3	1	..
Kshatriya ..	109	317	2·91	289	912	5	16	69	18	1
Malayali ..	7	14	2·00	11	786	..	2	3	2	..
Others ..	102	303	2·97	278	917	5	14	66	16	1
Kudumi chetti ..	472	1,342	2·84	1,020	760	170	119	159		..
Kurukkal ..	13	41	3·15	24	585	2	5	5	1	..
Kusavan ..	116	408	3·52	285	699	27	19	44	23	3
Nambidi ..	12	26	2·17	23	885	1	4	6	1	..
Nanjanattu Pillai ..		5	1·67	4	800	..		1	..	..
Nayadi ..	3	7	2·33	4	571	1	..	2	..	..
Nayar ..	5,474	19,076	3·48	13,867	727	381	725	2,871	1,383	114
Odan ..	39	143	3·67	104	727	7	19		6	..
Otta-Naikan (Odde) ..	6	11	1·83	8	727	1	1	3	1	..
Panan ..	53	177	3·34	127	718	8	5	28	11	1
Pandaran ..	79	309	3·91	250	809	9	11	39	20	..
Panditattan ..	27	108	4·00	90	833	2	5	18	1	..
Pulayan ..	1,009	4,249	4·13	2,648	654	167	112	532	183	15
Pulluvan ..	1	6	6·00	5	833	1	..	..	..	..
Samantan ..	9	19	2·11	16	842	..	..	5	4	..
Sambavan (Parayan) ..	124	537	4·33	345	642	16	21	62	25	..
Tarakan ..	1	..	..	..	..	..	..	..	1	..
Ullatan ..	3	17	5·67	10	588	1	..	1	1	..
Vaisyan ..	37	132	3·57	76	576	13	8	15	1	..
Valan ..	256	1,084	4·23	751	693	3	57	134	33	1
Vaniyan ..	30	78	2·60	53	679	6	10	13	1	..
Vannan ..	19	98	5·16	57	582	6	1	7	5	..
Velakkattalavan ..	107	367	3·43	258	70	8	20	57	20	2
Velan ..	230	852	3·70	578	678	30	41	122	34	3
Vellalan ..	4	4	1·00	2	500	1	1	1	1	..
Veluttedan ..	118	432	3·66	291	674	14	28	58	17	1
Vettuvan ..	243	906	3·73	634	700	22	36	126	58	1
Vilkurup ..	8	35	4·38	25	715	3	1	3	1	..
Caste unspecified ..	331	1,154	3·49	732	635	56	50	171	51	3
No-caste ..	5	28	5·60	12	429	2	..	3	..	..
MUSLIM ..	**1,919**	**8,006**	**4·17**	**5,636**	**704**	**265**	**362**	**962**	**298**	**32**
Jonakan ..	17	68	4·00	43	632	1	3	8	5	..
Others ..	1,902	7,938	4·17	5,593	70	264	359	954	293	32
CHRISTIAN ..	**10,862**	**42,690**	**3·93**	**32,134**	**753**	**1,287**	**1,801**	**6,384**	**1,302**	**88**
Anglo-Indian ..	76	338	4·45	262	776	3	7	52	13	1
Indian Christian ..	10,786	42,352	3·93	31,872	753	1,284	1,794	6,332	1,289	87
JEW ..	**62**	**223**	**3·60**	**161**	**722**	**9**	**22**	**26**	**5**	..
ZOROASTRIAN ..	**2**	**2**	**1·00**	**1**	**500**	**1**	**1**	..	..	..

V.—Average size of Family correlated with age of Wife at Marriage.

Age of wife at marriage	Number of families	Number of children born alive	Average observed	Number of children surviving	Average observed
1	2	3	4	5	6
All ages	**33,471**	**125,878**	**3·76**	**92,458**	**2·76**
0—12	3,854	17,126	4·44	12,776	3·31
13—14	5,502	22,177	4·03	16,682	3·03
15—19	18,177	65,446	3·60	48,454	2·67
20—29	5,528	19,844	3·59	13,716	2·48
30 and over	410	1,285	3·13	830	2·02

VI.—Proportion of Fertile and Sterile Marriages.

Age of wife at marriage	Duration of marriage years							
	0—4		5—9		10—14		15 and over	
	Fertile	Sterile	Fertile	Sterile	Fertile	Sterile	Fertile	Sterile
1	2	3	4	5	6	7	8	9
All ages	**3,337**	**2,505**	**5,311**	**433**	**5,315**	**205**	**15,959**	**406**
0—12	45	159	258	58	523	27	2,718	66
13—14	303	375	728	110	990	24	2,919	53
15—19	2,115	1,565	3,264	178	2,862	86	7,919	188
20—29	811	370	993	68	870	59	2,268	89
30 and over	63	36	68	19	70	9	135	10

Note.—Sex Table VII has not been prepared.

CHAPTER VI.—CIVIL CONDITION.

PART A of Imperial Table VII gives the number of unmarried, married and widowed persons of each sex by age and by religion for the whole State, and Part B gives like figures for all municipal towns. The statistics of civil condition for selected castes are contained in Imperial Table VIII. There are five Subsidiary Tables appended to this chapter, which present these statistics in proportional forms as shown below: **Reference to statistics**

Subsidiary Table I shows the distribution by civil condition of 1,000 of each sex, religion and main age-period at each of the last five censuses;

Subsidiary Table II shows the distribution by civil condition of 1,000 of each sex at certain ages in each religion;

Subsidiary Table III shows the distribution by main age-periods and civil condition of 10,000 of each sex and religion ;

Subsidiary Table IV gives the proportion of the sexes by civil condition and religion at certain ages; and

Subsidiary Table V shows the distribution by civil condition of 1,000 of each sex at certain ages for selected castes.

2. The instructions in the enumeration books regarding the returns of civil condition were: **Meaning of statistics**

"*Column 6 (Married, etc)*.—Enter each person, whether infant, child or grown up, as either *married*, *unmarried* or *widowed*. Divorced persons who have not remarried should be entered as widowed, and dancing girls as married or unmarried according as they return themselves".

The following supplementary instructions also were issued to supervisors:—

"Note that this column should never be blank, not even for infants. If when asked if he is married, a man says 'yes,' he should next be asked whether his wife is living, as the answer in the vernacular to the former question does not show whether he is married or a widower. In filling up this column, neither you nor the enumerators should question the validity of any marriage or be guided by your own notions of what is or is not a marriage, but should accept the statements made by the person, or, in the case of children, by their relatives. Every person who has a wife or husband living at the time of the census should be entered as '*married*'. Persons who have been divorced, and who have not married again, should be entered as '*widowed*'. Enumerators must be careful not to use the same vernacular word for '*unmarried*' and '*widowed*'."

The necessity for these elaborate instructions arises from the well-known fact that marriage among the Hindus has not the same meaning as in the West, because it is not necessarily accompanied immediately by cohabitation, one or both of the contracting parties being often children or, at times, even infants. Further there are various forms of marriage having different degrees of validity and repute, and the marriage customs of one community differ from those of another. It was therefore necessary to take special precautions against the returns being influenced by the personal views and prejudices of the enumerators.

3. In the light of the detailed instructions issued to all census officers, the statistics of civil condition collected at the census may be accepted as an accurate classification of the population in the three prescribed classes, namely, **and their accuracy**

the unmarried, the married and the widowed; and though dancing girls, unmarried prostitutes or kept women might at times return themselves as married in their desire to appear respectable, their numbers in this State are so few as to be utterly negligible.

General conditions of marriage

4. The rites, customs and institutions connected with marriage among the various communities in Cochin have been described in detail in the Report on the Census of 1901 and in Mr. L. K. Ananthakrishna Ayyar's *Cochin Tribes and Castes.* The Notes for Report issued by the Census Commissioner for India direct that "the matter to be discussed in the chapter on civil condition should be primarily based on the statistics and should be confined to such aspects of the general subject as arise out of the figures or are connected with them as influences explanatory of the variations. It will therefore be relevant and even necessary to discuss any modifications during the last 10 years in the attitude of the public or of special communities towards marriage, widowhood, divorce and so forth which may have influenced the trend of the figures or may be likely to influence them in future." We have therefore to note here that the attitude of the people in general, and of some of the Malayali communities in particular, towards marriage has been for some time undergoing a gradual change chiefly because of the progress of English education and the increasing contact with western ideals. We find this change reflected in more than one direction. Thus some of the educated members of the orthodox communities of the Tamil and Konkani Brahmans, among whom pre-puberty marriage is (was?) compulsory, and who visited violations of this custom with social degradation, have assumed the role of social reformers and are putting off the marriage of their daughters till they are old enough to enter upon the duties of married life. Thus too the Nayars, who comprise the largest section of the *Marumakkathayam* communities among the Malayali Hindus, which form a considerable proportion of the State's population, and which never followed the custom of pre-puberty marriage, have mostly given up the *talikettu* ceremony (the tying of the *tali*, the sacred symbol of marriage), or the mock marriage as it has been aptly called, the first of the two forms of marriage which all girls of the *Marumakkathayam* communities had to go through. Educated opinion justly looked upon this custom as a senseless imitation or a costly mockery of the pre-puberty marriage prevalent among non-Malayali Hindus—a mockery as it brought no husband to the girl who was married. But scruples are hard to die particularly when they have a religious flavour about them as in this affair, marriage being a religious ceremony among the Hindus, and the transition period has its humorous side also. Educated and well-to-do parents, for instance, who dare not violate the time-honoured custom, but who at the same time are too sensitive to bear the scorn that would be directed against them if they openly performed a *talikettu* ceremony of the orthodox and aristocratic type, take their daughters to temples where the mother herself ties the *tali* round her daughter's neck in the presence of the deity. This obviates the necessity for the usual rites and marriage feasts. Others avoid the awkward situation by combining the *talikettu* and *sambandham* or the real adult marriage, the *tali* being tied by the bridegroom at the time of the real marriage. As the *talikettu* marriage fell into discredit, the *sambandham* grew in importance in more than one respect. This form of marriage, which was not recognised in law though socially it was as valid and as much respected as any other form of Hindu marriage, was legalised by the Cochin Nayar Regulation which was enacted in 1920 as a result of the representations made to the Darbar by the enlightened section of the

community. From the simple ceremony of ancient days unaccompanied by religious rites, the *sambandham** has been growing into an elaborate and costly affair with many innovations, both social and religious, introduced into it.

5. Similar developments are seen in other Malayali Hindu communities also, and marriage is generally regarded now as a sacrament to be attended by religious rites even among those to whom it was of old not more than a solemn social contract in respect of its form. The Iluvans, for instance, who form the second largest community in the State's population, have introduced many reforms in this direction. The *talikettu* marriage has been discredited in both the *Marumakkathayam* and *Makkathayam* sections of the community, and only very few girls go through this form of marriage at present. Some combine it with the real adult marriage which, under the guidance of their religious heads, has been transformed into a strictly religious ceremony in the progressive section of the community. In spite of the large and mostly avoidable increase in expenditure involved in these reforms, the innovations adopted by the Iluva and Nayar communities are regarded in some quarters as a move in the right direction in that they are supposed to invest the union between man and wife with an air of greater sanctity and respectability than of old. Some of the educated young men among the Iluvans do not, however, seem to be much in love with these forms and appearances. They are too independent to be priest-ridden and they want that the form of marriage should be that of a simple social contract.

6. Other significant changes too in the customs and institutions connected with marriage have followed in the wake of the enlightenment of modern education. Polyandry, which was once prevalent here to a certain extent in some of the communities, has long since been given up even by the lowest classes. Polygamy also was not unknown in this State and the Nambudiri Brahmans resorted to it, often in the past but only rarely of late, since they always lacked bridegrooms on account of their peculiar custom according to which only the eldest son of a Nambudiri family could marry within the caste, while the Nambudiri maidens could not be given in marriage to members of any other community. The younger and bolder spirits among the Nambudiris, who have come into contact with modern ideals through English education, have set up a strong agitation against this custom and bills have been introduced in the State Legislative Council in order that a radical social reform might be effected in the community. Polygamy among Nambudiris, therefore, appears to be doomed. The Nayar Regulaiton penalised polygamy among Nayars, when economic if not moral considerations had already sounded its death-knell in most communities including the Nayars. Restrictions on marriage like hypergamy have been fast disappearing as much under the influence of English education and the contact with western ideals as perhaps on account of the paucity of eligible bridegrooms for the maidens of high caste families; and we find girls from higher sub-castes among the Nayars often marrying young men of lower sub-castes without undergoing any social degradation thereby.

To what extent the statistics of civil condition have been influenced by the new tendencies and changing ideals of the times will be seen from the review of these statistics in the subsequent paragraphs of this chapter.

---

* Of the several Malayalam words denoting marriage among the *Marumakkathayam* Nayars, *sambandham* was the principal one. Of late this word, though harmless in itself and though it conveys the best of meanings (*Sam*=*Samyuk*=good, fast, and *bandham*=tie, union), has been discredited and is not now generally used in this State.

Summary of statistics

7. Of the 1,205,016 persons enumerated in Cochin at the census of 1931, 633,669 were returned as unmarried, 461,763 as married and 109,584 as widowed, the proportion of the three classes per mille of the population being 526, 383 and 91 respectively. The corresponding figures for 1921 were 515, 385 and 100 respectively. There are 830 females per 1,000 males among the unmarried against 803 in 1921. The proportion of wives is seen to be 1,067 per thousand husbands while it was only 1,053 at the previous census ; and there are as many as 4,470 widows for every 1,000 widowers, the ratio in 1921 being only 3,945. The rise in the proportion of widows during the last decade must probably be attributed to a greater proportion of widowers getting re-married than during the previous decade, and not to a higher death-rate among husbands since the death-rate during the intercensal period was but normal. A growing volume of emigration will account for the increase in the ratio of wives to husbands and of unmarried women to bachelors. When the emigration is not of a permanent character, men as a rule leave their families behind them. The marginal figures reveal a slight rise in the proportion of unmarried persons in the State's population during the decade. This increase is to be attributed to the change in the age constitution of the population and the growing influence of western ideals in some of the populous and educationally advanced communities.

Distribution by civil condition of 1,000 persons

		Unmarried	Married	Widowed
1921	Persons ..	515	385	100
	Males ..	578	381	41
	Females ..	452	390	158
1931	Persons ..	526	383	91
	Males ..	587	379	34
	Females ..	467	387	146

Comparison with Madras and Travancore

8. The proportion of the unmarried, married and widowed per mille of the total population of each sex is given in the following table together with the corresponding figures for Travancore and Madras for purposes of comparison.

	Males per 1,000			Females per 1,000		
	Unmarried	Married	Widowed	Unmarried	Married	Widowed
Madras ..	527	433	40	377	445	178
Travancore ..	584	387	29	475	406	119
Cochin ..	587	379	34	467	387	146

The difference between the Malabar coast and the rest of India in respect of the customs of marriage and widowhood is illustrated by the difference between the figures for Travancore and Cochin on the one hand and those of Madras on the other. The Malayali communities including Indian Christians and Muslims do not observe the custom of compulsory pre-puberty marriage. Nor do they prohibit the re-marriage of widows (the Malayali Brahmans, who form but a very small and altogether negligible fraction of the population, being excepted). Religious compulsion to marry, the obligation to marry girls before they attain puberty and the prohibition of the re-marriage of widows are the factors that determine the character of the statistics of the civil condition of a vast majority of the Indian population. It is only the non-Malayali caste Hindus, who comprise but a very insignificant proportion of the State's population, that are directly affected by these factors. For these reasons the

Proportion of Unmarried, Married & Widowed

per 1,000 of each sex, in each main age group & in each main religion

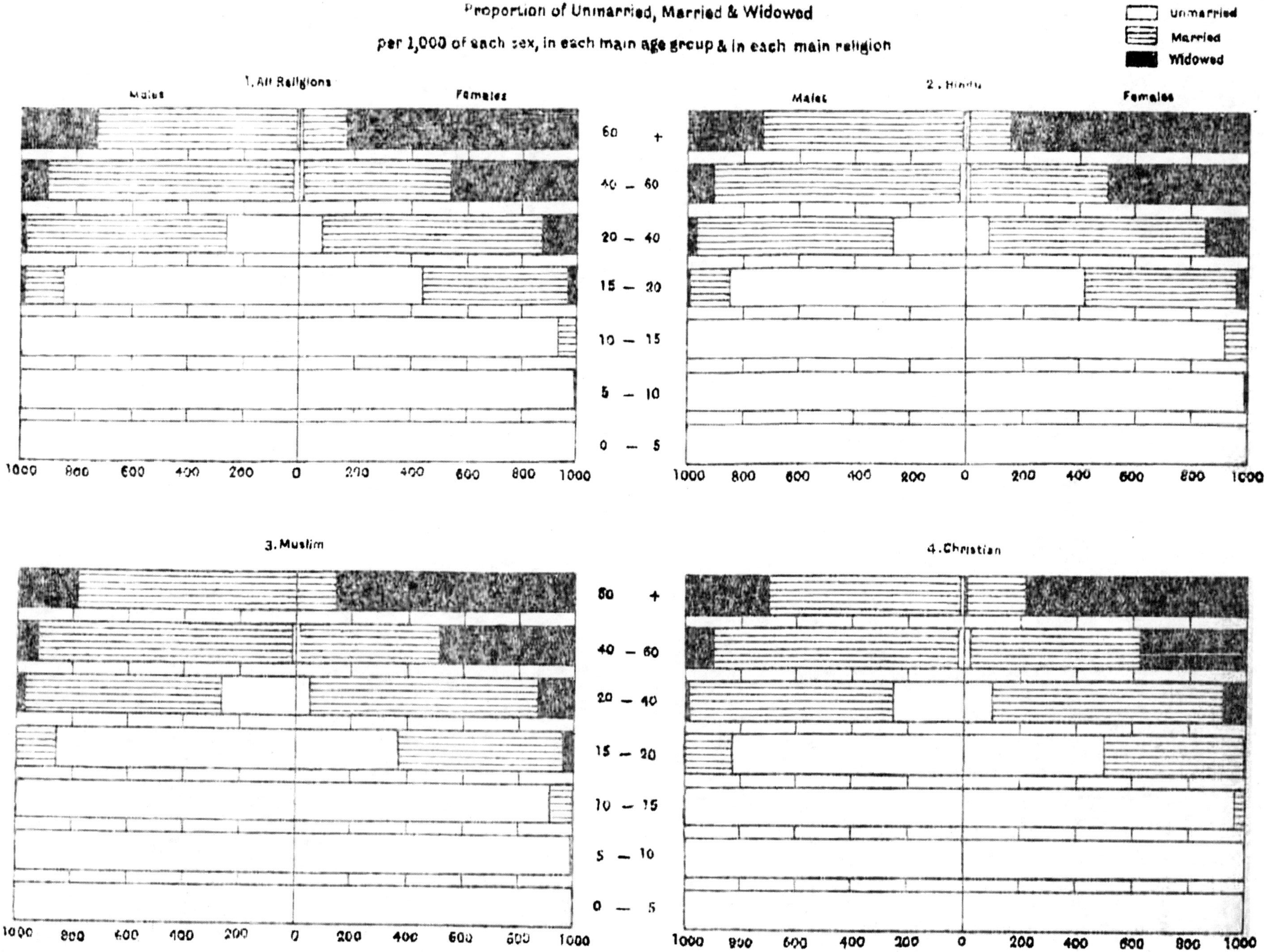

three most striking features of the Indian statistics, namely, the universality of marriage, the early age of marriage and the large proportion of widows, are not as prominent in Cochin and Travancore as elsewhere in India.

9. Diagrams 1 to 4 and the three tables given below will illustrate the universality of marriage. **Universality of marriage**

1. Distribution by civil condition of 1,000 of each sex by age-periods.

Age	Males per 1,000			Females per 1,000		
	Unmarried	Married	Widowed	Unmarried	Married	Widowed
0—5 ..	1,000	..	..	1,000	..	..
5—10 ..	1,000	..	..	993	7	..
10—15 ..	997	3	..	930	67	3
15—20 ..	846	148	6	439	530	31
20—40 ..	260	712	28	82	793	125
40—60 ..	23	883	94	14	525	461
60 and over ..	13	714	273	7	161	832

2. Distribution by civil condition of 1,000 of each sex by religion.

Religion	Males per 1,000			Females per 1,000		
	Unmarried	Married	Widowed	Unmarried	Married	Widowed
Hindus ..	583	381	36	450	387	163
Muslims ..	598	377	25	470	397	133
Christians ..	593	376	31	507	385	108

3. Distribution by civil condition of 1,000 of each sex aged 15 and above.

		1931			1921
		Madras	Travancore	Cochin	England and Wales
Unmarried	Males ..	229	276	277	365
	Females ..	55	107	120	368
Married	Males ..	705	674	664	584
	Females ..	658	687	636	520
Widowed	Males ..	66	50	59	51
	Females ..	287	206	244	112

How the Hindu belief that a man must beget a son if his soul is to attain salvation has influenced the attitude of the people towards marriage; how economic considerations are never taken into account when a man or a boy marries a girl; how, perhaps, they look only at the brighter side of the picture where a wife is depicted as a valuable economic asset; how the fashion set by the higher castes among Hindus has been followed by others including Muslims and Christians, have all been explained in the Reports of previous censuses. The figures in the first of the three statements given above show that as many as 154 (including 6 widowed) in every 1,000 males aged 15—20 are married, that the proportion of married men in the age group 20—40 rises to 740 (including 28 widowed) and that, after 40, there are but few that remain unmarried. This tendency is even more prominent among females, and it will be observed that there are only 82 in every 1,000 women aged 20—40 that remain unmarried. That the followers of the different religions do not differ to any great extent in this respect will be seen from the second of the three tables. The Christians alone show a considerably higher proportion of unmarried women and lower proportion of widows. The difference between Indian and western ideals is revealed in the last of the three tables, the proportion of unmarried men and women above 15 years in England and Wales serving to illustrate the unnatural restraint which the artificial social and economic conditions of western civilization have exercised on the natural instinct influencing Indian conditions that marriage is indispensable and inevitable. We have already seen from the preceding paragraph that the difference between the figures for Cochin and those for Madras reflects the difference between the two in respect of the customs of marriage and widowhood. And the fact that English education has made greater progress in this State than in Madras has tended to make the difference wider.*

Early age of marriage

10. The following table contains the proportions of the unmarried, married and widowed by main age-periods in the population of Cochin, Travancore and the Madras Presidency.

---

*In the Census Report of India for 1921 (Page 156, Part I, Vol. I,) the relatively high proportion of the unmarried in Travancore and Cochin is attributed to the influence of Christianity. It is well known that the factors that are responsible for the higher proportion of unmarried persons in Cochin are (1) the peculiar customs of the Malayali communities referred to in paragraph 8 of this chapter, and (2) the ever-increasing contact with western ideals consequent on the rapid progress of English education. Thus several indigenous Malayali Hindu castes in Subsidiary Table V are seen to have *a higher proportion of unmarried males than even the Christians.* Further Subsidiary Table I shows how the proportion of the unmarried in the Christian community also was much lower in the past like that of the Hindus and how it has been rising steadily under the influence of the forces mentioned above. It is also significant that there is no steady or perceptible rise in the proportion of the unmarried among the Muslims who have been least influenced by English education. In these circumstances the explanation given in the Census Report of India for 1921 can hardly be accepted as correct so far as Cochin is concerned. (Please see paragraph 13 of this chapter where the influence of higher education is examined in detail).

			Age-groups						
			0—5	5—10	10—15	15—20	20—40	40—60	60 and over
Unmarried	Males	Madras ..	997	981	958	747	219	26	19
		Travancore ..	1,000	999	991	813	265	32	21
		Cochin ..	1,000	1,000	997	846	260	23	13
	Females	Madras ..	987	906	769	219	37	9	7
		Travancore ..	1,000	992	920	388	72	14	10
		Cochin ..	1,000	993	930	439	82	14	7
Married	Males	Madras ..	3	18	41	248	750	863	712
		Travancore ..	..	1	9	182	713	888	743
		Cochin ..	..	..	3	148	712	883	714
	Females	Madras ..	12	93	224	744	805	444	150
		Travancore ..	..	8	78	592	835	582	212
		Cochin ..	..	7	67	530	793	525	161
Widowed	Males	Madras ..	..	1	1	5	31	111	269
		Travancore ..	..	..	..	5	22	80	236
		Cochin ..	..	..	..	6	28	94	273
	Females	Madras ..	1	1	7	37	158	547	848
		Travancore ..	..	..	2	20	93	404	778
		Cochin ..	..	..	3	31	125	461	832

It will be observed from the figures that the age of marriage is higher in Cochin and Travancore than in the Madras Presidency, the reasons being identical with those that have made marriage less universal in the two States than in most other parts of India. Between Cochin and Travancore the former is seen to have proportionately fewer early marriages. All the same 3 in every 1,000 boys under 15 and 7 in every 1,000 girls under 10 years are married in this State. When we turn to adolescent males aged 15—20 and girls between 10 and 15, the proportion of the married is seen to rise sharply to 154 (including 6 widowed) and 70 (including 3 widowed) respectively. The difference between the conditions in Cochin and those in Western Europe will be clear from the fact that in England and Wales there is no boy or girl under 15 who is married and that the proportion of married males and females is only 4 and 18 respectively per 1,000 of each sex in the age-group 15—19.*

The appended table shows that the Muslims and the Christians do not differ from the Hindus in respect of early marriages. Indeed, it will be noticed that early marriages among males are more common in the two communities than among the Hindus. But the Christians have the lowest and the Muslims the highest proportion of early marriages among females.

* The proportions are according to the census of 1921.

			Age-groups 0—5	5—10	10—15	15—20	20—40	40—60	60 and over
Unmarried	Males	Hindu ..	1,000	1,000	997	851	263	25	13
		Muslim ..	1,000	997	996	858	270	15	5
		Christian ..	1,000	1,000	997	831	251	23	15
	Females	Hindu ..	1,000	991	920	421	78	11	6
		Muslim ..	1,000	991	913	367	50	6	4
		Christian ..	1,000	998	958	499	100	23	9
Married	Males	Hindu ..	..	..	3	142	704	880	719
		Muslim ..	..	1	4	136	704	914	784
		Christian ..	..	..	3	168	732	880	687
	Females	Hindu ..	..	9	76	540	779	498	146
		Muslim ..	..	9	83	594	818	505	136
		Christian ..	..	2	41	493	821	600	206
Widowed	Males	Hindu ..	..	..	..	7	33	95	268
		Muslim ..	..	..	..	6	26	71	211
		Christian ..	..	..	..	1	17	97	298
	Females	Hindu ..	..	..	4	39	143	491	848
		Muslim ..	..	..	4	39	133	489	860
		Christian ..	..	..	1	8	79	377	785

Proportion of widows

11. Widowed males number 34 and widowed females 146 per 1,000 of each sex in the State's population. There is not much difference between India and the West so far as the proportion of widowers is concerned, but the difference in respect of widows is striking, though inevitable in view of the general prohibition of the re-marriage of widows among Hindus. We have already seen that the Malayali communities (excluding Malayali Brahmans) permit the re-marriage of these women and, for this reason, their ratio in Cochin is relatively low. But it is not clear why this State should compare unfavourably with Travancore where they have only 119 widows per 1,000 women. The highest proportion of widowed women is naturally to be found among the Hindus. The Brahmans prohibit their re-marriage and many of the non-Brahman castes imitate them in order to rise in their social status, the custom being held to be a mark of social respectability. The Christians have the lowest figures for widowed women.

Married persons of reproductive ages and sex ratio.

Religion	Number of females to 1,000 males in: Total Population (all ages)	Population of reproductive ages: All classes	Married persons only
State: all religions ..	1,043	1,267	1,203
Hindus ..	1,065	1,296	1,225
Muslims ..	962	1,163	1,156
Christians ..	1,015	1,229	1,167

12. It will be interesting to examine the civil condition of the population at reproductive ages with special reference to their sex proportion, because it is these ages that count with regard to the increase or decrease of the future population. In paragraph 7 of the preceding chapter we had occasion to study the sex ratio at different age periods, and it was seen that the ratio of women to men was highest in the age groups 15—40. The inset table compares the number of women of

reproductive ages (15—45) with the number of men of like ages (20—50), the figures for the different religions being shown separately; and the sex proportion in the total population at reproductive ages is compared with the proportion among married persons only of the same ages. The figures show that the sex ratio is very much higher in the reproductive periods than it is in the total population, the increase being 224 women per 1,000 men for all religions combined. The ratio among Hindus has risen by 231, among Muslims by 201 and among Christians by 214, and the three classes are seen to maintain the same relative position in respect of their sex ratio at reproductive ages as in the total population. When the category of married persons alone of reproductive ages is examined separately, a similar rise in the sex ratio is seen, but it is slightly lower than in the case of the total population at these ages. And it is noteworthy that, as between different religions, the ratio among Muslims of this class shows the highest increase of 194 women per 1,000 men against 160 and 152 among Hindus and Christians respectively.

Comparison with previous censuses

13. In the first of the two following tables is given the distribution by civil condition of 1,000 persons of each sex and religion at each of the last five censuses.

Year		All Religions		Hindu		Muslim		Christian	
		Males	Females	Males	Females	Males	Females	Males	Females
Unmarried	1931	587	467	583	450	598	476	593	507
	1921	578	452	576	439	595	467	580	482
	1911	562	435	563	423	583	460	553	459
	1901	579	456	584	450	598	484	562	467
	1891	535	425	532	408	560	464	535	465
Married	1931	379	387	381	387	377	397	376	385
	1921	381	390	380	387	377	394	382	396
	1911	400	407	397	402	391	407	411	419
	1901	383	387	378	380	376	385	400	[illegible]
	1891	439	460	443	473	422	425	436	432
Widowed	1931	34	146	36	163	25	133	31	168
	1921	41	158	44	174	28	139	38	122
	1911	38	158	40	175	26	133	36	122
	1901	38	157	38	120	26	131	38	128
	1891	20	115	25	119	18	113	29	103

The figures show a slow but gradual rise in the proportion of the unmarried from decade to decade balanced by a corresponding fall in the ratio of the married. There is a definite set-back to this movement noticed between 1901 and 1911, the reasons for which have not been explained in the Report on the Census of 1911. Further, though this movement is general, it is more marked among the Hindus and the Christians than among the Muslims. The figures for the different age-periods given in Subsidiary Table I make it clear that the increase in the number of unmarried persons is shared by most of the age-groups during the decade preceding 1921. A comparison of the statistics of civil condition for selected castes presented in proportionate forms in Subsidiary Table V with the corresponding statistics of previous censuses will afford an explanation for the movement noticed above.

		Males per 1,000			Females per 1,000		
		Unmarried	Married	Widowed	Unmarried	Married	Widowed
				Educationally advanced communities.			
Indian Christian	1931	593	376	31	506	386	108
	1921	579	383	38	481	396	123
Nayar	1931	647	311	42	443	340	217
	1921	630	324	46	417	367	216
				Intermediate communities.			
Ilavan	1931	590	379	31	479	377	144
	1921	588	376	36	454	383	163
Kammalan	1931	575	398	27	474	386	140
	1921	582	383	35	468	387	145
				Backward communities.			
Muslim (Jonakan)	1931	597	377	26	472	401	127
	1921	603	375	22	503	356	141
Pulayan	1931	546	419	35	446	418	136
	1921	547	407	46	492	365	143
*Sambavan (Parayan)	1931	524	437	39	458	429	113
	1921	540	405	55	449	421	130

From the statistics presented in the statement given above, we find that the increase in the number of the unmarried attended by a corresponding decline in the number of the married is mostly characteristic of such Malayali castes or communities as are advanced in English education. Those that are educationally backward or occupy the lowest position in society do not as a rule show any similar tendency. On the other hand there is at times a rise in the proportion of the married among them. The intermediate castes or communities are seen to continue without any appreciable change; and such variations as we find in their figures are calculated to reduce the distance between them and the advanced communities. It is therefore clear that the influence of western ideals imbibed through the medium of English education has an important part to play in this connection. The standard of life has been steadily rising among the educated classes and the artificial social conditions of western civilization, which determine the character of the statistics of civil condition in the West, are slowly invading the Malayali society. Economic considerations, therefore, influence the attitude of these classes towards marriage. A wife, who is a valuable economic asset among the labouring classes, often proves a costly luxury in the higher circles on account of the changing ideals and rising standards of life, and an educated man must be assured of a sufficient income before he can encumber himself with the dear article. Likewise an educated woman also must have some assurance that she will be able to keep up her ideals and high standards in her new sphere of life before she agrees to take a partner. The movement revealed by the statistics, therefore, signifies a gradual deviation from the Indian standards and a growing approximation to the standards of the West.

* The seven communities in this table together form 80 per cent of the State's total population. The statistics of the civil condition of these communities must, therefore, determine the character of the statistics of the civil condition of the State's population as a whole.

5

Proportion of Unmarried, Married & Widowed per 1,000 of each sex for selected castes

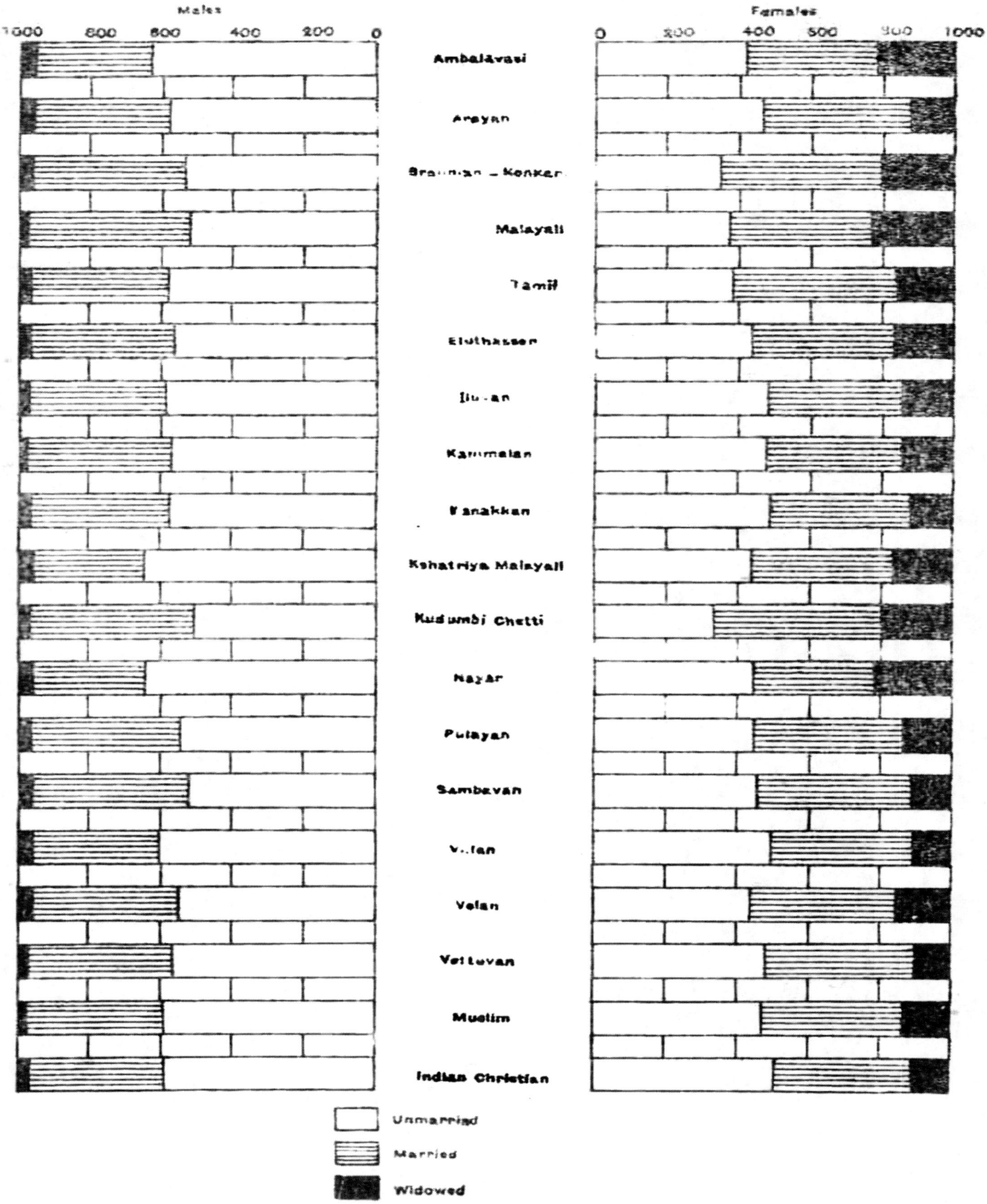

That English education and western ideals should influence the statistics of civil condition in this State to a greater extent than elsewhere will be clear from the chapter on Literacy where it is shown that Cochin is considerably in advance of other States and Provinces in respect of higher education.

14. There is, however, another important cause for the increase in the numbers of the unmarried during the past decade. We have already seen from Chapter IV that the age-constitution of the population has changed during the decade and that a large increase in the earlier age-groups was recorded. The change must necessarily affect the statistics of civil condition, raising the proportion of the unmarried and lowering that of the married for the obvious reason that the earlier age-groups are almost wholly in the category of the unmarried. When we turn to the individual age-periods of 1921 and 1931, it is seen that the ratio of the unmarried in the adult groups has actually decreased in many cases during the last ten years, while that of the married has increased. It is therefore clear that the higher figures for the unmarried in 1931 are partly to be attributed to the change in the age-constitution of the population. At the same time the present ratio of the unmarried in the adult groups of educationally advanced communities like those of the Christians and Nayars is lower than that of 1921, so much so that the influence of western ideals is seen to be still at work. **Variation, 1921—1931**

15. The figures for married females in the age-groups 5—15 and for married males in the group 15—20 are perceptibly higher than in 1921 so that it will appear that the age of marriage has actually been *lowered* during the past decade. More than the usual number of infant and child marriages are reported to have been conducted in British India towards the close of the last decade in order that the operation of the Sarda Act of 1929 might be forestalled. There was no corresponding social legislation in this State to influence the statistics. The set-back, which is as much evident in the Christian community as among the Hindus and Muslims, is perhaps to be accounted for by the economic prosperity of the decade that must have led to a relatively large number of marriages among the lower orders. **Age of marriage**

16. If we now turn to Subsidiary Table V and examine the figures given there for different castes, we shall find that the proportion of the married (particularly of married women) is highest among non-Malayali groups like the Konkani and Tamil Brahmans, Kudumi Chettis, Kusavans, Ambattans, etc. It is high among the lower classes of the indigenous Malayali population like the Pulayas, Sambavans and Vettuvans (all depressed classes), and also among communities like the Muslims and Jews. The Indian Christians and Iluvans have a lower ratio of married women, but the lowest figures are found among the *Marumakkathayam* communities like the Ambalavasis and Nayars. The largest proportion of widows is to be found among the Nambudiri and Konkani Brahmans and the *Marumakkathayam* communities. The Indian Christians, Muslims and Jews and many of the Malayali castes show a high ratio of unmarried women. But the figures for single women in the effective age-groups 17—23 and 24—43 in the populous communities of the Nayars and Indian Christians are specially noteworthy. The bulk of English-educated women in the State is from these two communities and we have already seen from paragraph 13 above in what direction the statistics of civil condition are influenced by higher education. These women in increasing numbers live in single blessedness, earning their own livelihood by service in aided girls' schools or in the Education, Medical or other departments of the Government. **Civil condition by caste**

Civil condition in urban population

17. A statement showing the distribution by civil condition of 1,000 persons of each sex and main age-period from the population of the municipal towns is given below. The distribution of 1,000 persons from the population of the State as a whole is also shown side by side for purposes of comparison.

Age-period		Males per 1,000			Females per 1,000		
		Unmarried	Married	Widowed	Unmarried	Married	Widowed
0—5	State	1,000	..	..	1,000	..	..
	Urban	1,000	..	..	1,000	..	..
5—10	State	1,000	..	..	993	7	..
	Urban	999	1	..	987	12	1
10—15	State	997	3	..	930	67	3
	Urban	997	3	..	906	92	2
15—20	State	846	148	6	439	530	31
	Urban	873	123	4	424	549	27
20—40	State	260	712	28	82	793	125
	Urban	332	643	25	99	771	130
40—60	State	23	883	94	14	525	461
	Urban	40	867	93	22	491	487
60 and over	State	13	714	273	7	161	832
	Urban	26	706	268	10	145	845
All ages	State	587	379	34	467	387	146
	Urban	589	378	33	457	390	153

The urban statistics are seen to possess certain characteristics which distinguish them from the statistics of the State's total population. Thus early marriages appear to be more common in towns and the age of marriage for girls is decidedly lower. Accordingly the proportion of married females in the age-periods below 20 is higher in the urban population. The fact that the non-Malayali Hindus like the Tamil and Konkani Brahmans, among whom pre-puberty marriage is compulsory, are mostly residents of towns will afford an explanation for this difference in the urban statistics. The ratio of unmarried males aged 15—20 in the urban population is seen to be higher, and it must probably be attributed to the student population in these towns. But the figures for unmarried males and females in the population of town in all age-periods above 15—20 constitute perhaps the most interesting feature of the urban statistics. They are decidely higher than the corresponding figures for the State's population as a whole; and they reveal in an unmistakable manner the influence of the new ideals and changing standards of life referred to in paragraph 13 above. Urban society is the starting point for new tendencies of the kind, and it is therefore but natural that they should influence the statistics of the urban population to a greater extent.

There are only 736 females for every 1,000 males among the unmarried and 981 wives for every 1,000 husbands in the population of the towns. The corresponding proportions in the State's population are, as we have already seen, 830 and 1,067 respectively. The difference shows that the towns contain a larger proportion of males, both married and unmarried, 'a condition which is generally recognised as characteristic of urban life'.

SUBSIDIARY TABLES.

I.—*Distribution by civil condition of 1,000 of each sex, religion and main age-period at each of the last five censuses.*

Religion, sex and age	Unmarried					Married					Widowed				
	1931	1921	1911	1901	1891	1931	1921	1911	1901	1891	1931	1921	1911	1901	1891
1	2	3	4	5	6	7	8	9	10	11	12	13	14	15	16
ALL RELIGIONS (Males)															
0—5	1,000	1,000	1,000	1,000	1,000	..	..	..	..	..	..	..	..	..	..
5—10	1,000	1,000	1,000	1,000	999	..	..	..	..	1	..	..	..	..	..
10—15	997	997	995	995	985	3	3	5	5	15	..	..	..	..	..
15—20	846	925	894	903	849	148	73	102	95	150	6	2	4	2	1
20—40	260	255	214	251	163	712	705	753	718	821	28	40	33	31	16
40—60	23	26	21	36	26	883	862	869	852	902	94	112	107	112	72
60 and over	13	20	15	17	28	714	696	673	673	719	273	290	302	310	253
Not stated	..	..	..	386	541	..	..	..	523	432	..	..	..	91	27
All ages	**587**	**578**	**562**	**579**	**535**	**379**	**381**	**400**	**383**	**439**	**34**	**41**	**38**	**38**	**26**
ALL RELIGIONS (Females)															
0—5	1,000	1,000	1,000	1,000	997	..	..	..	..	3	..	..	..	..	..
5—10	993	999	997	998	983	7	1	3	2	16	..	..	..	..	1
10—15	930	944	910	920	851	67	55	88	78	148	3	1	2	2	1
15—20	439	488	402	432	327	530	490	574	547	666	31	22	24	21	7
20—40	82	59	47	76	41	793	813	821	800	890	125	128	132	124	69
40—60	14	16	11	18	34	525	501	479	455	571	461	483	510	527	395
60 and over	7	12	8	4	39	161	150	139	117	184	832	838	853	879	777
Not stated	..	..	..	241	472	..	..	..	426	361	..	..	..	333	167
All ages	**467**	**482**	**435**	**456**	**425**	**387**	**390**	**407**	**387**	**460**	**148**	**158**	**158**	**157**	**118**

I.—Distribution by civil condition of 1,000 of each sex, religion and main age-period at each of the last five censuses.—(contd.)

Religion, sex and age	Unmarried 1931	Unmarried 1921	Unmarried 1911	Unmarried 1901	Unmarried 1891	Married 1931	Married 1921	Married 1911	Married 1901	Married 1891	Widowed 1931	Widowed 1921	Widowed 1911	Widowed 1901	Widowed 1891
1	2	3	4	5	6	7	8	9	10	11	12	13	14	15	16
HINDU (Males)															
0—5	1,000	1,000	1,000	1,000	1,000	..	..	..	..	..	..	..	..	..	..
5—10	1,000	1,000	1,000	1,000	998	..	..	..	..	2	..	..	..	..	..
10—15	997	997	996	995	985	3	3	4	5	15	..	..	..	..	..
15—20	851	933	909	915	863	142	65	87	83	136	7	2	4	2	
20—40	263	269	235	280	178	704	687	728	687	807	33	44	37	33	15
40—60	25	28	25	44	30	880	856	868	817	902	95	116	107	109	68
60 and over	13	20	15	18	32	719	693	681	673	718	268	287	301	309	250
Not stated	..	..	..	387	308	..	..	..	484	692	..	..	..	129	..
All ages	**583**	**576**	**563**	**584**	**532**	**381**	**380**	**397**	**378**	**443**	**36**	**44**	**40**	**38**	**25**
HINDU (Females)															
0—5	1,000	1,000	1,000	1,000	995	..	..	..	..	5	..	..	..	..	..
5—10	991	998	997	998	979	9	2	3	2	21	..	..	..	..	..
10—15	920	934	903 416	912	823	76	64	91	86	176	4	2	3	2	1
15—20	421	496	49	447	317	540	478	551	529	676	39	26	30	24	7
20—40	78	66	11	88	43	779	781	801	775	888	143	153	150	137	69
40—60	11	15		21	33	498	480	459	438	575	491	595	530	541	392
60 and over	6	12	7	4	40	146	138	123	111	185	848	850	870	885	775
Not stated	..	..	..	289	333	..	..	..	294	467	..	..	..	316	200
All ages	**450**	**439**	**423**	**450**	**408**	**387**	**387**	**402**	**380**	**473**	**163**	**174**	**175**	**120**	**119**

I.—Distribution by civil condition of 1,000 of each sex, religion and main age-period at each of the last five censuses.—(cont.)

Religion, sex and age	Unmarried					Married					Widowed				
	1931	1921	1911	1901	1891	1931	1921	1911	1901	1891	1931	1921	1911	1901	1891
1	2	3	4	5	6	7	8	9	10	11	12	13	14	15	16
MUSLIM (Males)															
0—5	1,000	1,000	1,000	1,000	1,000	..	..	..	..	..	..	..	..	..	..
5—10	999	1,000	1,000	1,000	1,000	1	..	..	..	..	..	..	..	..	..
10—15	996	997	998	995	996	4	3	2	5	4	..	..	..	..	..
15—20	858	948	926	945	893	136	50	70	54	106	6	2	4	1	1
20—40	270	277	255	258	176	704	691	718	711	811	26	29	27	31	11
40—60	15	12	13	18	11	914	914	917	909	913	71	74	70	73	46
60 and over	5	12	5	11	15	784	763	759	780	781	211	225	236	209	204
Not stated	..	..	..	600	834	..	..	..	400	83	..	..	..	..	83
All ages	**598**	**595**	**583**	**598**	**560**	**377**	**377**	**391**	**376**	**422**	**25**	**28**	**26**	**26**	**18**
MUSLIM (Females)															
0—5	1,000	1,000	1,000	1,000	1,000	..	..	..	..	..	..	..	..	..	..
5—10	991	998	1,000	999	995	9	2	..	1	5	..	..	..	..	..
10—15	913	948	924	947	919	83	51	73	52	81	4	1	3	1	..
15—20	367	436	390	414	381	594	535	583	556	609	39	29	27	30	10
20—40	50	50	41	61	50	818	824	838	827	869	132	126	121	112	81
40—60	6	14	11	18	27	505	492	498	481	542	489	494	489	501	431
60 and over	4	12	9	3	41	136	142	157	107	136	860	846	834	890	823
Not stated	..	..	..	..	667	..	..	..	333	..	..	..	..	607	333
All ages	**470**	**467**	**460**	**484**	**464**	**397**	**394**	**407**	**385**	**423**	**133**	**139**	**133**	**131**	**113**

I.—Distribution by civil condition of 1,000 of each sex, religion and main age-period at each of the last five censuses.—(cont.)

Religion, sex and age	Unmarried					Married					Widowed				
	1931	1921	1911	1901	1891	1931	1921	1911	1901	1891	1931	1921	1911	1901	1891
1	2	3	4	5	6	7	8	9	10	11	12	13	14	15	16
CHRISTIAN (Males)															
0—5	1,000	1,000	1,000	1,000	1,000	..	..	..	..	..	..	..	..	..	..
5—10	1,000	1,000	999	1,000	998	..	..	1	..	2	..	..	..	..	..
10—15	997	996	992	993	982	3	4	8	7	18	..	..	..	..	..
15—20	831	910	846	861	798	168	88	152	138	201	1	2	2	1	1
20—40	251	211	152	167	113	732	758	825	808	869	17	31	23	25	18
40—60	23	23	22	20	10	880	865	860	853	900	97	112	118	127	90
60 and over	15	21	18	14	20	687	665	657	646	702	298	314	325	340	278
Not stated	..	..	..	250	500	..	..	..	750	500	..	..	..	..	..
All ages	**593**	**580**	**553**	**562**	**535**	**376**	**382**	**411**	**400**	**436**	**31**	**38**	**36**	**38**	**29**
CHRISTIAN (Females)															
0—5	1,000	1,000	1,000	1,000	1,000	..	..	..	..	..	..	..	..	..	..
5—10	998	1,000	996	998	995	2	..	4	2	5	..	..	..	..	..
10—15	958	963	921	934	907	41	37	78	65	93	1	..	1	1	..
15—20	499	483	363	394	343	493	509	628	597	654	8	8	9	9	3
20—40	100	55	42	46	30	821	851	873	861	905	79	94	85	90	65
40—60	23	20	15	12	35	600	559	529	499	569	377	421	456	489	396
60 and over	9	12	10	3	35	206	187	185	141	192	785	801	805	856	773
Not stated	..	..	..	200	533	..	..	..	600	400	..	..	..	200	67
All ages	**507**	**482**	**459**	**467**	**468**	**385**	**396**	**419**	**405**	**432**	**108**	**122**	**122**	**128**	**103**

I.—Distribution by civil condition of 1,000 of each sex, religion and main age-period at each of the last five censuses.—(cont.)

Religion, sex and age	Unmarried					Married					Widowed				
	1931	1921	1911	1901	1891	1931	1921	1911	1901	1891	1931	1921	1911	1901	1891
1	2	3	4	5	6	7	8	9	10	11	12	13	14	15	16
JAIN (Males)															
0—5	1,000	1,000	1,000	1,000	..	..	..	..	..	..	..	..	..	..	..
5—10	1,000	1,000	1,000	..	..	..	..	..	..	..	..	..	..	..	..
10—15	1,000	800	929	..	..	..	..	71	..	..	..	200	..	..	..
15—20	1,000	714	1,000	..	..	..	286	..	..	..	..	..	..	..	..
20—40	280	261	146	500	..	700	696	781	500	..	20	43	73	..	..
40—60	..	..	..	1,000	..	750	625	875	..	..	250	375	125	..	..
60 and over	..	..	..	..	..	..	1,000	500	..	..	1,000	..	500	..	..
All ages	**534**	**500**	**345**	**750**	..	**398**	**414**	**586**	**250**	..	**68**	**86**	**69**	..	..
JAIN (Females)															
0—5	1,000	1,000	1,000	..	..	..	..	..	..	..	..	..	..	..	..
5—10	1,000	1,000	1,000	..	..	..	..	..	..	..	..	..	..	..	..
10—15	900	1,000	400	..	..	100	..	600	..	..	..	..	..	..	..
15—20	..	..	..	..	..	889	1,000	1,000	1,000	..	111	..	..	..	..
20—40	..	71	..	..	..	906	929	885	..	..	94	..	115	..	..
40—60	..	..	..	..	..	182	400	..	..	..	818	600	1,000	..	..
60 and over	..	..	..	..	..	..	..	..	..	..	1,000	1,000	1,000	..	..
All ages	**391**	**395**	**225**	..	..	**435**	**512**	**673**	**1,000**	..	**174**	**93**	**102**	..	..

I.—Distribution by civil condition of 1,000 of each sex, religion and main age-period at each of the last five censuses.—(cont.)

Religion, sex and age	Unmarried					Married					Widowed				
	1931	1921	1911	1901	1891	1931	1921	1911	1901	1891	1931	1921	1911	1901	1891
1	2	3	4	5	6	7	8	9	10	11	12	13	14	15	16
JEW (Males)															
0—5	1,000	1,000	1,000	1,000	1,000	..	..	..	..	..	..	..	..	..	..
5—10	1,000	1,000	1,000	1,000	1,000	..	..	..	..	..	..	..	..	..	..
10—15	1,000	1,000	1,000	1,000	1,000	..	..	..	..	..	..	..	..	..	..
15—20	951	966	942	1,000	1,000	49	34	58	..	..	..	..	..	..	..
20—40	330	406	377	396	337	638	563	586	573	639	32	31	17	13	24
40—60	63	29	60	..	40	854	811	810	854	871	83	140	130	146	89
60 and over	..	..	28	25	..	723	688	694	825	860	277	312	278	150	1,0
All ages	**571**	**555**	**566**	**573**	**555**	**386**	**387**	**380**	**381**	**412**	**43**	**58**	**54**	**46**	**33**
JEW (Females)															
0—5	1,000	1,000	1,000	1,000	1,000	..	..	..	..	..	..	..	..	..	..
5—10	1,000	1,000	1,000	1,000	988	..	..	..	..	12	..	..	..	..	..
10—15	952	933	969	996	958	36	67	31	4	42	12	..	..	..	..
15—20	500	500	583	422	546	500	500	400	547	436	..	..	17	31	18
20—40	142	128	150	79	48	805	823	767	820	894	53	49	83	101	58
40—60	48	14	10	10	11	627	534	670	529	652	325	452	320	461	337
60 and over	25	30	25	..	21	146	182	150	135	333	829	788	825	865	646
All ages	**457**	**469**	**442**	**418**	**401**	**422**	**412**	**422**	**412**	**471**	**121**	**119**	**136**	**170**	**128**

II.—*Distribution by civil condition of 1,000 of each sex at certain ages in each religion and natural division.*

Cochin State—Natural Division: 'Malabar and Konkan'

Males.

Religion	All ages			0—5			5—10			10—15			15—40			40 and over		
	Unmarried	Married	Widowed	Unmarried	Married	Widowed	Unmarried	Married	Widowed	Unmarried	Married	Widowed	Unmarried	Married	Widowed	Unmarried	Married	Widowed
1	2	3	4	5	6	7	8	9	10	11	12	13	14	15	16	17	18	19
All religions ..	**587**	**379**	**34**	**1,000**	..	..	**1,000**	..	..	**997**	**3**	..	**407**	**570**	**23**	**21**	**847**	**132**
Hindu ..	583	381	36	1,000	..	..	1,000	..	..	997	3	..	398	565	37	22	846	132
Muslim ..	598	377	25	1,000	..	..	999	1	..	996	4	..	416	563	21	13	889	98
Christian ..	593	376	31	1,000	..	..	1,000	..	..	997	3	..	402	585	13	21	838	141
Jain ..	534	398	68	1,000	..	..	1,000	..	..	1,000	..	..	368	614	18	..	632	368
Jew ..	571	386	43	1,000	..	..	1,000	..	..	1,000	..	..	484	492	24	47	822	131

Females.

Religion	All ages			0—5			5—10			10—15			15—40			40 and over		
1	2	3	4	5	6	7	8	9	10	11	12	13	14	15	16	17	18	19
All religions ..	**467**	**387**	**146**	**1,000**	..	..	**993**	**7**	..	**930**	**67**	**3**	**170**	**728**	**102**	**12**	**440**	**548**
Hindu ..	450	387	163	1,000	..	..	991	9	..	920	76	4	161	721	118	9	415	576
Muslim ..	470	398	132	1,000	..	..	991	9	..	915	81	4	130	761	109	5	430	565
Christian ..	507	385	108	1,000	..	..	998	2	..	958	41	1	204	736	60	20	507	473
Jain ..	391	435	174	1,000	..	..	1,000	..	..	900	100	..	..	902	98	..	143	857
Jew ..	457	422	121	1,000	..	..	1,000	..	..	952	36	12	232	728	40	42	509	449

III.—Distribution by main age-periods and civil condition of 10,000 of each sex and religion.

Religion and age	Males			Females		
	Unmarried	Married	Widowed	Unmarried	Married	Widowed
1	2	3	4	5	6	7
ALL RELIGIONS						
0—10	3,028	..	..	2,848	8	..
10—15	1,265	4	..	1,108	79	3
15—40	1,538	2,152	85	692	2,955	414
40 and over	41	1,632	255	23	832	1,038
HINDU						
0—10	2,993	..	..	2,762	10	..
10—15	1,253	4	..	1,059	88	4
15—40	1,543	2,135	101	662	2,953	484
40 and over	44	1,667	260	19	820	1,139
MUSLIM						
0—10	3,039	2	..	2,998	12	1
10—15	1,282	5	..	1,149	103	5
15—40	1,638	2,217	82	547	3,204	457
40 and over	23	1,543	169	9	654	860
CHRISTIAN						
0—10	3,108	..	..	3,017	3	..
10—15	1,280	4	..	1,215	53	1
15—40	1,407	2,176	48	800	2,891	237
40 and over	40	1,573	265	35	904	842
JAIN						
0—10	2,342	..	..	2,935	..	..
10—15	1,087	..	..	978	109	..
15—40	1,780	2,966	85	..	4,022	435
40 and over	..	1,017	593	..	717	1,304
JEW						
0—10	2,829	..	..	2,435	..	..
10—15	1,110	..	..	1,096	41	14
15—40	1,650	1,678	83	959	3,014	164
40 and over	125	2,178	347	96	1,164	1,027

IV.—Proportion of sexes by civil condition at certain ages for religions and natural divisions.

Cochin State—Natural Division: 'Malabar and Konkan'.

Religion	Number of Females per 1,000 Males														
	All ages			0—10			10—15			15—40			40 and over		
	Unmarried	Married	Widowed	Unmarried	Married	Widowed	Unmarried	Married	Widowed	Unmarried	Married	Widowed	Unmarried	Married	Widowed
1	2	3	4	5	6	7	8	9	10	11	12	13	14	15	16
All religions ..	**850**	**1,067**	**4,470**	**981**	**23,318**	**22,000**	**914**	**19,618**	**15,846**	**469**	**1,432**	**5,107**	**579**	**532**	**4,248**
Hindu ..	822	1,083	4,797	983	51,250	16,000	900	23,006	18,778	457	1,473	5,107	459	524	4,662
Muslim ..	757	1,015	5,062	949	6,375	..	862	19,565	..	321	1,391	5,344	363	408	1,892
Christian ..	867	1,042	3,499	985	8,667	..	957	12,333	3,500	542	1,350	5,019	913	583	3,223
Jain ..	571	851	2,000	900	..	..	750	..	..	..	1,057	4,000	..	167	1,714
Jew ..	811	1,108	2,839	868	..	..	1,000	..	..	588	1,818	2,000	778	541	3,[illegible]00

V.—Distribution by civil condition of 1,000 of each sex at certain ages for selected castes.

Caste	Distribution of 1,000 males of each age by civil condition																				
	All ages			0—6			7—13			14—16			17—23			24—43			44 and over		
	Unmarried	Married	Widowed	Unmarried	Married	Widowed	Unmarried	Married	Widowed	Unmarried	Married	Widowed	Unmarried	Married	Widowed	Unmarried	Married	Widowed	Unmarried	Married	Widowed
1	2	3	4	5	6	7	8	9	10	11	12	13	14	15	16	17	18	19	20	21	22
HINDU																					
Ambalavasi ..	631	321	48	1,000	..	..	1,000	..	..	993	7	..	894	100	6	321	626	53	71	748	181
Ambattan ..	581	376	43	1,000	..	..	1,000	..	..	1,000	..	..	667	324	9	127	817	56	25	800	175
Arayan ..	581	376	43	1,000	..	..	1,000	..	..	1,000	..	..	864	129	7	123	815	62	7	835	158
Brahman—Konkani ..	536	424	40	1,000	..	..	1,000	..	..	982	18	..	707	291	2	115	857	28	44	801	155
Do Malayali ..	525	448	27	1,000	..	..	1,000	..	..	1,000	..	..	785	215	..	231	743	26	82	836	82
Do Tamil ..	581	386	33	1,000	..	..	1,000	..	..	991	9	..	763	231	6	88	891	21	14	848	138
Chakkan ..	552	416	32	1,000	..	..	1,000	..	..	986	14	..	842	158	..	168	799	23	11	860	129
Chaliyan { Chaliyan ..	595	351	54	1,000	..	..	1,000	..	..	1,000	..	..	774	226	..	204	735	61	26	763	211
Chaliyan { Pattariyan ..	574	384	42	1,000	..	..	1,000	..	..	1,000	..	..	800	190	10	133	816	51	13	826	161
Eluthassan ..	563	402	35	1,000	..	..	1,000	..	..	994	6	..	763	219	18	77	887	36	8	850	142
Iluvan ..	590	379	31	1,000	..	..	1,000	..	..	991	9	..	754	234	12	91	874	35	9	852	139
Kaikolan ..	518	417	65	1,000	..	..	1,000	..	..	989	11	..	690	293	17	99	826	75	44	726	230
Kammalan ..	575	398	27	1,000	..	..	999	1	..	988	12	..	755	234	11	83	887	30	6	877	117

V.—Distribution by civil condition of 1,000 of each sex at certain ages for selected castes.—(cont.)

Caste		All ages			0—6			7—13			14—16			17—23			24—43			44 and over	
	Distribution of 1,000 males of each age by civil condition																				
	Unmarried	Married	Widowed	Unmarried	Married	Widowed	Unmarried	Married	Widowed	Unmarried	Married	Widowed	Unmarried	Married	Widowed	Unmarried	Married	Widowed	Unmarried	Married	Widowed
1	2	3	4	5	6	7	8	9	10	11	12	13	14	15	16	17	18	19	20	21	22
HINDU (*cont.*)																					
Kanakkan ..	575	387	38	1,000	..	..	999	1	..	992	6	2	740	247	13	83	879	38	7	813	180
Kaniyan ..	591	372	37	1,000	..	..	1,000	..	..	1,000	..	..	815	185	..	145	814	41	19	832	149
Kshatriya—Malayali ..	649	305	46	1,000	..	..	990	10	..	1,000	..	..	1,000	..	..	321	630	49	74	756	170
Kudumi Chetti ..	511	452	37	1,000	..	..	1,000	..	..	969	31	..	582	411	7	80	876	44	7	849	144
Kusavan ..	490	454	56	1,000	..	..	1,000	..	..	850	141	..	383	598	19	29	890	81	3	808	189
Nayar ..	647	311	42	1,000	..	..	1,000	..	..	996	1	..	924	73	3	266	684	50	53	769	179
Pandaran ..	539	427	34	1,000	..	..	1,000	..	..	988	12	..	664	304	32	65	898	37	63	818	119
Panditattan ..	582	385	33	1,000	..	..	996	..	4	1,000	..	..	827	163	10	153	826	21	28	819	153
Pulayan ..	546	419	35	1,000	..	..	1,000	..	..	980	18	2	618	355	27	51	906	43	7	859	134
Sambavan (Parayan) ..	524	437	39	1,000	..	..	999	1	..	960	40	..	532	441	27	50	906	44	12	836	152
Valan ..	610	351	39	1,000	..	..	1,000	..	..	1,000	..	..	794	194	12	159	802	39	11	811	178
Velakkattalavan ..	614	340	46	1,000	..	..	1,000	..	..	985	15	..	819	170	11	200	749	51	15	777	208
Velan ..	548	411	41	1,000	..	..	1,000	..	..	989	11	..	591	377	32	83	869	48	28	823	149
Vellalan ..	558	389	53	1,000	..	..	1,000	..	..	1,000	..	..	839	145	16	183	765	52	25	771	204

V.—Distribution by civil condition of 1,000 of each sex at certain ages for selected castes.—(cont.)

Caste	Distribution of 1,000 males of each age by civil condition																				
	All ages			0—6			7—13			14—16			17—23			24—43			44 and over		
	Unmarried	Married	Widowed	Unmarried	Married	Widowed	Unmarried	Married	Widowed	Unmarried	Married	Widowed	Unmarried	Married	Widowed	Unmarried	Married	Widowed	Unmarried	Married	Widowed
1	2	3	4	5	6	7	8	9	10	11	12	13	14	15	16	17	18	19	20	21	22
HINDU—(cont.)																					
Veluttedan ..	580	368	52	1,000	..	..	1,000	..	..	993	7	..	784	216	..	130	809	61	3	790	207
Vettuvan ..	569	397	34	1,000	..	..	1,000	..	..	985	12	3	657	327	16	67	894	39	5	844	151
MUSLIM																					
Jonakan ..	597	377	26	1,000	..	..	999	1	..	991	9	..	767	223	10	120	849	31	13	870	117
Ravuttan ..	586	392	22	1,000	..	..	999	1	..	995	5	..	729	261	10	79	891	30	4	894	102
Others ..	608	367	25	1,000	..	..	997	3	..	987	13	..	822	172	6	168	796	36	12	887	101
CHRISTIAN																					
Anglo-Indian ..	651	317	32	1,000	..	..	1,000	..	..	1,000	..	..	905	95	..	251	711	38	65	817	118
European ..	586	414	..	1,000	..	..	1,000	..	..	..	..	..	833	167	..	464	536	..	529	471	..
Indian Christian ..	593	376	31	1,000	..	..	1,000	..	..	988	11	1	733	265	2	103	872	25	18	819	163
JAIN ..	534	398	68	1,000	..	..	1,000	..	..	1,000	..	..	1,000	..	..	196	784	20	..	500	500
JEW ..	571	386	43	1,000	..	..	1,000	..	..	1,000	..	..	949	51	..	149	811	40	43	810	147

V.—*Distribution by civil condition of 1,000 of each sex at certain ages for selected castes.*—(*cont.*)

Caste	Distribution of 1,000 females of each age by civil condition																				
	All ages			0—6			7—13			14—16			17—23			24—43			44 and over		
	Unmarried	Married	Widowed	Unmarried	Married	Widowed	Unmarried	Married	Widowed	Unmarried	Married	Widowed	Unmarried	Married	Widowed	Unmarried	Married	Widowed	Unmarried	Married	Widowed
1	2	3	4	5	6	7	8	9	10	11	12	13	14	15	16	17	18	19	20	21	22
HINDU																					
Ambalavasi ..	419	364	217	1,000	..	..	991	9	..	745	245	10	254	668	78	43	723	234	14	313	673
Ambattan ..	417	442	141	1,000	..	..	977	23	..	535	448	17	143	800	57	24	805	171	..	388	612
Arayan ..	465	411	124	1,000	..	..	1,000	..	..	822	173	5	186	781	13	8	877	115	4	402	594
Brahman—Konkani ..	340	449	202	999	1	..	941	58	1	53	940	7	17	935	48	3	786	211	2	303	695
Do Malayali ..	373	400	227	1,000	..	..	991	9	..	786	214	..	344	623	33	40	788	172	2	336	662
Do Tamil ..	383	458	159	1,000	..	..	922	78	..	115	869	16	10	937	53	2	833	165	1	417	582
Chakkan ..	396	432	172	1,000	..	..	970	30	..	536	464	..	143	837	20	10	789	201	..	353	647
Chaliyan { Chaliyan ..	438	375	187	1,000	..	..	1,000	..	..	800	200	..	241	724	35	22	739	239	..	368	632
Chaliyan { Pattariyan ..	474	395	131	1,000	..	..	1,000	..	..	864	136	..	336	634	30	29	826	145	6	453	541
Eluthassan ..	437	394	169	1,000	..	..	994	6	..	741	242	17	180	746	74	19	805	176	5	344	651
Iluvan ..	479	377	144	1,000	..	..	996	4	..	859	134	7	293	660	47	33	798	169	9	382	609
Kaikolan ..	358	422	220	1,000	..	..	968	32	..	503	497	..	80	872	48	7	735	258	5	285	710
Kammalan ..	474	386	140	1,000	..	..	991	8	1	814	178	8	275	691	14	44	801	155	16	385	599

V.—Distribution by civil condition of 1,000 of each sex at certain ages for selected castes.—(cont.)

Caste	Distribution of 1,000 females of each age by civil condition																				
	All ages			0—6			7—13			14—16			17—23			24—43			44 and over		
	Unmarried	Married	Widowed	Unmarried	Married	Widowed	Unmarried	Married	Widowed	Unmarried	Married	Widowed	Unmarried	Married	Widowed	Unmarried	Married	Widowed	Unmarried	Married	Widowed
	2	3	4	5	6	7	8	9	10	11	12	13	14	15	16	17	18	19	20	21	22
HINDU.—(cont.)																					
Kanakkan ..	487	394	119	1,000	..	..	995	5	..	829	164	7	246	719	35	30	834	136	7	408	585
Kaniyan ..	468	367	165	1,000	..	..	1,000	..	..	908	85	7	416	533	51	66	752	182	15	401	584
Kshatriya—Malayali ..	441	395	164	1,000	..	..	992	8	..	840	140	20	262	719	19	19	824	157	7	365	628
Kudumi Chetti ..	331	46	197	1,000	..	..	840	159	1	61	901	38	19	916	65	7	740	253	7	264	729
Kusavan ..	406	485	109	1,000	..	..	888	112	..	480	520	..	86	871	43	13	878	109	11	466	520
Nayar ..	443	340	217	1,000	..	..	994	6	..	814	175	11	335	588	77	52	688	260	8	299	693
Pandaran ..	412	429	159	1,000	..	..	949	51	..	580	415	5	144	827	29	14	817	169	..	348	652
Panditattan ..	386	437	177	1,000	..	..	995	5	..	667	320	13	110	856	34	5	825	170	4	327	669
Pulayan ..	446	418	136	1,000	..	..	990	9	1	680	298	22	160	784	56	18	832	150	7	396	597
Sambavan (Parayan) ..	458	429	113	1,000	..	..	991	9	..	737	258	5	159	803	38	21	862	117	4	438	558
Valan ..	491	399	110	1,000	..	..	993	7	..	838	162	..	197	760	43	14	872	114	8	458	534
Velakkattalavan ..	419	363	218	1,000	..	..	983	17	..	653	339	8	208	720	72	41	713	246	14	250	736
Vilan ..	441	403	156	1,000	..	..	990	10	..	793	188	19	210	723	67	18	803	179	13	368	619

V.—Distribution by civil condition of 1,000 of each sex at certain ages for selected castes.—(cont.)

Caste	Distribution of 1,000 females of each age by civil condition																				
	All ages			0—6			7—13			14—16			17—23			24—43			44 and over		
	Unmarried	Married	Widowed	Unmarried	Married	Widowed	Unmarried	Married	Widowed	Unmarried	Married	Widowed	Unmarried	Married	Widowed	Unmarried	Married	Widowed	Unmarried	Married	Widowed
1	2	3	4	5	6	7	8	9	10	11	12	13	14	15	16	17	18	19	20	21	22
HINDU—(cont.)																					
Vellalan ..	390	391	219	1,000	..	..	980	16	4	738	255	7	132	833	30	5	735	260	4	264	732
Veluttedan ..	402	365	231	1,000	..	..	990	10	..	729	250	21	235	679	86	27	664	309	13	307	680
Vettuvan ..	481	416	103	1,000	..	..	998	1	1	814	181	5	163	788	49	13	873	114	6	466	528
MUSLIM																					
Jonakan ..	472	401	127	1,000	..	..	991	9	..	753	235	12	172	773	55	16	817	167	7	378	615
Ravuttan ..	430	404	166	1,000	..	..	960	40	..	481	496	23	83	865	52	8	783	209	1	241	758
Others ..	486	383	131	1,000	..	..	990	9	1	802	192	6	221	725	54	18	819	163	2	387	611
CHRISTIAN																					
Anglo-Indian ..	565	323	112	1,000	..	..	1,000	..	..	911	89	..	702	298	..	130	761	109	100	437	463
European ..	685	259	56	1,000	..	..	1,000	..	..	1,000	..	..	625	375	..	655	345	..	428	143	429
Indian Christian ..	506	386	108	1,000	..	..	997	3	..	863	136	1	291	607	12	42	845	113	17	453	530
JAIN ..	391	435	171	1,000	..	..	1,000	..	..	500	500	..	..	882	118	..	920	80	..	77	923
JEW ..	457	422	121	1,000	..	..	1,000	..	..	854	125	21	333	667	..	82	841	77	37	433	530

CHAPTER VII.—INFIRMITIES.

Reference to statistics

As at previous censuses, four infirmities were recorded at the present census also, namely, insanity, deaf-mutism, total blindness and leprosy. The statistics of these infirmities are presented in Parts I and II of Imperial Table IX, in State Table III and in the three Subsidiary Tables appended to this chapter, as shown below:

Imperial Table IX—Part I—contains the actual figures of the afflicted by age-periods.

Imperial Table IX—Part II—gives their distribution by taluks.

State Table III shows the actual figures of the afflicted for selected castes.

Subsidiary Table I presents the number afflicted in every 100,000 of the population at each of the last five censuses.

Subsidiary Table II shows their distribution by age per 10,000 of each sex for five censuses.

Subsidiary Table III gives the number afflicted per 100,000 persons of each age-period, and the number of females afflicted per 1,000 males.

Accuracy of statistics

2. In his Notes for Report, Chapter VII.—Infirmities, the Census Commissioner for India comments thus on the accuracy of the statistics presented in Infirmities Tables: "Owing partly to the difficulties in the way of an accurate diagnosis, and partly to intentional concealment, the statistics in these tables are far less reliable than the other Census figures. It has seriously been proposed to drop this enquiry altogether. But in India there are few ordinary means of obtaining statistics of any kind on these subjects and as the errors are to some extent constant the statistics of distribution and variation are of some comparative interest."

The instructions issued to census officers in this connection were clear enough. The last column of the enumeration schedule intended for infirmities had for its heading "Insane, deaf-mute, totally blind or leper." The schedule contained these additional directions: "If any person be insane, or blind of *both* eyes, or suffering from corrosive leprosy, or deaf and dumb, enter the name of the infirmity in this column. Do not enter those who are blind of one eye only, or who are suffering from white leprosy only or who are deaf without being dumb." After all the inmates of a family had been enumerated, the enumerator was to read out the heading of the last column and ask the principal member of the family if there were any persons in it suffering from any of the infirmities specified; and if an affirmative answer was received, the necessary entries were to be made against the persons afflicted.

As pointed out in the Census Commissioner's Note, it has been fully recognised that, of all statistics collected at the census, the figures relating to infirmities are the least free from errors of omission as well as commission. It will, however, be clear from the discussion of the subject in the subsequent paragraphs of this chapter that, so far as Cochin is concerned, the returns for the infirmities other than blindness are vitiated chiefly, if not wholly, by deliberate concealment from a sense of shame or by unintentional omission on account of ignorance. It is extremely doubtful whether any one will volunteer to return a weak-minded person in his family as insane when the general tendency is to conceal cases of real madness through false shame. For the same reason, there is no likelihood of persons who developed deafness late in life being returned as deaf-mutes or of any kind of skin disease being returned as leprosy. Indeed, there is an additional reason for the omission of lepers in that, according to medical opinion, it is almost impossible to detect the presence of the disease in its earlier stages before pain, disfigurement and other inconveniences set in. We have therefore to look for omissions on a large scale of genuinely afflicted persons from these returns, and not for the erroneous inclusion of those that are really free from these infirmities.

Proof of omissions: low proportion of women and children among the afflicted

3. A comparison of the number of males and females suffering from the same infirmity usually serves as a guide to the extent to which the statistics of that infirmity are vitiated by intentional concealment. The motive for secrecy being strongest when the afflicted person is a woman—it is particularly so when she is a member of a respectable family—, the proportion of females among the sufferers will be lower than that of males where there is deliberate concealment. And this is what we actually find in the marginal figures taken from Subsidiary Table III which shows the sex proportion of the afflicted by age-periods. The disparity between the figures of male and female lepers is particularly striking and unmistakably points to omissions of the latter on a large scale even after due allowance is made for the fact that the disease attacks males more frequently than females. The low proportion of children among the afflicted revealed in Subsidiary Table III is another proof of omissions. Parents generally refuse to recognize the presence of the disease in their children and, when the infirmity is deaf-mutism, they fondly persuade themselves that it is but a case ot retarded development.

Infirmity	No. of females afflicted per 1,000 males
Insanity ..	779
Deaf-mutism ..	724
Blindness ..	1,104
Leprosy ..	347

Accuracy of statistics of blindness

4. Blindness is free from the odium that attaches itself to the other three infirmities. It evokes sympathy without raising disgust. Hence the motive for concealment is absent here. The specific figures of the blind, their sex proportion and their distribution by age-periods alike prove that the value of the returns has not been affected by omissions. If there are errors in the statistics of blindness, they must rise chiefly, if not wholly, from the inclusion in the returns of persons who were but partially blind. But, in the light of the clear and precise instructions issued to enumerators, it is not likely that many mistakes of this nature have crept into the statistics.

Variation for the decade

5. Since it will serve no useful purpose to explain, or to draw inferences from, statistics that are admittedly inaccurate, all that is necessary is to set out the figures for the four infirmities in turn with such comments as may be called for in each case. The actual and proportional figures of the afflicted for five censuses are given in the margin. The total number of the infirm according to the statistics of the present census is 3,459 against 2,586 returned at the census of 1921. This represents an increase of 34 per cent for the decade

Infirmity	No. afflicted according to the statistics of				
	1931	1921	1911	1901	1891
Insanity	637	381	393	197	213
	*53	*39	*32	*24	*29
Deaf-mutism	488	504	331	549	397
	*40	*51	*36	*68	*55
Blindness	1,595	1,250	1,185	886	863
	*132	*128	*129	*109	*109
Leprosy	745	466	461	334	350
	*62	*48	*50	*41	*48

* These figures represent the proportion of the afflicted per 100,000 of the population.

under review. Insanity has increased by 67 per cent, blindness by 28 per cent, and leprosy by 60 per cent. Deaf-mutism alone shows a decrease of 3 per cent. Of the total number of afflicted persons, 18·4 per cent are insane, 14·1 per cent are deaf-mute, 46·1 per cent are blind and 21·4 per cent are lepers. The corresponding proportions in 1921 were 14·5, 19·3, 48·2 and 18·0.

Variation and distribution of the insane. Lunatic Asylum

6. At the present census 61 persons in every 100,000 males and 45 in every 100,000 females were returned as insane against 44 and 34 respectively in 1921. The increase is fairly general, being shared by all taluks except Chittur as seen from the margin. The highest increase (190 per cent) is recorded by Trichur taluk because the Government Lunatic Asylum is located at Trichur. There were only 24 patients in this Asylum at the beginning of the decade, but the number rose to 136 in 1931. Be it remembered at the same time that only the poorest or the most destitute are sent to the Asylum.

Taluk	Variation per cent of the insane for the decade 1921—1931. [Increase (+) Decrease (—)]
COCHIN STATE ..	+ 67
Cochin-Kanayannur ..	+ 47
Cranganur ..	+ 43
Mukundapuram ..	+ 60
Trichur ..	+ 190
Talapilli ..	+ 53
Chittur ..	— 11

Insanity by age and sex

7. Diagram A shows that the incidence of insanity among children below ten years is very low either because intentional omissions are most common in this age-period or because the disease is not determined till the age of ten. From the tenth year upwards the curve rises gradually till forty and then declines. Adult age, which is more exposed to the storms and stress of life and the buffets of Fortune than any other period of existence, is naturally most affected and, as the insane are generally short-lived, the more advanced ages show a lower proportion of the afflicted. The figures indicate that the disease is less prevalent among women, but the male and female curves overlap each other in the age-periods 40—50 and 50—60. It is not unlikely that the motive for greater secrecy regarding female sufferers disappears when they are advanced in age.

Deaf-mutism: variation and distribution

8. Of the four infirmities deaf-mutism alone records a decrease during the decade. The proportion of the afflicted is 48 in every 100,000 among males and 33 among females. The corresponding figures for 1921 were 57 and 47 among males and females respectively. The statement in the margin shows how each taluk has fared in this respect. Chittur, the only taluk which registered a fall in the number of lunatics, reveals the highest percentage of decline. If these statistics are reliable it may perhaps appear that malarial fever which distinguishes Chittur from the other taluks acts as a remedy for insanity and deaf-mutism ! * The reasons for the increase in

Taluk	Variation per cent of deaf-mutes for the decade 1921—1931 [Increase (+) Decrease (—)]
COCHIN STATE ..	— 3
Cochin-Kanayannur ..	+ 2
Cranganur ..	+ 186
Mukundapuram ..	+ 29
Trichur ..	— 18
Talapilli ..	— 11
Chittur ..	— 65

* We have heard that malaria acts as a cure for certain diseases but it remains to be proved that the malarial parasite is an enemy of insanity and deaf-mutism.

A

Diagram showing the No. of Insane per 100,000 persons of each decennial age - period

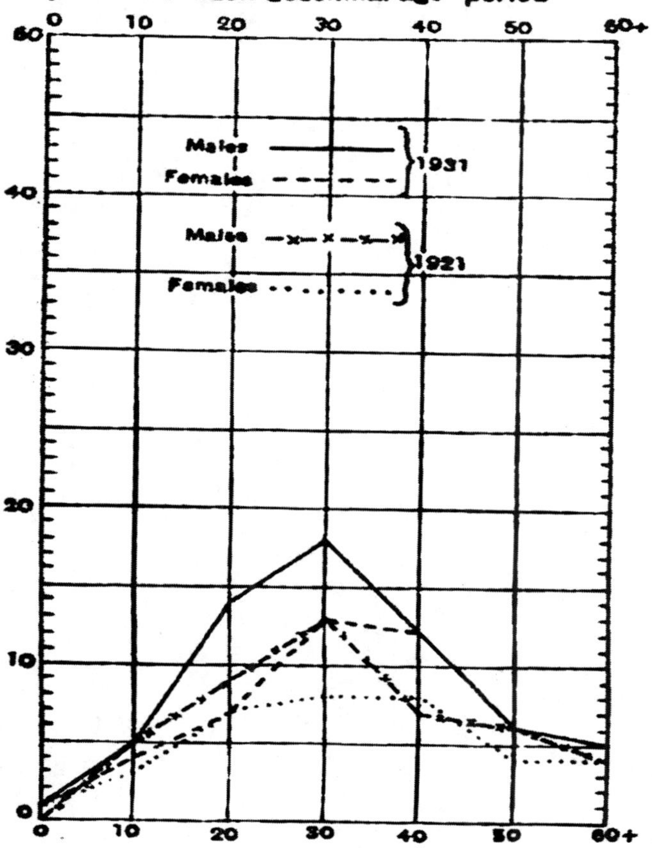

B

Diagram showing the No. of Deaf - mutes per 100,000 Persons of each decennial age - period

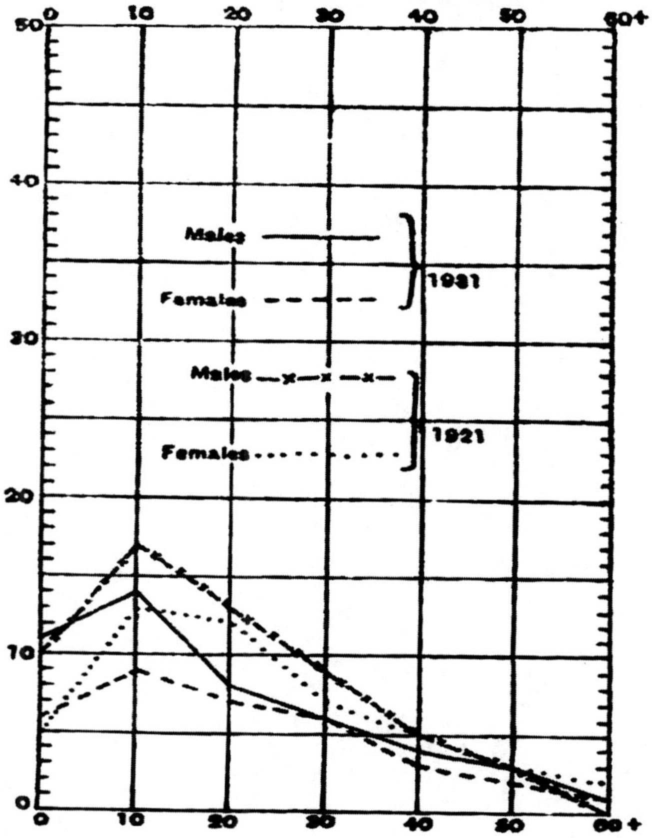

C

Diagram showing the No. of Blind per 100,000 Persons of each decennial age - period

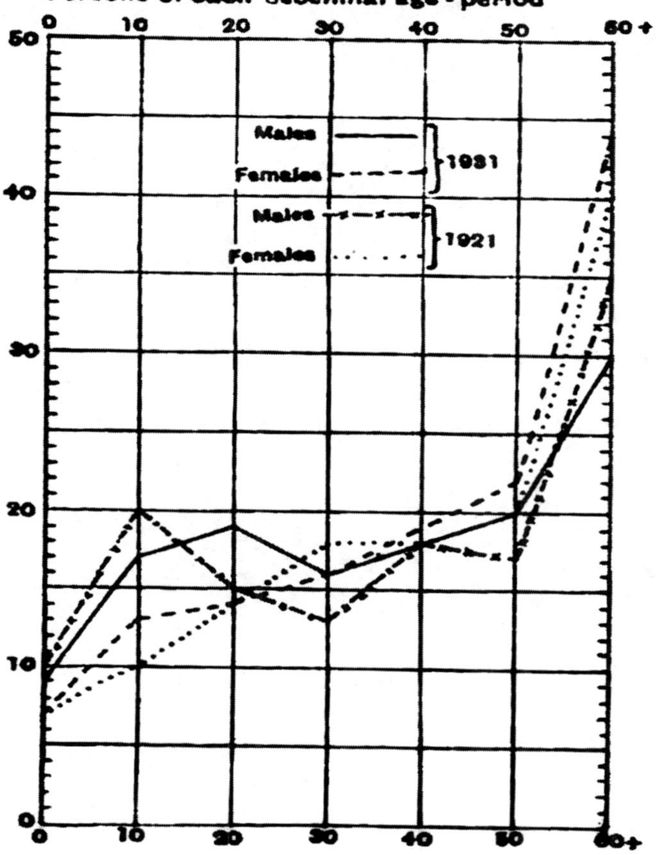

D

Diagram showing the No. of Lepers per 100,000 persons of each decennial age - period

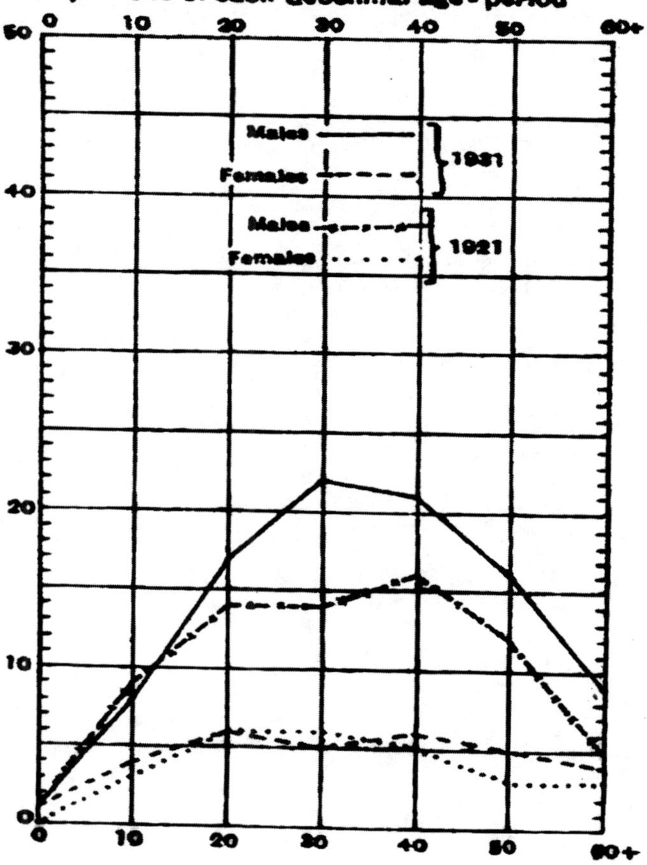

Cranganur and Mukundapuram are as obscure as the reasons for the decrease in Trichur, Talapilli and Chittur.

Deaf-mutism by age

9. Deaf-mutism being a congenital affliction, the proportion of the sufferers must be highest in the earliest age-periods; but Diagram B illustrates how the period most affected is 10—20. After 20 the curves fall steadily through each succeeding age-period. The reluctance of parents to recognize the infirmity in their children is no doubt responsible for the low proportion of deaf-mutes in the population aged 0—10 years. It is not likely that persons who lost their hearing late in life have been wrongly included in the returns, for the infirmity is seen to be least prevalent in the oldest age-periods.

Blindness: variation and distribution

Decade	Increase per cent of the blind
1891—1901	2·7
1901—1911	33·7
1911—1921	5·5
1921—1931	27·6

Taluk	Increase per cent of the blind for the decade 1921—1931
COCHIN STATE ..	28
Cochin-Kanayannur ..	9
Cranganur ..	16
Mukundapuram ..	35
Trichur ..	41
Talapilli ..	26
Chittur ..	26

10. The statistics of blindness, which are far more reliable than those of the other infirmities, show that the affliction is steadily on the increase. The rate of this increase for four decades is given in the margin. According to the returns of 1931, the proportion of the blind is 129 in every 100,000 males and 136 in every 100,000 females. The corresponding figures for 1921 were 127 among males and 128 among females. Though the increase is shared by all taluks, the coastal taluks (Cochin-Kanayannur and Cranganur) record a lower rate than the interior taluks (Mukundapuram, Trichur, Talapilli and Chittur) as seen from the margin.

Blindness by age and sex

11. Diagram C illustrates the sex proportion of the blind and their distribution by age-periods. Blindness being chiefly a disease of old age, the curves rise steadily from age-period to age-period except for a slight decline of the male curve between 30 and 50. From the fortieth year upwards the female curve rises higher than the male curve. The explanation generally offered for this higher proportion of the blind among women is that they spend a good deal of their time in the kitchen, cooking over smoky fires.

Leper Asylum

12. At the beginning of the decade there were 168 inmates in the Government Leper Asylum at Venduruthi (a small island in the backwaters between Ernakulam and Mattancheri). A more healthy and less objectionable site for the institution was selected at Adoor near Chalakkudi in Mukundapuram taluk, and the new Leper Asylum buildings were formally opened, and the management of the institution was handed over to the Salvation Army, early in 1931. Including 116 new admissions in the course of the year, the Asylum had 234 patients in 1931. The number represents but a small fraction of the afflicted and gives us no idea of the extent to which the disease has spread in the State, because it is only the most destitute lepers that seek refuge in the Asylum. Quite recently the cures effected at the Leper Hospital in Chingleput near Madras have led a few sufferers from the well-to-do classes to place themselves under the treatment of the medical experts at Chingleput.

Leprosy: variation and distribution

13. There are 94 male and 31 female lepers in every 100,000 persons of the respective sex according to the statistics collected at the present census. In 1921 the proportion was 70 among males and 25 among females. The percentage of the decade's variation for each taluk is shown in the margin. The small decrease of 19 per cent in Cochin-Kanayannur taluk resulting from the removal of the Leper Asylum to Mukundapuram is balanced by the large increase of 302 per cent in the latter taluk. It is not known why Talapilli, a healthy taluk of the interior, should record an increase of 134 per cent in the number of its lepers. The omissions in the returns from this taluk were probably less numerous than in 1921. The same remark will perhaps apply to Cranganur also.

Taluk		Variation per cent of lepers for the decade 1921—1931 [Increase (+) Decrease (—)]
COCHIN STATE	..	+ 60
Cochin-Kanayannur	..	— 19
Cranganur	..	+ 108
Mukundapuram	..	+ 302
Trichur	..	+ 55
Talapilli	..	+ 134
Chittur	..	+ 50

Leprosy by sex and age

14. The distribution of lepers by decennial age-periods and their sex proportion are illustrated in Diagram D, and the extent of concealment among women sufferers becomes apparent from the distance that separates the male and female curves. According to the available statistics, the highest proportion of lepers among males is between the ages of thirty and fifty and among females between twenty and sixty. Omissions on a very large scale, intentional or unintentional, will account for these and other differences.*

Infirmities by caste

15. The regional distribution of the afflicted, and their caste statistics shown in State Table III, prove nothing. The statistics being unreliable, they throw hardly any light on the causes of these infirmities. How unsafe it is to draw inferences from these inaccurate figures will be seen from the following instances. The Malayan hill tribe shows the very low proportion of 6 insane persons in every 10,000, though the tribesmen have deteriorated physically through long residence in fever-haunted tracts. Intellectually developed communities like the Tamil Brahmans who are fully exposed to the stress of life in modern towns, and among whom, therefore, a high incidence of insanity may be expected, also reveal a low proportion of insane persons, though unspecified minor groups of Brahmans (Others) have by far the highest figure. Castes like the Chakkans (oil-pressers), Kaikolans (weavers) and Kanakkans (boatmen and fishermen) have a relatively high proportion of insane persons, whereas other castes, living under

Caste		Proportion of afflicted persons per 10,000
INSANITY		
Brahman—Others	..	36
Chakkan	..	14
Kaikolan	..	11
Kanakkan	..	11
Brahman—Tamil	..	8
Malayan	..	6
Pulayan	..	2
Devangan	..	..
Vettuvan	..	..
DEAF-MUTISM		
Ambattan	..	13
Pandaran	..	10
Kusavan	..	9
BLINDNESS		
Eluthassan	..	32
Ambalavasi	..	30
Malayan	..	28
Malayali Kshatriya	..	27
Kammalan	..	15
Panditattan	..	..
LEPROSY		
Malayali Kshatriya	..	20
Challiyan	..	17
Malayan	..	13
Ottanaikan (Odde)	..	11
Panan	..	11
Sambavan (Parayan)	..	9

similar conditions and leading much the same life. have very low figures. According to our statistics, deaf-mutism is most widely prevalent among the Ambattans (barbers), Kusavans (potters) and Pandarans (engaged in making *pappadoms*, the crisp pulse cakes of the Malayali). Socially these castes occupy a low position. They are, however, to be found in many localities, living side by side with other socially inferior castes that have but a much lower proportion of deaf-mutes. The caste statistics of blindness appear perplexing. The highest incidence of the disease is among the Eluthassans who are mostly agriculturists, the Ambalavasis (temple servants), a socially high and educated caste, and the Malayali Kshatriyas who are much higher than the Ambalavasis in social status and education. The wide prevalence of syphilis in the community will perhaps explain why our Malayan friend the child of Nature, living for the most part in the green glades of his shady and cool forests, should be a member of this blind brotherhood. The Kammalans including blacksmiths, goldsmiths and leatherworkers (shoe-makers), whose occupations are exacting to the eyes, have strangely enough a much lower proportion of the blind among them, while the Panditattans (Tamil goldsmiths) are wholly free from this affliction! The caste statistics of leprosy are no less puzzling. The high incidence of the disease among the Malayans, the Sambavans (Parayans), the Panans, the Ottanaikans etc. may perhaps be explained on the ground of want of personal cleanliness, of dirty and unwholesome food, and other evils that characterise these socially inferior castes. There are, however, other castes whose habits of life are almost identical, but they are much less affected by the infirmity. It is not clear why the Chaliyans (weavers) who are far superior in social status and in their standard of life to the castes mentioned above should have a much higher proportion of the afflicted among them. Nor can one understand how the educated Malayali Kshatriyas, who are models of neatness and simplicity in their habits of life, came to have the highest proportion of lepers in their community. The vagaries of these statistics appear to be really inexplicable.

SUBSIDIARY TABLES.

I.—Number afflicted per 100,000 of the population at each of the last five censuses.

Natural Division "Malabar and Konkan"	Insane										Deaf-mutes									
	Males					Females					Males					Females				
	1931	1921	1911	1901	1891	1931	1921	1911	1901	1891	1931	1921	1911	1901	1891	1931	1921	1911	1901	1891
1	2	3	4	5	6	7	8	9	10	11	12	13	14	15	16	17	18	19	20	21
COCHIN STATE	**61**	**44**	**34**	**27**	**32**	**45**	**34**	**30**	**23**	**27**	**48**	**57**	**39**	**77**	**66**	**33**	**47**	**33**	**60**	**43**
Cochin-Kanayannur	57	53	40	..	36	53	41	32	..	26	41	46	39	..	58	31	46	41	..	34
Cranganur	57	28	6	..	43	37	52	18	..	43	57	28	18	..	21	37	12	6	..	29
Mukundapuram	42	37	23	..	25	33	23	30	..	27	69	60	46	..	95	41	48	31	..	41
Trichur	106	43	44	..	38	63	30	28	..	31	56	77	41	..	70	35	62	32	..	45
Talapilli	46	34	30	..	27	32	26	31	..	13	41	49	45	..	51	27	41	35	..	63
Chittur	48	59	42	..	31	42	55	30	..	37	13	65	18	..	57	18	37	25	..	42

Natural Division "Malabar and Konkan"	Blind										Lepers									
	Males					Females					Males					Females				
	1931	1921	1911	1901	1891	1931	1921	1911	1901	1891	1931	1921	1911	1901	1891	1931	1921	1911	1901	1891
	22	23	24	25	26	27	28	29	30	31	32	33	34	35	36	37	38	39	40	41
COCHIN STATE	**129**	**127**	**133**	**113**	**133**	**136**	**128**	**125**	**107**	**105**	**94**	**70**	**73**	**57**	**66**	**31**	**25**	**28**	**25**	**31**
Cochin Kanayannur	81	102	108	..	88	76	73	81	..	55	93	139	123	..	106	22	42	43	..	29
Cranganur	123	137	71	..	113	84	81	24	..	101	90	68	59	..	128	28	..	31	..	22
Mukundapuram	128	115	119	..	125	191	128	117	..	107	131	35	52	..	71	49	21	27	..	47
Trichur	172	161	193	..	191	197	169	161	..	149	48	36	42	..	28	15	14	19	..	26
Talapilli	167	165	175	..	177	191	175	195	..	126	135	66	66	..	40	54	29	24	..	29
Chittur	125	89	98	..	114	111	120	103	..	124	27	15	36	..	26	13	14	15	..	20

Note:—Taluk-war figures for 1901 are not available.

II.—Distribution of the infirm by age per 10,000 of each sex.

Age	Insane									
	Males					Females				
	1931	1921	1911	1901	1891	1931	1921	1911	1901	1891
1	2	3	4	5	6	7	8	9	10	11
0—5 ..	113	47	..	..	..	35	119	73	..	..
5—10 ..	112	47	64	182	256	107	60	73	426	208
10—15 ..	167	235	192	273	256	215	119	73	213	208
15—20 ..	612	845	513	909	342	573	655	365	532	417
20—25 ..	922	939	1,090	1,182	598	717	833	1,022	852	1,042
25—30 ..	1,369	1,033	1,538	1,192	1,453	789	1,131	511	1,276	1,042
30—35 ..	1,536	1,502	1,218	1,454	1,881	1,290	952	1,605	1,276	1,771
35—40 ..	1,369	1,549	1,731	1,182	1,111	1,470	1,369	584	557	1,354
40—45 ..	1,257	986	1,218	1,091	1,453	1,362	1,071	1,460	1,489	1,771
45—50 ..	754	657	769	364	..	1,290	1,369	1,387	532	..
50—55 ..	513	798	513	727	1,197	789	714	949	745	1,354
55—60 ..	419	517	385	727	..	430	417	657	213	..
60 and over ..	838	845	769	727	684	932	1,191	1,241	1,489	833
Not stated ..	..	..	..	..	769	..	..	..	..	..
Total ..	10,000	10,000	10,000	10,000	10,000	10,000	10,000	10,000	10,000	10,000

Age	Deaf-mutes									
	Males					Females				
	1931	1921	1911	1901	1891	1931	1921	1911	1901	1891
	12	13	14	15	16	17	18	19	20	21
0—5 ..	671	356	281	160	167	439	173	457	241	127
5—10 ..	1,696	1,394	1,011	1,090	1,000	1,415	909	654	1,097	956
10—15 ..	1,696	1,429	1,461	1,442	917	1,463	1,428	1,111	1,219	764
15—20 ..	1,201	1,502	1,573	1,250	1,458	1,122	1,299	1,438	1,504	1,783
20—25 ..	1,025	1,245	899	1,282	1,083	1,171	1,256	1,438	732	1,083
25—30 ..	636	1,026	1,461	1,058	875	927	1,428	1,438	1,098	1,210
30—35 ..	707	916	730	897	1,042	829	1,169	784	1,220	701
35—40 ..	636	659	674	705	708	829	300	588	569	637
40—45 ..	530	513	562	385	1,042	634	649	523	591	956
45—50 ..	339	366	449	417	..	342	346	458	406	..
50—55 ..	389	366	281	449	833	341	433	523	366	573
55—60 ..	141	147	225	288	..	244	130	65	..	..
60 and over ..	283	73	393	557	875	244	390	523	854	1,210
Not stated ..	..	..	..	..	..	..	..	..	..	..
Total ..	10,000	10,000	10,000	10,000	10,000	10,000	10,000	10,000	10,000	10,000

II.—Distribution of the infirm by age per 10,000 of each sex (*cont.*)

Age	Blind									
	Males					Females				
	1931	1921	1911	1901	1891	1931	1921	1911	1901	1891
	22	23	24	25	26	27	28	29	30	31
0—5 ..	211	261	246	197	124	167	188	243	206	105
5—10 ..	488	555	640	482	602	358	393	382	549	368
10—15 ..	620	734	650	502	757	466	267	434	458	553
15—20 ..	686	816	673	724	663	478	457	573	549	684
20—25 ..	739	620	476	614	973	454	518	607	847	870
25—30 ..	778	571	755	768	1,035	585	597	781	709	790
30—35 ..	632	376	805	855	849	574	706	799	664	805
35—40 ..	594	655	903	680	849	585	675	660	801	789
40—45 ..	786	751	755	724	1,357	609	879	851	824	947
45—50 ..	726	636	437	789	..	801	550	573	549	..
50—55 ..	77[illegible]	701	772	1,100	1,077	751	863	955	778	1,394
55—60 ..	765	620	608	526	..	872	659	642	595	..
60 and over ..	2,206	2,724	2,250	2,040	1,656	3,298	3,218	2,500	2,471	2,605
Not stated ..	..	..	..	..	..	..	..	..	..	..
Total ..	10,000	10,000	10,000	10,000	10,000	10,000	10,000	10,000	10,000	10,000

Age	Lepers									
	Males					Females				
	1931	1921	1911	1901	1891	1931	1921	1911	1901	1891
	32	33	34	35	36	37	38	39	40	41
0—5 ..	36	29	..	43	42	52	..	77	97	90
5—10 ..	90	59	30	173	42	208	159	155	388	90
10—15 ..	217	618	211	303	377	417	317	543	388	451
15—20 ..	615	618	753	606	335	938	714	543	971	991
20—25 ..	759	912	964	433	711	885	1,349	698	1,262	541
25—30 ..	1,013	1,118	753	1,429	1,088	885	873	1,085	1,262	1,171
30—35 ..	1,121	1,147	1,144	952	1,255	833	1,508	1,395	777	1,171
35—40 ..	1,212	824	1,235	1,082	1,171	781	873	1,473	680	811
40—45 ..	1,230	1,588	1,265	1,212	2,385	938	794	1,085	874	2,342
45—50 ..	1,031	735	934	953	..	990	1,032	698	485	90
50—55 ..	940	1,029	964	779	1,297	938	714	698	1,068	991
55—60 ..	741	647	904	909	..	781	556	698	583	..
60 and over ..	995	676	843	1,126	1,297	1,354	1,111	852	1,165	1,261
Not stated ..	..	..	..	..	..	..	..	..	..	..
Total ..	10,000	10,000	10,000	10,000	10,000	10,000	10,000	10,000	10,000	10,000

III.—Number afflicted per 100,000 persons of each age-period and number of females afflicted per 1,000 males.

Age	Number afflicted per 100,000								Number of females afflicted per 1,000 males			
	Insane		Deaf-mutes		Blind		Lepers		Insane	Deaf-mutes	Blind	Lepers
	Male	Female	Male	Female	Male	Female	Male	Female				
1	2	3	4	5	6	7	8	9	10	11	12	13
0—5 ..	4	1	19	9	16	14	2	1	250	474	875	500
5—10 ..	5	4	61	38	47	39	6	5	750	604	811	800
10—15 ..	8	8	64	41	63	53	16	11	1,000	625	830	667
15—20 ..	41	26	61	37	93	65	61	29	696	676	769	529
20—25 ..	66	34	58	41	113	64	84	29	606	828	679	405
25—30 ..	116	45	43	38	140	99	133	34	449	1,056	831	304
30—35 ..	137	81	50	38	120	108	155	36	655	850	1,200	258
35—40 ..	141	117	52	48	130	140	193	43	837	944	1,089	224
40—45 ..	146	125	49	42	160	167	221	59	844	867	981	265
45—50 ..	114	152	46	30	232	284	240	80	1,333	636	1,218	333
50—55 ..	88	109	54	35	238	313	254	89	1,222	636	1,068	346
55—60 ..	104	81	28	34	401	494	284	102	800	1,250	1,259	366
60 and over ..	124	95	33	18	719	1,009	227	95	867	625	1,586	473
All ages ..	**61**	**45**	**48**	**33**	**129**	**136**	**94**	**31**	**779**	**724**	**1,104**	**347**

CHAPTER VIII.—OCCUPATION.—PART I.—GENERAL.

Introductory

THE record of the occupation or means of livelihood of the population of a country is as important as it is interesting. There are, however, serious difficulties in the collection and compilation of occupation statistics. Incomplete, vague or misleading answers render the enumeration stage of the work difficult; and the tabulation stage has its own complications in that the imperfect and vague returns of occupation recorded in the enumeration schedules have to be identified and assigned to the respective orders and groups in the classification scheme.

Occupation columns in enumeration schedule

2. Commensurate with the importance of the subject, as many as four columns in the enumeration schedule were set apart for the questionnaire of occupations at the present census. The columns were headed as shown in the margin. The cover of the enumeration book contained these instructions regarding the four columns:

Earner or Dependent	Occupation or means of Subsistence of actual workers		For organized workers, the industry in which employed
	Principal	Subsidiary	
9	10	11	12

"*Column 9* (*Earner or dependent*).—Enter 'Earner' (E) or 'Dependent' (D). *Earners* are all those who have a distinct individual means or partial means of livelihood. *Dependents* are all those who have not.

Column 10 (*Principal occupation*).—Enter the principal means of livelihood of all earners only. If a person is temporarily out of work he should be shown as following his previous occupation. Enter the exact occupation and avoid vague terms such as 'service' or 'writing' or 'labour.' For example, in the case of labour, say, whether in the fields, or in a coal mine or jute factory, or cotton mill or lac-factory, or earthwork, etc. In the case of agriculture distinguish between landowners and tenants, cultivators, and non-cultivators, farm servants (whose labour is hired for considerable period) and casual or daily field labourers. If a person makes the articles he sells he should be entered as 'maker and seller' of them. For dependents, only a X should be put in column 10.

Column 11 (*Subsidiary occupation*).—Enter here any occupation which earners pursue at any time of the year in addition to their principal occupation. Thus if a person lives principally by his earnings as a cultivating landowner, but partly also by bandy-driving the words 'cultivating landowner' will be entered in column 10 and 'bandy-driver', in column 11. If an earner has no additional occupation a X should be put in column 11. Any occupation pursued by dependents should be entered in this column; e.g., a woman who keeps house for her husband has the occupation 'house-keeping' in this column.

Only one such occupation (the most important) should appear in this column for any one person.

Column 12 (*Industry in which employed*).—Only those persons are to be entered in this column who are employed by other persons or by a company or firm and paid wages for the work they do and who work in company with others similarly paid. For such persons, e. g., managers, clerks, operatives or workmen employed in a factory or any employer enter the name of the industry, e. g., coal-mining, biscuit making, soap making. For individual workers not employed by others put a X."

Instructions to enumeration staff

3. The Manual for Supervisors supplemented these instructions in elaborate detail, giving numerous and apt illustrations for the guidance of the enumeration staff. The shades of difference between *earners* and *dependents*—, for purposes of the occupation returns, *dependent* practically meant *non-earner*—, between *working dependents* and *non-working dependents*, and between *subsidiary occupation* and *principal occupation* were carefully explained and illustrated. The

attention of the enumeration staff was particularly directed to those points where they were most likely to go wrong and, in the many census classes held at different centres, the subject of occupation returns in the four columns of the schedule received special and careful treatment.

4. The enumerators appear to have understood the instructions on the whole and done their work very creditably, and it is not their fault if the returns are not more accurate and statisfactory than they actually are. The distinction between the *principal occupation* and *subsidiary occupation* of an earner was to be based on the amount of the income derived from either, but earners were generally inclined to return that occupation as their principal one, which was regarded as more honourable or respectable; and I myself have seen several instances of earners personally known to me, who carried on quite a lucrative trade in private, lending money for short terms on high interest, but who did not return this calling either as their *principal* or as their *subsidiary occupation* for the obvious reason that the descendants of Shylock are not objects of affection or esteem even in these days of rank materialism. Again it was far from easy to decide where a dependent ceased to be non-working and passed into the working class. The difficulty in drawing the line between a woman who was an earner and another who was only a working dependent was equally great, if not greater; because thousands of women of the lower-middle and lowest classes in the State are actual workers who, in addition to the solid help they often render to their menfolk in the latters' avocations, are engaged regularly, periodically, or at irregular intervals, in more or less profitable pursuits like the collection of firewood and fodder for sale, the manufacture of coir-yarn, mats, baskets and scores of other articles, the preparation and sale of sweetmeats, domestic and menial service and a hundred other occupations of a like nature. These inherent and inevitable difficulties of enumeration were considerably aggravated by the very nature of the questions which the enumerators had to ask of all householders for eliciting in full the information required for the occupation columns of the schedule. Some of these questions might even convey a suggestion of unwarranted curiosity if not impertinence on the part of the innocent and much-enduring enumerator, whose only payment for the arduous work would then be the resentment or ire of the householders concerned. It is for such reasons that competent and experienced authorities on the subject maintain that, if accurate and really useful statistics of occupation are to be collected, agencies with better qualifications and more time at their disposal than the untrained and temporary staff of census enumerators should be employed for the purpose.

Difficulties of enumeration

5. The statistics of occupation compiled from the returns in columns 9, 10 and 11 of the enumeration schedule are presented in the following tables :

Reference to statistics

i. Imperial Table X—Occupation or Means of Livelihood, showing the number of earners, working dependents, etc., in each group of occupation in the classification scheme ;

ii. Imperial Table XI—Part A—Occupation of Selected Castes, Tribes or Races, showing the variety of occupation followed by each of the castes with particular reference to their traditional occupation ;

iii. State Table IV showing the subsidiary occupations of earners who returned agriculture (general cultivation) as their principal occupation ;

iv. Subsidiary Table I (a) showing the general distribution by occupation of earners (principal occupation) and working dependents ;

v. Subsidiary Table I (b) showing similar distribution of subsidiary earners only;

vi. Subsidiary Table II giving the distribution by Sub-classes of

(a) earners (principal occupation) and working dependents, and

vii. (b) earners (subsidiary occupation);

viii. Subsidiary Table III giving the occupation of females by Sub-classes, and selected orders and groups;

ix. Subsidiary Table IV—Selected occupations, giving comparative figures for 1911, 1921 and 1931;

x. Subsidiary Table V showing the occupations of selected castes; and

xi. Subsidiary Table VI giving the number of persons employed in Railways, Posts and Telegraphs, Irrigation etc.

The all-India Table of Organized Industries that was to have been compiled from the returns in column 12 of the enumeration schedule was given up along with a few other Imperial Tables for reasons of economy. State Table V contains the statistics of organized industries in the State compiled from the returns in column 12. That the figures are unfortunately misleading and that they do not correctly represent the growth of organized industries in Cochin will be shown in the course of the review of these statistics.

Part I of Imperial Table XII shows educated unemployment by class, and Part II by degrees. The special census of educated unemployment taken along with the general census was not successful and the figures give but a poor idea of the extent of unemployment among English-educated persons of both sexes in the State. The subject is treated in paragraphs 36 to 39 of this chapter.

Accuracy of statistics

6. It does great credit to the patient and conscientious work of the honorary census staff that the occupation statistics collected in the face of the many difficulties referred to in paragraph 4 above are on the whole not unsatisfactory in that they represent to a very large extent the normal functional distribution of the State's population. This will be evident from the review of these statistics in the subsequent paragraphs of this chapter and particularly from the relatively small proportion of vague and ambiguous returns such as labourer, cooly, clerk, shop-keeper and so forth. Sub-class XI (Insufficiently described occupations) shows 28,415 persons as the total following such occupations. This represents but 4·6 per cent of the total number of earners and working dependents in the State. We find from the inset table that the corresponding figures for Travancore, Mysore, Baroda and the Madras Presidency are all higher. The occupation statistics of Cochin do not, therefore, compare unfavourably with those of other States and Provinces in respect of accuracy.

Province or State	Total following occupation	Total (including subsidiary earners) following Sub-class XI (Insufficiently described occupations)	Proportion per cent
Cochin ..	614,051	28,415	4·6
Travancore ..	2,408,132	128,977	5·4
Mysore ..	2,986,230	157,431	5·3
Baroda ..	1,210,475	72,099	6·0
Madras ..	26,195,421	2,784,836	10·6

7. The Classification Scheme of Occupations adopted at the present census does not differ from that of 1921 in respect of the main divisions or Classes and the Sub-classes. Accordingly all occupations were classified as shown below : **Classification scheme of occupations**

CLASS A. PRODUCTION OF RAW MATERIALS.

SUB-CLASS I. Exploitation of Animals and Vegetation.
" II. Exploitation of Minerals.

CLASS B. PREPARATION AND SUPPLY OF MATERIAL SUBSTANCES.

SUB-CLASS III. Industry.
" IV. Transport.
" V. Trade.

CLASS C. PUBLIC ADMINISTRATION AND LIBERAL ARTS.

SUB-CLASS VI. Public Force.
" VII. Public Administration.
" VIII. Professions and Liberal Arts.

CLASS D. MISCELLANEOUS

SUB-CLASS IX. Persons living on their income
" X. Domestic service.
" XI. Insufficiently described occupations.
" XII. Unproductive.

The Sub-classes are divided into 55 orders and 195 groups as against 56 orders and 191 groups in 1921. This difference arises from the fact that some of the groups in the old scheme of classification were amplified while others were compressed. A few re-groupings also have been made.

8. It is further to be observed that the returns of occupation recorded at this census differ in certain important respects from those of 1921 on account of the changes introduced in the enumeration schedule. The returns of 1921 showed *the population supported by each group of occupation under the heads of actual workers and dependents*, but the returns of the present census do not give the distribution of dependents by occupation. They merely record *the number of workers engaged in each group under the heads of earners and working dependents.* The actual workers of 1921 correspond not only to the earners but also to a strong section of the working dependents of 1931, while the dependents of the last census represent both the non-working, and the other section of the working, dependents of the present census. There is therefore no precise or exact correspondence between the figures in the occupation tables of 1921 and those in the tables of 1931, so much so that it is not possible to institute just comparisons between the two sets of figures. **Changes in occupation returns**

9. From Imperial Table X it is seen that 466,726 persons, representing 38·7 per cent of the total population in the State, have returned themselves as earners and 147,325 persons or 12·2 per cent of the total population as working dependents. The number of non-working dependents is seen to be 590, 965 (49 per cent of the population). In other words, one half of the population consists of workers and the other of non-workers. An analysis of the non-working dependents will show that there are 270,173 males and 320,792 females among them. The male population aged 0—15 and 55 and over numbers 292,163 or 21,990 more than the non-working male dependents. It will thus appear that many boys below 15 and elderly men above 55 years are either earners or working dependents; and when due allowance is made for the student population aged 15—20, there will apparently be but few, if any, adult males among the non-workers, eating the bread of idleness. **General distribution of population into workers and dependents**

Meaning of 'actual workers'

10. Here is a rosy and pleasant picture which is very likely to mislead people if the full significance of these returns is not grasped by them. Let it therefore be understood at the very outset that the 'actual workers' include the rich and leisurely aristocratic class, lolling at their lazy length, content to vegetate on the rent received from their lands leased out to tenants, because these lotus-eaters also are *earners*. For the same reason, people living on pensions or similar allowances, and holders of stipends or scholarships are also included in the working population. If the income of the earners is taken into consideration, we shall find that the princely merchant who earns a monthly income of Rs. 10,000 and the beggarly sweeper who cleans the court-yard of the merchant's mansion for a regular monthly wage of but one or two rupees are both clubbed together as earners. Nor is it all. For, as irony would have it, people temporarily (i. e., for any indefinite period of time,) out of job and suffering the most acute distress on this account are also returned as earners in those groups of occupation in which they had last worked! And we may be certain that considerable numbers belong to this category. Allowance should also be made for the important factor of sentiment influencing these returns; because to be without a respectable calling is regarded as a great disgrace to an adult male. The working population returned at the census therefore contains a not insignificant proportion of persons who have been unemployed for indefinite periods of time, of people whose earnings, though regular and steady, are next to nothing, and of those whose name is Retired Leisure or Idle Luxury. It this composition of the active workers and earners of the occupation tables is not carefully borne in mind, we may very likely form an utterly false picture of the whole affair, a picture of a happy land where the people are all industrious and have plenty to do and plenty to get, where they live in economic sufficiency and independence and where, therefore, the struggle for existence is almost unknown.

Comparison of actual workers, 1921 and 1931

11. At the census of 1921, 44 per cent of the total population were returned as actual workers and 56 per cent as dependents. We have already seen that the actual workers of the past census roughly correspond to the earners and a considerable proportion of the working dependents of the present census. The proportion of actual workers in 1931 will, therefore, be somewhere between 38·7 per cent (earners) and 51 per cent (earners and working dependents combined) of the total population. In other words, it will be very near, or perhaps a little higher than, the old 44 per cent, and therefore does not appear to vary to any considerable extent from the proportion of workers in 1921. The actual workers formed 41 per cent of the total population at the census of 1911.

Comparison with other States and Provinces

12. Perhaps it will be more interesting to compare the distribution of the population of Cochin into workers and dependents with similar distributions in other States and Provinces. The inset table gives the figures for Travancore, Mysore, Baroda and the Madras Presidency. The proportion of earners in this State (38·7 per cent *) is almost identical with their proportion in Madras (38·3 per cent) and Baroda (39·3 per cent). Mysore has a slightly lower figure (35·8 per cent), but Travancore comes last with only 29 per cent. It will, however, be noticed that

Province or State	Percentage in total population of		
	Earners	Working dependents	Non-working dependents
Cochin ..	38·73	12·23	49·04
Travancore ..	29·01	18·25	52·74
Mysore ..	35·84	9·70	54·46
Baroda ..	39·25	10·30	50·45
Madras ..	38·33	17·18	44·49

* The percentages in this paragraph are calculated on the total population of the State or Province.

Diagram 1
Distribution of the Working Population
(Earners & Working Dependents) by Occupation

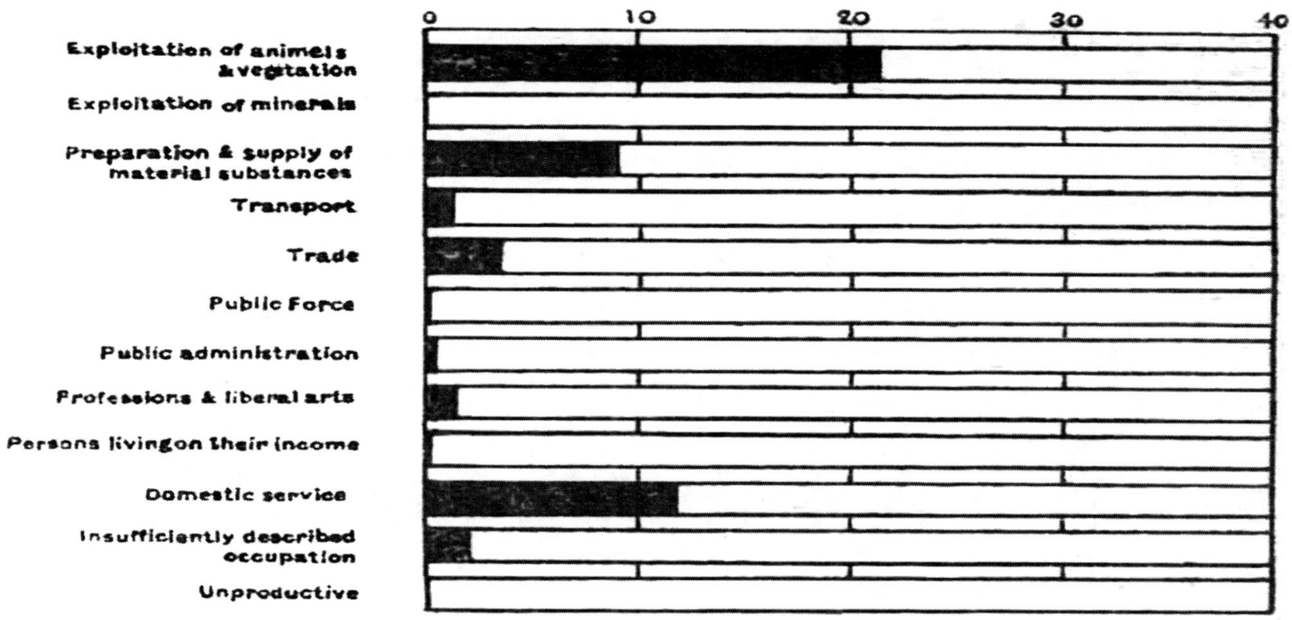

Diagram 2
Proportion of Working Dependents to Earners in certain occupations

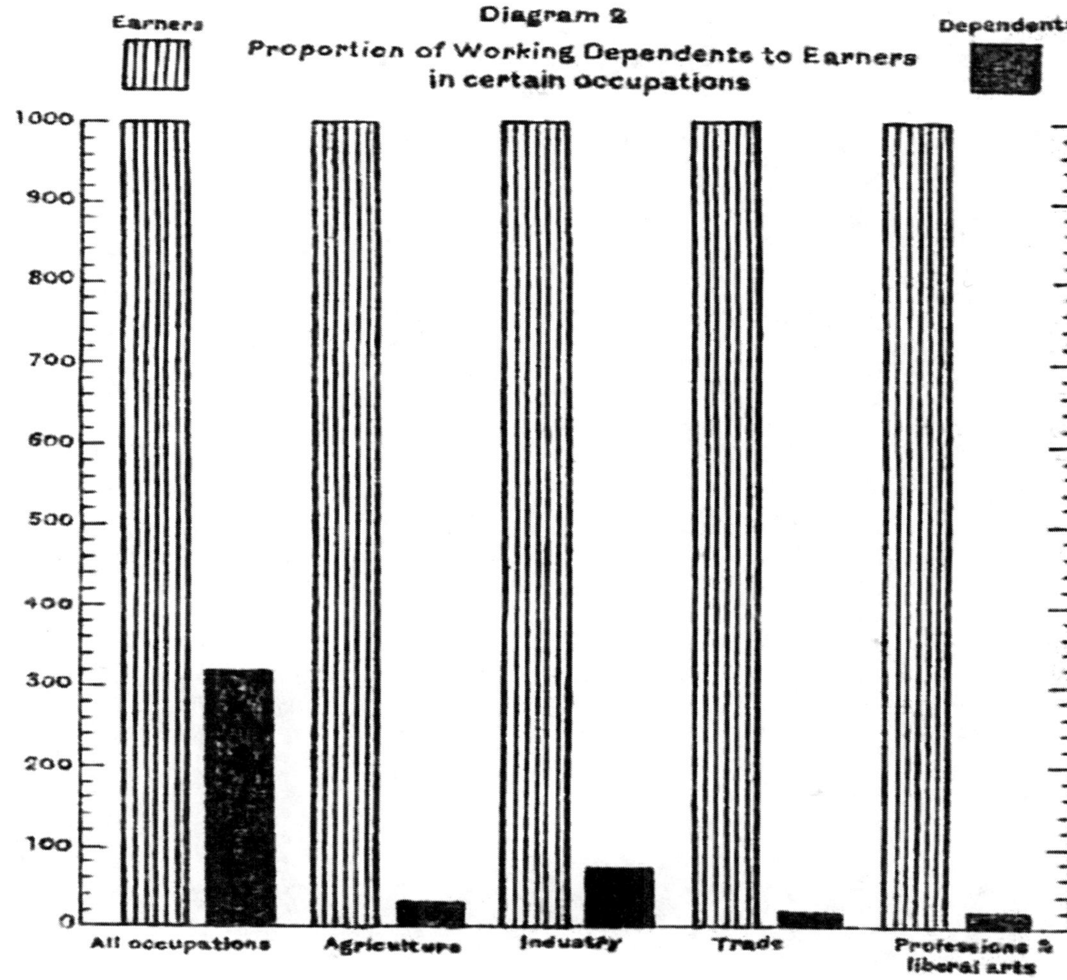

Province or State	Proportion of females per 1,000 males among		
	Earners	Working dependents	Non-working dependents
Cochin ..	498	17,476	1,187
Travancore ..	323	4,749	1,090
Mysore ..	213	4,038	1,766
Baroda ..	348	4,638	1,457
Madras ..	404	7,667	1,215

the figures for working dependents are highest in Travancore (18·3 per cent). Madras comes next with 17·2 per cent and Cochin, Baroda and Mysore follow in due order at some distance. The highest ratio of non-working dependents is to be found in Mysore and the lowest in Madras. Turning to the sex ratio of workers and dependents, we find that Cochin has the largest proportion of females among earners and working dependents. Mysore takes the last place in this respect and, obviously for this very reason, has the highest figures for non-working female dependents.

Distribution of the working population by Sub-class of occupation

13. The distribution of the working population (earners and working dependents) in each of the 12 Sub-classes of occupation is illustrated in diagram 1 facing this page; and the marginal table contains the figures for earners and working dependents combined in each Sub-class side by side with the corresponding figures for some of the other States and Provinces. Sub-class I, mainly representing Agriculture, claims 41·8 per cent of the total number of earners and working dependents in Cochin. The statement shows that Travancore and Cochin depend to a much smaller extent on this occupation than Baroda and Mysore. Sub-class II (Exploitation of Minerals) may be omitted altogether so far as this State is concerned. 17·6 per cent of earners and working dependents are to be found in Sub-class III (Industry), 2·4 per cent of the working population in Sub-class IV (Transport) and 6·8 per cent in Sub-class V (Trade). It is interesting to note from the marginal statement that, in all the three Sub-classes, and particularly in Sub-classes III and IV, Cochin returns a much larger proportion of population than the other States and Provinces. Sub-classes VI (Public Force), VII (Public Administration), VIII (Professions and Liberal Arts) and IX (Persons living on their income) claim ·2, ·8, 2·8 and ·4 per cent respectively of the working population. As many as 22·9 per cent of the working population find a place in Sub-class X (Domestic service). The proportion does not differ materially from that of Travancore and Madras, but the figures for Mysore and Baroda are very much lower. It is also noteworthy that in Madras, Travancore and Cochin the vast majority of those who have returned Domestic service as their occupation are female working dependents. The difference in local conditions alone will hardly account for this wide disparity

Sub-class	Proportion per cent of working population in each Sub-class.				
	Cochin	Travancore	Mysore	Baroda	Madras
I. Exploitation of Animals and Vegetation ..	41·8	39·1	76·3	70·7	48·6
II. Exploitation of Minerals ..	..	·1	·4	·2	·1
III. Industry ..	17·6	14·6	7·0	10·7	8·7
IV. Transport ..	2·4	1·6	·8	1·3	1·1
V. Trade ..	6·8	6·5	4·5	5·5	4·0
VI. Public Force..	·2	·1	·6	1·2	·2
VII. Public Administration ..	·8	·7	1·1	1·0	·6
VIII. Professions and Liberal Arts ..	2·8	2·4	1·2	2·4	1·2
IX. Persons living on their income ..	·4	·1	·2	·5	·1
X. Domestic service ..	22·9	29·7	1·6	·7	24·8
XI. Insufficiently described occupations ..	4·2	4·9	8·8	5·4	10·0
XII. Unproductive..	·2	·2	·6	·4	·6

between Mysore and Baroda on the one hand and Madras and the two Malayali States on the other in respect of the numbers engaged in this calling, and a probable explanation for it is to be sought for in the definition and classification of working dependents adopted by each State or Province.

4·2 per cent of the working population are returned in Sub-class XI (Insufficiently described occupations), and ·2 per cent in Sub-class XII (Unproductive).

Proportion of workers in Sub-classes I, III and V

14. It will be seen from the above distribution that the population of Cochin depends chiefly on Sub-classes I, III and V for its subsistence. These three classes alone claim as many as 83 8 per cent of the total number of earners (working dependents being excluded). Besides, most of those returned in Sub-class XI really belong to one or other of these same three divisions. The earners in Sub-class XI should therefore be included in I, III or V for all practical purposes. The three divisions will then contain no less than 89·1 per cent of the total number of earners in the State, the remaining nine divisions together showing but less than 11 per cent. From the inset table we find that Travancore, Mysore, Baroda and Madras do not differ from Cochin to any great extent in this respect.

Province or State	Percentage of earners in Sub-classes.		
	I, III and V	XI	II, IV, VI, VII, VIII, IX, X and XII
Cochin ..	83·81	5.32	10·87
Travancore ..	83·76	6·95	9·29
Mysore ..	86·46	5·70	7·84
Baroda ..	83·75	6·78	9·47
Madras ..	80·24	12·94	6·82

and in VII and VIII

15. The figures for earners in the intellectual Sub-classes VII and VIII (Public Administration and Professions and Liberal Arts) are of particular significance. The marginal statement will show that, among the States and Provinces selected for comparison, the highest proportion of population engaged in these intellectual occupations is to be found in Cochin. The proportion would certainly have been higher but for the fact that the intellectual Sub-classes offer but very limited scope in this Lilliput of a State, so much so that many of her educated sons and even daughters have either to remain unemployed or to emigrate to more promising climes. It will be seen from the next chapter how truly these figures reflect the measure of the progress achieved by the State in the sphere of modern education.

Province or State	Number per 10,000 of the total population working as earners in Sub-classes VII and VIII combined
Cochin ..	177
Travancore ..	139
Mysore ..	104
Baroda ..	169
Madras ..	96

Sub class I, order 1, Agriculture

16. Turning to the working population returned in Sub-class I, we find from the margin that the proportion of earners and working dependents calculated on the total population of the State is almost identical with that of the actual workers of 1921 and 1911. According to the occupation statistics of these two previous censuses, about half the population of the State is seen to have been supported by

	Sub-class I (Exploitation of Animals and Vegetation)	Proportion per 10,000 of the total population	Variation per cent between 1921 and 1931
Earners and working dependents 1931 ..	256,709	2,230	+ 20·2
Actual workers 1921 ..	213,569	2,181	
Actual workers 1911 ..	188 319	2,051	

agriculture; and because there is no appreciable variation between 1921 and 1931 in the ratio of the working population in this Sub-class, it may perhaps be safely concluded that agriculture still supports almost the same proportion of population. It must, however, be noted in this connection that the earners who returned agriculture as their principal occupation together with the working dependents under the same order show an increase of only 19·6 per cent over the actual workers in the same order in 1921, while the State's population has increased by more than 23 per cent. At the same time the non-agriculturists who returned agriculture as their subsidiary source of income in 1931 number 18,692, whereas the partially agricultural population of 1921 numbered but 9,659. These statistics show that agriculture is gaining in popularity at least as a subsidiary source of income if not as one of the principal means of earning. In any case, agriculture still continues to be the predominent occupation of the people in Cochin also, though, as we have already seen, not to the same extent as in most other States and Provinces.

Order	Earners and working dependents	Actual workers		Variation per cent between 1921 and 1931
	1931	1921	1911	
1. Pasture and Agriculture ..	247,400	206,895	181,984	+19·6

17. The principal divisions of the agricultural population in Sub-class I are non-cultivating proprietors taking rent in money or kind (group 1), meaning the land-owners who do not themselves cultivate their lands but lease them out to tenants for fixed rents, cultivating owners (group 5) who farm their lands themselves with hired labour, cultivating tenants (group 6 a) who themselves cultivate the lands leased out to them, non-cultivating tenants (group 6 b) who engage sub-tenants for farming the lands they hold on lease, and who receive rent in their turn, and agricultural labourers (group 7). The specific figures for these groups are given in the margin side by side with the figures of actual workers in 1921 and 1911. The most populous groups are seen to be those of cultivating owners, cultivating tenants and agricultural labourers. As the actual workers of 1921 roughly correspond to the earners and working dependents of 1931, the non-cultivating proprietors and the cultivating owners will appear to have registered a large increase during the last 10 years. The fall in the numbers of cultivating tenants must, in all probability, be attributed to many of them being now in the class of land-owners. Agricultural labourers have increased very considerably in numbers. It is evident from the figures shown in the margin that there is no waning of interest in agriculture despite the growing enthusiasm for industrial pursuits characteristic of modern times.

Divisions of agricultural population

Group	Earners and working dependents	Actual workers		Variation per cent between 1921 and 1931
	1931	1921	1911	
1 Non-cultivating proprietors taking rent in money or kind..	6,547	3,093	2,834	+111·7
5 Cultivating owners ..	23,413	11,508	11,499	+103·4
6 a. Cultivating tenants ..	49,480	74,427	60,648	−33·5
b. Non-cultivating tenants .	764	1,045	543	−26·9
7 Agricultural labourers ..	129,788	101,815	95,373	+27·5

18. Under order 1 (a) (Cultivation), rice is the chief crop of cultivation throughout the State. Next in importance to rice are cocoanut (group 10) in the southern taluks and arecanut (included in group 16) in the northern taluks,

Special crops: cocoanut

both groups falling under order 1 (b), dealing with the cultivation of special crops. Group 10 is of particular interest and importance. It shows that the working population (including subsidiary earners) engaged in the cultivation of the cocoanut numbers over 21,000 persons or a little less than 2 per cent of the total population of the State. Obviously the numbers supported by this group must be still greater. From Sub-class III (Industry) we find how this valuable special crop peculiar to the Malabar coast gives work to many more people who earn their livelihood from the multiple industries connected with the produce of the cocoanut palm. The following extract from the Census Report of 1901 will be read with interest in this connection.

"So multifarious are the uses to which the various parts and products of the cocoanut palm are applied that it is, like the Mexican *agave*, a tree which encloses within a compact form many of the elements of human comfort and civilization, and naturally its cultivation furnishes a corresponding multiplicity of occupations to the people in the regions of its special growth. Moreover, its products have all along been at the root of the commercial prosperity of the seaboard taluks and the material well-being of the people thereof. The manufacture of oil from the kernels, the drawing of toddy from the unexpanded flower spathes, and the distillation of arrack † from the fermented toddy occupy a considerable number of people under 'food, drink and stimulants', while the preparation of the husk into fibre and its fabrication into ropes, cordage, mats, etc., similarly engage innumerable hands under 'textile fabrics'. Dealing in shells, trunk, plaited leaves and other minor products also gives subsistence to many poor people. Confining our attention to 'agriculture', the cultivation of the cocoanut palm forms the means of livelihood of 19,027 or 4·6 per cent of the total agricultural population. * * * * * * * * * Income derived from the cultivation of cocoanut, where it is not the chief means of subsistence, is, throughout the seaboard taluks, almost invariably a subsidiary source in the family means of livelihood, while it is the sole resource to many in the same area."

Order 2, Fishing and Hunting

19. The numbers returned in group 27 under order 2 (Fishing and Hunting) are also noteworthy. They show that the rich facilities for fishing which exist in the State are being availed of to an increasing extent.

Sub-class III, Industry

20. Sub-class III (Industry) must be regarded as the most important occupation of the people after Sub-class I, even though the industrial population stands below the working population returned in Sub-class X (Domestic service) in respect of its numerical strength. As remarked in paragraph 13, Cochin has a larger proportion of people engaged in industrial pursuits than Mysore, Baroda or Madras. The explanation for this is to be found in the following extract from the Census Report of 1911.

"This comparative preponderance of industrial population in these two ‡ States is due not to the infertility of the soil or its unsuitability to agriculture but to certain natural advantages possessed by them, which have diverted a larger proportion of people than in most other parts of India from agriculture to industrial occupations. Among these may be mentioned the existence of a large extent of backwaters and canals teeming with fish life and providing occupation to a large number of fishermen, fish-curers and dealers, and boat and bargemen; of valuable forests covering nearly one-half of the States and providing employment to numbers of wood cutters, sawyers, carpenters and collectors of forest produce; and of facilities for the cultivation of the cocoanut palm, the raw produce of which affords scope for important and extensive industries, such as toddy drawing, jaggery making, arrack distilling, oil pressing, coir making, etc."

† This has since been prohibited.

‡ Travancore and Cochin.

21. The figures for such groups in this Sub-class of occupation, as are taken up for discussion here, are given in the margin of the respective paragraphs together with the figures of actual workers in the corresponding groups in 1921 and 1911. Groups 43 (cotton spinning, sizing and weaving) and 45 (rope, twine, string and other fibres) are the most important divisions under order 5 (Textiles). Cotton weaving has been growing both as a cottage and as a factory industry, and we find that the numbers engaged in this group have increased by 42·7 per cent. It was observed in paragraph 11 of Chapter I that the spinning and weaving mills at Trichur had developed into a flourishing and important concern. Weaving colonies on a small scale started by private enterprise are also thriving in several parts of the State. **Order 5, Textiles**

Group	Earners and working dependents	Actual workers		Variation per cent between 1921 and 1931
	1931	1921	1911	
43 Cotton spinning, sizing and weaving ..	6,099	4,274	3,177	+42·7

22. Group 45 is mostly concerned with the manufacture of cocoanut fibre and yarn and gives work to as many as 34,673 persons (nearly 3 per cent of the State's population), and subsistence to many more. The numbers in this group show an increase of 35·4 per cent during the decade.

Group	Earners and working dependents	Actual workers		Variation per cent between 1921 and 1931
	1931	1921	1911	
43 Rope, twine, string and other fibres ..	34,673	25,605	24,833	+35·4

23. Groups 54, 55 and 56 in order 7 (Wood) find employment for 23,007 persons (below 2 per cent of the total population). The actual workers in this order numbered 20,798 in 1921. The rich and extensive forest area in the State and its systematic exploitation are responsible for the relatively large proportion of the population working in this order. Group 54 (sawyers) shows a decrease in numbers probably because of the growing competition of sawing mills worked by steam power. **Order 7, Wood**

Group	Earners and working dependents	Actual workers		Variation per cent between 1921 and 1931
	1931	1921	1911	
54 Sawyers ..	3,283	4,352	9,348	—24·6
55 Carpenters, turners and joiners, etc. ..	7,781	7,474	9,348	+ 4·1
56 Basket makers and other industries of woody materials, etc. ..	11,943	8,972	8,872	+33·1

24. So far as Cochin is concerned, the two most important groups under order 8 (Metals) are 59 (blacksmiths etc.) and 60 (workers in brass etc.). The marginal figures show a very considerable decline in the numerical strength of group 59. The disparity between 1921 and 1911 in respect of the numbers returned in this group gives rise to doubts regarding the accuracy of the figures recorded in 1921. The blacksmith community has increased by 15·5 per cent during the **Order 8, Metals**

Group	Earners and working dependents	Actual workers		Variation per cent between 1921 and 1931
	1931	1921	1911	
59 Blacksmiths, other workers in iron, makers of implements, etc. ..	2,824	3,908	2,406	—27·7
60 Workers in brass, copper and bell metal.	1,085	1,017	556	+ 6·7

past decade and most of the workers of this class still pursue their hereditary occupation. It must, however, be observed in this connection that the demand for articles like locks, bolts, nails etc. of local manufacture has been gradually decreasing, because imported articles of foreign make have flooded the market.

Order 9, Ceramics

25. Group 63 representing potters and makers of earthen-ware in order 9 (Ceramics) is another industry showing signs of decline. The standard of living has risen among most classes of the population and the use of earthen-ware is now restricted to the very lowest orders among the people, metal utensils having largely replaced earthen ones. The rise in the number of brick and tile factories referred to in paragraph 11 of Chapter I will account for the large increase observed in group 64. It is satisfactory to note that most of the factories are thriving.

Group	Earners and working dependents	Actual workers		Variation per cent between 1921 and 1931
	1931	1921	1911	
63 Potters and makers of earthen-ware ..	2,172	2,245	1,935	− 3·3
64 Brick and tile makers ..	836	451	239	+ 85·4

Order 10 Chemical products etc.

26. The manufacture and refining of vegetable oils is the only group of importance under order 10 (Chemical products etc.). Though there are numerous oil mills worked by steam power where the extraction chiefly of cocoanut oil is carried on as a factory industry, oil-pressing as a cottage industry still gives work to many people.

Group	Earners and working dependents	Actual workers		Variation per cent between 1921 and 1931
	1931	1921	1911	
68 Manufacture and refining of vegetable oils ..	2,008	2,067	1,351	+ 40·7

Order 11. Food industries

27. The groups that deserve special notice under order 11 (Food industries) are 71 (rice pounders, huskers etc.), 75 (sweetmeat makers etc.), 76 (toddy drawers) and 78 (manufacturers of tobacco). The increase in the number of rice hulling mills employing steam power is reflected in the figures returned in group 71. Rice mills were first opened in the decade 1901—1911 and the workers in this group fell from 13,816 to 9,790 during the period. The industry was pursued almost exclusively by women of the poorer classes, and thousands of them have now been driven to other callings. Though the excise revenue of the State in 1931 shows a considerable increase over that of 1921, toddy drawers are seen to have decreased by no less than 52·4 per cent during the decade. We do not know what proportion of this decrease is to be attributed to the unwillingness of people to return the disreputable pursuit of toddy drawing as their occupation; but it may be safely assumed that there has been a fall in the consumption of toddy in as much as certain sections of the labouring classes—toddy is the favourite drink of these classes—have been persuaded to give it up in favour of tea.

Group	Earners and working dependents	Actual workers		Variation per cent between 1921 and 1931
	1931	1921	1911	
71 Rice pounders and huskers and flour grinders ..	2,472	10,083	9,790	− 75·5
75 Sweetmeat and condiment makers ..	1,281	1	2	?
76 Toddy drawers ..	4,573	9,605	6,985	− 52·4
78 Manufacturers of tobacco ..	531	52	147	+921·2

The fact that tobacco manufacturers have registered a very large increase must show the growing prevalence of the snuff and smoking habits.

Order 12, Industries of dress and the toilet

28. One wonders whether the numbers returned in some of the most important groups under order 12 (Industries of dress and the toilet) do not reflect certain interesting aspects of modern fashions. The working population in group 85 (washing and cleaning) shows a slight increase over the figures of 1921. But the tailors of group 83 and the barbers of group 86 have both declined in their numerical strength. Obviously these groups must depend on the patronage chiefly of the upper classes for their subsistence. The girls of these classes learn needle-work at school and have dispensed with the services of tailors for such articles of dress as the women folk of their classes require. Group 83 appears to have therefore suffered an appreciable loss. Likewise the golden age for barbers seems to have come to an end when English education introduced western fashions in its wake. Of old the males in the Christian and Muslim communities had the whole of their crown, and those in the Hindu communities, the whole of their crown with the exception of a round patch at the top or back reserved for a tuft, shaved clean at frequent and short intervals. But now they have their hair cropped after the fashion of the West, and most men have their daily shave attended to by themselves. The two groups therefore have but little reason to be in love with modern ways and fashions. *

Group	Earners and working dependents	Actual workers		Variation per cent between 1921 and 1931
	1931	1921	1911	
83 Tailors, milliners etc.	1,551	2,114	1,891	—26.6
85 Washing and cleaning ..	6,002	5,819	5,502	+ 3·1
86 Barbers etc.	2,295	2,478	2,451	+ 7·4

Order 14, Building industries and order 17, Miscellaneous industries

29. Group 90 (lime burners, cement workers etc.) under order 14 and group 98 (makers of jewellery etc.) under order 17 complete the list of the important divisions in Sub-class III. Both groups show a fall in numbers, but the decrease in group 98 is very considerable. One hopes that the craze for ornaments and jewellery characteristic of our women is generally on the decline.

Group	Earners and working dependents	Actual workers		Variation per cent between 1921 and 1911
	1931	1921	1911	
90 Lime burners, cement workers etc. ..	8,228	9,616	4,532	—14·4
98 Makers of jewellery and ornaments ..	2,875	3,953	2,228	—27·3

Sub-class III reviewed as a whole

30. The 19 groups reviewed above account for 95·9 per cent of the earners and working dependents in this important Sub-class. The remaining 32 groups of the Sub-class, for which returns have been received, together contain but 4·1 per cent of the working population engaged in industries.

It is further to be observed that the numbers in Sub-class III as a whole have slightly declined during the period under review. As already explained, the largest decrease is in group 71 (rice pounders, huskers etc.) Groups 59 (blacksmiths etc.), 76 (toddy drawers), 90 (lime burners, cement workers etc.) and 98 (makers of jewellery etc.) have also contributed much to this tall. Most of the remaining groups reveal a substantial increase.

Sub class	Earners and working dependents	Actual workers		Variation per cent between 1921 and 1931
	1931	1921	1911	
III. Industry	107,835	108,945	89,644	—1·0

* It is suggested that the barbers will not complain when ladies take to modern hairdressing.

Sub-class IV, Transport

31. We have already seen that Sub-class IV (Transport) gives work to 14,594 persons (excluding subsidiary earners) or 1·2 per cent of the total population. The extensive waterways possessed by the State provide exceptional facilities for transport by water. All important groups in this division record a large rise in numbers, the percentage of increase for the Sub-class as a whole being no less than 55 for the decade. Group 107 relating to mechanically driven vehicles is particularly noteworthy. It shows the new development of transport by road by mechanical means with special reference to motor vehicles. The rural and out-lying parts of the State have been opened out as never before and brought within very easy reach of all important towns by this means. At the same time the more primitive forms of inland transport like the ancient bullock-carts are still kept up in connection with trade. Group 108 which deals mainly with such forms of transport actually records an increase of 8·6 per cent. In the northern taluks of the State the transport of goods to and from commercial centres in Malabar and Coimbatore is still effected to a large extent by these bullock-carts. The increase in road traffic is reflected in the numbers returned in group 106 (labourers employed on roads etc.) In the southern taluks the primitive *vallums* (native boats for carrying goods and passengers) and the modern steam and motor boats mostly take the place of the bullock-carts and motor buses of the northern taluks.

Group	Earners and working dependents	Actual workers		Variation per cent between 1921 and 1931
	1931	1921	1911	
102 Ship-owners, boat-owners etc. ..	4,186	3,164	2,916	+ 32·3
106 Labourers employed on road, etc. ..	1,256	541	..	+ 132·2
107 Owners, etc., connected with mechanically driven vehicles ..	1,371	79	2,706	+ 1635·4
108 Owners, etc. connected with other vehicles ..	3,898	3,588		+ 8·6

32. Subsidiary Table VI gives the numbers of persons employed in Railways, Posts and Telegraphs, Irrigation and other departments. An abstract of the figures is given in the margin. Sections A (Railways), B (Postal department) and E (Anchal department) record an increase over the corresponding figures of 1921. The decrease noticed in sections C (Irrigation department) and D (Forest Tramway) is only apparent, because the returns of 1931 do not include the coolies working in the departments, whereas those of 1921 contain coolies also.

Departments	Persons employed			
	1931		1921	
	Europeans and Anglo-Indians	Indians	Europeans and Anglo-Indians	Indians
A Railways ..	4	649	1	471
B Postal department ..	2	148	1	124
C Irrigation do ..	..	96	..	175
D Forest Tramway ..	3	310	4	406
E Anchal department ..	..	250	..	232

Sub class V. Trade

33. Sub-class V (Trade) which deals with the commercial population is seen to occupy the third place in importance, when the proportion of earners in the various Sub-classes is taken into consideration. The figures for the division as a whole have risen by 9 per cent during the period even though all

orders do not share in this increase. Trade was flourishing till almost the close of the decade, and the commercial population enjoyed considerable prosperity. These circumstances are revealed to a certain extent by the appreciable increase noticed in group 115 under order 23, which represents bank managers, money lenders etc. The reasons for the fall in the numbers of those trading in textiles (group 117) are not quite obvious. Perhaps many of them have been returned as workers in groups 43 and 45 under Sub-class III (Industry), in as much as they are but petty dealers who themselves sell the articles they manufacture. The growing restrictions imposed on the sale of liquor will partly account for the decrease in group 126 (vendors of wine, liquors, etc.), the number of liquor shops having fallen from 789 in 1921 to 560 in 1931. The fall in the consumption of toddy alluded to in paragraph 27 above may also be recalled in this connection. But it is doubtful whether the decrease in group 126 points to any reduced demand for the more harmful varieties of drink like arrack and foreign liquors. The phenomenal increase in group 127 (owners and managers of hotels, cook shops, etc.), and perhaps also in group 150 (general store-keepers and shop-keepers otherwise unspecified), is most probably to be attributed to the habit of tea-drinking which is now very widely prevalent among most classes of the people. This habit has led to the opening of hundreds of tea-shops in all parts of the State.

Sub-class and groups	Earners and working dependents	Actual workers		Variation per cent between 1921 and 1931
	1931	1921	1911	
V. Trade	41,964	38,513	35,967	+ 9·0
115 Bank managers etc. ..	2,488	2,037	1,430	+ 22·1
117 Trade in piecegoods etc. ..	2,041	2,541	1,898	− 19·7
126 Vendors of wine etc. ..	1,124	2,739	2,397	− 59·0
127 Owners and managers of hotels etc. ..	3,927	1,801	1,760	+ 118·0
150 General Store-keepers etc. ..	5,484	2,028	4,315	+ 170·4

The abnormal variations between 1921 and 1931 in almost all groups under order 32 (Other trade in food stuffs) arise chiefly from the re-grouping of occupations in the classification scheme and call for no special comment.

Sub-classes VI, Public Force, VII, Public Administration, and VIII, Professions and Liberal Arts

34. Sub-classes VI and VII (Public Force and Public Administration) are seen to employ more people than in 1921. The former deals chiefly with the State Police and the latter with the Sirkar and municipal services. The professional population is represented by Sub-class VIII (Professions and Liberal Arts). Orders 45 (Religion) and 47 (Medicine) both return larger numbers than in 1921, but group 170 in order 47 contains more quacks than qualified physicians following the *Ayurvedic* or other indigenous systems of medicine. The fall in numbers under order 48 (Instruction) must be due to

Sub-class	Earners and working dependents	Actual workers		Variation per cent between 1921 and 1931
	1931	1921	1911	
VI. Public Force	1,027	975	700	+ 5·3
VII. Public Administration	4,665	3,421	3,731	+ 36·4

Sub-class and order	Earners and working dependents	Actual workers		Variation per cent between 1921 and 1931
	1931	1921	1911	
VIII. Professions and Liberal Arts	16,970	16,708	11,073	+ 1·6
45 Religion ..	4,331	4,055	4,422	+ 6·8
47 Medicine ..	2,861	2,022	1,475	+ 41·5
48 Instruction ..	6,203	7,523	2,597	— 17·5
49 Letters, arts and sciences etc. ..	2,751	2,067	1,994	+ 33·1

the disappearance of many unrecognised indigenous schools referred to in paragraph 19 of the next chapter, from which it will be seen that the decrease does not signify any set-back in education. The increase under order 49 (Letters, arts etc.) is partly to be accounted for by the re-groupings of occupations in the classification scheme, an instance of which is seen in witches and wizards being transferred from group 189 in Sub-class XII of the old scheme to group 181 under order 49 "where they are at least as suitably kennelled as astrologers and mediums."

Intellectual occupations and educated classes

35. The working population in the two Sub-classes VII and VIII represent the intellectual and educated classes, and together they absorb 3·5 per cent of the total working population of the State. The corresponding figure in 1921 was 4·7 per cent. It will be seen from the next chapter that English education has made remarkable progress during the past decade, so much so that a higher proportion of the working population ought to have been returned in the professional Sub-classes, if all educated persons had found suitable employment within the State itself. Instead of the expected rise in the proportion of workers found in the two classes, we have an actual fall of 1·2 per cent, even though the specific numbers employed show a slight increase over the figures of 1921. The fact is that the scope for employment in the professional sphere is strictly limited. Trade, Industry and even Agriculture can afford to absorb an increasing number of workers, but Public Administration and the Professions cannot. For this reason considerable numbers of English-educated persons, who ought to have during the last 10 years joined the ranks of those pursuing intellectual callings, have been subjected to much distress through unemployment. This aspect of the subject is treated in greater detail in the next chapter which deals with literacy.

Accuracy of statistics of educated unemployment

36. The statistics of educated unemployment presented in the two parts of Imperial Table XII may be briefly reviewed here. It was remarked in paragraph 5 above that the census of educated unemployment was unfortunately a failure. Special schedules were distributed by the enumerators with suitable instructions to the English-educated persons of their respective blocks, but the response was poor and the schedules were not returned in a majority of cases. We have seen that the average man views unemployment and dependence as a disgrace. He is naturally unwilling 'to hold a candle to his own shame' by returning himself as unemployed. This unwillingness will be all the greater on the part of educated young men with their high ideals of independence and honour. Disappointment and dejection too might have been partly responsible for the poor response. In any case the special census has been a failure everywhere and the Census Commissioner proposed that Imperial Table XII might be dropped and the results of the enquiry shown in a Subsidiary Table appended to this chapter. The Table was, however, compiled before the proposal was received and hence it has been retained.

Review of statistics

37. Turning to the figures in the Table, we find that 444 persons between the ages of 20 and 40, with educational qualifications ranging from a

*Please see paragraph 26 of Chapter IX.—Literacy.

pass in the secondary school-leaving certificate (matriculation) examination to the highest degrees of the Madras University, returned themselves as unemployed or unsuitably employed at the special census. 4 persons over 40 and 74 persons under 20 years, with like attainments are also to be added to this list, so that the total number of the unemployed will stand at 522 according to these returns. That unemployment is not confined to graduates in Arts will be seen from Part II of the Table. It is no exaggeration to state that scores of our legal practitioners (graduates in Law) have so little work that they should strictly be grouped with the unemployed. Qualified medical practitioners also have been hit hard. 80 out of the 444 unemployed persons aged 20—40 are Masters or Bachelors of Arts, but as many as 351 are only holders of completed secondary school-leaving certificates. 25·5 per cent of the unemployed are Brahmans, 53·2 per cent are "other Hindus" and 20·9 per cent are from all other classes combined. Almost all the Brahmans are from the Tamil Brahman class and the "other Hindus" from the Nayar community. Indian Christians form the majority in "all other classes." A knowledge of the local conditions will show that, though the returns are far from complete, this distribution of the unemployed by class reflects with much truth the relative proportion of the extent of educated unemployment in the three communities. Other communities are backward in English education, and are therefore much less affected.

Educated unemployment among women

38. The distress to which educated women are subjected as a result of the growing extent of unemployment in their ranks is the saddest part of the whole affair. Though very few returns were received from English-educated women, it is but too well known that several graduates and many intermediates in Arts, and scores of school-leaving certificate holders (matriculates) in the State are forced to remain idle against their will, for the Education department can absorb but a very small proportion of their ever-increasing numbers. Other departments can help them even less. For reasons explained in paragraphs 13 and 16 of Chapter VI, most of these women are likely to remain unmarried. Unemployment in their case, therefore, means the most acute distress.

Problem of educated unemployment

39. In any case the problem of educated unemployment has already assumed serious proportions and it is high time that effective remedial measures are devised to relieve the situation, and purge the communities affected of the unhealthy and growing element of discontent.

Sub-class X, Domestic service, and XI, Insufficiently described occupations

40. Of the remaining Sub-classes, X (Domestic service) and XI (Insufficiently described occupations) alone deserve any notice. The proportion of the working population engaged in Sub-class X has already been commented on in paragraph 13 above. Only 7·8 per cent of this population are earners, the rest being working dependents; and among these working dependents 99·1 per cent are women. According to the instructions issued to the census staff, such dependents as contributed to the support of the household were to be shown as workers in column 11 of the schedule. Where female dependents regularly performed actual manual work like cooking, thereby obviating the necessity for employing paid cooks or domestic servants, they were to be treated as working dependents and the work they did was to appear in column 11. These instructions are responsible for the returns under this Sub-class.

Sub-class X. Domestic service		
Earners	Males	4,241
	Females	6,763
Working dependents	Males	1,104
	Females	128,635

We have already seen that the numbers in Sub-class XI represent no more than 4·2 per cent of the total working population. 97·5 per cent of the workers in this Sub-class are earners engaged in one or other of the three principal occupations, namely, Agriculture, Industry and Trade. But it is not possible to assign these workers to their respective groups in these Sub-classes because of the defective nature of the returns.

Sub-class XI. Insufficiently described occupations	
Earners ..	24,845
Working dependents ..	635

Proportion of working dependents to earners

41. The marginal table shows the proportion of working dependents to earners in each Sub-class of occupation and diagram 2 illustrates this proportion in some of the principal occupations. For reasons already explained in the preceding paragraph, Sub-class X may be excluded when the ratio of working dependents to earners is examined. Likewise the negligible numbers in Sub-class XII where beggars, vagrants etc. were returned as working dependents may also be ignored. Turning to the remaining Sub-classes, we find that the figures for working dependency are as a rule very low. In the important section dealing with Agriculture, there are but 29 working dependents for every 1,000 earners. Industry receives more help, the ratio here being 74. Professions and Liberal Arts have 18 and Trade but a poor 16 helpers to 1,000 earners. Public Force and Public Administration have naturally no working dependents. Sub-class XI (Insufficiently described occupations) shows a ratio of 26.

Sub-class	Total earners (principal occupation)	Total working dependents	Proportion of working dependents per 1,000 earners
All occupations ..	466,726	147,325	316
I. Production of raw materials ..	249,467	7,242	29
III. Industry ..	100,379	7,456	74
IV. Transport ..	14,464	130	9
V. Trade ..	41,322	642	16
VI. Public Force ..	1,026	1	1
VII. Public Administration ..	4,654	11	2
VIII. Professions and Liberal Arts ..	16,676	294	18
IX. Persons living on their income ..	2,667	39	15
X. Domestic service ..	11,004	129,829	11,798
XI. Insufficiently described occupations ..	24,845	635	26
XII. Unproductive ..	200	1,046	5,230

Comparison with other States and Provinces.

42. The statement in the margin gives the proportion of working dependency in selected Sub-classes of occupation for other States and Provinces. The disparity between Cochin on the one hand and these States and Provinces on the other in this respect is seen to be so wide that we cannot but attribute it to a difference in the basis of the census returns. It does not appear likely that many working dependents in Cochin were erroneously returned as earners, because the ratio of earners will hardly support this view. In all probability many persons who were qualified to be treated as working dependents have been included in the class of non-working dependents.

Proportion of working dependents per 1,000 earners.

Sub-class	Cochin	Madras	Travancore	Mysore	Baroda
I Exploitation of Animals and Vegetation ..	29	115	149	336	353
III. Industry ..	74	86	277	171	165
V. Trade ..	16	51	84	58	137
VIII. Professions and Liberal Arts ..	18	30	46	21	23
XI. Insufficiently described occupations ..	26	121	149	77	1

Province or State	Number of females per 1,000 males in the working population	Number of females per 1,000 males in the working population excluding Sub-class X (Domestic service)
Travancore ..	883	248
Madras ..	896	451
Cochin ..	921	506

Working population by sex

43. The proportion of women in the working population of the State is relatively high. If Sub-class X (Domestic service) is also included, we shall find 921 female workers per 1,000 male workers in the two classes of earners and working dependents combined; and even when Domestic service is left out of consideration, there will be 506 women per 1,000 men.

Sex ratio among earners.

44. Among earners taken separately, the female ratio is found to be 498. The following table gives the figures for selected Sub-classes and groups and it is satisfactory to note that they testify to the general accuracy of the returns.

Occupation		Earners: Males	Earners: Females	Proportion of females per 1,000 males
I Exploitation of Animals and Vegetation	..	159,622	89,845	563
1. Non-cultivating proprietors taking rent etc.	..	3,607	2,923	815
5. Cultivating owners	..	18,454	4,617	250
6a. Cultivating tenants	..	39,433	8,965	226
7. Agricultural labourers	..	60,309	65,983	1,094
27. Fishing and Pearling	..	8,155	846	104
III. Industry	..	59,673	41,306	693
43. Cotton spinning, sizing and weaving	..	3,918	1,938	495
45. Rope, twine, string and other fibres	..	9,247	20,190	2,183
56. Basket makers and other industries etc.	..	3,343	7,770	2,324
63. Potters and makers of earthenware	..	1,157	986	852
71. Rice pounders and huskers etc.	..	128	2,164	16,906
78 Toddy drawers	..	4,500	34	8
85. Washing and cleaning	..	1,604	4,222	2,63
100. Scavenging	..	167	560	3,35
IV. Transport	..	13,919	545	39
V. Trade	..	33,475	7,847	234
130. Dealers in sweetmeats, sugar and spices	..	3,115	1,767	567
131. Dealers in dairy products, eggs and poultry	..	625	783	1,253
VII. Public Administration	..	4,617	37	8
VIII. Professions and Liberal Arts	..	13,890	2,786	201
169. Registered medical practitioners etc.	..	208	15	72
172. Midwives, Vaccinators, Compounders etc.	..	199	381	1 915
174. Professors and teachers of all kinds	..	4,323	1,374	31
175. Clerks and servants connected with education	..	451	34	75
IX. Persons living on their income	..	1,495	1,172	784
X. Domestic service	..	1,241	6,763	1 595
XI. Insufficiently described occupations	..	20,158	4,687	233
XII. Unproductive	..	140	60	429

In Agriculture, the ratio among non-cultivating proprietors is naturally much higher (810) than among cultivating owners (250) or tenants (226). Agricultural labourers correctly show an actual excess of female workers. Women of the lower classes are engaged for field labour in large numbers, the harvesting of crops in particular being almost their monopoly. Under Industry, Textiles attract considerable numbers of females, but they are far in excess of males in the industries connected with cocoanut fibre. Thousands of women of the lower orders in the coastal taluks are engaged in these light and profitable pursuits which could be conveniently plied during their leisure intervals. The same remark applies to group 56 (basket makers etc.), the only difference being that it is not confined to the coastal taluks. The cottage industry of earthenware has almost as many women as men workers. It has already been remarked that rice pounding and husking are occupations pursued almost exclusively by women. Washing and cleaning and scavenging are other industries where they predominate. The presence of a few women among toddy drawers can only mean that their income is derived from toddy drawing, the actual work being performed by their paid agents or servants. Sub-class IV (Transport) naturally shows a very low ratio of the weaker sex, but Sub-class V (Trade) affords more scope for women in groups like 130 (dealers in sweetmeats etc.) and 131 (dairy products etc.). Public Force still retains its male sex, but Public Administration is no longer the close preserve of men though, as yet, the female element in it is very weak. In another decade we may expect from this Sub-class of occupation more tangible evidence of the progress of female education and the general awakening of women. Professions and Liberal Arts have been fairly overrun by the fair sex, the female ratio in groups 169 (registered medical practitioners etc., representing qualified physicians and surgeons trained in modern medical colleges and schools), 172 (midwives, nurses etc.), 174 (professors, teachers etc.) and 175 (clerks etc.) being particularly noteworthy. Domestic service naturally employs more women than men. It is to be observed that the sex ratio in the various Sub-classes and groups of occupation is in strict accord not only with the peculiar social and economic conditions of this densely peopled Malayali State, but also with the comparatively high level of education, enlightenment and freedom enjoyed by the women of Cochin.

and among working dependents

45. Among working dependents females are far in excess of males for the obvious reason that the latter will generally pass into the class of earners as soon as they are able to work, and we find the most remarkable ratio of 17,476 women for every 1,000 men in this class of the working population. Even when Domestic service with its legions of women is excluded from our calculations, this ratio will be as high as 1,581. The table given at the end of this paragraph shows the figures for selected occupations. The working dependents in Sub-class I as a whole are seen to have 930 women for every 1,000 men; cultivating tenants showing a proportion of 907 and agricultural labourers 2,222. The ratio in Sub-class II reaches the high figure of 4,380, group 56 (basket makers etc.) being almost monopolised by women. Several other groups and orders also are dominated by them. Domestic service of course heads the list with the proportion of 107,735 females for every 1,000 males!

Occupation	Working dependents		Proportion of females per 1,000 males
	Males	Females	
ALL OCCUPATIONS ..	7,974	139,351	17,476
Sub-class I. Exploitation of Animals and Vegetation ..	3,753	3,489	930
Group 6. a. Cultivating tenants ..	599	543	907
,, 7. Agricultural labourers ..	1,085	2,411	2,222
,, 27. Fishing and Pearling ..	120	170	1,417
Sub class III. Industry ..	1,386	6,070	4,380
Group 43. Cotton spinning, sizing and weaving ..	110	133	1,209
,, 45. Rope, twine, string and other fibres ..	796	4,440	5,578
,, 56. Basket makers and other industries etc...	51	779	15,275
Order 11. Food Industries ..	29	245	8,448
,, 12. Industries of dress and the toilet ..	65	210	3,231
Group 85. Washing and cleaning ..	28	148	5,286
Sub-class IV. Transport ..	120	10	83
,, V. Trade ..	341	301	883
,, X Domestic service ..	1,194	128,635	107,735

46. Subsidiary Tables I (b) and II (b) deal with the proportion, in the total population, of earners who have returned a subsidiary occupation; and we find that, of the total earning population of 466,726 persons, 99,763 or 21·4 per cent have returned a subsidiary calling in addition to their principal occupation. The comparative statement in the margin shows that Travancore has relatively a larger number of subsidiary earners. The figures for Mysore and Baroda are, however, very low. Perhaps the two West Coast States offer greater facilities for workers to pursue more than one occupation at a time. The numbers returned under Domestic service are also partly responsible for the higher proportion in Travancore and Cochin.

Subsidiary occupations

Province or State	Proportion per cent of total earners having a subsidiary occupation
Travancore ..	33·3
Cochin ..	21·4
Madras ..	15·1
Mysore ..	10·3
Baroda ..	6·9

The statement given below shows the numbers and proportion of earners who follow each of the Sub-classes as their subsidiary occupation.

Sub-classes	Subsidiary earners. Actual figures	Number per cent in each Sub-class
I. Exploitation of Animals and Vegetation	35,106	35·2
III. Industry	10,741	10·8
IV. Transport	2,325	2·3
V. Trade	7,896	7·9
VI. Public Force	29	..
VII. Public Administration	253	·3
VIII. Professions and Liberal Arts	2,638	2·6
IX. Persons living on their income	1,123	1·4
X. Domestic service	36,167	36·3
XI. Insufficiently described occupations	2,935	2·9
XII. Unproductive	202	·2

Of the three important Sub-classes, Agriculture is naturally the most popular, and as many as 35·2 per cent of the subsidiary earners are engaged in this congenial pursuit. Industry and Trade also are seen to claim appreciable numbers.

Subsidiary occupations of agriculturists

47. More interesting than the above distribution of subsidiary earners by Sub-classes of occupation is their classification based on their principal occupation. For this purpose we shall divide the total earning population into two classes, the first showing agricultural, and the second non-agricultural, vocations as their principal source of income. There are 206,142 earners following order 1 (a), Cultivation, under Sub-class I as their chief occupation, and out of this number 57,850 persons representing 28·1 per cent of the earners in the above order, and 58 per cent of the total number of subsidiary earners in the State, have returned a second occupation as a subsidiary source of their income. Of the earners in the remaining 54 orders (numbering 260,584 persons), only 41,913 or 16·1 per cent are seen to have more than one occupation. The proportion of subsidiary earners among agriculturists is thus higher than among non-agriculturists, but it must be remembered in this connection that the agriculturists who have non-agricultural subsidiary occupations number only 42,757, the rest (15,093) having returned one of the groups of their own order (1 [a], Cultivation,) as their subsidiary calling. When due allowance is made for this section among agricultural earners, there will be only 207 for every 1,000 earners of order 1 (a) having a non-agricultural subsidiary occupation. Among the non-agricultural earning population, the proportion of those who pursue agricultural callings as a subsidiary source of income is as low as 72 per 1,000.

	Number per mille of earners
Agriculturists having subsidiary occupations ..	281
Non-agriculturists having subsidiary occupations ..	161
Agriculturists with non-agricultural subsidiary occupations ..	207
Non-agriculturists with agricultural subsidiary occupations ..	72

The following table gives the distribution by occupation of subsidiary earners among agriculturists.

Sub-class	Agricultural earners (order 1 [a]) with subsidiary occupation	Number per cent in each Sub-class
ALL OCCUPATIONS	57,850	
I. Exploitation of Animals and Vegetation	15,724	27·2
II. Exploitation of Minerals	44	·1
III. Industry	6,048	10·5
IV. Transport	1,145	2·0
V. Trade	4,244	7·4
VI. Public Force	14	..
VII. Public Administration	182	·3
VIII. Professions and Liberal Arts	1,212	2·1
IX. Persons living on their income	771	1·3
X. Domestic service	26,505	45·8
XI. Insufficiently described occupations	1,824	3·2
XII. Unproductive	37	·1

If Sub-classes I and X are omitted, there will remain but a fourth for all other occupations combined. In the circumstances it may not be wrong or unfair to conclude that the great majority of agricultural workers who have much more leisure on their hands than workers in other spheres are not making proper use of their spare time. They reveal a sad disinclination to take to subsidiary occupations for improving their economic condition. And their attitude seems to be characterised by a placid, but pathetic, contentment with their present lot, however unenviable it may be.

48. The extent to which different castes are retaining their traditional occupations or have taken to other pursuits will be seen from Imperial Table XI and Subsidiary Table V. The following extracts from the Census Report of 1901 will be found to be highly interesting and instructive in this connection. The searching and historical analysis of the whole subject and the fullness of its treatment justify the long quotation. **Occupation by castes**

"*Occupation and Caste.*—We have seen that caste has flourished most luxuriantly on this coast, and that the differentiation has been carried on with a degree of elaboration that has hardly any parallel elsewhere. Subsidiary Table XI has been compiled only for certain selected castes, but it reflects with sufficient clearness the practical economic life of the society and the partially occupational basis of caste, which we have traced to the double source of race and occupation. The ancient customs and institutions of the land subsisting with greater or less vitality, the various castes, as we have elsewhere shown, socially remain almost in the places assigned to them ages ago. In respect of occupations, few, if any, of the castes are now seen as being bound to any particular calling by which they live, nor were they perhaps at any time so exclusively bound. Interest in land, or some occupation or other connected with agriculture, has been a source of livelihood to most castes that have other traditional occupations. Besides being landlords, the different groups of Nambudris have most of them distinct functions to discharge, and tradition similarly assigns complex callings to several other castes. But as only a few families and individuals of a caste are so circumstanced, this fact of complex functions may be ignored, and we may confine our attention to the predominant occupation of a caste, assigned to it by tradition and generally implied in its current appellation.

The movement of the groups from their traditional moorings is regulated by a variety of circumstances, the most important of which is the supporting power of the occupations. The Nambudris or Malayali Hindu priestly class and the Ambalavasis or temple servants represent two communities, each divided into groups upon a system of religious functions, and owing to the continuance of these functions, such systems of occupations have had a prolonged existence. It is instructive in this connection to institute a comparison between the Nambudris and the Tamil Brahmans. The latter are found in almost all walks of life, having overflowed the limits of their traditional occupation in all available directions These and the Konkani Brahmans form here, as do their brethren elsewhere, two prosperous communities full of enterprise and activity. They have indeed each gone through different social experiences and arrived at different practical conclusions, while the Nambudris, hampered by the traditions of the past, have yet to recognize that matters relating to economics are 'a body of practical expedients to be amended from time to time'. As we have said elsewhere, they have not as yet begun to feel the pressure of material wants. But though their material existence has been so far agreeable and may not in the near future become insupportable, there are indications that it is gradually ceasing to be agreeable to the extent it used to be. Their economic existence is practically in a state of numbness and inactivity, and in other respects too, they present few of the characteristics of a progressive community. The faculties of this superior race have been so far of little practical use to the progress of the Malayalis as a nation in modern times, but, if, as of yore, their energies had been diverted into proper channels, a sensible addition would have been made to the intellectual wealth of the Malayali community, which would have reacted with effect in the sphere of material advancement.

Recognition of function in relation to caste is least possible in the case of high caste Nayars. As a relic of former times, we find that the small force of Infantry (the Nayar Brigade) maintained by the State still goes by the name of the ancient military caste of Kerala. Aristocratic military leaders of the feudal ages, who then derived their income chiefly from landed property, all appear in an enfeebled state in these times of uninterrupted peace and tranquillity. Some of them are almost penniless, and while a few families keep up their ancient position, most of them have lost their prestige and influence. Besides the governing and military classes, there are among Nayars sub-castes of potters, weavers, oil-mongers, copper-smiths, etc. Not only are none of these castes found engaged in any of these industries, but they even consider it a disgrace to be known by their traditional callings. Hence it is only natural that they are not seen in great numbers under industrial and commercial groups. There are again some classes of Nayars who are to do personal services to the Nambudris or to their own community, but the tendency has been to discontinue these services and take to other and more respectable callings. The community muster strong in the order of agriculture as occupiers and cultivators of land. Their partiality for agriculture and their reluctance to take to manufacture and commerce are in harmony with the sentiments generated by feudalism and caste, and with the rigid conservatism which marks the mass of the society in so many forms. They are well represented in the civil service and professions, as in the race of progress, they march at the head of the Malayali community. Contrasted with the Nayars are the Native Christians, who with their eminent practical genius, skill and ability, lead the van in the industrial occupations and compete with the Tamil Brahmans in quasi-commercial callings. Not being bound to any traditional occupation, they are found in all walks of life. Owing to the distinctions of caste, the different groups of Nayars still remain as incohesive elements, while, in spite of the difference of sects, there is among Christians much co-operation and union. Among the Eurasians in the State, there is an appreciable proportion having some vested interest in land, and while there are a few in the civil service of the State, and a few others again in the learned and artistic professions, the majority of them are engaged in industrial pursuits. Like the Native Christians, the Jonaka Mappilas take kindly to industrial and commercial occupations, but lag behind them in all intellectual callings. The Kudumi Chetties, who came here originally as the personal servants of the Konkanis, have almost transformed themselves into a labouring class, and they are found well represented in all occupations which demand an active life of physical exertion, earning comparatively more wages than other classes of labourers. The Kaduppattans,* a purely local group, appear among those least touched by the spirit of progress. Their traditional calling of making and selling salt has long ceased to be a local industry, and they have been mostly occupiers and cultivators of the soil. The numerous body of Iluvans, with the traditional occupation of toddy drawing and selling, seem, by choice as well as by pressure, to have from the first taken to agriculture, general labour, and some minor industrial occupations. As for the rest, the low caste Nayars (the barbers and washermen), the Kammalans (the artisan classes), the Valans (fishermen and boatmen), the Pulayans, Paraiyans, etc., (the agrestic serfs of old), and most of the intermediate castes that have not been brought into the Table, are all more or less rigidly tied to their respective time-honoured trades and pursuits.

Summary and Conclusion.—The fundamental condition of the social union obtaining among Malayali Hindus is based upon the supremacy of the Nambudri Brahmans, and on the interest of religion. In respect of occupations, the Nambudris from the circumstances of their colonization seem to have hit at the outset upon a self-sufficing state political and

*Ezhuthassans (new style).

economical, no less than social, in order mainly to protect and preserve themselves from unnecessary contact with foreign populations. In a land with abundant natural resources and inhabited by classes competent to supply the material wants of man, they found it easy to arrange the economic life of the community just as they wished, and seem to have tried from the first to base the system on an invariable foundation. While they pursued the learned and artistic professions, and the Nayars were generally entrusted with the tasks of war and protection, other groups in the population already enumerated, the mechanics, the artisans, the immediate cultivators of the soil and others, supplied the different wants of society. The system became organized as a fully developed theocracy, 'the classes or castes maintaining the degree of division of labour, which had been reached in early periods', with the sacerdotal caste having the regulation of life in most of its departments. In a word, under special ethnographic and territorial conditions, a system of social economy was adopted carrying with it a notion of fixity and self-sufficiency. Though it settled the conditions of life, we know that the land was not for long let alone by foreigners, and consequently, notwithstanding the geographical isolation, articles from foreign parts began to come in from very early times, and steadily continued to pour in with the increased activity of immigration, which gradually tended to affect the economic basis of society. The wants of society outgrew what used to be supplied by indigenous resources and labour. Few arts and industries have however found their way from elsewhere and gained location here, nor has any caste ever risen to the situations called into existence by the changing order of things; on the other hand, there has been throughout a tendency to yield in the struggle for existence in economic matters, so that, instead of development, we notice successive phases of decline and deterioration in the pursuit of their respective industries by indigenous castes. They were perhaps destined to meet with this vicissitude from the first. The castes engaged in the immediate prosecution of industries were, as they still mainly are, destitute of intellectual culture, and naturally enough, the industries have remained in the crude and undeveloped state, in which they were in very early times. Moreover, as they have been pursued mostly by low castes, there has prevailed among the higher orders a contempt for such occupations. The Nambudris of early times might indeed be presumed to have given some thought to the theoretical study of industries, as they had in some measure to furnish the various classes with their traditional stock of conceptions to supply their own peculiar wants. But, in course of time, they have by degrees left off even that partial association with such occupations. Most of the orders immediately below them also have extended but a feeble hand of support to the labouring castes, who under a theocracy were naturally regarded more as means to the ends of society than as its members. After the decay of Brahman supremacy in political matters, feudalism, which took definite shape with the establishment of monarchy (that is, after the advent of the Perumals), also worked against the growth of freedom and collective life, by the government becoming practically vested in caste, class or local chieftains. In fact, it became grafted on to the caste system with its complicated fetters and restrictions, and tended to intensify the isolation of the groups and to perpetuate in particular the degradation of the lower orders. Whatever advantages caste in its relation to occupation might have had at a certain stage of development in giving regularity, certitude and tranquillity to society, it rendered the industries practically stagnant. As for feudalism, it no doubt suited the warlike circumstances of the times, but, when its historical function disappeared, the rank and file of the military orders did not direct their energies to industrial arts and commerce, for they regarded these as unworthy and demeaning. Nor could they, even if they had wished, have achieved much success, for the trade of the country, both internal and foreign, had long before fallen into the hands of foreigners, so that after the great political change, which marked the close of the 18th century, they concerned themselves with their ancient pursuit of agriculture, and became at the same time devoted aspirants to offices under the new *regime*. Thus, when feudalism died hard before the dawn of the last century, among the general body of the people social and economic ideas did not liberate themselves from its influence, or from caste fetters. The result has been that, of the three great spheres of human activity—agriculture, manufacture and commerce—agriculture has been

almost the only means of livelihood of most of the Malayali castes, and we mark among them the phenomena characteristic of an agricultural community, *viz.*, 'stagnation, want of enterprise, and the maintenance of antiquated prejudices'."

The effect of three decades of change

49. Conditions have changed since 1901, but it is more than doubtful whether they have changed to that extent which one might have reasonably expected from the remarkable progress made by the State in the sphere of modern education during the past 3 decades. For instance we find that most of those castes that had well known occupations assigned to them by tradition are almost as much attached to these vocations as they were of old. Be it remembered at the same time that stagnation, deterioration and decline have overtaken several of the indigenous industries during the period owing as much to an ever-increasing foreign competition as to the lack of that support, enterprise and progress which were demanded by a rapidly changing order of things, so much so that many of these callings are now much less profitable than in the past.

Departure from traditional occupations

50. The marginal statement gives the proportion among earners of persons who returned their hereditary occupation as their principal source of income. Wherever available, the figures for 1911 are also given side by side for purposes of comparison. It is significant that there are but five castes among the selected ones in which less than 50 per cent of the earners are engaged in their traditional occupation. Of the five, the Tamil Brahmans are the most educated, advanced, enterprising and practical. Only a negligible fraction (6 per cent) of the earners in this class still retains the traditional occupation of priesthood, a fraction just sufficient to minister to the spiritual needs of the community, the rest having wisely taken to other pursuits. Imperial Table XI will show that there is no Sub-class of occupation except the disreputable last one (Beggars, Vagrants, etc.) that has not considerably benefited from the energetic contribution of this intellectual and superior race. The numbers engaged in Trade, Public Administration and Professions and Liberal Arts are particularly noteworthy. The Konkani Brahmans (not included in the marginal list) too are like their Tamil brethren so far as their attachment to their traditional calling of priesthood is concerned, but they have for long devoted themselves almost exclusively to Trade. The Ambalavasis and Nayars under the influence of English education have been deserting their hereditary

Caste		Proportion per cent of earners following traditional occupation as their principal calling	Proportion per cent of actual workers following their traditional occupation 1911
Brahman—Tamil	..	6	..
Iluvan	..	38	..
Nayar	..	40	..
Kaniyan	..	44	..
Ambalavasi	..	48	56·2
Kudumi Chetti	..	51	..
Vellalan	..	51	..
Pandaran	..	54	..
Kanakkan	..	57	68·6
Velan	..	57	71·8
Velakkattalavan	..	63	83·4
Chaliyan	..	65	..
Chakkan	..	66	61·6
Brahman—Malayali	..	67	..
Kaikolan	..	68	..
Valan	..	73	77·4
Vettuvan	..	76	..
Arayan	..	79	65·2
Ambattan	..	81	..
Panditattan	..	85	..
Kammalan	..	86	90·9
Pulayan	..	87	93·2
Veluttedan	..	87	91·1
Sambavan (Parayan)	..	93	94·6
Kusavan	..	94	00·1

occupations in increasing numbers in favour of Public Administration and Professions and Liberal Arts. Their reluctance to take to manufacture and commerce has not yet been overcome, and hence their poor representation in other Sub-classes like Industry and Trade. It is doubtful whether toddy drawing and the industries connected with it alone gave work to all Iluva workmen even in ancient times. The numbers engaged in this calling form but a very small fraction of the earning population in the community. Even when agriculture too is included in their hereditary occupation —it is well known that the Iluvans took to agriculture from very early days—, only 38 per cent of the Iluva earners will be seen to be following their traditional vocation. The remaining workers are distributed in the other Sub-classes. A large proportion of the agricultural, industrial and general labour in the State is recruited from among the Iluvans.

51. The figures for the remaining castes reveal but little change. A few like the Vellalans, Velans, Pandarans, Kudumi Chettis and Kanakkans would appear to have drifted to a considerable distance from their old moorings, but most of them are so distributed in agricultural, industrial or general labour that we may well question the accuracy of the proportions shown against them.

52. Comparing the ratios of 1931 with those of 1911, we observe the remarkable fact that the changes of two eventful decades of modernisation in most spheres of our activities have not affected to any appreciable extent the traditional occupations of a large majority of communities, a fact which cannot but testify to the singular strength of the system of social economy instituted in ancient times to suit the then conditions of society. Of the 12 castes compared, 3 (the Arayans, Chakkans and Kusavans) actually show a higher proportion of earners following their hereditary occupation. The Veluttedans, Valans, Pulayans, Sambavans (Parayans) and Kammalans reveal a slight fall in the ratio, which may be ignored in view of the fact that the working dependents and subsidiary earners of 1931 are not included in the figures. The proportion in the remaining 4 castes has fallen perceptibly. We have already seen how the Velakkattalavans or barbers were affected by modern fashions. The primitive washing of the Velans is growing less popular every day, and the Velans' priestcraft and tonsorial skill too are much less in demand among the classes served by them of old. And it has already been explained how English education has affected the ratio of the Ambalavasis and how general labour has upset the figures for the Kanakkans.

Occupations of Indian Christians and Muslims

53. The occupations of Indian Christians and Muslims deserve special notice. Neither of these communities is hampered by hereditary prejudices or predilections, and the result is seen in the economic progress of the two classes, and of the Indian Christians in particular. Imperial Table XI will show how this community is strongly represented in all the Sub-classes. As remarked in the third paragraph of the extract from the Census Report of 1901 quoted above, the Indian Christians compete with the Tamil Brahmans in quasi-commercial callings and lead the van in industrial occupations. Indigenous banking which was once the monopoly of the Tamil Brahmans has now passed mostly into the hands of Christians. The progress of higher education in the community has enabled them to compete successfully with others in Public Administration and Professions and Liberal Arts. The catholicity of Indian Christians in the choice of occupations, which has been rightly emphasised in previous Census Reports, is once more revealed by the occupation statistics of 1931. The Muslims are well represented in industrial and commercial pursuits and appear to be economically sound. But their representation in intellectual

callings is poor owing to a general disinclination to take to literary pursuits, which characterised the community till very recent times.

Organized Industries

54. Before concluding this chapter, the figures compiled from the returns for organized industries recorded in column 12 of the schedule may be briefly reviewed. It was remarked in paragraph 5 above that these statistics did not truly represent the growth of organized industries in the State. According to the instructions issued to the census staff, any organized concern employing at least 4 persons was to be returned, but it is clear from the available figures that even more ambitious concerns have been omitted, apparently because the instructions were not properly understood. A few instances of short returns may be cited from State Table V embodying the statistics collected from column 12. There are 1,537 persons engaged in the cultivation of tea in group 15 of Sub-class I in Imperial Table X; but we find only a smaller number recorded under tea plantations in State Table V. The fish-curing yards at Narakkal employ considerable numbers, but only 2 persons are seen under this head in the State Table. That the figures for soda water factories are simply ridiculous will be testified to by any one acquainted in the least with local conditions. Tobacco, snuff, bidi and cigarette factories, tailoring works, motor transport, tramways and motor and steam boats are other items that furnish instances of short returns. It is also noteworthy that no figures have been recorded in Sub-class V (Trade).

55. The basis of the returns in 1931 being different from that of 1921, comparisons with the figures of 1921 will serve no useful purpose. The statistics exhibited in the State Table will at best give an idea of some of the important organized industries in the State and the lines of possible development in the future. The subject is treated in Part II of this chapter, which Mr. V. K. Achyutha Menon, M. A., B. Com., Superintendent of the Government Trades School, Trichur, has kindly contributed.

CHAPTER VIII.—OCCUPATION.—PART II.—INDUSTRIES AND INDUSTRIAL RESOURCES.

[*Contributed by Mr. V. K. Achyutha Menon, M. A., B. Com., Superintendent, Government Trades School, Trichur.*]

State and industries

THE problem of industrial development in Cochin does not differ materially from the same problem as it has presented itself in other parts of India. During the period succeeding the Industrial Commission Report (1916—18), when the British Provinces and some of the Indian States initiated an era of industrial development by their active participation in industrial ventures, and by extending State help to industries started by private enterprise, Cochin also took stock of her industrial resources and adopted various measures for their development. Thus the Government of the State directly undertook some pioneering work in this field not only by offering financial assistance to private enterprises but also by taking a proprietory interest in industrial concerns.

Government Stoneware Factory and the Cochin Tanneries, Limited

2. The Government Stoneware Works at Chalakkudi and the Cochin Tanneries, Limited, owed their origin to this new policy. Of these the former is a purely Government concern which is yet to emerge out of the experimental stage, while a substantial portion of the capital for the Tanneries has been subscribed by the Government. It is however unfortunate that this concern had to stop work when it had carried on manufacture for about a year and a half only (1923—1924). The following remarks, among others, of Mr. Guthrie, sometime Principal of the Leather Trade Institute, Madras, who studied the question on the spot, will be pertinent in this connection: "Considering all things I think it is good business for the Cochin Durbar who are the chief share-holders of the company to increase their advance to the company so as to make it possible for regular work to be carried on in the tannery. If this advance is not made I see nothing for it but to wind up the company."

Industrial finance: Joint stock companies

3. At the end of August 1930—31, there were 202 joint stock companies registered in Cochin and 12 companies registered outside, working in the State. The aggregate paid-up capital of the 202 companies was Rs. 41,67,824 Only 8 of these companies are manufacturing concerns. Evidently investment of savings in large scale industries is not popular. What little confidence the people had in industrial concerns has been rudely shaken, because the shareholders of certain joint stock companies, for the shares of which there was a real scramble to begin with, have found that their realisations fell very far short of their expectations. It is uphill task to restore the lost confidence. One principle which, however, promoters may learn with advantage from experience of company promotion in Cochin is to expand from small beginnings. Another feature to be noted in this connection is that joint stock ventures are here taking a communal turn as a result of which industrial and business concerns are either individual enterprises or joint stock companies completely managed and financed by one community. This is hardly desirable and it is to be hoped that it will soon disappear in the light of a broad outlook or spirit of 'State development.'

Banks

4. Cochin cannot be said to be underbanked. Of the 202 companies registered in the State, 162 were banking institutions. Besides, banks registered in British India and Travancore have opened branches in the State and there are also indigenous money lending concerns. But they are all commercial banks and do not provide finance for block capital for industries. The registered banks

of the State fail even to provide working capital apparently because they are not conversant with the financial side of industries in general.

Banking Regulation

5. It may not be out of place to refer here to a question of considerable importance which affects the credit structure of the State. 'Banks have an influence on the economic life of the people as they are repositories of cash resources of all classes of individuals and institutions.' Of late there has been a 'wild' increase in the number of joint stock banks in the State. Whether this growth is healthy and the institutions are sound cannot but require the most careful examination; and, in the interests of the public, legislation for regulating banking business, on the lines recommended by the Indian Central Banking Enquiry Committee in its report, may have to be introduced sooner or later.

Government loans

6. To return to our point, banks in the State justifiably refuse to provide industrial finance. Joint stock companies are yet to get popular. And there is want of initial capital which has stood in the way of the development of industries in the State. To remove this difficulty at least in part, the Government have been extending State aid by the grant of industrial loans, and loans to the extent of about six lakhs of rupees have been disbursed to different industrial concerns. A system of rules to regulate such aid is yet to be framed and the loans are now being granted on the merits of individual applications. The question of liberal and organized financial assistance is under consideration and a State Aid to Industries Act may be placed in the Statute Book at no distant date.

Commercial intelligence and statistics

7. The collection and publication of statistics and other information relating to trade and industry form an important function of all modern Governments. These give the basis for an active Governmental policy. They are also helpful to producers and traders. So far as Cochin is concerned, much statistical information of general interest is at present filed in each department of the Government, but it serves no useful purpose. The question of the systematic collection and intelligible presentation of statistics has been under the consideration of the Government for some time, and recently they have passed orders sanctioning the constitution of an agency to deal with the subject. The collection and dissemination of other commercial information also will be undertaken by this agency which is expected to materialise as soon as financial conditions improve.

Economic survey

8. The formulation of a definite policy of industrial development presupposes a knowledge of the facts of the present situation. For this an intensive survey of the economic resources of the State seems to be essential. A scheme has been worked out and sanctioned by the Government, which is at present held in abeyance owing to the existing financial stringency.

Previous surveys

9. Here it may be noted that a survey of 'cottage and household industries' was undertaken in 1910 and a general economic survey was conducted along with the census of 1921. They have indicated certain general lines of progress, but they lack intensity for the initiation of definite action. It must however be said to their credit that it was the 1910 survey that brought to the forefront the working defects of our artisans, and it led to the opening of industrial schools for the demonstration of the advantages of improved tools and methods. There are 43 of these schools at present, 24 Government institutions and 19 private ones. The 1921 survey emphasised the waste that resulted from the isolated action of the different Development departments of the Government.

Industrial schools

It was realised that it would be more profitable if the activities of the several departments were co-ordinated. The Industrial Advisory Board remedied this defect to some extent. But a wider organization with a larger sphere of activity was considered desirable and an Economic Development Committee was constituted in 1926 to formulate suggestions for the improvement of the economic resources of the State. Economic Development Committee

10. The coast line of the State (35 miles in length) is unbroken and near the shore water is shallow. Hence steamers which touched the ports of the State had to lie at anchor in open roadsteads about two and a half miles away from the coast. During the south-west monsoon from the end of May until the middle of August even this was impossible because of the heavy seas, and shipping was almost at a standstill. The few steamers that came in during the period took refuge in the smooth water anchorage known as the Narakkal mud banks, a geological formation of mud and oil, which, by the action of oil on water, keep the waters smooth. Port facilities

11. Cochin, 90 miles south of Calicut, is the most important port between Bombay and Colombo. It is nearer to Aden and Durban than Bombay, and is the natural outlet for South India. A full development of these natural facilities should ensure a very great increase in her trade. Between Cochin and Ernakulam is a stretch of backwaters connected to the sea by a natural opening and capable of developing into a first class harbour safe at all seasons of the year for ocean-going steamers. But before steamers could enter this inner harbour the bar at the opening had to be removed and the backwaters made sufficiently deep for them. This in fact comprised the initial stages of the present development of the Cochin harbour*. The scheme assumed practical shape in 1920—22 when successful experimental dredging of the outer bar was conducted. Regular dredging was then started and a deep channel 540 feet wide and 34 feet deep at low water was dredged out. By 1928 it was possible for steamers to enter the inner harbour. The spoils of the dredgings have been utilised for the reclamation of a considerable area from the backwaters. The fourth stage of the harbour development recently sanctioned involves further improvements such as the construction of wharves, jetties, warehouses, etc., in the reclaimed area, and the extension of the railway from the mainland right up to the wharves. To facilitate railway transport, work has already been started for the conversion of the metre-gauge Shoranur-Ernakulam railway into a broad-gauge one. The number of steamers that cleared the port in 1913—14 was 1,211 with an aggregate tonnage of 834,213. In 1928—29, when the inner harbour was open for ocean traffic, the number of ships that cleared the port was 1,146 with an aggregate tonnage of 1,194,512. In 1930—31, the latest year for which figures are available, it was 1,066 and 1,386,235 respectively**. These figures are significant. One notices a decrease in the number of steamers that clear the port; but their aggregate tonnage is seen to be on the increase in spite of the existing depression. This emphasises a principle of the economics of marine navigation that, provided there are harbour facilities, big steamers pay more than small ones. Harbour development

12. The statistics of half a century show that the trade of Cochin has steadily been growing from decade to decade. During the period, 1870—71 to 1879—80, the aggregate value of trade, including imports and exports, was Rs. 1,49,49,525. During the last decade this rose to Rs. 10,48,67,922, an increase of over 700 per cent within the last 60 years! The following statements showing, for the last 5 Trade of the port of Cochin.

* The inset in the Map of the Cochin State inserted at the beginning of this volume will give an idea of the situation of this harbour.

** These figures are taken from the Annual Report of the Cochin Chamber of Commerce for 1930—31.

years, the quantity of certain selected commodities that enter into the sea-borne trade of Cochin are instructive.* The selected commodities will show that organized effort may tend to increase our exports and reduce our imports.

EXPORTS

Commodity		Year				
		1925—26	1926—27	1927—28	1928—29	1929—30
Coffee	cwt. ..	799	101	461	2,703	108
Coir (unmanufactured)	cwt. ..	406	360	814	2,222	515
Coir (manufactured)	tons ..	31,943	29,342	32,176	33,501	31,938
Nux-vomica	cwt. ..	10,500	17,766	15,550	13,357	14,464
Dye and tanning substances	cwt. ..	5,028	1,182	4,423	4,747	5,173
Oils essential—Lemongrass	lbs. ..	545,212	560,346	630,541	813,461	632,552
Oils vegetable—cocoanut	cwt. ..	283,251	396,126	299,918	312,257	372,680
Do Others	cwt. ..	14,764	24,236	22,182	12,448	4,628
Oilcakes	tons ..	9,425	12,899	8,093	10,726	12,507
Rubber	lbs. ..	8,066,861	6,872,133	8,506,410	9,251,674	9,068,598
Spices	cwt. ..	34,763	27,136	52,093	30,118	36,761
Tea	lbs. ..	11 549,029	11,545,923	14,037,978	17,416,121	17,984,874
Wood and timber	c. tons ..	735	2,254	1,939	1,540	1,130
Cordage and ropes of vegetable fibres	cwt ..	66,122	65,043	58,426	64,265	64,961
Hemp (raw)	cwt. ..	2,681	3,347	1,583	1,426	2,600

IMPORTS

Commodity		Year				
		1925—26	1926—27	1927—28	1928—29	1929—30
Cement	tons ..	1,472	1,728	2,509	3,253	2,556
Machinery and Millwork (value)	Rs. ..	3,29,317	2,95,268	15,72,504	6,22,291	4,17,038
Manures	tons ..	1,654	1,745	3,029	4,157	3,079
Paper and paste board (value)	Rs. ..	2,92,540	3,14,769	2,59,454	3,56,759	3,96,250
Soap	cwt. ..	4,710	4,809	5,025	6,320	7,881
Stationery (except paper) (value)	Rs. ..	1,14,487	72,077	53,225	1,17,382	1,28,498
Textiles (twist and yarn)	lbs. ..	30,400	800	3,000	4,593	20,708
Textiles (piecegoods)	yds. ..	4,807,939	7,184,247	6,682,932	6,845,984	12,291,569
Paddy (rice in husk)	tons ..	56,741	37,983	54,628	63,786	66,356
Rice (not in husk)	tons ..	153,898	166,643	137,001	126,818	121,957
Gums and resins	cwt. ..	8,954	10,300	6,979	4,965	4,372
Matches gross of	boxes ..	179,800	177,550	227,510	704,775	378,060
Mineral oil—Kerosine	galls. ..	6,753,672	6,790,861	7,838,458	3,938,058	8,906,819
Oil—vegetable	cwt. ..	541	1,986	2,571	2,581	931

* The figures have been taken from "Imports and Exports at each principal port of the Presidency of Madras", 1925—26 to 1929—30.

The following explanation may be helpful in this connection:

(a) Travancore and British Malabar have a considerable share in the trade of Cochin port; but this does not detract from the value of the figures in so far as they apply to Cochin, because all the three regions present the same trade features. It is not possible to get separate figures for this State only. This fact has to be borne in mind whenever reference is made to the sea-borne trade figures of Cochin.

(b) A careful study of the figures will show that the depression in trade has not led to any appreciable fall in the figures for individual commodities given in the statements. Indeed some of the items are seen to have registered an actual increase. This goes to prove that the trade demand of Cochin port is inelastic as it deals more in necessaries than in luxuries.

Transport: waterways

13. Till the middle of the last century there were no good roads in the State and inland trade was carried on almost entirely by backwaters and rivers and connecting canals. There are 120 miles of these waterways extending from far off Ponnani in the north to distant Trivandrum in the south. They provided excellent means of transport for conveying the commodities of the interior to the ports and thus contributed to the early economic development of the State. With the coming in of the 'road mania' the canals began to be neglected, though even to-day a considerable amount of traffic passes through them.

Roads

14. It was in the forties of the last century that a vigorous policy of road and bridge construction was inaugurated in the State. Ever since the Government have paid the closest attention to the question of the building and improvement of roads, and miles of roads have been opened from time to time. To-day the State is well served with a net-work of good metalled roads of which about 500 miles are maintained by the Public Works department and the four municipalities, and about 600 miles by the 86 Village Panchayats. Within the last five or six years there has been an astonishing growth in motor traffic and this finds its way into almost all the villages of the State. This has once again necessitated the construction of numerous bridges and the maintenance of the roads in good condition. The Panchayat roads are for the most part unmetalled, but they allow motor traffic. Recently a permanent Road Board of officials and non-officials has been constituted to study the question of roads and their useful extension.

Railway

15. The Cochin State Railway is a metre-gauge line running for 65 miles from Shoranur to Ernakulam. It is completely owned by the State, but it is managed by the South Indian Railway Company, Limited, under an agreement. The State's share of profits on its working has been increasing and in recent years it has been paying a return of 7 to 8 per cent on the capital investment of about 76 lakhs of rupees. We have already seen that the line is being converted into a broad-gauge one in connection with the development of the Cochin harbour. There are other schemes also of railway extension to the interior under Government consideration.

Forest Tramway

16. The chief means of transport for working the forests were elephant labour, pack bullocks, carting, floating and rafting. These could not give access to some of the thick virgin-forest regions where the extractable quantity of timber was found out by a survey to be enormous. Accordingly the scheme of constructing a Forest Tramway was put through and it was opened for traffic in 1905. The Cochin State Forest Tramway is 52 miles in length and taps about 128 square miles of forest area. By its means large quantities of valuable species of timber are being extracted and transported to sale depots in the plains

and sold there to the best advantage. The extension of the line to the British Anamalai hills may further strengthen the port of Cochin as the principal outlet for the rubber, tea and timber of the hinterland.

Power resources

17. Wood serves as the main fuel supply for all the steam engines working in the State. It is only the railway that has replaced it by coal. The lower calorific value of wood fuel is, however, compensated for by its comparative cheapness. It is possible that the harbour improvements would make the transport of coal into Cochin cheap. In that case wood fuel is not unlikely to be confined to household use in the future. Even otherwise the world tendency to replace wood and coal by the more economic and convenient oil-fuel has affected Cochin also, which accordingly has begun to show a preference for oil engines.

Hydro-electricity

18. There is one other potential source of power which, if fully developed, could make it very cheap in the State. The physical features and rainfall condition of the State are such that there are waterfalls in the Chalakkudi river which can be profitably harnessed to generate electric power. Up on the hills 30 miles from Chalakkudi station on the Cochin Railway are the waterfalls of Poringalkuttu, a fall of about 500 feet, which can generate without storage some 3,500 horse power. The project was investigated in detail by experts 15 years ago and again during the last year and a regular scheme complete with sketches and estimates has been placed in the hands of the Government. If the necessary finances are forthcoming, it can be launched immediately. A survey of the existing load market has shown that it can be put on a profitable working basis as soon as power is made available.

Forests and forest products

19. Fully exposed to the force of the Arbaian sea branch of the south-west monsoon, the State has a normal rainfall of 117·8″. Precipitation increases in intensity as we proceed towards the ghat area in the east which supports a thick growth of luxuriant natural vegetation. This constitutes the forests of the State, an extent of 582·25 square miles (about 39 per cent of the total area of the State). In the first decade of the present century the forests represented about 43 per cent of the total area. It is evident that the forests are being cleared for cultivation purposes under the pressure of increasing population.

Timber

20. The forests abound in such valuable timbers as teak, rose-wood and ebony and common jungle woods like *irul* (Xylia dolabriformis), *vedan korna* (Bignomia xylocarpa), *kunni vaka* (Albizza odoratizzima) and many other well-known timbers. There are innumerable species awaiting further exploitation. The total outturn of timber during the period August 1930—31 was 27,975 candis of $12\frac{10}{27}$ cubic feet each. In addition a quantity of 4,500 tons of fuel was also removed. Teak wood and rose wood are established timbers and costly. Jungle wood on the other hand is comparatively cheap because of its supposed inferiority, though it is being used as a useful substitute for teak for furniture and house-building purposes. Wood technologists are demonstrating that by chemical treatment jungle wood could be used for all kinds of structural work. In the light of this new process the rich supply of jungle wood in the State Forests is likely to prove a source of growing industrial wealth.

Minor forest produce

21. Minor forest produce like cardamom, honey, bees-wax, nux vomica, etc., worth thousands of rupees, are being removed from the State forests every year. A scientific survey of the forests may perhaps bring into economic importance many minor products that are now being wasted, because they are but imperfectly known.

Match manufacture

Soft wood for match making is known to exist in the State forests. There are two match factories in Trichur employing on an average 400 persons daily in addition to finding part time occupation on a piece-work system for scores of families employed in making the empty boxes. The two factories are between them producing about 90,000 gross of match boxes annually, and protected by a heavy import duty there is scope for further expansion. Thousands of gross of boxes are being imported into the State every year while the local matches are finding a market in the dry regions of the Madras Presidency. The factories should be improved to produce matches that can stand the most moist days of the monsoon months, before they can find a local market. The most common timbers used at present are *poola* (Bombax malabaricum) and *elavu* (Eriodendron anfractuosum) while there are other varieties which could be chosen with equal success. The most suitable timber has to be experimented upon and its production concentrated in regular plantations.

Paper manufacture

22. Bamboo pulp after exhaustive experiments has been found to be equal to wood pulp for paper manufacture. The strength of bamboo paper has been tested and found to be actually greater than that of paper made out of *sabai* grass, the most common raw material used in North Indian paper factories. Bamboos grow in plenty in our forests and two to three lakhs of these are being cut and removed from the forests annually. In 1930—31 Cochin imported 34,491 cwts. of paper and paste-board valued at Rs. 1,91,151*. When the contemplated hydro-electric scheme materialises, the possibilities of a paper factory seem to deserve special investigation.

Agricultural products

23. Rainfall in Cochin is not only heavy but regular as to time and quantity. The net area sown in the State is 507,836** acres, representing about 53 per cent of the total area. The following statement gives a general idea of the area under some of the important crops which supply most of the raw materials for the industries of the State.

Rice	307,434	acres.
Millets and Ragi	7,699	,,
Pulses and other food grains	46,600	,,
Cocoanut	47,986	,,
Ground-nut	16,571	,,
Other oil seeds	10,668	,,
Sugar-cane	682	,,
Fruit and vegetables including root crops	74,287	,,

The State is not at all self-sufficient regarding its food products. In 1930—31, 56,486 tons of unhusked paddy valued at Rs. 36,05,332 and 183,206 tons of rice (husked), the staple food of the State, valued at Rs. 1,76,54,331 were imported into the port of Cochin in addition to 27,954 tons of other grains valued at Rs. 41,71,856. During the same period Calicut and Aleppy imported 60,605 and 25,147 tons of rice respectively and it might therefore be assumed that a considerable proportion of the imports into Cochin was for State use. This leaves out of account the large quantity of paddy and rice imported by road. It was during the war-period when imports suffered that the problem of food scarcity was brought home to the State and, as stated in Chapter I, all possible measures are being adopted to increase the area under cultivation. The

* The quantity imported by rail is not included here.

**These statistics refer to 1927—28 and are taken from the Agricultural statistics of India, Part II issued by the department of Commercial Intelligence and Statistics, India. The total area under occupation and cultivation in 1930—31 was 508,357 acres.

present international position of agriculture is one of over-production and fall in the price of commodities. When cheap foreign grains are flooding the market, it is not worth while for Cochin to be self-sufficient. Further the census returns show that, of the total population, 247,000 persons are directly employed on land. In other words there is one person to every 2·5 acres of cultivated land. When compared with 1921, there is to be noted a decrease in the area of the average individual holdings. Land for cultivation is limited in the State; and there is therefore a limit to the extent to which agriculture can afford to absorb increasing numbers of workmen. The adoption of intensive and improved methods of cultivation may ease the situation to a certain extent; and the raising of suitable raw materials for the building up of small industries in agricultural villages, which will give subsidiary occupation to agriculturists, and thus partly alleviate the evils of over-crowding, will also be a move in the right direction.

Census statistics

24. Trade and Industries in Cochin are getting organized. We have seen that in 1930—31 there were 214 joint stock companies working in the State. Of these 8 are industrial concerns. In addition there are 96 factories* that come under the Factory Regulation. There are no official statistics available, showing the number of operatives employed in them. According to certain figures supplied by the Inspector of Factories, the total number of persons employed in 67 of the 104 factories is seen to be about 10,000. If the remaining 37 factories also are taken into consideration, the number employed in organized industries of the regulated factory type only should be much more than that returned at the census. In addition there are the joint stock trading concerns and small unregulated factories, which for census purposes are all organized. As such it does not pay us to study the census figures for organized industries as they cannot give us a helping lead. The fact is occupational analysis in census returns is on the most restricted scale and only tendencies of a very general character could be indicated. Even this is made difficult as there are no official statistics to act as checks. But the very increase in numbers is striking. At the end of the intercensal period the population of the State has increased by 23 per cent. There are 187,371 more earners and working dependents in 1931 than actual workers in 1921 and the decade has had to find increased occupational accommodation for these additional numbers. How this new demand as represented by the increased population has been met by the different occupations is fully explained in Part I of this chapter. We have only to observe that the decade has registered an absolute decrease in the number employed in industries which is for the most part explained by the transition from the domestic to the factory system of production, which always throws out of adjustment a number of cottage workers. Even this has a redeeming feature in that most of those thus displaced are women. But woman 'wage-earner' as distinct from woman 'home-worker' is assuming importance in the State. There is also acute unemployment among the educated middle classes. And the remedy that suggests itself to provide means of living for the increasing numbers is rapid industrialisation by the multiplication of factories and industrial establishments.

25. Having considered the more important factors on which the development of industries in general depends, we may broadly review the present condition of industries in the State.

---

* These are not registered joint stock companies and are therefore not included in the 214 joint stock companies referred to above.

Cocoanut oil pressing is an important organized industry. The coastal taluks of Cochin, with a well distributed rainfall and their sandy soil containing plenty of decayed vegetable matter, are particularly suitable for the growth of the cocoanut palm. The dry kernal of the nut gives an oil which is edible and at the same time suitable for making soaps and margarine. The increasing demand for the oil and the consequent increased prices have stimulated the activity of the people in planting trees and in expressing oil.* Malabar *copra* (dried kernal of the cocoanut) in general yields a high quality oil and, under the trade name of 'Cochin oil', it has always commanded a good price in the world's markets. Oil pressing was a cottage industry from time immemorial. But the heavy demand for the oil has been displacing the country *chucks* by mills worked by power, of which there are 13 oil mills and 8 combined rice and oil mills. In 1930—31 ten of the mills are reported to have produced about 3½ million gallons of oil. The total export of oil during the same period from the port of Cochin was 4,441,156 gallons valued at Rs. 68,81,189. During the last decade the highest figure of Rs. 1,54,99,596 was reached in 1921—22. The decrease noted in the value of exports is solely due to fall in price. Cochin mills depend for their raw material on the State production as well as imports from Travancore. In 1907 the Travancore Government imposed a heavy export duty on *copra*. At the same time there was an increasing export of *copra* to the continental countries of Europe from Cochin. And the Cochin mills received a set back. In fact several mills were transferred to Travancore. During the closing years of the last decade the export of *copra* from Cochin was hardly anything. In 1930—31 it was only 46 tons valued at Rs. 8,826. On the other hand the low prices prevailing in Ceylon have made it possible for oil-millers in Cochin to import Ceylon copra. There is no knowing whether these tendencies will continue. The mills with the exception of the Tatas are comparatively small concerns and they are following an individualistic policy. By a system of 'rationalisation' the industry can be put on a more profitable basis. **Organized industries: cocoanut oil pressing**

26. *Poonac* or oilcake is also an important item of export. 10,665 tons of this article valued at Rs. 8,57,508 was exported from the port of Cochin in 1930—31. This is the lowest figure for the last ten years. Evidently the depression has affected this trade. The largest quantity exported during the decade was in 1922—23 when *poonac* valued at Rs. 22,21,438 was shipped from the port of Cochin. **Oilcake**

27. Some of the mills have also taken to other oil seeds like *marowtti*, castor, gingelly, etc. Gingelly is cultivated as a second crop in single crop wet lands. The cultivation of gingelly and the extraction of its oil on a scale which is more extensive than the present cannot but be profitable since gingelly oil has a local demand and thousands of maunds of it are being imported annually into the State. **Other oils**

28. Malabar has almost the monopoly for lemon-grass (Andropogon Schœnanthus) oil which is largely in demand in Europe and America for the manufacture of soaps and scents. From the port of Cochin a quantity of 41,886 gallons of this oil valued at Rs. 5,25,512 was exported in 1930—31. The contribution of this State towards the trade is quite insignificant. Lemon-grass is growing wild in our forests. Its regular cultivation and the organized production of oil from it will be profitable industries. But nothing could be done immediately as there is a heavy slump in this trade. **Lemon-grass oil**

29. The different oils expressed in the State can serve as raw materials for the manufacture of soaps. The Tatas have already taken to this industry **Soap**

* The present depression has seriously affected this industry, and several oil mills have been temporarily closed down.

and their soaps have begun to command markets. There are a few other small soap-works also doing unorganized business. In spite of this we find that there is actually an increasing import of this toilet necessity into Cochin. This chemical industry deserves to be organized on a sound basis since both the raw materials and the market are at hand.

Coir manufacture

30. Coir is the fibre extracted from the husk that encloses the cocoanut. The extraction of this fibre and the preparation of coir yarn have been essential Cochin industries as far back as can be traced. The husk is soaked in water for about 6 to 12 months and the fibre is beaten out by hand. The 'retting' that is necessary localises the industry in the coastal regions, though in the interior tracts unsoaked fibre which is inferior to the soaked in strength and colour is prepared. Europe was a market for unmanufactured coir; but with the increase in the manufacture of coir in Cochin and Travancore export of fibre has been decreasing. At the same time exports of manufactured coir are on the increase. In 1930—31 manufactured coir, including yarn, mats and matting, weighing 539,480 cwts. and valued at Rs. 86,34,681, was exported from Cochin. The highest value of export during the last decade was in 1921—22 when manufactured coir worth Rs. 1,15,37,502 was shipped from the port. The large decrease in the value of export is due to the fall in the price of the commodity.

During the same period a quantity of 51,484 cwts. of cordage and rope also was exported. Most of this goes to the other Indian ports and the average quantity of export has been kept up. It may do well to tap foreign markets for these articles as coir ropes are found to possess good wearing qualities in water. The manufacture of coir has always been a domestic occupation in the coastal districts. With the increasing demand for coir products factories are springing up and there are six of them in operation to-day.

Other fibres

31. There are many other fibrous plants growing wild in the State, out of which ropes of varying thickness, intensity and strength and mats and mattings are being manufactured. In 1930—31, 570,842 square yards of such mats and mattings were shipped from the port of Cochin. Hemp is grown in the State but its fibre is now used only to provide warp for grass mats. *Vakka* (Sterculia villosa) gives a stout and strong rope. Wild in the plains and forests grows the sedge grass (Cyprous corimbosus) with which are made mats of excellent quality for every day use and as cheap substitutes for carpets (the ordinary size being 6″ × 3″). Their prices range from a few annas to twenty-five rupees or even more. Mats of any and every kind of design are worked out of the grass by the Kakkalans, a sort of gypsies of the State, of whom there are 732.

Similarly mats made out of the screw-pine leaves (Pandanus oderatisimus) are also meeting household and coarse packing requirements. The manufacture of these mats is now a cottage industry and those engaged in the pursuit are doing things off and on according to their convenience. There is a market for these articles, if they could be supplied in a business-like fashion. Private capitalists would do well to open small factories to collect weavers of these mats and thus organize the trade.

Cotton weaving

32. One other vegetable fibre, which the soil and heavy rainfall of the State do not permit of successful cultivation, but on which an industry has grown up, deserves special mention. As in other parts of India, so here also cotton weaving has been a hereditary occupation, the castes in Cochin engaged in this trade being chiefly the Chaliyans, Kaikolans and Chedars (Devangans of the Caste Table), together numbering about 9,000. The importance of the industry in the economy of the State is very much of a local character. It must be said to the credit of the weavers that in the manufacture of certain varieties

of cloth favoured by the local people they stand unrivalled, but when it comes to cloth in competition with that manufactured in power mills they must acknowledge defeat. The present "Buy Indian" mentality is an opportunity to organize them as well as those engaged in other industries. It is a happy sign of the times that, under the *Swadesi* stimulus, small weaving factories equipped with improved appliances are being opened by enterprising private individuals. There is also one large scale factory, the Sitaram Spinning and Weaving Mills, Limited, Trichur, equipped with up-to-date machineries and employing on an average 1,300 persons a day. Their total production of cloth in 1931—32 was 7,471,279 yards. That there is scope for the expansion of this industry in the State is evidenced by the large import of cheap mill made cloth. A quantity of 13,207,091 yards of piece-goods valued at Rs. 65,33,963 was landed at the port of Cochin in 1930—31. Most of this belongs to the coasting trade, though it is noteworthy that the import of foreign cloth into Cochin is increasing while other Indian ports are recording a decrease.

Leather industry

33. The Chakkiliyans and Tolkollans who together number more than 2,400 at the present census follow leather industry as their traditional occupation. Of late, however, enterprising Christians, Muslims and Jews have been organizing small workshops for the manufacture of sandals, slippers, boots, shoes, suit-cases, brief-bags, irrigation buckets, etc. There are several of these shops employing a dozen or more workmen in the important towns of the State, and it is estimated that the quantity of tanned hides and skins consumed by them is between 4 and 5 thousand cwts. annually. This is now imported from outside, while the raw hides and skins available in the State are collected and exported by small dealers. There is therefore scope for a successful tannery in Cochin, though past attempts have been failures. Thus a small concern started at Trichur in 1904 failed because of bad management and lack of technical knowledge; and we have seen from paragraph 2 above that the ambitious project of the Cochin Tanneries, Limited, shared the same fate. Here the best part of the capital was locked up in land and buildings and plant and machinery, so much so that the company had not even the minimum necessary working capital when work was to be started. Even now it is not perhaps too late to begin work on a small scale and carry the project to ultimate success as Mr. Guthrie has suggested.

Ceramic industry

34. The geology of the State is such that it provides materials for building purposes and for the successful conduct of a ceramic industry. This has been a cottage industry with the hereditary potters (Kusavans and Odans), of whom there are about 4,800 in the State. They supply common earthen vessels for the domestic use of the poorer classes. Cheap metal-ware is rapidly displacing earthen-ware and hence this industry is on the decline.

The red clay deposits in certain parts of the State have been tested and found to be highly suitable for the manufacture of bricks, terracottah and tiles, and an expanding industry in the manufacture of tiles and bricks has already been built up. There are at present 34 brick and tile factories in the State and this industry has accordingly been completely taken out of the potters' hands. Correct figures showing the output of these factories are not available, but about 21 of them, together employing a 1,000 labourers, are known to have manufactured 8,646,600 tiles and bricks in 1930-31. If the outturn of the other 12 factories also are included, the total must exceed 10 millions. These tiles and bricks are very much in demand in the State and the supply is also sufficient to meet in part the requirements of South Malabar, Travancore and some of the eastern districts of the Madras Presidency.

The economic occurrence of various kinds of raw material for a ceramic industry in the State has not yet been fully ascertained. The Government Stoneware Factory at Chalakkudi was started with the object of manufacturing glazed wares. The factory did not succeed in this particular line and now it is making minton tiles, drainage pipes, firebricks and vitrified stable-bricks; which compare very favourably with similar articles of standard specification. Some experts opine that for the particular variety of glazed wares, for which the factory was opened, the necessary raw materials do not occur in the State. In the circumstances a survey of them seems essential.

Building industries

35. Interested promoters are very sanguine about a cement factory in the State. We are importing about 5,000 tons of portland cement a year, about half of which comes from abroad and the other half from Indian cement factories. As we have no successful cement works in Southern India, the prospects of a cement factory in Cochin are worth investigation. Shells are gathered in large quantities from the backwaters and they are burnt in lime-kilns to supply cement for pointing and plastering.

Laterite which is peculiar to Malabar and which is particularly suitable for building purposes is used for the masonry work of all substantial structures. Likewise granite is used for the foundations of buildings, for walls, road-metalling and the preparation of concrete. The quarrying of laterite and granite is thus an industry of importance which supports considerable numbers.

Plantation industries

36. The Malabar coast below the Western Ghats has climatic conditions and surface features favourable for the cultivation of coffee, tea and rubber. Plantations of these are growing in importance in the State. The Nelliampathi hills attracted foreign capitalists from early times as a suitable area for coffee cultivation, and between the years 1862 and 1870 about 9,470 acres were leased out to various companies and private individuals. Most of the coffee is exported, and owing to want of transport facilities, the acreage under cultivation has been decreasing and to-day there are only about 6,000 acres under coffee. The Nelliampathi ghat road recently opened is likely to overcome transport difficulties, and it may have a happy reaction in increasing the acreage under coffee and tea (for tea is displacing coffee to a certain extent). Rubber among plantation industries has the greatest acreage to-day. The first rubber plantation was started in 1905 in Palapilli hills. Ever since the number of plantations has been increasing and to-day there are seven of them with an aggregate area of about 10,000 acres. In 1930—31, 8,462,303 lbs. of raw rubber valued at Rs. 51,41,690 was exported from Cochin. The highest figures during the last decade were reached in 1925—26, when 8,666,861 lbs. of rubber valued at Rs. 1,03,83,349 was exported. The difference between the two sets of figures is remarkable and it gives an idea of the extent to which the price of rubber has fallen. As a result there has been a set back in the production of rubber and the factories are busy getting inactive. The prices are so low that they do not meet the cost of production, not to speak of interest on capital and profit.

Metal industries

37. The growth of factories equipped with machineries worked by power has necessitated the import of machinery and mill-work. This has been an expanding import commodity, and the depression is responsible for the low value of imports in 1930—31, which amounted to Rs. 2,94,730 only. But the import of iron and steel as raw materials for the manufacture of spare parts is not encouraging. There are a few foundries in Trichur and Mattancheri, but they cannot cope with the existing demand. The increase in motor traffic and the development of the harbour are sure to call for the services of more and better equipped foundries and smithy shops than there are to-day.

Metal industries remind us of Moosaris, the hereditary bell-metal workers of Cochin. There are about 1,500 of them in the State. They make all kinds of vessels, from 'a tiny cup to a cauldron thirty feet in diameter and weighing 10 hundred weights' and lamps, bells, etc. Though the methods employed by them are old-fashioned, the articles turned out are of the best quality. A search of old aristocratic family houses will bring to light from the 'rubbish heap' precious jewels of the Moosaris' art like bell-metal mirrors of the highest polish and beautiful images of every description. A few small factories for the manufacture and sale of bell-metal articles opened at convenient centres and worked on improved methods would surely succeed financially. Cheap aluminium wares have affected the Moosaris' trade very adversely. Sheet metal work they can pursue with advantage. It is pertinent to note here that the bell-metal workers of Katavalloor in Talapilli taluk, who do plates by the hammering process, are prospering much better than other Moosaris because of the comparative cheapness of the articles they make. Trade in Katavalloor is also better organized than elsewhere.

Wood-work and carpentry

38. This is one of the few industries in Cochin where machinery has yet to force access. True there are saw-mills in the State, but all branches of wood-work are in the hands of hereditary carpenters (Asaris), of whom there are more than 23,000. They are good workmen and some of them excel as carvers. But the latter lack encouragement, and therefore they do carving only as a subsidiary occupation without making any attempt to specialise in the art. Their development is typical of the development of cottage workers in general, and after a reference to the problem of the cottage worker, we shall close this article.

Problem of cottage industries

39. We have seen how there is a tendency on the part of industries in Cochin to get organized on modern factory lines. It is remarkable that, in spite of this tendency, the State is in 'substantial possession' of its cottage industries, even though cheap machine-made goods are everywhere available. More than 80 per cent of those engaged in industries as earners and working dependents are pursuing them on a domestic basis. In paragraph 32 above, it was stated that the artisan weaver was supreme in the manufacture of certain special varieties of cloth favoured by the locality. It is such specialised products that have kept them going in the face of competition. At the same time, competition is leaving its mark on the earning capacity of the unorganized cottage workers. A two-fold remedy suggests itself for the removal of the defects of the present situation. It is education and organization. The artisans have to be trained in the use of improved tools and methods and sub-division of processes, so that their technical skill may improve. Further, they have also to be taught to be business-like. This cannot but lead to enhanced efficiency, cheap production and increased demand. If new markets for the various products are also captured through advertisement, the cottage industries will be assured of a bright future. The Industrial Exhibitions held by the Government at regular intervals in different centres have been of some assistance in this connection. But the real solution for the problem lies in the organization of Industrial Co-operative Societies for the production and sale of the artisans' products. An individual debt-ridden artisan is helpless, and if he is left to himself, he can only move in a vicious circle, and be exploited by enterprising middlemen. It is here that the help of the Co-operative Societies is required. In the initial stages the opening of Government stores for the sale of cottage industry products may also be of considerable use. The results achieved by such stores in some of the Indian States like Mysore and Hyderabad are encouraging. A store may be organized here also. Even if this involves some risk in the early stages, it is justifiable in view of the supreme importance of the whole question relating to the economic progress and well-being of the artisan classes.

SUBSIDIARY TABLES

I (a)—General distribution by occupation

[Earners (principal occupation) and working dependents]

Class, Sub-class and Order	Number per 10,000 of total population	Percentage recorded	
		In cities and urban industrial areas	In rural areas
1	2	3	
NON-WORKING DEPENDENTS ..	4,904	12	88
ALL OCCUPATIONS:			
[EARNERS (PRINCIPAL OCCUPATION) AND WORKING DEPENDENTS] ..	5,096	11	89
A PRODUCTION OF RAW MATERIALS ..	2,131	3	97
I. Exploitation of Animals and Vegetation ..	2,131	3	97
1. Pasture and Agriculture ..	2,053	2	98
(a) Cultivation ..	1,753	2	98
(b) Cultivation of special crops, fruit, etc. ..	213	3	97
(c) Forestry ..	25	5	95
(d) Stock raising ..	62	3	97
(e) Raising of small animals and insects ..	..	..	100
2. Fishing and Hunting ..	78	5	95
II. Exploitation of Minerals ..	..	18	82
4. Non-Metallic Minerals ..	..	18	82
B. PREPARATION AND SUPPLY OF MATERIAL SUBSTANCES ..	1,364	15	85
III. Industry ..	895	11	89
5. Textiles ..	339	7	93
6. Hides, skins and Hard materials from the animal kingdom ..	4	25	75
7. Wood ..	191	10	90
8. Metals ..	36	17	83
9. Ceramics ..	26	3	97
10. Chemical products, properly so called and analogous ..	31	30	70
11. Food Industries ..	74	10	90
12. Industries of dress and the toilet ..	83	12	88
13. Furniture Industries ..	1	93	7
14. Building Industries ..	68	11	89
15. Construction of means of transport ..	1	31	69
16. Production and transmission of Physical force ..	..	95	5
17. Miscellaneous and undefined Industries ..	41	22	78
IV. Transport ..	121	28	72
19. Transport by water ..	38	31	69
20. Transport by road ..	73	27	73
21. Transport by rail ..	8	18	82
22. Post Office, Telegraph and Telephone services ..	2	37	63
V. Trade ..	348	22	78
23. Banks, establishments of credit, exchange and insurance ..	21	34	66

I (a)—General distribution by occupation
[Earners (principal occupation) and working dependents].—(cont.)

Class, Sub-class and Order	Number per 10,000 of total population	Percentage recorded	
		In cities and urban industrial areas	In rural areas
1	2	3	4
24. Brokerage commission and export ..	1	34	66
25. Trade in textiles ..	17	26	74
26. Trade in skins, leather and furs ..	1	57	43
27. Trade in wood ..	6	16	84
28. Trade in metals ..	2	55	45
29. Trade in pottery, bricks and tiles ..	3	7	93
30. Trade in chemical products ..	5	33	67
31. Hotels, cafes, restaurants, etc. ..	42	26	74
32. Other trade in food-stuffs ..	172	15	85
33. Trade in clothing and toilet articles ..	1	63	37
34. Trade in furniture ..	5	20	80
35. Trade in building materials ..	3	4	96
36. Trade in means of transport ..	7	37	
37. Trade in fuel ..	7	10	90
38. Trade in articles of luxury and those pertaining to letters and the arts and sciences ..	3	51	49
39. Trade of other sorts ..	52	30	70
C. PUBLIC ADMINISTRATION AND LIBERAL ARTS..	158	25	75
VI. Public Force ..	8	39	61
40. Army ..	..	1	99
43. Police ..	8	42	58
VII. Public Administration ..	30	35	65
44. Public Administration ..	39	35	65
VIII. Professions and Liberal Arts ..	141	22	78
45. Religion ..	36	15	85
46. Law ..	7	47	53
47. Medicine ..	24	22	78
48. Instruction ..	51	24	76
49. Letters, arts and sciences ..	23	19	81
D. MISCELLANEOUS ..	1,413	18	82
IX. Persons living on their income ..	23	27	73
50. Persons living principally on their income ..	23	27	73
X. Domestic Service ..	1,169	16	84
51. Domestic service ..	1,169	16	84
XI. Insufficiently described occupations ..	211	30	70
52. General terms which do not indicate a definite occupation ..	211	30	70
XII. Unproductive ..	10	22	78
53. Inmates of Jails, asylums and alms houses ..	2	6	94
54. Beggars, vagrants, prostitutes, etc. ..	8	25	75
55. Other unclassified non-productive industries ..	..	100	..

I (b)—General distribution by occupation (Earners as subsidiary occupation).

Class, Sub-class and Order	Number per 10,000 of total population	Percentage recorded	
		In cities and urban industrial areas	In rural areas
1	2	3	4
ALL OCCUPATIONS :			
(EARNERS AS SUBSIDIARY OCCUPATION)	828	4	96
A. PRODUCTION OF RAW MATERIALS	292	3	97
I. Exploitation of Animals and Vegetation	291	2	98
1. Pasture and Agriculture	280	2	98
(a) Cultivation	169	3	97
(b) Cultivation of special crops, fruit, etc.	99	2	98
(c) Forestry	7	..	100
(d) Stock raising	5	2	98
(e) Raising of small animals and insects	..	..	100
2. Fishing and Hunting	11	2	98
II. Exploitation of Minerals	1	..	100
3. Metallic Minerals	..	..	100
4 Non-Metallic Minerals	1	..	100
B. PREPARATION AND SUPPLY OF MATERIAL SUBSTANCES	174	5	95
III. Industry	89	3	97
5. Textiles	25	2	98
6. Hides, skins, and Hard materials from the animal kingdom	..	..	100
7. Wood	28	2	98
8. Metals	1	16	84
9. Ceramics	1	36	64
10. Chemical products properly so called and analogous	4	5	95
11. Food Industries	17	3	97
12. Industries of dress and the toilet	6	4	96
13. Furniture Industries	..	69	31
14 Building Industries	6	4	96
15. Construction of means of transport	..	30	70
16 Production and transmission of Physical force	..	100	..
17. Miscellaneous and undefined Industries	1	10	90
IV. Transport	19	7	93
19. Transport by water	7	9	91
20. Transport by road	12	5	95
21. Transport by rail	..	36	64
22. Post Office, Telegraph and Telephone services	..	6	94
V. Trade	66	6	94
23. Banks, establishments of credit, exchange and insurance	10	16	84
24. Brokerage commission and export	..	6	94

I (b)—General distribution by occupation.—(cont.)
(Earners as Subsidiary occupation)

Class, Sub-class and Order	Number per 10,000 of total population	Percentage recorded	
		In cities and urban industrial areas	In rural areas
	2	3	4
V. Trade—(cont.)			
25 Trade in Textiles ..	4	6	94
26 Trade in skins, leather and furs ..	..	10	90
27 Trade in wood ..	2	8	92
28 Trade in metals ..	..	34	66
29 Trade in pottery, bricks and tiles ..	..	2	98
30 Trade in chemical products ..	1	7	93
31 Hotels, cafes, restaurants, etc. ..	4	5	95
32 Other trade in food stuffs ..	27	3	97
33 Trade in clothing and toilet articles ..	..	30	70
34 Trade in furniture ..	1	3	97
35 Trade in building materials ..	..	..	100
36 Trade in means of transport ..	3	9	91
37 Trade in fuel ..	2	9	91
38 Trade in articles of luxury and those pertaining to letters and the arts and sciences ..	1	12	88
39 Trade of other sorts ..	1	4	96
C. PUBLIC ADMINISTRATION AND LIBERAL ARTS ..	2	7	93
VI. Public Force ..	..	28	72
43 Police ..	..	28	72
VII. Public Administration ..	2	6	94
44 Public Administration ..	2	6	94
VIII. Professions and Liberal Arts ..	22	7	93
45 Religion ..	6	6	94
46 Law ..	1	12	88
47 Medicine ..	4	6	94
48 Instruction ..	4	7	93
49 Letters, arts and sciences ..	7	8	92
D. MISCELLANEOUS ..	338	5	95
IX. Persons living on their income ..	12	19	81
50 Persons living principally on their income ..	12	19	81
X. Domestic Service ..	300	4	96
51 Domestic Service ..	300	4	96
XI. Insufficiently described occupations ..	24	3	97
52 General terms which do not indicate a definite occupation ..	24	3	97
XII. Unproductive ..	2	..	100
53 Inmates of Jails, asylums and alms houses ..	..	..	100
54 Beggars, vagrants, prostitutes, etc. ..	1	..	100
55 Other unclassified non-productive industries ..	1	..	100

II.—Distribution of occupation by sub-classes in Natural Divisions.

(a) Earners (principal occupation) and working dependents.

NATURAL DIVISION "Malabar and Konkan"	Total 1,000			Number per mille of the total population occupied as Earners (principal occupation) and working dependents in											
	Non-working Dependents	Working Dependents	Earners (principal occupation)	Sub-class I—Exploitation of Animals and Vegetation	Sub-class II—Exploitation of Minerals	Sub-class III—Industry	Sub-class IV—Transport	Sub-class V—Trade	Sub-class VI—Public Force	Sub-class VII Public Administration	Sub-class VIII—Professions and Liberal Arts	Sub-class IX—Persons living on their income	Sub-class X—Domestic service	Sub-class XI—Insufficiently described occupations	Sub-class XII—Unproductive
1	2	3	4	5	6	7	8	9	10	11	12	13	14	15	16
COCHIN STATE ..	491	122	387	213	..	89	12	35	1	4	14	2	117	21	1

(b) Earners (Subsidiary occupation.)

NATURAL DIVISION "Malabar and Konkan"	Number per mille of total population, of earners having a subsidiary occupation in											
	Sub-class I—Exploitation of Animals and Vegetation	Sub-class II—Exploitation of Minerals	Sub-class III—Industry	Sub-class IV—Transport	Sub-class V—Trade	Sub-class VI—Public Force	Sub-class VII—Public Administration	Sub-class VIII—Professions and Liberal Arts	Sub-class IX—Persons living on their income	Sub-class X—Domestic service	Sub-class XI—Insufficiently described occupations	Sub-class XII—Unproductive
1	2	3	4	5	6	7	8	9	10	11	12	13
COCHIN STATE ..	29	..	9	2	7	..	..	2	1	30	2	..

III—Occupation of females by sub-classes, and selected orders and groups.

Group No.	Occupation	Number of Earners (principal occupation) and working dependents — Males	Number of Earners (principal occupation) and working dependents — Females	Number of females per 1,000 males
1	2	3	4	5
	I. EXPLOITATION OF ANIMALS AND VEGETATION ..	163,375	93,334	571
	1. Pasture and Agriculture ..	155,082	92,318	595
1	Non-cultivating proprietors taking rent in money or kind ..	3,619	2,928	809
5	Cultivating owners ..	18,698	4,715	252
6	Tenants ..	40,497	9,747	241
7	Agricultural labourers ..	61,394	68,394	1,114
10	Cocoanut cultivation ..	13,407	3,342	249
13	Pan-vine cultivation ..	1,571	328	209
14	Rubber plantation ..	1,223	339	277
15	Tea plantation ..	1,000	539	539
16	Market gardeners, flower and fruit growers ..	2,683	775	289
18	Wood cutters and charcoal burners ..	1,900	88	46
21	Cattle and buffalo breeders and keepers ..	2,444	194	79
23	Herdsmen, shepherds and breeders of other animals ..	4,447	359	81
	2. Fishing and Hunting ..	8,293	1,016	123
27	Fishing and pearling ..	8,275	1,016	123
	II. EXPLOITATION OF MINERALS ..	10	12	1,200
	4. Non-metallic minerals ..	10	12	1,200
37	Building materials (including stone, materials for cement-manufacture and clay) ..	10	12	1,200
	III. INDUSTRY ..	60,459	47,376	784
	5. Textiles ..	14,107	26,714	1,894
43	Cotton spinning, sizing and weaving ..	4,028	2,071	514
45	Rope, twine, string and other fibres ..	10,043	21,630	2,452
	7. Wood ..	14,405	8,602	597
54	Sawyers ..	3,277	6	2
55	Carpenters, turners and joiners, &c. ..	7,734	47	6
56	Basket makers and other industries of woody materials, including leaves and thatchers and builders working with bamboo, reeds or similar materials ..	3,394	8,549	2,519
	8. Metals ..	3,920	379	97
59	Blacksmiths, other workers in iron, makers of implements ..	2,567	257	100
	9. Ceramics ..	1,881	1,251	665
63	Potters and makers of earthen-ware ..	1,170	1,002	856
	10. Chemical products properly so called and analogous ..	3,328	461	139
68	Manufacture and refining of vegetable oils ..	2,566	342	133
	11. Food industries ..	5,836	3,093	530
71	Rice pounders and huskers and flour grinders ..	130	2,342	18,015

III.—Occupation of females by sub-classes, and selected orders and groups.—(cont.)

Group No.	Occupation	Number of Earners (principal occupation) and working dependents		Number of females per 1,000 males
		Males	Females	
1	2	3	4	5
	11. Food industries—(*cont.*)			
75	Sweet-meat and condiment makers ..	597	684	1,146
76	Toddy drawers ..	4,514	59	13
	12. Industries of dress and the toilet ..	4,788	5,154	1,076
83	Tailors, milliners, dress-makers and darners ..	1,305	246	189
85	Washing and cleaning ..	1,632	4,370	2,678
86	Barbers, hair-dressers and wig-makers ..	1,767	528	299
	14. Building industries ..	7,586	642	85
90	Lime burners, cement workers; excavators and well-sinkers; stone cutters and dressers; brick layers and masons; builders (other than buildings made of bamboo or similar materials), painters, decorators of houses, tilers, plumbers, etc. ..	7,586	642	85
	17. Miscellaneous and undefined industries ..	3,908	1,068	273
98	Makers of jewellery and ornaments ..	2,803	72	26
99	Other miscellaneous and undefined industries (toy-making, taxidermy, etc.) ..	94	421	4,479
100	Scavenging ..	167	573	3,431
	IV TRANSPORT ..	14,039	555	40
	19. Transport by water ..	4,603	10	2
102	Ship-owners, boat-owners and their employees, officers, mariners, etc., ships brokers, boatmen and towmen ..	4,176	10	2
	20. Transport by road ..	8,406	379	45
106	Labourers employed on roads and bridges ..	1,087	169	155
107	Owners, managers, and employees (excluding personal servants) connected with mechanically driven vehicles (including trams) ..	1,341	30	22
108	Owners, managers and employees (excluding personal servants) connected with other vehicles ..	3,875	23	6
111	Porters and messengers ..	1,654	147	89
	V. TRADE ..	33,816	8,148	241
	23. Banks, establishments of credit, exchange and insurance ..	1,630	858	526
115	Bank managers, money lenders, exchange and insurance agents, money changers and brokers and their employees ..	1,630	858	526
	25 Trade in textiles ..	1,935	106	55
117	Trade in piece-goods, wool, cotton, silk, hair and other textiles ..	1,935	106	55
	31. Hotels, Cafes, restaurants, etc. ..	4,389	662	151
127	Owners and managers of hotels, cook-shops, sarais, etc. (and employees) ..	3,384	543	160
	32. Other trade in food stuffs ..	15,556	5,128	329
129	Grain and pulse dealers ..	5,773	939	163
130	Dealers in sweet-meets, sugar and spices ..	3,160	1,824	577

III.—Occupation of females by sub-classes, and selected orders and groups.—(cont.)

Group No.	Occupation	Number of Earners (principal occupation) and working dependents — Males	Females	Number of females per 1,000 males
1	2	3	4	5
	32. Other trade in food stuffs—(*cont.*)			
131	Dealers in dairy products, eggs and poultry ..	644	815	1,266
132	Dealers in animals for food ..	1,407	743	528
134	Dealers in other food stuffs ..	3,834	649	169
	39. Trade of other sorts ..	5,709	547	96
150	General store-keepers and shop-keepers otherwise unspecified ..	5,026	458	91
	VI. PUBLIC FORCE ..	1,027	...	...
	VII. PUBLIC ADMINISTRATION ..	4,627	38	8
	44. Public Administration ..	4,637	38	8
159	Service of the State ..	3,473	21	6
	VIII. PROFESSIONS AND LIBERAL ARTS ..	14,048	2,922	208
	46. Religion ..	3,554	777	219
163	Priests, ministers, etc. ..	1,272	15	12
166	Servants in religious edifices, burial and burning grounds, pilgrim conductors, circumcisers, etc. ..	1,621	656	405
	47. Medicine ..	2,382	479	201
170	Other persons practising the healing arts without being registered ..	1,955	62	32
172	Midwives, vaccinators, compounders, nurses, masseurs, etc. ..	201	402	2,000
	48. Instruction ..	4,788	1,415	296
174	Professors and teachers of all kinds ..	4,337	1,379	318
	49. Letters, arts and sciences (other than 44. Public Administration) ..	2,500	251	100
182	Musicians (composers and performers other than military), actors, dancers, etc. ..	1,319	163	124
	IX. PERSONS LIVING ON THEIR INCOME ..	1,524	1,182	776
	50. Persons living principally on their income ..	1,524	1,182	776
185	Proprietors (other than agricultural land), fund and scholarships holders and pensioners ..	1,524	1,182	776
	X. DOMESTIC SERVICE ..	5,435	135,398	4,912
	51. Domestic service ..	5,435	135,398	24,912
187	Other domestic service ..	5,163	135,398	26 194
	XI. INSUFFICIENTLY DESCRIBED OCCUPATIONS ..	20,477	5,003	244
	52. General terms which do not indicate a definite occupation ..	20,477	5,003	244
189	Cashiers, accountants, book-keepers, clerks and other employees in unspecified offices and warehouses and shops ..	2,683	35	13
191	Labourers and workmen otherwise unspecified ..	16,378	4,967	303
	XII. UNPRODUCTIVE ..	803	443	552
	55. Other unclassified non-productive industries ..	..	6	..
195	Other unclassified non-productive industries ..	..	6	..

IV.—Selected occupations.

Group No.	Occupation		Earners showing occupation as principal and working dependents 1931	Actual workers 1921	Actual workers 1911
1	2		3	4	5
	I. EXPLOITATION OF ANIMALS AND VEGETATION		256,759	213,509	188,319
	1. Pasture and Agriculture	..	247,400	206,895	181,984
2	Non-cultivating proprietors taking rent in money or kind	..	6,547	3,093	2,854
5	Cultivating owners	..	22,413	11,508	11,499
6	Tenants	..	50,244	75,472	61,191
7	Agricultural labourers	..	139,788	101,815	95,373
10	Cocoanut cultivation	..	16,749	..	..
13	Pan-vine cultivation	..	1,899	..	..
14	Rubber plantation	..	1,562 }		
15	Tea plantation	..	2,539 }	1,352	1,641
16	Market gardeners, flower and fruit growers	..	3,458	8,918	5,278
18	Wood cutters and charcoal burners	..	1,088	1,967	1,812
21	Cattle and buffalo breeders and keepers	..	2,638	124	84
23	Herdsmen, shepherds and breeders of other animals	..	4,806	1,323	1,483
	2. Fishing and Hunting	..	9,309	6,614	6,335
27	Fishing and pearling	..	9,291	6,582	6,315
	II. EXPLOITATION OF MINERALS	..	22	..	..
	III. INDUSTRY	..	107,835	103,945	89,644
	5. Textiles	..	40,821	29,949	28,013
43	Cotton spinning, sizing and weaving	..	6,099	4,274	3,177
45	Rope, twine, string and other fibres	..	24,673	25,625	24,833
	7. Wood	..	23,007	20,798	18,220
54	Sawyers	..	3,283	4,352 }	9,348
55	Carpenters, turners and joiners, &c.	..	7,781	7,474 }	
56	Basket makers and other industries of woody materials, including leaves and thatchers and builders working with bamboo, reeds or similar materials	..	11,913	8,072	8,872
	8. Metals	..	4,299	5,056	3,215
57	Blacksmiths, other workers in iron, makers of implements	..	2,824	3,908	2,406
62	Workers in brass, copper and bell-metal	..	1,085	1,017	556
	9. Ceramics	..	3,132	2,701	2,185
63	Potters and makers of earthen-ware	..	2,172	2,245	1,925
	10. Chemical products properly so called and analogous	..	3,789	2,145	1,407
68	Manufacture and refining of vegetable oils	..	2,908	2,067	1,351
	11. Food industries	..	8,928	20,820	17,566
71	Rice pounders and huskers and flour grinders	..	2,472	10,083	9,790

IV.—Selected occupations.—(cont.)

Group No.	Occupation	Earners showing occupation as principal and working dependents 1931	Actual workers 1921	Actual workers 1911
1	2	3	4	5
	11. Food industries—(cont.)			
75	Sweet-meat and condiment makers ..	1,281	1	2
76	Toddy drawers ..	4,571	9,605	6,985
	12. Industries of dress and the toilet ..	9,912	10,652	9,959
83	Tailors, milliners, dress-makers and darners ..	1,551	2,114	1,891
85	Washing and cleaning ..	6,002	5,819	5,502
86	Barbers, hair-dressers and wig-makers ..	2,295	2,478	2,451
	14. Building industries ..	8,228	9,616	4,532
90	Lime burners, cement workers, excavators, and well-sinkers, stone cutters and dressers, brick layers and masons, builders (other than buildings made of bamboo or similar materials), painters, decorators of houses, tilers, plumbers, etc. ..	8,228	9,616	4,532
	17. Miscellaneous and undefined industries ..	4,976	6,341	..
98	Makers of jewellery and ornaments ..	2,875	3,953	2,228
	IV. TRANSPORT ..	14,594	9,118	7,639
	19. Transport by water ..	4,613	3,350	2,921
102	Ship-owners, boat-owners and their employees, officers, mariners, etc., ships brokers, boatmen and towmen ..	4,186	3,164	2,916
	20. Transport by road ..	8,785	4,707	3,873
106	Labourers employed on roads and bridges ..	1,256	541	..
107	Owners, managers and employees (excluding personal servants) connected with mechanically driven vehicles (including trams) ..	1,371	79 }	
108	Owners, managers and employees (excluding personal servants) connected with other vehicles ..	3,898	3,588 }	2,706
111	Porters and messengers ..	1,801	141	252
	V. TRADE ..	41,964	38,513	38,967
	23. Banks, establishments of credit exchange and insurance ..	2,488	2,037	1,439
115	Bank managers, money lenders, exchange and insurance agents, money changers and brokers and their employees ..	2,485	2,037	1,439
	25. Trade in Textiles ..	2,041	2,541	1,898
117	Trade in piece goods, wool, cotton, silk, hair and other textiles ..	2,041	2,541	1,898
	31. Hotels, cafes, restaurants, etc. ..	5,051	4,540	3,757
126	Vendors of wine, liquors, aerated waters and ice ..	1,124	2,739	2,397
127	Owners and managers of hotels, cookshops, sarais etc. (and employees) ..	3,927	4,801	1,360
	32. Other trade in food stuffs ..	20,714	22,324	23,123
129	Grain and pulse dealers ..	6,712	5,355	5,827
130	Dealers in sweet-meats sugar and spices ..	4,984	682	1,815

IV.—Selected occupations.—(cont.)

Group No.	Occupation	Earners showing occupation as principal and working dependents 1931	Actual workers 1921	Actual workers 1911
1	2	3	4	5
	32. Other trade in food stuffs—(*cont.*)			
131	Dealers in dairy products, eggs and poultry ..	1,459	1,343	779
132	Dealers in animals for food ..	2,150	107	158
134	Dealers in other food stuffs ..	4,483	9,017	..
	36. Trade in means of transport ..	906	213	347
	39. Trade of other sorts ..	6,256	2,713	4,670
150	General store-keepers and shop-keepers otherwise unspecified ..	5,484	2,028	4,345
	VI. PUBLIC FORCE ..	1,027	975	700
	VII. PUBLIC ADMINISTRATION ..	4,665	3,421	3,731
	44. Public Administration ..	4,665	3,421	3,731
159	Service of the State ..	3,494	2,291	2,026
160	Service of Indian and foreign State ..	14		
	VIII. PROFESSIONS AND LIBERAL ARTS ..	16,970	16,708	11,672
	45. Religion ..	4,331	4,055	4,422
163	Priests, ministers, etc ..	1,287	1,029	983
166	Servants in religious edifices, burial and burning grounds, pilgrim conductors, circumcisers, etc. ..	2,277	2,527	2,943
	47. Medicine ..	2,861	2,022	1,475
169	Registered medical practitioners including occulists ..	223	..	..
170	Persons practising the healing arts without being registered ..	2,617	..	..
	48. Instruction ..	6,203	7,523	2,597
174	Professors and teachers of all kinds ..	5,716	6,173	..
	49. Letters, arts and sciences (other than 44. Public Administration) ..	2,731	2,067	1,994
181	Horoscope casters, astrologers, fortune tellers, wizards, witches and mediums ..	773	370	..
182	Musicians (composers and performers other than military), actors, dancers, etc. ..	1,482	586	1,323
	IX. PERSONS LIVING ON THEIR INCOME ..	2,706	589	342
	50. Persons living principally on their income ..	2,706	589	342
185	Proprietors (other than agricultural land), fund and scholarships-holders and pensioners ..	2,705	589	342
	X. DOMESTIC SERVICE ..	140,833	3,852	3,867
	51. Domestic Service ..	140,833	3,852	3,867
187	Domestic servants other than private motor drivers and cleaners ..	140,567	3,799	3,867

IV.—*Selected occupations.*—(*cont.*)

Group No.	Occupation	Earners showing occupation as principal and working dependents	Actual workers	
		1931	1921	1911
1	2	3	4	5
	XI. INSUFFICIENTLY DESCRIBED OCCUPATIONS ..	25,450	23,390	29,351
	52. General terms which do not indicate a definite occupation ..	25,480	23,390	29,351
188	Manufacturers, businessmen and contractors otherwise unspecified ..	957	786	260
189	Cashiers, accountants, book-keepers, clerks and other employees in unspecified offices and warehouses and shops ..	2,718	3,033	1,725
191	Labourers and workmen otherwise unspecified ..	21 315	19,561	27,357
	XII. UNPRODUCTIVE.	1,246	7,362	1,880
	54. Beggars, vagrants, etc. ..	1,028	1,298	1,765
193	Beggars and vagrants ..	1,028	1,298	1,765

Note.— (1) The figures in 1921 against group 16 include growers of pan vine.

(2) The number of cocoanut cultivators is probably included in the number of tenants (group 6) in 1921 and 1911.

(3) The figures in 1911 against group 68 include manufacturers of mineral oils.

V.— Occupation of Selected Castes (1931 and 1921.)

Caste and occupation	Number per 1,000 earners engaged in each occupation	Number of female earners per 100 male earners
1	2	3
HINDU		
Ambalavasi—		
Income from rent of land	92	58
Cultivators of all kinds	113	30
Agents and managers of landed estates, planters, forest officers and their clerks, rent collectors, etc.	27	8
Trade	34	13
Public administration	34	1
Arts and professions	588	49
Persons living on their income	26	183
Domestic service	19	63
Contractors, clerks, cashiers, etc., otherwise unspecified	17	12
Other occupations	40	38
Ambattan—		
Cultivators of all kinds	22	18
Field labourers, wood cutters, etc.	67	1,900
Industries	815	19
Arts and professions	37	144
Domestic service	20	500
Labourers unspecified	12	250
Other occupations	27	23
Arayan—		
Cultivators of all kinds	25	19
Fishing and hunting	787	14
Industries	136	541
Trade	16	11
Labourers unspecified	17	710
Other occupations	19	20
Brahman, Konkani—		
Cultivators of all kinds	125	16
Raisers of live-stock, milkmen and herdsmen	10	900
Industries	74	70
Trade	428	7
Public administration	14	..
Arts and professions	122	3
Persons living on their income	15	163
Domestic service	48	63
Contractors, clerks, cashiers, etc., otherwise unspecified	81	..
Labourers unspecified	60	3
Other occupations	23	8
Brahman, Malayali—		
Income from rent of land	667	5
Cultivators of all kinds	94	4

V.—*Occupation of Selected Castes (1931 and 1921).—(cont.)*

Caste and occupation	Number per 1,000 earners engaged in each occupation	Number of female earners per 100 male earners
1	2	3
Brahman, Malayali—(*cont.*)		
Agents and managers of landed estates, planters, forest officers and their clerks, rent collectors, etc. ..	20	..
Trade ..	31	20
Arts and professions ..	39	..
Persons living on their income ..	87	71
Domestic service ..	19	14
Contractors, clerks, cashiers, etc., otherwise unspecified ..	25	..
Other occupations ..	16	9
Brahman, Tamil—		
Income from rent of land ..	112	27
Cultivators of all kinds ..	61	10
Agents and managers of landed estates, planters, forest officers and their clerks, rent collectors, etc. ..	26	..
Industries ..	18	1
Transport ..	32	..
Trade ..	197	24
Public administration ..	88	..
Arts and professions ..	250	8
Persons living on their income ..	83	52
Domestic service ..	48	20
Contractors, clerks, cashiers, etc. otherwise unspecified ..	62	..
Labourers unspecified ..	11	4
Other occupations ..	12	73
Chakkan—		
Cultivators of all kinds ..	61	25
Field labourers, wood cutters, etc. ..	72	110
Industries ..	689	34
Transport ..	10	..
Trade ..	103	50
Domestic service ..	15	333
Labourers unspecified ..	31	50
Other occupations ..	19	13
Chaliyan (Chaliyan)—		
Cultivators of all kinds ..	39	17
Field labourers, wood cutters, etc. ..	240	95
Raisers of live-stock, milkmen and herdsmen ..	6	..
Industries ..	519	39
Transport ..	33	..
Trade ..	11	100
Public force ..	6	..
Public administration ..	6	..
Persons living on their income ..	6	..

V.—*Occupation of Selected Castes (1931 and 1921).—(cont.)*

Caste and occupation	Number per 1,000 earners engaged in each occupation	Number of female earners per 100 male earners
1	2	3
Chaliyan (Chaliyan)—(cont.)		
Domestic service ..	61	1,000
Labourers unspecified ..	73	..
Chaliyan (Pattariyan)—		
Cultivators of all kinds ..	65	45
Field labourers, wood cutters, etc. ..	13	11
Industries ..	719	72
Transport ..	15	..
Trade ..	92	3
Public administration ..	26	..
Arts and professions ..	22	7
Domestic service ..	20	300
Labourers unspecified ..	15	200
Other occupations ..	13	21
Eluthassan—		
Income from rent of land ..	18	6
Cultivators of all kinds ..	328	7
Agents and managers of landed estates, planters forest officers and their clerks, rent collectors, etc. ..	19	1
Field labourers, wood cutters, etc. ..	410	129
Raisers of live-stock, milkmen and herdsmen ..	15	11
Industries ..	35	10
Transport ..	22	2
Trade ..	33	11
Arts and professions ..	16	5
Domestic service ..	17	282
Labourers unspecified ..	69	67
Other occupations ..	17	14
Iluvan—		
Cultivators of all kinds ..	27	44
Field labourers, wood cutters, etc. ..	191	110
Raisers of live-stock, milkmen and herdsmen ..	17	6
Industries ..	586	63
Transport ..	39	6
Trade ..	58	23
Arts and professions ..	11	12
Labourers unspecified ..	48	39
Other occupations ..	23	65
Kaikolan—		
Income from rent of land ..	16	23
Cultivators of all kinds ..	39	13
Field labourers, wood cutters, etc. ..	81	305
Industries ..	701	68
Trade ..	103	32

V.—Occupation of Selected Castes (1931 and 1921).—(cont.)

Caste and occupation	Number per 1,000 earners engaged in each occupation	Number of female earners per 100 male earners
1	2	3
Kaikolan—(cont.)		
Domestic service ..	19	1,750
Labourers unspecified ..	21	116
Other occupations ..	20	8
Kammalan—		
Cultivators of all kinds ..	19	34
Field labourers, wood cutters, etc. ..	67	687
Industries ..	873	15
Labourers unspecified ..	15	300
Other occupations ..	26	129
anakkan—		
Cultivators of all kinds ..	14	24
Field labourers, wood cutters, etc. ..	16	54
Raisers of live stock, milkmen and herdsmen ..	12	7
Fishing and hunting ..	51	3
Industries ..	186	474
Transport ..	34	4
Trade ..	66	102
Labourers unspecified ..	52	19
Other occupations ..	579	62
aniyan—		
Cultivators of all kinds ..	82	20
Field labourers, wood cutters, etc. ..	118	156
Industries ..	42	32
Transport ..	11	..
Public administration ..	18	..
Arts and professions ..	687	33
Domestic service ..	13	167
Other occupations ..	29	17
Kshatriya, Malayali—		
Income from rent of land ..	61	76
Cultivators of all kinds ..	32	109
Agents and managers of landed estates, planters, forest officers and their clerks, rent collectors, etc. ..	17	..
Industries ..	72	2,500
Trade ..	32	15
Public force ..	117	52
Public administration ..	50	..
Arts and professions ..	79	26
Persons living on their income ..	450	108
Domestic service ..	72	108
Labourers unspecified ..	11	40
Other occupations ..	7	95

V.—Occupation of Selected Castes (1931 and 1921).—(cont.)

Caste and occupation	Number per 1,000 earners engaged in each occupation	Number of female earners per 100 male earners
	2	3
Kudumi chetti—		
Cultivators of all kinds ..	163	4
Field labourers, wood cutters, etc. ..	63	74
Fishing and hunting ..	32	3
Industries ..	56	262
Transport ..	18	..
Trade ..	82	13
Domestic service ..	48	3,273
Labourers unspecified ..	515	31
Other occupations ..	23	14
Kusavan—		
Field labourers, wood cutters, etc. ..	10	217
Industries ..	946	82
Trade ..	25	1,533
Other occupations ..	19	20
Nayar—		
Income from rent of land ..	59	100
Cultivators of all kinds ..	21	146
Agents and managers of landed estates, forest officers and their clerks, rent collectors, etc. ..	22	..
Field labourers, wood cutters, etc. ..	107	206
Raisers of live-stock, milkmen and herdsmen ..	11	8
Industries ..	35	106
Transport ..	18	4
Trade ..	75	35
Public administration ..	52	..
Arts and professions ..	70	21
Persons living on their income ..	14	77
Domestic service ..	76	216
Contractors, clerks, cashiers, etc., otherwise unspecified ..	15	1
Labourers unspecified ..	20	42
Other occupations ..	402	44
Pandaran—		
Cultivators of all kinds ..	60	25
Field labourers, wood cutters, etc. ..	200	143
Industries ..	79	69
Transport ..	24	2
Trade ..	38	41
Arts and professions ..	19	..
Other occupations ..	580	97
Panditattan—		
Field labourers, wood cutters, etc. ..	24	200

V.—Occupation of Selected Castes (1931 and 1921).—(cont.)

Caste and occupation		Number per 1,000 earners engaged in each occupation	Number of female earners per 100 male earners
1		2	3
Panditattan—(*cont.*)			
Industries	..	901	2
Trade	..	13	86
Domestic service	..	27	2 690
Other occupations	..	35	75
Pulayan—			
Cultivators of all kinds	..	11	18
Field labourers, wood cutters, etc.	..	876	89
Raisers of live-stock, milkmen and herdsmen	..	25	6
Industries	..	49	557
Labourers unspecified	..	20	55
Other occupations	..	19	190
Sambavan (Parayan)—			
Raisers of live stock, milkmen and herdsmen	..	14	2
Industries	..	20	43
Labourers unspecified	..	37	84
Other occupations	..	929	94
Valan—			
Cultivators of all kinds	..	19	23
Industries	..	119	213
Transport	..	31	3
Trade	..	54	284
Arts and professions	..	10	29
Other occupations	..	767	22
Velakkattalavan—			
Cultivators of all kinds	..	179	25
Field labourers, wood cutters etc.	..	87	215
Industries	..	639	35
Arts and professions	..	42	663
Labourers unspecified	..	10	36
Other occupations	..	43	66
Velan—			
Cultivators of all kinds	..	54	7
Field labourers, wood cutters, etc.	..	84	8
Industries	..	107	29
Transport	..	11	..
Arts and professions	..	131	1
Labourers unspecified	..	33	23
Other occupations	..	580	418
Vellalan—			
Income from rent of land	..	10	82

V.—*Occupation of Selected Castes (1931 and 1921).—(cont.)*

Caste and occupation	Number per 1,000 earners engaged in each occupation	Number of female earners per 100 male earners
1	2	3
Vellalan—(*cont.*)		
Agents and managers of landed estates, planters, forest officers and their clerks, rent collectors, etc. ..	12	4
Field labourers, wood cutters, etc. ..	194	120
Raisers of live-stock, milkmen and herdsmen ..	18	5
Industries ..	87	6
Transport ..	24	..
Public administration ..	17	9
Arts and professions ..	48	2
Persons living on their income ..	17	61
Contractors, clerks, cashiers, etc., otherwise unspecified ..	25	..
Labourers, unspecified ..	28	24
Other occupations ..	530	38
Veluttedan—		
Income from rent of land ..	9	24
Cultivators of all kinds ..	65	27
Field labourers, wood cutters, etc. ..	15	106
Industries ..	878	138
Other occupations ..	33	16
Vettuvan—		
Cultivators of all kinds ..	17	23
Field labourers, wood cutters, etc. ..	36	80
Raisers of live-stock, milkmen and herdsmen ..	11	..
Fishing and hunting ..	765	85
Industries ..	43	325
Labourers unspecified ..	111	40
Other occupations ..	17	102
MUSLIM		
Jonakan—		
Cultivators of all kinds ..	189	18
Field labourers, wood cutters, etc. ..	233	89
Raisers of live-stock, milkmen and herdsmen ..	10	7
Fishing and hunting ..	15	1
Industries ..	106	61
Transport ..	70	2
Trade ..	220	12
Arts and professions ..	24	2
Domestic service ..	22	175
Labourers unspecified ..	83	7
Other occupations ..	18	10
Ravuttan—		
Cultivators of all kinds ..	92	13

V.—Occupation of Selected Castes (1931 and 1921).—(cont.)

Caste and occupation	Number per 1,000 earners engaged in each occupation	Number of female earners per 100 male earners
1	2	3
Ravuttan—(*cont.*)		
Field labourers, wood cutters, etc. ..	295	100
Raisers of live-stock, milkmen and herdsmen ..	75	12
Industries ..	62	19
Transport ..	61	12
Trade ..	156	11
Arts and professions ..	18	7
Domestic service ..	16	103
Labourers unspecified ..	51	37
Other occupations ..	23	9
Others—		
Cultivators of all kinds ..	139	29
Agents and managers of landed estates, planters, forest officers and their clerks, rent collectors, etc. ..	15	4
Field labourers, wood cutters, etc. ..	129	48
Fishing and hunting ..	52	..
Industries ..	210	218
Transport ..	43	..
Trade ..	245	5
Arts and professions ..	26	5
Domestic service ..	26	282
Contractors, clerks, cashiers, etc., otherwise unspecified ..	16	..
Labourers unspecified .	72	13
Other occupations ..	27	21
CHRISTIAN		
Anglo-Indian		
Cultivators of all kinds ..	101	21
Agents and managers of landed estates, planters, forest officers and their clerks, rent collectors, etc. ..	11	..
Field labourers, wood cutters, etc. ..	11	..
Fishing and hunting ..	18	..
Industries ..	438	11
Transport ..	55	..
Trade ..	70	10
Public administration ..	20	..
Arts and professions ..	142	183
Persons living on their income ..	33	29
Domestic service ..	17	300
Contractors, clerks, cashiers, etc., otherwise unspecified ..	61	..
Other occupations ..	17	33
European—		
Agents and managers of landed estates, planters, forest officers and their clerks, rent collectors, etc. ..	279	..

V.—Occupation of Selected Castes (1931 and 1921).—(cont.)

Caste and occupation		Number per 1,000 earners engaged in each occupation	Number of female earners per 100 male earners
		2	3
European—(cont.)			
Industries	..	164	11
Transport	..	16	..
Public force	..	16	..
Public administration	..	49	..
Arts and professions	..	410	108
Persons living on their income	..	49	59
Domestic service	..	17	..
Indian Christian—			
Cultivators of all kinds	..	253	19
Field labourers, wood cutters etc.	..	156	81
Fishing and hunting	..	21	2
Industries	..	248	62
Transport	..	46	1
Trade	..	133	14
Arts and professions	..	34	33
Domestic service	..	28	147
Labourers unspecified	..	45	26
Other occupations	..	36	25
JAIN			
Trade	..	301	..
Arts and professions	..	14	..
Persons living on their income	..	41	..
Contractors, clerks, cashiers, etc., otherwise unspecified	..	617	..
Labourers unspecified	..	27	..
JEW			
Cultivators of all kinds	..	138	49
Industry	..	55	28
Transport	..	33	..
Trade	..	627	10
Public administration	..	19	33
Arts and professions	..	26	22
Persons living on their income	..	14	..
Domestic service	..	31	..
Contractors, clerks, cashiers, etc., otherwise unspecified	..	21	..
Labourers unspecified	..	26	..
Other occupations	..	10	33

VI.—Number of persons employed on the 26th February, 1931, in the Railway, Post and Telegraph, Irrigation, etc., departments as compared with those employed on the 18th March, 1921.

Class of persons employed	1931		1921	
	Europeans and Anglo-Indians	Indians	Europeans and Anglo-Indians	Indians
1	2	3	4	5
(A) RAILWAYS				
Total persons employed ..	4	649	1	471
ersons directly employed				
Officers ..	..	1	1	..
Subordinates drawing more than Rs. 75 per mensem ..	4	36	..	3
Subordinates drawing from Rs. 20 to Rs. 75 per mensem ..	..	202	..	55
Subordinates drawing under Rs. 20 per mensem ..	..	407	..	308
Persons indirectly employed				
Contractors ..	..	3	..	1
Contractors' regular employees ..	..	..	..	4
Coolies ..	..	..	..	100
(B) POSTAL DEPARTMENT				
Total persons employed ..	2	148	2	124
Supervising officers (including probationary Superintendents, etc.) ..	..	1	..	1
Post Masters, including Deputy, Assistant Sub and Branch Post Masters ..	1	9	1	28
Miscellaneous agents, school masters, station masters, etc. ..	1	37	..	..
Clerks of all kinds ..	..	19	..	16
Postmen ..	..	38	..	39
Unskilled labour establishment including line coolies, cable guards, batterymen, telegraph messengers, peons and other employees ..	..	17	..	22
Road establishment consisting of overseers, runners, clerks and booking agents, syces, coachmen, bearers and others ..	..	27	..	18
(C) IRRIGATION DEPARTMENT				
Total persons employed ..	..	96	..	175
Persons directly employed				
Officers ..	..	..	..	1
Upper subordinates ..	..	..	..	1
Lower subordinates ..	..	1	..	3
Clerks (Work Superintendent) ..	..	1	..	3
Peons and other servants ..	..	94	..	20
Coolies ..	..	..	..	84
Persons indirectly employed				
Contractors ..	..	..	..	3
Coolies ..	..	..	..	60
(D) COCHIN FOREST TRAMWAY				
Total persons employed ..	3	310	4	406

VI.—Number of persons employed on the 26th February, 1931, in the Railway, Post and Telegraph, Irrigation, etc., departments as compared with those employed on the 18th March, 1921.—(cont.)

Class of persons employed	1931		1921	
	Europeans and Anglo-Indians	Indians	Europeans and Anglo-Indians	Indians
1	2	3	4	5
(D) COCHIN FOREST TRAMWAY—(cont.)				
Persons directly employed				
Officers ..	1	..	2	4
Subordinates drawing more than Rs. 75 per mensem ..	2	3	2	4
Subordinates drawing from Rs. 20 to Rs. 75 per mensem ..	..	44	..	58
Subordinates drawing under Rs. 20 per mensem ..	..	260	..	261
Persons indirectly employed				
Contractors ..	..	3	..	3
Contractors' regular employees ..	..	..	..	3
Coolies ..	..	..	..	2
(E) COCHIN ANCHAL DEPARTMENT				
Total persons employed ..	..	250	..	232
Supervising officers including Inspectors ..	..	2	..	3
Anchal masters of all grades ..	..	61	..	58
Miscellaneous agents ..	..	..	..	3
Clerks of all kinds ..	..	22	..	21
Sorters and other mail service men ..	..	3	..	..
Anchalmen and other servants ..	..	122	..	109
Road establishment ..	..	39	..	38

Note.—There are no employees in the Telegraph department in 1931 or 1921.

CHAPTER IX.—LITERACY.

Statistics of literacy: their meaning

IN a country where illiteracy has been the rule and literacy the exception, statistics of the growth of literacy from decade to decade should naturally be of more than ordinary interest and importance in that they will show "how far the progressive efforts of educational agencies have been able to dispel ignorance and bring the minimum knowledge of letters to the doors of the people". Two columns were provided in the census schedule as on previous occasions, one for recording literacy in general and the other for literacy in English in particular, and the instructions issued in 1911 and 1921, defining the standard of literacy as the ability "to write a letter to a friend and read the answer to it" in any language, were adopted at the present census also. Besides, an attempt has been made for the first time to secure special information regarding the numbers of those persons among literates who have attended schools and completed their primary education. And statistics of children between the ages of 6 and 12 years, who are attending school, who have attended school for some time but left it, and who have not attended any school at all, have also been collected separately in accordance with the instructions of the local Government.

Reference to Tables

2. These statistics are presented in two Imperial Tables and fourteen Subsidiary Tables as explained below:

i. Imperial Table XIII giving the figures of literacy by religion and age;

ii. Imperial Table XIV giving the figures of literacy by castes, tribes or races;

iii. Subsidiary Table I giving the proportional figures of literacy by age, sex and religion;

iv. Subsidiary Table II giving specific figures of literacy by sex and locality;

v. Subsidiary Table III giving proportional figures of literacy by sex and locality;

vi. Subsidiary Table IV giving similar figures of English literacy by sex and locality;

vii. Subsidiary Table V giving similar figures of literacy by caste (1931 and 1921);

viii. Subsidiary Table VI showing the progress of literacy since 1881;

ix. Subsidiary Table VII showing the proportion of literacy at certain ages;

x. Subsidiary Table VIII and VIII (a) showing the number, kind, management etc. of institutions and the number of pupils according to the returns of the Education department;

xi. Subsidiary Table IX showing the results of the University and Public examinations in 1931;

xii. Subsidiary Table X showing the numbers of literates who have completed their Primary education *;

---

* The statistics presented in this Subsidiary Table are not reviewed in the chapter. Provinces in British India were asked to collect the information as it was required by the Franchise Committee in connection with the question of adding a literacy to a property qualification for the exercise of a vote. Similar information was collected for the State also in accordance with the instructions of the Darbar. The returns are far from complete, the absence of a special column in the schedule for recording the information leading to omissions on a large scale. Moreover a considerable section of the literates who do not possess this qualification must be regarded as much more learned than those that have merely completed their primary school course. The Nambudiri with his vedic lore, the Kaniyan well-read in Astrology, the Ayurvedic physician and the old type of Sanskrit Pandits will illustrate the point.

xiii. Subsidiary Tables XI, XII and XIII showing the number of children of school-going age (6 to 12 years) who are attending school, by taluks, religion and selected castes;

xiv. Subsidiary Table XIV showing the number and circulation of periodicals.

Diagrams have been added to illustrate

(i) the number of literates by sex in each taluk of the State;

(ii) the progress of literacy in Cochin (1901—1931);

(iii) the progress of English literacy in Cochin (1901—1931);

(iv) literacy by religion and sex;

(v) literacy in Cochin compared with literacy in other States and Provinces; and

(vi) literacy in selected castes.

Extent of literacy

3. The main fact to be learnt from these statistics is that of 1,205,016 persons in the State 339,653 (of whom 225,669 are males and 113,984 are females,) have been returned as satisfying the test of literacy and are therefore to be regarded as being able to read and write. The marginal figures will show that there are at present 158,243 more literates than in 1921. Literate persons have thus increased by 87·2 per cent while the increase in the general population is only 23·1 per cent. It is a relief to note that the corresponding rise in the illiterate population is only 8·5 per cent. And the fact that literate women have multiplied by no less than 131·1 per cent is particularly gratifying.

	1931	1921	Percentage of increase
Literates (Total)	339,653	181,410	87·2
Illiterates ,,	865,363	797,670	8·5
Literates (Males)	225,669	132,090	70·8
Illiterates ,,	364,144	350,869	3·8
Literates (Females)	113,984	49,320	131·1
Illiterates ,,	501,219	446,801	12·2

Comparison with other States, Provinces, etc.

4. In spite of this large increase we find that only 282 per mille of the population (383 per mille amongst males and 185 amongst females) are literate. But the proportion of the literate population will be seen to be slightly higher when children in the age-period 0—5, who cannot be expected to satisfy the test of literacy, are excluded from the total population. According to this calculation 337 in every 1,000 of the population claim to have attained the minimum standard of literacy set by the census, the proportion of literates among males being 460 per mille and among females 220. Low as this proportion is, the statistics compare very favourably with those of other Provinces and States as shown in the margin. Burma as usual takes the first place in literacy among the Provinces and States in the Indian Empire, the indigenous system of free education, evidently of a

Province or State	Number per mille who are literate (5 years and above)		
	Persons	Males	Females
Burma ..	368	560	165
Cochin ..	**337**	**460**	**220**
Travancore ..	289	408	168
Baroda ..	209	331	79
Delhi ..	163	226	72
Pudukkottai ..	127	244	21
Ajmer Merwara ..	125	203	35
Bengal ..	110	180	32
Madras ..	108	188	30
Mysore ..	106	174	33
Gwalior ..	47	78	11
Hyderabad ..	47	83	10

Literacy in Cochin Compared with that in other Provinces & States

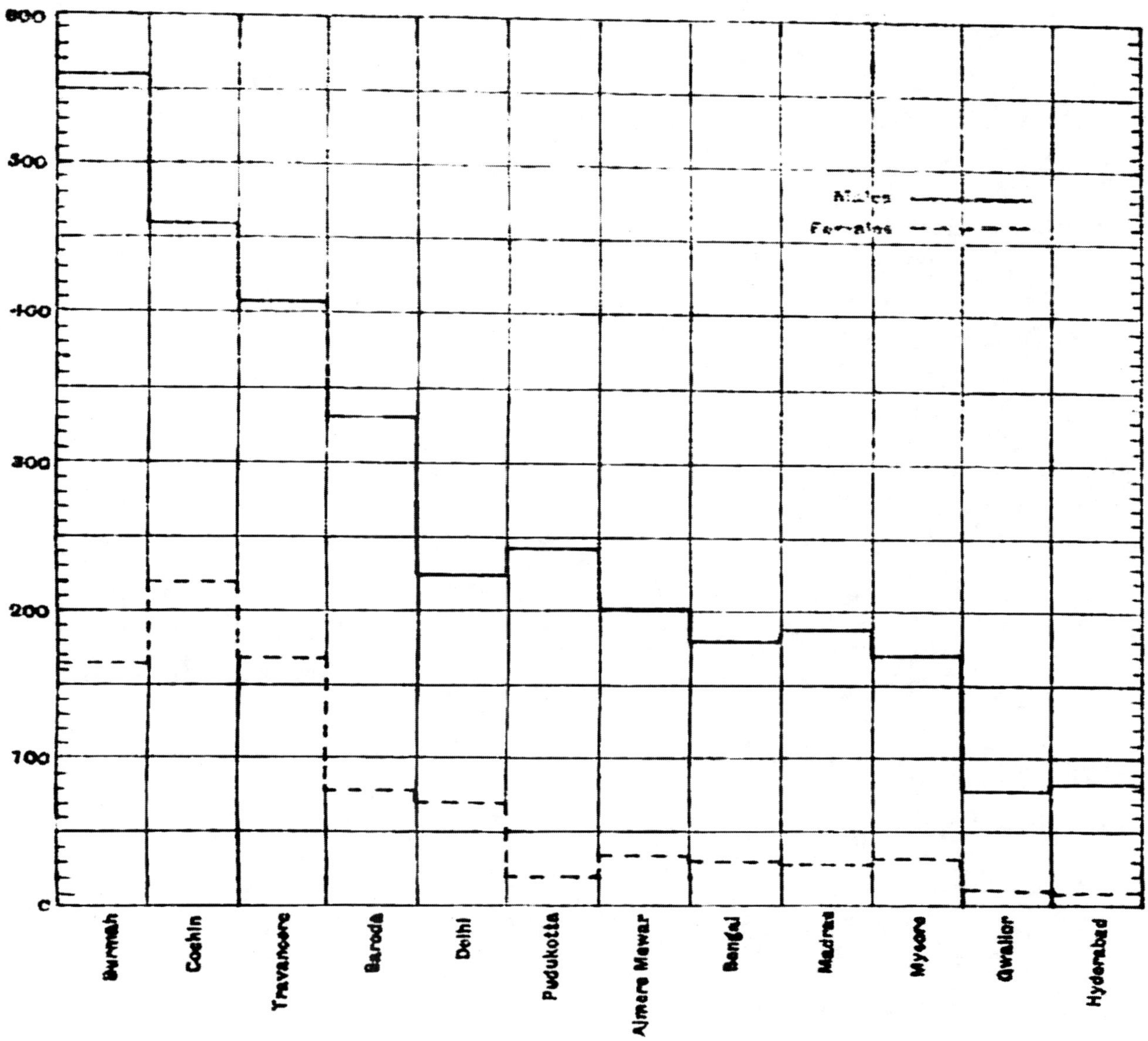

Diagram showing literacy by religion & sex

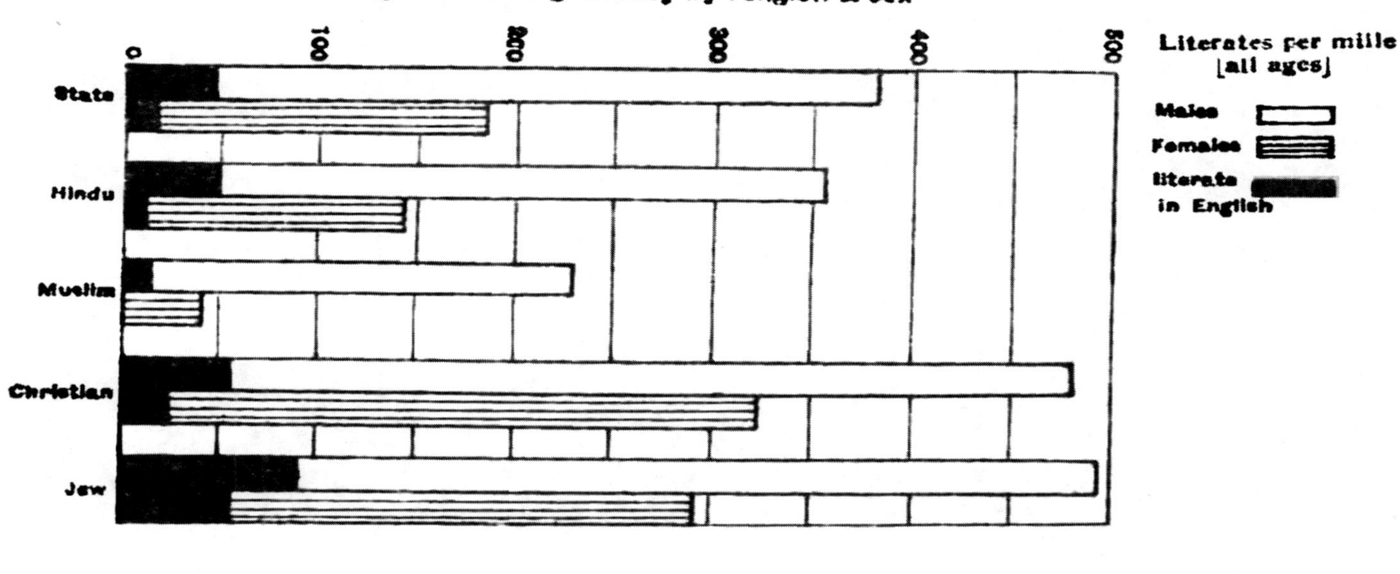

religious character, imparted in monasteries, being no doubt responsible for this enviable position of the Province. Cochin takes the second place followed at some distance by Travancore. Baroda where the compulsory system of primary education prevails to a certain extent takes but the 4th place and is separated from Cochin and Travancore by a long distance. In respect of female literacy, however, our State stands first and enjoys the proud and honoured distinction of having the most literate female population in the Indian Empire. If the comparison is restricted to units of smaller area, it will still be seen that the position of Cochin is not materially altered. Thus the most highly literate districts of the Madras Presidency stand far below this State, while even the city of Madras, the capital of the Presidency and the educational centre of South India, has but a lower proportion of literate females, though it occupies a slightly higher position than Cochin in male literacy.

District	Number per mille who are literate (5 years and above)		
	Persons	Males	Females
Madras (City) ..	349	487	194
Cochin ..	337	460	220
Tinnevelly ..	173	300	55
Malabar ..	170	273	75
Tanjore ..	161	299	35
Madura ..	131	241	23
Trichinopoly ..	125	223	31
Chingleput ..	123	211	32

5. Indeed, the rapid growth of literacy among women must justly be regarded as the most hopeful feature of these statistics. Whereas there were but 25 literate females in 1911 and 37 in 1921 to every 100 literate males, there are as many as 51 at the present census. And out of every 100 literates in the State 34 are seen to be women, the corresponding figure for 1921 being only 27. The disparity in numbers between male and female literates is thus growing less though the literate population among males is fast increasing. If we now turn to the figures and proportions of the literate population contained in Imperial Table XIII and Subsidiary Table I, and study the ratios given in the appended statements, it will be seen that the disparity is less evident in the earlier age-periods and grows more and more prominent with the older ages. And the proportion of females in the literate population aged 5—20 is much higher than in more advanced age-groups. Likewise the percentage of literates in the female population is higher in the earlier periods than in the later ones. And of the total number of female literates only 39·4 per cent are in the age-group 24 and above, while 21·6 per cent are aged 17—23 — Literacy by sex and age

Age-period	Proportion of literate females to 100 literate males		Proportion of females in every 100 literates	
	1931	1921	1931	1921
5—10	72	64	41	39
7—13	70	..	41	..
10—15	69	58	40	37
14—16	63	..	38	..
15—20	62	49	38	33
17—23	61	..	38	..
20 and above	38	30	29	23
24 and above	37	..	27	..
All ages	51	37	34	27

Age-period	Percentage of literates in the female population		Percentage of literates in the male population	
	1931	1921	1931	1921
5—10	19	5	26	7
10—15	30	15	44	25
15—20	32	17	57	36
20 and over	12	11	50	40
All ages (5 years and above)	20	11	46	32

years, 13·4 per cent are aged 14—16 years and 25·6 per cent, below 14 years. The figures show that the younger ages predominate and that a generation of literate women is coming into existence. The percentages for the corresponding age-groups among male literates are 53·1, 17·7, 10·8 and 18·4.

The age-period 15—20 contains those that have been under effective instruction during the past quinquennium and it therefore represents the educational effort of the decade more fully than any other age-group. Here 575 per mille of the male population and 321 per mille of the female population are literate as shown in Subsidiary Table I, while 112 in every 1,000 males and 41 in every 1,000 females in this group are literate in English also. And the pace at which literacy has been progressing and the degree of success that has attended the activities of the educational agencies of the State will be clear from the margin where the number and proportion returned as literate at this age-period on the present as well as on previous occasions are given for purposes of comparison.

Year	No. of literates in the age-period 15—20		Proportion per mille of the population aged 15—20	
	Males	Females	Males	Females
1931	32,166	19,872	575	321
1921	16,696	8,240	359	174
1911	13,755	4 776	303	104
1901	11,067	3,070	224	45

Literacy by locality

6. From Subsidiary Tables II and III we find that the most favoured taluks are, as in other respects, Cochin-Kanayannur and Trichur and the proportion of literates, both male and female, in these taluks is higher than the State average as seen from the margin. The following statement will show that the two taluks are better equipped in respect of educational institutions than the other taluks.

Percentage of literates

Taluk	Persons	Males	Females
COCHIN STATE ..	28·2	38·3	18·5
Cochin-Kanayannur ..	33·8	45·0	22·3
Cranganur ..	25·5	36·0	15·1
Mukundapuram ..	25·3	34·8	16·4
Trichur ..	33·0	43·6	23·1
Talapilli ..	24·1	33·0	16·1
Chittur ..	15·0	22·7	7·7

Taluk	Area	Population	Colleges		High Schools		Lower Secondary Schools		Primary Schools		Total
			Boys	Girls	Boys	Girls	Boys	Girls	Boys	Girls	
COCHIN STATE ..	1,480·28	1,205,016	2	1	30	12	47	13	554	72	731
Cochin-Kanayannur ..	158·52	350,268	1	1	12	5	18	4	180	26	247
Cranganur ..	17·51	42,531	..	..	1	1	1	..	14	..	17
Mukundapuram ..	510·00	263,722	..	..	2	2	11	2	130	11	158
Trichur ..	245·50	239,257	1	..	8	2	7	5	95	21	139
Talapilli ..	256·00	202,424	..	..	5	1	7	2	108	10	133
Chittur ..	292·75	106,814	..	..	2	1	3	..	27	4	37

I

Diagram showing the no. of literates in each Taluk

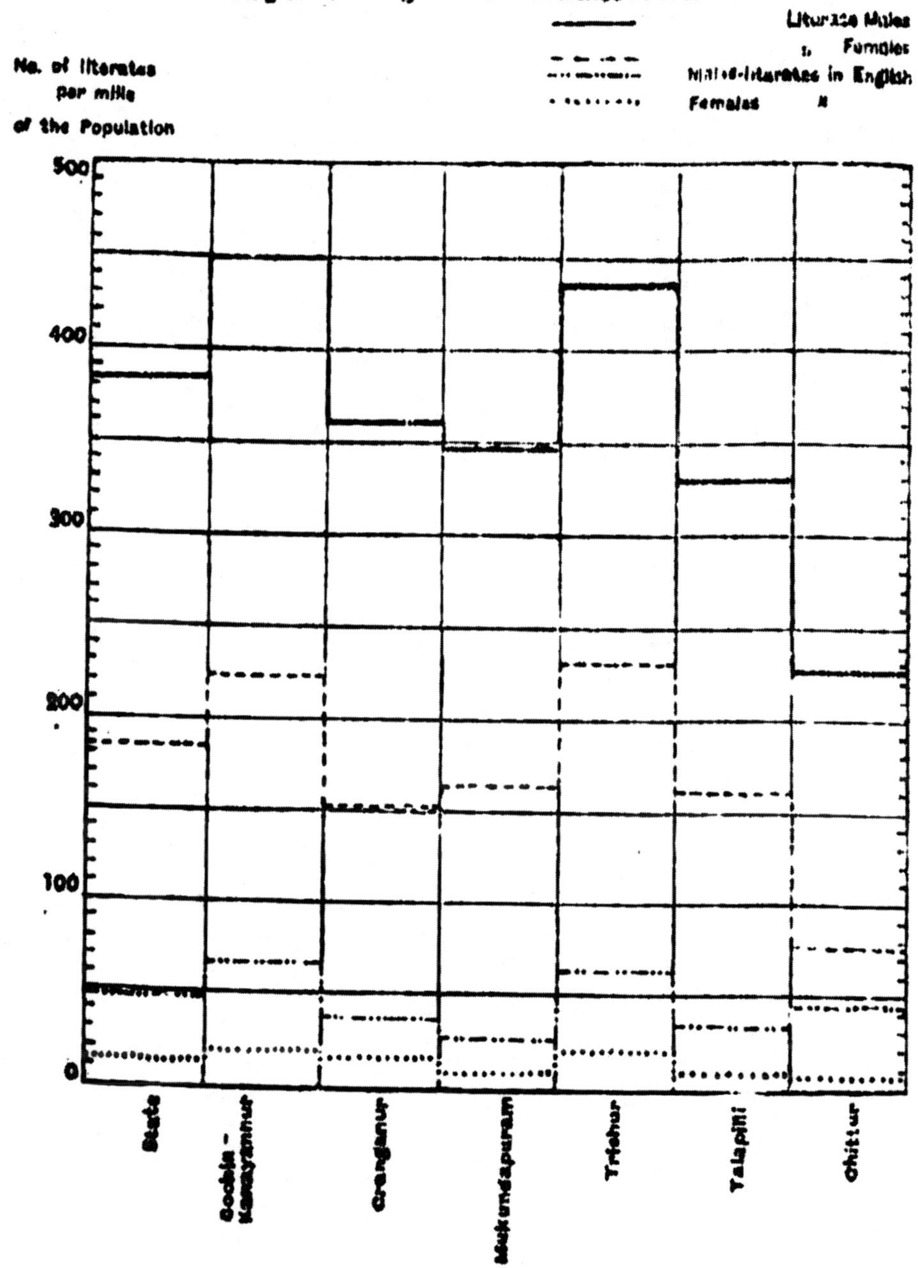

II

Diagram showing the progress of literacy in Cochin 1901-1931

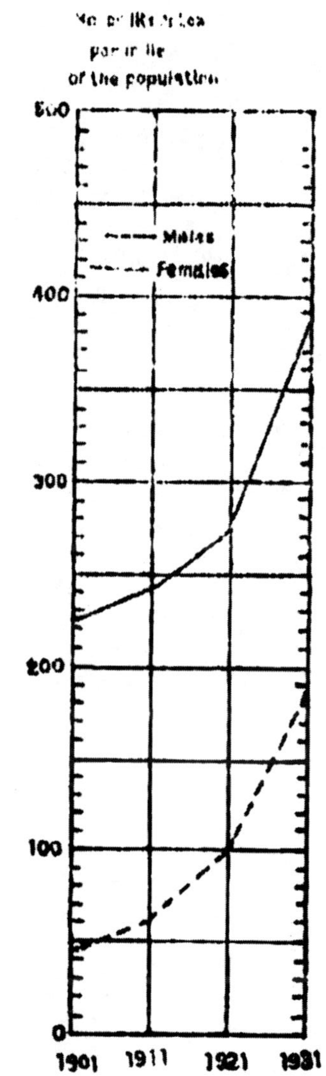

III

Diagram showing the progress of literacy in English 1901-1931

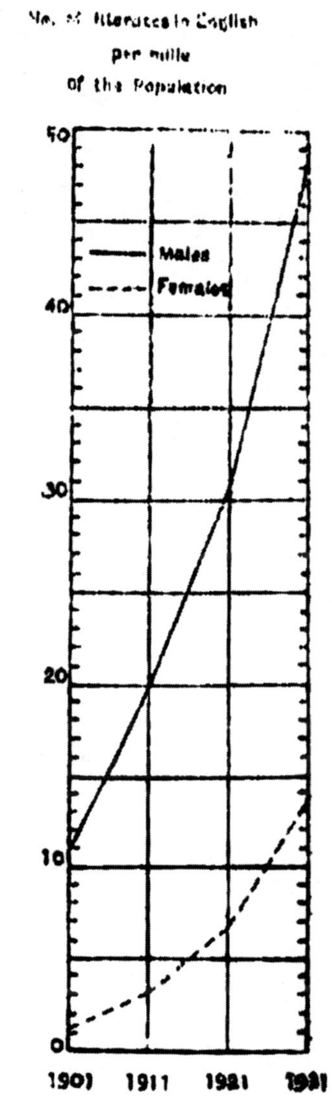

Ernakulam and Trichur are the two educational centres of the State, with their first-grade colleges and numerous high schools, and facilities for modern education were available in Cochin-Kanayannur and Trichur long before the other taluks came to possess them. There are other reasons also for the low proportion of literacy in Cranganur, Mukundapuram, Talapilli and Chittur. In Cranganur the proportion of Muslims who are backward in literacy is far higher than in other places and there are but very few Christians to restore the balance of the literate population. Mukundapuram, Talapilli and Chittur have an essentially agricultural population and these taluks have a high percentage of such Hindu communities as are very much backward in literacy, if not entirely illiterate. Chittur, in particular, lying almost wholly detached from the literate West Coast, has a population of a highly mixed character in which backward and illiterate communities predominate, and even the very small proportion of Christians in this taluk is mostly illiterate. The wide disparity between Chittur and other taluks in the number of educational institutions is also significant. No wonder that Chittur has the lowest figures and stands at the bottom.

Literacy by religion: Christians

7. The actual figures of the literates of each religion by age-periods are to be found in Imperial Table XIII, while proportional figures are given in Subsidiary Table I. Likewise Imperial Table XIV contains the figures of literates aged 7 years and over for each caste, tribe or race and the figures are condensed into proportional forms in Subsidiary Table V. Turning to those religions that have the largest following, we find that the Christians, who returned the highest proportion of literates at previous censuses, still maintain their precedence both in male and female literacy. The influence of the Indian clergy and the educational activities of Christian missions, which won for them their high position, have enabled them to retain it, while helping the followers of other religions also on the road to literacy and progress. Though the Indian Christians form but 27·6 per cent of the State's population, 39 per cent of the literate population are from this community. And the fact that 47·4 per cent of the female literates of the State are Indian Christians shows more than anything else the degree of their pre-eminence in literacy.

Religion	Literates (all ages) per mille of the population		
	Persons	Males	Females
All religions ..	282	383	185
Hindus ..	247	357	143
Muslims ..	137	230	41
Christians ..	401	480	323
Jews ..	391	491	289

Literacy among Christians by sect

8. Among the Indian Christians themselves, the Protestants and Syrians have a slight advantage over the Roman Catholics and Romo-Syrians between whom there is little to choose. The numerical strength of the Roman Catholics and Romo-Syrians combined with the fact that they have large numbers of converts among them from the depressed and illiterate Hindu communities must account for this difference, particulars of which will be seen from the statement given below. As the figures of 1921 are not available for comparison, those of 1911 have been taken for this purpose.

	Population (1931)	1931 Percentage of literates (all ages)			Population (1911)	1911 Percentage of literates (all ages)		
		Persons	Males	Females		Persons	Males	Females
Indian Christians ..	333,041	40	48	32	230,568	21	31	11
Roman Catholics ..	108,013	39	47	31	95,397	21	30·5	11
Romo-Syrians ..	183,418				100,166	21·4	31·6	11·2
Syrians (Jacobite, Mar Thoma, Chaldean etc.) ..	36,165	47	56	39	32,776	21	31·5	10·6
Protestants ..	5,445	45	48	43	2,229	25	37·9	13·2

Literacy among Hindus by caste

9. The progress in literacy from decade to decade among the Christians as compared with the progress of other communities is shown below :

	Census Year		Hindus	Muslims	Christians	Jews
Proportion per cent in the total population ..	1931		64·8	7·3	27·8	..
	1921		66·0	7·0	26·8	..
	1911		67·1	7·0	25·1	..
	1901		68·3	6·7	24·4	..
Proportion per cent in the total number of literates ..	1931	Persons	56·7	3·5	39·6	..
		Males	59·9	4·6	35·4	..
		Females	50·4	1·5	47·8	..
	1921	Persons	58·7	3·2	37·9	..
		Males	60·9	4·1	34·9	..
		Females	52·7	1·1	46·0	..
	1911	Persons	60·4	3·4	36·0	..
		Males	62·4	4·0	33·3	..
		Females	52·2	0.7	46·9	..
	1901	Persons	64·8	3·3	31·6	..
		Males	65·9	3·8	30·1	..
		Females	59·7	0·9	39·3	..
Percentage of literates in each religion (all ages) ..	1931		24·7	13·7	40·1	37·1
	1921		16·5	8·5	26·2	27·8
	1911		13·6	7·4	21·5	19·7
	1901		12·7	6·7	17·4	20·8

Diagram showing the literacy of selected Castes
(literates per mille of the Population)
[7 years and above.]

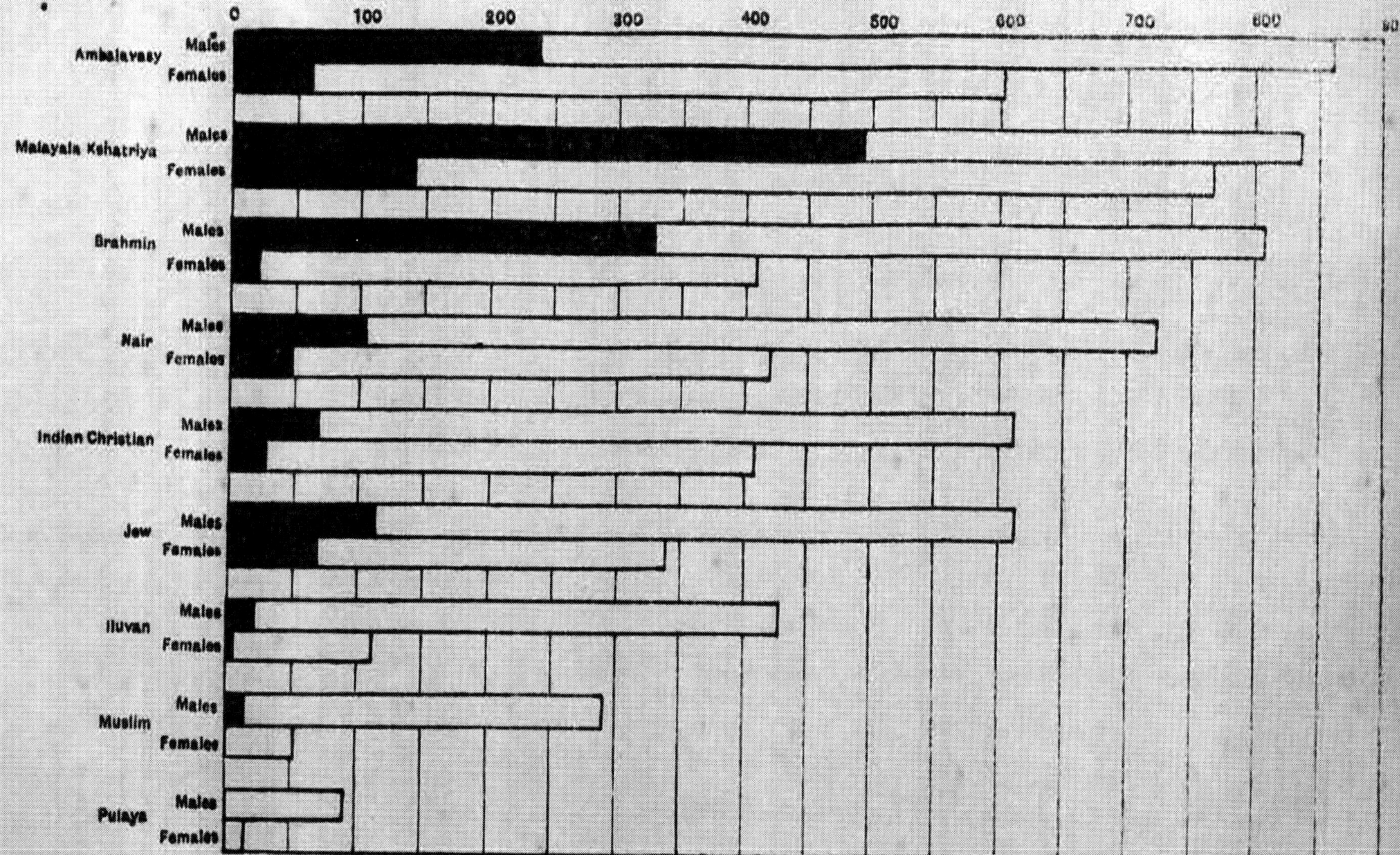

The black portion indicates literacy in English

Caste or community (arranged according to rank in literacy.)	Percentage of literates (7 years and over for 1931 and all ages for the previous years.)			
Both Sexes	1931	1921	1911	1901
Hindu-Malayali Kshatriya	80	58	61	47
,, Ambalavasi	73	48	40	40
,, Brahman (Tamil)	69	49	43	40
,, ,, (Malayali)	68	47	43	47
,, Nayar	56	31	27	27
Indian Christian	51	26	21	17
Jew	47	28	20	21
Hindu Brahman (Konkani)	45	24	29	24
Males.				
Hindu-Brahman (Tamil)	87	71	68	69
,, Ambalavasi	86	61	55	61
,, Brahman (Malayali)	85	63	63	70
,, Malayali Kshatriya	84	66	72	62
,, Brahman (Konkani)	72	37	50	44
,, Nayar	72	43	41	43
Jew	61	38	31	38
Indian Christian	61	35	31	27
Females.				
Hindu-Malayali Kshatriya	77	51	49	32
,, Ambalavasi	60	33	25	25
,, Brahman (Tamil)	50	25	15	8
,, ,, (Malayali)	49	27	20	23
,, Nayar	42	20	14	12
Indian Christian	41	17	11	6
Jew	34	18	9	5
Hindu-Brahman (Konkani)	18	8	4	2

Whereas the contribution of the Christians to the literate population, which is proportionately much higher than that of the Hindus, has been steadily increasing, the contribution of the Hindus shows an equally steady decline. The gradual fall in the strength of the Hindu element in the total population of the State is not the only reason for this diminishing contribution. For it is seen from the variation in the percentage of literates in each religion from decade to decade that the Hindus as a whole have not been progressing at the same pace as the Christians. The explanation for this state of affairs is that more than 50 per cent of the Hindu population is made up of communities which, on account of extreme poverty, or the want of facilities resulting from the social disabilities* inherent in the rigid caste system of Malayali Hindus, or from both causes, are very much backward in literacy if not wholly illiterate. The statement in the margin will show that the so-called caste Hindus among the purely Malayali section of the population rank among the most literate classes in India, that the proportion of literates among them, both male and female, is far higher than among the Indian Christians, and that the pace of their progress is second to that of none. The statement includes the Tamil and Konkani Brahmans also who, though non-Malayalis, are prominent Hindu castes in the State.

Literacy among caste Hindus.

10. Illiteracy among males is practically unknown in communities like the Tamil and Malayali Brahmans, the Ambalavasis and the Malayali Kshatriyas. Literacy among their women also is high, but the Malayali Kshatriyas enjoy an unassailable pre-eminence in this respect. And it is only in the fitness of things that the community to which the Ruling Family of the State belongs should set this worthy example to others. The Nayars, the third largest community in the State (coming after the Indian Christians and the Iluvans), occupy a high rank, the proportion of literates among their males being particularly high; and though they form but 11·8 per cent of the State's population, 19 per cent of the total number of literates and 23·2 per cent of the female literates in the State are Nayars, who thus contribute a proportionately higher percentage to the male

*This refers to the past. So far as the present is concerned, the disabilities have disappeared to a very considerable extent.

and female literate population than the Christians. In the light of the figures for English literacy discussed below, it will further be seen that the standard of literacy among these castes is higher than among others.

non-caste Hindus.

11. Imperial Table XIV and Subsidiary Table V are of special interest and importance in that they show the figures and ratios for the literates of each caste and tribe separately. But a detailed examination of all these castes and tribes is out of the question because of considerations of space. It may however be noted that, among the non-caste Hindus, the Kaniyans—astrologers by profession—are one of the most literate castes in the State, 81 per cent of the males and 50 per cent of the females (aged 7 years and above) among them being literate: The Iluvans, the second largest community in the State forming 23 per cent of its total population, who were educationally backward, have been making such rapid and creditable progress that they have as many as 262 literates in every 1,000 of their population aged 7 years and above, the proportion for males being 429 and for females 111, so much so that 17 per cent of the literate population in the State belong to their fold. The Eluttassans, the Ambattans and Arayans, the Kanakkans and Kudumi Chettis, the Valans and Velans and the Velakkattalavans and Veluttedans are some of the other castes that show very considerable progress in literacy during the decade. And communities that are backward in literacy—most of the above belong to this class—enjoy special concessions in the matter of fees in all educational institutions in the State.

and depressed classes and hill tribes

12. In literacy, as in other matters, the depressed brother figures but poorly. Living in abject poverty and, for the most part, outside the pale of society, the unapproachable castes of the Pulayans, the Vettuvans, the Sambavans (Parayans, old style), the Ullatans and the Nayadis for long rivalled the hill tribes in illiteracy and ignorance. But the times are changed, and the social disabilities to which these people were subjected under the most rigid and exacting of caste systems are gradually disappearing. A sympathetic Government has been actively exerting itself for the improvement of their miserable lot. Still the depressed classes have hardly shown that progress which one might have expected from the very liberal measures adopted by the Darbar for the amelioration of their condition in general and for the removal of their illiteracy in particular. Heroic attempts have been made by the Education department to storm the citadel of their ignorance and to hoist the flag of learning within it. The weapons used in this warfare, if novel, are the most effective that can be employed for the purpose, and they recall to our mind the story of the Red Indian Chief who, in the midst of the impassioned address of the English Missionary on the greatness and glory of Christianity, quietly got up from his seat among the audience and told the inspired speaker to his utter discomfiture that what he and his brethren wanted was not eloquence or fine words but brandy and tobacco! A free meal at noon or a small money payment instead, and the free distribution of clothing, to depressed pupils in all schools appealed more powerfully to the ill-fed and ill-clad children of these communities than the richest literary repast served out to them gratis for their intellectual delectation. Many schools have been opened in localities where the depressed classes are found in large numbers. The children of these classes are given free tuition and free supplies of school requisites. Besides, special scholarships are awarded to them in all secondary schools and colleges in addition to a full remission of fees.* Many night schools, chiefly intended for the adult members of these communities, have also been started in suitable centres. And yet, in spite of

*For a full account of the concessions extended to depressed class pupils in the matter of education, please see paragraph 10 of Appendix II.—Depressed classes, and the footnotes to the paragraph.

these attractions, concessions and facilities, the depressed classes do not appear to be taking kindly to education; and the statistics of depressed pupils in schools given in the Administration Report of the State show a deplorable fall in their numbers during the year 1930—31.* This does not however mean that there has been no progress in literacy among them, and the figures contained in the following statement testify to the degree of success attained by the Education department during the decade under review.

Caste (arranged according to numerical strength)	Literates per mille of the population					
	1931 (7 years and above)			1921 (all ages)		
	Persons	Male	Female	Persons	Male	Female
1. Pulayan ..	53	91	17	9	16	3
2. Vettuvan ..	55	85	24	3	4	2
3. Sambavan (Parayan) ..	31	54	8	7	12	3
4. Ullatan ..	44	55	34	..	..	..
5. Nayadi ..	56	113	..	..	..	..

A similar campaign against illiteracy started recently among the primitive tribes of the hills has produced 9 male and 2 female literates among the 267 Kadars and 16 male and 1 female literates among the 3,185 Malayans.

13. The Muslims have always occupied the last place in literacy among the followers of different religions in the State. They form 7·3 per cent of the State's population but only 3·5 per cent of the literate population are Muslims. The restrictions enjoined by the *purdha* system must to a great extent account for the fact that there are but very few Muslim women able to read and write, and the disparity between the sexes in literacy is greatest among Muslims who have 230 literates in every 1,000 males but only 41 literates in the same number of females. And for every 100 male literates among them there are but 17 female literates. **Literacy among Muslims**

The Census Report of 1901 contains the following observations regarding the extreme illiteracy of the Muslims: "The nature of their occupations in life and their general disinclination to take kindly to literary pursuits have always stood in the way of their progress, and they are likely to continue in the same state, unless, by some bold resolve, they themselves make up their minds to better their condition in this respect. Some acquaintance with scraps of the Koran, even the study of which is not compulsory, is all the knowledge that they can boast of. The condition of the fair sex amongst them is most deplorable in the matter of education." Apparently 'the bold resolve' was lacking for a long time. In any case, judging from the progress hitherto made, it would appear that the Muslims did not avail themselves to the fullest extent of the many facilities open to them in the field of education. They had not even the excuse of social disabilities or of abject poverty which the depressed brother could bring forward; and yet the Government extended to them more concessions ** in educational matters than to other communities backward in literacy.

* In the Administration Report this fall in numbers is attributed to the severe economic depression of the period.

** Some of these concessions are given below:

(1) Every Muslim girl in the Primary classes of English schools received a monthly stipend of Rs. 2. Recently this amount has been reduced to 8 annas.

But their progress has hardly been in proportion to the special concessions enjoyed by them. For instance, we find that the disparity between the Muslims and the followers of other creeds in the ratio of literate persons in the earlier age-periods in Subsidiary Table I is no less great than in the later periods, though a slight improvement is seen in the proportion of female literates in the earlier age-groups. And the Muslims lag far behind the other communities, thanks probably to their "general disinclination to take kindly to literary pursuits."

It is, however, to be observed in this connection that recently there has been a general awakening among the Muslims as among others, so much so that the community is now well organized with its communal associations systematically working for safeguarding its interests and promoting its welfare. Accordingly the Muslims have begun not only to avail themselves to the fullest extent of the existing facilities for the education of their children but also to secure further concessions* from the Government by means of organized representation. And we may be more or less certain that the Census Superintendent of 1941 will have a much more satisfactory account to give of the Muslims' progress in literacy.

Literacy among Jews

14. The Jews have always ranked high in literacy, but their numbers are so few that no detailed examination of their figures is called for. It is, however, strange that they find a place in the list of communities backward in education though they rival the Christians in general literacy and far surpass them in English literacy. And yet the Jews, shrewd and practical as they are, have apparently no desire to be classed with the advanced communities, probably for the reason that they will forfeit the solid benefits accruing from the concessions extended to backward communities by the Education department, if they go in for a hollow, unprofitable title.

English education

15. In respect of English education and English literacy also Cochin enjoys the same pre-eminence as in general literacy. Except Delhi, there is no Province or State, big or small, in the Indian Empire, which possesses an equally high proportion in its population of persons literate in English. It is only the Province of Delhi, the seat of the Imperial Government, and cities like Madras, Bombay and Calcutta, that have, for obvious reasons, a higher proportion of literates in English. Progressive Travancore, which is educationally very much advanced, and which takes the next place to Cochin in general literacy, is seen to lag far behind our State in English education.

Province or State	Number per mille who are literate in English (5 years and above)		
	Persons	Males	Females
Delhi ..	60	90	18
Cochin ..	**37**	**58**	**16**
Ajmer Merwara ..	27	45	7
Bengal ..	25	43	5
Travancore ..	19	31	7
Mysore ..	16	27	5
Baroda ..	15	28	2
Madras ..	14	26	

(2) Muslim girls in the Lower and Upper Secondary classes are each given monthly stipends of Rs. 3 and Rs. 5 respectively.

(3) Muslim boys in the Upper Secondary and College classes are each given monthly stipends of Rs 3 and Rs. 6 respectively.

(4) Remission of half the standard rate of fees is granted to Muslim pupils who are too poor to prosecute their studies.

(5) There are also special scholarships for Muslim students in the College classes.

* For instance, the Government recently sanctioned the appointment of Quran teachers in all schools where there are Muslim pupils in sufficient numbers.

District	Number per mille who are literate in English (5 years and above)		
	Persons	Males	Females
Madras (City) ..	168	256	70
Cochin ..	**37**	**58**	**16**
Tanjore ..	21	41	2
Chingleput ..	19	33	5
Trichinopoly ..	18	33	4
Malabar ..	17	30	6
Tinnevelly ..	17	30	5

And the model States of Baroda and Mysore are still further off. The great disparity between Travancore and Cochin in this respect is perhaps to be attributed to the fact that the secondary schools in Cochin are all Anglo-vernacular, whereas there are both vernacular and Anglo-vernacular secondary schools in Travancore, and the pupils of the vernacular secondary schools have little or nothing to do with English. In the Madras Presidency, even those favoured districts that have for long been the centres of English education stand far below our State.

Progress of English education by sex and locality

16. The high proportion of English literates in Cochin is not the result of any strong European or Anglo-Indian element in the State's population, for these communities are so small in numbers that they can be safely ignored. But it is to be attributed to the steady progress of English education in the State from decade to decade. The marginal figures indicate that the proportion of English-educated persons among literates has been rising apace. They further show that the progress in English literacy has been shared in an increasing measure by the female section of the population, so much so that the disparity between the sexes in English literacy is now much less than in the past. The taluks that take precedence in English education are, as in general literacy, Cochin-Kanayannur and Trichur where the proportion of English literates exceeds the State average. The explanation for the low average in the other taluks is the same as the one advanced in connection with the disparity that was noticed in respect of general literacy. Chittur is more advanced in English education than Talapilli and Mukundapuram, though it takes the last place in general literacy. The proportion of English-educated persons among literates is higher in this taluk than elsewhere. This is so because most of the literates of Chittur are Tamil Brahmans and Nayars who, as we shall presently see, have a high proportion of English literates among them.

Census year	Literates per 1,000 (all ages)		Literates in English per 10,000 (all ages)	
	Males	Females	Males	Females
1931 ..	383	185	484	137
1921 ..	274	99	305	66
1911 ..	243	61	199	31
1901 ..	224	45	108	12
1891 ..	246	39	26	3

Taluks	Number per mille who are literate in English (all ages)		
	Persons	Males	Females
Cochin State ..	**30·7**	**48·4**	**13·7**
Cochin-Kanayannur ..	43·0	66·2	19·2
Cranganur ..	25·7	36·4	15·3
Mukundapuram ..	16·7	26·0	8·0
Trichur ..	40·4	62·5	19·7
Talapilli ..	20·1	33·1	8·3
Chittur ..	25·1	44·3	7·0

17. It is noteworthy that the Christians who were behind the Hindus in English literacy three decades ago, overtook them in the course of a decade and

outstripped them in another. That they are still maintaining the pace of their progress will be clear from the figures in the statement given below.

English education by religion

Literates in English in every 1,000.

Religion	1931		1921		1911		1901	
	Males	Females	Males	Females	Males	Females	Males	Females
Hindu ..	50	11	33	5	21	2	11·5	·5
Muslim ..	13	1	6	·5	4	..	1·9	..
Indian Christian ..	51	22	31	10	19	5	9·5	2
Jew ..	90	58	53	21	53	15	27·4	..

The Muslims, of course, occupy their unenviable position at the very bottom, several decades behind the Christians and Hindus. The Jews on the other hand stand far above the rest with 74 literates in English in every 1,000 (both sexes combined) against 37 among the Indian Christians. And 58 per mille of their female population are literate in English, while the Christians have but 22, the Hindus 11 and the Muslims 1 in every 1,000 women, able to read and write English.

and by caste and sex

18. Columns 8, 9 and 10 of Subsidiary Table V tell the interesting story of the progress made in higher education by the different castes and communities. Those that started early in the race for English education which, for many years, led to respectable if not lucrative careers, are to be distinguished by the high proportion of English literates among them. The marginal list gives the ratios for the Indian Christians, Iluvans and Nayars, the three largest communities in the State. The proportion of English literates among the Indian Christians is only one half of that among the Nayars and the disparity is more prominent in the male than in the female population. Of the English literates in the State 29·8 per cent are Nayars who form but one-ninth of the total population, while the Indian Christians who number more than a fourth of the State's population contribute but 33·6 per cent, and the Iluvans only 7 per cent, of the English-educated population of the State. About 85 per cent of our English-educated women belong to these three communities, the Nayars claiming 35·4 per cent, the Christians 43·3 per cent and the Iluvans only 5·4 per cent. The highest places for English education are, however, monopolised by some of the smaller communities among the Hindus. There are but 41,324 Brahmans in the State—a mere 3·4 per cent of its population—, but no less than 16·7 per cent of the English-educated population belong to this aristocracy of intellect. The enterprising Tamil Brahman enjoys an astonishing pre-eminence in this respect in as much as 49 per cent of the male population in this community aged 7 years and above are able to read and write English. The Konkani Brahman also stands high, but far below his Tamil brother. The head of this order of aristocracy, the orthodox and conservative Nambudiri, who for decades looked upon the language of the 'foreign heretic' as an object of intellectual if not moral

Community	Literates in English in every 1,000 (7 years and above)		
	Persons	Males	Females
Indian Christian ..	48	68	28
Iluvan ..	13	21	5
Nayar ..	96	154	48

Community		Literates in English in every 1,000 (7 years and above)		
		Persons	Males	Females
Brahman	Tamil	264	494	35
,,	Konkani	149	280	18
,,	Nambudiri	43	83	1
Malayali Kshatriya		296	493	142
Ambalavasi		147	237	61

pollution, is at long last moving with the times and already showing excellent results. The Ambalavasis are behind the Tamil Brahmans though their rank is high. But even the Tamil Brahman has to yield the palm to the Malayali Kshatriyas, who enjoy the same distinction in English as in general literacy, and among whom 49 per cent of the males and 14 per cent of the females aged 7 years and above are English-educated.

The Brahmans' supremacy is confined to the male section of their population. Child marriages among the Tamil Brahmans, the conservatism of the Konkanis and the *purdha* system and orthodoxy of the Nambudiris account for the comparatively low proportion of English-educated women among them. But the Time Spirit has affected even the Nambudiri women in their *purdha*, and the ghosts of their grandsires must be stirring uneasily in their graves to see Nambudiri maidens discarding their umbrella-veils and going to public schools, and Srimati Parvathi Antharjanam* presiding over public meetings and joining the deliberations in the State Legislative Council over the Nambudiri Bill which is to pave the way for the emancipation of her sisters.

Subsidiary Table V shows that almost all communities including the backward ones have taken to English education and are showing considerable progress in it. It is no doubt a sign of the times that even the depressed classes of the Pulayans, Vettuvans and Sambavans have a few English literates among them. And the sight of the undergraduate Pulaya girl in the Maharaja's College at Ernakulam must certainly inspire sentiments of awe and wonder in the elderly members of her community, sentiments not much different from those which Captain Cuttle's mother would have entertained if she had lived to see her worthy offspring translated into a dealer in nautical instruments and "a man o' science."

Statistics of the Education department and progress of education

19. The statistics of the Education department are given in Subsidiary Tables VIII, VIII A and IX. A comparison of the figures of educational institutions returned in 1931 with the figures of 1921, 1911 and 1901 is likely to lead to the inference that there is gradual retrogression in the field of education.

---

*Srimati Nenmanimangalam Parvathi Antharjanam is an enlightened Nambudiri lady who has discarded her veil. She has been nominated as a special member of the State Legislative Council in connection with the Nambudiri Bill now before the Council.

The following account of a meeting of the Select Committee for the Nambudiri Bill, supplied to the Madras daily, *the Hindu*, by its Trichur correspondent, is not without humour:

"There were some interesting incidents when the Select Committee of the Cochin Nambudiri Bill recorded evidence recently.

The majority of the young Nambudiris were in favour of the Bill for marriage of all males in their community (instead of the eldest alone so marrying at present leaving the rest to resort to a sort of marriage with females of the Nayar and Ambalavasi communities), for stopping polygamy, for stamping out dowry practice, and for family management of a responsible nature. But the few elder, the orthodox of the community, who appeared before the Committee, were against such progressive change and refused to look at Mrs. Nenmanimangalam Parvathi (lady Nambudiri member specially nominated for the Bill), or to answer her questions. The President had even to stop examining one Mr. Thuppan Nambudiri in the circumstance. Another, Mr. Kally Thamarapilly Nambudiri, preferred to be under a veil (of his own make) to avoid the sight of Mrs. Nenmanimangalam who had discarded the *purdha*."

(" The veil of his own make" is reported to have been a piece of cloth which the gentleman held stretched out before him like a curtain or screen, hiding his upper half from the audience.)

But the number of pupils under instruction will give a more just and correct idea of the situation. Collegiate education has made remarkable progress during the past decade. The two second grade colleges of 1921 were raised to the first grade, and another first grade college for women, an aided institution run by the St. Teresa's Convent at Ernakulam, was opened. Accordingly the strength of the college classes rose by 129 per cent (from 438 to 1,003) during the period. Besides, the first grade college at Alwaye in Travancore territory is so situated that it is of as much service to Cochin as to Travancore. Statistics are not available of the many scores of Cochin students * pursuing higher studies in arts and professional colleges at educational centres like Madras, Trichinopoly, Trivandrum, Madura, Chidambaram, Bombay, Calcutta and Benares, and in foreign universities. Secondary education too has kept pace with collegiate education and there are now 42 high schools (of which 12 are exclusively for girls,) with a strength of 6,105 pupils against 28 high schools and 2,574 pupils in 1921, the increase in the number of pupils being 137 per cent. Lower secondary schools also have increased in numbers and their strength rose from 6,781 to 10,701 or by 58 per cent. Nor has primary education lagged behind, for the returns show that there are as many as 121,266 pupils under instruction in the primary classes against 79,381 in 1921. The figures represent an increase of 53 per cent. There is a good deal of confusion in regard to the number of primary schools returned at the previous censuses. The 503 schools shown against 1931 in Subsidiary Table VIII are purely literary schools, whereas the 1,026 primary schools of 1921 include 576 unaided, indigenous institutions and other special schools. In 1923 a special census of the indigenous schools was taken, when it was seen that there were only 289 such schools with 6,921 pupils in them instead of the 576 schools and 11,437 pupils returned by the Education department in 1921. Though this department has included the 289 indigenous schools and 6,921 pupils in its returns for 1931, it is not known whether these institutions exist now and, if they do, what their strength is. This unknown and uncertain quantity has been excluded from the figures for 1931 in Subsidiary Table VIII, and hence the great disparity between 1921 and 1931 in the number of primary schools and the total number of educational institutions. That there has been an actual rise in the number of primary schools during the decade under review is clear enough from the increase of 53 ** per cent in the number of pupils.

Ratio of literates to learners: correlation of census figures with the figures of the Education department

20. In the marginal statement an attempt is made to correlate the census figures of literates under 15 years with the returns of pupils obtained from the Education department. According to these returns the strength of the primary schools is 121,266 and that of the Special schools 10,089. But the average boy or girl who has completed 14 years will be at least in the highest class of the lower secondary school if not in the upper secondary classes, and therefore we have to add the 10,701 pupils of the lower secondary schools also to the above

	No. of pupils returned by the Education department (excluding upper secondary and collegiate sections)	No. of literates under 15 returned at the census	Proportion per cent of literates to learners
1931	142,056	91,116	64·1
1921	87,203	32,710	37·5
1911	49,894	19,813	39·7
1901	38,739	14,539	37·5

* The University examination results in Subsidiary Table IX are incomplete because they do not include the results of the students referred to here.

** The percentage of increase will be 68 if the pupils of the indigenous schools and the special (Night) schools are included as in 1921.

numbers since our calculation is to include all literates under 15. The approximate number of children under 15 years attending schools will thus be 142,056 according to the statistics of the Education department, while the census returns give 91,116 literates under 15. The proportion per cent of literates to learners therefore works out at 64. The results of our calculation show that the statistics of the Education department are in agreement with the census statistics. For, out of the 121,266 pupils in the primary schools we have to select only those that have attained the census standard of literacy. The instructions issued to enumerators in this connection in consultation with the educational authorities were to the effect that only such pupils were to be returned as literate as had completed at least three out of their four years' primary course at the time of the final census, and in view of the high standard maintained in the State schools, these instructions were considered as strict enough. The pupils of the fourth and third standards, who had just completed four and three years respectively of their primary course, were accordingly returned as literate, and the pupils of the first and second standards were treated as illiterate. About 40 per cent of the primary school pupils, and all the pupils of the special and lower secondary schools, numbering in all about 70,000, should therefore be included in the group of literates under 15. There will then be a difference of about 20,000 to be accounted for, the total number of literates under 15 being 91,116. The explanation for this difference is to be sought for in the numbers of those pupils of the upper secondary classes that are under 15, of those who left school during or after their lower secondary course and who are still under 15* and of those who left school after their primary course and who too are still under 15 years (see column 11 of Subsidiary Table XI). The fact that the educational statistics of 1931 disclose a fall of more than 6,000 in the number of pupils during the academic year 1930—31 is of special significance in this connection.

The ratio of literates to learners is high enough to testify to the effective character of the education imparted to them; and the ratio for 1931 compares very favourably with the ratios for past years.

Educational policy

21. The results of the educational efforts of the past decade reviewed in paragraph 19 above may be summed up in the statement that there are 149,164 pupils (excluding the uncertain figure of 6,921 belonging to the 289 unaided, indigenous institutions) under instruction at the end of the period against 90,215 at its beginning. This represents an increase of no less than 65 per cent. The progress revealed by these figures has been achieved in spite of the fact that the Darbar has not yet adopted any system of compulsory primary education. But an enlightened policy was pursued in educational matters and private institutions were supported with liberal grants. Education in vernacular primary schools is free to all, and we have already seen that substantial concessions are extended to the backward and depressed communities. Facilities for elementary education have been provided in all parts of the State, and even the Kadars of the forests have their school on the top of the hills. From the statement appended to paragraph 6 above it will be seen that all taluks except Chittur are well equipped in the matter of educational facilities, so much so that, if all the schools in the State are evenly distributed, each village will have an average of almost three schools in it.

Wastage in primary education

22. And yet from Subsidiary Table XI we find that out of a total population of 178,516 children aged 6 to 12 years as many as 87,226 or 48·8 per cent

---

*Columns 11 and 14 of Subsidiary Table XI show that about 8,800 pupils aged 6 to 12 years left school during or after their primary course. In the same way a considerable number (all literates) must have left school during or after their lower secondary course.

(42·3 per cent of boys and 55·6 per cent of girls,) have never attended any school; and to this number must be added 3,610 boys and 3,216 girls who left school before they completed their primary course, and who therefore represent the wastage in primary education.* The percentage of children aged 6 to 12 years who are at school (including the few that have left school after successfully completing their primary course) is but 47. These figures will form a proper basis on which the question of compulsory primary education may be discussed and the educational policy of the Darbar revised if necessary.

Expenditure on education

23. The expenditure on education has naturally kept pace with the progress of educational activities and has increased by more than 50 per cent during the past ten years. In the financial year 1930—31 it was Rs. 14,03,360 (more than 16 per cent of the gross revenue, and 17·4 per cent of the total expenditure). The corresponding expenditure in 1920—21 was only Rs. 8,92,231 (14·8 per cent of the gross revenue and 14·7 per cent of the total expenditure).

Statistics of periodicals

24. Subsidiary Table XIV shows the statistics of the periodicals published in the State and the extent of their circulation. Though the figures indicate perceptible progress since 1921, they are very far indeed from erring on the side of superfluity. Nor do they give a true idea of the extent to which literacy has spread among the lower orders at least in urban areas, or to which newspapers are in demand among them. It is not a very uncommon sight to see the Rikshawalla, who waits for his hire in the street, purchasing a copy of the day's *Gomati*** hawked about in the streets and selling like ho cakes at 3 pies a copy, and deciphering the articles on the political situation and civil disobedience in British India! Verily Cochin is not far from "the realization of the visions of the journalist, who saw, as in a glass darkly, Ramaswami leaning at even in intellectual contemplation on the five-barred gate of his paddy field, or deciphering the daily newspapers in the village smithy".

Modern education and its achievements

25. This chapter may be closed with a few observations on the vital problems connected with the progress of modern education in the State. It is now four decades since the old and popular *pyal* schools were superseded in favour of schools of the modern type, and throughout this period the course of the new system of education has been marked by steady and uninterrupted progress. The statistics reviewed in this chapter prove that the primary object of education—that of conquering ignorance and bringing the minimum knowledge of letters to all—is being fulfilled in an ever increasing measure. The achievements of the educational agencies in the State, both Sirkar and private, have been such as any State or Province can justly be proud of. They have

---

* These figures give but a very imperfect idea of the actual wastage in primary education. As no special column was provided for these returns, omissions were very common. Besides, they give no information regarding those pupils of the primary classes who do not fall within the age period 6—12. Reliable statistics of the wastage, which a batch of pupils would be subjected to during their four years' course in the primary classes, were therefore collected from the Education department.

In August, 1927, there were 45,293 pupils in class I of all primary schools in the State put together. In August, 1928, we find only 28,847 pupils in class II. Of these, only 18,660 are seen in class III in August 1929. And when we turn to class IV in August, 1930, only 15,230 pupils are seen remaining.

Here is a batch of pupils losing *two thirds* of their numbers before they completed their primary course. It may be argued that a considerable number of those that failed to secure promotion at the first chance might have continued in the same class and won promotion at the second chance. Let us grant that a *third* of the loss is recovered in this way. Still there is an appalling wastage of no less than 45 per cent—50 per cent will perhaps be nearer the mark—of our children attending primary schools. A great majority of these children will be destined to be illiterate throughout their life.

** A Malayalam weekly newspaper, recently converted into a daily.

placed Cochin in the very forefront of all progressive and educated States in the Indian Empire. But the present system of education is also responsible for bringing in its wake many dark and baffling problems that defy all attempts at solution.

26. "The main point to which attention is now directed is the study of English. The material prosperity or progress of a community or of any part of India is even gauged by the degree of advance made in the same. It is likewise regarded by the people themselves as the one central hope of salvation for them".

"The value set at present on English education is so great that only one who possesses it now passes for a man of learning. That English education is a great leveller cannot be questioned, and its effect is markedly felt in the increasing cordiality of the relations between men of various castes and creeds. While the study of English stimulates intelligence and supplies a common medium of culture, it is also slowly renovating social conditions and modifying domestic relations, so that all over the country the old order of ideas is by degrees yielding place to new. The circumstance that females are taking to it in steadily increasing numbers, and that they also are yearning for a better state of things is a propitious sign that the new civilization will finally settle itself without violence to domestic tranquillity and social happiness".

Problems of modern education: educated unemployment

Thus wrote the Census Superintendent of 1901 in the chapter on Education in his Report, and it may be conceded that his anticipations have been realized to a considerable extent within the brief period of 30 years that have since elapsed. But little did he dream that the new order of civilization, the dawn of which appeared so rosy and refreshing to him, would usher in trials of the kind we are experiencing at present and that the very thing which the people regarded as their one central hope and salvation would ere long prove their chief despair and damnation. The high price set on English education was chiefly because of "the direct attachment of graduated pecuniary values to the passing of each and every examination" and, as English-educated persons were shown preference in the public service, a race began for higher education in which one community after another competed. The pecuniary value attached to the examinations began to decline because English-educated persons soon overstocked their own market. By the beginning of the decade we are dealing with, the supply far exceeded the demand. The public service was full and could not absorb more. The literary professions were all overcrowded. Those that had received English education at much cost and labour now found themselves unemployed or unsuitably employed on absurdly low salaries.* Nor could they turn to other walks in life since by temperament and training they were fit only for such pursuits as called for nothing more than a purely literary type of education. And thus arose the thorny problem of "educated unemployment", a problem that grows more complicated from year to year, because each year sends its new recruits to swell the ranks of the army of unemployed young men who are chiefly to be distinguished by an air of discontent and listlessness that sits heavy on their dejected features.

Paragraphs 36 to 39 of the last chapter, in which the results of the special census of educated unemployment have been reviewed, may be recalled in this connection.

---

* A single instance will suffice to show the gravity of the problem in this State. Graduates of the Madras University have joined the Police department as recruits. During the period of their training they will receive *a monthly allowance of Rs. 10.* After training they will develop into regular police constables on *a monthly salary of Rs. 12!* And yet there are many—graduates, undergraduates and School Finals—who envy these graduate-recruits for their extraordinary good luck in getting employed!!

Disturbing signs and outlook

27. Comparing the statistics of the Education department for the two years 1930 and 1931, one wonders whether the fall in the number of pupils referred to in paragraph 20 above, and shown in the margin, is to be attributed merely to the economic depression of the times as done by the educational authorities. Does it not also show that at least some people have begun to entertain misgivings about the utility of the kind of education their children are receiving? It is significant that the decrease in strength is confined to the lower secondary and primary classes alone. The pupils of the upper secondary and college departments are not proof against the economic depression and yet their numbers show no decline but an actual increase. The probable explanation is that they have reached a stage in higher education at which it will be unwise on their part to withdraw. Be the reasons what they may, the fall in the strength of pupils particularly of the primary classes is not a happy sign. Should it continue in future years also, the progress of literacy during the next decade cannot but be seriously affected.

Year	Number of literary institutions	Number of pupils
1930	751	152,132
1931	731	145,992

Vocational education

28. The steady increase in the number of industrial institutions will show that the educational authorities have been alive to the situation and adopting remedial measures against the growing evil. Vocational instruction is being gradually introduced in literary schools also. It is, however, extremely doubtful whether the opening of a few more industrial schools or the teaching of a few vocational subjects in the literary schools will solve the mighty problem before us. When the present system of literary education is overhauled from top to bottom; when in its place a more useful and popular system, based on and in harmony with the normal lives and the intimate needs of the people, and imparting both theoretical and practical instruction in vocational subjects which will thoroughly equip the pupils for agricultural, industrial or other useful pursuits in life that help in the production of wealth, is developed; and when the people freely take to the new system realizing in full that the higher English education of the prevalent type must be left to the rich and leisured, or intellectually gifted, few; when the present order changes giving place to a new and more practical one on the above or similar lines, then indeed shall we hope to see the dawn of a new era of contented progress in the light of which the dark trials of the present are bound to disappear.

Year	Number of industrial institutions	Number o pupils
1921	19	1,125
1930	41	3,039
1931	42	3,172

SUBSIDIARY TABLES.

I.—Literacy by age, sex and religion.

Religion	Number per mille who are literate													Number per mille who are illiterate			Number per mille who are literate in English		
	All ages			0—5		5—10		10—15		15—20		20 and over							
	Total	Males	Females	Males	Females	Males	Females	Males	Females	Males	Females	Males	Females	Total	Males	Females	Total	Males	Females
1	2	3	4	5	6	7	8	9	10	11	12	13	14	15	16	17	18	19	20
All religions ..	**282**	**383**	**185**	**2**	**2**	**264**	**191**	**439**	**303**	**575**	**321**	**498**	**187**	**718**	**617**	**815**	**31**	**48**	**14**
Hindu ..	247	357	143	2	1	248	157	411	245	578	248	461	139	753	643	857	30	50	11
Muslim ..	137	230	41	1	1	136	64	236	97	331	71	316	26	863	770	959	7	13	1
Christian ..	401	480	323	4	3	333	298	553	480	731	556	632	353	599	520	677	39	54	24
European ..	911	931	889	..	..	..	333	1,000	1,000	1,000	1,000	1,000	1,000	89	69	111	866	916	815
Anglo-Indian ..	620	629	573	10	8	282	262	772	794	863	733	792	702	355	371	341	303	351	260
Indian-Christian ..	400	479	322	4	3	333	298	552	478	730	551	631	350	600	521	679	37	51	22
Jain ..	419	619	163	..	77	214	286	333	300	857	333	870	87	581	381	837	24	42	..
Jew ..	391	494	289	18	22	376	298	563	381	639	487	625	293	609	506	711	74	90	58
Buddhist ..	667	725	600	91	..	800	571	857	750	833	1,000	955	684	333	275	400	354	490	200
Zoroastrian ..	1,000	1,000	1,000	..	..	..	..	..	..	..	1,000	1,000	1,000	..	..	..	667	1,000	500

II.—Specific figures of literacy by sex and locality.

Taluks		Number of persons		Number literate (all ages)		Literate in English (all ages)	
		Males	Females	Males	Females	Males	Females
1		2	3	4	5	6	7
COCHIN STATE	..	**589,813**	**615,203**	**225,669**	**113,984**	**28,557**	**8,442**
Cochin-Kanayannur	..	177,242	173,026	79,743	38,559	11,738	3,329
Cranganur	..	21,099	21,432	7,593	3,234	787	327
Mukundapuram	..	127,738	135,984	44,394	22,296	3,317	1,085
Trichur	..	115,523	123,734	50,402	28,574	7,225	2,441
Talapilli	..	96,173	106,251	31,721	17,094	3,187	879
Chittur	..	52,038	54,776	11,816	4,227	2,303	381

III.—Proportional figures of literacy by sex and locality.

Taluks		Number per mille who are literate (all ages)		
		Persons	Males	Females
1		2	3	4
COCHIN STATE	..	**282**	**383**	**185**
Cochin-Kanayannur	..	338	450	223
Cranganur	..	255	360	151
Mukundapuram	..	253	348	164
Trichur	..	330	436	231
Talapilli	..	241	330	161
Chittur	..	150	227	77

IV.—Proportional figures of English literacy by sex and locality.

Taluks		Number of persons literate in English in every 10,000		
		Persons	Males	Females
1		2	3	4
COCHIN STATE	..	**307**	**484**	**137**
Cochin-Kanayannur	..	430	662	192
Cranganur	..	257	364	153
Mukundapuram	..	167	260	80
Trichur	..	404	625	197
Talapilli	..	201	331	83
Chittur	..	251	443	70

V.—Literacy by caste (1931, 7 years and over and 1921, all ages.)

Caste	Number per 1,000 who are literate						Number per 10,000 who are literate in English					
	1931			1921			1931			1921		
	Persons	Male	Female	Persons	Male	Female	Persons	Male	Female	Persons	Male	Female
1	2	3	4	5	6	7	8	9	10	11	12	13
HINDU												
Agamudaiyan ..	161	313	27	..	..	..	47	101	..	..	..	..
Ambalavasi ..	728	861	602	482	636	327	1,468	2,369	608	759	1,268	246
Adikal ..	636	1,000	..	..	..	..	455	714	..	..	..	..
Chakkiyar ..	615	882	409	..	..	..	513	1,176	..	..	..	..
Chakkiyar Nambiyar ..	754	804	632	..	..	..	2,000	2,825	..	..	..	..
Chengazhi Nambiyar ..	538	732	329	..	..	..	886	1,585	132	..	..	..
Kallattu Kurup ..	548	762	386	..	..	..	411	714	181	..	..	..
Marar ..	675	801	555	..	..	..	1,363	1,856	890	..	..	..
Nambiyassan ..	715	884	541	..	..	..	949	1,865	..	..	..	..
Pisharodi ..	719	872	580	..	..	..	1,628	2,712	631	..	..	..
Pushpakan Nambiyar ..	743	879	601	..	..	..	1,496	2,832	119	..	..	..
Putuval ..	796	872	739	..	..	..	1,859	2,983	1,009	..	..	..
Tiyyattunni ..	889	1,000	750	..	..	..	2,222	4,000	..	..	..	..
Unni ..	790	870	697	..	..	..	2,028	2,468	1,515	..	..	..
Variyar ..	788	903	678	..	..	..	1,662	2,753	620	..	..	..
Ambattan ..	299	410	194	..	..	..	192	348	47	..	..	..
Arayan ..	283	428	118	122	202	26	93	139	41	23	39	4
Baniya ..	496	697	286	..	..	..	543	1,061	..	..	..	..
Boya ..	5	10	..	..	..	..	..	..	..	..	..	..
Brahman ..	613	828	409	422	598	211	1,841	3,381	233	1,061	1,849	120
Embran ..	525	659	292	..	..	..	425	621	82	..	..	..
Gauda ..	198	272	83	..	..	..	494	683	194	..	..	..
Gujarati ..	488	716	192	..	..	..	952	1,684	..	..	..	..
Konkani ..	450	723	175	239	369	84	1,492	2,800	176	709	1,238	79
Marathi ..	497	728	213	..	..	..	2,095	3,696	133	..	..	..
Malayali — Elayad ..	720	882	526				517	949	..			
Malayali — Muttad ..	806	869	742	465	629	273	1,550	3,000	78	266	488	7
Malayali — Nambudiri ..	664	845	477				425	831	8			
Tamil ..	686	869	503	489	712	246	2,644	4,742	349	1,468	2,677	149
Telugu ..	783	920	619	..	..	..	4,130	7,200	476	..	..	..
Others ..	540	662	182	353	453	140	805	1,077	..	837	1,109	257
Chakkan ..	233	378	87	114	190	24	158	301	11	108	198	..
Chakkiliyan ..	28	31	22	..	..	..	15	..	31	..	..	..
Chaliyan — Chaliyan ..	240	302	169	151	254	47	158	118	203	105	169	40
Chaliyan — Pattaryan ..	413	581	260				383	648	139			

V.—Literacy by caste (1931, 7 years and over and 1921, all ages.)—cont.

Caste	Number per 1,000 who are literate						Number per 10,000 who are literate in English					
	1931			1921			1931			1921		
	Persons	Male	Female	Persons	Male	Female	Persons	Male	Female	Persons	Male	Female
1	2	3	4	5	6	7	8	9	10	11	12	13
HINDU—cont.												
Chavalan ..	83	154	10	..	..	..	..	..	..	..	..	..
Chetti ..	181	335	56	79	157	14	155	334	9	105	230	2
Dasi ..	442	664	330	..	..	..	1,128	2,364	505	..	..	..
Devangan ..	204	371	39	227	456	57	121	229	15	514	1,013	142
Eluthassan ..	289	462	127	126	219	39	161	286	44	40	72	10
Eravalan ..	2	4	..	..	..	..	..	..	..	..	..	..
Idaiyan ..	373	472	263	..	..	..	740	1,288	135	..	..	..
Iluvan ..	262	429	111	105	186	33	118	205	49	38	71	7
Kadan ..	54	81	22	..	..	..	..	..	..	..	..	..
Kaikolan ..	92	186	10	89	201	7	86	172	6	71	163	4
Kakkalan ..	181	277	76	..	..	..	52	99	..	..	..	..
Kallan ..	229	427	55	..	..	..	..	..	..	..	..	..
Kammalan ..	296	511	95	129	238	25	43	82	8	12	23	2
Kallasari ..	313	576	55	..	..	..	24	48	..	..	..	..
Kollan ..	156	334	63	..	..	..	30	58	3	..	..	..
Marasari ..	307	548	85	..	..	..	39	75	6	..	..	..
Moosari ..	260	412	105	..	..	..	43	86	..	..	..	..
Tattan ..	438	671	217	..	..	..	105	185	29	..	..	..
Tolkollan ..	194	343	57	..	..	..	..	..	..	..	..	..
Kanakkan ..	103	171	35	44	76	8	11	16	6	..	..	..
Kaniyan ..	656	808	504	371	531	237	169	313	25	46	101	..
Kavara ..	10	20	..	..	..	..	15	29	..	..	..	..
Kavundan ..	133	247	17	48	60	31	68	129	7	..	..	..
Kootan ..	11	22	..	..	..	..	..	..	..	.	..	..
Kshatriya ..	648	728	577	..	..	..	2,175	3,506	1,001	..	..	..
Gujarati ..	479	762	167	..	..	..	917	1,746	..	..	..	..
Karnataka ..	227	369	18	..	..	..	213	357	..	..	..	..
Marathi ..	86	111	76	..	..	..	..	..	..	..	..	..
Malayali ..	797	830	767	579	658	507	2,964	4,931	1,422	1,583	2,419	822
Rajput .	244	444	87	..	..	..	976	2,222	..	..	..	..
Others ..	583	583	583	..	..	..	833	1,042	..	..	..	..
Kudumi chetti ..	146	260	24	85	169	6	49	91	5	9	14	4
Kurukkal ..	257	500	23	..	..	..	153	313	..	..	..	..
Kusavan ..	41	79	10	23	48	1	..	..	..	26	56	..

V.—*Literacy by caste (1931, 7 years and over and 1921, all ages.)—cont.*

Caste	Number per 1,000 who are literate						Number per 10,000 who are literate in English					
	1931			1921			1931			1921		
	Persons	Male	Female	Persons	Male	Female	Persons	Male	Female	Persons	Male	Female
1	2	3	4	5	6	7	8	9	10	11	12	13
HINDU—*cont.*												
Malayan ..	7	12	1	..	..	..	..	..	..	..	..	..
Nambidi ..	599	769	484	..	..	..	994	2,231	156	..	..	..
Nanjanattu Pillai ..	556	686	333	..	..	..	1,516	2,229	294	..	..	..
Nayadi ..	56	113	..	..	..	..	..	..	..	..	..	..
Nayar ..	557	722	420	310	420	200	960	1,541	477	396	633	176
Odan ..	83	156	12	..	..	..	..	..	..	..	..	..
Ottanaikan (Odde) ..	49	81	15	62	114	12	51	92	9	..	..	..
Panan ..	172	248	98	100	186	32	..	..	..	..	..	..
Pandaran ..	168	294	48	64	107	24	48	94	5	39	69	11
Pandltattan ..	309	494	110	288	478	39	165	294	26	92	109	71
Pulayan ..	53	91	17	9	16	3	8	14	2	..	1	..
Pulluvan ..	230	386	72	..	..	..	72	143	..	..	..	..
Samantan ..	654	882	512	..	..	..	992	1,955	157	..	..	..
Sambavan (Parayan) ..	31	54	8	7	12	3	4	9	..	1	..	3
Do. Tamil ..	65	119	8	..	..	..	36	70	..	..	..	..
Tarakan ..	302	484	139	..	..	..	515	978	98	..	..	..
Tottiyan ..	58	78	45	..	..	..	..	..	..	..	..	..
Ullatan ..	44	55	34	..	..	..	..	..	..	..	..	..
Vadukan ..	55	114	5	..	..	..	36	77	..	..	..	..
Vaisyan ..	410	644	127	..	..	..	858	1,538	39	..	..	..
Valan ..	307	461	144	117	208	42	168	258	73	25	52	4
Valluvan ..	6	12	..	..	..	..	..	..	..	..	..	..
Vaniyan ..	339	615	64	..	..	..	377	754	..	..	..	..
Vannan ..	59	105	11	..	..	..	..	..	..	..	..	..
Velakkattalavan ..	352	501	214	165	254	86	139	197	85	31	27	35
Velan ..	287	519	77	181	335	23	32	60	7	13	25	..
Vellalan ..	333	545	122	241	324	100	566	1,042	95	401	604	59
Veluttedan ..	310	471	179	144	222	75	138	266	34	24	45	6
Vettuvan ..	55	85	24	3	4	2	11	15	7	..	..	..
Vilkurup ..	258	429	114	..	..	..	7	15	..	..	..	..
Minor castes ..	172	266	72	..	..	..	328	584	52	..	..	..
Caste unspecified ..	330	511	170	..	..	..	742	1,353	63	..	..	..
No caste ..	714	833	..	..	..	..	2,143	2,500	..	..	..	..

V.—Literacy by caste (1931, 7 years and over and 1921, all ages.)—cont.

Caste	Number per 1,000 who are literate						Number per 10,000 who are literate in English					
	1931			1921			1931			1921		
	Persons	Male	Female	Persons	Male	Female	Persons	Male	Female	Persons	Male	Female
1	2	3	4	5	6	7	8	9	10	11	12	13
MUSLIM												
Jonakan ..	156	265	45	68	128	7	51	96	5	15	29	1
Ravuttan ..	158	280	27	129	227	12	111	210	5	64	110	10
Others ..	234	377	85	..	..	..	180	330	22	..	..	..
CHRISTIAN												
Anglo-Indian ..	725	790	667	288	235	350	3,736	3,565	3,886	1,389	1,219	1,586
European ..	962	982	939	909	007	913	9,231	9,091	9,388	8,485	8,605	8,261
Indian Christian ..	508	612	407	262	351	172	475	678	277	205	309	101
JAIN ..	503	745	178	356	569	70	291	510	..	495	517	465
JEW ..	471	612	339	278	380	176	899	1,127	685	368	528	207
BUDDHIST ..	808	923	692	..	..	..	4,359	6,410	2,308	..	..	..
ZOROASTRIAN ..	1,000	1,000	1,000	..	..	..	6,667	10,000	5,000	..	..	..

Note.—Figures for columns left blank under 1921 are not available.

VI.—Progress of Literacy since 1881.

NATURAL DIVISION "Malabar and Konkan"	Number of literates per mille											
	All ages (10 and over)											
	Male						Female					
	1931	1921	1911	1901	1891	1881	1931	1921	1911	1901	1891	1881
1	2	3	4	5	6	7	8	9	10	11	12	13
Cochin State ..	497	365	329	302	376	..	225	127	79	59	62	..

Number of literates per mille															
15—20								20 and over							
Male				Female				Male				Female			
1931	1921	1911	1901	1931	1921	1911	1901	1931	1921	1911	1901	1931	1921	1911	1901
14	15	16	17	18	19	20	21	22	23	24	25	26	27	28	29
575	359	303	282	321	174	104	77	498	392	367	343	187	113	73	56

Note.—Out of a population of 600,278 there were 10,752 persons returned as literate in 1881. Figures by sex and age are not available. Figures for 1891 for the age periods of 15—20 and 20 and over are also not available.

VII.—Proportion of Literacy at certain ages.

Age-group	Total population			Total literate			Total literate in English		
	Persons	Males	Females	Persons	Males	Females	Persons	Males	Females
1	2	3	4	5	6	7	8	9	10
7—13 years	209,925	106,543	103,382	70,424	41,310	29,114	2,443	1,621	822
14—16 „	86,288	43,187	43,101	39,634	24,382	15,252	5,973	4,114	1,859
17—23 „	149,526	68,741	80,785	64,451	39,951	24,500	11,572	8,398	3,174
24 years and over	509,868	245,980	263,888	164,289	119,550	44,739	16,986	14,399	2,587
Total	955,607	464,451	491,156	338,798	225,193	113,605	36,974	28,532	8,443

VIII.—(a) Classification of Educational Institutions into Literary and Industrial.

Agency	1929—30				1930—31			
	Number of institutions	Number of pupils			Number of institutions	Number of pupils		
		Boys	Girls	Total		Boys	Girls	Total
1	2	3	4	5	6	7	8	9
LITERARY INSTITUTIONS								
Government ..	171	29,623	16,363	45,966	168	27,649	16,707	44,416
Church Mission Societies or Protestant Missionaries ..	21	2,356	1,334	3,690	16	2,111	1,101	3,212
Roman Catholic Missionaries ..	22	4,672	2,676	7,348	17	3,374	1,605	4,979
Indian Priests ..	196	23,015	17,017	40,032	163	18,026	14,881	32,907
Indian Gentlemen and Ladies ..	280	32,170	15,826	47,996	326	34,934	20,166	55,100
Masters themselves ..	61	5,300	1,900	7,200	41	3,825	1,553	5,378
Total ..	751	97,016	55,136	152,152	731	89,919	56,073	145,992
INDUSTRIAL INSTITUTIONS								
Government ..	22	1,187	724	1,911	22	1,150	760	1,910
Church Mission Societies or Protestant Missionaries ..	1	..	32	32	1	..	35	35
Roman Catholic Missionaries ..	..	..	..	..	..	..	..	..
Indian Priests ..	11	154	601	755	11	160	632	792
Indian Gentlemen and Ladies ..	7	164	177	341	8	195	240	435
Masters themselves ..	..	..	..	..	..	..	..	..
Total ..	41	1,505	1,534	3,039	42	1,505	1,667	3,172
Grand Total ..	**792**	**98,521**	**56,650**	**155,171**	**773**	**91,424**	**57,740**	**149,164**

VIII.—(b) The number of institutions and pupils according to the returns of the Education Department.

Class of Institution	1931		1921		1911		1901	
	No. of Institutions	No. of Scholars	No. of Institutions	No. of Scholars	No. of Institutions	No. of Scholars	No. of Institutions	No. of Scholars
1	2	3	4	5	6	7	8	9
First Grade Colleges ..	3	1,003	..	..	..	..	..	..
Second Grade Colleges ..	..	..	2	438	1	172	1	57
High Schools ..	42	*6,105	28	2,574	13	1,246	8	804
Lower Secondary Schools ..	60	† 10,701	61	6,781	21	[illegible]	19	1,696
Primary Schools ..	503	‡ 121,266	1,026	79,381	969	[illegible]	875	29,139
Night Schools ..	111	6,099						
Special Schools, such as technical, Industrial and Religious Schools ..	54	3,990	21	1,041	11	[illegible]	386	7,904
Total ..	778	149,164	1,138	90,215	1,015	51,322	1,289	39,600

* Strength of upper secondary classes only.

† Includes the strength of the lower secondary classes (1) of the 60 Lower Secondary Schools and (2) of the 42 High Schools.

‡ Includes the strength (1) of the 503 Primary Schools (2) of the primary classes of the 60 Lower Secondary Schools and (3) of the primary classes of the 42 High Schools.

IX.—Main results of University Examinations.

Examination	1931		1921		1911		1901	
	Candidates	Passed	Candidates	Passed	Candidates	Passed	Candidates	Passed
1	2	3	4	5	6	7	8	9
Entrance Examination ..	1,941	490	532	234	378	102	133	41
Intermediate Examination ..	279	149	156	80	55	27	17	11
B. A. Examination ..	170	68	..	..	..	..	..	..
Total ..	2,390	707	688	314	433	129	150	52

X.—Statement showing the number of persons among literates who have successfully completed their Primary course in schools according to the Census of 1931.

TALUK			Number of persons who have successfully completed the Primary course by Religion																
			All Religions			Hindu		Christian		Muslim		Jew		Jain		Buddhist		Zoroastrian	
			Persons	Males	Females	Males	Females	Males	Females	Males	Females	Males	Females	Males	Females	Males	Females	Males	Females
1			2	3	4	5	6	7	8	9	10	11	12	13	14	15	16	17	18
Cochin State	..	..	**116,394**	**78,848**	**37,546**	**46,280**	**18,747**	**30,226**	**18,388**	**2,185**	**322**	**102**	**76**	**24**	**2**	**28**	**12**	**1**	**1**
Cochin-Kanayannur	..	..	43,639	30,575	13,064	16,874	6,169	12,702	6,738	873	75	102	76	24	2	1	3	1	1
Cranganur	..	..	2,992	2,025	967	1,647	820	165	109	213	38	..	..	..	..	..	..	..	..
Mukundapuram	..	..	17,266	11,387	5,879	5,993	2,412	5,026	3,180	363	85	..	..	..	..	5	2	..	..
Trichur	..	..	31,748	20,808	10,940	11,395	5,093	9,020	5,792	379	48	..	..	..	..	14	7	..	..
Talapilli	..	..	13,787	8,922	4,865	5,657	2,491	3,085	2,311	180	63	..	..	..	..	..	..	..	..
Chittur	..	..	6,962	5,131	1,831	4,724	1,762	230	56	177	13	..	..	..	..	..	..	..	..

XI.—Statement showing the number and literacy of children of school-going age (6—12) in the State.—(1) by Taluks.

TALUKS	Total number of children of school-going age (between 6 and 12 years of age)			Number of children who are now attending school						Number of children who have left school						Number of children who have not attended any school		
				Above Primary classes			In Primary classes			After completing Primary course			Before completing Primary course					
	Total	Boys	Girls	Total	Boys	Girls	Total	Boys	Girls	Total	Boys	Girls	Total	Boys	Girls	Total	Boys	Girls
1	2	3	4	5	6	7	8	9	10	11	12	13	14	15	16	17	18	19
COCHIN STATE	**178,516**	**90,865**	**87,651**	**4,168**	**2,621**	**1,547**	**78,300**	**45,025**	**33,275**	**1,996**	**1,132**	**864**	**6,826**	**3,610**	**3,216**	**87,226**	**38,477**	**48,749**
Cochin-Kanayannur	51,458	26,176	25,282	1,542	972	570	26,320	14,760	11,560	684	372	312	2,265	1,106	1,159	20,647	8,966	11,681
Cranganur	6,509	3,306	3,203	105	63	42	2,417	1,383	1,034	47	27	20	198	117	81	3,742	1,716	2,026
Mukundapuram	40,250	20,663	19,587	453	285	168	17,701	10,506	7,195	333	183	150	1,720	977	743	20,043	8,712	11,331
Trichur	34,857	17,735	17,122	1,217	752	465	17,399	9,803	7,596	471	279	192	1,269	624	645	14,501	6,277	8,224
Talapilli	29,701	14,983	14,718	442	285	157	11,189	6,413	4,776	370	253	117	1,145	666	479	16,555	7,366	9,189
Chittur	15,741	8,002	7,739	409	264	145	3,274	2,160	1,114	91	18	73	229	120	109	11,738	5,440	6,298

XII.—Statement showing the number and literacy of children of school-going age (6—12) in the State.—(2) by Religion.

RELIGIONS	Total number of children of school-going age (between 6 and 12 years of age)			Number of children who are now attending school						Number of children who have left school						Number of children who have not attended any school		
				Above Primary classes			In Primary classes			After completing Primary course			Before completing Primary course					
	Total	Boys	Girls	Total	Boys	Girls	Total	Boys	Girls	Total	Boys	Girls	Total	Boys	Girls	Total	Boys	Girls
1	2	3	4	5	6	7	8	9	10	11	12	13	14	15	16	17	18	19
ALL RELIGIONS ..	**178,516**	**90,865**	**87,651**	**4,168**	**2,621**	**1,547**	**78,300**	**45,025**	**33,275**	**1,996**	**1,132**	**864**	**6,826**	**3,610**	**3,216**	**87,226**	**38,477**	**48,749**
Hindu ..	113,348	58,066	55,282	2,565	1,707	858	45,005	27,149	17,856	1,043	577	466	4,098	2,189	1,909	60,637	26,444	34,193
Christian ..	50,418	25,649	24,769	1,496	859	637	29,737	15,802	13,925	866	512	354	2,165	1,140	1,025	16,164	7,336	8,828
Muslim ..	14,504	7,016	7,488	102	51	51	3,428	1,986	1,443	85	43	42	559	279	280	10,330	4,657	5,673
Jew ..	202	114	88	3	2	1	107	72	35	1	..	1	3	2	1	88	38	50
Jain ..	32	17	15	2	2	..	24	14	10	1	..	1	..	..	..	5	1	4
Buddhist ..	12	3	9	..	..	..	9	2	7	..	..	..	1	..	1	2	1	1

XIII.—Statement showing the number and literacy of children of school-going age (6—12) of selected Hindu castes.

Castes	Total number of children of school-going age (between 6 and 12 years of age)			Number of children who are now attending school. Above Primary classes			Number of children who are now attending school. In Primary classes			Number of children who have left school. After completing Primary course			Number of children who have left school. Before completing Primary course			Number of children who have not attended any school		
	Total	Boys	Girls	Total	Boys	Girls	Total	Boys	Girls	Total	Boys	Girls	Total	Boys	Girls	Total	Boys	Girls
1	2	3	4	5	6	7	8	9	10	11	12	13	14	15	16	17	18	19
Advanced in Literacy																		
Ambalavasi ..	1,257	642	615	93	63	30	737	406	331	22	12	10	51	17	34	354	144	210
Brahman-Konkani ..	1,461	709	752	92	66	26	718	426	292	24	9	15	35	14	21	592	194	398
Do Tamil ..	3,648	1,881	1,767	487	353	134	2,341	1,224	1,117	62	22	40	99	26	73	659	256	403
Nayar ..	19,555	9,912	9,643	1,052	654	398	11,130	6,020	5,110	312	173	139	697	317	380	6,364	2,748	3,616
Total ..	25,921	13,144	12,777	1,724	1,136	588	14,926	8,076	6,850	420	216	204	882	374	508	7,969	3,342	4,627
Backward in Literacy																		
Ilavan ..	42,934	20,792	20,142	474	310	164	16,508	10,174	6,334	332	185	147	1,480	800	680	22,140	9,323	12,817
Kammalan ..	6,431	3,262	3,169	49	32	17	2,471	1,568	903	91	30	61	281	160	121	3,539	1,472	2,067
Kanakkan ..	1,919	969	950	1	1	..	582	357	225	1	1	..	63	85	28	1,272	575	697
Kudumi chetti ..	2,076	1,102	974	5	5	..	604	457	147	2	2	..	70	48	22	1,395	590	805
Pulayan ..	12,167	6,184	5,983	20	18	2	2,312	1,469	843	5	3	2	459	274	185	9,371	4,420	4,951
Sambavan ..	1,633	833	800	5	5	..	235	189	46	6	6	..	55	36	19	1,332	597	735
Valan ..	1,843	955	888	30	17	13	858	508	350	24	20	4	107	54	53	824	356	468
Velan ..	1,476	744	732	7	6	1	444	286	158	20	15	5	56	31	22	949	402	546
Vettuvan ..	1,785	926	859	7	6	1	432	289	143	3	1	2	95	54	41	1,248	576	672
Total ..	70,264	35,767	34,497	598	400	198	24,446	15,297	9,149	484	263	221	2,066	1,495	1,171	42,070	18,312	23,758

XIV.—Number and circulation of newspapers, etc.

Language	Class of newspaper (daily, weekly, etc.)	1931		1921		1911		1901	
		Number	Circulation	Number	Circulation	Number	Circulation	Number	Circulation
1	2	3	4	5	6	7	8	9	10
Malayalam ..	Bi-weekly	1	850	..	..	..	..	..	..
Do ..	Weekly	6	4,400	7	5,850	3	2,675	..	..
English ..	do	..	..	1	400	..	..	..	..
Anglo-Vernacular ..	do	7	5,000	1	500	..	..	..	..
Do ..	Tri-monthly	1	500	..	..	..	..	..	..
Malayalam ..	Bi-monthly	..	..	..	..	1	280	..	..
Do ..	Monthly	17	8,700	10	4,875	7	5,200	..	..
Latin ..	do	..	..	1	1,000	..	..	..	..
Anglo Vernacular ..	do	5	5,200	..	..	..	..	..	..
Latin and Malayalam ..	do	1	800	..	..	..	..	..	..
English and Latin ..	do	..	..	1	1,000	..	..	..	..
Malayalam and Sanskrit ..	do	..	..	..	..	1	600	..	..
Anglo-Vernacular and Latin ..	do	..	..	1	300	..	..	..	..
Malayalam ..	Once in two months	..	..	..	..	1	320	..	..
Do ..	Quarterly	1	500	..	..	..	..	..	..
English ..	do	..	..	1	650	..	..	..	..
Anglo-Vernacular ..	do	5	3,300	..	..	..	..	..	..
Anglo-Vernacular and Latin ..	At intervals	1	150	..	..	..	..	..	..
	Total	**45**	**29,400**	**23**	**14,475**	**13**	**9,075**	..	..

CHAPTER X.—LANGUAGE.

Reference to statistics

STATISTICS of the languages spoken in the State are given in Part I of Imperial Table XV. Part II of this Table together with its supplement deals with bi-, tri- and poli-lingualism. Of the two Subsidiary Tables appended to this chapter, the first shows the distribution of the total population by mother tongue, the languages being arranged according to the revised scheme of classification of Indian languages based on Sir George Grierson's scheme. The second Subsidiary Table gives the distribution by language of the State's population, only the more important local languages being shown.

Accuracy of language returns

2. The enumeration schedules contained two columns for recording language returns, in the first of which the enumerators were asked to "enter each person's mother tongue, i. e. the language as first spoken from the cradle." Where the person enumerated was an infant or a deaf-mute, the language of the mother was to be given. In the other column intended for subsidiary languages the enumerators were to "enter the language or languages habitually spoken by each person in addition to his mother tongue in daily or domestic life." The popular languages spoken in the State are so well known that the returns of mother tongue in the first column are on the whole accurate, the errors being very few and quite negligible. But the returns of subsidiary languages appear to be less satisfactory for reasons explained in paragraph 10 of this chapter.

Distribution of population by language

3. According to these statistics, twenty-nine languages were returned at the present census against seventeen* at the census of 1921; and Subsidiary Table I shows that thirteen of them are vernaculars of India, seven are vernaculars of other Asiatic countries and Africa and nine are European languages. Cochin like other parts of South India is pre-eminently Dravidian in respect of its languages. The West Coast in particular is the home of Malayalam, one of the members of the Dravida group in the Dravidian family of languages, and the parent tongue of as many as 90·3 per cent of the State's population is Malayalam. Tamil, Kanarese and Tulu, three other members of the Dravida group, form the mother tongue of 5·9 per cent of the population, while Telugu, the Andhra language of the Dravidian family, is claimed by 1 per cent. Thus 97·2 per cent of the total population have Dravidian languages as their mother tongue. The remaining twenty-four languages together form the parent tongue of only 2·8 per cent of the State's population.

Language	Proportion of speakers per mille of the total population during the census year			
	1931	1921	1911	1901
Malayalam	903·0	901·7	893·3	881·6
Tamil	54·9	58·8	60·2	66·7
Konkani	18·5	18·0	23·0	23·7
Telugu	10·0	9·1	12·2	15·6
Kanarese	3·7	3·9	4·5	5·1
Tulu	0·6	0·5	0·6	0·8
Total	990·7	992·0	993·8	993·5

Malayalam, the vernacular of the State

4. Malayalam is the vernacular and official language of the State and elementary education is imparted through its medium. The proportion of those who return Malayalam as their mother tongue has been steadily increasing, so much so that it has risen from 88·2 per cent of the total population in 1901 to 90·3 per cent in 1931. This increase is made up by a corresponding decrease in the proportion of those who have returned other languages as their parent tongue and the marginal table shows how Tamil, the most widely spoken language after

*The new languages returned at the present census are 13 in number: Pashto, Bengali, Marwari (Rajasthani), Singhalese, Persian, Chinese, Japanese, Italian, French, Welsh, Gaelic, Flemish and German.

Malayalam, and some other languages have been gradually though slowly losing ground. It is further to be noted in this connection that Malayalam is the language of literacy for a great majority of those who have returned Tamil and Konkani as their mother tongue. 95·7 per cent of the population in Mukundapuram taluk, 96 per cent in Trichur, 93·9 per cent in Talapilli and 92·4 per cent in Cranganur speak Malayalam as their parent language. But the proportion in Cochin-Kanayannur with its strong Konkani element and with the mixed population of Mattancheri is slightly lower, being only 90 per cent. The Tamil-Malayalam cultural border zone in Chittur taluk has naturally the lowest proportion of Malayalam speakers, their percentage being but 57·7 in the population of the taluk as a whole. The statistics for the North-East and South-West blocks of Chittur were compiled separately for the inset in the Linguistic map inserted in this chapter, and they show that the proportion of Malayalam speakers in the North-East block bordering the Tamil district of Coimbatore is as low as 52·2 per cent. The distribution by taluks of the more important languages of the State is shown in the appended table.

Taluk	Number per 10,000 of the total population in each taluk whose mother tongue is										
	Malayalam	Tamil	Konkani	Kanarese	Tulu	Telugu	Marathi	Kachchhi	Gujarati	Hindi	English
COCHIN STATE ..	9,030	549	185	37	6	101	43	6	10	21	5
Cochin-Kanayannur ..	8,996	253	466	15	14	9	117	20	36	20	12
Cranganur ..	9,243	263	329	4	3	3	148	2	..	..	..
Mukundapuram ..	9,568	246	118	9	3	30	11	..	..	7	2
Trichur ..	9,598	298	17	8	4	42	6	..	..	15	6
Talapilli ..	9,389	395	..	71	1	133	1	..	..	8	..
Chittur ..	5,773	3,235	3	195	2	685	3	..	..	101	2

Other Dravidian language

5. 66,164 persons representing 5·5 per cent of the State's population have returned Tamil as their mother tongue. For reasons stated in the last paragraph, Chittur taluk is the stronghold of Tamil and as many as 34,557 of these Tamil speakers (52·2 per cent of their total strength) are to be found in this taluk, and their proportion in the population of Chittur is as high as 32·4 per cent. In the North-East block alone this proportion rises to 36·9 per cent. Telugu has been returned by 12,142 persons (1 per cent of the State's population) and it is again Chittur with its mixed population that claims more than half this number. Kanarese is the mother tongue of 4,493 persons, about half this number being found in Chittur. Tulu is spoken by a very small number (731) of Tulu Brahmans or Embrans as they are called.

Other Indian languages

6. Of the other Indian languages, Konkani is the parent tongue of 22,350 persons (1·9 per cent of the total population), Marathi of 5,210, Hindi of 2,565, Gujarati of 1,261 and Kachchhi (Sindhi) of 714. Most of these people with the exception of the Hindi speakers are to be found in Cochin-Kanayannur taluk. The non-Malayali section of the population in Chittur taluk claims about half the number of Hindi speakers.

Dutch was returned by 2 persons in 1921, whereas we have no returns for Dutch in 1931. The 13 new languages together claim but 33 speakers.

7. Of the European languages, English has been returned as the mother tongue of 630 persons, Portuguese of 114, and all other languages together of 26. The figures for English are noteworthy. Imperial Table XVII shows that there are 112 Europeans and 1,717 Anglo-Indians in the State's population. It is therefore obvious that most of the Anglo-Indians have returned Malayalam as their parent language. These returns are correct in as much as Malayalam is the home speech of a great majority of the Anglo-Indians in the State. **English and other European languages**

8. A comparison of the language statistics of Part I of Imperial Table XV with the statistics of Race, Tribe or Caste given in Imperial Table XVII will throw light on wrong or misleading returns of mother tongue in as much as the latter table enables us to classify the population into linguistic groups like the Malayalam-speaking indigenous Malayali castes, the Tamil-speaking Tamil castes and other castes speaking other languages. A statement showing the numerical strength of the more prominent communities according to Imperial Table XVII side by side with the strength of these communities according to Part I of Imperial Table XV is given in the margin. It is seen from the figures that the number of persons who have returned languages other than Malayalam as their mother tongue is lower than the number of persons in the respective communities according to the Caste Table, while the position is reversed so far as Malayalam is concerned. Wrong or misleading returns of mother tongue and the displacement of the languages of foreign minorities by the language of the local majority are the two reasons for this disparity. The total strength of the Konkani castes is 27,016, but only 22,338 persons have returned Konkani as their parent language. Many Konkani Brahmans consider it an honour to call their mother tongue Marathi, and accordingly we find Marathi returned by 5,210 persons though the Marathi castes according to Imperial Table XVII number but a few hundreds. There are 1,571 Tulu Brahmans according to the Caste Table but only 731 persons speak Tulu. It is to be feared that many Tulu Brahmans wrongly returned Kanarese as their mother tongue, and this will partly account for the difference in numbers. Hebrew was entered as the parent language of as many as 266 Jews; but, even though a few among them have some knowledge of the language, Malayalam is now their mother tongue. The parent language of the original Hebrew immigrants to Cochin was displaced centuries ago by the most widely spoken language of their new home. **Wrong or misleading returns of mother tongue**

Community classified by language	* Numerical strength according to Caste Table (XVII)	Number of speakers of the language according to Part I, Imperial Table XV
Malayalam ..	1,082,000	1,088,081
Tamil ..	70,000	66,164
Konkani ..	27,016	22,338
Telugu ..	14,000	12,142
Tulu ..	1,571	731

* The figures are only approximately correct since only the approximate numbers of Tamils, Telugus etc. among Indian Christians, certain sections of Muslims, minor castes and castes unspecified were available.

9. While wrong or misleading returns thus account for part of the difference between the two sets of figures in the margin of the foregoing paragraph, the process of the displacement of the languages spoken by foreign minorities by the chief language of the State is responsible for this discrepancy to a much greater extent. It was remarked in paragraph 4 above that the proportion of Malayalam speakers in the State's population was slowly increasing against a corresponding decrease in the number of speakers of other languages. Malayalam speakers have increased by 23·5 per cent during the past decade while those who have returned Tamil as their mother tongue record an increase **Displacement of alien languages by Malayalam**

of only 14·9 per cent, and the figures in the margin of paragraph 4 reveal the gradual decline not only of Tamil but of other languages as well. Alien communities like those of the Nanjanattu Pillais and Tharakans, which were originally Tamil-speaking castes that had immigrated from the Tamil districts, have been domiciled in the Malayalam country for such a long time that they have adopted Malayali customs, manners and speech with the result that they can no more be distinguished from indigenous Malayali castes. Here, therefore, we have living instances of a change not merely of the mother tongue but of the very culture of a people brought about by the necessary adaptation of immigrant minorities to their altered environment. For purposes of the marginal table in the last paragraph, such communities have been treated as Malayalam-speaking castes in Imperial Table XVII. But there are other communities like the Panditattans (Tamil goldsmiths), Pandarans and Chakkans (oil-pressers), that are still treated as Tamil castes; and though a few among them like the Panditattans still pretend to speak Tamil as their home language—their speech is Tamil in name but Malayalam in substance—, most of them are now Malayali in several respects including that of their mother tongue. What is true of the Tamil castes is equally true of other non-Malayali castes. In a census class held at Vadakkancheri in Talapilli taluk for the training of census officers, certain Tulu Brahmans who happened to be present on the spot were enumerated. They returned Malayalam as their parent tongue, and I was surprised to learn from them that they did not know Tulu and that there were several families of Tulu Brahmans in Talapilli who had given up their original mother tongue in favour of Malayalam. This is one of the reasons why the number of Tulu Brahmans exceeds the number of those that have returned Tulu as their parent language.

Bi-lingualism and accuracy of returns of subsidiary languages

10. The first stage in the process of this displacement of alien languages by the home language is the prevalence of bi-lingualism among the alien minorities who are compelled by the exigencies of their residence to learn the language of their new home. To illustrate this aspect of the subject, Part II of Imperial Table XV—Bi-lingualism—has been compiled from the returns of subsidiary languages collected at the census. As remarked in paragraph 2 above, these returns are less accurate than the returns of mother tongue. In some cases it was found that people returned all the languages they knew (including dead languages and languages that were not spoken by any section of the population in Cochin), irrespective of the fact that they had no occasion to speak them; while, in other cases, they did not return even those languages which they generally used in their daily intercourse with others. For instance, in the North-East block of Chittur taluk, where the Tamil and Malayalam zones meet, considerable numbers of the Malayalam-speaking section of the population know Tamil and have occasion to speak it in their daily life. The returns, however, give but a poor idea of the numbers of these people.

Malayalam as subsidiary language

11. The Bi-lingualism Table, and the Linguistic map inserted in this chapter, illustrate how the non-Malayali communities in the State, with very few and quite insignificant exceptions, speak Malayalam as a subsidiary language. Thus 79·7 per cent of the non-Malayali section of the population have returned Malayalam as a subsidiary language. In important communities like the Tamil, Konkani, Telugu, Kanarese, Marathi etc., the proportion ranges between 75 and 90 per cent. In other words, excluding children, almost all persons belonging to these communities know, and have occasion to speak, Malayalam. The Linguistic map together with its key gives the exact proportions of the bi-lingual population for the more important languages. The very low proportion of persons speaking Indian subsidiary languages among those who have returned Malayalam as their mother tongue is significant in this connection.

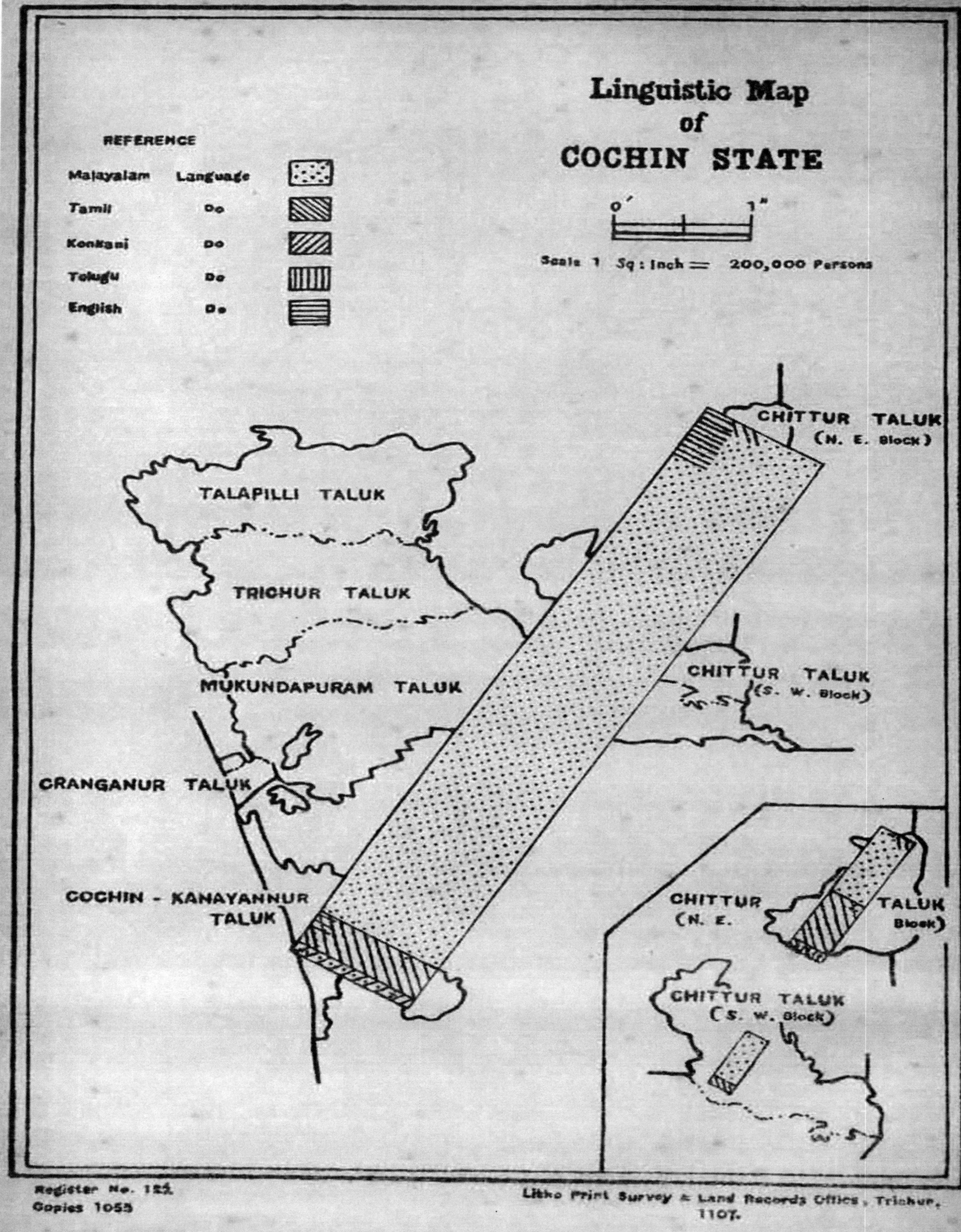

Register No. 125
Copies 1055

Litho Print Survey & Land Records Office, Trichur,
1107.

KEY TO LINGUISTIC MAP.

Cochin State: Population 1,205,016.

Malayalam: 1,088,081 (90·3%)

Of these 29,342 (2·7%) speak English,
3,440 (less than 1%) speak Tamil, and
971 (less than 1%) speak both English and Tamil.

Tamil: 66,164 (5·5%)

Of these 45,597 (68·9%) speak Malayalam, and
4,729 (7·1%) speak both Malayalam and English.

Konkani: 22,338 (1·9%)

Of these 18,086 (81%) speak Malayalam,
315 (1·4%) speak English, and
715 (3·2%) speak both English and Malayalam.

Others: (each under 1%) not shown.

Inset—Chittur Taluk (Tamil-Malayalam cultural border zone.)

South-west block—Population 25,060.

Malayalam: 18,967 (75·7%)

Of these 463 (2·4%) speak English (not shown) and
305 (1·6%) speak Tamil (not shown).

Tamil: 4,387 (17·5%)

Of these 3,463 (78·9%) speak Malayalam, and
308 (7%) speak both English and Malayalam. (English not shown.)

Others: (each less than 1%) not shown.

North-east block, bordering the Tamil District of Coimbatore—Population 81,754.

Malayalam: 42,700 (52·2%)

Of these 1,388 (3·3%) speak Tamil,
825 (1·9%) speak English, and
148 (less than 1%) speak Tamil and English.

Tamil: 30,170 (36·9%)

Of these 21,804 (72·3%) speak Malayalam and
771 (2·6%) speak both Malayalam and English.

Telugu: 6,164 (7.5%)

Of these 3,030 (49·2%) speak Malayalam,
2,875 (46·6%) speak both Malayalam and Tamil, and
259 (4·2%) speak Tamil (not shown).

Others: (each less than 1%) not shown.

English as subsidiary language: influence of English education

12. Next to Malayalam, English is the most popular subsidiary language in the State, and for this reason it is shown separately in the Bi-lingualism Table, Subsidiary Table II and the Linguistic map. It is often the common medium of conversation and intercourse between English-educated persons even when they belong to the same community and have the same mother tongue. They write their letters in English and not uncommonly speak English even in their home circles. Indeed, it is no exaggeration to state that many of them are in the habit of thinking in English. As a result, English-educated persons speak their mother tongue with a large admixture of English words, and most of them find it very difficult, if not impossible, to express with accuracy or fluency all their ideas in their parent language in its unadulterated form. This is but the natural outcome of the practice hitherto in vogue of imparting secondary and collegiate education through the medium of English. Recently, however, Malayalam too has been recognised as an alternative medium for secondary education. It remains to be seen whether this new departure will lead to any appreciable change in the vocabulary and form of Malayalam as now spoken by the English-educated section of the Malayali population.

Malayalam of popular speech and literary Malayalam

13. The example of the educated classes and the contact with new ideas received through the medium of English have alike influenced the Malayalam of popular speech whose vocabulary has been enriched to a considerable extent by the English element absorbed into it. Unfortunately, however, written Malayalam, the language of journalism and of literary works, has not been benefited by English to the same extent. This is because of a regrettable tendency on the part of modern writers to borrow words from classical Sanskrit to serve as the vehicle of new ideas for which the vocabulary of Malayalam contains no suitable words.* It passes one's understanding how any person, least of all a literary man, could seek help from a dead language, utterly unfamiliar to 99 out of every 100 readers, for conveying unfamiliar ideas to them. Even when these learned writers have to express ideas from modern science or politics, they seldom or never turn to English and borrow the words which first gave them the new ideas and which would be understood by a majority of readers. Instead, they dig into their Sanskrit vocabulary, unearth strange roots and coin uncouth compound words whose meaning will be as easily intelligible to their readers as the hieroglyphics of Egypt or the language of birds.** This leaning towards classical Sanskrit is conspicuous in a particular class of present-day writers who measure the excellence of their style by the degree of Sanskrit scholarship exhibited in their vocabulary. Their language is highly artificial and has little in common with the language of the people. It is not therefore easily intelligible to those that have not deliberately studied it.

---

* It is not intended here to ignore the very heavy debt which Malayalam owes to Sanskrit. Indeed it is well known that Malayalam has borrowed largely from Sanskrit, so much so that its vocabulary contains a considerable proportion of Sanskrit words which are easily assimilated to Malayalam.

Literary Malayalam of the present day contains a small proportion of English words. These were borrowed in the early days of its contact with the English language, when new ideas were received through the medium of the latter. But modern writers, who want to express new ideas received through the medium of the English language, have recourse to Sanskrit; and even when Sanskrit has no suitable words for these ideas (e. g., ideas relating to modern science and politics), they coin strange words from Sanskrit roots, which they prefer to the English words that first gave them the ideas. It is this tendency on the part of modern writers that is to be regretted.

** It is pointed out that English writers seek the help of Latin and Greek when they want to express new ideas in connection with their scientific discoveries or inventions. On this ground the procedure adopted by modern Malayalam writers is supported by some critics. We may imitate the English writers when we too begin to make scientific discoveries or inventions; but when we borrow the idea from English, the safest course to adopt is to borrow the word also from that language, so that at least English-educated readers may be in a position to understand the writers' meaning.

One often hears this language used also on the platform for set speeches on social, political and literary subjects. The attempts of these litterateurs and orators to sanskritise Malayalam and make it develop on artificial lines instead of helping it to grow unfettered, enriching itself by the free absorption of words from modern living languages through the medium of which new ideas are received, do not appear to have been very successful hitherto. It remains to be seen whether the popular language will ever be influenced to any serious extent by the artificial literature produced by these people.

Lingua franca of India

14. The claims of Hindi to be the *lingua franca* of India have been more or less recognised in the State, and Hindi has been introduced as an optional language in some of the State schools. A local *Hindi Prachar Sabha* is doing propaganda work on a small scale. These are recent developments and it is much too early to expect any tangible results therefrom.

SUBSIDIARY TABLES.

I.—Distribution of total population by mother tongue.

Family, Sub-Family, Branch and Sub-Branch	Group and Sub-group	Language	Total number of speakers 1931	Total number of speakers 1921	Number per mille of the population of the State
1	2	3	4	5	6
Languages of India					
DRAVIDIAN FAMILY					
	Dravida group	Tamil	65,164	57,574	54·91
		Malayalam	1,088,051	882,822	902·96
		Kanarese	4,493	3,772	3·73
		Tulu	731	453	0·61
	Andhra language	Telugu	12,142	8,901	10·1
INDO-EUROPEAN FAMILY					
ARYAN SUB-FAMILY					
Eranian Branch	Eastern group	Pashto	3	..	..
Indo-Aryan Branch					
Outer Sub-Branch	Southern group	Marathi	5,212	3,013	4·32
		Goanese	12	8	..
		Konkani	22,338	17,604	18·54
	Eastern group	Bengali	3	..	..
	North-Western group	Kachchhi (Sindhi)	714	622	·59
Inner Sub-Branch	Central group	Gujarati	1,253	1,342	1·04
		Parsi	5	..	..
		Hindustani (Hindi)	2,486	2,387	2·06
		Hindustani (Urdu)	79	2	..
		Marwari (Rajasthani)	1	..	..
Unclassed languages		Indian unspecified	13	..	..
Vernaculars of other Asiatic Countries and Africa					
INDO-EUROPEAN FAMILY					
ARYAN SUB-FAMILY					
Indo-Aryan Branch					
Outer Sub-Branch	Southern group	Singhalese	7	..	..
Eranian Branch	Persian group	Persian	1	..	..
TIBETO-CHINESE FAMILY					
TAI CHINESE SUB-FAMILY					
Chinese Branch	Chinese group	Chinese	1	..	..

I.—Distribution of total population by mother tongue.—(cont.)

Family, Sub-Family, Branch and Sub-Branch	Group and Sub-group	Language	Total number of speakers		Number per mille of the population of the State
			1931	1921	
1	2	3	4	5	6
SEMITIC FAMILY		Arabic	236	53	0·2
		Hebrew	266	50	0·22
		Syriac	3	92	..
MONGOLIAN FAMILY					
	Japanese group	Japanese	1	..	..
European Languages					
INDO-EUROPEAN FAMILY	Romance group	Italian	9	..	..
		French	1	..	..
..		Spanish	6	9	..
		Basque	4	..	..
		Portuguese	114	50	..
	Celtic group	Welsh	1	..	..
		Gaelic	1	..	..
.. ..	Teutonic group	English	630	324	0·52
		Flemish	2	..	..
		German	2	..	..

Note : (1) Figures for Hindi and Hindustani in 1921 have been clubbed together and given against "Hindi" in column 5 this time.

(2) The figure for "Dutch" in 1921 has been omitted in column 5 as there are no persons speaking that language in 1931.

II.—Distribution by Language of the population of each District.

Natural Division "Malabar and Konkan"	Number per 10,000 of the total population speaking									
	Malayalam as mother tongue					Tamil as mother tongue				
	as mother tongue only	with Tamil as subsidiary	with Konkani as subsidiary	with English as subsidiary	Total	as mother tongue only	with Malayalam as subsidiary	with Konkani as subsidiary	with English as subsidiary	Total
1	2	3	4	5	6	7	8	9	10	11
COCHIN STATE ..	9,698	41	..	270	10,009	2,382	7,606	..	725	10,713

Natural Division "Malabar and Konkan"	Number per 10,000 of the total population speaking									
	Konkani as mother tongue					English as mother tongue				
	as mother tongue only	with Malayalam as subsidiary	with Tamil as subsidiary	with English as subsidiary	Total	as mother tongue only	with Malayalam as subsidiary	with Tamil as subsidiary	with Konkani as subsidiary	Total
1	12	13	14	15	16	17	18	19	20	21
COCHIN STATE ..	1,422	8,417	51	461	10,351	1,968	7,429	841	238	10,476

II.—Distribution by Language of the population of each District.—(cont.)

Natural Division "Malabar and Konkan"	Number per 10,000 of the total population speaking											
	Telugu as mother tongue						Marathi as mother tongue					
	as mother tongue only	with Malayalam as subsidiary	with Tamil as subsidiary	with Konkani as subsidiary	with English as subsidiary	Total	as mother tongue only	with Malayalam as subsidiary	with Tamil as subsidiary	with Konkani as subsidiary	with English as subsidiary	Total
1	22	23	24	25	26	27	28	29	30	31	32	33
COCHIN STATE ..	307	8,960	3,909	..	155	13,331	1,491	8,426	109	8	520	10,554

Natural Division "Malabar and Konkan"	Number per 10,000 of the total population speaking											
	Kanarese as mother tongue						Other languages as mother tongue					
	as mother tongue only	with Malayalam as subsidiary	with Tamil as subsidiary	with Konkani as subsidiary	with English as subsidiary	Total	as mother tongue only	with Malayalam as subsidiary	with Tamil as subsidiary	with Konkani as subsidiary	with English as subsidiary	Total
1	34	35	36	37	38	39	40	41	42	43	44	45
COCHIN STATE ..	1,157	8,320	4,605	20	178	14,280	1,462	7,803	1,413	7	829	11,514

Note: The excess over 10,000 in columns 6, 11, 16, 21, 27, 33, 39 and 45 is due to the fact that there are 975; 4,719; 784; 30; 4,044; 289; 1923; and 902 persons respectively, speaking more than one subsidiary language.

Subsidiary Table III has not been prepared as there are no distinct tribal languages.

CHAPTER XI.—RELIGION.

Reference to statistics

We have already seen from the previous chapters that religion is used as a basis of classification of most of the statistics presented in the Imperial Tables. But, for purposes of this chapter, the most important Tables are

i. Imperial Table XVI showing the religious distribution of the State's population and containing on the title page a summary of the returns regarding the sects of Christians; and

ii. State Table II (Population of Taluks by Religion and Literacy) in which the depressed classes in the Hindu community are shown separately.

There are also four Subsidiary Tables appended to this chapter, of which the first two show in proportional form the general distribution of the population by religion, the third gives the number and variations of Christians, and the fourth deals with the religions of the urban and rural population.

The social map inserted at the end of this chapter represents graphically the proportion of Hindus, Muslims and Christians in the total population of each taluk.

Accuracy of statistics

2. The cover of the enumeration book contained the following instructions for the entry of religion in the schedule :

Column 4 (Religion).—Enter here the religion which each person returns, *e g., Hindu, Muhammadan, Christian, Sikh, Jain, Parsi*. It is essential to give the sect also where Christians are concerned and enumerators must pay particular attention to this point. The sect should be entered below the entry 'Christian' thus, Roman Catholic, Anglican, South India United Church, Wesleyan, Lutheran, etc.

In the case of aboriginal tribes who are not Hindus, Muhammadans, Christians, etc., the name of the tribe should be entered in this column

These instructions were expanded and explained according to local requirements. Moreover, the main religions of the State and their followers are sufficiently well known, so much so that the returns for these religions may be accepted as accurate *from the census point of view*.

Meaning of figures

3. The above qualification regarding the accuracy of our statistics is necessary in view of the fact that 'we are concerned in this chapter with the numbers of those who have been returned as professing certain religions, rather than with their tenets except in so far as these influence the figures'. Of the various aspects of religion such as the philosophical, doctrinal, ethical, ceremonial, spiritual or personal and communal, the census deals only with the last, its aim being 'to record religion in its communal aspect, merely distinguishing those who lay claim to one or other of the recognised sectional labels without looking too closely into the validity of their claims.' This is easy enough in the case of creeds like Islam, Christianity and Judaism, for their doctrinal basis and cultural outlook are fairly distinct from those of others. But when we turn to Hinduism, the community of faith or of culture characteristic of the other main religions will be seen to be absent. In Cochin, as elsewhere in India, Hinduism embraces within its fold 'heterogeneous multitudes, whose chief claim to inclusion in the faith is that its wide tolerance has never definitely cast them out.' And when we assert that a large proportion of the State's population consists of Hindus, it is well for us to bear in mind the composition of the Hindu community described in the following extract from the Census Report of 1901.

"The structure of the Malayali section of the Hindu community consists of a closely related series of social strata rising by infinitesimal gradations from the degraded and servile Cherumans and Paraiyans at the base to the dignified and venerated hierarchy of the Nambudiri Brahmans at the top; and from the Hinduism of the Paraiyan to the Hinduism of the Nambudiri, there is an advance step by step from 'the most ignorant and degrading cults to the purest and loftiest heights of philosophic speculation'. Though the mental and moral interval between the Nambudiri and the Paraiyan is vast, the break is nowhere abrupt or absolute. We have already remarked that, out of policy, the Nambudiris absorbed into their religious system, ideas of God and forms of worship foreign to their own, and such of them as were at first adopted probably out of convenience or necessity were insensibly grafted on to their own creed, and became part and parcel of their daily worship, practice and belief"

Religion as a basis of statistical classification

4. Here too we may examine the question relating to the validity and utility of religion's being used as a basis of classification of most of the census statistics. It has been pointed out that the religious label does not now represent any homogeneity of race, tradition or custom, that a difference of creeds will not necessarily imply any dissimilarity in the customs which relate to the age of marriage, seclusion of women, treatment of children etc., and which, therefore, influence the growth of communities, but that it is the social and economic condition of the people which is the primary factor in regulating customs of demological importance. For these reasons it is held that the census statistics should be classified on the basis of divisions not by religion but by social and economic condition.

There is a good deal to be said in favour of these arguments so far as the Malabar coast is concerned. The chapters on Age, Sex and Civil Condition will show that the difference here is not so much between Hindus and Christians, Hindus and Muslims or Christians and Muslims as between one caste and another in the Hindu community belonging to different strata in society. A classification based on caste would have been far more illuminating and satisfactory, but unfortunately 'caste is too complex, too local and too controversial a factor to form a basis for a social and economic division even of Hindu society'. Similar or even more insuperable difficulties will have to be encountered if occupation is to be adopted as our principle for differentiation. Religion will therefore have to be retained as a basis for statistical classification in the absence of a more satisfactory alternative, particularly in view of the fact that these are days of communal representation in all spheres of our public life and activities and that the attitude of the public in almost all matters is deeply tinted with the communal hue.

General religious distribution

5. Subsidiary Table I gives the general distribution of the population by religion and locality, the proportion of the followers of each creed per 10,000 of the total population and the variations for four censuses. An abstract of the figures of the present census for the main religions is given in the margin. It shows that the Hindus form 64·77, the Christians 27·79, and the Muslims 7·29, per cent of the State's population. All other religions together claim but 15 persons in every 10,000 of the population. Perhaps the most interesting feature in this distribution is the relative strength of the Christian element, a

Religion	Actual figures	Proportion per 10,000 of the population
Hindu ..	780,484	6,477
Muslim ..	87,902	729
Christian ..	334,870	2,779
Jew ..	1,451	12
Others ..	309	3

feature which is peculiar to Travancore and Cochin and which has no parallel anywhere else in India. Nor is it surprising that the hospitable shores where Christianity found the necessary facilities for establishing its first and earliest home in India should continue to have a higher proportion of Christians than other parts of the country. The marginal figures compare Travancore and Cochin with Malabar, Madras and India in this respect. They show that the Hindus are proportionately less numerous in the two States and in British Malabar than in Madras or India as a whole. But in British Malabar it is the Muslims that take the place of Christians. This is so because the Muslim traders from Arabia had their earliest dealings with Calicut where they were specially favoured by the Zamorin Raja. Their rivalry stood in the way of the Christians making much progress in the Zamorin's territory. Moreover the invasion of Malabar by Tippu strengthened the sway of Islam still further, while it weakened the position of other creeds to a proportionate extent.

Province or State	Proportion per 10,000 of the total population		
	Hindus	Muslims	Christians
Travancore ..	6,152	693	3,149
Cochin ..	6,477	729	2,779
Malabar ..	6,519	3,292	186
Madras ..	8,813	706	380
India ..	6,824	2,216	180

Distribution of religions by locality

6. Turning to the distribution of the main religions by locality, we find that the proportion of the Hindus rises above the State average of 64·77 per cent in the interior taluks of Trichur, Talapilli and Chittur and in the small coastal taluk of Cranganur. The border zone taluk of Chittur in particular has no fewer than 8,598 Hindus in every 10,000 of the taluk's population and is more like a Tamil district of the Madras Presidency than a taluk of this Malayali State in respect of the religious distribution of its population. Cochin-Kanayannur and Mukundapuram show far lower figures, the former having only 5,266 Hindus per 10,000 of the population. Here the balance of the Hindu proportion has been upset by Christians who are numerically stronger in this taluk than in others. The religious propaganda carried on by the Portuguese at Cochin during the 16th and 17th centuries will account for this large Christian element in Cochin-Kanayannur. Mukundapuram has the next largest proportion of Christians. In Trichur too their numerical strength is high, but Chittur and Cranganur have only few adherents of this creed. It is strange that Cranganur where the gospel of Christ is believed to have been first preached in India should have the lowest proportion of Christians among the six taluks. The Muslims show the highest ratio in Cranganur where they form 26·23 per cent of the population, while the strength of the community in the State's population as a whole is but 7·29 per cent. Talapilli taluk bordering on the Mappila (Muslim) centres of British Malabar also shows a high figure (11·2 per cent). In the other taluks the proportion of the Muslims is about, or below, the average for the State. Most of the Jews are residents of Mattancheri and Ernakulam in Cochin-Kanayannur, while a few are to be found in Mukundapuram taluk also. The Jains are confined to Mattancheri.

Taluk	Proportion per 10,000 of the total population		
	Hindus	Muslims	Christians
Cochin-Kanayannur ..	5,266	663	4,028
Cranganur ..	6,780	2,623	597
Mukundapuram..	6,278	502	3,213
Trichur ..	6,771	320	2,837
Talapilli ..	7,301	1,182	1,517
Chittur ..	8,598	796	606

Urban and rural proportion

7. The distribution of urban and rural population by religion, given in Subsidiary Table IV, may be examined in this same connection. The marginal figures show the difference between the urban and rural proportions. It was explained in paragraph 6 of Chapter II that the Malayali Hindu was averse to the crowded life and close neighbourhood of towns. Further the Hindus as a class are more agricultural than other communities. For these reasons their proportion in the population of towns is very considerably lower, and in the rural population perceptibly higher, than that in the State's population as a whole. Chittur and Cranganur taluks are exceptions to this rule. We have already seen from Chapter II that Chittur has a strong non-Malayali element in its Hindu population, which will account for the difference in Chittur. The only town in Cranganur owes its existence to the famous *Kali Temple* of the place, round which it has grown. It is therefore a centre of the so-called caste Hindus.

Religion	Proportion per 10,000 of		
	Urban population	Rural population	Total population
Hindu ..	5,479	6,683	6,477
Muslim ..	893	695	729
Christian ..	3,564	2,617	2,779
Jain and Jew ..	62	4	14

The Muslims, Christians, Jews and Jains have not that partiality for rural life which the Malayali Hindus cherish. They are engaged more in industrial or commercial pursuits than in agriculture, and therefore their proportional strength in the urban population is greater, and in the rural population smaller, than their average strength in the State's population. Indeed the Jains and the Jews are almost wholly urban.

Hindus. (1) Primitive tribes

8. We may now take the figures of each religion for detailed review, starting with the primitive tribes. It was at the census of 1921 that the term 'Animism' was deleted from the Table dealing with religion because 'it does not represent the communal distinction which is the essence of the census aspect of religion'. It was also misleading, both in its content and its extent, as a description of a definite religious category distinct from the other religions recorded at the census. 'Animism' was therefore replaced by 'Tribal Religions'. Imperial Table XVI shows that no figures have been entered under Tribal Religions at the present census so far as Cochin is concerned. The omission was deliberate and not the result of any oversight. As a matter of fact, all the selected tribes in Imperial Table XVIII are primitive enough to be classified under the heading Tribal Religions. But with very few exceptions they were returned as Hindus in column 4 of the schedule. Nor is it to be wondered at. For these classes, including the hill tribes of the Kadars and Malayans, have been in contact with their more sophisticated neighbours of the plains and open country for a sufficiently long period for them to have acquired an indefinite position on the outskirts and border-land of Hinduism. And a kind of negative recognition as Hindu outcastes has been extended to these tribes from olden times. It must not be forgotten in this connection that Hinduism, though non-proselytizing, is in a sense acquisitive. 'If it strains at the individual gnat it can swallow with cheerfulness the tribal camel: some slight profession of faith and moderate proficiency in the nice conduct of ceremony are sufficient to secure for an aspiring Animistic tribe (gods included) admission within the pale'. For these reasons the returns of these tribes as Hindus in column 4 are in accord with accepted notions and usage, and should not be viewed as inaccurate.

9. Though Tribal Religions do not find a place in Imperial Table XVI, it will be interesting to review separately the statistics of those tribes which

stand on the fringe, if not absolutely outside the pale, of Hinduism in their practices and methods of life. Imperial Table XVIII deals with their statistics. The religion of the six tribes* included in the Table and shown in the margin consists of beliefs and practices of a very primitive character. They number in all 5,163 persons and form ·43 per cent of the State's population and ·7 per cent of the Hindu community. The Eravalans and Irulans are non-indigenous classes found in the half-Tamil Chittur taluk. The caste statistics of previous censuses do not contain any Irulans. At the present census they were returned from the estates of the Nelliampathi and other hills, where they were working as estate coolies. The wide disparity between 1921 and 1931 in respect of the numerical strength of these tribes should in all probability be attributed to short-counting at the census of 1921, as explained in paragraphs 16 to 21 of Chapter I. The statistics reveal that the Malayans and Ullatans are progressive and have been growing in numbers, but the Kadars and Nayadis do not share in this progress; and Appendix I dealing with the Forest tribes will show how the Kadars are actually decaying.

and their statistics

Tribe		Population		
		1931	1921	1911
Eravalan	..	541	..	503
Irulan	..	240	..	..
Kadan	..	267	274	447
Malayan	..	3,185	594	2,461
Nayadi	..	152	119	220
Ullatan	..	778	413	537
Total	..	5,163	1,400	4,168

10. If the six selected tribes of Imperial Table XVIII are to be treated as denizens of the dim border-land of Hinduism, there are several others that are to be located in their close neighbourhood on the border, though within the pale. Columns 10 and 11 of State Table II show the numbers of the so-called depressed classes as 126,652. In addition to the six classes specified in the preceding paragraph, there are eight included in the list.** Their names and numerical strength for three censuses are given in the following statement:

(2) Other depressed classes

Caste		Population			Variation per cent	
		1931	1921	1911	1921—31	1911—21
Kootan	..	228	..	..	..	..
Kavara	..	790	260	537	+ 203·8	− 51·6
Kanakkan	..	13,193	8,424	7,527	+ 56·6	+ 11·9
Valluvan	..	212	30	502	+ 606·7	− 94·0
Vettuvan	..	11,797	4,750	5,261	+ 147·9	− 9·5
Sambavan (Parayan)	..	11,562	7,145	8,340	+ 61·8	− 14·3
Do Tamil	..	351	90	16	+ 290·0	+ 462·5
Pulayan	..	82,043	69,423	72,737	+ 18·2	− 4·6
Total	..	120,176	90,131	94,970	+ 33·3	− 5·1

*In the social map only the two hill tribes of the Kadars and Malayans are shown separately in red as Animists.

**The total strength of the fourteen classes is 125,339, while the total for the depressed classes in State Table II is 126,652. The difference of 1,313 rises from the fact that the Vadukan caste was inadvertently included in the depressed communities when the State Table was prepared. According to the old order of social precedence, the Vadukans of Chittur taluk occupied a social position which was slightly superior to that of the Ilavans.

In their beliefs, practices and methods of life, there is not that marked difference between the two sections* of the depressed classes, which would entitle them to be labelled as followers of two different and distinct creeds. But the Pulayans, Sambavans, Vettuvans, etc., differ widely from most of the other Hindu castes. All the same they have never been grouped with the Animists, but always included in the Hindu fold. The eight castes together number 120,176 persons, representing about 10 per cent of the total, and 15·4 per cent of the Hindu, population. According to the figures shown above, they appear to have increased by 33·3 per cent during the past decade. The aboriginal population is no doubt exceedingly prolific under ordinary circumstances, but we do not know to what extent the rate of increase recorded here may be accepted as accurate. On the one hand there is the obvious short-counting of 1921, evident in the figures for castes like the Sambavans and Vettuvans, pointing to a much lower rate of growth. On the other, there is the important consideration that the depressed communities, and particularly the Sambavans and Pulayans, provide the chief field for Christian missionary propaganda. The loss by conversion to the Christian creed sustained by these classes during the decade under review will imply a higher rate of increase, and this may partially cancel the effect of the short-counting referred to above.

and (3) non-caste and caste Hindus

11. We may now turn to the third section of the Hindu community consisting of all castes other than the 14 reviewed in the two preceding paragraphs. The fact that the remaining castes are all grouped together should not lead us to the conclusion that they have common beliefs, practices or methods of life, or the same communal outlook. As pointed out in the extract from the Census Report of 1901 quoted in paragraph 3 above, there are infinitesimal, almost imperceptible, gradations from 'the most ignorant and degrading cults (of the primitive tribes) to the purest and loftiest heights of philosophic speculation' characteristic of the religion of the Nambudiri Brahmans; and perhaps it will be far easier for the Darwinians to find out where the Ape ends and Man begins than for us to detect where the Animism of the aboriginal classes loses itself in the Demonolatry of the next higher groups, or where the cult of Demonolatry merges into the theistic ideas of the topmost classes.

Modern tendencies in Hinduism

12. To explain in detail the tenets of Hinduism in its varying grades will be not only outside the scope of this chapter but also superfluous in view of the exhaustive accounts of all the main religions given in the Census Report of 1901. It may not, however, be altogether irrelevant if we were to examine here the modern tendencies and developments in the religion of each of the three sections into which we have divided the Hindu community. Broadly speaking, a two-fold movement is discernible in this connection. Among those placed in the lower grades of Hindu society it is a movement for the purification and elevation of their religious rites and practices; while those born in the higher grades reveal a growing indifference in all matters connected with religion. Thus the depressed classes are being persuaded to give up their degrading rites and practices, and temples or *Bhajana Matoms*, wherein they could pray and offer worship like the caste Hindus, have been erected in some of the colonies opened for them by the Government. Thus too, among the so-called non-caste Hindus, the populous Iluva community under the leadership of an able *Guru*** effected several healthy reforms in its practices both in the religious and socio-religious spheres of life. But when we turn to the Brahmans and

*The first comprises the six selected tribes of Imperial Table XVIII and the second consists of the eight castes in the marginal table.

**The late Sri Narayana Guru Swami.

Kshatriyas, the Ambalavasis and Nayars, and the other so-called caste Hindus, to whom religion was, of old, 'like an all-embracing heavenly canopy, like an atmosphere and life-element, which is not spoken of, which in all things is presupposed without speech,' we find a remarkable change of outlook which, if difficult to applaud or commend, is easy enough to understand and explain. To the generality of English-educated persons—be it remembered in this connection that the caste Hindus have progressed much more than all others in English education—religion is now a matter of utter indifference or unconcern, and its rites and practices are a mass of superstition to be derided and condemned by all right-thinking people. Nor is this attitude to be wondered at. For, there being no provision for religious instruction* in the curriculum of our modern schools, the children of the educationally advanced Hindu classes **grow up as complete strangers to even the most elementary principles of their creed, so much so that our educated Hindu youth is as a rule grossly ignorant of the essence of Hindu religion and philosophy and of the inner meaning of its rituals. He is not prepared to accept things blindly, 'believing where we cannot prove'. Apart from this, the attitude of a great majority of the English-educated young men of caste Hindu communities towards their religion is now one of veiled hostility because, in these days of communal demand for equal representation of all creeds and classes in the Public service in which the caste Hindus are already over-represented, they find that the unlucky accident of their birth within the Hindu fold is an almost impassable barrier against their entry into government or quasi-government service the only career for which they are fit by training and temperament alike.

13. The example of educated persons has very widely affected all the upper classes with the result that laxity and indifference in religious matters are the order of the day. If the forms of religion are still observed by a majority, it is but a matter of mere formality, the spirit or inner significance of these forms being entirely lost sight of. And if considerable numbers still pray and offer worship in temples, the practice may serve at most as a discipline of the mind, but can hardly lead to a chastening of the spirit. Much less can it raise the Inner Self to higher planes of spiritual existence, or lead the Self to communion with the Infinite. The poet truly sang: "Love had he found in huts where poor men live". The philosopher can preach with equal truth that faith too is now found almost exclusively among the ignorant, illiterate and lowly. It is to be feared that the western ideals of materialism ushered in under the auspices of modern education are chiefly to be held responsible for this change. Pursuit of material comforts, pleasures and happiness is the Ideal or Religion of the higher classes at present. Even the priestly and pious Nambudiri Brahman has been affected by this Ideal owing to his constant contact with his educated neighbours. The austere purity of life and simplicity of habits which reigned supreme in olden times are rapidly disappearing. Costly and unwholesome luxuries have invaded the life of the higher classes. And the plain living and high thinking which once distinguished these Malayali castes more than all others have been giving way to high living and low thinking, because the old religious basis of their life has been utterly undermined.

Religious ideal of high class Hindus

---

* Moral instruction classes common to pupils of all creeds were opened in schools in the recent past The question of introducing formal religious instruction in schools is being considered by the Government.

**The Christians and Muslims are much better off than the Hindus in the matter of religious education. If public schools make no provision for religious instruction, they have their own private arrangements for this. Moreover, there are catechism and scripture classes for Christian pupils in schools run by Christian missions. As in other matters connected with education, the Muslims are the most favoured party in the matter of religious instruction also. Quran teachers are appointed in all schools (aided or Government) where there are Muslim pupils in sufficient numbers, so much so that formal religious instruction has been introduced in schools so far as the Muslims are concerned.

Their attitude towards depressed classes

14. Here is indeed a gloomy picture, but it has certainly its bright side as well. This is seen in the present attitude of caste Hindus towards the so-called depressed classes. Educated opinion favours the removal of the social disabilities to which these classes have been subjected for centuries; and though the caste Hindus as a class are too indolent and indifferent to take an active part in the work of reform, their passive approval, or at least the absence of opposition from them, cannot but prove helpful to the cause. In any case the status of the depressed classes has been gradually changing for the better during the past decade.

Statistics of non-caste and caste Hindus and their variation (1921—31)

15. We may now turn to the numerical strength of the third section of the Hindu community comprising all Hindu castes other than the fourteen treated as depressed and included in the first and second groups. They number in all 655,145, forming more than half the total population of the State, their exact proportion being 5,437 in every 10,000. Their numbers in 1921 were 554,969. They have therefore increased by 100,176 or 18·1 per cent during the past decade. If we make some allowance for the short-counting of 1921, this rate of growth must show a slight decline. Even as it is, the rate is considerably lower than the average of 23·1 per cent for the State as a whole and, as we shall see from the next paragraph, far below the increase recorded by the Muslims and the Christians. Both natural and artificial causes operate to produce this result. It is well known that the higher grades of society are on the whole less prolific than others. We have also seen from the chapters on Age, Sex, and Civil Condition that old communities like that of the Nambudiris are more or less stationary, showing little or no growth. It was also explained in Chapter III dealing with migration that the majority of emigrants are from the Hindu community. These are some of the important factors that will account for the low rate of increase noticed above.

Variations (all religions) since 1891

16. The following statement gives the proportion of Hindus (including the primitive tribes), Muslims, Christians and Jews per 10,000 of the population for five censuses.

Religion	Proportion per 10,000 of population in					Net variation 1891—1931	
	1931	1921	1911	1901	1891	Actual numbers	Per cent
All religions ..	10,000	10,000	10,000	10,000	10,000	+ 482,110	+ 66·7
Hindu ..	6,477	6,603	6,752	6,872	6,938	+ 278,940	+ 55·6
Muslim ..	729	702	695	671	642	+ 41,513	+ 89·5
Christian ..	2,779	2,682	2,539	2,441	2,405	+ 161,039	+ 92·6
Jew ..	12	12	13	14	16	+ 309	+ 27·1

It is seen from above that the Hindus have increased by 55·6, the Christians by 92·6, the Muslims by 89·5, and the Jews by 27·1, per cent during the space of four decades. Here the Jews may perhaps be disposed of first. The analysis of the age constitution of the Jews in Chapter IV indicated that the community had ceased to be progressive, and we shall not be wrong if we conclude that the Jews are actually decaying. Where a small group of people, numbering little more than a 1,000, lives in isolation trying to preserve its racial purity by marrying invariably within the community, the result cannot be different from the one we see before us. Turning to the three main religions, we find that the oldest of the three records the lowest increase. In addition to the reasons already specified in the foregoing paragraph for this relatively low growth of the Hindu population, it has to be remembered that, while the creed receives no additions to itself through conversions, its lower grades form the main field for the missionary labours of other creeds and particularly of Christianity. The younger communities of the Muslims and Christians, full of the energy and vigour of early manhood, have naturally increased at a far higher rate. Even though conversions in modern days are effected only on a much smaller scale than of old, still their cumulative effect must also be taken into consideration when the growth of the Christian population is examined. It is also significant that the Hindus who form the bulk of the population have increased at a rate which is considerably lower than the mean for the State, while the rate for the minority groups of the Muslims and Christians is far above the average.

The accumulated results of this process for four decades, as revealed in the above table, are noteworthy. The Hindus who in 1891 numbered 6,938 in every 10,000 of the State's population have sustained a loss of no less than 461 in their proportion during the period, their strength having fallen to 6,477. What the Hindus have lost the Christians have gained, their proportional strength in every 10,000 of the population having risen by 374 (from 2,405 to 2,779) within the same period. The corresponding gain of the Muslims has been but 87.

17. Turning to the creed of Islam, we find that its adherents have multiplied by 27·9 per cent during the decade under review. In view of the fact that conversions to Islam are at present almost, if not wholly, unknown so far as Cochin is concerned, this increase, which is slightly higher than even that of the Christians, is to be attributed to natural causes. A very small proportion of it may perhaps be accounted for by immigration also from British Malabar. In any case the Muslim population is decidedly progressive and growing rapidly. **Muslims**

An attempt was made to record the sects of Muslims, but it proved a failure. The illiterate section of the community knew nothing of sects, while educated Muslims insisted that they should not be shown as belonging to any particular sect as they did not recognize sectarian differences. They further objected to the terms *Muhammadan* and *Muhammadanism* and maintained that their religion should be called *Islam* and that they should be returned as *Muslims*.

18. Of the 334,870 Christians returned at the present census, 333,041 are Indians, 1,717 are Anglo-Indians and 112 are Europeans and allied races. Distributed racially, 9,946 in every 10,000 Christians are therefore Indians, 51 are Anglo-Indians and only 3 are Europeans. The mixed or foreign element in the community is thus quite negligible so far as Cochin is concerned. **Christians**

The distribution of the Christian population by locality and its uniformly high rate of growth in the past have already been commented on. During the last 10 years the Christians are seen to have registered an increase of 27·5 per cent, and even when due allowance is made for any short-counting of the Christian population in 1921 and for the numbers* converted from other creeds to

*Accurate statistics of conversions are unfortunately not available. The authorities of the Roman Catholic (Latin) archdiocese of Veropoly furnished the information that the number of converts to their sect

Christianity during the intercensal period—it is to be noted in this connection that the labours of Christian missionaries in the recent past have been much less successful than before—, this increase may safely be fixed at about 24 per cent. It therefore follows that the natural rate of growth of the Christian population, like that of the Muslims, is certainly higher than the rate at which the Hindu community as a whole has been growing.

Christian sects

19. We have seen that the attempt to record the sects of Muslims proved unsuccessful. So far as the Hindus of this State are concerned, there is no occasion to secure returns of their sects, because the Malayali Hindu observes no sectarian differences. As at previous censuses, Christianity is the only religion in the case of which statistics of sects were collected in full. The most populous of the Christian sects in Cochin are the Romo-Syrian or Syrian Catholic, the Roman or Latin Catholic and the Jabobite Syrian. Of these the first flourishes in Mukundapuram and Trichur, the second is chiefly confined to Cochin-Kanayannur and the third is found in considerable numbers both in Talapilli and Cochin-Kanayannur. The Chaldean Syrians or Nestorians who are confined to Trichur, the Mar Thoma or Reformed Syrians who are mostly to be found in Talapilli, and the Anglicans whose chief centres are Trichur and Ernakulam, are smaller communities. Besides these, there are several minor sects also returned at the census.

A detailed history of the Malabar Church is given in the Census Report of 1901, in which the origin and development of the various Christian sects in Cochin are clearly traced. It is not therefore necessary to deal with the subject here except in so far as later changes or developments are concerned. In the circumstances we shall more or less confine our attention to the growth of each of these sects reflected in the figures before us.

Inaccuracy of statistics

20. Careful and minute instructions were issued to the enumeration staff in order that accurate returns might be secured. The spiritual heads of the important Christian denominations are so well known that the enumerators were expected to be able to identify easily the sect of any Christian by ascertaining which Archbishop, Bishop or Metropolitan he followed. There was apparently no reason why the returns should not have been correct in every respect.

The following statement shows the numerical strength of the different Christian sects recorded at 5 censuses together with their variations from decade to decade.

---

might *approximately* be fixed at 1,000 for the last 10 years. The information supplied by the Roman Catholic diocese of Cochin was identical. If we assume (as we may safely do in the light of the above information) that the Romo-syrian archdiocese of Ernakulam and diocese of Trichur have like figures to show during the period, it will follow that the two archdioceses of Ernakulam and the dioceses of Cochin and Trichur together have secured about 4,000 converts to Christianity in the decade under review. Converts to the Roman Catholic (Latin) sect in Chittur Taluk which is included in the Roman Catholic diocese of Coimbatore, and to other sects throughout the State, must also be taken into consideration According to these calculations. the total number of converts to Christianity during the last 10 years may perhaps be fixed at about 5,000. If we deduct this number from the Christian population returned in 1931, the natural increase of this population over the figures recorded in 1921 will be seen to be as high as 25·7 per cent on the not unjustifiable assumption that the factor of migration does not influence the Christian figures to any perceptible extent.

Christian sects	Actual figures					Variation per cent for			
	1931	1921	1911	1901	1891	1921 to 1931	1911 to 1921	1901 to 1911	1891 to 1901
Romo-Syrian ..	183,632	120,372	100,166	90,142	56,326	+ 52·6	+ 20·2	+ 11·1	+ 60·0
Roman (Latin) Catholic ..	109,503	108,739	97,789	79,221	93,903	+ ·7	+ 11·2	+ 23·4	— 15·6
Chaldean Syrian ..	6,809	1,822	12,157	8,884	..	+273·7	— 85·0	+ 36·9	..
Jacobite Syrian ..	25,849	24,325	20,025	17,408	12,436	+ 6·3	+ 21·5	+ 15·0	+ 40·0
Mar Thoma Syrian ..	2,005	3,692	596	514	..	— 45·7	+519·5	+ 16·0	..
Unspecified Syrian ..	1,505	..	..	..	..	..	..	..	..
Others ..	5,567	3,645	2,361	2,070	1,818	+ 52·7	+ 54·4	+ 14·1	+ 13·9

According to the returns of 1931, the Romo-Syrians appear to have increased by no less than 52·6 per cent, their numbers having risen from 120,372 to 183,632 in the course of 10 years. The populous and prolific community of the Roman Catholics, who numbered 108,739 according to the census returns of 1921, shows an increase of only 764 persons or ·7 per cent during the same period. The Chaldeans who were almost wiped out of existence by the census of 1921 have apparently recovered a good deal of their lost ground and multiplied at the very modest and easily intelligible rate of 273·7 per cent! The Jacobite Syrians register an increase of only 6·3 per cent, while the Mar Thoma or Reformed section has lost 45·7 per cent according to the figures of 1931. A goodly company of 1,505 unspecified Syrians remains as a reserve force to be used at the strategic points of our statistical conflict. Here is the last and most convincing proof of the accuracy of the returns of the various Christian sects!

21. A study of the figures of past censuses given in the statement appended above will enable us to arrive at the correct explanation for these discrepancies. According to these figures, in 1891 the Roman Catholics outnumbered the Romo-Syrians by more than 37,000, but in 1901 the former registered a decrease of 15·6 per cent for the intercensal period, while the Romo-Syrians showed an increase of 60 per cent, exceeding the Roman Catholics by 11,000 in their specific numerical strength. The Jacobite Syrians had at the same time multiplied by 40 per cent and the Chaldeans were returned separately for the first time. In the Census Report of 1901, the Superintendent explained that thousands of Syrians (Romo, Jacobite, and Chaldean) were wrongly returned as Roman Catholics in 1891, and expressed much satisfaction at the accuracy of his own figures. The Census of 1911, however, showed a much lower rate of growth for the Romo-Syrians than for the Roman Catholics and Chaldeans, and the Superintendent maintained a discreet silence on the subject in his Report. During the next decade the Romo-Syrians appeared to have once again grown more prolific than the Roman Catholics, while the Chaldean minority was all but extinct. At the same time the Mar Thoma sect showed a sudden and remarkable rise of 519·5 per cent in their numbers. The only explanation offered by the Superintendent for these anomalies is that the disappearance of the Chaldeans was to be attributed to large numbers of the community having joined the Romo-Syrian sect 'out of social necessities.' **Variations since 1891**

22. From this review of the statistics for five censuses, we cannot but draw the conclusion that the figures of Christian sects recorded at every census (including the present) are utterly inaccurate, unreliable and worthless. Apparently the returns of sects are vitiated in two ways. Ignorance on the part of **Probable reasons for inaccuracy**

the enumerator and his victims will no doubt account for a very large proportion of the errors. When the census figures were published in 1921, the Chaldeans lodged a protest with the Government to the effect that their numbers were understated by several thousands. They maintained that interested enumerators belonging to the Romo-Syrian community had deliberately falsified the returns. There has been in the past, as there is at present also, some rivalry between the two sects, and the Romo-Syrian majority may naturally desire to absorb the small group of Christians who still continue to be independent of Rome. The Chaldeans being a weak minority have very often to contract marriage alliances with their Romo-Syrian brethren in whose midst they live, and on all such occasions the Chaldean party concerned has to join the Romo-Syrian Church. In this way their numerical strength has been steadily declining from decade to decade, so much so that it is only a question of time when the sole remnant of Nestorianism on the Malabar coast will be wholly absorbed by the Romo-Syrians. All the same the returns of Chaldeans at the census of 1921, according to which they numbered only 1,822, were palpably wrong in view of the fact that they had at the time more than 1,800 children aged 5 to 15 years in their catechism classes as seen from their records. We are not, however, in a position to find out whether deliberate falsification of returns is responsible to any extent for the strange fluctuations in the numerical strength of the various sects seen in the statement appended to paragraph 20 above.

That conversions have but little to do with these fluctuations will be clear from the foot-note to paragraph 18 of this chapter. It is true that considerable numbers from the depressed classes were converted to Christianity in the past chiefly because most of the social disabilities to which these classes were subjected within the Hindu community disappeared with the change of their creed. The Catholic sects in particular might have gained many adherents in this way. But, for the last two or three decades, conversions could certainly have had but little influence on the rate of increase of the most populous Christian sects.

Nor can these fluctuations be attributed to members of one sect joining another. With the exception of the Chaldeans noticed above, instances of such defection are generally rare. In any case they cannot affect the figures of the major sects to any perceptible extent.

Census statistics compared with figures furnished by Churches

23. To gauge the probable extent of inaccuracy in the census returns of 1931, information was sought of the authorities of some of the important Churches regarding the numbers of the different sects. The figures which these authorities very obligingly furnished are shown in the margin side by side with the statistics compiled from the census returns. According to these figures the Romo-Syrians and the Roman Catholics, numbering 135,000 and 123,000 respectively, will show an increase of only 12 to 13 per cent over their numerical strength as recorded at the census of 1921. This rate of growth is certainly too low to be accepted as

Sect	Numerical strength (1931) according to the	
	Census returns	Figures* from the church records
Romo-Syrian or Syrian Catholic ..	153,632	135,000
Roman (Latin) Catholic ..	109,503	123,000
Chaldean Syrian (Nestorian) ..	6,800	7,000

* These figures are, of course, only approximate, but they serve to give us a rough idea of the extent of inaccuracy in the census figures.

correct, but we have already seen that the census figures of 1921 for the two sects are as inaccurate and unreliable as those of 1931. Comparing the figures furnished by the authorities of the Churches with the census statistics of 1931, we find that, as a result of defective enumeration at the census, the Romo-Syrians have gained more than 48,000 persons whereas the Roman Catholics have lost from 13 to 14 thousand. Obviously, all these Roman Catholics have been wrongly returned as Syrian Catholics. It is suggested in this connection that Roman Catholics frequently try to pass for Syrian Catholics because the latter community (excluding modern converts from the lower classes of Hindus) is regarded as superior in social status in the light of their generally recognized claim that they are the descendants of the original Syrian settlers in Malabar and of the high-caste Hindu converts (including Nambudiris) who believed in the gospel of Christ when it was first preached in this country. The Roman Catholics, on the other hand, are mostly the descendants of those converted during and after the Portuguese period in Cochin, and these converts were obtained chiefly from the lower grades of the Hindu community. It is however doubtful whether these social distinctions are observed at present as strictly as they were in the past. Modern education has been a great leveller, and the educated sections of both denominations appear to be above these time-honoured prejudices.

24. The remaining 34,000 Christians (in round figures) who have been wrongly returned as Romo-Syrians and the 1,505 unspecified Syrians have now to be assigned to their respective denominations. But it has not been possible to ascertain the approximate strength of the other Christian sects (with the exception of the Chaldeans) from the authorities of the Churches concerned. The Chaldeans do not appear to have sustained any noticeable loss on the present occasion. As for the others, we can only guess that the Jacobite and Mar Thoma Syrians and the several minor sects of Protestants have really many more followers than are seen in the census statistics and that the balance of more than 34,000 mentioned at the beginning of this paragraph should be distributed among these denominations. Enquiries on the subject go to show that there have been no defections from the Mar Thoma community but that it has been gaining recruits in small numbers from other sects. Instead of a decrease of 45·7 per cent, this community must therefore show a substantial increase over its strength as recorded in 1921.

Jacobite Syrians

25. It will be remembered that a split in the Jacobite Syrian camp in the first half of the 19th century led to the formation of the two parties now known as Jacobite Syrians and Mar Thoma or Reformed Syrians. The latter seceded from the authority of the Patriarch of Antioch and set up a Church of their own, owing no allegiance to any foreign ecclesiastical authority, while the former continued to acknowledge the spiritual supremacy of the Patriarch. History repeats itself, and we find the Jacobite Syrians once again splitting into two sections in the recent past. Their churches were independent of the authority of Antioch in the management of their temporal affairs, but the Patriarch of Antioch who visited Malabar in 1910 wanted to interfere in temporal matters also. The Metropolitan Mar Dionysius who was opposed to this policy of the Patriarch was excommunicated, and another Metropolitan installed in his stead. Large numbers of Jacobite Syrians, who afterwards came to be known as the *Metropolitan's party*, were alienated from the Patriarch as a result of this procedure. The rest followed the Patriarch and formed the *Patriarch's party*. The alienated section succeeded in persuading the rival

Ex-Patriarch of Antioch to visit Malabar and grant them a *Catholicos*, a dignitary with powers to ordain their Metropolitan and Bishops. This *Catholicos* has not been recognized by the present Patriarch, but is still continuing. The *Metropolitan's party* is bent upon having the *Catholicos*, so much so that a situation seems to have arisen where, in the event of the Patriarch's persistent refusal to recognize the *Catholicos*, the spiritual supremacy of Antioch may no longer be acknowledged by the *Metropolitan's party*. The Patriarch's followers now form but a weak minority, and it is expected that they may reunite with the stronger section sooner or later. Hopes are also entertained in some quarters that a reunion may perhaps be effected with the Mar Thoma section too, in view of the fact that there will be no interference hereafter from any foreign authority.

The unsettled state of affairs in the Jacobite Syrian community might perhaps have led to ambiguous, misleading or wrong, returns of this sect at the census. But we are not in a position to find out what proportion of those wrongly included in the Romo-Syrian category belongs to the Jacobite Syrian group.

Minor sects

Sect	Numbers	Sect	Numbers
Others ..	**5,567**	American Mission ..	1
Anglican ..	2,783	London Mission ..	90
Lutheran ..	195	Church of Scotland ..	4
Salvation Army ..	299	Methodist ..	1
Protestant—unspecified ..	540	Presbyterian ..	7
Basel Mission ..	14	Unspecified ..	523
Baptist Mission ..	40		
* Brethren ..	1,070		

26. The last entry in column 2 of the statement in paragraph 20 above against *Others* includes various sects. They are shown in the margin together with their numerical strength as found in the returns. It is not unlikely that the numbers of some of these sects also have been under-estimated. The Anglican authorities, for example, claim more adherents than are assigned to them in the marginal list.

South India United Church

27. Though the South India United Church, which appeared as a distinct denomination at the census of 1921 for the first time, and which is composed of the followers of the London Mission, the American Madura Mission, the United Free Church of Scotland Mission, etc., has apparently but very few followers in Cochin at present, still it is likely to secure many more adherents, and to wield greater influence in the near future. It is understood that the negotiations for a union between this Church and the Anglican Church, alluded to on page 121, Chapter IV.—Religion, of Part I of the Census Report of India (Volume I) for 1921, are about to terminate satisfactorily. Several minor Protestant sects that now stand aloof are also likely to merge into the United Church. The promoters of the union are not without hopes that the Mar Thoma Syrians may join them. We have already seen how the Jacobite Syrians are casting longing eyes at the Mar Thoma section. Time alone can show how these things will shape themselves in the end.

Desirability of dropping the enquiry about Christian sects

28. The statistics of the different Christian denominations are 'of value chiefly to the missionary bodies and to students specially interested in the progress of the Christian religion in India'. The experience of the past censuses proves beyond the shadow of a doubt that the information collected by the census agency is absolutely worthless. The time, labour and expenses involved in the enumeration, tabulation and compilation of the Christian sects

* They were known as the Nagal Mission in the past, but they objected to the use of this name, stating that they accepted 'no names but such as are applicable to all true Christians'. They suggested that they might be called *Brethren*, if they were to be shown as a separate sect. It is however interesting to note that only 188 persons returned themselves as *Brethren*, the remaining 882 having returned the old name *Nagal Mission*.

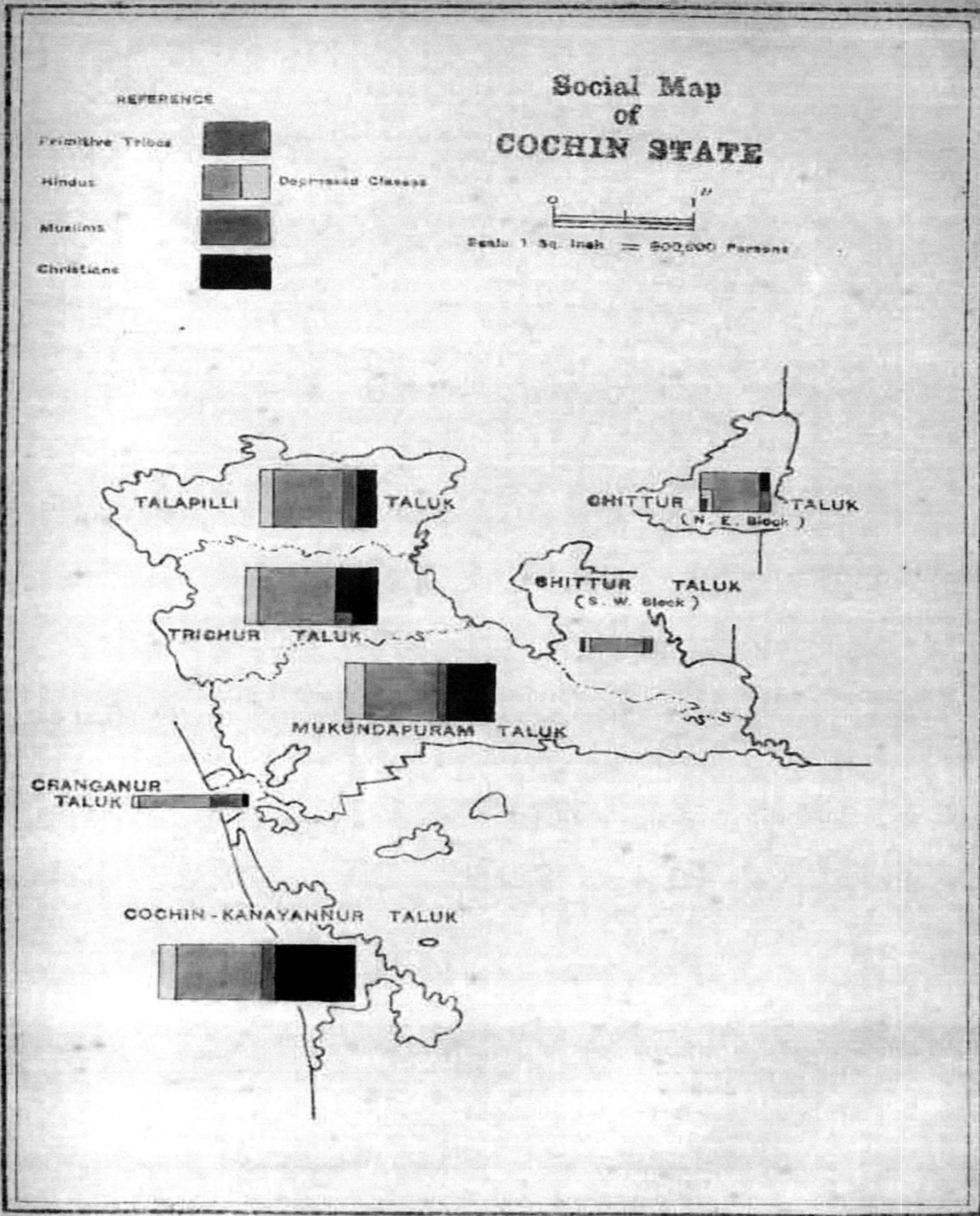

Register No. 121
Copies 1065

Litho Print Survey & Land Records Office, Trichur
1107

KEY TO SOCIAL MAP.

Taluk.	Total Population.	Communities.	Specific figures.	Percentage
Cochin-Kannyannur.	350,268	Hindus, depressed classes	28,009	8·0
		Hindus, others	156,428	44·7
		Muslims	23,213	6·6
		Christians	141,092	40·3
		*Others	1,526	0·4
Cranganur.	42,531	Hindus, depressed classes	2,877	6·8
		Hindus, others	25,962	61·0
		Muslims	11,155	26·2
		Christians	2,537	6·0
Mukundapuram.	263,722	Hindus, depressed classes	33,102	12·6
		Hindus, others	132,459	50·2
		Muslims	13,228	5·0
		Christians	84,745	32·2
		*Others	188	..
Trichur.	239,257	Hindus, depressed classes	23,091	9·6
		Hindus, others	138,922	58·1
		Muslims	7,885	3·3
		Christians	69,315	29·0
		*Others	44	..
Talapilli.	202,424	Hindus, depressed classes	25,977	12·8
		Hindus, others	121,814	60·2
		Muslims	23,919	11·8
		Christians	30,713	15·2
		*Others	1	..
Chittur. (South-west)	25,060	Primitive Tribes	1,282	5·1
		Hindus, depressed classes	2,754	11·0
		Hindus, others	18,603	74·2
		Muslims	2,128	8·5
		*Others	293	1·2
Chittur (North-east)	81,754	Primitive Tribes	2,057	2·5
		Hindus, depressed classes	7,503	9.2
		Hindus, others	59,644	72·9
		Muslims	6,374	7·8
		Christians	6,176	7·6

*Not shown in the map.

have been a sheer waste since the figures arrived at are palpably wrong and misleading. The records of the missions or Churches concerned contain much more reliable and approximately accurate information on the subject. In the circumstances we may well question the wisdom and necessity of retaining the record of Christian sects at future censuses.

Jews, Jains and Buddhists

29. Turning to the remaining religions in Imperial Table XVI, we find that the small and stationary or decaying community of the Jews shows an increase of 284 persons in their numerical strength during the past decade, but it may after all mean nothing in the face of the short-counting in 1921. The Jains are immigrants from Bombay, engaged in commercial pursuits in Mattancheri. Of the 96 Buddhists in the State, 7 are Singhalese, 1 Chinese and 1 Japanese. Most of the others are educated Malayali Iluvans who, disgusted with the social disabilities to which their caste is subjected within the Hindu fold, have become Buddhist converts along with their dependents. Though their numbers are so few as to be altogether ignored, still they point to a new tendency. In the light of the recent very favourable change in the attitude of the caste Hindus towards the question of the removal of the social disabilities of their non-caste brethren, it is doubtful whether this movement is destined to live long or gain in strength.

SUBSIDIARY TABLES.

I.—General distribution of the population by Religion.

Religion and locality	Actual number in 1931	Proportion per 10,000 of population in				Variation per cent (Increase +, Decrease —)			Net variation 1901—1931	
		1931	1921	1911	1901	1921—1931	1911—1921	1901—1911	Actual number	Per cent
1	2	3	4	5	6	7	8	9	10	11
HINDU										
Cochin State ..	**780,484**	**6,477**	**6,603**	**6,752**	**6,872**	**+ 20·7**	**+ 4·3**	**+ 11·1**	**+ 222,332**	**+ 39·8**
Cochin-Kanayannur ..	184,437	5,266	5,353	5,479	5,579	+ 23·3	+ 3·1	+ 10·6	+ 53,275	+ 40·6
Cranganur ..	28,839	6,780	6,888	6,961	7,006	+ 20·3	+ 3·8	+ 13·2	+ 8,421	+ 41·2
Mukundapuram ..	165,561	6,278	6,371	6,602	6,701	+ 24·5	+ 3·8	+ 18·1	+ 57,101	+ 52·6
Trichur ..	162,013	6,771	6,863	7,031	7,146	+ 23·7	+ 9·7	+ 15·1	+ 58,303	+ 56·2
Talapilli ..	147,791	7,301	7,424	7,579	7,691	+ 17·0	+ 0·9	+ 7·5	+ 31,400	+ 27·0
Chittur ..	91,843	8,598	8,691	8,672	8,711	+ 11·0	+ 4·5	+ 1·5	+ 13,832	+ 17·7
MUSLIM										
Cochin State ..	**87,902**	**729**	**702**	**695**	**671**	**+ 27·9**	**+ 7·7**	**+ 17·1**	**+ 33,410**	**+ 61·3**
Cochin-Kanayannur ..	23,213	663	626	593	540	+ 32·7	+ 11·3	+ 23·7	+ 10,512	+ 82·7
Cranganur ..	11,155	2,623	2,557	2,523	2,470	+ 25·4	+ 6·2	+ 16·3	+ 3,955	+ 54·9
Mukundapuram ..	13,228	502	495	505	489	+ 28·1	+ 5·5	+ 23·6	+ 5,308	+ 67·0
Trichur ..	7,885	320	321	331	339	+ 28·6	+ 9·1	+ 14·1	+ 2,960	+ 60·1
Talapilli ..	23,919	1,182	1,097	1,033	961	+ 25·1	+ 9·5	+ 17·2	+ 9,374	+ 64·4
Chittur ..	8,502	796	756	796	804	+ 18·1	— 1·0	+ 0·9	+ 1,301	+ 18·0
CHRISTIAN										
Cochin State ..	**334,870**	**2,779**	**2,682**	**2,539**	**2,441**	**+ 27·5**	**+ 12·7**	**+ 17·6**	**+ 136,631**	**+ 68·9**
Cochin-Kanayannur ..	141,092	4,028	3,979	3,881	3,836	+ 26·9	+ 8·1	+ 14·0	+ 50,913	+ 56·4
Cranganur ..	2,537	597	555	561	522	+ 31·2	+ 12·8	+ 12·5	+ 1,015	+ 66·6
Mukundapuram ..	84,745	3,213	3,130	2,857	2,802	+ 29·7	+ 16·7	+ 23·4	+ 39,392	+ 86·8
Trichur ..	69,315	2,897	2,816	2,638	2,513	+ 29·0	+ 20·0	+ 22·8	+ 32,846	+ 90·1
Talapilli ..	30,713	1,517	1,479	1,388	1,346	+ 22·0	+ 9·8	+ 12·5	+ 10,334	+ 50·7
Chittur ..	6,468	606	553	532	484	+ 22·8	+ 8·5	+ 11·9	+ 2,131	+ 49·1

I.—General distribution of the population by Religion.—(cont.)

Religion and locality	Actual number in 1931	Proportion per 10,000 of population in				Variation per cent (Increase +, Decrease —)			Net variation 1901—1931	
		1931	1921	1911	1901	1921—1931	1911—1921	1901—1911	Actual number	Per cent
1	2	3	4	5	6	7	8	9	10	11
JAIN										
Cochin State ..	**210**	**2**	**1**	**1**	..	**+ 107·9**	**— 21·7**	**+ 24·8**	**+ 205**	**+ 4,100·0**
Cochin-Kanayannur ..	209	6	4	5	..	+ 113·3	— 23·4	+ 24·6	+ 204	+ 4,080·0
Talapilli ..	1	..	..	..	..	..	..	..	1	..
JEW										
Cochin State ..	**1,451**	**12**	**12**	**13**	**14**	**+ 24·3**	**— ·6**	**+ 3·3**	**+ 314**	**+ 27·6**
Cochin-Kanayannur ..	1,294	37	38	40	44	+ 21·9	— ·2	+ 2·5	+ 257	+ 24·8
Mukundapuram ..	156	6	5	6	6	+ 47·2	— 3·6	+ 10·0	+ 56	+ 56·0
Trichur ..	1	..	..	..	..	..	..	..	1	..
BUDDHIST										
Cochin State ..	**96**	**1**	..	..	..	..	..	..	**+ 96**	..
Cochin-Kanayannur ..	20	..	..	..	..	..	..	..	+ 20	..
Mukundapuram ..	32	1	..	..	..	..	..	..	+ 32	..
Trichur ..	43	2	..	..	..	..	..	..	+ 43	..
Chittur ..	1	..	..	..	..	..	..	..	+ 1	..
ZOROASTRIAN										
Cochin State ..	**3**	..	..	..	..	..	..	..	**+ 3**	..
Cochin-Kanayannur ..	3	..	..	..	..	..	..	..	+ 3	..

II.—*Distribution by districts of the main Religions.*

NATURAL DIVISION "Malabar and Konkan"	Number per 10,000 of the population who are											
	Hindus				Muslims				Christians			
	1931	1921	1911	1901	1931	1921	1911	1901	1931	1921	1911	1901
1	2	3	4	5	6	7	8	9	10	11	12	13
Cochin State ..	6,477	6,599	6,706	6,825	729	702	695	671	2,779	2,682	2,539	2,441

Number per 10,000 of the population who are															
Jains				Jews				Buddhists				Zoroastrians			
1931	1921	1911	1901	1931	1921	1911	1901	1931	1921	1911	1901	1931	1921	1911	1901
14	15	16	17	18	19	20	21	22	23	24	25	26	27	28	29
2	1	1	..	12	12	13	14	1	..	..	..	..	..	..	..

III.—Christians.—Number and variations.

NATURAL DIVISION "Malabar and Konkan"	Actual number of Christians in				Variation per cent			
	1931	1921	1911	1901	1921—1931	1911—1921	1901—1911	1891—1901
1	2	3	4	5	6	7	8	9
Cochin State ..	**334,870**	**262,595**	**233,092**	**198,239**	**27·5**	**12·7**	**17·6**	**14·0**
Cochin-Kanayannur ..	141,092	111,174	102,834	90,179	26·9	8·1	14·0	12·8
Cranganur ..	2,537	1,933	1,713	1,522	31·2	12·8	12·5	6·7
Mukundapuram ..	84,745	65,321	55,990	45,353	29·7	16·7	23·5	14·6
Trichur ..	69,315	53,729	44,775	36,460	29·0	20·0	22·8	16·0
Talapilli ..	30,713	25,170	22,927	20,379	22·0	9·8	12·5	15·4
Chittur ..	6,468	5,268	4,853	4,337	22·8	8·6	11·9	13·3

IV.—Religions of urban and rural population.

NATURAL DIVISION "Malabar and Konkan"	Number per 10,000 of urban population who are					Number per 10,000 of rural population who are				
	Hindu	Muslim	Christian	Jain and Jew	Buddhist and Zoroastrian	Hindu	Muslim	Christian	Jain and Jew	Buddhist and Zoroastrian
1	2	3	4	5	6	7	8	9	10	11
Cochin State ..	**5,479**	**893**	**3,564**	**62**	**2**	**6,683**	**695**	**2,617**	**4**	**1**
Cochin-Kanayannur ..	4,841	1,244	3,776	137	2	5,420	451	4,120	9	..
Cranganur ..	8,769	938	293	..	..	6,398	2,947	655	..	..
Mukundapuram ..	5,130	501	4,369	..	..	6,357	502	3,134	6	1
Trichur ..	4,896	390	4,711	..	3	7,214	315	2,469	..	2
Talapilli ..	4,666	729	4,605	..	..	7,574	1,223	1,198	..	..
Chittur ..	8,959	881	160	..	..	8,491	771	738	..	..

CHAPTER XII.—RACE, TRIBE AND CASTE.

Reference to statistics

THE last chapter of the Report deals with the interesting, if complex, subject of the Race, Tribe or Caste to which the population enumerated at the census belongs. We have already seen that statistics of selected castes, tribes and races are combined with those of age and civil condition in Imperial Table VIII, of occupation in Imperial Table XI, of literacy in Imperial Table XIV, and of infirmities in State Table III. But for purposes of this chapter Imperial Tables XVII, XVIII and XIX are the most important. Table XVII shows the general caste return and XVIII the variations in the numerical strength of certain selected tribes for five censuses. Table XIX deals with the statistics of Europeans and allied races and Anglo-Indians. The Subsidiary Table at the end of this chapter gives the variations in numbers since 1901 in important castes and the proportion of each such caste to the population of the State.

State Table II shows separately the numbers of the depressed classes* in the Hindu community, and the social map given at the end of the last chapter represents the proportional strength of these classes in the Hindu, as well as the total, population of each taluk.

Definitions

2. *Race* denotes "'a main division of mankind the numbers of which have important physical characters in common' and is usually applied to stocks of considerable antiquity." According to Dr. Haddon, a *tribe* is "'a group of a simple kind occupying a concentrated area, having a common language, a common government and a common action in warfare.' If we add the words 'a tradition of common origin' and interpret the words 'government' and 'warfare' as representing respectively the internal organization and the external attitude towards other communities, the definition may roughly apply to our ideas of the aboriginal tribe." The term *caste* was defined at the census of 1911 as an "endogamous group or collection of groups bearing a common name and having a common traditional occupation, who are so linked together by these and other ties, such as the tradition of a common origin and the possession of the same tutelary deity, and the same social status, ceremonial observances and family priests, that they regard themselves, and are regarded by others, as forming a single homogeneous community."

Necessity of caste return

3. The necessity or advisability of retaining a return of caste has often been questioned on various grounds. For one thing it is suggested that 'the distribution of various castes and tribes in the population changed only at large intervals and that it was not necessary to obtain figures at each decennial enumeration'. Again the collection of caste statistics at the census is regarded as undesirable in that it is tantamount to 'recognizing and perpetuating, by official action, the system of caste differentiation'. Lastly it is pointed out that the statistics thus secured are 'inaccurate and worthless, since the lower castes took the opportunity of passing themselves off as belonging to groups of higher status'. The Census Report of India for 1921 makes the following remarks in this connection :

> "Whatever view may be taken of the advantages or disadvantages of caste as a social institution, it is impossible to conceive of any useful discussion of the population questions in India in which caste would not be an important element. Caste is still 'the foundation of the Indian social fabric,' and the record of caste is still 'the best guide to the changes in the

---

* See foot-note to paragraph 10 in Chapter XI.

various social strata in the Indian society.' Every Hindu (using the term in its most elastic sense) is born into a caste and his caste determines his religious, social, economic and domestic life from the cradle to the grave. In western countries the major factors which determine the different strata of society, *viz.*, wealth, education and vocation are fluid and catholic and tend to modify the rigidity of birth and hereditary position. In India spiritual and social community and traditional occupation override all other factors. Thus, where in the censuses of western countries an economic or occupational grouping of the population affords a basis for the combination of demographic statistics, the corresponding basis in the case of the Indian population is the distinction of religion and caste. Whatever view may be taken of caste as a national and social institution it is useless to ignore it, and so long as caste continues to be used as one of the distinguishing features of an individual's official and social identity it cannot be claimed that a decennial enumeration helps to perpetuate an undesirable institution."

Accuracy of caste returns

4. Detailed instructions were issued to the census staff regarding the entry to be made in column 8 of the enumeration schedule, headed *Race, Tribe or Caste*. Almost every person's caste is known locally, and in the vast majority of cases the enumerators were local men. The caste column was not therefore likely to contain many wrong entries. There were, of course, instances of ambiguous returns. Thus, in some cases, sub-castes were entered instead of the main castes. Again vague terms, general names or caste titles were also found returned instead of the correct caste names. In a great majority of these cases the caste was easily identified, the entry in column 8 being carefully checked with the entries against occupation and mother tongue. The number of returns that could not be thus identified is only 1,635 or ·21 per cent of the total Hindu population, as seen from the figures for unspecified castes in Imperial Table XVII. A few mistakes might have been committed in the returns particularly of some non-indigenous and little-known castes numbering but a few hundreds each. A few errors might have crept in in the course of slip-copying and sorting. But these mistakes must be so few as to be quite negligible, and the caste statistics, with very few exceptions, may therefore be accepted as substantially accurate and sufficient for all practical purposes.

Scope of the caste return

5. Though the caste of every person who was enumerated at the census was ascertained and recorded in column 8 of the schedule, all the castes thus returned have not been tabulated separately. Communities whose numerical strength falls below a certain percentage of the total population are generally clubbed together. Imperial Table XVII shows that 94 Hindu castes have been tabulated separately, though the proportional strength of some of them is but 2 or 3 in every 100,000 of the population. About 40 non-indigenous and little-known communities, numbering in all 1,404 persons, are shown together as minor castes.

Scope of the chapter

6. It is not the aim of this chapter to deal with the subject of caste from the ethnographic point of view or to discuss the origin of the institution. The Cochin Census Report of 1901 treats these aspects of the subject at some length. *The Cochin Tribes and Castes* by Mr. L. K. Ananthakrishna Ayyar, who carried out the Ethnographical Survey of the State, gives elaborate accounts of the castes and tribes of this State. *The Cochin State Manual* by Mr. C. Achyuta Menon also deals with the subject. And the *History of Kerala* by the late Mr. K. P. Padmanabha Menon is the latest and one of the most interesting of the publications that contain accounts of the Malabar castes.

A glossary containing brief notes on the castes mentioned in Imperial Table XVII is given at the end of this chapter. With very few exceptions, these notes are copied from the caste glossary in the Cochin Census Report of 1911.

The discussion in this chapter will be more or less confined to a review of the statistics of the more populous, important or interesting castes with special reference to the variations in their numbers since the last census. A few other aspects of interest and importance are also noticed in the course of this discussion.

Census and caste claims

7. Past experience has shown that the opportunity of the census is generally seized by all but the highest castes to press for recognition of claims for a higher social status and 'to secure, if possible, a step upwards in the social ladder'. If all the claims thus advanced are to be conceded, there may perhaps be no caste distinction among Hindus (so far as caste names in the census and Government records are concerned) in the course of a few censuses, for all Hindu communities may have to be classed as Brahmans by that time. It is obvious that caste names which have long been in vogue, which have been accepted and recognized widely, and which are significant in that they point to the origin, traditional occupation or history of the castes concerned, should not be lightly given up in favour of new names that are of ambiguous, uncertain or misleading significance, lest the past history of these castes should be shrouded in obscurity and irreparably lost.

Kallan, Panditattan and Visva Karma Brahman

8. The tendency on the part of socially inferior castes to claim a higher place in the social order with new names devoid of any degrading associations of the past is perhaps less marked in Cochin than elsewhere. At the census of 1921, there was but one change of caste name ordered by the Government, according to which the Kadupattans came to be called Eluthassans. Likewise at the present census the Parayans, one of the lowest of the depressed classes, have been re-christened Sambavans, the change having been adopted by the Government. There are two Tamil castes, hitherto known as Kallans (workers in granite) and Panditattans (Tamil goldsmiths), together numbering about 4,000 persons according to the returns of the present census. They are identical with the castes grouped under the main head *Kammalan*, *Kamsala*, *Panchala*, *Visva Brahman* or *Visva Karma Brahman* in the Tamil country. They wanted that their old names should be replaced by the new one of Visva Karma Brahman as in Madras, and it was ordered by the Government that the change might be adopted if a majority of them returned the new caste name. But the census returns showed that a great majority of them knew nothing of the proposed change, and the old names have accordingly been retained in the Tables.

Pattaryan versus Chaliyan

9. The Chaliyans, a Malayali caste whose traditional occupation is weaving, advanced a claim to be classed as 'Vaisyas of the Aryan stock' under the new name *Pattarya* (weavers of silk). The claim was based on the most flimsy and fanciful grounds. There is a Pattarya caste in South Travancore which is Tamil-speaking, and which takes after the Tamilians in point of dress, social customs, manners, ceremonials, etc. This caste is apparently of a higher social status than the Chaliyans of North Travancore and Cochin. The proposed change of name must lead to confusion in as much as the South Travancore Pattaryans and the North Travancore and Cochin Chaliyans, who form two distinct and separate castes, and between whom there is but very little in common, will get mixed up if both are to be called by the same name. It was therefore decided to retain the old nomenclature. All the same such Chaliyans as desired to return the new name at the census were allowed to do so and a great majority of them availed themselves of the concession. They are shown against the sub-head Pattaryans under the main head Chaliyans in the Tables dealing with castes.

Caste feeling

10. The question whether caste has now the same influence as it had in the past in determining the life of the individual may be examined before we proceed further. In the face of the modern economic and intellectual influences to which people are subjected, one should naturally expect a weakening of caste feeling and a loosening of caste bonds; and in a progressive State like Cochin, where these influences will be strongly felt on account of the rapid spread of modern education, the change must be more perceptible than in other places. But what we find in reality is that the modern forces alluded to above have not yet led to any weakening, much less the disappearance, of the caste feeling. In this connection it is significant that only 15 persons out of 780,484 Hindus have refused to return their caste, and these 15 belong to communities that are labouring under social disabilities. The organization of caste *sabhas* (also called *samajams*) or societies, whose purpose was to advance the status and promote the welfare of the castes concerned, was a new feature noticed in many Provinces and States at the census of 1921. This movement has been steadily gaining in strength during the past decade, so much so that many important castes and communities in Cochin, including the Muslims and the Christians, have at present their caste or communal associations systematically working for the furtherance of their interests. This has led to the development of 'a feeling for the caste as a corporate body and what may almost be called a caste patriotism'*, often accompanied by an ambition to rise in the social scale. It has also engendered a good deal of caste jealousy and antagonism. In short one aspect of the influence of the modern forces at work is seen in a strengthening of caste consciousness and an aggravation of the communal feeling of individual castes.

Caste restrictions of old times

11. There is, however, another aspect of this influence which is more pleasant and attractive to view. Thus a relaxation of the less essential rules of caste, by which the caste system is being brought into adjustment with modern conditions, is everywhere noticeable. It is notorious that the caste system of Malabar (including Travancore and Cochin) was the most rigid in all India. In no other part of the country did it flourish so luxuriantly as here. Its ramifications were wild and intricate, its ordinances drastic and numerous, and their observance rigorously enforced. Any infringement of even its less important rules had to be atoned for by the penalty of various kinds and degrees of purification; while the violation of its more important ordinances was visited with summary excommunication. Whereas other parts of India knew and observed only touch pollution, Malabar had** the distinction of strictly observing atmospheric pollution. The tiny plant of Untouchability grew into the mighty and many-branched tree of Unapproachability in its priest-ridden and fertile soil. There were untouchable castes and unapproachable, almost unseeable, castes.† Some castes polluted others by touch. Some others caused pollution to members of higher castes if they approached them within a distance of 24 feet. Some had to remain at a distance of 36 feet, some at a distance of 48 feet, while yet others could not approach the highest castes within a distance of 64 feet‡ without

* This remark is hardly applicable to the rising generations of the so-called caste Hindu classes which are over-represented in the Government service. As their caste makes it almost impossible for them to enter the State service, the sentiments they cherish for it are neither friendly nor flattering. Their attitude towards their religion alluded to in paragraph 12 of the last chapter may be recalled in this connection.

** The past tense is purposely used, for these observances are now practically dead.

† Malayali Hindus must have been much relieved to hear of the existence of an *unseeable* caste in the Tamil district of Tinnevelly on the other side of the Western Ghats. It is called by the name *Purada Vannan* and its members are washermen to depressed classes. This community was unearthed recently by the Anti-Untouchability Leaguers. It is reported to be a *night-caste*, for its unfortunate members are allowed to step out of their miserable huts only after nightfall when the caste Hindus, ([illegible]), who consider themselves polluted by their sight, have all retired for the night !!

‡ According to other versions, the polluting distance for some of the unapproachables was much greater. For instance, it was 300 ft. for the Nayadis !

polluting them. The distance in each case was regulated by the depth of degradation, wretchedness and squalor into which the caste had sunk.* Birth pollutions, death pollutions and many other allied ceremonial pollutions were to be religiously observed, and purificatory ceremonies had to be performed at their termination. The restrictions regarding inter-dining and inter-marriage were equally rigorous. The following extracts from the Cochin Census Report of 1911 will be read with interest in this connection :

"Inter-marriage, inter-dining and pollution by touch or proximity are the tests by which caste status is determined in Cochin. The meals prepared by persons belonging to higher castes can be partaken of by those belonging to the lower ones, but the converse is strictly prohibited, especially in the case of females. A high class Nambudiri male may eat the food cooked by low class Nambudiris, and even by Tirumulpads, but their females cannot. Similarly Nayar males can partake of the meals prepared by any Nayar without distinction of sub-caste; but a female belonging to a higher sub-caste cannot eat the food prepared by one belonging to a lower. All Nayar females can eat together in the same room, but those of higher sub-castes may not sit in the same row for the purpose with those of a lower one. Similar rules are observed also among the lower castes. Inter-marriage also is generally governed by the same rules as those of inter-dining. A Nambudiri female can of course be married only in her own class, but a Nambudiri male can form *Sambandham* union in any caste below his, but not below that of Nayars. As a rule, women belonging to the Nayar and intermediate castes may marry only where they eat, that is, with equals and superiors, but these rules are not so strictly observed in these days as formerly, especially by the Nayars. Pollution is another element for caste differentiation, and there are some features of it which are peculiar to this part of India. A Nambudiri is polluted by the touch of any one below him in the social scale, while Kammalans and the castes below them pollute him, if they approach within a prescribed radius. Similarly, the members of any other castes are polluted by the touch or approach, as the case may be, of the castes below them.

Caste rules and restrictions are in some respects more rigid and severe among the Malayalis than among most other classes in India. The rules regarding pollution by touch or proximity, which has already been referred to, are strictly enforced. Such pollution can be removed only by complete immersion in water either in a tank or a river. Besides this pollution, there is what may be called ceremonial pollution. A death or birth in a family causes such pollution to all members of the family in all its branches, and a similar pollution is also entailed on women during their monthly periods and after delivery. The duration of the ceremonial pollution varies according to the status of the different castes, the highest having the shortest period, but in the case of monthly periods, the duration is three days uniformly. Pollution of all kinds, however acquired, can be removed only by complete immersion in water. In the case of death pollution and women's special pollutions, certain purificatory ceremonies, besides immersion in water, are necessary to remove the taint. Similar ceremonies are also required if a Brahman or a Kshatriya is touched by members of castes below them when under death, monthly or delivery pollution. Again, the extreme penalty of formal excommunication is enforced here more regularly and rigidly than elsewhere in serious cases of violation of caste rules. The member of any main caste partaking of the meals prepared by one of a lower caste; any member of a twice-born caste eating flesh or fish or drinking intoxicating liquor ; a Nayar or a member of any higher caste having sexual connection with a female of any caste below that of Nayars ; a male member of any caste having similar connection with a woman of any higher main caste ; the non-observance of ceremonial pollution and the non-performance of funeral rites ; these are some of the offences punishable with formal excommunication, and such offences are seldom

* A classification of castes based on considerations of pollution is given on pages 181 and 182 in the Cochin Census Report for 1901.

overlooked. Similar offences, if committed between members of sub-castes are treated as minor ones, and punishment in such cases is a fine, or expulsion from the *enangu or *tara* association. The eating of flesh and fish and the use of distilled or fermented liquors are prohibited only in the case of Brahmans, Kshatriyas and Ambalavasis, while in the case of Nayars and those below them beef is the only prohibited article of food. The re-marriage of widows is prohibited only among the Brahmans, while the marriage of girls before puberty is not enforced among any of the Malayali castes."

12. Modern influences have wrought a remarkable change in the attitude of people towards most of these caste rules and restrictions. In respect of marriages the caste ordinances are still potent, and the day of inter-caste marriages is yet to dawn. At the same time the restrictions regarding marriages between sub-castes within the same main caste are not observed now-a-days, and it was noted in paragraph 6 of Chapter VI that hypergamy among such Malayali castes as observed it of old had all but disappeared. But if the caste ordinances regarding inter-marriage between main castes are still very much alive and active, those regarding commensality, pollution and other matters are more dead than alive. The tendency to ignore these restrictions started many years ago, and it was commented on in the Cochin Census Report of 1911 thus: **Modern tendencies**

"The caste system still continues to reign supreme over the Hindu community of Cochin, but signs of disintegration have begun to make themselves visible on all sides, more especially in towns. Among the more important forces that are working towards the relaxation of caste rules are English education, the public school system, the railways and the enactment of equal laws for all, and their impartial administration without distinction of caste or creed. English education has given a new turn to the ideas and aspirations of the people, and is working a change in the national frame of mind, which has hitherto accepted all that exists among the Hindus as divinely ordained and consequently as being beyond question or investigation. Public schools and railways are open to all castes and creeds, and high castes and low are thrown together there, where it is impossible for a casteman to preserve that aloofness which he maintains in his own village, or to purify himself as often as he should, or to be as particular as he should be in regard to what he eats and drinks. Equal laws and their impartial administration have considerably affected the supremacy of one caste over another in some respects, and are leading the people to question why there should be such supremacy in other respects as well. A Nayar could in the good old days take into his own hands the punishment of a Pulaya who polluted him by approaching within the prohibited distance, but he can no longer do it with impunity. This leads him to ask himself why he should accept without question the mandates of the Brahman as he used to do formerly. Traditional occupation was another force making for caste exclusiveness and caste preservation. But the advent of railways and the introduction of machinery have made it impossible for many to confine themselves to their traditional occupations. Many of the old village industries have become unprofitable, while a great and growing demand is springing up for labour in mills, plantations and workshops. Numbers of people are therefore deserting their traditional means of livelihood in favour of new and more profitable vocations, and a man's caste is no longer, as it once was, a fairly certain index to his occupation. Again, the organisations which take cognizance of minor caste offences have also begun to undergo disintegration. Respect for the authority of elders, which is essential for the maintenance of the *enangu* and *tara* organisations, is very much on the decline in the altered political and social conditions of these days, and these organisations

* Caste tribunal of Nayars.

have therefore almost entirely disappeared from towns and are gradually disappearing from villages also. It must however be admitted that the great majority of the people, especially in the villages, are still as particular as ever they were in regard to caste observances. But the influence of the small but powerful minority, who are bidding a lingering farewell to them, is surely, if slowly, permeating the masses. This minority honour caste rules nowadays more by their breach than by their observance, especially when they are away from home, although in their own homes the fear of giving offence to their more orthodox relatives and friends leads them to make a show of observing the established rules and proprieties. In return for this show their lapses elsewhere are tacitly condoned. While disintegration is thus in progress now, certain relaxations permissible in the old days have ceased to be in operation. In the case of caste offences meriting excommunication, Sudras and persons inferior to them in caste could be saved from that penalty by the Raja of Cochin by presenting to them with his own hands a *kindi* or vessel of water to drink. A Tamil Sudra could be made a Nayar, and any one could be raised to a superior sub-caste by the same means. This has however become obsolete in these days."

Relaxation of caste rules

13. It is not possible to give within the limited scope of this chapter a full account of the changes which have taken place during the 20 years that have lapsed since the above remarks were made. Suffice it to say that the forces that were noticed in 1911 as working towards the relaxation of caste rules have been steadily and rapidly gathering strength throughout the last two decades, so much so that most of the old restrictions are now practically dead. Distance and touch pollutions are not generally observed in these days; and if any old, orthodox and conservative members of the higher castes (like aged Nambudiris) still desire to observe the rules about atmospheric pollution, they must either remain within doors or frequently undergo the purificatory ceremonies for pollution, for the unapproachable castes are no longer prepared to fly before the approach of the orthodox in public places as they did in the past. Ceremonial pollutions also have shared much the same fate. Though instances of formal inter-dining between caste and caste are rare, the restrictions regarding commensality are violated almost daily by very considerable numbers from all Hindu castes. At social gatherings and other parties, members of both sexes of the highest* and lowest castes and of different religions sit at the same table and partake of refreshments. And the most significant part of the whole affair is that nobody thinks of the penalties that obtained of old for such violations of caste rules. The fact is these practices are no longer looked upon as caste offences and hence they are openly tolerated. The infliction of penalties for infringements of caste rules has not been heard of for a very long time. The caste tribunals which took cognizance of offences against caste rules in olden days have long ceased to function and they do not exist even in name at the present day. Should there be a modern Rip Van Winkle belonging preferably to one of the approachable or touchable castes, who fell asleep at the end of the last century in some Sleepy Hollow of the Western Ghats, and should he wake up one of these fine mornings and return to his old haunts, he must be so much shocked at the changes noticed above that he would most probably go to his last sleep without the slightest delay!

Caste statistics and variations

14. Turning to the figures contained in Imperial Table XVII, we find that there are only 10 castes or communities, the numerical strength of each of which exceeds one per cent of the total population. Their actual numbers and variations are shown in the following statement.

* Nambudiri women to be excepted.

Caste		Strength (actual figures)			Variation per cent 1921—31
		1931	1921	1911	
Indian Christian	..	333,041	260,347	230,568	+ 27·9
Iluvan	..	276,649	224,008	208,453	+ 23·5
Nayar	..	142,637	131,054	121,206	+ 8·8
Muslim	..	87,901	68,717	63,822	+ 27·9
Pulayan	..	82,043	69,423	72,787	+ 18·2
Marasari	..	23,430	18,555	17,779	+ 26·3
Tamil Brahman	..	21,754	21,836	18,923	— 0·4
Elathassan	..	18,536	15,197	14,323	+ 22·0
Kudumi Chetti	..	16,104	10,328	12,371	+ 55·9
Kanakkan	..	13,192	8,424	7,527	+ 56·6

Of the ten communities, all but the Tamil Brahmans, Kudumi Chettis and a small proportion of Muslims are Malayalis. Together they form 84·3 per cent of the State's population. The rate of increase among Muslims and Indian Christians has already been commented on in the previous chapter. We had occasion to note that the Tamil Brahmans were both prolific and long-lived in the course of the analysis of their age constitution in Chapter IV. Here, however, an actual decrease is seen in their numbers. An explanation for this is to be sought for in the statistics of emigration collected at the special enquiry, which were reviewed in Chapter III. According to these statistics, the bulk of the emigrants was seen to consist of Hindus. It was also remarked that the Brahmans in Special Emigration Table I were, with few or no exceptions, Tamils.

In this connection we have to note that the small and well-organized community of Tamil Brahman immigrants in Cochin for long held a unique position in the public life of the State. They led the van in all intellectual pursuits and learned professions. With the Ambalavasis and Nayars they virtually monopolised the State service in the last century. We have seen from the chapter on Occupation that they were the pioneers in indigenous banking and that they flourished in other walks of life also. But now times are changed and the keen competition they have to face at every turn from other enterprising communities, and particularly from the Christians, has much reduced the scope for their activities. As the Tamil Brahmans are already very much over-represented in the State service, and as other communities also are pressing their claims for proportional representation, educated members of the community find no opening for suitable careers in the State. It is no wonder therefore that they are emigrating in considerable numbers.

15. Of the other castes shown in the statement, the Eluthassans, Marasaris and Iluvans need no comment, their decennial increase being about

the average recorded for the State as a whole. If the figures for the Kudumi Chettis and Kanakkans are far above the average, the explanation for this is most probably to be found in faulty enumeration at the census of 1921. A higher rate of growth might perhaps have been expected among the primitive Pulayans, but the loss sustained by them through conversion to Christianity has also to be taken into consideration in this connection. So far as the Nayars are concerned, the increase of 8·8 per cent seems to be almost normal, the corresponding increase for 1911 to 1921 and 1901 to 1911 being 8·1 and 8·3 per cent respectively. Emigration also has probably influenced the rate to a slight extent in as much as considerable numbers of educated Nayars, finding no scope for employment in the State, have emigrated to other places like the Tamil Brahmans. The statistics in Special Emigration Table I in Chapter III support this view.

16. Each of the 8 castes shown in the following statement numbers between 5 and 10 per mille of the total population of which they together comprise but 6·7 per cent.

Caste	Actual numbers			Variation per cent 1921—1931
	1931	1921	1911	
Vettuvan ..	11,797	4,759	5,261	+ 147·9
Valan ..	11,684	9,507	7,827	+ 22·9
Sambavan (Parayan) ..	11,562	7,145	8,340	+ 61·8
Velan ..	10,895	6,232	9,322	+ 74·8
Konkani ..	9,661	8,080	8,522	+ 19·6
Kollan ..	9,276	8,029	7,156	+ 15·5
Ambalavasi ..	9,211	8,079	7,804	+ 14·0
Arayan ..	6,574	5,580	4,766	+ 17·8

With the exception of the Konkani Brahmans, these castes are all indigenous Malayalis. The Ambalavasis have several distinct sub-castes which do not inter-dine or inter-marry. They do not differ much from the Nayars and the increase of 14 per cent seen in their numbers may be regarded almost as normal for the decade under review. The rise in the numbers of the Arayans, Kollans and Valans may also be taken as normal for the period. It is not unlikely that the strength of the Konkani Brahmans was underestimated at the census of 1921, for they are shown to have suffered a loss of 5·2 per cent during the decade 1911 to 1921. Hence the increase of 19·6 per cent seen in their numbers during the last 10 years may be considerably above their average. The abnormal rate of growth recorded by the Vettuvans, Velans and Sambavans cannot but be attributed to defective enumeration in 1921.

17. The appended statement contains 17 castes which together form but 5·7 per cent of the total population. The proportional strength of each of them varies from 2 to 5 per 1,000 of the population.

Caste	Actual numbers			Variation per cent 1921—1931
	1931	1921	1911	
Tattan ..	5,956	5,602	4,309	+ 6·3
Nambudiri ..	5,918	5,427	5,520	+ 9·0
Chetti ..	5,339	9,163	4,606	— 41·7
Vellalan ..	5,259	4,587	6,044	+ 15·5
Pandaran ..	4,860	3,560	3,715	+ 36·5
Veluttedan ..	3,922	3,347	3,381	+ 17·2
Kallasari ..	3,852	2,436	3,101	+ 58·1
Kaniyan ..	3,841	2,393	3,244	+ 60·5
Kaikolan ..	3,714	4,805	4,121	— 22·7
Velakkattalavan ..	3,699	3,185	3,271	+ 16·1
Kavundan ..	3,680	6,354	1,095	— 42·1
Panan ..	3,603	2,642	2,902	+ 36·4
Kusavan ..	3,295	3,442	3,557	— 4·3
Malayan ..	3,185	594	2,461	+ 436·2
Devangan ..	3,055	370	2,349	+ 725·7
Panditattan ..	2,964	1,299	2,456	+ 128·2
Otta-naikan (Odde) ..	2,765	2,437	2,815	+ 13·5

Among these castes 8, namely, the Nambudiris, Kallasaris, Tattans, Kaniyans, Malayans, Panans, Velakkattalavans and Veluttedans are Malayalis and the others non-Malayalis. The increase recorded by the Kallasaris, Kaniyans, Malayans and Panans among the Malayali castes, and Pandarans among the alien castes, is far above the average and has to be accounted for by the short-counting of 1921. The rise in numbers among Velakkattalavans and Veluttedans, and perhaps among Nambudiris also, may be regarded as normal. The variation (+ 6·3 per cent) in the strength of the Malayali Tattans is to be examined side by side with that of the Tamil or Panditattans (+ 128·2 per cent). It is significant that the latter showed a fall of 47 per cent, whereas the former registered an increase of 30 per cent at the census of 1921. Be it noted at the same time that the artisan classes (of which the Tattans form one) showed an average rise of only 3·9 per cent in 1921. The natural inference from this is that many Tamil Tattans were wrongly returned as Malayali Tattans at the previous census. The variations in the figures of Chettis, Devangans and Kavundans are apparently perplexing, but they are easily explained. They are all non-Malayalis, and Malayali enumerators are not as well acquainted with the alien castes as with the indigenous ones. To make matters more complicated, Chetti is the name of a distinct caste as also the title affixed to the names of members of several castes. Thus there are Devanga Chettis, Vala Chettis, etc. Kavundan is not the name of a caste but only a title assumed by certain castes like the Vellalans. For these reasons the numbers shown against the three names must be as faulty at the present census as at previous ones. The decrease in the strength of the Kaikolans and Kusavans requires explanation. It cannot be that these castes declined in numbers during a decade which was prosperous for all classes and creeds. Perhaps many of them have emigrated to the neighbouring British territory. In the absence of such emigration, defective enumeration or wrong returns of caste names at the present census* must be responsible for the decrease.

18. It is hardly necessary to review the statistics and explain the variations of each of the remaining castes separately. They are but of little importance in that they together form less than 3 per cent of the State's population in which the proportional strength of each of them is below 2 per mille. Where any of them shows an increase which is much above the average, it is most probably to be attributed to short-counting in 1921. In the case of alien castes immigration or faulty returns of caste names may be responsible to a certain extent. Where, however, we find any very low increase or an actual decrease, we have to seek for its explanation chiefly in emigration and, in the case of non-Malayali castes, in wrong returns of caste names also.

Muslims

19. Islam recognizes no caste distinctions, but its followers are divided into 'four large families, Pathans, Moghuls, Saiyids and Sheikhs, and into sectional or functional groups such as the Boras, Khojas and Memons of Bombay', the Mappillas of Malabar etc. The Muslims of Cochin have been classified under 10 sub-divisions as seen from Imperial Table XVII. Of these the Jonakans or Jonaka Mappillas are the most numerous. The educated and advanced section among them did not want any class name and insisted on their being returned as Muslims in column 8 of the schedule. Hence the sub-division *others* has been swollen and it is seen to contain no less than 15,985 persons. Although the distinction between one division and another is very much looser than in the case of the Hindu castes, some restrictions about inter-marriage are still observed among them. The question of social position also naturally comes into play in this connection. A very large proportion of the Muslim population of the State consists of the descendants of converts from the various grades of Hindu society. The influence of the Hindu caste system to which they were subjected as a result of their descent and of their environment does not appear to have vanished altogether.

From the chapter on Literacy we have seen that there has been a general awakening among the Muslims of the State in recent times. For this reason they are now well-organized and progressive as a community. They have their communal organizations working efficiently for safeguarding and promoting the interests of their class.

Europeans and allied races

20. The number returned as Europeans or of allied races has risen from 66 to 112 since 1921. The increase is in the number of European British subjects. There were but 23 of them in 1921 whereas there are 72 at present. The statistics of birth place in Imperial Table VI will give us an idea of their nationality. They represent England, Wales, Scotland, Ireland, East Africa, Natal, New Zealand and Sumatra. Alien subjects are seen to hail from Belgium, Germany, Greece, Italy, Spain, Switzerland, Turkey and the United States of America.

The Europeans thus form but a very small community in the State. Among them the planters and the Christian missionaries are the most numerous. The former are represented in the Legislative Council.

The Odans (a class of potters) are not shown separately either in 1921 or in 1911. It seems very likely that they were clubbed with Kesavans (also potters). If this is so, the present decrease among Kusavans is easily explained. At the present census the Odans are shown separately and they number 1,514.

21. Apparently there has been a fall in the number of Anglo-Indians from 2,182 to 1,717 during the past decade. This is no doubt to be attributed to many Firingis being returned as Indian Christians at the present census. Originally descended from Portuguese traders who married women of the country, the great majority of the Firingis have at present next to no admixture of foreign blood. They differ very little from Indian Christians. Those that are well-to-do wear clothes of European fashion, while the dress of others differs but little from that of Indians. Many of them wrongly return themselves as Anglo-Indians, while considerable numbers return Firingi or Indian Christian as their race. The Firingis are not shown separately in the Tables, but are included with the Indian Christians. The statistics of Anglo-Indians are therefore inaccurate and misleading. **Anglo-Indians**

The Europeans and allied races and the Anglo-Indians are separately classified by age and sex in Imperial Table XIX.

22. Christianity like Islam has nothing to do with caste as a socio-religious institution. But the social life of the Indian Christians is influenced to a certain extent not only by the caste prejudices of their Hindu brethren but also by sectarian differences. We have already seen from the chapter on Religion how the Syrians consider themselves superior to the Latin Catholics in social status. Likewise recent converts from the lower classes of Hindus are assigned but an inferior position in the Christian society, and no Christian family of any standing or status will enter into marriage relations with these converts. **Indian Christians**

The Indian Christians are by far the best organized community in the State. Their communal organizations and journals have been working with remarkable success and promoting their interests in all directions, so much so that they have, within the space of a decade or two, risen from comparative insignificance to a position which, if not the first, is second to that of none in the public life of the country.

23. Some account has already been given of the aboriginal tribes and other depressed classes in the preceding chapter. More about them will be found in the two appendices at the end of this chapter, the first dealing with the hill tribes (Kadars and Malayans) and the second with the depressed classes. The principle followed in the selection of the classes included in the category of the depressed is explained below **The aboriginal tribes and other depressed classes**

Outside Malabar untouchability is generally regarded as the [dis] qualification for a community to be classed as depressed. Obviously this will not fit in with the peculiar conditions obtaining here, as may be seen from paragraph 11 above. Nor can we adopt unapproachability as the standard in the place of untouchability. The 64 feet castes were unapproachable not only to the higher or non-polluting castes but also to unapproachable castes of 24 feet, 36 feet etc.; and the different castes in each group of unapproachables of the same polluting distance were mutually untouchable. Among the non-polluting or approachable communities, each was untouchable to all the castes above it. Thus the Velakkattalavans, Veluttedans and Chaliyans, while they were mutually untouchable, were all untouchable to the Nayars, Ambalavasis, etc. The latter were untouchable to the Kshatriyas and Nambudiris. Most non-Malayali Hindu castes below the rank of Brahmans were untouchable to the higher Malayali Hindu castes to whom the Christians, Muslims, Jews, etc. were, of course, very much untouchable, though not unapproachable. In this dark wilderness or neo-pandemonium of untouchability and unapproachability, no safe standard based on touch or distance pollution could be adopted for any castes to be treated as depressed, and therefore the selection of communities to be included in the column for the depressed in State Table II was based on the classification adopted by the Government. The question of the amelioration of the social and economic condition of such communities as occupied the lowest rungs of the social ladder, and as had no access whatsoever to civilized society, was taken up by the Government some twelve years ago; and when work was actually started in this direction, the communities selected as the most depressed and helpless were the Kanakkans, Vettuvans, Pulayans, Sambavans, Nayadis and Ullatans. To these were added the two hill tribes, the Kadars and Malayans, though they could be depressed neither socially nor economically so long as they chose to live in their forests, uncontaminated by the civilized, approachable or touchable castes of the plains. The depressed classes in State Table II include not only the above communities recognized as depressed and helped by the Government but also five others *shown in the margin, whose social and economic condition does not differ much from that of the former. But they are not indigenous castes and their numbers are very few. The appendices make no mention of them.

Caste or tribe	Strength 1931 (actual figures)
Eravalan ..	541
Irulan ..	240
Kootan ..	228
Kavara ..	790
Valluvan ..	212

Reform among Iluvans

24. The statistics reviewed in paragraphs 14 to 18 above will show that, from the point of view of numerical strength, there are but 5 castes and communities that deserve special notice in this chapter. They are the Christians, Iluvans, Nayars, Muslims and Pulayans, and they comprise more than 75 per cent of the total population of Cochin. Of the five, the Muslims and the Christians have already been noticed in sections 19—22 above, and the Pulayans are treated in the appendix dealing with the depressed classes. Here it is proposed to record a few observations regarding the present condition of the Iluvans and Nayars with special reference to the modern attitude towards caste rules and restrictions described in paragraphs 12 and 13 of this chapter. Taking the Iluvans first into consideration, we find that changes that might well be described as revolutionary have taken place in their social, socio-religious and religious spheres of life. The first decade of the 20th century saw the community in its old dormant condition, content to take things lying down and meekly submitting to the social disabilities it was subjected to under the rigours of the Malayali caste system which had branded it with an unapproachability of 36 degrees (36 feet distance). There was no leadership, no organization, no union. But now the Iluvans are wide awake; and, what is more, they seem to have no idea of going to sleep hereafter. Within the short space of two decades the Iluvans have been transformed into a well-organized community with their *samajams* or associations successfully working for their social, moral and spiritual uplift and waging war against their social disabilities. At the same time they were setting their own house in order. We have seen from the last chapter how a religious reformation tending towards the purification and elevation of their religious beliefs, rites and forms of worship was effected in the community. The Iluvans have virtually abolished touch and distance pollution with reference to the castes

* The foot-note to paragraph 1c in Chapter XI explains how another caste (the Vadukans) has been wrongly included in the depressed classes of State Table II.

below them. They opened many temples for themselves as they had no access to the temples of the non-polluting castes, and several of these Iluva temples now admit the lower castes like the Pulayas who were of old unapproachables to Iluvans.

25. The modern tendencies referred to in paragraphs 12 and 13 above are fully reflected in this community. The changes introduced in the marriage rites and customs of the Iluvans have been already noticed in the chapter on Civil Condition. Ceremonial pollutions and other observances have lost much of their old rigidity. The periods of pollution as also the cost of the ceremonies have been considerably reduced. The advanced (English-educated) section is giving up these observances altogether. And yet no caste tribunal passes sentence of excommunication on the delinquents. The *Sahodara Sangham*, an association formed in the recent past, advocated inter-dining and inter-marriage with lower castes like the Pulayans and, in spite of the strenuous opposition it encountered in the beginning from the orthodox and conservative section of the community, has achieved its object to a considerable extent. The restrictions on inter-dining with lower castes are widely ignored and a few instances of inter-marriage also have taken place. In short the Iluvans are fast developing into a progressive and enlightened community.

Influence of their late Guru

26. The one force behind these changes and reforms was the unique personality of the late Sri Narayana Guru Swami whose teachings and influence galvanized the dormant community into vigorous activity, and whose enlightened leadership, more than anything else, was responsible for these achievements. A self-made man, the Guru came to be recognized as the spiritual head of the community in virtue of the solid work he did for its uplift. Like Poet Tagore, he preached the message of universal brotherhood, proclaiming that there was but "One God, one religion and one caste." For the spiritual, moral and social regeneration of his community, he started the *Sanyasi Sangham* and the *S. N. D. P. Yogam*, two associations that functioned with efficiency and success for a long time. Truly the Iluvans are indebted to their great Guru for whatever progress they have made.

Iluva caste sabhas

27. The *Thiyya Mahajana Sabha* and other *Yogams* of the Iluvans are now doing active propaganda work. Social reform and uplift of the community are their chief aims. Organized representations for the removal of social disabilities are made by them, social legislation is advocated and the claims of the Iluvans for appointment in the Government service are advanced. A Thiyya bill was recently enacted which legalized the system of partition evolved by the *Marumakkathayam* section of the community—there are both *Makkathayam* and *Marumakkathayam* sections among the Iluvans—,according to which sons and daughters were given equal shares of the parent's properties. The new regulation penalises bigamy and provides for inter-marriage with other classes. The *Marumakkathayam* section seems to be gradually tending towards *Makkathayam*.

Nayars

28. Turning to the Nayars, we find that the present-day tendencies and developments of caste are revealed to a very great extent in the social life of this community. The changes that have taken place in the rites and customs relating to marriage among Nayars have already been alluded to in the chapter on Civil Condition. Pollutions of all kinds, touch, atmospheric and even ceremonial, are very seldom observed except perhaps by the oldest generations in rural areas. The educated section of both sexes, which comprises a very

considerable proportion of the community's numerical strength, ignores all restrictions on inter-dining, and the example of this section is copied by others also. Up to this point the movement is parallel among the Iluvans and Nayars, the only difference being that the changes among Nayars referred to above have followed in the wake of higher education and the western ideals imbibed through its medium. But it is in the religious sphere that we find a real difference between the Nayars and Iluvans, and the reasons for this we had occasion to examine in the chapter on Religion. It is significant that the small English-educated section among the Iluvans also shares the same indifference and laxity in religious matters as characterise the Nayars and other educated classes.

Influence of the Nayar Regulation

29. The influence of the Nayar Regulation, a piece of social legislation enacted 10 years ago, may perhaps be gauged here in the light of a decade's experience. It cannot be denied that the new legislation has proved an able auxiliary to the forces of disintegration that have been actively at work in the Nayar community for more than a century. The Nayar Regulation fulfilled the aims of its promoters in that it legalized marriage among Nayars, deprived the managing proprietors of joint *Marumakkathayam* families of their despotic powers, safeguarded the interests of the junior members, and made due provision for those who wanted to follow the *Makkathayam* system of inheritance. And, as a matter of fact, the tendency towards *Makkathayam* is fast developing in the community. But the regulation facilitated the partition of joint families and hundreds of these have been divided during the past decade. Many who were at least theoretically in affluent circumstances as members of well-to-do families, and who would never have become destitute but for the partition of their family properties, have thereby been reduced to the verge of poverty and misery. Obviously small branches or individuals, separating from a rich joint family of numerous branches and members, and setting up by themselves, must naturally find their shares too small to keep them above want. On the whole it almost looks like a period of transition for the Nayars from the *Marumakkathayam* to the *Makkathayam* system, a period of uncertainty, gloom and general distress. Time alone can reveal how the transition will affect the character, disposition and material condition of this ancient community.

Caste patriotism among Nayars

30. Here too it must be remarked that, as a community, the Nayars in this State are not organized or united like the Iluvans, Muslims or Christians. Nayar *Samajams* or associations have been formed recently, but they do not function well in Cochin. Not that there is any dearth of educated and able Nayars to lead. Indeed there are many who have distinguished themselves in intellectual pursuits, learned professions and other walks of life. But they appear to be above communal considerations and evince but very little interest or concern in matters affecting their community. If caste patriotism is looked upon as a weakness or an evil passion in that it leads to communal jealousy and antagonism, then happily the Nayars of this State have one weakness less than other classes, because there is practically no caste patriotism among them! In any case the Nayar *Sabhas* in Cochin will compare very unfavourably with the corresponding associations of other communities like the Iluvans. And the few who desire to serve the community's interests through the medium of these *Samajams* find themselves handicapped by the general spirit of indiscipline, indifference and indolence, which perhaps constitute some of the distinguishing traits of the present-day Nayars of Cochin.*

---

* Most of the observations about Nayars in sections 28, 29 and 30 will apply to the Ambalavasis also who differ but very little from the Nayars; and though the Nayar Regulation does not apply to the Ambalavasi classes, they are not much behind the Nayars in their attempts to partition their joint *Marumakkathayam* families and reduce themselves to poverty and misery.

Nambudiris

31. Though the Nambudiris form but an insignificant minority in respect of their numerical strength—their proportion in the total population is but less than 5 per mille—, their unique position of old as the head of the intellectual and landed aristocracy of the State entitles them to special notice in this chapter. We had occasion to remark in the chapter on Literacy that the Time Spirit had at long last battered down the strongholds of orthodoxy and conservatism in which the Nambudiris had dwelt safely for centuries, uncontaminated by modern influences, and that a general awakening was visible in the community. The reform movement started but a couple of decades ago. The example of other classes like the Tamil Brahmans, Ambalavasis and Nayars, that had taken to English education, learned professions and Government service and thereby won honour and distinction, naturally fired the younger generation of Nambudiris with the laudable ambition of emulating them. The *Yoga Kshema Sabha* was organized by them, and the *Yoga Kshemam* and *Unni Nambudiri* journals were started as the organs of the *Sabha*, the chief aim of the promoters being the reformation or rather the rejuvenation of the old and worn out Nambudiri caste by means of social and other reforms calculated to bring the life of the community into adjustment with modern conditions. The reformers advocated English education for Nambudiri boys and girls and wanted that Nambudiris also should take an active part in the public life of the country like other educated classes. *Purdha* was to be abolished and the younger sons also of a father should be allowed to marry within the caste whereas, according to long-established custom, only the eldest son had this privilege. Rational changes were to be introduced in the management of the joint family, which was most often conducted on despotic lines by the managing proprietor, the interests of the younger members being neglected.

Progress of reform movement

32. The reforms advocated were so much opposed to all established and accepted usages that they appeared revolutionary and gave rise to a storm of protest from a great majority of the Nambudiri population. But the reformers who were prepared for all contingencies persevered, and gradually the no-changers began to lose ground. Time was against them, for they were the older of the two parties and their ranks were soon thinned by Death whom the reformers considered as their best ally. A few Nambudiri boys took to English education and, by the time they returned from their colleges, they were radicals who delighted in violating all caste rules and restrictions. The reform party rapidly gained in strength and the orthodox and conservative section has all but admitted defeat. The rising generations are now taking to English education in larger numbers. A few Nambudiri girls are attending public schools, having discarded their *Purdha*. The younger generations of women are in full sympathy with the movement. There are Nambudiri members in the Legislative Council; and we have seen from the chapter on Literacy that a Nambudiri lady has been nominated to the Council in connection with the Nambudiri Bill now under consideration. Things are moving fast and the whole Nambudiri world is in a ferment, anxiously watching the fortunes of the bill which, if enacted, must revolutionize the life of the community.

Reformers versus caste rules

33. The Nambudiris were the reputed authorities on, and in a sense the guardians of, all caste rules and restrictions so far as the higher Malayali castes were concerned. It is perhaps an irony of fate that the aged and orthodox among them should live to see the most sacred rules binding their own caste violated with impunity by their own children. The advanced section seldom, if ever, observes the touch or distance pollution. There is laxity in the observance even of ceremonial pollutions. Restrictions regarding inter-dining which were of the most rigorous character are defied in many cases. According

to these caste rules, a Nambudiri cannot take even a drink of water from any caste below the Kshatriyas, and if he is under pollution by touching any one of a lower caste or by approaching any unapproachable caste, he should undergo the ceremonial purification prescribed for such pollutions before he can take food or drink. The Nambudiri boys at school now take pleasure in sitting at the same table as members of other castes and creeds (including untouchables and unapproachables) and partaking of all kinds of refreshments in their company at social gatherings. Nambudiris of the reform party oppose untouchability and unapproachability with more ardour than English-educated Nayars who are perhaps too indolent to take any active interest in such matters; and advanced Nambudiris advocate temple entry for the untouchables and unapproachables with more enthusiasm than social reformers of other castes*. The example of the Nambudiris cannot but influence all other Malayali Hindus. If the highest caste could thus discard the rules and restrictions binding it, the others need have no hesitation to follow suit. Indeed it looks very doubtful whether any of these caste ordinances (except perhaps those relating to inter-marriage between one main caste and another) will be in force when the Census Report of 1941 comes to be written.

Neglect of religion

34. The progressive party has made a serious omission in its enthusiasm for an all-round reform. Religious study, pursuits and practices constituted not merely the traditional occupation but the very life-mission of the Nambudiris in olden times. Nambudiri boys were initiated into the study of sacred literature at an early age and they devoted their boyhood and adolescence to this pursuit. Now, however, their sacred mission is woefully neglected. The remarks made in the last chapter on the ignorance of caste Hindus regarding the most elementary principles of their religion are unfortunately applicable to the younger generation of the Nambudiris also to a very great extent. Of old the Nambudiris were looked upon by all who knew them as the visible and living embodiment of the Hindu religion in its highest and purest aspects. Perhaps no section of the Hindu population of India followed the religious precepts of Hinduism with such devotion and care, or lived so spiritual a life as the Nambudiri Brahmans. Their religious traditions are, therefore, of the noblest and most sacred character. Thus their community produced in the past some of the greatest and most authoritative exponents of Hindu religion and philosophy, and it is to the eternal glory of this community that it gave birth to the renowned Sri Sankaracharya. When a people with such traditions behind them grows indifferent about their religion and begins to neglect religious study and religious observances and rites, it must certainly be regarded as a day of evil omen not only for them or the other Hindu castes of Malabar but for the whole of Hindu India. It therefore behoves the reformers to remedy this most serious defect in their programme of work so that they may save themselves and their ancient religion from disaster.

Old order changeth

35. In the reforms and changes advocated by the rising generations, pessimists and conservatives see but irretrievable ruin to the community as a whole. But, despite man's conservatism,

> "The old order changeth, yielding place to new,
> And God fulfils Himself in many ways,
> Lest one good custom should corrupt the world."

---

* The influence of Gandhism and of the national movement in India is perhaps less perceptible in Cochin than in other Indian States. In any case it is almost nothing here when compared with the movement in Northern India. And yet Gandhism appears to have given an impetus to the reform movement among Nambudiris. Most of the young Nambudiris are ardent nationalists. Other caste Hindus also have been affected by this influence, but only to a much less extent. Communities other than caste-Hindus hardly show any trace of this influence.

SUBSIDIARY TABLE.

Variation in Caste, Tribe or Race since 1901.

Caste Tribe or Race	Persons				Percentage of variation Increase +, Decrease—			Net variation	Number per mille of the population in 1931
	1931	1921	1911	1901	1921—1931	1911—1921	1901—1911	1901—1931	
1	2	3	4	5	6	7	8	9	10
HINDU ..	780,484	646,132	615,708	554,255	+ 20·8	+ 4·9	+ 11·0	+226,229	648
Ambalavasi ..	9,311	8,079	7,804	7,483	+ 14·0	+ 2·5	+ 4·3	+ 1,728	8
Ambattan ..	1,570	1,032	1,101	1,240	+ 52·1	— 6·3	— 11·2	+ 330	1
Arayan ..	6,574	5,580	4,766	4,081	+ 17·8	+ 17·1	+ 16·8	+ 2,493	5
Brahman—Konkani ..	9,661	8,080	8,522	7,250	+ 19·6	— 5·2	+ 17·5	+ 2,411	8
Do Nambudiri ..	5,918	5,427	5,520	5,290	+ 9·0	— 1·7	+ 4·3	+ 628	5
Do Tamil ..	21,754	21,836	18,923	16,017	— 0·4	+ 15·4	+ 18·1	+ 5,737	18
Chakkan ..	2,162	463	2,101	1,525	+ 367·0	— 78·0	+ 37·8	+ 637	2
Chaliyan { Chaliyan .. / Pattaryan .. }	397 / 1,921	2,003	1,693	1,608	+ 15·7	+ 18·3	+ 5·3	+ 710	2
Chetti ..	5,339	9,163	4,606	5,143	— 41·7	+ 98·9	— 10·4	+ 196	4
Devangan ..	3,055	370	2,349	3,557	+ 725·7	— 84·2	— 34·0	— 502	3
Eluthassan ..	18,536	15,197	14,323	13,063	+ 22·0	+ 6·1	+ 9·6	+ 5,473	15
Ilavan ..	276,649	224,008	208,453	185,464	+ 23·5	+ 7·5	+ 12·4	+91,185	230
Kaikolan ..	3,714	4,805	4,121	3,616	— 22·9	+ 16·6	+ 13·9	+ 98	3
Kallan ..	1,096	1,135	945	1,067	— 3·4	+ 20·1	— 11·4	+ 29	1
Kammalan ..	45,546	35,917	34,558	29,809	+ 26·8	+ 3·9	+ 15·9	+15,737	38
Kanakkan ..	13,192	8,424	7,527	5,917	+ 56·6	+ 11·9	+ 27·2	+ 7,275	11
Kaniyan ..	3,841	2,393	3,244	2,547	+ 60·5	— 26·2	+ 27·4	+ 1,294	3
Kshatriya—Malayali ..	1,467	1,232	1,015	892	+ 19·1	+ 21·4	+ 13·8	+ 575	1
Kudumi chetti ..	16,104	10,328	12,371	10,843	+ 55·9	— 16·5	+ 14·1	+ 5,261	13
Kusavan ..	3,295	3,442	3,557	3,231	— 4·3	— 3·2	+ 10·0	+ 64	3
Nayar ..	142,637	131,054	121,206	111,837	+ 8·8	+ 8·1	+ 8·3	+ 30,800	118
Odan ..	1,514	..	..	..	..	..	..	+ 1,514	1
Otta-naiken ..	2,765	2,437	2,815	2,066	+ 13·5	— 13·4	+ 36·3	+ 699	2
Panan ..	3,603	2,642	2,902	2,781	+ 36·4	— 9·0	+ 4·4	+ 822	3

Variation in Caste, Tribe or Race since 1901.—(cont.)

Caste, Tribe or Race	Persons				Percentage of variation Increase +, Decrease —			Net variation	Number per mille of the population in 1931
	1931	1921	1911	1901	1921—1931	1911—1921	1901—1911	1901—1931	
1	2	3	4	5	6	7	8	9	10
HINDU—*cont.*									
Pandaran ..	4,860	3,560	3,715	2,735	+ 36.5	— 4.2	+ 35.8	+ 2,125	4
Panditattan ..	2,964	1,299	2,456	3,648	+ 128.2	— 47.1	— 32.7	— 684	2
Pulayan ..	82,043	69,423	72,787	59,840	+ 18.2	— 4.6	+ 21.6	+22,203	68
Sambavan (Parayan) ..	11,562	7,145	8,340	8,841	+ 61.8	— 14.3	— 5.6	+ 2,721	10
Valan ..	11,684	9,507	7,827	7,564	+ 22.9	+ 21.5	+ 3.4	+ 4,120	10
Velakkattalavan ..	3,699	3,185	3,271	2,761	+ 16.1	— 2.6	+ 18.4	+ 938	3
Velan ..	10,895	6,232	9,322	8,243	+ 74.8	— 33.1	+ 13.1	+ 2,652	9
Vellalan ..	5,299	4,587	6,014	8,242	+ 15.5	— 24.1	— 26.6	— 2,943	4
Veluttedan ..	3,922	3,347	3,381	3,152	+ 17.2	— 1.0	+ 7.2	+ 770	
Vettuvan ..	11,797	4,759	5,261	6,349	+ 147.9	— 9.5	— 17.1	+ 5,448	10
MUSLIM ..	**87,902**	**68,717**	**63,822**	**54,492**	**+ 27.9**	**+ 7.7**	**+ 17.1**	**+33,410**	**73**
Jonakan ..	57,371	56,018	51,469	43,604	+ 2.4	+ 9.0	+ 18.0	+13,767	48
Ravuttan ..	10,927	6,544	8,430	8,160	+ 67.0	— 22.4	+ 3.3	+ 2,767	
Others ..	19,604	6,155	3,923	2,728	+ 218.5	+ 56.9	+ 43.8	+16,876	16
CHRISTIAN ..	**334,870**	**262,595**	**233,092**	**198,239**	**+ 27.5**	**+ 12.7**	**+ 17.5**	**+136,631**	**278**
Anglo-Indian ..	1,717	2,182	2,446	4,033	— 21.3	— 10.8	— 39.3	— 1,316	1
European British Subjects ..	72	23	47 }	55	+ 213.0	— 51.1 }	+ 41.8	+ 57	..
Do Others ..	40	43	31 }		— 7.0	+ 38.7 }			..
Indian Christian ..	333,041	260,347	230,568	194,151	+ 27.9	+ 12.9	+ 18.7	+138,890	276
JAIN ..	**210**	**101**	**129**	**5**	**+107.9**	**— 21.7**	**+2,480.0**	**+ 205**	..
JEW ..	**1,451**	**1,167**	**1,178**	**1,137**	**+ 24.3**	**— 0.7**	**+ 3.3**	**+ 314**	**1**

GLOSSARY OF CASTES, TRIBES AND RACES.

(Those included in Table XVII.)

Note.—1. Names printed in antique type as **Ambalavasi** *are those of indigenous Malayali castes, and names printed in capitals are those of non-indigenous castes.*

2. Indigenous castes marked with an asterisk follow the Marumakkathayam system of marriage and inheritance, and the rest Makkathayam.

3. In the case of indigenous castes where the period of pollution is not mentioned, it is to be assumed to be fifteen days, and where it is not mentioned how their women are called, it is to be understood that the usual feminine affix has only to be added to the male names.

4. The figures entered after each name show the total strength of the caste.

Adikal (25).—A class of Ambalavasis. They are said to have been Brahmans originally, but were degraded for having officiated as priests in Bhadrakali temples and made offerings of flesh and liquor. They wear the holy thread, officiate as priests in minor temples and do other temple services. They follow Makkathayam, and their pollution period is ten days. Their women are called Adiyammas.

AGAMUDAIAN (264).—A Tamil cultivating caste. They are found only in the eastern-most villages of the Chittur taluk.

* **Ambalavasi** (9,211).—The word means temple-resident, and is the generic name of a group of castes whose hereditary occupation is temple service. They are mostly either degraded Brahmans or the offspring of hypergamy. The castes to which this name is applied in Cochin are the Adikal, Chakkiyar, Chakkiyar Nambiyar, Chengazhi Nambiyar, Kallattu Kurup, Marar, Nambiyassan, Pisharodi, Puduval, Thiyyattunni and Variyar. These castes will be found treated separately in alphabetical order. They follow the Marumakkathayam law, all except the Adikal, Thiyyattunnis and Nambiyassans; the first two follow the Makkattayam system, while among the last some follow the one system and the rest the other. Marars eat the food cooked by other Ambalavasis, and Pisharodi and Variyar males dine with each other. With these exceptions there is no inter-dining or inter-marriage between the several sections of Ambalavasis.

AMBATTAN (1,570).—Tamil barber caste.

ANGLO-INDIAN (1,717).—The name now officially given to Europeans of mixed Indian descent, hitherto known as Eurasians. The great majority of the Eurasians of Cochin are how ever of Portuguese and Dutch descent and there is nothing "Anglo" about them.

Arayan (6,574).—They are fishermen and boatmen like the Valans, but while the latter fish only in the backwaters and lagoons, the former engage themselves in sea fishing. They are therefore also called Kadalarayans (or sea Arayans). Their approach within 32 feet of high caste Hindus polluted the latter according to the old caste rules. Though Arayans and Valans are of equal status in the eyes of other castes, they neither inter-marry nor inter-dine with each other. They observe birth and death pollution only for eleven days. Amukkuvans, who are a sub-caste of Arayans, are their priests as well as those of Valans.

BANIYA (153).—Vaisya immigrants from the Bombay Presidency residing chiefly in Mattancheri and its neighbourhood for trade.

BLACK JEW (1,307).—One of the two divisions of local Jews. They are considered the offspring of mixed unions or converts from the lower classes of Hindus. They themselves claim, however, that they were the first settlers on this coast, the White Jews being later immigrants, and that the darkness of their complexion was due chiefly to their long residence in the tropics.

BORA (74).—Muslim converts from the Bombay side.

BOYA (231).—A shikari tribe in the Deccan Districts, who subsist on game and forest produce.

BRAHMAN (41,324).—In Table XVII Brahmans are classified by the parent tongues returned by them. The classes are Embran, Gouda, Gujarati, Konkani, Marathi, Malayali, Tamil, Telugu and others. Malayali Brahmans are again divided into Nambudiris, Elayads and Muttads. The reader is referred to the notes given under the respective heads.

CHAKKAN (2,162).—A Tamil caste of oil pressers locally called by this name, *Chakku* meaning an oil mill. Elsewhere they are called Vaniyans. Though they wear the sacred thread, their touch pollutes Nayars and the higher castes, and they are also not allowed access to the Brahmanical temples. The reason for this seems to be that Manu has for some unknown reasons classed oil pressing as a low occupation. A class of Tamil Brahmans officiate as their priests.

CHAKKILIYAN (839).—A Telugu caste of leather workers.

• **Chakkiyar** (50).—A class of Ambalavasis. They are the offspring of adulterous Nambudiri women born after the commencement of their guilt but before its discovery and their expulsion from caste. Boys so born, who have already been invested with the sacred thread, become Chakkiyars, and those who have not been so invested become Chakkiyar Nambiyars, the girls joining either caste indifferently. Their females are called Illodammas, and those of Chakkiyar Nambiyars, Nangiyars. The traditional occupation of the Chakkiyar is the *kuttu*, or the recitation of passages from the Puranas, with commentaries interspersed with witty allusions to current events and to the members of the audience. The Nambiyar accompanies the performance on a metal drum called *Mizhavu* and the Nangiyar keeps time with a cymbal. The Nangiyars also perform on occasions another kind of *kuttu*, which is a pantomimic performance on the Chakkiyar's stage. This stage is a consecrated one built within the premises of important temples. The Chakkiyar wears the holy thread, but the Nambiyar does not. The former may marry a Nangiyar, while the latter cannot marry an Illodamma. Their pollution period is eleven days.

• **Chakkiyar Nambiyar** (76).—*See* Chakkiyar above.

• **Chaliyan (Pattaryan)** (397+1,021).—A Malayali caste of cotton weavers. They are considered as a low class of Sudras, but are not allowed access to the Brahmanical temples. According to the old Malayali caste system, their touch polluted the higher castes. Most of them follow Marumakkathayam, and to a great extent resemble the Nayars in their customs and usages, but some among them follow Makkathayam. They have their own temples, in which their barbers officiate as priests. They are the only indigenous people that live in streets, which probably points to the fact of their being comparatively recent settlers from the East Coast.

•**Chengazhi Nambiyar** (185).—A class of Ambalavasis. They wear the sacred thread and resemble Nambiyassans in their customs and usages, except that they all follow Marumakkathayam.

CHETTI (5,339).—This is a titular or occupational term, meaning trader, and not the name of caste. The members of several Tamil and Telugu castes tack this title on to their names to denote, though not in all cases, that trade is their occupation.

CHUNNAMBOTTAN (115).—A Telugu caste of people who deal in *Chunnam*.

DASI (395).—Devadasis attached to the Konkani temples in Cochin-Kanayannur taluk, and recruited mainly from Konkani Sudras. They speak the Konkani dialect.

DEVANGAN (3,055).—A weaving caste found only in the Chittur taluk and the eastern portion of the Talapilli taluk, more commonly known here as Chetans. They are immigrants from Mysore, and speak Kanarese. They wear the holy thread, and Chetti is their agnomen.

Elayad (941).—A class of Malayali Brahmans who have suffered social degradation for having officiated at the funeral rites of the Nayars, which is now their hereditary occupation.

In regard to marriage, inheritance, pollution, etc., they closely follow the usages of Nambudiris. Their women are called Flormas.

Eluthassan (18,536).—Low class Malayali Sudras, popularly supposed to have been the descendants of Pattar Brahmans degraded for having eaten *kadu*, a kind of fish. They were known as Kadupattans, a name which they have given up as degrading. Like Brahmans they observe pollution only for ten days, but they are not allowed access to Brahmanical temples. There is a peculiarity in their system of inheritance, *viz.*, that in the absence of sons the father's property does not descend to his daughters, but to his nearest male relatives. In former times they were largely employed as village school masters. The manufacture and sale of salt were among their chief occupations, when salt was not a Sirkar monopoly. They are now chiefly engaged in agriculture and general labour.

EMBRAN (1,571).—Tulu Brahman immigrants from South Canara. They are treated on a footing of equality by the Nambudiris, who however will not inter-marry with them. They are mostly employed as officiating priests in the temples of the State.

ERAVALAN (541).—A Tamil speaking forest tribe, immigrants from Coimbatore. In Cochin they are mostly agricultural labourers in the plains.

GAUDA (627).—A class of Brahman mendicants wandering from place to place. They speak Telugu and it is not clear why they are called Gaudas.

HANEVI (54) —A Musalman sect.

IDAIYAN (385).—The great shepherd caste of the Tamil country.

Iluvan (276,649).—They are called also Chogans in Cochin, and correspond to the Tiyyans of British Malabar and the Shanans of the Tamil Districts. They are believed to have immigrated from Ceylon and introduced the cultivation of the cocoanut palm. Cocoanut growing and toddy drawing were their hereditary occupation, but as they were numerically one of the strongest castes in Cochin, a great many of them had to take to other occupations, chiefly agriculture. The Iluvans in Cochin-Kanayannur follow Marumakkathayam and those in the rest of the State Makkathayam. Among the former divorce and widow marriage are allowed. The headmen of the Iluvans are called Tandans, and are appointed to that position by the Ruler of the State. They are to perform certain specified functions, and are entitled to fees, at marriage and other ceremonies. Kavutiyans or Vattis are their priests and barbers, and form a distinct sub-caste inferior to them in status. According to the old caste rules, Iluvans polluted the higher castes by approach within 24 Malabar feet.

Jonakan (57,371).—Malayalam-speaking Muslims, also called Mappilas or Jonaka Mappilas, to distinguish them from Native Christians, who are locally known as Nasrani (Nazarene) Mappilas. They are the descendants of the offspring of mixed unions or converts from the lower classes of Hindus. They are all Sunis, and polygamy prevails among them.

KACHCHI (684).—A class of Muslims, more commonly known as Kachchi Memons. They are so called here as they come from Cutch and its neighbouring Districts.

Kadan (267)—A hill tribe confined to the Nelliampatis and Parambikolam, from which other hill tribes are excluded. They are a short, muscular people, of a deep black colour with thick lips and curly hair, and speak a *patois* more akin to Malayalam than to Tamil. They are good trackers and tree climbers, and are useful in the collection of minor forest produce. During the working season they live on the rice supplied by forest contractors, and at other times on such animals as they are able to trap and on wild yams and other forest produce.

KAIKOLAN (3,714).—A caste of Tamil weavers found only in Chittur and Talapilli taluks. Some of them speak Malayalam, and wear their tuft in front like the Nayars. Most of them still follow their hereditary occupation.

KAKKALAN (732).—A gipsy tribe, whose males are tailors, mat makers, jugglers and snake charmers, and whose females are professional beggars and palmists. They speak a corrupt Tamil. They are called Kuravans in the northern taluks.

KALLAN (1,096).—A Tamil caste of workers in granite. They wear the sacred thread and are not distinguishable from Pandi Tattans (Tamil goldsmiths) in any respect except their occupation. They are not allowed access to Brahmanical temples in Cochin.

Kallasari (3,852).—A division of Kammalans, who are masons by occupation. They work only in laterite. *See* Kammalan.

***Kallattu Kurup** (370).—The lowest division of Ambalavasis.

Kammalan (45,546).—The artisan class, divided into a number of endogamous sub-castes—Marasari (carpenter), Kallasari (mason), Musari (brazier), Kollan (blacksmith), Tattan (goldsmith) and Tolkollan (leather-worker). As their services are much in requisition and as they earn better wages than unskilled labourers, they are still engaged in their hereditary occupations. The first five groups are socially on a par with each other. They all inter-dine, but do not inter-marry. But the Tolkollans are considered inferior in status to the rest, and cannot touch them without causing pollution, probably on account of their work in leather, which in its raw state is considered impure. Polyandry of the fraternal type was prevalent among them, several brothers marrying one wife and the children being treated as common to all. This practice is now extinct. The Kurups, who form a sub-caste among them, are their priests as well as barbers, and officiate at their marriage and funeral ceremonies. The Kammalans polluted the higher castes by approach within 24 feet.

Kanakkan (13,192).—A class of fishermen and boatmen, who polluted the higher castes by approach within a radius of 48 feet. They are also engaged in agriculture and general labour. They are a very poor class, and very backward in point of education.

Kaniyan (3,841).—Also called Kanisan. They are professional astrologers, whose services are in constant requisition for casting horoscopes and for fixing propitious hours for marriage and other ceremonies. Many among them are employed as village school masters. They are the most literate among the polluting castes. Their pollution distance was 24 feet.

KAVARA (790).—A Telugu caste of basket makers.

KAVUNDAN (3,680).—A title of Kongu Vellalas.

Kollan (9,276).—A class of Kammalans, who are hereditary blacksmiths. They are called Karuvans in the northern taluks. *See* Kammalan.

KONKANI BRAHMAN (9,661).—A branch of the Saraswat sub-division of Pancha Gaudas. They are so called because they are immigrants from Konkan. They speak the Konkani dialect of Marathi, and are found only in the southern taluks. They are Vaishnavites, and have well-endowed temples of their own in the State. The Nambudiris and other Brahmans will not treat them as Brahmans; not only will they not inter-dine with them, but they will not even allow them access to their temples and tanks. The Konkanis return the compliment by refraining from dining with other Brahmans and by refusing them admission to their temples. By occupation they are mostly traders and shop-keepers, but there are landholders also among them.

***Kshatriya** (2,128).—Kshatriyas are grouped under several classes in the caste Table. Of these, the indigenous Malayali Kshatriyas are known as either Tampurans, Tampans or Tirumulpads: this is a sub-division not by caste but by position. The Tampurans are members of ruling families, while Tampans are those who were once ruling chiefs but have since lost their political power. All the rest are Tirumulpads. Their women are called Tampurattis, Tampattis and Nambashtaris respectively. Brahman males partake of the meals prepared by them. In their personal habits, observances and ceremonies they are very like the Nambudiris, who act as their priests in all ceremonies. They observe pollution for eleven days, follow the Marumakkathayam law of succession, and have two marriages like the Nayars, the *Tali* and the *Sambandham*.

KUDUMI CHETTI (16,104).—Konkani Sudras, who serve Konkani Brahmans as their domestic servants, live in their midst and speak their language. They are among the most illiterate classes of the population, but for capacity for continued hard work they are unrivalled. They are employed in all kinds of unskilled labour, and they are also good boatmen. Their headman, styled Muppan, who was appointed by the Ruler of the State, directed all their social concerns. Konkani Brahmans officiate as their priests.

***Kurukkal** (319).—A sub-division of Nayars, who take part in the worship of non-Aryan tutelary deities in village temples called *Kavus*.

KUSAVAN (3,295).—Tamil potters.

Malayan (3,185).—A hill tribe found chiefly in the Kodasseri and Palapilli forests. They do not differ much in appearance and habits from the Kadans, except that they are less wild and less averse to manual labour than the latter. Besides collecting minor forest produce like the Kadans, they make good bamboo mats and baskets. They are also good trackers and tree climbers.

***Marar** (2,016).—A division of Ambalavasis, who are temple musicians. They eat the food cooked by the other Ambalavasis, but none of the latter will partake of the meals prepared by them.

Marasari (23,430).—A class of Kammalans, who are carpenters by occupation. *See* Kammalan.

Musari (1,460).—A division of Kammalans, whose hereditary occupation is work in bell-metal. *See* Kammalan.

Muttad (304).—Malayali Brahmans who are said to have suffered social degradation for having tattooed their body with figures representing the weapons of Siva and for partaking of offerings made to that god. They perform some of the duties in the temples which Ambalavasis perform and are therefore considered by some to belong to the latter class, but they also carry the idols when taken out in procession, which no Ambalavasi is entitled to do, and, like the Elayads, they follow the usages of Nambudiris. Their women are called Manayammas, who are goshas like the Nambudiri women.

***Nambidi** (410).—An intermediate caste between Nambudiris and Nayars. They are said to be the descendants of certain Brahmans who were degraded for assassinating one of the Perumals. They wear the sacred thread, and observe pollution only for ten days like the Brahmans, and Nambudiris officiate as priests in all their ceremonies. Their women are called Manolpads. Nambidi is also the title of some Nayar aristocrats.

Nambiyassan (1,327).—A class of Ambalavasis. Pushpakan is the generic name of this class, the particular local names being Nambiyassan, Nambiyar and Unni. Their duty consists in collecting flowers and making garlands for decorating idols, while their women, who are called Pushpanis or Brahmanis, sing certain songs in Bhadrakali temples and at the *tali* marriage ceremonies of Nayars and others. Among them some follow Makkathayam and others Marumakkathayam. They are the only Ambalavasis, except Chakkiyars, Thiyyattunnis and Chengazhi Nambiyars, who wear the sacred thread. Their pollution period is ten days.

Nambudiri (5,918).—The Brahmans of Kerala. They follow the Makkathayam system of marriage and inheritance, but as a rule only the eldest sons marry in their own caste, while the other members form Sambandham union with Kshatriya, Ambalavasi and Nayar women. Their women are goshas and are called Antarjanams or Akattammars (in-doors ladies). They generally marry after puberty. and their chastity is jealously guarded. The Nambudiris are divided, on the basis of certain sacerdotal rights and privileges enjoyed by them, into ten social groups. The highest class enjoy all the ten privileges, the next only nine and so on. The first six groups have the privilege of studying the Vedas, while the last four have not. The Vedic Nambudiris again are divided into three groups, of which the Adhyans occupy the highest position, the Asyans, the intermediate, and the Samanyans, the lowest. The Asyans are entitled to perform *Yagams* or sacrifices, and the Samanyans are not, while the Adhyans are above it. Among Vedic Nambudiris some are hereditary Tantris, who are the highest temple priests and whose authority is final in all matters of temple ritual, Vadhyans, who preside over the Yogams and Vedic schools at Trichur and Tirunavaya, Vaidikans, who decide all matters relating to caste, and smartans, who preside over caste tribunal. The non-Vedic Nambudiris also are divided into various groups Among them are the Mussads or Ashtavaidyans, whose hereditary occupation is the study and practice of medicine. the Sastrangakars, or more correctly Kshatrangakars (military Brahmans), who are believed to be the descendants of the Brahmans who were engaged in military service in former days, and the Graminis, who were engaged in administering *gramams* or Nambudiri colonies. All the Nambudiris are divided, like other Brahmans, into exogamous *gotras*. Their pollution period is ten days.

NANJANATTU PILLAI (330).—Tamil Vellalas long domiciled in the country and therefore partaking of the character of the Nayars to some extent. The men wear the fore-tuft, and dress themselves like the Nayars, while the women's dress looks more like that of Vellala women. They follow a system of marriage and inheritance, which is partly Tamil and partly Malayali. The *tali* marriage is the regular marriage, but divorce is freely permitted. Divorced women and widows cannot marry, but can form *Sambandham* alliance with men of their own caste. The sons are entitled to inherit a fourth of their father's property, while the rest goes to his sister's children. Nanjanattu Pillais and Nayars do not inter-marry or inter-dine with each other, at least in Cochin.

* Nayar (142,637).—Once a military class of people who, with the Nambudiris and Ambalavasis, form the most characteristic section of the people of Cochin. Their martial spirit however has during a century of unbroken peace died out, but its traces still remain in some of their titles, games, etc. They are however making considerable advance in other respects. English education has made considerable progress among them, and they are found in all the literate walks of life in large numbers. The great majority of the Nayars however are petty farmers and agricultural labourers, though there are several land-holders and substantial farmers among them. Domestic servants in well-to-do caste Hindu families are almost entirely recruited from this caste. The Nayars are divided into a number of sub-castes, most of which are known by different names in British Malabar, Cochin and Travancore. The highest sub-caste, for instance, is known as Kiriyam in Malabar, while in Cochin it is generally called Vellayma. Next comes the Sudra Nayar, who is attached to Nambudiri and Kshatriya houses for certain services, religious and domestic : if attached to the former, he is called Illattu Nayar and, if to the latter, Swarupattil Nayar. Charna Nayars are attendants on Rajas and chiefs, but the sub-caste is not indigenous to Cochin. Pallichans are the palanquin bearers of Brahmans and Rajas, and Vattekadans are oil mongers for temples and Nambudiri houses. Odattu Nayars tile temple buildings and Anduru Nayars make earthen vessels for the temples, while Attikurussi Nayars or Chitikans act as purifiers and quasi priests to the other Nayars. These are the main sub-divisions, but there are shades of differences within each sub-caste which are too numerous and too subtle to be dealt with here. Every Nayar has a title affixed to his name, which is conferred upon him by the Raja as a hereditary or personal distinction, while those who have received no title affix the title Nayar to their names. The title does not indicate one's position in the caste hierarchy, as the Raja can confer any of these titles without reference to the sub-caste of the recipients. Acchan, Karta, Kaimal and Mannadiyar are among the titles of nobility, while Panikkar, Kurup and Kuruppal are the titles of those who maintained *Kalaris*, or military gymnesia, as a hereditary profession. Menon is the title which was in the old days generally

conferred on the Nayars who followed literate occupations and which is now most in use among the middle classes. It is the only title now conferred by the Raja as a personal distinction, but in these days many Nayars assume it without any such formality.

Nayadi (152).—An animistic tribe living in the outskirts of the jungles. Begging, watching crops in the plains, beating for game in the jungles and collecting forest produce are their chief occupations. They are the laziest and the most uncleanly people in the State, and eat the most dirty reptiles and vermins. Their approach within 72 feet polluted caste Hindus. Even Pulayans and Parayans considered themselves polluted by their approach.

OTTA NAIKAN, OR ODDE (2,765).—Telugu tank diggers and earth workers. They are among the most illiterate classes in Cochin, but for earth work they are unrivalled. They are probably the most law abiding people in the State.

Panan (3,603).—A polluting caste according to the old caste system, whose hereditary occupation is sorcery and exorcism. Some of them still exercise that profession, but the great majority of them are agriculturists and umbrella makers. Fraternal polyandry once prevailed among them. Their pollution distance was 24 feet.

PANDARAN (4,860).—A caste of Tamil priests and beggars. The Pandarans who have long been domiciled in Cochin are however neither priests nor beggars. Most of them are engaged in making *pappadams*, the crisp pulse cakes much affected by the Malayalis. The men have their tuft in front and dress like the Nayars, while the women dress like Tamil Sudras. Their home language here is Malayalam.

PANDITATTAN (2,964).—Tamil goldsmith caste. They wear the sacred thread, but are not allowed access to Brahmanical temples and public tanks in Cochin. Their touch polluted the higher castes.

PATHAN (2,275).—Muslims of Afghan descent. The name is also assumed by many who have no right to it. Here they are employed chiefly in subordinate Government service especially as peons and constables.

***Pisharodi** (1,459).—A division of Ambalavasis. They make garlands for idols and do other menial services in temples. Their women are called Pisharasyars. They are said to be the descendants of a Brahman novice who, when about to be ordained a *sanyasi*, ran away after he was divested of the holy thread but before his head was completely shaved. In memory of this they are buried like sanyasis in a sitting position and the grave filled with salt and paddy. They inter-dine with Variyars, but not with any other division of Ambalavasis. Their pollution period is 12 days.

Pulayan (82,043).—Agrestic serfs emancipated in 1854. They are also called Cheramans. They are all engaged in field labour—ploughing, sowing, crop-watching and reaping—and are generally paid in kind. They are all poor and illiterate, and live in the confines of paddy flats in miserable huts. They polluted the higher castes by approach within 64 feet. Parayans polluted them by touch, and Nayadis, Vettuvans, Ullatans, etc., by approach.

Pulluvan (170).—A polluting caste according to old caste rules. They are professional beggars. They also sing in serpant groves to the accompaniment of a quaint musical instrument called *Pulluvakkudam.*

***Putuval** (471).—A division of Ambalavasis, who are stewards of temples. They do not dine or inter-marry with other Ambalavasis, nor the latter (except Marars) with them. Their women are called Puduvalasyars.

RAVUTTAN (10,927).—Muslims like Jonaka Mappilas, who are the descendants of mixed unions or converts from the lower classes. They are immigrants from the east coast, and speak Tamil. They are mostly petty shop-keepers.

SAIVID (43).—A Musalman tribe from Upper India. They are regarded as the direct descendants of the Prophet, and are therefore the highest sect of Musalmans.

*Samantan (571).—This caste is not indigenous to Cochin, and those who have returned themselves as Samantans are either natives of British Malabar or are Nayar aristocrats who have of late begun to like to be considered to be superior to the ordinary Nayars in caste. Samantans are said to have sprung from the union of Kshatriya males and Nayar females. Like the Kshatriyas, they observe pollution for 11 days, but do not wear the sacred thread.

Sambavan (Parayan, old style) (11,914).—An agricultural labourer caste, the lowest in the social scale. They polluted the higher castes by approach within 72 feet. Many among them live by making mats and baskets and practising witchcraft. As magicians they are much feared, especially by the lower classes. Their principal cult is the *odi*, the patron goddess of which is Nili of Kalladikod. They are the only caste in Cochin that eat beef. The Tamil Parayans are superior to them in status.

SHABI (287).—A Muslim sect.

SHEIK (202).—A Muslim tribe from Upper India. They are the descendants of the first three Caliphs or successors of the Prophet, and are therefore second only to the Saiyids in racial purity and social precedence.

TAMIL BRAHMAN (21,754).—They are locally known as Pattars, and are more numerous in the State than the Nambudiris. They are immigrants from the neighbouring Tamil Districts and settled in the State at different periods. They retain the customs and the usages of the east coast, but many among them, especially the earlier immigrants, have by their contact with the Malayalis for centuries made some change in their manners and customs, such as the wearing of *mundus* by many of their males, the observance of pollution by touch, approach, &c. By their intelligence, education and enterprise they have attained a prominent position everywhere. They are employed in all grades of Government service, and are conspicuous in all the learned professions. A good many of them are traders, money-lenders, land-holders and farmers, while the poorer among them are engaged in domestic service. They have rendered their personal service indispensable to all the princely and aristocratic families, where large numbers of them are employed in various capacities, especially as cooks. They are as good Brahmans as the highest class of Nambudiris from a spiritual point of view, but the latter will not admit such equality. Nambudiri women, for instance, will not take the meals cooked by Pattar Brahmans, nor will the men allow them to take part in their religious ceremonies. They are also not allowed access to the inner shrines of Nambudiri temples. Nor are they permitted to touch the Nambudiris when engaged in their devotions and ceremonies.

TARAKAN (929).—A trading class of Tamil Sudras, who settled on this side of the Palghat gap to act as trade medium between the Malayalam and Tamil countries, Tarakan meaning literally a broker. They gradually adopted the customs and usages of the Nayars except in regard to marriage and inheritance, and have in recent years been practically assimilated with them.

Tattan (5,956).—A division of Kammalans who are gold and silver-smiths. *See* Kammalan.

Thiyyattunni (11).—A division of Ambalavasis, whose occupation is the performance of ceremonies in Bhagavati temples called *Tiyyattam*, in which they paint the image of the goddess on the floor and chant certain propitiatory songs, especially to check the spread of small-pox. They are also called Tiyyattu Nambiyars. Some among them follow Makkattayam and others Marumakkathayam. Their pollution period is ten days. Their women are called Pushpinis or Brahmanis.

Tolkollan (1,572).—A division of Kammalans, who work in leather. *See* Kammalan.

TOTTIYAN (196).—A Telugu cultivating caste.

Ullatan (778).—A hill tribe living in the outskirts of jungles. They are chiefly engaged in felling trees, in scooping out logs for boats and in agricultural labour. Their approach pollutes Pulayans and Parayans.

Vadukan (1,313)—Found chiefly in the Chittur Taluk. They are slightly superior to the Iluvans in social status. They pursue agriculture and general labour.

Valan (11,684).—A caste of fishermen and boatmen. The fishermen and boatmen of this coast are divided into four endogamous groups, *viz.*, Sankhan, Bharatan, Amukkuvan and Mukkuvan. Of these, Arayans belong to the first group, and Valans to the second. Amukkuvans, who form a sub-caste of Arayans, are the priests of Valans as well as of Arayans. Among the Valans again there are four exogamous divisions called *Illoms*. They are Alayakad, Ennalu, Vaisyagiriyam and Vazhapilli. Each division has its own headman, called Arayar, who is appointed by the Ruler of the State. Under each headman there are subordinate social heads called Ponambans, who are appointed by the Arayar himself. The Valans had the exclusive privilege of fishing in the backwaters and rowing His Highness' escort snake boats. Their pollution distance was 32 feet.

VALLUVAN (212).—A Tamil caste of priests to Parayans. They consider themselves superior to Parayans and will not dine or inter-marry with them.

VANIYAN (856).—Konkani Vaisyans. They wear the sacred thread, and resemble Konkani Brahmans in their habits. They have their own priests, who are called Panditans. They are mostly petty traders. These Vaniyans are to be distinguished from Chakkans, who are also called by that name. Their pollution period is twelve days.

VANNAN (443).—Tamil washerman

* **Variyar** (3,221).—The most numerous division of Ambalavasis. Their hereditary occupation is making flower garlands for idols and sweeping temple premises. They inter-dine with Pisharodis, but with no other division of Ambalavasis. Their women are called Varasyars, and their pollution period is 12 days. The Variyars are the most progressive among Ambalavasis in point of English education.

* **Velakkattalavan** (2,699).—Low caste Sudras, who are hereditary barbers to the Nayars and the higher castes. They are like the Nayars in their customs and usages, but are not allowed access to Brahmanical temples and public tanks. They inter-dine but not inter-marry with Veluttedans. Unlike the Nayars and other low class Sudras, Velakkattalavans observe birth and death pollution only for ten days, and Brahmans give them holy water for purification after pollution. Their touch pollutes Nayars and those above them.

Velan (10,895).—Washermen to the higher polluting castes, whose services are also required by Nayar and other caste women for purification after delivery and monthly periods. There are several herbalists and exorcists among them. Plucking cocoanuts is one of their chief occupations in the south. Their pollution distance was 32 feet.

VELLALAN (5,299).—The great cultivating caste of the Tamil countries and the highest division among the Tamil Sudras. The great majority of Vellalans in Cochin belong to the eastern villages of the Chittur Taluk bordering Coimbatore.

***Veluttedan** (3,922).—Low caste Sudras, who are hereditary washermen to the Nayars and the higher castes. They are like the Velakkattalavans in all respects except in regard to the period of pollution.

Vettuvan (11,797).—Emancipated agricultural serfs, who live mainly in the outskirts of the jungles. They are, as their name implies, hunters by occupation. The great majority of them however are now agricultural labourers and collectors of forest produce. Vettuvans and Pulayans polluted each other by approach. Their pollution distance for the higher castes was 72 feet.

Vilkurup (1,779).—The same caste as Tolkollans Some of them were in the old days engaged in making bows and arrows: hence the name.

WHITE JEW (144).—One of the two divisions of the local Jews. They are considered the only Jews here of pure and unmixed origin. They preserve their racial purity and light complexion to a remarkable extent, notwithstanding their being here for many centuries.

APPENDICES.

APPENDIX I.

THE FOREST TRIBES OF COCHIN.

[*Contributed by Mr. K. Govinda Menon, M. A. (Oxon), Retired Conservator of Forests, Cochin State.*]

There are three forest tribes in Cochin. They are the Kadars, * the Nattu Malayans and the Kongu Malayans. **Forest tribes of Cochin**

2. The name *Kadars* signifies *forest-dwellers.* They inhabit the interior forest tracts and never the outskirts or areas adjoining plains. They are invariably dark coloured, have pouting thick lips and frizzly hair and are stout and muscular. Dr. Keane, in his *Living Races of Mankind* says: **Kadars**

"There is good evidence to show that the first arrivals in India were a black people, most probably Negritos, who made their way from Malayasia round the Bay of Bengal to the Himalayan foot hills, and then spread over the Peninsula without ever reaching Ceylon. At present there are no distinctly Negrito communities in the land, nor has any clear trace of a distinctly Negrito language yet been discovered. But distinctly Negrito features crop up continually in all the uplands from the Himalayan slopes to Cape Comorin over against Ceylon. The Negritos, in fact, have been absorbed or largely assimilated by the later intruders, and, as of these there are four separate stocks, we call these Negritos the submerged fifth. There is ample evidence for the submergence since they arrived, if not in the early, certainly in the Tertiary period many thousands of years ago." The Kadars have Negrito characteristics blended with those of other races and are not racially pure in any sense of the word.

3. The dress of the Kadars in old days consisted of a white or coloured loin-cloth for men and a coloured cloth and bodice for women. The latter wore glass bangles, coloured beads, couri necklaces and *oda* ear-rings. They also stick into their hair, which is tied into a knot at the back, combs of bamboo or *oda* for ornamentation. Males too grew their hair in full and did it into a knot at the back like females, smoothening it with a gloss of cocoanut or gingelly oil. Of late they get their hair cropped in imitation of the people of the plains. They have scarcely any hair on their face except a little on the chin and on the upper lip, which they never shave. **Dress, ornamentation, etc.**

Both males and females file the incisor teeth of the upper and lower jaws. The origin of this custom is lost in obscurity and we can only make conjectures about it. The Kadan himself says that it is done for beauty.

4. "Without weapons man is but a feeble creature: the most powerful athlete or even a company of athletes would stand but a poor chance against the tiger of the jungle." Except his root-digger or *kooran-kole* and bill-hook the Kadan has no weapon at all. These two instruments meet all his requirements whether of offence or of defence. He is not much given to offence, being gentle and inoffensive by nature, and his occasions of defence are also very rare. His keenness of hearing and smell saves him from all danger. The distant approach of his enemy, the elephant, the tiger, the bear, the panther and other wild animals, is conveyed to him by his sense of smell and hearing; and he gives a wide berth to these enemies. Casualties through wild animals coming upon the **Weapons**

* *Kadan* is the singular and *Kadar* is the plural in the Malayalam language. But *Kadars* is generally used as the plural on the analogy of English plurals, and from this a new singular *Kadar* (which is strictly the Malayalam plural) has also been formed.

Kadars unaware are very rare. Their children shoot birds with bow and arrows and with catapult; * but these pastimes are not cultivated beyond adolescence. The axe has lately been introduced in connection with wood-cutting; but its use has not yet become common.

Habitations

5. The Kadars live in huts, 15 to 20 of which are grouped together to form a village. The selection of the site for the village is based on considerations of food and water supply; and a spot where there is a perennial supply of water close by to quench their thirst, and where they could, without distant journeys or other difficulties, procure jungle roots and tubers to appease their hunger, is chosen for locating their huts. These huts are but temporary structures, easily improvised of readily available materials like saplings and poles of various forest growths, bamboos, *odas*, fibres of various climbers and llianes and leaves of *oda* and teak and *punna* (** *Dillenia pentagyna*). But they are very artistic and neat, and the *oda* leaf thatching lasts half a decade. The floor is sometimes slightly raised, earth being dumped in and beaten down hard for the purpose. Of furniture there is practically nothing in the modern sense of the word. Some coarse grass mats made by themselves and a few cots of bamboo posts and split bamboo rods or *thazhuthals* are the sole appurtenances to their dwellings. Food is cooked in a corner of the hut in earthen-ware vessels or tins.

Utensils

6. It is not a matter of great concern to the Kadars to abandon their huts when they want to shift to a new area. They have but few possessions of value to take with them. A few earthen-ware vessels, mats, their carrying-basket called *pooni* made by themselves of *oda* or rattan, their bill-hooks and digging poles and their fire-making implements which they call *chakkumukki* are the only things they have to remove to their new abode. There is another utensil used for carrying water. It is a tube consisting of a few nodes of the thick bamboo (*Bambusa arundinacea*) with the internode plates knocked out. But this is a cheap and easily procurable article, so much so that it is left behind in the abandoned hut when they migrate†.

Fire-making Implements

7. The fire-making implements of the Kadars comprise a piece of steel, a bit of quartz and the floss from the fronds of *Borassus flabellifer* (palmyra palm or brab tree) carried in a scooped out seed of *Entada scandens*. With these the Kadars produce fire easily whenever and wherever they want it.‡ There is no religious significance or any other kind of importance attached to this affair.

Food

8. In olden days the Kadars lived chiefly on jungle roots and tubers. They are not vegetarians and they like all sorts of game and fish, but the bison and the bear are two animals which no Kadan will touch living or dead. They are very fond of honey and the honey-gathering season is accordingly a jolly time for them.

Marriage customs

9. Marriages among the Kadars are usually arranged by the parents of the contracting parties; but instances of the contracting parties themselves coming to an understanding are not rare. Exogamy is the usual custom but endogamy

---

* This is a typical catapult, the shooting contrivance of boys, consisting of a forked stick and elastic (India rubber) cord. The Kadars got it from the Tramway employees after the Forest Tramway was opened. Their boys used the ordinary sling before they got the catapult.

** In his account of the Kadars in *The Cochin Tribes and Castes*, Mr. L. K. Ananthakrishna Ayyar has made several mis-statements of facts. Here, for instance, he refers to the *Calophyllum Inophyllum* instead of *Dillenia pentagyna*.

† Mr. Ananthakrishna Ayyar makes them carry this utensil also with them when they migrate.

‡ Mr. Ananthakrishna Ayyar seems to think that it is a difficult process for the Kadars to produce fire and that they therefore preserve it carefully when once it is built up. The idea is wrong and misleading.

also is not unknown. Marriage with one's sister or her daughter or with one's brother's daughter is entirely forbidden; but marriages between sister's or brother's children are allowed. Girls are never married before puberty and boys rarely before 25. The best marriages are those contracted between members of different villages (*pathies*) and not between members of the same village. As a token of betrothal the contracting parties through their parents or near kinsmen exchange some forest produce. Dowries consist of forest produce or articles made by themselves. Of late years money transactions also have been introduced to the detriment of the tribe. This unhappy development is to be attributed to their contact with civilization from the plains. The real marriage ceremony consists of feasting at the huts of the bride and bridegroom for a day, or two at the most. *Thali* tying which was unknown in old days has been introduced lately; and gold chains and bangles which also were unknown are now substituted for their primitive ornaments. The marriage tie is very loose and either party is free to sever it whenever he or she wants to do so. But instances of such desertion or divorce were practically unknown so long as the lust of civilized man from the plains was content to leave these innocent and harmless people to themselves.

Sexual intercourse

10. Sexual intercourse among the Kadars is not effected within their huts but at a trysting place in the jungle agreed to between husband and wife. They go different ways and meet at the agreed place in the course of the day. After the intercourse both take a bath, completely immersing themselves under water, and return home. This custom is of peculiar significance in view of the fact that the Kadars do not bathe daily even though they have perennial streams in their midst. The males bathe every other day or even less frequently, while the females have their baths at longer intervals. The advent of men from the plains has brought about a radical change in these sexual habits of the Kadars. The former do not leave the Kadar women alone; and, according to their usage, they have connection with these women within their huts, making it a matter of daily routine. The Kadars in their original state had sexual connections few and far between as they never knew their wives in their huts. Comparisons are odious; but one fears that civilized man does not stand to gain much when he is compared with these primitive people in the above respect.

Pregnancy and child-birth

11. During the period of pregnancy the Kadar women go about their usual vocations in their ordinary dress.* The accouchement takes place in a small hut built for the purpose and removed from the usual abode. There are no professional midwives among the Kadars but elderly dames attend the lying-in. A decoction of certain medicinal herbs and roots is taken both morning and evening during the lying-in period, and they partake of the usual diet. The mother suckles the baby for as long as she cares to, after which the baby is gradually given adult's food. Though women are considered unclean for three months after child-birth, the period of actual birth pollution is limited to ten days after which the mother and baby are bathed and admitted into the family circle. The temporary abode is then consigned to flames. Likewise the monthly period also is observed by them with great strictness. The woman dwells in a small hut put up for the purpose at a short distance from the usual abode. Food and drink for her are left at some distance from the hut and she takes it. On the morning of the 4th day she bathes in the river close by, immersing herself completely under water, and sets fire to the temporary hut.

---

* The women do not change their costume during the period as stated by Mr. L. K. Ananthakrishna Ayyar.

Naming ceremony

12. The ceremony of naming the new born infant is usually performed on the 10th day after childbirth, but it may be postponed to any later date before the expiry of six months. Generally it is the father that performs this ceremony but sometimes it is done by the *Mooppan* (the village headman). The performer sprinkles some cold water over the baby and calls out its name three times. A feast on a small scale is usually held on the occasion. The ceremony has apparently no religious significance. The ceremonies of the ear-boring and nose-boring of the infant are also performed on the naming day but may sometimes be postponed to any other convenient date. The operations are most commonly undertaken by the *Mooppan*; but in his absence they are done by the father or by any other male member of his village. A lighted lamp is placed before the child and ancestral blessing is invoked before the operations.

Conjugal attachment

13. The marriage tie among the Kadars, as stated elsewhere, is very loose. Either party is at liberty to quit the other whenever he or she likes to do so, but this privilege was very seldom, if ever, resorted to in old days. The divorced wife or husband could easily take another mate. No council of elders is called in nor does any expulsion from the community take place in connection with divorces.* The divorced party lives with his or her parents or separately according to choice, and attends to all usual vocations. If there are any children from the dissolved union, they usually remain under the father's protection.

Polygamy and Polyandry

14. The institutions of polygamy and polyandry are absolutely unknown among the Kadars. During my 29 years' service in the Forest department, not a single instance has come to my knowledge of any one man keeping more than one wife or woman, or of any one woman having more than one man at a time. It is true that the marriage tie is very loose among them, but the wholesome principle of "one mate at a time" is rigidly adhered to.†

Family life

15. The father is the head of the family and he controls and directs everything. His wife and children are obedient to his behests. The work of food-gathering is shared by all. No one is a drone in the family circle except children, very old people and invalids.

Inheritance and organization

16. The son inherits the father's possessions, if any. After the father's death the son or sons are bound to look after the widow so long as she remains single. Widowed girls go to the parental roof for protection. The civic life of the village is under the control of the *Mooppan* who is appointed by His Highness the Maharaja on the recommendation of the head of the Forest department. *Mooppanship* is generally inherited by the sister's son. The *Mooppan's* position carries no material advantages with it, but there are certain distinct disadvantages accompanying it. Thus manual labour is considered derogatory to a *Mooppan's* dignity and prestige and, as Kadars cannot escape starvation if they do no manual work, the unfortunate *Mooppan* finds himself condemned to honourable idleness and its unpleasant sequel. For this reason no one is willing to accept this strange honour and the tribe is now without their *Mooppan* or chief. The symbol of this dignitary's authority is a walking stick mounted with silver bearing the Cochin coat-of-arms. When the chief's place is vacant, the stick is returned to the Conservator of Forests. In rare cases disputes among the villagers used to be settled by *Mooppans*; but ordinarily they are taken for adjudication to the Forest department whose decision is accepted as final.

---

* Mr. Ananthakrishna Ayyar's statement to the contrary is wrong.

† Mr. Ananthakrishna Ayyar's statement that, among the Kadars, "polygamy is indulged in with a view to increase the numerical strength of the tribe" is an egregious error and does much injustice to these people.

17. The Kadars worship demons of various denominations, tree-spirits, *Malavazhi* (hill-ruler), and *Ayyappan*. They revere these spirits and demons, patrons of villages, protectors of springs and dwellers in forests and caves. The blessings of departed ancestors are invoked in all their undertakings besides the blessings of spirits and demons. A stone set up at the base of a tree is all their temple. Offerings of various sorts are made to it. The *poojari* (priest) is usually the headman of the village and, in his absence, any male member takes the place. Priests skilled in driving off demons and spirits are got from the plains whenever their services are required. Religion

18. The dead are buried with the head always towards the south. The body is washed and covered with a piece of new cloth before being taken to the grave dug some distance from the village. A handful of rice is thrown over the dead body in the grave before it is covered with earth. Near relatives and other members of the village weep when any one dies. No kind of memorial or mark is erected over the grave. Nor is any article which was owned by the deceased buried with the dead body. The Kadars observe no death pollution. If the dead person happened to be an elderly male (past middle age), he will find a place in the niche of ancestor worship and his blessings will be invoked in all future undertakings. Barring this, there will be no vestige of the deceased remaining. There are many *Cromlechs* and *Dolmens* lying scattered about in the forests of Cochin, but they appear to be connected in no way with the burial or any other ceremony of the Kadars. Indeed these people have not the remotest idea as to how or when these things came into existence. Disposal of the dead

19. The Kadars are engaged in the collection of the minor produce of the forests like honey, wax, cardamoms, etc. They also help in elephant-capturing operations and take part in other activities too of the Forest department. Without their help this department and the contractors who work under it will certainly find it very difficult to do their work satisfactorily. In old days the wages of the Kadars were paid in kind and not in cash, the payment being limited to the day's rations. The Forest department then did its work departmentally and only Kadars were employed for the purpose. Later on, with the introduction of the contract system of working, contractors arrived and they brought labour from the plains. The employment of workmen from the plains involved payment of wages in money; but these labourers did not displace the Kadars altogether, for the latter were indispensable for certain kinds of work. The system of paying one set of labourers in kind and another in cash was found to be unsatisfactory; and therefore the wages of the Kadars also began to be paid in money. The latter now claim and obtain the same rate of wages as is paid to workmen from the plains. That the Kadars have not gained by this change will be clear when we examine their present condition. Occupation

Though the Kadars are allowed by the State to cultivate forest lands free of any tax, they do not take much advantage of this concession. One reason for their apathy is that they do not like to take to any pursuit which their ancestors did not follow. Another reason is that they have no protective measures against the damage caused by wild elephants. Cultivation on a large scale will therefore mean sheer waste of labour. And their activities in this sphere are therefore limited to a few bananas, yams and kitchen vegetables planted round their huts.

Some of the Kadars keep a few head of cattle and goats now-a-days, for they are allowed free grazing of their cattle by the Government. Cattle-rearing is not, however, likely to thrive among them, for it will be very difficult for them to market their dairy products.

Relation with the State

20. The Kadars are thus allowed free cultivation of land and grazing of cattle. They are also permitted to travel, free of charges, by the State Forest Tramway. And once every year, during the Malabar festival of *Onam*, the State distributes presents of clothes, trinkets, tobacco, etc., to all Kadars through the agency of the Forest department. In return for these concessions and presents, the Kadars are bound to serve the State when called upon to do so. But they will be paid due wages for their services.

Games and pastimes

21. Both males and females indulge in a sort of dance, but they never have it mixed. The females' dance is a sort of merry-go-round to the accompaniment of singing, drumming and a monotonous tune from a sort of flute. There is no keeping time. The body is swayed backwards and forwards with occasional clapping. The drummers and musicians are males. The males' dance is a sort of chase of game by tiger or panther accompanied, as in the females' dance, by drumming and fluting. There is no religious significance attached to either dance. The usual season for these dances is the hot weather (April and May) when the collection of honey and wax is at its highest. This is the "harvest time" of the Kadars when they get a good return for their labour from the minor produce contractor. And they generally enjoy a good feed of honey, grabbing it from the tree tops before the comb is taken to the contractor.

Contact with civilization

22. We have seen how contractors and labourers from the plains arrived when the Forest department introduced the contract system of work. The opening of the State Forest Tramway not only facilitated communication between the hills and the plains but also led considerable numbers of people (working in the Tramway department) to reside up the hills. In this way the Kadars were brought into direct, almost intimate, contact with the people of the low country. Unfortunately most of the latter were labourers belonging to the lower classes. What the influence of this contact has been and how the conditions of the Kadars' life have been altered as a result of this clash between the primitive culture of the hills and the higher and more developed culture of the plains are questions that should be examined in this connection.

Physical decay

23. It has already been remarked that, of old, the food of the Kadars was simple, nourishing, and natural to their surroundings and circumstances. They were accordingly a strong, sturdy and muscular set of people possessed of great powers of endurance, so much so that they could easily carry loads of substantial weight on their backs (they never carried loads on their heads) for long distances. The contact with people from the plains has wrought a most lamentable change in the Kadars. Rice was introduced from the low country and the Kadars preferred rice diet to their wholesome roots and tubers. The contractors also took with them arrack and opium to tempt the Kadars and get the most out of the poor people for the lowest possible payment. And the Kadars fell. They now drink hard and spend the greater part of their earnings in arrack and opium. Rice diet and coffee (for they have taken to coffee also in imitation of their civilized brethren of the low country), *arrack and opium have made them physical wrecks, subject to ailments and diseases which were of old unknown in their primitive domains. Cholera and small-pox have made their unwelcome appearance among them. Diabetes and albuminuria, which were powerless against the Kadars so long as they lived their old life of simplicity,

*An arrack shop was opened in the Forest area and this aggravated the evil beyond measure. This has now been in existence for many years. Representations were repeatedly made to the Government regarding the urgent necessity for closing this shop, but no action was taken in the matter. The pittance of revenue derived from this shop is nothing when compared with the dreadful havoc this shop has played on the life of the Kadars.

activity and wholesome diet, have already cast their baneful eye on these fallen people. And the vitality of the Kadars having been lowered to a dangerous extent, they are not in a position to withstand these diseases.

The opening of a dispensary on the hills has not tended to better their condition but has, on the other hand, made it worse. They are fast forgetting their knowledge of indigenous roots and herbs and at the same time they have not much faith in allopathic medicines. If at all they attend the dispensary, it is chiefly for the surgical dressing of wounds and not for ordinary ailments.

Moral deterioration

24. If the physical health of the Kadars has been undermined and ruined almost permanently as a result of their contact with the people of the low country, their moral health also has been deeply tainted by the same influence. When the dark avenues of the primeval forests echoed under the tread of the greedy contractor and his assistants, and the screech of the steam engine of the Forest Tramway first reverberated through the hills and vales, they proclaimed that the Civilized Man, the Destroyer, had set his foot within the fair precincts of the Kadars' domains. It was observed that the lust of the people from the plains did not leave the Kadar women alone. Promiscuous intercourse for years between the new arrivals and these women has infected the whole tribe with syphilis, the first fruits of civilization. The primitive purity of the Kadar women was tainted for ever and their ideals of chastity have been brought into adjustment with those of the low class people of the plains with whom they were brought into touch. Moral and physical deterioration has followed and the rising generations show mixed and tainted blood. The employment of Kadar labour in the coffee estates of the Nelliampathi hills has very much aggravated the evil. In the estates the Kadars come into contact with Tamil labourers of the lowest classes. The surroundings, food, and other influences in this new sphere are entirely different from those the Kadars are generally accustomed to. There is free scope to indulge in arrack and opium in the estates, and the Kadars try to ape the filthy ways of the dissolute Tamil labourers. The Kadar children born in the estates are all tainted and cannot be distinguished from the puny and sickly progeny of the Tamil labourer.

Discontent and changed outlook

25. In other directions also the Kadars have lost heavily by their contact with civilization. Their outlook on life seems to have been affected detrimentally by this. They were one of the happiest groups of people, because they were supremely cotented with their lot. For one thing, they always lived above want, and all were equally rich or equally poor so that there was no room for envy, heart-burn and the allied plagues of civilized society. No economic depression could blight their prosperity. They were free from many of the diseases that levy their daily toll from civilized regions and they had their effective herbs and other remedies for the few ailments that visited them. Their wants were few and simple and these were easily satisfied.

Now, however, they have partaken of the forbidden fruit, and new desires and ambitions beyond their reach have been kindled in their humble breasts. The Kadars began to compare their habits and ways of life with those followed by people who were supposed to be superior to them, and in their simplicity and innocence they thought that progress for them lay in the direction of becoming civilized by imitating the ways of their bogus superiors. They accordingly went in for things which served only to ruin them. Thus the old simplicity in their dress began to disappear and they became acquainted with Tinnevelly *saries*, Benares silk banyans and Manchester twill shirts. The women wanted gold chains and bangles, gold or gilt ear-rings and rings for their fingers. They compared their lot with that of their civilized brethren and in their ignorance thought that the latter were ideally happy whereas they themselves were destined to be supremely miserable. The blessed contentment which made their life a long and happy holiday to them in days of old deserted them and with it departed their happiness. And the discomfort which rises from vague desires impossible to fulfil and from the absence of a definite purpose in life is now the distinguishing feature of a Kadan's life.

Dishonesty

26. Another baneful result of the contact with men from the plains is that the Kadars have lost their primitive simplicity and honesty and taken to ways of deceit and hypocrisy. They were of old as innocent and truthful as little children. Violence and crimes were practically unknown among them, their character being essentially gentle and peace-loving. But their association with their low country compatriots has made them adepts in lying and cheating. Originally it was very difficult to get the truth from a Kadan not because he liked to prevaricate or hide it, but because he was naturally shy. He is least inclined to displease or offend anybody, so much so that his answers depended on the way in which the questions were put to him. If he were approached properly, he became frank and gave candid replies to all enquiries.

Education

27. Naturally the Kadan had no education in the sense in which we use the word. But he might perhaps have justly claimed a higher kind of education in that

> 'His daily teachers had been woods and rills,
> The silence that is in the starry sky,
> The sleep that is among the lonely hills.'

A philanthropic missionary, who had unfortunately the ideas of proselytism in his head, started a primary school some years ago and the institution throve pretty well. But one morning the missionary's agent, the school master, put into the hands of the pupils a book of catechism on Jesus Christ's Nativity, Crucifixion and Resurrection, when the pupils in a body left and never again crossed the threshold of the school, which had therefore to be closed for good. The Kadars are included among the so-called depressed classes*, and the Protector of the depressed classes accordingly opened a school for them on the hills. But the school does not appear to be worked on proper lines. It is not a knowledge of the three "R"s that the Kadars chiefly want. If at all they are to be educated, it is vocational knowledge that should be imparted to them. The training given to them must enable them to make the best use of the raw materials of the forest. If they could be taught to convert these materials into marketable products of utility, it will benefit them as well as others. Literacy among Kadars even of the most rudimentary type is not, in my opinion, conducive to their welfare. Their education should not wean them away from their ancestral and original callings but should supplement them. Any education which is calculated to turn the Kadan's mind and inclination to paths other than those which his ancestors were accustomed to, and which he also should legitimately and naturally follow, is bound to throw him out of gear with his environment, so much so that he will become unfit for the Kadar society. At the same time he will not be an acquisition to any other society. In short, he will lose his Kadar moorings and will not get into any safer haven. As a matter of fact, the boys who attend the Kadar school are known to develop a dislike for their ancestral pursuits. They want to live like the officers of the Forest and Tramway departments!

---

*The Kadars were in no way depressed to start with. But now they may be regarded as depressed, thanks to the arrack shop and the other influences already explained.

28. The sum total of the influences to which the Kadars have been subjected in their contact with civilization is that they have undergone an all-round deterioration. A spirit of restlessness or discomfort has invaded their life. Their adaptation to their environment has been seriously impaired because the new conditions of their life are incompatible with the environment. In the circumstances they must deteriorate and decay. And what we actually find is that they have been decaying. The returns of Kadars at 3 successive censuses shown in the margin conclusively prove this. As matters stand at present the tribe is doomed, and its utter extinction is but the question of a few decades. **Decay in numbers**

Year	Actual strength
1911	417
1921	274
1931	267

29. The wisest policy in the circumstances would appear to be to leave the Kadars alone. They have to be saved both from their friends and their enemies. The type of education that is now imparted to the Kadar boys must be forthwith changed. If we have nothing better to give them than the education which is given to our boys, let us at least desist from thrusting an unsuitable system of instruction on them. Let us also banish arrack and opium from the Kadars' domains. While absolute non-interference with their habits and ways of life is essential, active and stern interference is urgently required to ensure the safety of Kadar women from the ravages of the syphilis-breeding wretches of the plains. And effective medical treatment must at once be resorted to so that the venereal diseases, which are now widely prevalent among the Kadars, and which have very much lowered their vitality and fertility, might be eradicated once for all. If these or similar measures are urgently adopted, perhaps these people may be saved from their impending doom of speedy extinction, and they may once more develop their innate qualities of natural nobility and simplicity and child-like goodness, gentleness, and innocence to thrive once again in their native home. **Preventive measures**

30. The Kadars maintain that they are superior to the Malayans, but the latter contend that they are of a higher status than the Kadars. As their name implies, the Malayans are hill tribes, but they inhabit the forests skirting the plains. Owing to their proximity to the plains, they have been for long in contact with the inhabitants of the low country, and are practically one with the low country population. There is a good deal of admixture in their blood and they have more or less the same physical features and complexion as their low country neighbours, whom they try to imitate in their manners, customs and habits, and with whom they have begun to form open alliances, so much so that in a decade or two it will be almost impossible to come across a Nattu Malayan except in name. They have lost much of their primitive condition. They profess a mixture of Animism and Hinduism, and the latter element is gradually becoming more and more predominant. Their habitations are semi-permanent or even permanent and they are getting rid of their wandering habits gradually. They are taking to agriculture which leads them to adopt a settled life in permanent abodes. They also rear cattle, goats and poultry, the produce of which they sell to their low country neighbours. The Malayans have grown as deceitful and cunning as their low country neighbours whose daily influence on them cannot but leave its impress on them. Rice is the chief article of their diet with jungle roots and tubers to supplement. They observe all the ceremonies of their low country neighbours but in a cheaper style owing to their poverty. The Forest **Nattu Malayans**

department does not find the services of the Malayans indispensable, because their low country neighbours have taken their place.

The census statistics show that the tribe has been steadily increasing in numbers. It is therefore obvious that the Malayans have adapted themselves successfully to the new conditions arising from their contact with the plains. And for this reason they may be expected to thrive.

Year	Actual strength †
1911	2,461
1921	594*
1931	3,185

Kongu Malayan

31. The Kongu Malayans hail from the forests of the Tamil country. Their habits, customs and manners are similar to those of the Tamil Sudras except in respect of their marriage ceremony which is very peculiar. After the selection of the bride by the parents of the bridegroom, the latter goes for the first time to the house of the bride. There the bride's parents receive in the presence of four or more witnesses, a sum not less than 3 rupees from the bridegroom as the price of their daughter. After the usual feasting and merry-making the bride is escorted to the house of the bridegroom. Subsequently, if at any time a divorce is resorted to on any account whatever, the bridegroom returns his wife to her parents after receiving back, in the presence of the same four witnesses if possible, the price-money he gave at the time of his marriage. Marriage is, therefore, considered as a mercantile business in which the commodity, if found unfit for the purchaser, is returned to the owner and the purchase money thereof taken back. Instances of this practice are very rare though sanctioned by the society. The Nattu Malayans and Kadars do not mix with these people. They have no objection to eat all sorts of carrion. They are a filthy race occupying almost the lowest rung of the social ladder. They are professional thieves and burglars in certain parts of the country.

---

† Includes both Nattu Malayans and Kongu Malayans.

* This decrease, as explained elsewhere, is to be attributed to short-counting in 1921.

APPENDIX II.

DEPRESSED CLASSES *

Introductory

Some account has already been given of the depressed population of Cochin in the last two chapters of this Report. In paragraphs 9 and 10 of Chapter XI, for instance, the claims of these classes to be included within the fold of the Hindu religion were examined; and in paragraph 23 of Chapter XII the principle followed in the selection of the tribes or communities to be included in the category of the depressed was explained. In this appendix it is proposed to give a brief account of the past condition of this section of the State's population and of the measures adopted by the Government of the State for its social, material and moral uplift.

Depressed communities

2. As stated in paragraph 23 of Chapter XII, when organized work was started for the amelioration of the conditions of life of the social outcastes among Hindus, 8 classes which occupied the lowest rungs of the social ladder were selected by the Government as degraded enough to be included in the category of the depressed. They were the Kadars and Malayans (the two hill tribes), the Nayadis and Ullatans, the Sambavans (Parayans), Vettuvans, Pulayans and Kanakkans. Of these the Kadars and Malayans are treated separately in Appendix I. They do not therefore require any special notice here.

Their statistics

3. The statistics of the remaining six classes for four censuses are given in the inset table. Together they number 119,876, and form 15·4 per cent of the Hindus and 9·9 per cent of the State's population. The figures show that all except the Nayadis have been growing in their numerical strength. Indeed, these communities must be regarded as prolific in that the statistics in the marginal table do not represent their increase in full, because they do not include the numbers converted to Christianity. Be it remembered at the same time that the depressed population provided the chief field for the labours of Christian missionaries who got the largest number of converts from the ranks of those that laboured under the humiliating social disabilities inherent in the caste system of Malayali Hindus. If the Nayadis, who form but a very small group, do not reveal any steady or substantial rise in their numerical strength, it is probably to be attributed to the loss they have sustained in their numbers through conversions to Christianity.

Classes	Numerical strength			
	1931	1921	1911	1901
Kanakkan ..	13,192	8,424	7,527	5,917
Pulayan ..	82,043	*69,423	72,787	59,840
Vettuvan ..	11,797	*4,759	*5,261	6,349
Sambavan (Parayan) ..	11,914	*7,235	*8,356	8,841
Ullatan ..	778	*413	537	439
Nayadi ..	152	119	220	215

*Defective enumeration or wrong classification of castes is most probably responsible for these low figures.

Atmospheric pollution

4. According to the usages of the orthodox Malayali caste Hindu society of old, these six classes polluted the so-called caste Hindus if they approached them within distances ranging from 48 feet for the Kanakkans

*I am very much indebted to M. R. Ry. Rao Sahib C. Matthai Avl., B. A., L. T., Retired Director of Public Instruction and Protector of Depressed Classes, Cochin State, for the notes he kindly furnished on the work done by the Government for the uplift of the depressed communities. Paragraphs 10 to 19 of the appendix in particular are almost wholly based on these notes.

to 300* feet for the Nayadis. Even non-caste Hindus (other than the depressed communities), who were themselves treated as unapproachables by caste Hindus, observed atmospheric pollution in their dealings with these out-castes, the only difference in their case being that the range of pollution was considerably less. Among themselves the depressed classes observed varying degrees of pollution. Thus the Kanakkans, whose contamination had a radius of only 48 feet, considered themselves polluted by the approach, within specified distances, of the other five classes whose infection had a much wider range. Thus too the Pulayans and Vettuvans treated the Nayadis and Ullatans as unapproachables and, like the higher castes, had purificatory ceremonies to perform when they were under pollution. A Vettuvan, for instance, who was polluted by a Nayadi or an Ullatan, had not only to take purificatory baths but also "to fast for seven days, subsisting on water, tender cocoanuts and toddy" before he could get rid of the taint. A Pulayan in like predicament, not to be outdone by his Vettuvan brother, had to bathe seven times (immersing himself completely under water on each occasion in a different tank), and then shed the pollution by shedding a few drops of his blood from his finger which was deliberately cut for the purpose. The Sambavan was an untouchable to the Pulayan and Vettuvan; while, as between the last two, each claimed to be socially superior to the other, so much so that they wisely decided to err on the safe side, and accordingly treated each other as unapproachables!

Social disabilities

5. The natural result of all this was that the unfortunate communities were subjected to social disabilities of a severe and humiliating character. Segregated in localities which were often unhealthy and removed far from villages and towns, and condemned to live in miserable hovels that were unfit for human occupation, they were shut out from almost all civilizing influences and had no access generally to the amenities of civilized life. Materially and metaphorically their existence was dark, steeped as they were in filth and wretchedness, ignorance and superstition.

Poverty: occupation of Kanakkans, Pulayans, Vettuvans and Sambavans

6. Poverty, abject and undiluted, was the birth right of the depressed classes, and their last moments in life were perhaps never embittered by thoughts of the many good things they had to leave behind. With the exception of the Nayadis and Ullatans, they were originally agrestic serfs attached to estates as agricultural labourers, and were bought and sold with the land. Slavery was abolished in the middle of the last century, but the emancipation of the depressed communities did not lead to any perceptible improvement in their social or economic condition. So long as orthodoxy reigned supreme among caste Hindus, they had to labour under all the disabilities which unapproachability involved and to depend chiefly on their old occupations for their subsistence. The Kanakkans, however, gradually took to fishing and boat service and the Sambavans found an additional occupation in the manufacture of baskets and bamboo mats.

and of Nayadis and Ullatans. Conversion to other religions, only redemption for the depressed

7. The Nayadis and Ullatans were in a worse plight than the others. The former were a wandering tribe and had no settled abode or occupation. They were as a class averse to manual labour and preferred to live on the charity of the higher castes. At times they were engaged in petty handicrafts like crude rope making or in the collection of the minor produce of forests like honey and bees' wax. The Ullatans too earned what they could from the collection and sale of forest produce and supplied agricultural labour when there

*This is the most orthodox version of the range of a Nayadi's pollution.

was a demand for it. But the social disabilities rising from unapproachability very much circumscribed the field of choice of all these classes, and their only redemption was conversion to other religions. "Their conversion to Christianity or Islam gives them a passport to tread over the field forbidden to them up to that time; their approach no longer pollutes castes above them; in fact, they find themselves in a position much better than they ever were in. By becoming a convert, any one of the darkskinned sons of the soil rises by one leap from the most degraded position to one of equality with most others. But yesterday a slave, compelled to stand at a distance of 64 feet from his Brahman or Nayar master, and even from castes below these two, and always restricted to the limits of the field, from which he steps out but with loud warnings of his approach, to-day he walks on the public road almost shoulder to shoulder with the most orthodox Brahman, and approaches within reasonable distance of the sacred edifice of the latter. When thus metamorphosed, he is able to engage himself in whatever work he can do, earn higher wages and lead a comparatively easy and comfortable life." *

Depressed classes of Cochin and of other places compared

8. It must, however, be noted in this connection that the condition of the depressed classes of Cochin described above would have compared very favourably with the condition of their brethren outside Malabar. The old landlords were shrewd enough to realize that it was in their own interests to clothe and feed their workmen even during seasons of slack work, for they would thereby ensure the supply of cheap labour. And the proverbial charity of the Malayalis never failed to succour the distressed and the destitute. The barest necessaries of life the depressed classes therefore managed to secure at all times; and during seasons of sowing, harvest, etc., when their services were much in demand, they generally got a good supply of toddy also which was perhaps the only luxury they knew. The Pulayans in particular were so much addicted to this drink that they would rather forgo their meals than miss their daily potation. On the whole, these classes dragged on their weary and unenviable existence, satisfying their animal cravings as best they could and multiplying in their numbers at a rapid rate.

Change in attitude of superior castes and its sequel

9. Such then was the condition of the depressed classes at the beginning of this century. But the last three decades have, as indicated in Chapter XII of this Report, witnessed a remarkable change in the attitude of the socially superior castes towards untouchability, unapproachability and many a similar disability that had sprung from the Malayali caste system. One aspect of this change vitally affected the depressed classes. It was that atmospheric pollution ceased to be observed except perhaps by the ultra orthodox in rural areas. The unapproachables thus got access to public roads, hospitals, bazaars, etc. They were now in a position at least to see what civilized life was, though they had as yet no part in it. And it is particularly noteworthy that the change was wrought not through any social legislation but by the influence of modern education.

Measures for ameliorations education

10. When the prejudices of the higher castes were thus overcome to a great extent through the agency of education, the Government of the State began to organize measures for the amelioration of the condition of the depressed population. The task was far from easy, for the thick veil of ignorance and superstition beneath which they moved had to be lifted and they had to be taught to live a clean life, facilities for which did not as yet exist. Among the

* Page 173, Part I, Cochin Census Report, 1901.

various measures adopted by the Government, the earliest and the most effective have been in the field of education. Special concessions were extended to the children of the depressed classes by the Education department and the opposition of the higher castes against the admission of these children in schools was tactfully overcome, so much so that they are now freely admitted into all* educational institutions where they sit side by side with the children of the highest Hindu castes. Education, both English and vernacular, was made free for the depressed children and they were supplied with clothes and with books and other school requisites. In the earlier stages when the number of children attending schools was limited, they were also fed daily. But with the increase in their numbers the feeding was restricted to the last day in the week and to children who were regular in attendance throughout the week. Even this has been stopped now and the payment of an anna each substituted in its stead. Daily feeding is however continued in the schools for the children of the Kadar tribe up the hills.**

Schools

11. It has not been the policy of the Government to open separate schools for the depressed classes for the obvious reason that such a procedure might perpetuate the existing cleavage between them and the higher castes. But schools intended for all classes have been opened in localities where the depressed are found in large numbers. On behalf of adults, many night schools also have been started and they have contributed not a little to the general awakening of the depressed communities by the dissemination of much useful knowledge among them, particularly in temperance, co-operation and other kindred subjects.

Attendance at schools

12. That the children of the depressed communities do not take as kindly to literary studies as those of other classes is but natural, and many years of patient and persistent labour alone can produce any substantial results. The depressed children attend the lower classes in Primary schools in considerable numbers, but as they go higher they gradually drop off. And yet it is a hopeful sign that three Pulayans (including a girl) have reached the college classes.

Educational policy

13. Children attending school rapidly pick up habits of cleanliness and of decorous behaviour and speech by association with others, so much so that it would be hardly possible for an ordinary visitor to a school nowadays to distinguish them from the children of other classes. And if they do not show much keenness for literary studies, there are other directions in which they can thrive. As they have for long generations been dealing with Mother Earth, they have developed their powers of observation to a high degree and they show an intimate knowledge of the facts of nature so far as they come within their ken. For instance, there was a Pulaya boy who was employed as a cooly in the Government Central Farm some years ago.† He was put to the work of

---

* There are but four or five schools which, for special reasons, do not admit non-caste Hindus.

** The following concessions are now enjoyed by depressed class pupils in the matter of education:

i. Education, both English and vernacular, is free.
ii. Free supply of clothing and of books and other school requisites.
iii. Weekly payment of one anna to all regular pupils in the Primary classes.
iv. A monthly stipend of Rs. 2 to each pupil in the Lower Secondary classes.
v. A monthly stipend of Rs. 3 to each pupil in the Upper Secondary classes.
vi. Four scholarships of the monthly value of Rs. 10 tenable in the Intermediate (college) classes and Rs. 20 for initial expenses to each student joining the Intermediate class.
vii. Industrial stipends of Rs. 7 a month to each pupil in the Government Trades Schools and Girls' Industrial Schools.
viii. Daily feeding in the Kadar schools up the hills.

† It is understood that he is still on the menial staff of the Farm.

grafting and soon picked it up so well that the Superintendent used to say that he, illiterate as he was, was nearly cent per cent successful in grafting, whereas the others who worked with him, though more educated and experienced, could hardly score 50 per cent success. Such a boy with some literary education and technical training would develop into an efficient horticulturist and prove more useful in life than if he had been pushed through an Arts College against his natural bent of mind. Indeed it will be doing a positive disservice to the depressed classes if their children too are given the present type of higher education engendering the 'clerical' mentality, and are thus allowed to swell the already full ranks of the English-educated unemployed. But the intelligent ones among them may be given facilities for higher education so that they may qualify themselves for Government service or for other honourable and lucrative professions. Their example will then act as a stimulus to the whole community which must come to realise that birth need be no impassable barrier to their advancement. That the steps taken by the Government to educate the depressed classes have been hitherto attended with considerable success is indeed a hopeful feature, for there is no doubt that education will act as a potent lever for the humanisation and uplift of these degraded communities.

Depressed classes colonies

14. The efforts of the Government to ameliorate the condition of the depressed population have been extended in other directions also. Thus, in localities where these communities live in large numbers, tanks and wells are being provided where they do not exist. And colonies have been established in various parts of the State, because closer supervision is possible where they are grouped together, and effective measures can be taken for the improvement of their social and economic condition. There are as many as 41 colonies at present with 1,640 families settled in them under the supervision and care of the Protector of Depressed Classes. Here they are given house sites, and cottages and *Bhajana Matoms* (places of worship) are also built for them at Government cost. Lands for agricultural purposes are assigned to them, and agricultural implements, materials for fencing, seeds, etc., are supplied free of cost so that they might make an independent start in life. The ownership of a piece of land creates a new and permanent interest in their minds and provides a powerful incentive for honest work, which is absent in the case of those who live on lands from which they may be evicted at the will of the owners whereby they will be deprived of the fruits of their labour.

Co-operative Societies

15. To train them in habits of thrift "home-safe-boxes," in which they could deposit their small savings, were distributed among them. Co-operative societies also were opened and a Co-operative Inspector was specially appointed to organize and supervise these societies which were calculated to teach them self help and the habit of putting by what they could spare out of their earnings against times of need. The deposits in the "home-safe-boxes" were to be transferred to these societies periodically. There are 33 co-operative societies working at present and they have been doing much useful work. The depressed classes generally led a hand-to-mouth existence without any thought for the morrow. Owing to the lack of organizations for safe investment within their reach, they had no inducement to save anything from their daily earnings. They spent whatever they earned and contributed much to that portion of the excise revenue of the State which was derived from toddy shops. Their improvidence led to their being victimised by usurious money-lenders who often extorted cent per cent interest on the small sums lent to these helpless people, and thus sucked out their life blood. The co-operative societies are therefore of great help to them. With the progress of education and the growth of a sense of self-respect they may be expected gradually to free themselves from the evils of

drink and chronic indebtedness, and learn to appreciate the advantages of co-operative societies for the improvement of their economic condition.

Precautions necessary

16. If the colonies are worked on proper lines they are bound to exercise a very salutary influence on the depressed communities; and for this, particular care should be taken to see that there is demand for labour in localities where the colonies are opened. Much hardship will result in the absence of such demand. When, for instance, the first colony was established at Chalakkudi, the inmates found it very difficult to secure employment. The landlords in whose lands they had been living disowned them when they joined the colony; and it took a long time before other openings for work could be discovered. Efficient supervision also is necessary if the colonies are to thrive. Otherwise they are likely to become hotbeds of drink, dissipation, rioting and other vices, and the communities might, instead of showing any progress, deteriorate further.

Success of the scheme

17. The colonies have, on the whole, done much good to these people. The campaign against the vice of drunkenness carried on in these colonies is gradually producing beneficial results. The *Bhajana Matoms* have been instrumental in freeing them from many of their dark superstitions and in raising the general level of their cleanliness. Agricultural classes like the Pulayans and Sambavans are making good use of the lands assigned to them by the Government by planting fruit trees and raising seasonal crops which contribute substantially to the enhancement of their earnings and the improvement of their material condition. The Nayadis, however, have shown but poor progress hitherto. They have little inclination to till their lands, and find begging a far more congenial task than manual labour. But the possession of a homestead must make a settled life possible for them also. In any case it is a necessary foundation for progress towards civilization.

Communal associations

18. That the most important sections among the depressed communities have already begun to organize themselves on communal lines and form caste *sabhas* or *samajams* for safeguarding their interests and promoting their welfare is not without significance. The populous Pulaya community, for instance, have their *Pulaya Mahajana Sabha* and other associations functioning actively and doing yeomen service for the material and moral progress of the community.

Depressed classes and Franchise

19. There was no communal representation for the depressed classes in the first Legislative Council of the State, but since then a member from among them is always nominated to the Council. The nomination has hitherto been confined to the Pulaya community which is by far the largest. There is no doubt that the presence of a representative of the depressed classes in the Legislative Council is an acknowledgment on the part of the Government of the civic rights of these hitherto down-trodden people, and serves to raise their status in the estimation of the public. The depressed classes member has already done much good in voicing their grievances and the hardships to which they are subjected. They are entitled to vote in the general constituencies, but the number of those qualified to vote must be very small indeed. To increase their voting strength the best means would seem to be, as suggested by the Franchise Committee, to make literacy a qualification for voting and to fix a lower property (or tax) qualification in their case. In view of their heterogeneous character and of the fact that they are still steeped in ignorance and have not developed anything like a civic consciousness, a separate electorate for them will be of no use; and the present practice of nomination by the Government would appear to be the best course in the existing circumstances.

For the uplift of the depressed classes, an experiment of a unique character is being carried on by the Ramakrishna Mission in a village four miles to the west of Trichur. An account of this, published recently, is extracted below. It will be seen therefrom that the experiment is likely to achieve a large measure of success and that the methods adopted by the workers deserve to be copied by those who are interested in the uplift of the depressed communities.

SRI RAMAKRISHNA GURUKUL AND VIDYA MANDIR.

THE VILANGANS, TRICHUR.

Sri Ramakrishna Gurukul & Vidya Mandir

In response to the clarion call of Swami Vivekananda and with the idea of trying to work out his grand ideals the Sri Ramakrishna Ashram, Trichur, has, in all humility, taken up the service of *Daridra Narayana* as a part of spiritual *Sadhana*. It was during the days of the devastating floods in the Cochin State, in the year 1924, that the Ashram workers first came into close contact with the poor untouchables and realised their horrid plight. The relief operations in that year conducted under the inspiring leadership of Swami Atmaprakashananda, of the Belur Mutt, provided the first opportunity to serve them. This naturally took the shape of supplying their immediate necessities, such as rice, clothing, money and building materials. The workers, however, soon realised the need for a more permanent form of service to emancipate these unfortunates. After a series of experimental efforts in this direction, the Ashram opened in 1927 the Sri Ramakrishna Gurukul and Vidya Mandir in a suburban village, four miles to the west of Trichur Town, near the main road to the famous Guruvayur Temple. The village has a good number of Harijan* inhabitants which provides ample scope for service and uplift work.

Present strength

2. The Gurukul is the residential section, and the Vidya Mandir, the day school. Instruction is imparted free and covers the primary and secondary grades. The institutions are intended mainly for Harijans. But higher caste pupils are also freely admitted, and even encouraged to join, so as to give the children of the Harijans the benefit of equal association and comradeship with the children of the higher castes. There are at present 277 pupils on the rolls of the Vidya Mandir, of whom 262 are Harijans. 26 boys now live in the Gurukul ranging from 10 to 16 years of age. All are free boarders: 18 of them are Harijans and 8 belong to the higher castes. The boys live under the supervision of 10 teachers residing in the Gurukul all belonging to the higher castes. Two of them are Masters of Arts, one a Graduate and the rest Intermediates, and Matriculates and qualified teachers. The inmates lead a simple, open air life, following a daily routine of self-help and study that does not deprive them of their precious rural heritage of health, plain living and habits of hard work. As children of nature, the simple villagers have got many innate virtues and tendencies, to preserve which a special scheme of studies has been framed, suited to rural requirements and the needs of the masses.

Life in the Gurukul

3. The day begins at 4 30 a. m. in the Gurukul, with devotional songs and prayer after a cold plunge bath in the Ashram *Theertha*.** Then follow the recital of the *Geeta*, *Sandhya* and *Surya Namaskar*. The boys afterwards attend to their domestic work and home studies and are served with breakfast at 8. The school session begins at 9 and after three hours work breaks up for meals at 12 noon. The afternoon session begins at 1-30 and extends up to 4-30 p. m. After the dispersal of the school, the boys of the Gurukul divide themselves into two batches, one going out to play and the other attending to garden work alternately. Evening *Sandhya* and *Bhajana* are conducted between 6-30 and 7-30 p. m., after which meals are served. The boys gather at 8-30 to attend the Children's Republican Court which is presided over by a tribunal of three judges elected from among themselves. Here all complaints

* Old style, depressed classes.

** The tank attached to the Ashram.

preferred by boys against their mates are heard and disposed of with the help of their own advocates. There is also a juvenile police force to investigate complaints and prosecute delinquents. This is designed to give the boys practical training in citizenship and self-government. Appeals against the decrees of the Court are however heard and disposed of by the teacher in charge, who has also to approve all verdicts and punishments before they are executed. After the court, the daily papers are read. The boys are also regaled with stories till 9-30 p. m. when they retire for sleep.

Manual work

4. All work in the Gurukul like cleaning, cooking, washing, gardening and tending the cows is attended to by the boys themselves under the guidance of the teachers. Even in the erection of buildings and putting up of walls and fences, our practice is to entrust the boys with the major part of the labour. The boys also make their own furniture and weave and wash their own clothes. Hired labour is engaged only in cases of absolute necessity, where expert skill is wanted. This enables the boys to get practical training in these arts and crafts. They learn to love labour and feel its dignity. Besides, there is the joy and the satisfaction of creative effort which takes away much of the ordinary feelings of drudgery. Above all, this provides the most effective safeguard against the danger of the Harijan boys getting away with the idea that, by mere school-going they have risen above the level of their labouring brethren at home or in the field, or that their new found freedom from social tyranny has brought with it a corresponding freedom from honest work.

Culture of the Head and Heart

5. In thus laying special emphasis on manual labour, we have not minimised the importance of general intellectual training for Harijans. We have devised our special curriculum in such a way as to enable our boys to cover also the ordinary secondary school course and appear for the public examinations. Nor is the culture of the heart neglected. The boys are encouraged to observe and appreciate the beauties of nature and give free expression to their emotions through pictures and poems. Training in other fine arts such as music and folk-dance are also given their proper place in the curriculum.

General Education

6. Particular attention is paid to the study of the mother-tongue, *viz.*, Malayalam. A high level of proficiency is aimed at and special text books have been prepared to suit the purpose. Even in regard to the methods of instruction, particularly in the lower classes, we are trying to follow some of the old methods of orally mastering the alphabets and the rudiments of grammar and arithmetic. Sanskrit is taught compulsorily to all boys as the language of ancient Hindu culture and religion. A working knowledge of Hindi is imparted to all the boys as it is the common language of the nation. Instruction in English is given in the higher classes and the standard aimed at is sufficient to meet the requirements of the public examinations. The teaching of History, Geography and Civics is done in a manner calculated to cultivate in the boys love of the motherland and our ancient culture. There are at present 6 standards in the Vidya Mandir, but additional forms are opened every year and it is the intention of the Ashram to raise the institution to the status of a full-fledged High School.

Religious Instruction

7. Religious instruction is a special feature of the institution. Work in the Vidya Mandir begins and ends with prayer. Every day half an hour is set apart for regular religious classes. Regular *puja* and religious practices such as *Sandhya*, *Surya Namaskar* and *Swadhyaya* are part of the daily routine in the Gurukul. The birthdays of great prophets and saints belonging to the different religions are also celebrated. Every attempt is made to impress upon the boys the unity of all religions and remove from their minds narrow, sectarian prejudices. The birthday festivity of Sri Ramakrishna is specially marked by *Bhajana*, processions, poor feeding, public meeting and drama. The celebration attracts a large number of villagers belonging to all castes and creeds. On this occasion all ideas of high and low vanish, the 'touchables' freely mix with the 'untouchables' and an atmosphere of spiritual kinship prevails.

8. But, with the ignorant and poverty-stricken masses, the problem of bread-winning inevitably precedes that of culture. Only after the question of food, clothing and shelter is properly solved, will there be a sound basis for what are considered higher and more spiritual

things. We have therefore taken care to emphasise the earning value of education by starting an industrial school for vocational instruction. Here regular training is given in hand-spinning, weaving, carpentry and mat-making. As already referred to, the boys are also given training in such useful work as masonry, thatching, fencing, laundry and needlework. But for want of a well-equipped work-shop, we are at present unable to give instruction on modern scientific lines. We have also to provide for instruction in additional cottage industries that may be pursued with profit in the local village. The agricultural section gives practical training to the boys in agriculture, gardening, dairying, bee-culture and other farm work. We have also a small provision store for selling necessaries at cheap rates to the villagers. Here the Gurukul boys receive practical training in shop-keeping and accounts.

Industrial and agricultural Education

9. In framing this curriculum and scheme of uplift we have not hesitated to draw upon the valuable experiences of the American Negro pioneer, Booker T. Washington, the founder of the famous Tuskegee Institute. In his auto-biographical volume 'Up from Slavery', he says, "The great lesson which the Negro race needed to learn in freedom was to work. As a slave the Negro was worked till now; as a free man he must now learn how to work. There is a great difference between working and being worked. Being worked means degradation. Working means civilisation." This lesson, we are told, Tuskegee tries to emphasise very strongly. It teaches students to lift labour out of drudgery, and to place it on a plane where it would become attractive, where it would be something to be sought, rather than to be dreaded, and if possible to be avoided. More than this, Tuskegee also teaches men to put brains into their labour and to show that it is possible for one with the best mental training to work with the hands without feeling that he is degraded. The Sri Ramakrishna Gurukul and Vidya Mandir strive, in all humility, to do for the Harijans what Tuskegee has done and is doing for the Negroes of America. We, however, bear in mind the important distinction that, unlike the Negroes, the Harijans are not a separate race, but part and parcel, an organic limb of the Hindu society and that, therefore, their future depends on their complete assimilation in the Hindu fold. But, like the Negroes, the Harijans also have to learn in freedom, the great lesson to work willingly and efficiently. Accordingly, we try to infuse into the boys what may aptly be called the "Tuskegee spirit" of love of work and dignity of labour.

The Tuskegee spirit

10. This account will be incomplete whithout a brief reference to the numerous obstacles in the way of our unfortunate brethren fully availing themselves of the facilities provided for their benefit. To be indifferent to one's own welfare is one of the worst effects of prolonged slavery. This is true of Harijans as of no other community. They are utterly callous to the education of their children. It requires not a little effort to make them realise the value of education and to secure regular attendance of their boys at school. It is therefore doubly pitiable to see some of those who are willing to send their children to school prevented from doing so by their social and economic handicaps. The adults in the family have to be daily working in the fields from morn till eve, and children of school-going age are often the only ones left to look after the baby at home. The call of the crying brother or sister in the hut easily prevails over the distant call of the school bell. Often the landlords, on whose plots the poor Pulaya has put up his hovel, also add their domineering voice, sometimes with threats of eviction, to dissuade the parents from sending their children to school. Cases are not also rare of poor parents being forced even to pledge their children as security for loans taken from money lending landlords, for whom the boys have to work under conditions bordering on slavery. Needless to say that such boys cannot have any chance of freely attending schools. The few cases of such slavery that came to our notice were immediately redeemed and the boys taken to our school. Another difficulty arises from the fact that Harijan huts are situated in out of the way quarters, which makes it very hard for the children to go to school through circuitous and often thorny fields and foot-paths. Interested parties are also responsible for creating in the credulous minds of the Harijans the strange delusion that school-going is simply a prelude to recruitment in the army. Some at least of these difficulties could possibly be

Some difficulties

removed by opening a free colony for Harijans where they could live unmolested, easily accessible to progressive influences. The Ashram has in view the opening of such a colony and is in quest of some suitable plots for the purpose.

Adult Education

11. Experience has taught us that the education of the children of the suppressed communities cannot progress without a parallel programme of well-planned adult education. For, by that alone could the light of knowledge reach the Harijan homes and remove the ignorance and poverty prevailing there. An educated parent may be expected to value better the benefits of regular schooling to his children. Further, the children too who go to school will be better able to retain the benefits of school instruction if, as a result of adult education, their home life is improved and made to fairly approach the ideal presented at the school. But the difficulties in the way of the education of the elders are only greater than those in the case of the children. They cannot spare for that purpose the day time which they have to devote to work for their daily living. Nor is it easy to make them muster strong at nights after the day's toil. Any scheme of adult education should, therefore, provide attractions and utilities sufficient to rouse and keep up the interest of the elders. They have also to be weaned from the temptation of the toddy shop. The Ashram workers tried to hold night classes for the adults for some time, but the experiment had to be given up after a few months for want of attendance. We are sure to succeed better if we can provide ourselves with attractions like a gramophone or a radio set and a magic lantern with suitable slides.

Co-operation and Economic Relief

12. An attempt was also made to start a co-operative credit society. It was hoped thereby to make the members of the community more united and self-reliant. Many were very enthusiastic in the beginning, but they soon found it easier to use the society to take loans than to learn thrift or imbibe the co-operative spirit. Attendance at meetings grew poor; repayments became irregular in spite of the easy terms offered and the work of the society gradually came to a stand-still. We are attempting to devise means to bring it back to life. Since it was found very difficult to instil new ideas and new habits into the minds of the elders, we have started the movement among the school boys in the shape of the students' co-operative store for supplying school requisites. This and the provision stores already referred to, run by the boys themselves, are calculated to give them a good training in co-operative business methods and rudiments of commerce. In course of time, we hope to develop these into full-fledged co-operative societies. In the meanwhile, we are not refusing economic relief in cases of urgent necessity. Loans are given on sufficient security to be repaid in easy instalments. But the funds at our disposal being very small, we are not able to satisfy all applicants for help.

Medical Relief

13. One of the teachers in the Gurukul has some experience in the practice of the various branches of Ayurveda. His services have been freely availed of by many of the poor villagers. There is at present an average monthly attendance at the Ashram of about 1,000 patients belonging to all castes and creeds. We are sorry we have not been able as yet to freely supply medicines also. We have stocked a few medicines for emergent cases, such as snake-bite; but in the majority of cases our slender means compel us, much against our wish, to content ourselves with giving mere prescriptions. As more funds come in, we hope to be able to supply medicines also free. Cases are not rare where patients have to be kept in the school itself for days together for proper nursing and treatment. The need for an inpatient ward is thus keenly felt.

Want of accommodation

14. The school is now temporarily housed in a thatched shed which has also to provide accommodation for the residence of the Gurukul boys and workers. The industrial section and the stores are also accommodated there. This over-crowding causes not a little inconvenience. There are no retiring rooms for workers and visitors during day time, when the classes are in full swing. Nor is the available accommodation sufficient even for the classes. For want of funds, we are at present unable to provide additional accommodation. Our plan is to locate the literary section in a series of single room structures. With this object in view we have

already put up two such tiled buildings in which the lower secondary classes are now located. To similarly shift all the classes, eight more buildings of the same type have to be constructed; separate structures are also required for the office and the library. Residential quarters for the boys and teachers are also urgent necessities.

15. Besides meeting the recurring expenses to maintain the resident scholars and workers in the Gurukul, which now comes to nearly Rs. 400 per month, we have spent on capital outlay nearly Rs. 7,100 for the purchase of over 17 acres of land, the construction of five buildings, the digging of a tank and a well and other improvements. The following is a rough estimate of our immediate requirements :— Our Immediate needs

			Rs.
1.	For building residential quarters for 50 boys and 15 workers	..	12,000
2.	For constructing 8 single class room buildings at the rate of Rs. 500 per building	..	4,000
3.	For a shrine for Harijans	..	1,500
4.	For a dispensary with provision for in-patients	..	2,000
5.	For a building to accommodate the provision stores	..	250
6.	For fitting up a small workshop for vocational training	..	3,000
7.	For fitting up pump and pipes	..	750
8.	For a gramophone, a radio set with loud-speaker and a magic lantern with slides	..	1,500
9.	For educational equipments such as science apparatus, maps, globes, etc.	..	1,000

Free gifts of books and journals in the Vernacular and English for the Gurukul Library and Reading Room are also invited.

Recurring expenses come approximately to Rs. 10 per month for a residential scholar and Rs. 15 for a worker. Contributions, however small, will be gratefully received and acknowledged.

16. The above account will give the public an idea of our aims and ideals, our struggles and achievements. It is not yet time to measure the success of our endeavours which cover a wide field of rural reconstruction and social service. The problem of untouchability which is agitating the public mind so much at present is not going to be solved without intensive constructive work from within for the emancipation of the suppressed. We have to remove their age-long ignorance, uncleanliness and poverty that now keep them down as more or less willing slaves under the yoke of blind social tyranny. That their liberation could be brought about not so much by reform, as by growth from within, was also the view of Swami Vivekananda. "I do not believe in reform," he says, "I believe in growth. I do not dare to put myself in the position of God and dictate to our society, 'This way thou shoulds't move and not that.' My idea is growth, expansion, development on national lines." It is in this spirit that the Ashram strives to work and play its humble part in the building up of awakened India. Need for constructive work

17. The institution is still in its infancy, having only just completed its fifth year. It had to struggle against heavy odds to make headway in all directions. From humble beginnings the work has assumed dimensions that threaten to go beyond our limited energy and resources. We have reached a stage when we cannot advance further without substantial help from the public. The results attained so far embolden us to approach the public for support and sympathy, not merely on the merit of ideals, but also of achievements, however small. The few words of appreciation by distinguished patriots and high officials, who were good enough to visit our institution have also put cheer into our hearts and stimulated us to pursue our uphill work with vigour and hope. Above all, we have felt the Lord's infinite grace at every step and we rely on Him for strength and sustenance in future as in the past. May this humble offering of *Seva* be acceptable to His Lotus Feet! Appeal

APPENDIX III.

CENSUS OF AGRICULTURAL STOCK.

[*Contributed by Mr. I. Raman Menon, B. A., Dip: Agric: (Cantab), Retired Superintendent of Agriculture, Cochin State.*]

Introductory

As in other parts of India, cattle form the chief motive power in the State for agricultural and draught purposes. A census of cattle was taken along with the general census, the special schedules issued for the purpose being filled in at the time of the preliminary enumeration. The results of this census are exhibited in Statement I annexed.

A quinquennial census of cattle is taken by the Revenue department of the State. These figures are brought up-to-date from time to time by the village officers.

Variations between 1921 and 1931

2. In Statement II (annexed) the census figures of 1931 are given side by side with the figures of the Revenue department for 1921 and 1931 for purposes of comparison. It will be seen that the Revenue department figures of 1931 do not tally with those of the census. According to the departmental statistics, bulls, bullocks and bull calves together number 109,298, whereas the census shows but 104,982 of these animals. But the number of cows and cow calves returned at the census exceeds the number recorded by the Revenue department by 17,817. Indeed, according to the statistics collected by the village officers in 1921 and 1931, cows and cow-calves have decreased by about 5,000 during the last decade. A like difference is to be noticed in the number of she-buffaloes, the departmental figures being lower than the figures of 1921 and of the present census. The number of goats returned at the census is far in excess of the number recorded by the village officers. A similar discrepancy will be noticed in respect of ploughs also.

Of the two sets of figures, that of the census must be regarded as more accurate for obvious reasons. But no cattle census was taken along with the general census of 1921 and the only figures available for comparison are those collected by the Revenue department in that year. In examining the variations between 1921 and 1931, we have therefore to remember that the accuracy of the 1921 statistics cannot be vouched for.

Turning to the figures in Statement II, we find that stud bulls have decreased by 31 per cent during the decade, whereas bullocks (including calves) have increased by as many as 49 per cent during the same period if the Revenue department figures of 1921 are to be relied on. Cows (including calves) show an increase of about 12 per cent, buffaloes an increase of 15 per cent and she-buffaloes of 10 per cent. But it is among goats that we find the most remarkable rise in numbers, for these animals are seen to have multiplied by no less than 175 per cent during the last 10 years. The explanation for this abnormal increase is that of late goat's milk has come to be freely used in the place of cow's milk. There are very few sheep in the State. These few are found in the out-lying taluk of Chittur which adjoins the Coimbatore district. Late in the year (November—December) herds of sheep are taken from the Coimbatore district to the northern taluks of the State for grazing purposes. These are eventually taken back in January.

3. The census figures show that the total number of animals (bullocks and buffaloes) available for agricultural and draught purposes is 114,585. Leaving about 11,526 animals for purposes of carting (there are 5,763 carts returned at the census), it is found that the animals available for agricultural work alone is 103,059.

Inadequacy of agricultural livestock

The total extent of wet lands in the State is 207,686 acres. The major portion of the paddy lands in the Cochin-Kanayannur taluk is not generally ploughed. Tillage work in these lands is done by a special type of hoes. The kole lands in the Trichur taluk are also not usually ploughed at sowing time. Excluding these lands, the extent of lands in which tillage is done by bullock power is roughly 175,000 acres. On an average, one animal for every acre of wet land is required for the proper cultivation of paddy lands. The total number of animals available for agricultural work alone being only 103,059, the supply will be seen to be much below the actual requirements. The fact that the animals used for carting purposes are also used for ploughing whenever their services are available does not improve the position to any appreciable extent. On the other hand, when we take into consideration such areas of dry land under cultivation as have not been iucluded in the above calculation, the situation will be seen to be infinitely worse.

Farmers who own but small extents of lands, and who are too poor to maintain their cattle throughout the year, dispose of their animals soon after the cultivation season and again go in for new ones at the beginning of the next season. Likewise small garden owners also sell their cattle when their irrigation season is over, and purchase new animals when the next season commences. This arrangement is defective because, if the farms and gardens are not properly stocked, work is bound to be perfunctorily done. Further the supply of manure secured from the droppings of the animals will also be inadequate.

4. The number of ploughs returned at the census is 75,247 against 61,370 the Revenue figure of 1921, and 68,796 the Revenue figure of 1931. The decade has therefore recorded a considerable increase in the numbers of this agricultural implement.

Inadequacy of agricultural implements

The Cochin plough, like the typical Indian plough, is an implement which does not last for more than a season. Strictly speaking, it is no plough at all, but a cultivator in the true sense of the word. However, it is used as a general purpose implement, being made to serve the purpose of a plough, a cultivator, a clod-crusher and a harrow. For dry land work and for work in wet lands for the first sowings in April—May, the plough is perhaps the only implement used. The required tilth is secured by the land being ploughed 8 to 10 times. For transplanting work in paddy lands, two more implements, a clod crusher and a levelling board, are also used.

The holdings in Cochin, as in most other parts of the west coast, are generally small and scattered. The ryot therefore wants implements which can be conveniently carried from place to place on his shoulder. And for this reason the idea of the introduction of heavy labour-saving machines is out of the question.

The improved ploughs advocated by the Agricultural department are small iron ploughs (made in the workshop of the Government Central Farm), the shares of which can be replaced easily. These ploughs have wooden shafts.

Though slightly heavier than the local plough, they can be carried easily by the ploughman. They are gradually becoming popular and if their price is reduced from the present rate of Rs. 11 to Rs. 6 or 7, they may displace the old type of plough to a greater extent.

The local plough costs Rs. 2 to Rs. 2—8—0 each. The shaft and handle may cost 2 to 4 annas. The remaining portion of the plough is subject to such wear and tear that it does not last for more than a year, and therefore it is a certain loss to the farmer. The annual loss on account of the plough must thus be enormous. It should be observed at the same time that, under the prevailing conditions, the old type of plough can never be completely replaced by the improved plough. The advantage of the iron plough is that the entire surface of the land is cut and turned to one side with one round of ploughing. For the preparation of proper tilth the ryot has to fall back upon the local plough. The number of subsequent ploughings can however be reduced. There will thus be a saving of labour and my experience is that stocking also can be reduced by at least 20 per cent.

The pumping of water from the Kole lands used to be done with water wheels worked by man power. During the last two decades water wheels have been completely replaced by screw pumps worked by oil or steam engines.

Supply of milk

5. We have already seen that cows (including calves), she-buffaloes and goats have all increased in numbers during the decade. But when we turn to the question of milk supply, we find that it is utterly inadequate in spite of this increase in the number of animals. The total population of the State is over 1,200,000. A small proportion of this number living in the coastal tracts and by the side of the backwaters will have opportunities of taking a mixed diet consisting of rice and fish. With them milk is not an essential article of food. But in the interior, where fish is scarce and not within the reach of the poor, the people are underfed, their food being deficient in calcium. Good ghee and good butter-milk enter into the dietary only of the well-to-do classes in the vegetarian population, so much so that the poorer sections in this group are also subjected to the same defect (want of calcium) in respect of their food. There is indeed a very real shortage in the supply of milk which must necessarily form an essential article of diet. An ordinary cow of the west coast does not give more than 2 lbs. of milk at an average per day for 300 days in the year. Buffaloes are better milkers and the average yield of a buffalo is about 4 lbs. a day. On a rough calculation it is seen that the daily output of milk in the State (including the yield from the goats) cannot exceed 100,000 lbs. for a total population of over 1,200,000. The effect of this shortage on the population is vast. Children do not get good food during the growing period. And adults are not in a position to maintain their health.

Cattle breeding

6. The number of bulls recorded at the census is 1,641. This number is quite adequate for breeding purposes, seeing that there are but 72,834 cows. But the bulls are of an inferior type.

The typical Malabar cow is a worthless animal. It is undersized and is a very poor milker. Calves are invariably ill-fed. So long as the cow is a poor milker, there is no chance of rearing a good bull calf. Exotic types of animals are getting popular. These are Sindhi animals, Kangayams and Ongoles. The Government have stationed good breeding bulls in a few centres and are offering annual grants of Rs. 75 to 100 for each bull.

7. The existence of a few bulls or a few dozen bulls cannot however lead to any appreciable improvement in the breed of the cattle population of the

State. Drastic steps have to be taken if a change for the better is to be effected. All the worthless bulls should be got castrated, the bull calves reserved for breeding purposes should be got registered, and it should be made penal to own any uncastrated bull calf over two years old that has not been registered.

Suggestions for improved breeding

A sufficient number of good stud bulls of approved type and breed should be imported to replace the worthless ones castrated. A sound programme for a period of ten years, with a stock of 200 stud bulls and with a provision of 100 bulls every fourth year, will not cost more than Rs. 75,000 a year. The effect of this scheme on the cattle of the State cannot but be immense. After half a dozen years a good proportion of the present type of cattle will be replaced by a better type. Cows with a better frame and with better milking qualities and working animals of a bigger size able to turn out more work will come into existence. And the ryot population will be the richer in that they will be the owners of a better type of animals and will begin to take greater interest in livestock.

Private capital may not be available for this scheme of cattle improvement. The Government will therefore have to take the initiative. They may also persuade all Co-operative Societies and local administrations to move in the right direction.

The number of animals slaughtered for purposes of meat is not very large. The animals now slaughtered are either old or diseased and disabled. Meat from these emaciated animals is worthless and indigestible.

In countries where cattle are slaughtered in large numbers, there is unlimited scope for the selection and improvement of livestock. This may not be possible in very many places in India, much less in a State like Cochin where Hindus form a majority of the population. The method of castrating all bull calves found unfit for breeding purposes is the only alternative. Worked on proper lines, it will maintain the stock in fairly efficient condition, even though it may not be as effective as the method of wholesale slaughter.

Veterinary aid

8. There are 7 Veterinary Hospitals in the State located as shown below:

Taluk.	Location of Veterinary Hospitals.
Cochin-Kanayannur	Ernakulam
Mukundapuram	Irinjalakkuda
Trichur	Trichur
Talapilli	Vadakkancheri
	Kunnamkulam
Chittur	Tattamangalam
	Nemmara

The Trichur Hospital has two Veterinary Inspectors and the rest one each. The hospitals at Irinjalakkuda, Vadakkancheri, Kunnamkulam and Nemmara were opened during the last decade.

Statement III (annexed) shows the details of cases treated in these hospitals during the year 1106 (1930—1931).

As in other parts of South India, rinderpest occasionally accounts for a high rate of mortality amongst cattle in Cochin. The foot and mouth disease appears in an epidemic form once in a few years. Anthrax and Haemorrhagic scepticaemia appear at times in a sporadic form.

The Veterinary department has plenty of resources to combat these diseases, and the public have recognized the usefulness of the department.

Cattle trade

9. The State lies in the cattle trade route of the west coast. Cattle are generally taken from the adjoining eastern and northern districts to the various taluks of the State, and through the State to the northern taluks of Travancore. Hardly any cattle pass from the south to the north. The State Agricultural department has made arrangements with the officers in the adjoining British districts, by which timely intimation of any outbreak of contagious diseases will be received.

STATEMENT I.

STATISTICS OF AGRICULTURAL STOCK (CENSUS OF 1931).

TALUKS	Stud-bulls	Ploughing bullocks	Cart-bullocks	Bullock calves	Milch cows	Dry cows	Cow calves	Buffaloes	Buffalo calves	Milch she-buffaloes	Dry she-buffaloes	She-buffalo calves	Goats	Ploughs	Carts	Country boats
1	2	3	4	5	6	7	8	9	10	11	12	13	14	15	16	17
Cochin State ..	1,641	67,498	9,284	26,889	28,378	44,486	49,681	37,883	8,616	4,712	7,862	4,834	104,811	78,247	8,763	9,102
Cochin-Kanayannur ..	120	8,316	320	5,076	6,124	7,159	10,391	606	119	350	245	190	17,080	6,164	227	6,596
Cranganur ..	25	270	31	624	813	4,094	1,400	116	154	268	371	355	2,319	124	1	709
Mukundapuram ..	363	29,864	2,268	7,874	6,862	12,973	14,007	4,526	941	842	2,114	1,125	28,475	22,859	1,265	1,200
Trichur ..	178	9,619	2,157	4,567	5,070	9,277	10,106	7,289	904	1,376	1,857	1,352	15,999	10,890	1,433	492
Talapilli ..	313	13,014	1,132	5,436	6,484	9,485	9,383	16,750	1,298	120	784	459	28,115	20,396	879	94
Chittur ..	642	6,415	3,356	2,962	2,015	4,428	4,464	8,546	2,200	1,456	2,198	1,353	12,523	14,814	1,958	2

STATEMENT II.

STATISTICS OF AGRICULTURAL STOCK (CENSUS OF 1931 AND REVENUE DEPARTMENT FIGURES OF 1921 AND 1931.)

	Census figures 1931	Revenue department figures	
		1921	1931
Bulls ..	1,641	2,383	109,298
Bullocks ..	76,752	69,286	
Bull calves ..	26,589		
Cows ..	72,834	75,509	104,668
Cow calves ..	49,651	34,116	
Buffaloes ..	37,833	37,749	43,135
Buffalo calves ..	5,616		
She buffaloes ..	12,274	11,536	14,426
She-buffalo calves ..	4,834	4,037	
Goats ..	104,511	38,027	91,572
Ploughs ..	75,247	61,370	68,796
Carts ..	5,763	4,127	6,038
Boats ..	9,102	6,562	..
Water wheels ..	..	1,328	..

STATEMENT III.

CASES TREATED IN THE STATE VETERINARY HOSPITALS DURING THE YEAR 1106 M. E. (1930-1931 A. D.) (DEPARTMENT OF AGRICULTURE)

NAMES OF INSTITUTIONS	IN-PATIENT									OUT-PATIENT	
	Cattle	Sheep	Dogs	Horses	Fowls	Elephants	Cats	Other animals	Total	Cattle	Sheep
1	2	3	4	5	6	7	8	9	10	11	12
Veterinary Hospital, Ernakulam..	50	12	45	4	..	..	..	2	113	1,797	355
Do Vadakkancheri ..	30	..	..	..	..	..	..	1	31	1,429	386
Do Irinjalakkuda ..	..	..	..	..	..	..	..	..	..	1,186	157
Do Trichur ..	316	41	65	2	..	..	..	4	428	1,843	452
Do Kunnamkulam ..	..	..	..	..	..	..	..	..	..	1,252	270
Do Tattamangalam ..	..	..	..	..	..	..	..	..	13	678	46
Do Nemmara ..	..	..	..	..	..	..	..	..	..	763	323

OUT-PATIENT											OPERATIONS	
Dogs	Horses	Elephants	Pigs	Cats	Fowls	Turkeys	Monkeys	Other animals	Total	Grand Total	Castrations	Other operations
13	14	15	16	17	18	19	20	21	22	23	24	25
407	26	4	..	..	106	..	..	27	2,722	2,835	11	164
42	7	1	13	1	..	..	1	2	1,882	1,913	32	176
36	1	..	3	2	131	..	..	..	1,518	1,518	6	150
355	14	4	77	13	100	8	3	7	2,476	2,304	184	290
115	3	1	13	4	110	1	..	4	1,773	1,773	21	126
106	10	3	..	..	9	..	..	..	852	865	18	130
98	9	..	..	..	3	..	..	5	1,195	1,195	39	105

PART II

A.— IMPERIAL TABLES

TABLE I.

AREA, HOUSES AND POPULATION.

Note.—1. The total area of the State as furnished from the Land Records Office is 1,480·28 square miles as against 1,479 shown in the Census Report of 1921. The increase is on account of accretions from the Arabian Sea.

2. Column 4 shows the total number of Revenue Villages in the State excluding one village, Mattancheri, which has been wholly absorbed by the Municipal Town of that name.

3. 'Urban' population includes all persons enumerated in the places classed as towns for the purposes of Imperial Tables IV and V. 'Rural' means population enumerated in all other places (including the Forest Tramway area and the Forest tracts).

TABLE I.

AREA, HOUSES AND POPULATION.

TALUKS	Area in square miles	Towns	Villages	OCCUPIED HOUSES			POPULATION								
							Persons			Males			Females		
				Total	In Towns	In Villages	Total	Urban	Rural	Total	Urban	Rural	Total	Urban	Rural
1	2	3	4	5	6	7	8	9	10	11	12	13	14	15	16
Cochin State ..	**1,480·28**	**12**	**272**	**207,563**	**32,506**	**175,057**	**1,205,016**	**206,340**	**998,676**	**589,813**	**104,231**	**485,582**	**615,203**	**102,109**	**513,094**
Cochin-Kanayannur ..	**158·52**	4	36	**59,954**	14,335	45,619	**350,268**	93,475	256,793	**177,242**	48,894	128,348	**173,026**	44,581	128,445
Cranganur ..	**17·51**	1	5	**7,553**	1,097	6,456	**42,531**	6,866	35,665	**21,099**	3,381	17,718	**21,432**	3,485	17,947
Mukundapuram ..	**510·00**	2	60	**44,879**	2,559	42,320	**263,722**	16,933	246,789	**127,738**	8,330	119,408	**135,984**	8,603	127,381
Trichur ..	**245·50**	1	72	**39,261**	6,823	32,438	**239,257**	45,658	193,599	**115,523**	22,840	92,683	**123,734**	22,818	100,916
Talapilli ..	**256·00**	2	74	**35,314**	3,374	31,940	**202,424**	18,980	183,444	**96,173**	9,075	87,098	**106,251**	9,905	95,346
Chittur ..	**292·75**	2	25	**20,602**	4,318	16,284	**106,814**	24,428	82,386	**52,038**	11,711	40,327	**54,776**	12,717	42,059

TABLE II.

VARIATION IN POPULATION SINCE 1881.

TABLE II.

VARIATION IN POPULATION SINCE 1881.

TALUKS	PERSONS						VARIATION: INCREASE (+) DECREASE (—)				
	1931	1921	1911	1901	1891	1881	1921 to 1931	1911 to 1921	1901 to 1911	1891 to 1901	1881 to 1891
1	2	3	4	5	6	7	8	9	10	11	12
Cochin State ..	**1,208,016**	**979,080**	**918,110**	**812,025**	**722,906**	**600,278**	**+ 225,936**	**+ 60,970**	**+ 106,085**	**+ 89,119**	**+ 122,628**
Cochin-Kanayannur ..	**350,268**	279,381	264,828	235,081	207,615	178,605	+ **70,884**	+ 14,556	+ 29,744	+ 27,469	+ 29,010
Cranganur ..	**42,531**	34,808	33,193	29,140	27,965	20,950	+ **7,723**	+ 1,615	+ 4,053	+ 1,175	+ 7,015
Mukundapuram ..	**263,722**	208,713	193,930	161,833	145,690	115,212	+ **55,009**	+ 14,783	+ 32,097	+ 16,143	+ 30,478
Trichur ..	**239,257**	190,813	169,756	145,104	128,957	104,695	+ **48,444**	+ 21,057	+ 24,652	+ 16,147	+ 24,262
Talapilli ..	**202,424**	170,154	165,114	151,315	133,894	113,114	+ **32,270**	+ 5,040	+ 13,799	+ 17,421	+ 20,780
Chittur ..	**106,814**	95,208	91,289	89,549	78,785	67,702	+ **11,606**	+ 3,919	+ 1,740	+ 10,764	+ 11,083

Net variation in period 1881—1931. Increase (+) Decrease (—)	MALES						FEMALES					
	1931	1921	1911	1901	1891	1881	1931	1921	1911	1901	1891	1881
13	14	15	16	17	18	19	20	21	22	23	24	25
+ 604,738	**589,813**	**482,959**	**457,342**	**405,200**	**361,904**	**301,815**	**615,203**	**496,121**	**460,768**	**406,825**	**361,002**	**298,463**
+ 171,663	**177,242**	142,558	136,622	121,016	106,850	91,466	**173,026**	136,826	128,206	114,068	103,765	87,139
+ 21,581	**21,099**	17,558	16,856	14,710	14,111	10,634	**21,432**	17,250	16,337	14,430	13,854	10,316
+ 148,510	**127,738**	102,500	96,143	80,335	72,814	58,351	**135,984**	106,213	97,787	81,498	72,876	56,861
+ 134,562	**115,523**	92,587	83,520	71,647	63,980	51,766	**123,734**	98,226	86,236	73,457	64,077	52,929
+ 89,310	**96,173**	81,710	80,126	73,886	65,719	56,528	**106,251**	88,444	84,988	77,429	68,175	56,586
+ 39,112	**52,038**	46,046	44,075	43,606	38,430	33,070	**54,776**	49,162	47,214	45,043	40,355	34,632

TABLE III.

TOWNS AND VILLAGES CLASSIFIED BY POPULATION.

Note.—1. The number 283 in column 2 includes 12 towns and 271 out of the 272 villages shown in Table I. The remaining village (Punkunnam in the Trichur Taluk) has been omitted as the only house in it was unoccupied on the final census day.

2. Travellers enumerated in boats, trains, etc., were excluded from the total population of towns and villages before these were grouped into classes according to population. The travellers enumerated in a taluk are shown separately against that taluk in the last column.

TABLE III.

TOWNS AND VILLAGES CLASSIFIED BY POPULATION.

TALUKS	Total number of inhabited Towns and Villages	Population	Under 500		500—1,000		1,000—2,000		2,000—5,000		5,000—10,000		10,000—20,000		20,000—50,000		Encampments, boat and railway population unclassed
			Number	Population	Number	Population	Number	Population	Number	Population	Number	Population	Number	Population	Number	Population	
1	2	3	4	5	6	7	8	9	10	11	12	13	14	15	16	17	18
Cochin State ..	283	1,205,016	7	1,673	14	10,942	54	81,926	143	462,740	48	328,755	14	186,608	3	119,887	12,485
Cochin-Kanayannur ..	40	380,268	..	..	1	816	2	3,022	12	39,720	13	97,154	10	131,955	2	74,720	2,881
Cranganur ..	6	42,531	..	..	..	..	..	..	2	7,699	3	22,982	1	11,598	..	..	252
Mukundapuram ..	62	263,722	..	..	..	..	6	8,401	41	143,316	14	97,640	1	10,973	..	..	3,302
Trichur ..	72	239,287	4	1,048	3	2,324	20	30,329	37	113,767	7	44,728	..	..	1	45,167	1,854
Talapilli ..	76	202,424	1	8	7	5,417	22	33,256	40	122,046	5	26,730	1	13,618	..	..	1,349
Chittur ..	27	106,814	2	617	3	2,385	4	6,818	11	56,192	6	39,521	1	18,464	..	..	2,817

TABLE IV.

TOWNS CLASSIFIED BY POPULATION WITH VARIATIONS SINCE 1881.

Note.—1. Urban population was separately censused for the first time in 1891. The figures given in column 9 are only approximate.

2. Additions have been made to the areas of three Municipalities since 1921. The extent of these additions and the population in 1931 of the areas thus added are shown below.

Serial No.	Name of Municipality	Extent of the area added	Population of the area added
1	Trichur ..	1,025 acres.	13,752
2	Mattancheri ..	648 ,,	8,113
3	Ernakulam ..	549 ,,	5,669

3. Narakkal, Chalakkudi and Vadakkancheri have been treated as towns for the first time in this census.

4. Travellers are included in the population of the town in which they were enumerated.

TABLE IV.

TOWNS CLASSIFIED BY POPULATION WITH VARIATIONS SINCE 1881.

TOWNS	TALUKS	Municipality (M) or Town (T)	POPULATION						Variation: Increase (+) Decrease (—)					Variation in Period 1881 — 1931 Increase (+) Decrease (—)	MALES			FEMALES		
			1931	1921	1911	1901	1891	1881	1921 to 1931	1911 to 1921	1901 to 1911	1891 to 1901	1881 to 1891		1931	1921	1911	1931	1921	1911
1	2	3	4	5	6	7	8	9	10	11	12	13	14	15	16	17	18	19	20	21
Cochin State			**206,340**	**127,141**	**109,952**	**87,478**	**73,665**	**63,682**	**+79,199**	**+17,189**	**+22,474**	**+13,813**	**+ 9,983**	**+ 142,658**	**104,231**	**64,379**	**57,236**	**102,109**	**62,762**	**52,716**
Class III. (20,000 to 50,000)			**121,941**	**75,753**	**68,277**	**57,547**	**48,069**	**40,923**	**+46,188**	**+ 7,476**	**+10,730**	**+ 9,478**	**+ 7,146**	**+ 81,018**	**63,128**	**39,354**	**36,658**	**58,813**	**36,399**	**31,619**
Trichur ..	Trichur	M.	**45,658**	27,897	23,574	15,585	12,945	10,822	+17,761	+ 4,323	+ 7,989	+ 2,640	+ 2,123	**+ 34,836**	22,840	13,783	12,089	22,818	14,114	11,485
Mattancheri ..	Cochin-Kanayannur	M	**39,645**	24,661	23,508	20,061	17,254	14,634	+14,984	+ 1,153	+ 3,447	+ 2,807	+ 2,620	**+ 25,011**	20,925	12,930	12,625	18,720	11,731	10,883
Ernakulam ..	Do	M	**36,638**	23,192	21,195	21,901	17,870	15,467	+13,446	+ 1,997	— 706	+ 4,031	+ 2,403	**+ 21,171**	19,363	12,638	11,944	17,275	10,554	9,251
Class IV. (10,000 to 20,000)			**54,501**	**40,885**	**36,717**	**29,931**	**25,596**	**22,759**	**+13,616**	**+ 4,168**	**+ 6,786**	**+ 4,335**	**+ 2,837**	**+ 31,742**	**26,447**	**19,869**	**18,178**	**28,054**	**21,016**	**18,539**
Chittur-Tattamangalam ..	Chittur	M	**18,915**	18,150	14,706	14,317	12,630	11,165	+ 765	+ 3,441	+ 389	+ 1,687	+ 1,465	**+ 7,750**	9,120	8,673	7,010	9,795	9,477	7,696
Kunnamkulam ..	Talapilli	T	**13,822**	8,517	8,336	7,194	5,632	4,988	+ 5,305	+ 181	+ 1,142	+ 1,562	+ 644	**+ 8,834**	6,532	4,126	4,064	7,290	4,391	4,272
Irinjalakkuda ..	Mukundapuram	T	**11,047**	9,457	8,690	8,420	7,334	6,606	+ 1,590	+ 767	+ 270	+ 1,086	+ 728	**+ 4,441**	5,391	4,644	4,403	5,656	4,813	4,287
Trippunittura ..	Cochin-Kanayannur	T	**10,717**	4,761	4,976	..	..	..	+ 5,956	— 215	+ 4,976	..	..	**+ 10,717**	5,404	2,426	2,702	5,313	2,335	2,274
Class V. (5,000 to 10,000)			**29,898**	**10,503**	**4,958**	..	..	..	**+19,395**	**+ 5,545**	**+ 4,958**	..	..	**+ 29,898**	**14,656**	**5,156**	**2,400**	**15,242**	**5,347**	**2,558**
Cranganur ..	Cranganur	T	**6,866**	5,803	..	..	..	..	+ 1,063	+ 5,803	..	..	..	**+ 6,866**	3,381	2,930	..	3,485	2,873	..
Narakkal ..	Cochin-Kanayannur	T	**6,475**	..	..	..	..	..	+ 6,475	..	..	..	..	**+ 6,475**	3,202	..	..	3,273	..	..
Chalakkudi ..	Mukundapuram	T	**5,886**	..	..	..	..	..	+ 5,886	..	..	..	..	**+ 5,886**	2,939	..	..	2,947	..	..
Nemmara ..	Chittur	T	**5,513**	4,698	4,958	..	..	..	+ 815	— 260	+ 4,958	..	..	**+ 5,513**	2,591	2,226	2,400	2,922	2,472	2,558
Vadakkancheri ..	Talapilli	T	**5,158**	..	..	..	..	..	+ 5,158	..	..	..	..	**+ 5,158**	2,543	..	..	2,615	..	..

TABLE V.

TOWNS ARRANGED TERRITORIALLY WITH POPULATION BY RELIGION.

Note.—As in Table IV, travellers are included in the population of the town in which they were enumerated.

TABLE V.

TOWNS ARRANGED TERRITORIALLY WITH POPULATION BY RELIGION.

TALUKS	MUNICIPALITY (M) OR TOWN (T)	POPULATION			HINDU			MUSLIM			CHRISTIAN			JAIN			JEW			BUDDHIST			ZOROASTRIAN		
		Persons	Males	Females	Persons	Males	Females	Persons	Males	Females	Persons	Males	Females	Persons	Males	Females	Persons	Males	Females	Persons	Males	Females	Persons	Males	Females
1	2	3	4	5	6	7	8	9	10	11	12	13	14	15	16	17	18	19	20	21	22	23	24	25	26
Cochin State	..	**206,340**	**104,231**	**102,109**	**113,051**	**57,313**	**55,738**	**18,440**	**9,772**	**8,668**	**73,538**	**36,493**	**37,045**	**209**	**117**	**92**	**1,065**	**514**	**551**	**34**	**21**	**13**	**3**	**1**	**2**
Cochin-Kanayannur ..	Ernakulam (M) ..	**36,638**	19,363	17,275	18,170	9,853	8,317	2,406	1,381	1,025	15,391	7,779	7,612	4	3	1	644	335	309	20	11	9	3	1	2
Do ..	Mattancheri (M) ..	**39,645**	20,925	18,720	16,110	8,607	7,503	9,054	4,817	4,237	13,856	7,199	6,657	205	114	91	420	178	242	..	..	..	..	..	..
Do ..	Trippunittura (T) ..	**10,717**	5,404	5,313	8,614	4,329	4,285	155	85	70	1,948	990	958	..	..	..	..	..	..	..	..	..	..	..	..
Do ..	Narakkal (T) ..	**6,475**	3,202	3,273	2,357	1,183	1,174	14	13	1	4,104	2,006	2,098	..	..	..	..	..	..	..	..	..	..	..	..
Cranganur ..	Cranganur (T) ..	**6,866**	3,381	3,485	6,021	2,940	3,081	644	340	304	201	101	100	..	..	..	..	..	.	..	..	.	..	..	..
Mukundapuram ..	Irinjalakkuda (T) ..	**11,047**	5,391	5,656	5,880	2,872	3,008	571	281	290	4,594	2,245	2,349	..	..	..	..	..	..	..	..	..	..	..	..
Do ..	Chalakkudi (T) ..	**5,886**	2,969	2,917	2,806	1,415	1,391	275	154	121	2,804	1,369	1,435	..	..	..	1	1	..	..	..	..	.	..	..
Trichur ..	Trichur (M) ..	**45,658**	22,840	22,818	22,352	11,400	10,952	1,783	939	844	21,509	10,491	11,018	..	..	..	..	..	..	14	10	4	..	..	..
Talapilli ..	Kunnamkulam (T) ..	**13,822**	6,532	7,290	5,820	2,791	3,029	223	115	108	7,779	3,626	4,153	..	..	..	..	..	..	..	..	..	..	..	..
Do ..	Vadakkancheri (T) ..	**5,158**	2,543	2,615	3,035	1,511	1,524	1,161	553	608	962	479	483	..	..	..	..	..	..	..	..	..	..	..	..
Chittur ..	Chittur-Tattamangalam (M) ..	**18,915**	9,120	9,795	16,656	7,971	8,685	1,918	969	949	341	180	161	..	..	..	..	..	..	..	..	..	..	..	..
Do ..	Nemmara (T) ..	**5,513**	2,591	2,922	5,230	2,441	2,789	234	122	112	49	28	21	..	..	..	..	..	..	..	..	..	..	..	..

TABLE VI.

BIRTH PLACE.

IMPERIAL TABLE VI.

BIRTH PLACE.

BIRTH PLACE	POPULATION		
	Persons	Males	Females
1	2	3	4
COCHIN STATE	**1,205,016**	**589,813**	**615,203**
A.—BORN IN INDIA	**1,204,813**	**589,707**	**615,106**
I.—WITHIN THE PROVINCE OF ENUMERATION—COCHIN STATE	**1,117,599**	**553,453**	**564,146**
II.—PROVINCES AND STATES IN INDIA BEYOND THE PROVINCE OF ENUMERATION.	**87,214**	**36,254**	**50,960**
(a) *PROVINCES AND STATES ADJACENT TO THE PROVINCE OF ENUMERATION.*	**85,790**	**35,385**	**50,405**
1. **British Territory** (Madras Presidency)	**54,614**	**23,122**	**31,492**
Anantapur	6	6	..
Bellary	5	2	3
Chingleput	15	7	8
Chittoor	2	2	..
Coimbatore	4,909	2,268	2,641
Ganjam	3	3	..
Godavari	7	5	2
Guntur	1	1	..
Kurnool	3	2	1
Kistna	3	1	2
Madras	285	132	153
Madura	353	189	164
Malabar	46,415	18,972	27,443
Nellore	2	2	..
Nilgiris	82	42	40
North Arcot	31	20	11
Ramnad	15	11	4
Salem	470	261	209
South Arcot	10	3	7
South Canara	994	622	372
Tanjore	161	86	75
Tinnevelly	687	399	288
Trichinopoly	151	84	67
Vizagapatam	4	2	2
2. **Indian States.**	**31,176**	**12,263**	**18,913**
Travancore	31,167	12,257	18,910
Pudukkottai	9	6	3
(b) *OTHER PROVINCES AND STATES IN INDIA.*	**1,293**	**775**	**518**
1. **British Territory.**	**434**	**270**	**164**
Assam	3	..	3
Baluchistan	8	4	4
Bengal	33	17	16
Bombay	291	180	111
Burma	31	15	16
Central Provinces and Berar	11	8	3
Coorg	2	1	1
Delhi	1	1	..

IMPERIAL TABLE VI.—(*cont.*)

BIRTH PLACE.

BIRTH PLACE	POPULATION		
	Persons	Males	Females
1	2	3	4
1. British Territory *(cont.)*			
North West Frontier Province	2	2	..
The Punjab	19	15	4
United Provinces of Agra and Oudh	33	27	6
2. Indian States	**859**	**505**	**354**
Baroda State	3	1	2
Bombay States (Kathiawar)	491	312	179
Central India Agency (Bhopal)	1	..	1
Central Provinces (Udaipur)	2	2	..
Hyderabad	13	11	2
Kashmir	1	1	..
Mysore	127	62	65
Rajputana	12	4	8
Western India Agency (Cutch)	209	112	97
(c) FRENCH AND PORTUGUESE SETTLEMENTS.	**66**	**52**	**14**
1. French Settlements ..	**25**	**17**	**8**
Pondicherry	4	2	2
Karikal	4	1	3
Mahe	17	14	3
2. Portuguese Settlements	**41**	**35**	**6**
Goa	41	35	6
(d) UNSPECIFIED (INDIA) ..	**65**	**42**	**23**
B.—BORN IN OTHER ASIATIC COUNTRIES ..	**122**	**64**	**58**
I.—WITHIN BRITISH DOMINIONS ..	**110**	**55**	**55**
Ceylon	62	31	31
Straits Settlements and Malaya	48	24	24
II.—OUTSIDE BRITISH DOMINIONS ..	**12**	**9**	**3**
Afghanistan	3	3	..
Arabia	2	1	1
China	2	1	1
Japan	1	1	..
Nepal	2	1	1
Persia	2	2	..
C.—BORN IN EUROPE ..	**68**	**37**	**31**
I.—UNITED KINGDOM AND IRELAND ..	**38**	**22**	**16**
England and Wales	23	13	10
Scotland	13	8	5
Northern Ireland	2	1	1
II.—OTHER EUROPEAN COUNTRIES (Continental Europe). ..	**30**	**15**	**15**
Belgium	3	..	3
Germany	2	..	2
Greece	2	2	..
Italy	9	..	9

IMPERIAL TABLE VI.—(*cont.*)

BIRTH PLACE.

BIRTH PLACE	POPULATION		
	Persons	Males	Females
1	2	3	4
II.—OTHER EUROPEAN COUNTRIES (Continental Europe).—*cont.*			
Spain	11	10	1
Switzerland	1	1	..
Turkey	2	2	..
D.—BORN IN AFRICA (British Dominions.) ..	5	3	2
East Africa	4	2	2
Natal (South Africa)	1	1	..
E.—BORN IN AMERICA (Outside British Dominions.) ..	3	1	2
United States	3	1	2
F.—BORN IN AUSTRALASIA (Within British Dominions.) ..	4	1	3
New Zealand	2	..	2
Sumatra	2	1	1
G.—BORN AT SEA ..	1	..	1
Persian Gulf	1	..	1

TABLE VII.*

AGE, SEX AND CIVIL CONDITION.

Note:—This table has two parts A and B. Part A contains the State summary wherein statistics for every religion returned are given separately.

Part B deals with the four Municipal Towns and gives separate statistics for Hindus, Muslims and Christians only. *Others* comprise the remaining religions.

IMPERIAL TABLE VII.

PART A.—AGE, SEX AND CIVIL CONDITION.

1. ALL RELIGIONS.

Age	Population			Unmarried *			Married			Widowed		
	Persons	Males	Females	Persons	Males	Females	Persons	Males	Females	Persons	Males	Females
1	2	3	4	5	6	7	8	9	10	11	12	13
0— 1	40,043	20,083	19,960	40,043	20,083	19,960	..	..	..	..	..	..
1— 2	44,940	22,477	22,463	44,940	22,477	22,463	..	..	..	..	..	..
2— 3	41,802	20,933	20,869	41,802	20,933	20,869	..	..	..	..	..	..
3— 4	37,072	18,629	18,443	37,072	18,629	18,443	..	..	..	..	..	..
4— 5	34,240	17,304	16,936	34,238	17,304	16,934	1	..	1	1	..	1
Total 0— 5	198,097	99,426	98,671	198,095	99,426	98,669	1	..	1	1	..	1
5—10	156,302	79,218	77,084	155,746	79,195	76,551	534	22	512	22	1	21
10—15	148,115	74,899	73,216	142,762	74,607	68,155	5,134	249	4,885	219	13	206
15—20	117,905	55,964	61,941	74,518	47,350	27,168	41,171	8,307	32,864	2,216	307	1,909
20—25	108,729	49,736	58,993	41,905	30,630	11,275	62,990	18,413	44,577	3,834	693	3,141
25—30	91,521	42,145	49,376	9,807	7,686	2,121	75,276	33,282	41,994	6,438	1,177	5,261
30—35	84,494	40,050	44,444	5,006	3,705	1,301	71,793	35,092	36,701	7,695	1,253	6,442
35—40	69,702	34,646	35,056	2,012	1,325	687	57,476	31,849	25,627	10,304	1,562	8,742
40—45	61,286	30,793	30,493	1,441	896	545	48,574	28,186	20,388	11,271	1,711	9,560
45—50	47,363	23,748	23,615	865	549	316	33,801	21,170	12,631	12,697	2,029	10,668
50—55	40,625	20,478	20,147	658	429	229	27,074	17,800	9,274	12,893	2,249	10,644
55—60	29,219	14,448	14,771	356	225	131	16,258	11,797	4,461	12,605	2,426	10,179
60—65	23,256	11,174	12,082	255	160	95	11,593	8,768	2,825	11,408	2,246	9,162
65—70	12,410	5,871	6,539	114	79	35	5,142	4,191	951	7,154	1,601	5,553
70 and over	15,902	7,157	8,745	129	89	40	4,946	4,313	633	10,827	2,764	8,063
Grand total	1,205,016	589,813	615,203	633,669	346,342	287,327	461,763	223,439	238,324	109,584	20,032	89,552

2. HINDU.

Age	Persons	Males	Females	Persons	Males	Females	Persons	Males	Females	Persons	Males	Females
0— 1	25,406	12,645	12,761	25,406	12,645	12,761	..	..	..	..	..	..
1— 2	28,741	14,282	14,459	28,741	14,282	14,459	..	..	..	..	..	..
2— 3	26,741	13,308	13,433	26,741	13,308	13,433	..	..	..	..	..	..
3— 4	23,467	11,777	11,690	23,467	11,777	11,690	..	..	..	..	..	..
4— 5	21,606	10,925	10,681	21,604	10,925	10,679	1	..	1	1	..	1
Total 0— 5	125,961	62,937	63,024	125,959	62,937	63,022	1	..	1	1	..	1
5—10	98,770	50,177	48,593	98,337	50,168	48,169	417	8	409	16	1	15
10—15	93,838	47,514	46,324	89,963	47,351	42,612	3,697	154	3,543	178	9	169
15—20	75,492	35,365	40,127	47,002	30,107	16,895	26,648	5,000	21,648	1,842	258	1,584
20—25	70,234	31,535	38,699	26,721	19,572	7,149	40,394	11,379	29,015	3,119	584	2,535
25—30	60,100	27,257	32,843	6,520	5,149	1,371	48,572	21,175	27,397	5,008	933	4,075
30—35	55,628	25,972	29,656	3,390	2,571	819	46,434	22,457	23,977	5,804	944	4,860
35—40	46,388	22,703	23,685	1,318	923	395	37,526	20,681	16,845	7,544	1,129	6,415
40—45	40,818	20,183	20,635	925	623	302	31,724	18,384	13,340	8,169	1,174	6,995
45—50	31,703	15,619	16,084	535	378	157	22,037	13,891	8,146	9,131	1,350	7,781
50—55	27,250	13,458	13,792	409	289	120	17,639	11,689	5,950	9,202	1,480	7,722
55—60	19,648	9,452	10,196	225	151	74	10,516	7,699	2,817	8,907	1,602	7,305
60—65	15,768	7,344	8,424	167	111	56	7,540	5,746	1,794	8,061	1,487	6,574
65—70	8,359	3,842	4,517	75	51	24	3,342	2,755	587	4,942	1,036	3,906
70 and over	10,527	4,575	5,952	74	47	27	3,204	2,827	377	7,249	1,701	5,548
Grand total	780,484	377,933	402,551	401,620	220,430	181,190	299,691	143,845	155,846	79,173	13,658	65,515

3. MUSLIM.

Age	Persons	Males	Females	Persons	Males	Females	Persons	Males	Females	Persons	Males	Females
0— 1	2,822	1,462	1,360	2,822	1,462	1,360	..	..	..	..	..	..
1— 2	3,268	1,656	1,612	3,268	1,656	1,612	..	..	..	..	..	..
2— 3	3,127	1,596	1,531	3,127	1,596	1,531	..	..	..	..	..	..
3— 4	2,810	1,436	1,374	2,810	1,436	1,374	..	..	..	..	..	..
4— 5	2,664	1,360	1,304	2,664	1,360	1,304	..	..	..	..	..	..
Total 0— 5	14,691	7,510	7,181	14,691	7,510	7,181	..	..	..	..	..	..
5—10	11,905	6,110	5,795	11,843	6,102	5,741	59	8	51	3	..	3
10—15	11,191	5,766	5,425	10,696	5,743	4,953	473	23	450	22	..	22
15—20	8,945	4,386	4,559	5,434	3,761	1,673	3,304	598	2,706	207	27	180
20—25	8,369	3,950	4,419	3,072	2,520	552	4,961	1,378	3,583	336	52	284
25—30	7,013	3,368	3,645	763	689	74	5,742	2,588	3,154	508	91	417
30—35	6,403	3,223	3,180	335	295	40	5,486	2,832	2,654	582	96	486
35—40	5,045	2,707	2,338	90	71	19	4,247	2,533	1,714	708	103	605
40—45	4,255	2,323	1,932	54	40	14	3,463	2,177	1,286	738	106	632
45—50	3,062	1,685	1,377	30	21	9	2,253	1,553	700	779	111	668
50—55	2,481	1,367	1,114	26	21	5	1,685	1,231	454	770	115	655
55—60	1,722	921	801	16	12	4	993	795	198	713	114	599
60—65	1,306	683	623	7	4	3	694	577	117	605	102	503
65—70	657	363	294	3	2	1	327	288	39	327	73	254
70 and over	857	432	425	3	2	1	320	293	27	534	137	397
Grand total	87,902	44,794	43,108	47,063	26,793	20,270	34,007	16,874	17,133	6,832	1,127	5,705

IMPERIAL TABLE VII—(*cont.*)

PART A.—AGE, SEX AND CIVIL CONDITION.

4. CHRISTIAN.

Age	Population			Unmarried			Married			Widowed		
	Persons	Males	Females	Persons	Males	Females	Persons	Males	Females	Persons	Males	Femaels
1	2	3	4	5	6	7	8	9	10	11	12	13
0—1	11,763	5,950	5,813	11,763	5,950	5,813	..	..	..	..	..	..
1—2	12,881	6,509	6,372	12,881	6,509	6,372	..	..	..	..	..	..
2—3	11,881	5,999	5,882	11,881	5,999	5,882	..	..	..	..	..	..
3—4	10,752	5,392	5,360	10,752	5,392	5,360	...	..	..	..	..	..
4—5	9,918	4,991	4,927	9,918	4,991	4,927	..	..	..	..	.	..
Total 0—5	57,195	28,841	28,354	57,195	28,841	28,354	..	..	..	..	..	..
5—10	45,410	22,819	22,591	45,349	22,813	22,536	58	6	52	3	..	3
10—15	42,883	21,490	21,393	41,905	21,414	20,491	960	72	888	18	4	14
15—20	33,305	16,139	17,166	21,971	13,411	8,560	11,168	2,706	8,462	166	22	144
20—25	29,958	14,176	15,782	12,035	8,480	3,555	17,547	5,639	11,908	376	57	319
25—30	24,278	11,454	12,824	2,501	1,830	671	20,860	9,473	11,387	917	151	766
30—35	22,349	10,798	11,551	1,268	832	436	19,779	9,755	10,024	1,302	211	1,091
35—40	18,243	9,271	8,972	596	327	269	15,605	8,587	7,018	2,042	357	1,685
40—45	16,107	8,232	7,875	455	228	227	13,301	7,576	5,725	2,351	428	1,923
45—50	12,513	6,397	6,116	295	147	148	9,450	5,687	3,763	2,768	563	2,205
50—55	10,831	5,619	5,212	220	116	104	7,707	4,852	2,855	2,904	651	2,253
55—60	7,798	4,046	3,752	115	62	53	4,717	3,279	1,438	2,966	705	2,261
60—65	6,139	3,122	3,017	81	45	36	3,336	2,426	910	2,722	651	2,071
65—70	3,370	1,655	1,715	36	26	10	1,464	1,141	323	1,870	488	1,382
70 and over	4,491	2,136	2,355	51	31	20	1,414	1,185	229	3,026	920	2,106
Grand total	334,870	166,195	168,675	184,073	98,603	85,470	127,366	62,384	64,982	23,431	5,208	18,223

5. JAIN.

Age	Population			Unmarried			Married			Widowed		
	Persons	Males	Females	Persons	Males	Females	Persons	Males	Females	Persons	Males	Femaels
0—1	5	2	3	5	2	3	..	..	..	..	..	..
1—2	5	4	1	5	4	1	..	..	..	..	..	..
2—3	6	4	2	6	4	2	..	..	..	..	..	..
3—4	6	3	3	6	3	3	..	..	..	..	..	..
4—	7	3	4	7	3	4	..	..	..	..	..	..
Total 0—5	29	16	13	29	16	13	..	..	..	..	..	..
5—10	28	14	14	28	14	14	..	..	..	..	..	..
10—15	22	12	10	21	12	9	1	..	1	..	..	..
15—20	16	7	9	7	7	..	8	..	8	1	..	1
20—25	22	9	13	6	6	..	15	3	12	1	..	1
25—30	24	14	10	4	4	..	19	9	10	1	1	..
30—35	21	15	6	3	3	..	17	12	5	1	..	1
35—40	15	12	3	1	1	..	13	11	2	1	..	1
40—45	13	9	4	..	..	..	10	8	2	3	1	2
45—50	9	5	4	..	..	..	3	3	..	6	2	4
50—55	3	1	2	..	..	..	1	1	..	2	..	2
55—60	2	1	1	..	..	..	..	..	..	2	1	1
60—65	2	1	1	..	..	..	..	..	..	2	1	1
65—70	2	1	1	..	..	..	..	..	..	2	1	1
70 and over	2	1	1	..	..	..	..	..	..	2	1	1
Grand total	210	118	92	99	63	36	87	47	40	24	8	16

6. JEW.

Age	Population			Unmarried			Married			Widowed		
	Persons	Males	Females	Persons	Males	Females	Persons	Males	Females	Persons	Males	Femaels
0—1	41	20	21	41	20	21	..	..	..	..	..	..
1—2	42	24	18	42	24	18	..	..	..	..	..	..
2—3	45	24	21	45	24	21	..	..	..	..	..	..
3—4	36	20	16	36	20	16	..	..	..	..	..	..
4—5	40	23	17	40	23	17	..	..	..	..	..	..
Total 0—5	204	111	93	204	111	93	..	..	..	...	..	..
5—10	177	93	84	177	93	84	..	..	..	..	..	..
10—15	164	80	84	160	80	80	3	..	3	1	..	1
15—20	137	61	76	96	58	38	41	3	38	...	..	..
20—25	135	58	77	64	45	19	70	13	57	1	..	1
25—30	95	47	48	15	11	4	77	35	42	3	1	2
30—35	86	40	46	8	3	5	73	35	38	5	2	3
35—40	95	40	55	6	2	4	80	35	45	9	3	6
40—45	91	44	47	7	3	4	74	39	35	10	2	8
45—50	73	40	33	5	3	2	55	34	21	13	3	10
50—55	58	33	25	3	3	..	42	27	15	13	3	10
55—60	48	27	21	..	..	..	31	23	8	17	4	13
60—65	41	24	17	..	..	..	23	19	4	18	5	13
65—70	22	10	12	..	..	..	9	7	2	13	3	10
70 and over	25	13	12	1	..	1	8	8	...	16	5	11
Grand Total	1,451	721	730	746	412	334	586	278	308	119	31	88

IMPERIAL TABLE VII—(*cont.*)

PART A.—AGE, SEX AND CIVIL CONDITION.

7. BUDDHIST.

Age	Population			Unmarried			Married			Widowed		
	Persons	Males	Females	Persons	Males	Females	Persons	Males	Females	Persons	Males	Females
1	2	3	4	5	6	7	8	9	10	11	12	13
0—1	6	4	2	6	4	2	..	..	..	..	..	..
1—2	3	2	1	3	2	1	..	..	..	..	..	..
2—3	2	2	..	2	2	..	..	..	..	..	..	..
3—4	1	1	..	1	1	..	..	..	..	..	..	..
4—5	5	2	3	5	2	3	..	..	..	..	..	..
Total 0—5	17	11	6	17	11	6	..	..	..	..	..	..
5—10	12	5	7	12	5	7	..	..	..	..	..	..
10—15	17	7	10	17	7	10	..	..	..	..	..	..
15—20	9	6	3	8	6	2	1	..	1	..	..	..
20—25	11	8	3	7	7	..	3	1	2	1	..	1
25—30	11	5	6	4	3	1	6	2	4	1	..	1
30—35	7	2	5	2	1	1	4	1	3	1	..	1
35—40	5	2	3	1	1	..	4	1	3	..	..	..
40—45	2	2	..	..	..	..	2	2	..	..	..	..
45—50	3	2	1	..	..	..	3	2	1	..	..	..
50—55	1	..	1	..	..	..	..	..	..	1	..	1
55—60	1	1	..	..	..	..	1	1	..	..	..	..
60—65	..	..	..	..	..	..	..	..	..	..	..	..
65—70	..	..	..	..	..	..	..	..	..	..	..	..
70 and over	..	..	..	..	..	..	..	..	..	..	..	..
Grand total	96	51	45	68	41	27	24	10	14	4	..	4

8. ZOROASTRIAN.

Age	Population			Unmarried			Married			Widowed		
	Persons	Males	Females	Persons	Males	Females	Persons	Males	Females	Persons	Males	Females
0—1	..	..	..	..	..	..	..	..	..	..	..	..
1—2	..	..	..	..	..	..	..	..	..	..	..	..
2—3	..	..	..	..	..	..	..	..	..	..	..	..
3—4	..	..	..	..	..	..	..	..	..	..	..	..
4—5	..	..	..	..	..	..	..	..	..	..	..	..
Total 0—5	..	..	..	..	..	..	..	..	..	..	..	..
5—10	..	..	..	..	..	..	..	..	..	..	..	..
10—15	..	..	..	..	..	..	..	..	..	..	..	..
15—20	1	..	1	..	..	..	1	..	1	..	..	..
20—25	..	..	..	..	..	..	..	..	..	..	..	..
25—30	..	..	..	..	..	..	..	..	..	..	..	..
30—35	..	..	..	..	..	..	..	..	..	..	..	..
35—40	1	1	..	..	..	..	1	1	..	..	..	..
40—45	..	..	..	..	..	..	..	..	..	..	..	..
45—50	..	..	..	..	..	..	..	..	..	..	..	..
50—55	1	..	1	..	..	..	..	..	..	1	..	1
55—60	..	..	..	..	..	..	..	..	..	..	..	..
60—65	..	..	..	..	..	..	..	..	..	..	..	..
65—70	..	..	..	..	..	..	..	..	..	..	..	..
70 and over	..	..	..	..	..	..	..	..	..	..	..	..
Grand total	3	1	2	..	..	..	2	1	1	1	..	1

IMPERIAL TABLE VII.

PART B.—AGE, SEX AND CIVIL CONDITION.

1. ALL RELIGIONS.

Age	Population			Unmarried			Married			Widowed		
	Persons	Males	Females	Persons	Males	Females	Persons	Males	Females	Persons	Males	Females
1	2	3	4	5	6	7	8	9	10	11	12	13
0—1	4,023	1,996	2,027	4,023	1,996	2,027	..	..	..	..	..	..
1—2	4,448	2,240	2,208	4,448	2,240	2,208	..	..	..	..	..	..
2—3	4,368	2,214	2,154	4,368	2,214	2,154	..	..	..	..	..	..
3—4	4,011	2,008	2,003	4,011	2,008	2,003	..	..	..	..	..	..
4—5	3,791	1,905	1,886	3,789	1,905	1,884	1	..	1	1	..	1
Total 0—5	20,641	10,363	10,278	20,639	10,363	10,276	1	..	1	1	..	1
5—10	17,329	8,807	8,522	17,215	8,801	8,414	110	6	104	4	..	4
10—15	16,602	8,570	8,032	15,818	8,543	7,275	761	25	736	23	2	21
15—20	14,812	7,779	7,033	9,777	6,795	2,982	4,813	955	3,858	222	29	193
20—25	14,077	7,239	6,838	6,519	5,050	1,469	7,151	2,126	5,025	407	63	344
25—30	11,381	5,741	5,640	1,810	1,476	334	8,803	4,126	4,677	768	139	629
30—35	10,417	5,310	5,107	970	755	215	8,498	4,395	4,103	949	160	789
35—40	8,492	4,460	4,032	392	271	121	6,830	3,976	2,854	1,270	213	1,057
40—45	7,539	4,040	3,499	295	194	101	5,841	3,607	2,234	1,403	239	1,164
45—50	5,742	3,037	2,705	179	117	62	3,989	2,657	1,332	1,574	263	1,311
50—55	4,758	2,493	2,265	126	87	39	3,081	2,135	946	1,551	271	1,280
55—60	3,283	1,640	1,643	72	51	21	1,771	1,320	451	1,440	269	1,171
60—65	2,606	1,276	1,330	56	39	17	1,258	980	278	292	257	1,035
65—70	1,380	671	709	21	17	4	570	477	93	789	177	612
70 and over	1,797	822	975	26	17	9	563	497	66	1,208	308	900
Grand total	140,856	72,248	68,608	73,915	42,576	31,339	54,040	27,282	26,758	12,901	2,390	10,511

2. HINDU.

Age	Population			Unmarried			Married			Widowed		
	Persons	Males	Females	Persons	Males	Females	Persons	Males	Females	Persons	Males	Females
0—1	1,986	965	1,021	1,986	965	1,021	..	..	..	..	..	..
1—2	2,234	1,114	1,120	2,234	1,114	1,120	..	..	..	..	..	..
2—3	2,217	1,119	1,098	2,217	1,119	1,098	..	..	..	..	..	..
3—4	2,024	1,007	1,017	2,024	1,007	1,017	..	..	..	..	..	..
4—5	1,914	958	956	1,912	958	954	1	..	1	1	..	1
Total 0—5	10,375	5,163	5,212	10,373	5,163	5,210	1	..	1	1	..	1
5—10	8,763	4,471	4,292	8,675	4,470	4,205	86	1	85	2	..	2
10—15	8,385	4,395	3,990	7,851	4,385	3,466	520	9	511	14	1	13
15—20	7,630	4,106	3,524	4,794	3,586	1,208	2,694	502	2,192	142	18	124
20—25	7,320	3,842	3,478	3,270	2,687	583	3,798	1,113	2,685	252	42	210
25—30	5,949	3,041	2,908	951	815	136	4,532	2,140	2,392	466	86	380
30—35	5,502	2,827	2,675	526	441	85	4,410	2,288	2,122	566	98	468
35—40	4,557	2,415	2,142	205	168	37	3,608	2,115	1,493	744	132	612
40—45	4,042	2,188	1,854	148	118	30	3,065	1,930	1,135	829	140	689
45—50	3,114	1,638	1,476	81	67	14	2,087	1,420	667	946	151	795
50—55	2,619	1,353	1,266	59	51	8	1,634	1,144	490	926	158	768
55—60	1,833	894	939	36	32	4	946	708	238	851	154	697
60—65	1,460	695	765	31	27	4	670	523	147	759	145	614
65—70	766	368	398	10	9	1	304	260	44	452	99	353
70 and over	973	435	538	11	8	3	292	264	28	670	163	507
Grand total	73,288	37,831	35,457	37,021	22,027	14,994	28,647	14,417	14,230	7,620	1,387	6,233

3 MUSLIM.

Age	Population			Unmarried			Married			Widowed		
	Persons	Males	Females	Persons	Males	Females	Persons	Males	Females	Persons	Males	Females
0—1	343	182	161	343	182	161	..	..	..	..	..	..
1—2	408	212	196	408	212	196	..	..	..	..	..	..
2—3	406	215	191	406	215	191	..	..	..	..	..	..
3—4	387	201	186	387	201	186	..	..	..	..	..	..
4—5	381	193	188	381	193	188	..	..	..	..	..	..
Total 0—5	1,925	1,003	922	1,925	1,003	922	..	..	..	..	..	..
5—10	1,747	902	845	1,727	900	827	19	2	17	1	..	1
10—15	1,702	890	812	1,576	885	691	121	5	116	5	..	5
15—20	1,653	861	792	943	735	208	666	120	546	44	6	38
20—25	1,703	870	833	651	579	72	974	278	696	78	13	65
25—30	1,475	772	703	204	191	13	1,144	557	587	127	24	103
30—35	1,325	722	603	94	88	6	1,094	610	484	137	24	113
35—40	1,012	586	426	27	23	4	827	537	290	158	26	132
40—45	837	503	334	19	14	5	653	459	194	165	30	135
45—50	570	339	231	13	9	4	404	305	99	153	25	128
50—55	434	256	178	9	8	1	285	229	56	140	19	121
55—60	289	150	139	6	4	2	156	131	25	127	15	112
60—65	223	115	108	3	1	2	114	96	18	106	18	88
65—70	110	66	44	1	1	..	57	52	5	52	13	39
70 and over	156	81	75	1	1	..	62	57	5	93	23	70
Grand total	15,161	8,116	7,045	7,199	4,442	2,757	6,576	3,438	3,138	1,386	236	1,150

IMPERIAL TABLE VII—(*cont.*)

PART B.—AGE, SEX AND CIVIL CONDITION.

4. CHRISTIAN.

Age	Population			Unmarried			Married			Widowed		
	Persons	Males	Females	Persons	Males	Females	Persons	Males	Females	Persons	Males	Females
1	2	3	4	5	6	7	8	9	10	11	12	13
0— 1	1,661	831	827	1,661	831	827	..	..	..	..	..	..
1— 2	1,772	895	877	1,772	895	877	..	..	..	..	..	..
2— 3	1,707	860	847	1,707	860	847	..	..	..	..	..	..
3— 4	1,566	781	785	1,566	781	785	..	..	..	..	..	..
4— 5	1,461	735	726	1,461	735	726	..	..	..	..	..	..
Total 0— 5	8,167	4,105	4,062	8,167	4,105	4,062	..	..	..	..	..	..
5—10	6,661	3,353	3,308	6,655	3,350	3,305	5	3	2	1	..	1
10—15	6,369	3,213	3,156	6,248	3,201	3,047	118	11	107	3	1	2
15—20	5,404	2,756	2,648	3,954	2,419	1,535	1,415	332	1,083	35	5	30
20—25	4,924	2,472	2,452	2,537	1,739	798	2,312	725	1,587	75	8	67
25—30	3,860	1,875	1,985	637	455	182	3,051	1,392	1,659	172	28	144
30—35	3,502	1,717	1,785	339	220	119	2,924	1,461	1,463	239	36	203
35—40	2,836	1,420	1,416	154	78	76	2,323	1,289	1,034	359	53	306
40—45	2,575	1,306	1,269	121	59	62	2,057	1,181	876	397	66	331
45—50	1,992	1,025	967	80	38	42	1,453	903	550	459	84	375
50—55	1,656	857	799	56	26	30	1,129	740	389	471	91	380
55—60	1,126	577	549	30	15	15	649	466	183	447	96	351
60—65	892	450	442	22	11	11	459	349	110	411	90	321
65—70	486	228	258	10	7	3	201	159	42	275	62	213
70 and over	647	295	352	13	8	5	204	171	33	430	116	314
Grand total	51,097	25,949	25,148	29,023	15,731	13,292	18,300	9,182	9,118	3,774	736	3,038

5. OTHERS.

Age	Population			Unmarried			Married			Widowed		
	Persons	Males	Females	Persons	Males	Females	Persons	Males	Females	Persons	Males	Females
0— 1	33	15	18	33	15	18	..	..	..	..	..	..
1— 2	34	19	15	34	19	15	..	..	..	..	..	..
2— 3	38	20	18	38	20	18	..	..	..	..	..	..
3— 4	34	19	15	34	19	15	..	..	..	..	..	..
4— 5	35	19	16	35	19	16	..	..	..	..	..	..
Total 0— 5	174	92	82	174	92	82	..	..	..	..	..	..
5—10	158	81	77	158	81	77	..	..	..	..	..	..
10—15	146	72	74	143	72	71	2	..	2	1	..	1
15—20	125	56	69	86	55	31	38	1	37	1	..	1
20—25	130	55	75	61	45	16	67	10	57	2	..	2
25—30	97	53	44	18	15	3	76	37	39	3	1	2
30—35	88	44	44	11	6	5	70	36	34	7	2	5
35—40	87	39	48	6	2	4	72	35	37	9	2	7
40—45	85	43	42	7	3	4	66	37	29	12	3	9
45—50	66	35	31	5	3	2	45	29	16	16	3	13
50—55	49	27	22	2	2	..	33	22	11	14	3	11
55—60	35	19	16	..	..	..	20	15	5	15	4	11
60—65	31	16	15	..	..	..	15	12	3	16	4	12
65—70	18	9	9	..	..	..	8	6	2	10	3	7
70 and over	21	11	10	1	..	1	5	5	..	15	6	9
Grand total	1,310	652	658	672	376	296	517	245	272	121	31	90

TABLE VIII.

CIVIL CONDITION BY AGE FOR SELECTED CASTES.

Note.—While in Table VII—Part A—the whole population is dealt with, this Table deals only with selected castes, the minor ones being left out of account.

IMPERIAL

CIVIL CONDITION BY AGE

CASTE, TRIBE OR RACE	Sex	Population dealt with	Unmarried							
			Total	0–6	7–13	14–16	17–23	24–43	44 and over	Total
1	2	3	4	5	6	7	8	9	10	11
HINDU										
Ambalavasi	Males ..	**4,538**	2,864	882	755	295	471	402	59	1,456
	Females	**4,673**	1,958	842	678	225	143	56	14	1,702
Ambattan	Males ..	**776**	451	172	128	51	72	25	3	292
	Females	**794**	331	149	130	32	15	6	..	351
Arayan	Males ..	**3,457**	2,008	651	595	247	395	116	4	1,299
	Females	**3,117**	1,450	666	525	176	74	7	2	1,282
Brahman-Konkani	Males ..	**4,828**	2,587	881	806	326	388	141	45	2,046
	Females	**4,833**	1,686	909	747	14	10	4	2	2,171
Do Malayali	Males ..	**3,863**	1,922	526	481	256	336	249	74	1,640
	Females	**3,500**	1,305	509	459	158	136	41	2	1,401
Do Tamil	Males ..	**10,884**	6,327	2,318	2,173	770	829	207	30	4,202
	Females	**10,870**	4,161	2,297	1,775	70	12	5	2	4,976
Chakkan	Males ..	**1,085**	585	177	169	72	112	56	2	443
	Females	**1,097**	434	214	159	37	21	3	..	474
Chaliyan — Chaliyan	Males ..	**205**	122	76	41	10	24	10	1	72
	Females	**192**	84	44	20	12	7	1	..	72
Chaliyan — Pattarian	Males ..	**927**	532	202	157	53	84	34	2	356
	Females	**904**	471	205	155	57	45	8	1	393
Eluthassan	Males ..	**9,026**	5,070	1,863	1,542	649	828	185	12	3,631
	Females	**9,510**	4,150	1,839	1,544	490	218	51	8	3,750
Iluvan	Males ..	**132,875**	78,333	28,561	24,691	10,049	11,676	3,078	178	50,366
	Females	**143,774**	68,888	28,643	24,092	9,058	5,596	1,306	193	54,132
Kaikolan	Males ..	**1,820**	942	306	312	97	158	55	14	759
	Females	**1,894**	678	280	293	73	30	4	2	800
Kammalan	Males ..	**22,085**	12,693	4,597	3,876	1,708	2,021	478	19	8,784
	Females	**23,461**	11,123	4,527	3,741	1,328	890	280	57	9,058
Kanakkan	Males ..	**6,567**	3,776	1,459	1,336	192	533	149	7	2,539
	Females	**6,825**	3,224	1,448	1,135	368	211	56	6	2,613
Kaniyan	Males ..	**1,950**	1,152	384	321	157	216	67	7	725
	Females	**1,891**	855	318	285	128	114	35	5	694
Kshatriya-Malayali	Males ..	**673**	437	166	104	37	68	52	10	205
	Females	**794**	350	147	129	42	27	4	1	314
Kudumi Chetti	Males ..	**8,216**	4,198	1,618	1,297	475	603	196	9	3,713
	Females	**7,888**	2,636	1,675	882	32	22	16	9	3,697
Kusavan	Males ..	**1,880**	829	342	112	79	82	13	1	767
	Females	**1,885**	652	359	206	60	18	6	3	779
Nayar	Males ..	**86,225**	42,568	14,125	11,714	4,829	7,050	4,346	504	20,559
	Females	**78,412**	37,850	17,736	11,485	4,083	3,293	1,132	121	26,015
Pandaran	Males ..	**2,384**	1,256	471	391	162	150	44	25	1,017
	Females	**2,476**	1,021	466	391	109	45	10	..	1,061
Pandittattan	Males ..	**1,549**	502	123	238	101	167	66	7	596
	Females	**1,415**	547	273	198	50	23	2	1	618

TABLE VIII.

FOR SELECTED CASTES.

Married						Widowed						
0—6	7—13	14—16	17—23	24—43	44 and over	Total	0—6	7—13	14—16	17—23	24—43	44 and over
12	13	14	15	16	17	18	19	20	21	22	23	24
..	..	2	53	784	617	218	..	..	..	3	66	149
..	6	74	377	936	309	1,013	..	..	3	44	303	663
..	..	..	35	162	96	33	..	..	..	1	11	22
..	3	26	84	198	40	112	..	..	1	6	42	63
..	..	..	59	769	471	150	..	..	..	3	58	89
..	..	37	111	749	185	385	..	..	1	13	98	273
..	..	6	160	1,053	827	195	..	..	..	1	34	160
1	16	249	561	1,023	291	976	..	1	2	29	275	669
..	..	..	92	801	747	101	..	..	..	..	28	73
..	4	43	246	801	307	794	..	..	..	13	175	606
..	1	7	251	2,097	1,844	357	..	..	..	7	49	301
..	150	530	1,151	2,283	862	1,733	1	..	10	65	433	1,204
..	..	1	21	267	154	34	..	..	..	..	11	23
..	5	32	123	247	67	189	..	..	..	3	63	123
..	..	..	7	36	29	11	..	..	..	..	3	8
..	..	3	21	74	14	36	..	..	..	1	11	24
..	..	..	20	208	128	39	..	..	..	1	13	25
..	..	9	85	227	72	130	..	..	..	4	40	86
..	..	4	238	2,130	1,259	316	..	..	..	19	87	210
..	10	160	902	2,127	551	1,610	..	..	11	90	466	1,043
..	5	88	3,623	29,515	17,135	4,176	..	..	4	181	1,187	2,804
..	98	1,409	12,597	31,852	8,180	20,754	..	2	80	869	6,743	13,040
..	..	1	67	461	230	119	..	..	..	4	42	73
..	10	72	218	393	107	416	..	..	..	12	138	266
..	3	80	627	5,125	3,009	602	..	..	..	28	172	402
..	29	290	2,238	5,110	1,391	1,280	..	2	14	111	987	2,165
..	1	3	178	1,572	785	252	..	..	1	9	68	174
..	6	73	618	1,569	347	788	..	..	3	30	257	498
..	..	..	49	375	301	73	..	..	..	..	19	54
..	..	12	146	398	138	212	..	..	1	14	96	201
..	1	..	..	102	102	31	..	..	..	..	8	23
..	1	7	74	178	54	130	..	..	1	2	34	93
..	..	15	425	2,148	1,125	305	..	..	..	7	107	191
..	167	474	1,060	1,675	321	1,555	..	1	20	75	573	886
..	..	13	128	395	231	94	..	..	..	4	36	54
..	26	65	182	403	103	174	..	..	..	9	50	115
..	2	17	558	11,631	8,291	2,798	..	..	..	25	847	1,926
..	65	376	5,766	14,953	4,355	16,547	..	5	54	754	5,656	10,078
..	..	2	87	605	323	81	..	..	..	9	25	47
..	21	78	258	561	143	394	..	..	1	9	116	268
..	..	..	33	355	200	51	..	1	..	2	9	30
..	1	24	179	329	85	250	..	..	1	7	68	174

IMPERIAL

CIVIL CONDITION BY AGE

CASTE, TRIBE OR RACE	Sex	Population dealt with	Unmarried							
			Total	0—6	7—13	14—16	17—23	24—43	44 and over	Total
1	2	3	4	5	6	7	8	9	10	11
Pulayan ..	Males ..	**39,982**	21,815	8,692	7,253	2,788	2,463	578	41	16,772
	Females	**42,061**	18,764	8,933	6,805	1,906	862	214	44	17,561
Sambavan (Parayan)	Males ..	**5,734**	3,004	1,228	978	412	293	82	11	2,505
	Females	**5,828**	2,670	1,298	928	277	129	35	3	2,500
Valan ..	Males ..	**5,979**	3,645	1,328	1,088	397	582	240	10	2,101
	Females	**5,705**	2,801	1,327	1,606	300	141	21	6	2,377
Velakkattalavan ..	Males ..	**1,815**	1,114	297	328	132	154	99	4	617
	Females	**1,884**	790	318	287	77	52	21	5	683
Velan ..	Males ..	**5,205**	2,351	1,043	932	371	371	113	24	2,136
	Females	**5,090**	2,509	1,107	869	330	163	29	11	2,294
Vellalam ..	Males ..	**2,629**	1,467	431	478	169	267	151	11	1,023
	Famales	**2,670**	1,042	449	436	107	44	4	2	1,044
Veluttedan ..	Males ..	**1,816**	1,053	386	310	144	152	60	1	669
	Females	**2,106**	847	349	306	102	68	17	5	769
Vettuvan ..	Males ..	**5,943**	3,382	1,338	1,107	404	420	109	4	2,362
	Females	**5,854**	2,817	1,350	982	333	127	21	4	2,133
MUSLIM										
Jonakan ..	Males ..	**29,150**	17,407	6,287	5,300	2,184	2,631	954	51	10,995
	Females	**28,221**	13,327	6,020	4,865	1,605	683	130	24	11,323
Ravuttan ..	Males ..	**5,633**	3,300	1,153	1,089	405	525	125	3	2,209
	Females	**5,294**	2,276	1,089	950	164	60	12	1	2,140
Others ..	Males ..	**10,011**	6,086	2,105	1,744	761	1,017	440	19	3,670
	Females	**9,583**	4,667	2,031	1,766	557	274	46	3	3,670
CHRISTIAN										
Anglo Indian ..	Males ..	**820**	534	172	158	67	86	40	11	260
	Females	**897**	507	161	155	64	80	31	16	290
European ..	Males ..	**58**	34	3	4	...	5	13	9	24
	Females	**54**	37	5	3	2	5	19	3	14
Indian Christian ..	Males ..	**1,65,317**	98,035	36,146	30,498	12,104	14,560	4,262	465	62,100
	Females	**1,67,724**	84,926	35,374	30,139	10,618	6,351	1,826	418	64,678
JAIN ..	Males ..	**118**	63	30	19	5	9	10	..	47
	Females	**92**	36	19	16	2	..	..	..	40
JEW ..	Males .	**721**	412	144	119	41	75	26	7	278
	Females	**730**	334	117	119	41	35	17	5	308

TABLE VIII—*cont.*

FOR SELECTED CASTES (*cont.*)

Married						Widowed						
0—6	7—13	14—16	17—23	24—43	44 and over	Total	0—6	7—13	14—16	17—23	24—43	44 and over
12	13	14	15	16	17	18	19	20	21	22	23	24
..	1	51	1,415	10,234	5,071	1,395	..	..	5	110	489	791
..	61	835	4,215	10,079	2,351	5,736	..	9	63	303	1,817	3,544
..	1	17	243	1,485	759	225	..	..	..	15	72	138
..	8	97	650	1,403	342	658	..	..	2	31	190	435
..	..	..	143	1,207	752	233	..	..	..	9	59	165
..	7	58	545	1,302	365	627	..	..	..	31	170	426
..	..	2	32	370	213	84	..	..	..	2	25	57
..	5	40	182	368	90	411	..	..	1	18	127	265
..	..	4	237	1,177	718	215	..	..	..	20	65	130
..	9	76	562	1,329	316	887	..	..	8	52	296	521
..	..	...	46	633	344	139	..	..	..	5	43	91
..	7	37	280	589	131	584	..	2	1	10	208	363
..	..	1	42	374	252	94	..	..	..	..	28	66
..	3	35	197	412	122	490	..	..	3	25	192	270
..	..	5	209	1,451	697	199	..	..	1	10	63	125
..	1	74	613	1,411	334	604	..	1	2	38	185	378
..	7	20	764	6,748	3,456	748	..	..	..	36	246	466
..	42	500	3,080	6,466	1,235	3,571	..	2	26	220	1,316	2,007
..	1	2	188	1,406	612	124	..	..	..	7	47	70
..	40	169	623	1,133	169	878	..	..	8	38	302	530
..	5	10	213	2,085	1,357	255	..	..	..	7	94	154
..	17	133	501	2,139	480	1,256	..	1	4	67	426	758
..	..	..	9	113	138	26	..	..	..	..	6	20
..	..	4	34	182	70	150	..	..	..	..	26	74
..	..	..	1	15	8	...	..	..	..	..	..	..
..	..	..	3	10	1	3	..	..	..	..	..	3
..	9	136	5,264	15,094	20,697	5,182	..	..	6	39	1,012	4,127
..	100	1,672	15,213	36,617	11,076	18,120	..	5	18	223	4,877	12,937
..	..	..	..	40	7	8	..	..	..	..	1	7
..	..	1	15	23	1	16	..	..	..	2	2	12
..	..	..	4	142	132	31	..	..	..	..	7	24
..	..	6	70	174	58	88	..	..	1	..	16	71

TABLE IX.

INFIRMITIES.

PART I—DISTRIBUTION BY AGE.

PART II—DISTRIBUTION BY TALUKS.

Note.—1. Of the lepers, 1 Muslim male and 1 Christian female are blind, 1 Hindu female deaf-mute and 1 Hindu male insane.

Of the insane, 1 Hindu male is blind and 1 Christian female deaf-mute.

2. Persons suffering from more infirmities than one are included under each head and the double infirmities are 6 in number.

TABLE IX.

INFIRMITIES—Part I.—Distribution by Age.

AGE	POPULATION AFFLICTED			INSANE			DEAF-MUTES			BLIND			LEPERS		
	Persons	Males	Females	Persons	Males	Females	Persons	Males	Females	Persons	Males	Females	Persons	Males	Females
1	2	3	4	5	6	7	8	9	10	11	12	13	14	15	16
0—1	5	4	1	..	..	..	1	1	..	4	3	1	..	..	..
1—2	7	4	3	1	..	1	2	1	1	4	3	1	..	..	..
2—3	10	7	3	2	2	..	4	3	1	3	1	2	1	1	..
3—4	17	10	7	1	1	..	9	6	3	7	3	4	..	..	..
4—5	27	16	11	1	1	..	12	8	4	12	6	6	2	1	1
Total 0—5	66	41	25	5	4	1	28	19	9	30	16	14	3	2	1
5—10	160	94	66	7	4	3	77	48	29	67	37	30	9	5	4
10—15	196	113	83	12	6	6	78	48	30	86	47	39	20	12	8
15—20	240	143	97	39	23	16	57	34	23	92	52	40	52	34	18
20—25	259	160	99	53	33	20	53	29	24	94	56	38	59	42	17
25—30	288	182	106	71	49	22	37	18	19	108	59	49	73	56	17
30—35	302	185	117	91	55	36	37	20	17	96	48	48	78	62	16
35—40	301	179	122	90	49	41	35	18	17	94	45	49	82	67	15
40—45	299	179	120	83	45	38	28	15	13	103	52	51	86	68	18
45—50	278	150	128	63	27	36	18	11	7	122	55	67*	76	57	19
50—55	249	139	110	40	18	22	18	11	7	122	59	63	70	52	18
55—60	223	118	105	27	15	12	9	4	5	131	58	73	56	41	15
60—65	208	95	113	26	15	11	8	4	4	135	48	87	40	28	12
65—70	133	57	76	12	7	5	4	3	1	104	39	65	13	8	5
70 and over	257	114	143	18	8	10	1	1	..	211	87	124	28	19	9
Total 5—70 and over ..	3,393	1,908	1,485	632	354	278	460	264	196	1,568	742	823	742	551	191
GRAND TOTAL	3,459	1,949	1,510	637	358	279	488	283	205	1,598	758	837	745	553	192

Part II.—Distribution by Taluks.

TALUK	POPULATION AFFLICTED			INSANE			DEAF-MUTES			BLIND			LEPERS		
	Persons	Males	Females	Persons	Males	Females	Persons	Males	Females	Persons	Males	Females	Persons	Males	Females
1	2	3	4	5	6	7	8	9	10	11	12	13	14	15	16
COCHIN STATE	3,459	1,949	1,510	637	358	279	488	283	205	1,595	758	837	745	553	192
Cochin Kanayannur	801	485	316	192	101	91	131	72	59	275	144	131	206	168	38
Cranganur	108	68	40	20	12	8	20	12	8	44	26	18	25	19	6
Mukundapuram	819	472	347	99	54	45	144	88	56	343	163	180	233	167	66
Trichur	824	441	383	200	122	78	108	65	43	443	199	244	73	55	18
Talapilli	696	373	323	78	44	34	68	39	29	364	161	203	187	130	57
Chittur	211	110	101	48	25	23	17	7	10	126	65	61	21	14	7

TABLE X.

OCCUPATION OR MEANS OF LIVELIHOOD.

GENERAL TABLE.

Note.—Orders and groups for which there are no figures have been omitted.

IMPERIAL TABLE X.

OCCUPATION OR MEANS OF LIVELIHOOD.

GENERAL TABLE.

Total earners	466,726
„ Working dependents	147,325
„ Non-working dependents	590,965
„ Population	1,205,016

Class	Sub-class	Order	Group	Occupation	Total following Occupation	As principal occupation		As working dependents		As subsidiary to other occupation	
						Males	Females	Males	Females	Males	Females
1	2	3	4	5	6	7	8	9	10	11	12
A PRODUCTION OF RAW MATERIALS.	I. EXPLOITATION OF ANIMALS AND VEGETATION.	1		**Pasture and Agriculture.**	281,185	151,450	88,999	3,632	3,319	29,027	4,788
		(a)		*CULTIVATION.*							
			1	Non-cultivating proprietors taking rent in money or kind ..	7,882	3,607	2,923	12	5	1,128	207
			2	Estate Agents and Managers of owners ..	645	470	7	10	1	151	6
			3	Estate Agents and Managers of Government ..	123	74	..	..	..	47	2
			4	Rent Collectors, Clerks, etc. ..	823	597	3	2	25	155	41
			5	Cultivating Owners ..	27,463	18,454	4,617	244	98	3,622	428
			6	Tenants.							
				(a) Cultivating Tenants ..	55,804	39,433	8,905	599	543	5,922	402
				(b) Non-cultivating Tenants ..	862	463	297	2	2	98	..
			7	Agricultural labourers ..	137,945	60,309	65,983	1,085	2,411	5,639	2,518
		(b)		*CULTIVATION OF SPECIAL CROPS, FRUIT, ETC., (PLANTERS, MANAGERS, CLERKS AND LABOURERS).*							
			10	Cocoanut ..	21,284	13,312	3,328	95	14	4,055	480
			11	Coffee ..	510	329	177	4	..	..	..
			12	Ganja ..	2	..	..	..	..	..	2
			13	Pan-Vine ..	3,708	1,528	315	63	13	1,699	110
			14	Rubber ..	1,581	1,222	338	1	1	19	..
			15	Tea ..	1,607	998	539	2	..	67	1
			16	Market gardeners, flower and fruit growers ..	8,967	2,566	742	117	33	5,136	373
		(c)		*FORESTRY.*							
			17	Forest officers, rangers, guards, etc. ..	294	284	..	..	..	10	..
			18	Wood cutters and charcoal burners ..	2,652	1,890	82	10	6	622	42
			19	Collectors of forest produce ..	965	410	337	10	18	99	91
			20	Collectors of lac ..	2	..	..	..	..	2	..
		(d)		*STOCK RAISING.*							
			21	Cattle and buffalo breeders and keepers ..	3,059	1,967	152	477	42	381	40
			22	Breeders of transport animals ..	6	5	..	1	..	..	..
			23	Herdsmen, shepherds and breeders of other animals ..	4,996	3,549	252	898	107	175	15
		(e)		*RAISING OF SMALL ANIMALS AND INSECTS.*							
			24	Birds, bees, etc. ..	3	3	..	..	..	..	..
			25	Silkworms ..	2	..	2	..	..	..	..
		2		**Fishing and Hunting.**	10,630	8,172	846	121	170	1,138	183
			27	Fishing and Pearling ..	10,562	8,155	846	120	170	1,088	183
			28	Hunting ..	68	17	..	1	..	50	..
				Total Sub-Class I.	291,815	159,622	89,845	3,753	3,489	30,165	4,941
	II. EXPLOITATION OF MINERALS.	3		**Metallic Minerals.**	2	..	..	..	..	2	..
			29	Gold ..	2	..	..	..	..	2	..
		4		**Non Metallic Minerals.**	68	10	12	..	..	46	..
			37	Building materials (including stone, materials for cement-manufacture and clays) ..	68	10	12	..	..	46	..
				Total Sub-Class II.	70	10	12	..	..	48	..
				Total Class A. ..	291,885	159,632	89,857	3,753	3,489	30,213	4,941

IMPERIAL TABLE X—(*cont.*)

OCCUPATION OR MEANS OF LIVELIHOOD.

GENERAL TABLE.

Class	Sub-class	Order	Group	Occupation	Total following Occupation	As principal occupation		As working dependents		As subsidiary to other occupation	
						Males	Females	Males	Females	Males	Females
1	2	3	4	5	6	7	8	9	10	11	12
B. PREPARATION AND SUPPLY OF MATERIAL SUBSTANCES	III. INDUSTRY.	5		**Textiles.** ..	**43,882**	**13,196**	**22,141**	**911**	**4,573**	**1,753**	**1,308**
			42	Cotton ginning, cleaning and pressing ..	49	2	1	2	..	43	1
			43	Cotton spinning, sizing and weaving ..	6,324	3,918	1,938	110	133	175	50
			45	Rope, twine, string and other fibres ..	37,457	9,247	20,190	796	4,440	1,527	1,257
			46	Wool carding, spinning and weaving ..	49	28	11	3	..	7	..
			49	Dyeing, bleaching, printing, preparation and sponging of textiles ..	1	..	..	..	..	1	..
			50	Lace, crepe, embroideries, fringes, etc., and insufficiently described textile industries ..	2	1	1	..	..	..	..
		6		**Hides, skins and hard materials from the animal kingdom** ..	**520**	**464**	**12**	**9**	..	**34**	**1**
			51	Working in leather ..	510	457	12	9	..	31	1
			53	Bone, ivory, horn, shell, etc., workers (except buttons) ..	10	7	..	..	..	3	..
		7		**Wood.** ..	**26,330**	**14,251**	**7,814**	**154**	**788**	**1,503**	**1,820**
			54	Sawyers ..	3,574	3,263	6	14	..	291	..
			55	Carpenters, turners and joiners, etc. ..	8,007	7,645	35	89	9	225	1
			56	Basket makers and other industries of woody materials, including leaves and thatchers and builders working with bamboo, reeds or similar materials ..	14,749	3,343	7,770	51	779	987	1,819
		8		**Metals.** ..	**4,396**	**3,873**	**348**	**47**	**31**	**85**	**12**
			57	Smelting, forging and rolling of iron and other metals ..	40	29	..	..	..	11	..
			59	Blacksmiths, other workers in iron, makers of implements. ..	2,880	2,532	227	35	30	49	7
			60	Workers in brass, copper and bell metal ..	1,099	957	118	9	1	10	4
			61	Workers in other metals (except precious metals) ..	376	354	3	3	..	15	1
			62	Workers in mints, die-sinkers, etc ..	1	1	..	..	..	..	..
		9		**Ceramics.** ..	**3,234**	**1,865**	**1,230**	**16**	**21**	**69**	**33**
			63	Potters and makers of earthen-ware ..	2,211	1,157	986	13	16	35	4
			64	Brick and tile makers ..	897	646	186	2	2	32	29
			65	Other workers in ceramics ..	126	62	58	1	3	2	..
		10		**Chemical products properly so called and analogous.** ..	**4,204**	**3,264**	**480**	**64**	**53**	**384**	**31**
			66	Manufacture of matches, fireworks and other explosives ..	455	324	101	3	1	21	5
			67	Manufacture of aerated and mineral waters and ice ..	102	101	..	..	1	1	..
			68	Manufacture and refining of vegetable oils ..	3,288	2,505	303	61	39	354	26
			69	Manufacture and refining of mineral oils ..	305	295	4	..	..	6	..
			70	Others ..	53	39	..	..	12	2	..
		11		**Food Industries.** ..	**10,992**	**5,807**	**2,847**	**29**	**245**	**1,563**	**501**
			71	Rice pounders and huskers and flour grinders ..	2,962	128	2,164	2	178	27	463
			72	Grain parchers, etc. ..	22	15	7	..	..	..	..
			73	Butchers ..	46	33	..	..	..	13	..
			74	Makers of sugar, molasses and gur ..	3	..	..	..	..	3	..
			75	Sweetmeat and condiment makers ..	1,374	588	642	0	42	59	34
			76	Toddy drawers ..	6,009	4,500	34	14	25	1,432	4
			77	Brewers and distillers ..	2	..	..	..	..	2	..
			78	Manufacturers of Tobacco ..	558	529	..	2	..	27	..
			81	Others ..	16	14	..	2	..	..	..

IMPERIAL TABLE X—(*cont.*)

OCCUPATION OR MEANS OF LIVELIHOOD.

GENERAL TABLE.

Class	Sub-class	Order	Group	Occupation	Total following Occupation	As principal occupation		As working dependents		As subsidiary to other occupation	
						Males	Females	Males	Females	Males	Females
1	2	3	4	5	6	7	8	9	10	11	12
B. PREPARATION AND SUPPLY OF MATERIAL SUBSTANCES—(*cont.*)	III. INDUSTRY—(*cont.*)	12		**Industries of dress and the toilet** ..	**10,655**	**4,723**	**4,944**	**65**	**210**	**861**	**152**
			82	Boot, shoe, sandal and clog makers ..	21	..	..	..	..	18	3
			83	Tailors, milliners, dress-makers and darners ..	1,750	1,279	197	26	49	148	51
			84	Embroiderers, hat makers and makers of other articles of wear ..	89	63	9	..	1	16	...
			85	Washing and cleaning ..	6,187	1,604	4,222	28	148	117	68
..			86	Barbers, hair-dressers and wig-makers ..	2,564	1,756	516	11	12	246	23
..			87	Other industries connected with the toilet ..	44	21	..	..	..	16	7
		13		**Furniture Industries**	**142**	**124**	**1**	**1**	...	**16**	..
			88	Cabinet-makers, carriage painters, etc. ..	142	124	1	1	..	16	..
		14		**Building Industries.**	**8,948**	**7,542**	**596**	**44**	**46**	**677**	**43**
			90	Lime burners, cement workers; Excavators and well-sinkers; Stone cutters and dressers; Brick layers and masons; Builders (other than buildings made of bamboo or similar materials), painters, decorators of houses, tilers, plumbers, etc. ..	8,948	7,542	596	44	46	677	43
		15		**Construction of means of transport.**	**110**	**79**	..	**1**	..	**30**	..
			91	Persons engaged in making, assembling or repairing motor vehicles or cycles ..	44	36	..	..	..	8	..
			92	Carriage, cart, palki, etc., makers, and wheel wrights ..	51	32	..	1	..	18	..
			93	Ship, boat, aeroplane builders ..	15	11	..	..	..	4	..
		16		**Production and transmission of Physical force**	**27**	**22**	..	..	..	**5**	..
			94	Heat, light, electricity, motive power, etc., gas works and electric light and power ..	27	22	..	..	..	5	..
		17		**Miscellaneous and undefined Industries**	**5,136**	**3,863**	**965**	**45**	**103**	**134**	**26**
			95	Printers, engravers, book-binders, etc. ..	689	643	2	9	..	35	..
			96	Makers of musical instruments ..	6	5	..	..	..	1	..
			97	Makers of clocks and surgical or scientific instruments, etc. ..	194	187	..	..	..	7	..
			98	Makers of jewellery and ornaments ..	2,941	2,769	67	34	5	65	1
			99	Other miscellaneous and undefined industries (toy-making, taxidermy, etc.) ..	550	94	37	2	85	25	10
			100	Scavenging ..	756	167	560	..	13	1	15
				Total Sub-Class III ..	**118,576**	**59,073**	**41,306**	**1,386**	**6,070**	**6,814**	**3,927**
	IV. TRANSPORT.	18		**Transport by water.**	**5,400**	**4,545**	**9**	**58**	**1**	**782**	**5**
			102	Ship-owners, boat-owners and their employees, officers, mariners, etc. Ships brokers, boatmen and towmen ..	4,762	4,117	9	57	1	573	3
			103	Persons (other than labourers) employed in harbours, docks, rivers and canals, including pilots ..	382	241	..	..	..	139	2
	..		104	Labourers employed on harbours, docks, rivers and canals ..	256	185	..	1	..	70	..

IMPERIAL TABLE X—(*cont.*)

OCCUPATION OR MEANS OF LIVELIHOOD.

GENERAL TABLE.

Class	Sub-class	Order	Group	Occupation	Total following Occupation	As principal occupation: Males	As principal occupation: Females	As working dependents: Males	As working dependents: Females	As subsidiary to other occupation: Males	As subsidiary to other occupation: Females
1	2	3	4	5	6	7	8	9	10	11	12
B—PREPARATION AND SUPPLY OF MATERIAL SUBSTANCES—(*cont.*)	IV. TRANSPORT—*cont.*	20		**Transport by road.**	**10,254**	**8,346**	**372**	**60**	**7**	**1,443**	**26**
			105	Persons (other than labourers) employed on the construction and maintenance of roads and bridges ..	180	143	..	2	..	15	..
			106	Labourers employed on roads and bridges ..	1,437	1,082	167	7	2	162	19
			107	Owners, managers and employees (excluding personal servants) connected with mechanically driven vehicles (including trams) ..	1,445	1,334	30	7	..	74	..
			108	Owners, managers and employees (excluding personal servants) connected with other vehicles ..	4,612	3,856	23	19	..	713	1
			109	Palki, etc., bearers and owners ..	238	125	7	2	3	99	2
			110	Pack elephant, camel, mule, ass and bullock owners and drivers ..	314	176	..	1	..	137	..
			111	Porters and messengers ..	2,028	1,632	145	22	2	223	4
		21		**Transport by Rail.**	**924**	**738**	**163**	**1**	..	**22**	..
			112	Railway employees of all kinds other than coolies ..	199	187	2	..	..	10	..
			113	Labourers employed on railway construction and maintenance and coolies and porters employed on railway premises ..	725	551	161	1	..	12	..
		22		**Post Office, Telegraph and Telephone services.**	**341**	**290**	**1**	**1**	**2**	**47**	..
			114	Post Office, Telegraph and Telephone services ..	341	290	1	1	2	47	..
				Total Sub-Class IV	**16,919**	**13,919**	**545**	**120**	**10**	**2,294**	**31**
	V. TRADE.	23		**Banks, establishments of credit, exchange and insurance.**	**3,660**	**1,619**	**856**	**11**	**2**	**991**	**181**
			115	Bank managers, money lenders, exchange and insurance agents, money changers and brokers and their employees ..	3,660	1,619	856	11	2	991	181
		24		**Brokerage commission and export.**	**148**	**94**	**22**	..	..	**32**	..
			116	Brokers, commission agents, commercial travellers, warehouse owners and employees ..	148	94	22	..	..	32	..
		25		**Trade in textiles.**	**2,531**	**1,916**	**65**	**19**	**41**	**465**	**25**
			117	Trade in piece-goods, wool, cotton, silk, hair and other textiles ..	2,531	1,916	65	19	41	465	25
		26		**Trade in skins, leather and furs.**	**194**	**171**	**1**	**2**	..	**19**	**1**
			118	Trade in skins, leather, furs, feathers, horn, etc., and the articles made from these ..	194	171	1	2	..	19	1
		27		**Trade in wood.**	**905**	**634**	**71**	**6**	**3**	**184**	**7**
			119	Trade in wood (not fire-wood) ..	506	388	2	3	..	108	5
			120	Trade in barks ..	9	4	2	..	..	1	1
			121	Trade in bamboos and canes ..	246	130	56	1	3	55	1
			122	Trade in thatches and other forest produce ..	144	112	10	2	..	20	..
		28		**Trade in metals.**	**289**	**236**	**8**	..	**1**	**44**	..
			123	Trade in metals, machinery, knives, tools, etc ..	289	236	8	..	1	44	..
		29		**Trade in pottery, bricks and tiles.**	**405**	**179**	**187**	..	**17**	**33**	**19**
			124	Trade in pottery, bricks and tiles ..	405	179	157	..	17	33	19

IMPERIAL TABLE X—(*cont.*)

OCCUPATION OR MEANS OF LIVELIHOOD.

GENERAL TABLE.

Class	Sub-class	Order	Group	Occupation	Total following Occupation	As principal occupation		As working dependents		As subsidiary to other occupation	
						Males	Females	Males	Females	Males	Females
1	2	3	4	5	6	7	8	9	10	11	12
B. PREPARATION AND SUPPLY OF MATERIAL SUBSTANCES—(*cont.*)	V. TRADE—*cont.*	30		**Trade in chemical products.**	**726**	**620**	**26**	**5**	**3**	**70**	**2**
			125	Drugs, dyes, paints, petroleum, explosives, etc. ..	726	620	26	5	3	70	2
		31		**Hotels, cafes, restaurants, etc.**	**5,497**	**4,339**	**652**	**50**	**10**	**426**	**20**
			126	Vendors of wine, liquors, aerated waters and ice ..	1,149	884	94	13	3	145	10
			127	Owners and managers of hotels, cookshops, sarais, etc. (and employees) ..	4,204	3,352	542	32	1	267	10
			128	Hawkers of drink and food stuffs ..	144	103	16	5	6	14	..
		32		**Other trade in food stuffs.**	**24,017**	**15,416**	**4,939**	**170**	**189**	**2,891**	**412**
			129	Grain and pulse dealers ..	7,693	5,732	913	41	26	934	47
			130	Dealers in sweetmeats, sugar and spices ..	5,429	3, 15	1,767	45	57	250	95
			131	Dealers in dairy products, eggs and poultry ..	1,722	625	782	19	33	155	108
			132	Dealers in animals for food ..	2,372	1,390	694	17	49	192	30
			133	Dealers in fodder for animals ..	468	175	146	1	1	97	48
			134	Dealers in other food stuffs ..	5,656	3,790	626	44	23	1,089	84
			135	Dealers in tobacco ..	637	558	11	3	..	65	..
			136	Dealers in opium ..	29	23	..	..	..	6	..
			137	Dealers in ganja ..	11	8	..	..	..	3	..
		33		**Trade in clothing and toilet articles.**	**158**	**99**	**25**	**1**	**3**	**29**	**1**
			138	Trade in ready-made clothing and other articles of dress and the toilet (hats, umbrellas, socks, ready-made shoes, perfumes, etc.) ..	158	99	25	1	3	29	1
		34		**Trade in furniture.**	**665**	**373**	**166**	**6**	**1**	**84**	**35**
			139	Trade in furniture, carpets, curtains and bedding ..	354	178	111	2	..	32	31
			140	Hardware, cooking utensils, porcelain crockery, glassware, bottles, articles for gardening, etc. ..	311	195	55	4	1	52	4
		35		**Trade in building materials.**	**392**	**303**	**48**	**11**	**4**	**26**	..
			141	Trade in building materials (other than bricks, tiles and woody materials) ..	392	30,3	48	11	4	26	..
		36		**Trade in means of transport.**	**1,235**	**889**	**12**	**5**	..	**326**	**3**
			142	Dealers and hirers in mechanical transport, motors, cycles, etc. ..	56	18	..	..	..	38	..
			143	Dealers and hirers in other carriages, carts, boats, etc. ..	481	288	3	2	..	185	3
			144	Dealers and hirers of elephants, camels, horses, cattle, asses, mules, etc. ..	698	583	9	3	..	103	..
		37		**Trade in fuel.**	**994**	**543**	**251**	**7**	**7**	**80**	**106**
			145	Dealers in firewood, charcoal, coal, cowdung, etc. ..	994	543	251	7	7	80	106
		38		**Trade in articles of luxury and those pertaining to letters and the arts and sciences.**	**469**	**378**	**20**	**5**	**1**	**37**	**28**
			146	Dealers in precious stones, jewellery (real and imitation), clocks, optical instruments, etc. ..	159	141	1	1	..	16	..
			147	Dealers in common bangles, bead necklaces, fans, small articles, toys, hunting and fishing tackle, flowers, etc. ..	93	29	18	2	1	15	28
			148	Publishers, book-sellers, stationers, dealers in music, pictures, musical instruments and curiosities ..	217	208	1	2	..	6	[illegible]

IMPERIAL TABLE X—(*cont.*)

OCCUPATION OR MEANS OF LIVELIHOOD.

GENERAL TABLE.

Class	Subclass	Order	Group	Occupation	Total following Occupation	As principal occupation: Males	As principal occupation: Females	As working dependents: Males	As working dependents: Females	As subsidiary to other occupation: Males	As subsidiary to other occupation: Females
1	2	3	4	5	6	7	8	9	10	11	12
B. PREPARATION AND SUPPLY OF MATERIAL SUBSTANCES (*cont.*)	V. TRADE.—(*cont.*)	39		**Trade of other sorts.**	7,575	5,660	528	43	19	1,291	28
			149	Dealers in rags, stable refuse, etc. ..	12	3	..	2	..	3	4
			150	General store-keepers and shop-keepers otherwise unspecified ..	6,664	4,984	442	36	16	1,162	13
			151	Itinerant traders, pedlars and hawkers (of other than food, etc.) ..	308	271	22	..	..	15	..
			152	Other trades (including farmers of pounds, tolls and markets) ..	591	402	64	5	3	111	6
				Total Sub-Class V.	49,860	33,475	7,847	341	301	7,028	868
				Total Class B.	185,355	106,467	49,698	1,847	6,381	16,136	4,826
C. PUBLIC ADMINISTRATION AND LIBERAL ARTS.	VI. PUBLIC FORCE.	40		**Army.**	82	81	..	1	..	..	..
			153	Army (Imperial) ..	4	4	..	..	..	..	..
			154	Army (Indian States) ..	78	77	..	1	..	..	..
		42		**Police.**	974	945	..	..	..	29	..
			157	Police ..	953	924	..	..	..	29	..
			158	Village watchmen ..	21	21	..	..	..	..	..
				Total Sub-Class VI.	1,056	1,026	..	1	..	29	..
	VII. PUBLIC ADMINISTRATION.	44		**Public Administration.**	4,918	4,617	37	10	1	251	2
			159	Service of the State ..	3,904	3,463	20	10	1	109	1
			160	Service of Indian and Foreign States ..	23	14	..	..	..	9	..
			161	Municipal and other local (not village) service ..	147	373	16	..	..	57	1
			162	Village officials and servants other than watchmen ..	844	767	1	..	..	76	..
				Total Sub-Class VII.	4,918	4,617	37	10	1	251	2
	VIII. PROFESSIONS AND LIBERAL ARTS.	45		**Religion.**	5,077	3,460	695	88	82	698	48
			163	Priests, ministers, etc. ..	1,573	1,252	8	20	7	255	1
			164	Monks, nuns, religious mendicants ..	102	31	13	11	4	38	5
			165	Other religious workers ..	851	602	86	17	3	132	18
			166	Servants in religious edifices, burial and burning grounds, pilgrim conductors, circumcisers, etc. ..	2,551	1,581	588	40	68	243	24
		46		**Law.**	931	822	..	2	..	107	..
			167	Lawyers of all kinds including Quazis, Law Agents, and Mukhtiars ..	288	242	..	..	..	46	..
			168	Lawyers' clerks, petition writers, etc. ..	643	580	..	2	..	61	..
		47		**Medicine.**	3,406	2,361	451	21	28	507	38
			169	Registered medical practitioners including occulists ..	301	208	15	..	..	77	1
			170	Other persons practising the healing arts without being registered ..	2,414	1,936	55	17	7	420	7
			171	Dentists ..	3	2	..	..	..	1	..
			172	Midwives, Vaccinators, Compounders, Nurses, masseurs, etc. ..	670	199	381	2	21	7	30
			173	Veterinary Surgeons ..	18	16	..	..	..	2	..

IMPERIAL TABLE X.—(*cont.*)

OCCUPATION OR MEANS OF LIVELIHOOD

GENERAL TABLE.

Class	Sub-class	Order	Group	Occupation	Total following Occupation	As principal occupation Males	As principal occupation Females	As working dependents Males	As working dependents Females	As subsidiary to other occupation Males	As subsidiary to other occupation Females
1	2	3	4	5	6	7	8	9	10	11	12
C. PUBLIC ADMINISTRATION AND LIBERAL ARTS.—(*contd*).	VIII. PROFESSIONS AND LIBERAL ARTS.—(*contd*.)	48		**Instruction**	**6.639**	**4,774**	**1.408**	**14**	**7**	**405**	**31**
			174	Professors and teachers of all kinds ..	6,133	4,323	1,374	14	5	387	31
			175	Clerks and servants connected with education ..	505	451	31	..	2	18	..
		49		**Letters, arts and sciences (other than 44—Public Administration.)**	**3 555**	**2,467**	**232**	**33**	**19**	**788**	**16**
			176	Public scribes, stenographers, etc. ..	172	134	..	..	..	38	..
			177	Architects, surveyors, engineers and their employees (not being State servants) ..	80	77	..	..	..	3	..
			178	Authors, editors, journalists and photo-graphers ..	92	67	..	..	..	24	1
			179	Artists, sculptors and image-makers ..	89	65	..	2	..	20	2
			180	Scientists (astronomers, botanists, etc.) ..	21	8	9	..	..	4	..
			181	Horoscope casters, astrologers, fortune-tellers, wizards, witches and mediums ..	1,061	705	63	4	1	279	9
			182	Musicians (composers and performers other than military), actors, dancers, etc. ..	1,893	1,297	145	26	18	406	4
			183	Managers and employees of places of public entertainments, race courses, societies, clubs ..	68	59	..	..	..	9	..
			184	Conjurors, acrobats, reciters, exhibitors of curiosities and wild animals, etc. ..	80	56	15	1	..	5	..
				Total Sub-Class VIII.	**19,008**	**13,890**	**2,786**	**158**	**136**	**2,505**	**133**
				Total Class C.	**25.582**	**19.533**	**2.823**	**169**	**137**	**2.785**	**135**
D. MISCELLANEOUS.	IX. PERSONS LIVING ON THEIR INCOME.	50		**Persons living principally on their income.**	**4,129**	**1.495**	**1.172**	**29**	**10**	**1.087**	**336**
			185	Proprietors (other than agricultural land), fund and scholarships-holders and pensioners ..	4,129	1,495	1,172	29	10	1,087	336
				Total Sub-Class IX.	**4,129**	**1,495**	**1.172**	**29**	**10**	**1,087**	**336**
	X. DOMESTIC SERVICE.	51		**Domestic service.**	**177,000**	**4.241**	**6,763**	**1.194**	**128.635**	**804**	**35,363**
			186	Private motor-drivers and cleaners ..	271	252	..	14	..	5	..
			187	Other domestic service ..	176,729	3,989	6,763	1,180	128,635	799	35,363
				Total Sub-Class X	**177.000**	**4.241**	**6.763**	**1,194**	**128.635**	**804**	**35,363**
	XI. INSUFFICIENTLY DESCRIBED OCCUPATIONS.	52		**General terms which do not indicate a definite occupation.**	**28.415**	**20,158**	**4.687**	**319**	**316**	**2.490**	**445**
			188	Manufacturers, businessmen and contractors otherwise unspecified ..	1.056	956	..	1	..	98	1
			189	Cashiers, accountants, book-keepers, clerks and other employees in unspecified offices and warehouses and shops ..	2,938	2,656	35	27	..	206	14
			190	Mechanics otherwise unspecified ..	483	454	1	5	..	23	..
			191	Labourers and workmen otherwise unspecified ..	23,938	16,092	4,651	286	316	2,163	430
				Total Sub-Class XI.	**28,415**	**20,158**	**4,687**	**319**	**316**	**2,490**	**445**

IMPERIAL TABLE X—(*cont.*)

OCCUPATION OR MEANS OF LIVELIHOOD.

GENERAL TABLE.

Class	Sub-class	Order	Group	Occupation	Total following Occupation	As principal occupation		As working dependents		As subsidiary to other occupation	
						Males	Females	Males	Females	Males	Females
1	2	3	4	5	6	7	8	9	10	11	12
D. MISCELLANEOUS—(*cont.*)	XII. UNPRODUCTIVE	**53**		**Inmates of jails, asylums and alms houses**	**226**	**47**	..	**160**	**12**	**7**	..
			192	Inmates of Jails, Asylums and alms houses ..	226	47	..	160	12	7	..
		54		**Beggars, vagrants, &c.**	**1,074**	**93**	**54**	**503**	**371**	**35**	**18**
			193	Beggars and vagrants ..	1,074	93	54	503	371	35	18
		55		**Other unclassified non-productive industries**	**148**	..	**6**	..	..	**54**	**88**
			195	Other unclassified non-productive industries ..	148	..	6	..	..	54	88
				Total Sub-Class XII.	**1,448**	**140**	**60**	**663**	**383**	**96**	**106**
				Total Class D.	**210,992**	**26,034**	**12,682**	**2,205**	**129,344**	**4,477**	**36,250**
				Grand Total ..	**713,814**	**311,666**	**155,060**	**7,974**	**139,351**	**53,611**	**46,152**

TABLE XI.

OCCUPATION BY CASTE, TRIBE OR RACE.

PART A.—OCCUPATION OF SELECTED CASTES, TRIBES OR RACES.

Note.—Part B has not been prepared.

IMPERIAL

OCCUPATION BY CASTE.

PART A.—OCCUPATION OF SELECTED

	CASTE, TRIBE OR RACE	Traditional occupation	Population dealt with				
			Earners		Working dependents		Non-working dependents
			Males	Females	Males	Females	Both sexes
	1	2	3	4	5	6	7
	HINDU						
1	Ambalavasi ..	Temple servants	2,322	1,000	67	1,014	4,808
2	Ambattan ..	Barbers	448	147	10	212	753
3	Arayan ..	Fishermen and Boatmen	1,952	597	26	768	3,231
4	Brahman-Konkani ..	Merchants	2,514	342	38	1,838	4,929
5	Do. Malayali ..	Priests and Landed Aristocrats	1,963	167	49	962	4,022
6	Do. Tamil ..	Priests	4,651	589	54	3,682	12,778
7	Chakkan ..	Oil Pressers	626	249	20	282	985
8	Chaliyan						
	a. Chaliyan ..	Weavers	120	59	5	39	174
	b. Pattarian ..	do.	483	257	10	234	937
9	Eluthassan ..	Village school masters	5,040	2,839	191	2,385	8,081
10	Iluvan ..	Toddy drawers and agriculturists	69,888	41,682	1,917	29,690	133,472
11	Kaikolan ..	Weavers	1,179	810	20	258	1,447
12	Kammalan ..	Artisans	12,668	3,291	195	7,267	22,125
13	Kanakkan ..	Boatmen and Agricultural Labourers	3,699	2,769	82	780	5,862
14	Kaniyan ..	Astrologers and devil dancers	985	208	41	645	1,962
15	Kshatriya-Malayali.	Military and dominant	403	323	3	85	653
16	Kudumi Chetti ..	General labourers	4,694	1,614	114	2,133	7,549
17	Kusavan ..	Potters	1,033	885	19	79	1,279
18	Nayar ..	Military and Agricultural	32,022	17,921	918	17,343	74,433
19	Pandaran ..	Mendicants and Pappadam making	1,365	1,153	87	301	1,954
20	Panditattan ..	Goldsmiths	927	73	24	487	1,453
21	Pulayan ..	Agricultural labourers	23,404	21,252	484	3,412	33,491
22	Parayan ..	Basket makers and Agricultural labourers	3,421	3,071	67	349	4,654
23	Valan ..	Boatmen and fishermen	2,984	1,375	85	1,144	6,096
24	Velakkattalavan ..	Barbers	997	459	21	427	1,795
25	Velan ..	Barbers, priests and washermen	2,769	2,853	80	520	4,673
26	Vellalan ..	Agriculturists and merchants	1,582	603	27	672	2,415
27	Veluttedan ..	Washermen	1,018	1,179	22	144	1,559
28	Vettuvan ..	Hunters	3,301	2,631	64	522	5,279
	MUSLIM						
29	Jonakan ..		15,186	4,488	455	7,873	29,369
30	Ravuttan ..		3,105	965	72	1,577	5,208
31	Others ..		5,209	1,867	112	2,193	10,223
	CHRISTIAN						
32	Anglo-Indian ..		368	89	9	236	1,015
33	European ..		45	16	2	11	38
34	Indian Christian ..		84,374	29,899	2,494	44,562	171,712
35	JAIN		71	2	..	36	101
36	JEW		355	66	1	229	800

TABLE XI.

TRIBE OR RACE.

CASTES, TRIBES OR RACES.

	Number of earners whose traditional Caste occupation was returned as their — Principal means of livelihood		Subsidiary means of livelihood		No. of working dependents following the traditional occupation of their caste		No. of earners returning their traditional occupation as their principal means of livelihood who had some subsidiary occupation		Income from rent of land		Cultivators of all kinds		Agents and managers of landed estate, planters, forest officers and their clerks, rent collectors, etc.	
	Males	Females	Males	Females	Males	Females	Males	Females	Males	Females	Males	Females	Males	Females
	8	9	10	11	12	13	14	15	16	17	18	19	20	21
1	993	585	168	30	57	69	156	185	192	112	290	86	84	7
2	405	74	11	2	4	..	24	25	4	..	11	2	..	..
3	1,761	246	28	8	12	20	121	68	2	..	54	10	1	..
4	1,143	80	26	..	12	1	92	22	8	5	308	49	21	..
5	1,358	62	97	..	18	..	319	24	..	..	193	7	43	..
6	322	..	36	..	4	..	52	..	464	123	290	28	137	..
7	433	146	20	4	9	11	74	34	5	2	41	12	2	..
8														
a	58	18	2	1	2	1	5	3	..	..	6	1	..	..
b	306	173	20	6	4	4	28	42	1	1	33	15	..	..
9	40	4	1	..	1	..	5	1	135	8	1,974	610	151	2
10	30,831	14,400	2,207	1,099	454	841	8,241	4,705	106	88	2,093	927	305	73
11	814	535	53	..	2	11	72	235	26	6	69	9	1	..
12	11,996	1,861	166	35	119	134	1,104	321	16	6	219	75	14	8
13	2,257	1,412	205	74	27	20	197	359	2	..	72	17	2	..
14	512	8	50	..	5	..	113	1	5	1	82	16	2	..
15	56	29	..	..	..	..	2	3	25	19	11	12	12	..
16	2,458	757	209	75	38	177	177	141	1	12	991	40	45	..
17	985	820	10	..	8	20	57	211	..	4	16	..	..	..
18	13,058	6,088	918	172	243	175	2,941	2,395	1,172	1,770	427	625	1,082	5
19	659	701	66	17	32	27	120	207	9	5	120	30	3	..
20	839	7	4	..	16	..	25	1	..	1	5	2	..	..
21	20,597	18,276	374	451	131	368	1,694	3,996	5	2	396	73	36	2
22	2,983	2,895	102	47	37	70	1,068	1,161	..	..	23	5	..	..
23	2,394	784	68	18	53	64	140	269	..	2	69	16	3	..
24	680	231	108	12	2	5	92	75	3	3	208	52	1	..
25	575	2,610	53	22	7	82	110	711	2	2	285	21	10	5
26	803	306	2	1	6	7	77	60	12	10	4	1	26	1
27	803	1,116	71	19	16	29	75	275	17	4	112	30	6	..
28	2,441	2,083	89	42	23	59	308	427	..	..	84	19	..	..
29	..	..	..	..	..	..	..	..	27	42	3,144	575	137	3
30	..	..	..	..	..	..	..	..	15	5	332	44	4	..
31	..	..	..	..	..	..	..	..	22	18	760	224	99	4
32	..	..	..	..	..	..	..	..	1	1	37	9	5	..
33	..	..	..	..	..	..	..	..	..	..	..	..	17	..
34	..	..	..	..	..	..	..	..	564	525	24,410	4,555	235	10
35	..	..	..	..	..	..	..	..	..	..	..	..	..	..
36	..	..	..	..	..	..	..	..	1	1	39	19	..	..

IMPERIAL

OCCUPATION BY CASTE,

PART A.—OCCUPATION OF SELECTED

	CASTE, TRIBE OR RACE	Traditional occupation	Recorded Principal					
			Field labourers, wood cutters, etc.		Raisers of live-stock, milkmen and herdsmen		Fishing and hunting	
			Males	Females	Males	Females	Males	Females
			22	23	24	25	26	27
	HINDU							
1	Ambalavasi ..	Temple servants	11	11	8	20	..	..
2	Ambattan ..	Barbers	2	38	3	..	..	..
3	Arayan ..	Fishermen and Boatmen	2	1	..	1	..	..
4	Brahman-Konkani..	Merchants	4	..	3	27	..	..
5	Do Malayali ..	Priests and Landed Aristocrats	..	..	..	3	..	..
6	Do Tamil ..	Priests	2	..	10	27	..	..
7	Chakkan ..	Oil Pressers	30	33	5	..	..	..
8	Chaliyan							
	a. Chaliyan ..	Weavers	22	21	1	..	..	..
	b. Pattarian ..	do	9	1	..	1	..	..
9	Eluthassan ..	Village school masters	1,413	1,816	107	12	3	..
10	Iluvan ..	Toddy drawers and Agriculturists	10,131	11,194	1,839	109	270	8
11	Kaikolan ..	Weavers	40	122	10	1	..	..
12	Kammalan ..	Artisans	136	934	39	4	2	..
13	Kanakkan ..	Boatmen and Agricultural Labourers	67	36	74	5	322	9
14	Kaniyan ..	Astrologers and devil dancers	55	86	5	..	..	..
15	Kshatriya-Malayali	Military and dominant	1	..	..	1	..	..
16	Kudumi Chetti ..	General labourers	230	170	6	2	197	6
17	Kusavan ..	Potters	6	17	5	..	..	..
18	Nayar ..	Military and Agricultural	1 752	3,616	649	51	79	..
19	Pandaran ..	Mendicants and Pappadam making	207	296	23	..	..	..
20	Panditattan ..	Goldsmiths	8	16	..	..	..	..
21	Pulayan ..	Agricultural labourers	152	99	1,058	60	34	358
22	Parayan ..	Basket makers and Agricultural labourers	50	10	89	2	..	1
23	Valan ..	Boatmen and Fishermen	17	12	1	..	12	..
24	Velakkattalavan ..	Barbers	40	86	6	..	..	..
25	Velan ..	Barbers, Priests and Washermen	434	36	22	1	3	..
26	Vellalan ..	Agriculturists and Merchants	193	231	37	2	4	..
27	Veluttedan ..	Washermen	16	17	7	..	..	..
28	Vettuvan ..	Hunters	117	94	65	..	11	2
	MUSLIM							
29	Jonakan ..		2,422	2,150	181	13	291	3
30	Ravuttan ..		599	601	97	4	8	..
31	Others ..		621	295	32	1	368	..
	CHRISTIAN							
32	Anglo-Indian ..		5	..	1	1	8	..
33	European ..		..	..	..	..	..	..
34	Indian Christian ..		9,802	7,976	750	44	2,338	48
35	JAIN		..	..	..	..	..	..
36	JEW		..	..	..	..	2	..

TABLE XI.—(*cont.*)

TRIBE OR RACE.

CASTES, TRIBES OR RACES.

occupation of earners, other than traditional occupation of caste (by sub-classes.)

	Extraction of minerals				Industries				Transport				Trade	
	Owners, Managers, clerks, etc.		Labourers		Owners, Managers, clerks, etc.		Artisans, and other workmen		Owners, Managers, Ships' Officers, etc.		Labourers, boatmen, carters, palki-bearers, etc.			
	Males	Females	Males	Females	Males	Females	Males	Females	Males	Females	Males	Females	Males	Females
	28	29	30	31	32	33	34	35	36	37	38	39	40	41
1	3	..	..	..	1	..	17	3	8	..	21	..	101	13
2	..	..	..	..	..	..	4	2	..	..	1	..	2	3
3	..	..	..	..	2	..	52	292	..	..	8	..	38	4
4	..	..	..	..	36	18	88	69	3	..	24	..	..	..
5	..	..	..	..	7	..	3	..	1	..	5	..	54	11
6	1	..	..	..	33	..	61	1	87	..	82	..	834	198
7	..	..	..	..	2	..	15	7	1	..	8	..	60	30
8														
a	..	..	..	..	..	..	9	8	..	..	6	..	1	1
b	..	..	..	..	..	..	4	40	..	..	11	..	66	2
9	..	..	1	..	1	..	259	25	2	..	164	3	237	26
10	..	..	..	1	323	1	8,847	10,959	75	1	4,027	232	5,206	1,214
11	..	..	..	..	..	..	17	28	..	..	12	..	156	50
12	..	..	..	..	..	..	75	..	1	..	30	1	23	131
13	..	..	..	..	..	..	210	995	..	..	150	6	212	216
14	..	..	..	..	..	..	41	9	..	..	13	..	8	..
15	..	..	..	..	1	..	1	50	..	..	1	..	20	3
16	..	..	..	..	5	..	92	254	..	..	110	..	461	61
17	..	..	..	..	..	..	9	..	..	..	2	..	3	46
18	..	..	..	..	79	..	760	892	62	..	804	36	2,762	977
19	..	..	1	..	..	..	118	81	..	..	60	1	68	28
20	..	..	..	..	..	..	46	9	..	..	2	..	7	6
21	..	..	..	7	12	..	722	1,860	1	..	73	1	21	81
22	..	..	..	..	..	..	91	39	..	..	2	..	4	1
23	..	..	..	..	1	..	165	357	6	..	124	4	61	173
24	..	..	..	..	..	..	12	8	..	..	8	..	8	4
25	..	..	..	..	6	..	461	134	..	..	61	..	18	1
26	..	..	..	..	15	..	165	11	1	..	52	..	..	..
27	..	..	..	..	..	..	8	2	3	..	6	..	11	1
28	..	..	..	..	..	7	60	188	..	..	9	7	8	18
29	..	..	..	..	4	..	1,292	795	15	..	1,341	27	4,045	469
30	..	..	..	..	..	..	212	41	1	1	218	26	1,305	143
31	..	..	..	..	1	..	466	1,019	8	..	293	..	1,645	88
32	..	..	..	..	6	..	171	21	9	..	16	..	29	3
33	..	..	..	..	8	1	1	..	..	..	1	..	..	..
34	..	1	..	..	260	3	17,794	10,697	80	3	5,145	31	13,414	1,847
35	..	..	..	..	..	..	..	..	..	..	..	..	22	..
36	..	..	..	..	..	..	18	5	..	..	14	..	240	24

IMPERIAL

OCCUPATION BY CASTE,

PART A.—OCCUPATION OF SELECTED

	CASTE, TRIBE OR RACE	Traditional occupation	Recorded Principal							
			Public Force				Public administratoin			
			Commissioned and Gazetted Officers		Others		Gazetted Officers		Others	
			Males	Females	Males	Females	Males	Females	Males	Females
			42	43	44	45	46	47	48	49
	HINDU									
1	Ambalavasi	Temple servants	14	..	9	..	5	..	108	1
2	Ambattan ..	Barbers	..	..	..	..	..	..	1	..
3	Arayan ...	Fishermen and Boatmen	..	..	..	..	..	..	3	..
4	Brahman-Konkani..	Merchants	..	..	..	..	2	..	37	..
5	Do Malayali ..	Priests and Landed Aristocrats	..	..	..	..	1	..	10	..
6	Do Tamil ..	Priests	5	..	19	..	56	..	403	..
7	Chakkan ..	Oil Pressers	..	..	..	..	..	..	..	..
8	Chaliyan									
	a. Chaliyan ...	Weavers	..	..	1	..	..	..	1	..
	b. Pattarian ..	do	..	..	3	..	..	..	19	..
9	Eluthaasan ..	Village school masters	..	..	12	..	1	..	56	..
10	Iluvan ..	Toddy drawers and Agriculturists	5	..	33	..	6	..	224	8
11	Kaikolan ..	Weavers	..	..	..	..	..	..	2	..
12	Kammalan ..	Artisans	..	..	..	..	..	..	5	..
13	Kanakkan ..	Boatmen and Agricultural Labourers	..	..	..	..	..	..	3	8
14	Kaniyan ..	Astrologers and devil dancers	..	..	1	..	..	..	21	..
15	Kshatriya-Malayali	Military and dominant	..	..	..	..	2	..	34	..
16	Kudumi Chetti ..	General Labourers	..	..	6	..	..	..	14	1
17	Kusavan ..	Potters	..	..	..	..	..	..	..	..
18	Nayar ..	Military and Agricultural	27	..	201	..	42	..	2,557	10
19	Pandaran ..	Mendicants and Pappadam making	..	..	1	..	..	..	2	..
20	Panditattan ..	Goldsmiths	..	..	..	..	..	..	6	..
21	Pulayan ..	Agricultural Labourers	..	..	1	..	..	..	11	..
22	Parayan ..	Basket makers and Agricultural labourers	..	..	..	..	..	..	5	..
23	Valan ..	Boatmen and Fishermen	2	..	4	..	..	..	33	..
24	Velakkattalavan ..	Barbers	..	..	1	..	..	..	6	1
25	Velan ..	Barbers, Priests and washermen	..	..	1	..	..	..	3	..
26	Vellalan ..	Agriculturists and merchants	..	..	6	..	2	1	32	2
27	Veluthedan ..	Washermen	..	..	7	..	..	..	10	..
28	Vettuvan ..	Hunters	..	..	..	..	..	..	5	..
	MUSLIM									
29	Jonakan ..		..	..	27	..	3	..	32	..
30	Ravuttan ..		..	..	8	..	..	..	10	..
31	Others ..		1	..	29	..	1	..	51	1
	CHRISTIAN									
32	Anglo-Indian ..		..	..	3	..	..	..	9	..
33	European ..		1	..	..	..	2	..	1	..
34	Indian Christian ..		12	..	170	..	22	..	676	6
35	JAIN		..	..	..	..	..	..	..	..
36	JEW		..	..	..	..	..	..	6	2

TABLE XI.—(*cont.*)

TRIBE OR RACE.

CASTES, TRIBES OR RACES.

occupation of earners other than traditional occupation of caste (by sub-classes.)

	Arts and professions															
	Religions		Lawyers, doctors and teachers		Others		Persons living on their income		Domestic service		Contractors, clerks, cashiers, etc., otherwise unspecified		Labourers unspecified		Beggars, prostitutes, etc.	
	Males	Females	Males	Females	Males	Females	Males	Females	Males	Females	Males	Females	Males	Females	Males	Females
	50	51	52	53	54	55	56	57	58	59	60	61	62	63	64	65
1	..	..	287	52	35	2	42	77	38	24	51	5	4	2	..	..
2	..	..	8	2	1	11	..	..	2	10	2	..	2	5	..	..
3	4	..	11	1	5	1	1	..	3	4	..	..	5	37	..	..
4	140	..	143	6	49	4	16	26	84	53	233	..	166	5	..	..
5	..	..	68	..	14	..	111	79	36	5	54	..	3	..	..	..
6	..	..	887	11	84	8	286	149	209	42	323	..	56	2	..	..
7	..	..	2	..	..	..	..	..	3	10	1	..	18	9	..	..
8																
a.	..	..	..	..	..	..	1	..	1	10	..	..	13	..	..	.
b.	1	..	10	1	4	..	1	3	5	10	..	..	10	1	..	..
9	19	..	41	2	18	..	11	15	34	96	31	..	327	218	3	2
10	138	18	701	57	265	54	107	35	291	802	212	..	3,845	1,199	8	2
11	2	..	5	..	..	..	4	..	2	35	..	..	19	22	..	2
12	4	2	25	2	5	2	3	4	4	73	10	1	60	186	1	1
13	4	..	4	..	12	2	1	1	5	15	9	..	281	54	12	..
14	1	1	197	55	27	18	..	1	6	10	6	..	1	3	..	..
15	1	..	44	12	2	..	157	170	25	27	2	..	8	..	..	..
16	5	..	9	..	32	1	..	1	9	295	5	..	18	14	..	..
17	..	..	2	..	..	..	..	..	2	1	..	..	7	1	..	..
18	149	26	1,795	537	921	45	395	306	1,206	2,609	736	4	688	323	19	2
19	11	..	10	..	28	..	9	1	12	3	2	2	17	2	5	1
20	1	..	5	..	3	..	..	1	1	26	2	..	2	5	..	..
21	5	1	8	1	15	..	8	8	67	104	..	..	582	319	..	..
22	3	..	..	..	20	..	..	..	9	7	3	..	132	111	7	..
23	11	..	19	5	5	5	1	3	12	9	19	1	27	8	..	..
24	..	..	6	8	2	45	2	9	2	8	1	..	11	4	..	..
25	16	1	523	1	191	6	1	..	2	..	1	..	153	35	1	..
26	26	..	47	1	29	1	23	14	9	6	31	..	49	12	14	4
27	1	1	6	1	3		..	5	..	1	..	..	2	..	..	..
28	..	..	..	..	..	6	..	..	28	18	..	..	473	187	..	2
29	217	..	227	3	25	5	21	13	159	279	44	..	1,529	111	3	..
30	22	..	35	1	11	4	22	3	33	34	16	..	155	58	2	..
31	44	..	120	2	10	3	22	13	10	138	113	..	453	57	1	1
32	8	5	7	31	8	6	14	4	2	6	28	..	1	..	..	..
33	12	5	..	1	..	7	2	1	..	1	..	..	..	..	..	..
34	526	46	1,623	648	772	283	124	222	1,278	1,874	728	6	4,039	1,067	10	17
35	..	..	1	..	..	..	3	..	..	..	45	..	..	2	..	..
36	2	..	8	2	..	..	6	..	..	13	9	..	11	..	..	..

TABLE XII (i)

EDUCATED UNEMPLOYMENT (i) BY CLASS.

Note:—As there are no educated unemployed among Depressed Hindus and Muslims, these two classes are not given in column 1.

IMPERIAL TABLE XII (I).

EDUCATED UNEMPLOYMENT (I) BY CLASS.

CLASS	Total unemployed	Aged 20—24		Aged 25—29		Aged 30—34		Aged 35—39	
		Unemployed for							
		Less than one year	One year or more	Less than one year	One year or more	Less than one year	One year or more	Less than one year	One year or more
1	2	3	4	5	6	7	8	9	10
Brahmans ..	113	25	54	3	21	1	4	..	5
Other Hindus ..	236	47	120	7	43	6	12	..	1
Anglo-Indians ..	2	1	..	1	..	..	..	..	..
All other classes ..	93	11	33	9	26	..	10	..	4
Total ..	444	84	207	20	90	7	26	..	10

Total of English knowing unemployed under 20 years	**74**
.. .. over 40 years	**4**
Total number of educated unemployed whose fathers were Soldiers	**8**
.. .. .. Cultivators	**123**
.. .. .. Artizans	**4**
.. .. .. Menials or Servants	**11**
.. .. passed Matric or S. S. L. C. who though not totally unemployed failed to obtain employment with which they are satisfied	**74**

TABLE XII (ii)

EDUCATED UNEMPLOYMENT (ii) BY DEGREES.

Note:—There is no unemployment among those who have taken British, Continental, American or other Foreign degrees.

IMPERIAL TABLE XII (ii).

EDUCATED UNEMPLOYMENT (ii) BY DEGREES.

DEGREE	Total unemployed	Aged 20—24		Aged 25—29		Aged 30—34		Aged 35—39	
		Unemployed for							
		Less than one year	One year or more	Less than one year	One year or more	Less than one year	One year or more	Less than one year	One year or more
1	2	3	4	5	6	7	8	9	10
INDIAN DEGREES.									
Medical ..	6	1	..	1	..	..	3	..	1
Legal ..	2	..	..	1	..	..	1	..	1
M. A. ..	8	3	3	..	2	..	..	..	..
B. A. ..	72	23	23	8	14	..	3	..	1
L. T. ..	1	1	..	..	..	..	..	..	..
S. S. L. C. or Matric ..	351	55	180	10	73	7	19	..	7
Auto-Mechanism ..	3	1	1	..	1	..	..	..	..
Total ..	444	84	207	20	90	7	26	..	10

TABLE XIII.

LITERACY BY RELIGION AND AGE.

Note 1.—Of the 13.035 (9,044 males and 3.991 females) Christians returned as literate, in English 96 (50 males and 46 females) are Europeans and allied races 521 (235males and 286 females) are Anglo-Indians and the rest are Indian Christians.

2. Literacy among Indian Christians by Sect.

AGE	NUMBER LITERATE											
	INDIAN CHRISTIANS			PROTESTANT			ROMAN CATHOLIC			SYRIAN		
	Persons	Males	Females	Persons	Males	Females	Persons	Males	Females	Persons	Males	Females
Total	**13.2748**	**78.968**	**53.780**	**2,450**	**1,235**	**1,215**	**113.212**	**67,858**	**45.354**	**17.086**	**9,875**	**7,211**
0—5	193	103	90	8	5	3	144	77	67	41	21	20
5—10	14,139	7.512	6.627	282	143	139	12,070	6.156	5.914	1,787	913	874
10—15	21,869	11,745	10,124	413	205	208	18,776	10,137	8.639	2,680	1.403	1,277
15—20	20,930	11,512	9,418	340	156	190	18,092	10,014	8,078	2,492	1,342	1,150
20 & Over	75,617	48,096	27,521	1,401	726	675	64,130	41,174	22,956	10,089	6,199	3,890

IMPERIAL TABLE XIII.

LITERACY BY RELIGION AND AGE.

A. ALL RELIGIONS

AGE	POPULATION									LITERATE IN ENGLISH		
	TOTAL			LITERATE			ILLITERATE					
	Persons	Males	Females	Persons	Males	Females	Persons	Males	Females	Persons	Males	Females
1	2	3	4	5	6	7	8	9	10	11	12	13
0—5 ..	198,097	99,426	98,671	439	244	195	197,658	99,182	98,476	4	4	..
5—10 ..	156,302	79,218	77,084	35,648	20,897	14,751	120,654	58,321	62,333	1,240	820	420
10—15 ..	148,115	74,869	73,246	55,029	32,844	22,185	93,086	42,025	51,061	4,207	2,867	1,340
15—20 ..	117,905	55,964	61,941	52,038	32,166	19,872	65,867	23,798	42,069	8,774	6,259	2,515
20 and over ..	584,597	280,336	304,261	196,499	139,518	56,981	388,098	140,818	247,280	22,754	18,587	4,167
Total ..	1,205,016	589,813	615,203	339,653	225,669	113,984	865,363	364,144	501,219	36,979	28,537	8,442

B. HINDU.

AGE	Persons	Males	Females	Persons	Males	Females	Persons	Males	Females	Persons	Males	Females
0—5 ..	125,961	62,937	63,024	219	127	92	125,742	62,810	62,932	1	1	..
5—10 ..	98,770	50,177	48,593	20,043	12,422	7,621	78,727	37,755	40,972	793	563	230
10—15 ..	93,838	47,514	46,324	30,902	19,548	11,354	62,936	27,966	34,970	2,611	1,906	705
15—20 ..	75,492	35,365	40,127	29,000	19,030	9,970	46,492	16,335	30,157	5,345	4,055	1,290
20 and over ..	386,423	181,940	204,483	112,375	83,962	28,413	274,048	97,978	176,070	14,444	12,298	2,146
Total ..	780,484	377,933	402,551	192,539	135,089	57,450	587,945	242,844	345,101	23,194	18,823	4,371

C. MUSLIM.

AGE	Persons	Males	Females	Persons	Males	Females	Persons	Males	Females	Persons	Males	Females
0—5 ..	14,691	7,510	7,181	16	10	6	14,675	7,500	7,175	..	..	..
5—10 ..	11,905	6,110	5,795	1,205	834	371	10,700	5,276	5,424	18	13	5
10—15 ..	11,191	5,766	5,425	1,885	1,358	527	9,306	4,408	4,898	64	55	9
15—20 ..	8,945	4,386	4,559	1,772	1,450	322	7,173	2,936	4,237	149	143	6
20 and over ..	41,170	21,022	20,148	7,179	6,652	527	33,991	14,370	19,621	371	363	8
Total ..	87,902	44,794	43,108	12,057	10,304	1,753	75,845	34,490	41,355	602	574	28

D. CHRISTIAN.

AGE	Persons	Males	Females	Persons	Males	Females	Persons	Males	Females	Persons	Males	Females
0—5 ..	57,195	28,841	28,354	198	104	94	56,997	28,737	28,260	3	3	..
5—10 ..	45,410	22,819	22,591	14,325	7,599	6,726	31,085	15,220	15,865	423	241	182
10—15 ..	42,883	21,490	21,393	22,145	11,883	10,262	20,738	9,607	11,131	1,517	899	618
15—20 ..	33,305	16,139	17,166	21,172	11,636	9,536	12,133	4,503	7,630	3,248	2,041	1,207
20 and over ..	156,077	76,906	79,171	76,495	48,587	27,908	79,582	28,319	51,263	7,844	5,860	1,984
Total ..	334,870	166,195	168,675	134,335	79,809	54,526	200,535	86,386	114,149	13,035	9,044	3,991

F. JAIN.

AGE	Persons	Males	Females	Persons	Males	Females	Persons	Males	Females	Persons	Males	Females
0—5 ..	29	16	13	1	..	1	28	16	12	..	..	..
5—10 ..	28	14	14	7	3	4	21	11	10	..	..	..
10—15 ..	22	12	10	7	4	3	15	8	7	1	1	..
15—20 ..	16	7	9	9	6	3	7	1	6	1	1	..
20 and over ..	115	69	46	64	60	4	51	9	42	3	3	..
Total ..	210	118	92	88	73	15	122	45	77	5	5	..

IMPERIAL TABLE XIII.—(*cont.*)

LITERACY BY RELIGION AND AGE.

F. JEW.

AGE	POPULATION									LITERATE IN ENGLISH		
	TOTAL			LITERATE			ILLITERATE					
	Persons	Males	Females	Persons	Males	Females	Persons	Males	Females	Persons	Males	Females
1	2	3	4	5	6	7	8	9	10	11	12	13
0—5 ..	204	111	93	4	2	2	200	109	91	..	..	..
5—10 ..	177	93	84	60	35	25	117	58	59	4	1	3
10—15 ..	164	80	84	77	45	32	87	35	52	9	3	6
15—20 ..	137	61	76	76	39	37	61	22	39	23	14	9
20 and over ..	769	376	393	350	235	115	419	141	278	71	47	24
Total ..	1,451	721	730	567	356	211	884	365	519	107	65	42

G. BUDDHIST.

AGE	Persons	Males	Females	Persons	Males	Females	Persons	Males	Females	Persons	Males	Females
0—5 ..	17	11	6	1	1	..	16	10	6	..	..	..
5—10 ..	12	5	7	8	4	4	4	1	3	2	2	..
10—15 ..	17	7	10	13	6	7	4	1	3	5	3	2
15—20 ..	9	6	3	8	5	3	1	1	..	7	5	2
20 and over ..	41	22	19	34	21	13	7	1	6	20	15	5
Total ..	96	51	45	64	37	27	32	14	18	34	25	9

H. ZOROASTRIAN.

AGE	Persons	Males	Females	Persons	Males	Females	Persons	Males	Females	Persons	Males	Females
0—5 ..	..	..	..	..	..	..	..	..	..	..	..	..
5—10 ..	..	..	..	..	..	..	..	..	..	..	..	..
10—15 ..	..	..	..	..	..	..	..	..	..	..	..	..
15—20 ..	1	..	1	1	..	1	..	..	..	1	..	1
20 and over ..	2	1	1	2	1	1	..	..	..	1	1	..
Total ..	3	1	2	3	1	2	..	..	..	2	1	1

TABLE XIV.

LITERACY BY CASTES, TRIBES OR RACES.

IMPERIAL TABLE XIV.

LITERACY BY CASTES, TRIBES OR RACES.

CASTE, TRIBE OR RACE	Population (7 years and over)									Literate in English (7 years and over)		
	Total			Literate			Illiterate					
	Persons	Males	Females	Persons	Males	Females	Persons	Males	Females	Persons	Males	Females
1	2	3	4	5	6	7	8	9	10	11	12	13
Cochin State.	**955,607**	**464,451**	**491,156**	**338,798**	**225,193**	**113,605**	**616,809**	**239,258**	**377,551**	**36,974**	**28,532**	**8,442**
HINDU ..	**622,129**	**298,613**	**323,516**	**192,108**	**134,838**	**57,270**	**430,021**	**163,775**	**266,246**	**23,193**	**18,822**	**4,371**
Agamudaiyan ..	211	99	112	34	31	3	177	68	109	1	1	..
Ambalavasi ..	7,487	3,656	3,831	5,454	3,148	2,306	2,033	508	1,525	1,099	866	233
Adikal ..	22	14	8	14	14	..	8	..	8	1	1	..
Chakkiyar ..	39	17	22	24	15	9	15	2	13	2	2	..
Chakkiyar Nambiyar ..	65	46	19	49	37	12	16	9	7	13	13	..
Chengazhi Nambiyar ..	158	82	76	85	60	25	73	22	51	14	13	1
Kallattu Kurup ..	292	126	166	160	96	64	132	30	102	12	9	3
Marar ..	1,651	808	843	1,115	647	468	536	161	375	225	150	75
Nambiyassan ..	643	327	316	460	289	171	183	38	145	61	61	..
Pisharodi ..	1,155	553	602	831	482	349	324	71	253	188	150	38
Pushpakan Nambiyar ..	341	173	168	253	152	101	88	21	67	51	49	2
Putuval ..	382	164	218	304	143	161	78	21	57	71	49	22
Tiyyattunni ..	9	5	4	8	5	3	1	—	1	2	2	..
Unni ..	143	77	66	113	67	46	30	10	20	29	19	10
Variyar ..	2,587	1,264	1,323	2,038	1,141	897	549	123	426	430	348	82
Ambattan ..	1,249	604	645	373	248	125	876	356	520	24	21	3
Arayan ..	5,257	2,806	2,451	1,489	1,201	288	3,768	1,605	2,163	49	39	10
Baniya ..	129	66	63	64	46	18	65	20	45	7	7	..
Boya ..	193	104	89	1	1	..	192	103	89	..	..	..
Brahman ..	33,472	17,100	16,372	20,503	13,815	6,688	12,969	3,285	9,684	6,163	5,782	381
Embran ..	1,342	853	489	705	562	143	637	291	346	57	53	4
Gauda ..	526	320	206	104	87	17	422	233	189	26	22	4
Gujarati ..	168	95	73	82	68	14	86	27	59	16	16	..
Konkani ..	7,870	3,947	3,923	3,541	2,853	688	4,329	1,094	3,235	1,174	1,105	69
Marathi ..	167	92	75	83	67	16	84	25	59	35	34	1
Malayali — Elayad ..	793	432	361	571	381	190	222	51	171	41	41	..
Malayali — Muttad ..	258	130	128	208	113	95	50	17	33	40	39	1
Malayali — Nambudiri ..	5,077	2,575	2,502	3,369	2,176	1,193	1,708	399	1,309	216	214	2
Tamil ..	17,138	8,566	8,572	11,757	7,442	4,315	5,381	1,124	4,257	4,532	4,233	299
Telugu ..	46	25	21	36	23	13	10	2	8	19	18	1
Others .	87	65	22	47	43	4	40	22	18	7	7	..
Chakkan ..	1,771	888	883	413	336	77	1,358	552	806	38	37	1
Chakkiliyan ..	683	363	320	19	12	7	664	351	313	1	..	1
Chaliyan — Chaliyan ..	317	169	148	76	51	25	241	118	123	5	2	3
Chaliyan — Pattarian ..	1,514	725	789	626	421	205	888	304	584	58	47	11
Chavalan ..	779	396	383	65	61	4	714	335	379	..	..	..
Chetti ..	4,206	1,886	2,320	761	632	129	3,445	1,354	2,191	65	63	2
Chunnambottan ..	92	43	49	..	..	..	92	43	49	..	..	..
Dasi ..	328	110	218	145	73	72	183	37	146	37	26	11
Devangan ..	2,559	1,268	1,291	511	471	50	2,038	797	1,241	31	29	2

IMPERIAL TABLE XIV—(*cont.*)

LITERACY BY CASTES, TRIBES OR RACES.

CASTE, TRIBE OR RACE	Population (7 years and over)									Literate in English (7 years and over)		
	Total			Literate			Illiterate					
	Persons	Males	Females	Persons	Males	Females	Persons	Males	Females	Persons	Males	Females
1	2	3	4	5	6	7	8	9	10	11	12	13
HINDU (*cont.*)												
Eluthassan ..	14,834	7,163	7,671	4,285	3,307	978	10,549	3,856	6,693	239	205	34
Eravalan ..	467	245	222	1	1	..	466	244	222	..	..	..
Idaiyan ..	311	163	148	116	77	39	195	86	109	23	21	2
Iluvan ..	219,345	104,214	115,131	57,466	44,704	12,762	161,879	59,510	102,369	2,597	2,138	459
Irulan ..	176	89	87	..	..	..	176	89	87	..	..	..
Kadan ..	203	111	92	11	9	2	192	102	90	..	..	..
Kaikolan ..	3,128	1,514	1,614	297	281	16	2,831	1,233	1,598	27	26	1
Kakkalan ..	581	303	278	105	84	21	476	219	257	3	3	..
Kallan ..	881	412	469	202	176	26	679	236	443	..	..	..
Kammalan ..	36,122	17,488	18,634	10,708	8,936	1,772	25,414	8,552	16,862	157	143	14
Kalliasari ..	2,966	1,471	1,495	929	847	82	2,037	624	1,413	7	7	..
Kollan ..	7,366	3,615	3,751	1,443	1,207	236	5,923	2,408	3,515	22	21	1
Marasari ..	18,623	8,894	9,709	5,702	4,878	824	12,901	4,016	8,885	73	67	6
Moosari ..	1,152	580	572	299	239	60	853	341	512	5	5	..
Tattan ..	4,775	2,321	2,454	2,090	1,557	533	2,685	764	1,921	50	43	7
Tolkollan ..	1,260	607	653	245	208	37	1,015	399	616	..	..	..
Kanakkan ..	10,285	5,108	5,177	1,055	873	182	9,230	4,235	4,995	11	8	3
Kaniyan ..	3,139	1,566	1,573	2,058	1,265	793	1,081	301	780	53	49	4
Kavara ..	669	349	320	7	7	..	662	344	320	1	1	..
Kavundan ..	3,071	1,556	1,515	409	384	25	2,662	1,172	1,490	21	20	1
Kootan ..	187	92	95	2	2	..	185	90	95	..	..	..
Kshatriya ..	1,729	810	919	1,120	590	530	609	220	389	376	284	92
Gujarati ..	240	126	114	115	96	19	125	30	95	22	22	..
Karnataka ..	141	84	57	32	31	1	109	53	56	3	3	..
Marathi ..	93	27	66	8	3	5	85	24	61	..	..	..
Malayali ..	1,154	507	647	920	424	496	234	83	151	342	250	92
Rajput ..	41	18	23	10	8	2	31	10	21	4	4	..
Others ..	60	48	12	35	28	7	25	20	5	5	5	..
Kudumichetti ..	12,811	6,598	6,213	1,869	1,718	151	10,942	4,880	6,062	63	60	3
Kurukkal ..	261	128	133	67	64	3	194	64	130	4	4	..
Kusavan ..	2,594	1,348	1,246	107	94	13	2,487	1,254	1,233	..	..	..
Malayan ..	2,574	1,349	1,225	17	16	1	2,557	1,333	1,224	..	..	..
Nambidi ..	322	130	192	193	100	93	129	30	99	32	29	3
Nanjanattupillai ..	277	175	102	154	120	34	123	55	68	42	39	3
Nayadi ..	126	62	64	7	7	..	119	55	64	..	..	..
Nayar ..	114,776	52,100	62,676	63,978	37,634	26,344	50,798	14,466	36,332	11,017	8,028	2,989
Odan ..	1,179	582	597	98	91	7	1,081	491	590	..	..	..
Ottanaikan (Odde) ..	2,337	1,201	1,136	114	97	17	2,223	1,104	1,119	12	11	1
Panan ..	2,930	1,458	1,472	505	361	144	2,425	1,097	1,328	..	..	..
Pandaran ..	3,923	1,913	2,010	659	562	97	3,264	1,351	1,913	19	18	1

IMPERIAL TABLE XIV—(*cont.*)

LITERACY BY CASTES, TRIBES OR RACES.

CASTE, TRIBE OR RACE	Population (7 years and over)									Literate in English (7 years and over)		
	Total			Literate			Illiterate					
	Persons	Males	Females	Persons	Males	Females	Persons	Males	Females	Persons	Males	Females
1	2	3	4	5	6	7	8	9	10	11	12	13
HINDU (*cont.*)												
Panditattan ..	2,368	1,226	1,142	732	606	126	1,636	620	1,016	39	36	3
Pulayan ..	64,418	31,290	33,128	3,423	2,855	568	60,995	28,435	32,560	49	43	6
Pulluvan ..	139	70	69	32	27	5	107	43	64	1	1	..
Samantan ..	474	220	254	324	194	130	150	26	124	47	43	4
Sambavan (Parayan) ..	9,036	4,506	4,530	277	242	35	8,759	4,264	4,495	4	4	..
Sambavan (Parayan) Tamil ..	276	143	133	18	17	1	258	126	132	1	1	..
Tarakan ..	777	368	409	235	178	57	542	190	352	40	36	4
Tottiyan ..	139	51	88	8	4	4	131	47	84	..	..	..
Ullatan ..	630	311	319	28	17	11	602	294	308	..	..	..
Vadukan ..	1,125	519	606	62	59	3	1,063	460	603	4	4	..
Vaisyan ..	571	312	259	234	201	33	337	111	226	49	48	1
Valan ..	9,029	4,651	4,378	2,774	2,142	632	6,255	2,509	3,746	152	120	32
Valluvan ..	170	85	85	1	1	..	169	84	85	..	..	..
Vaniyan ..	717	358	359	243	220	23	474	138	336	27	27	..
Vannan ..	376	191	185	22	20	2	354	171	183	..	..	..
Velakkattalavan ..	2,054	1,418	1,536	1,040	711	329	1,914	707	1,207	41	28	13
Velan ..	8,745	4,162	4,583	2,513	2,159	354	6,232	2,003	4,229	28	25	3
Vellalan ..	4,419	2,198	2,221	1,470	1,198	272	2,949	1,000	1,949	250	229	21
Veluttedan ..	3,187	1,430	1,757	989	674	315	2,198	756	1,442	44	38	6
Vettuvan ..	9,109	4,605	4,504	500	390	110	8,609	4,215	4,394	10	7	3
Vil-kurup ..	1,447	659	788	373	283	90	1,074	376	698	1	1	..
Minor Castes ..	1,189	616	573	205	164	41	984	452	532	39	36	3
Caste unspecified ..	1,335	702	633	441	359	82	894	343	551	99	95	4
No caste ..	14	12	2	10	10	..	4	2	2	3	3	..
MUSLIM ..	**69,227**	**35,249**	**33,978**	**12,030**	**10,286**	**1,744**	**57,197**	**24,963**	**32,234**	**602**	**574**	**28**
Jonakan ..	45,064	22,863	22,201	7,039	6,049	990	38,025	16,814	21,211	228	219	9
Ravuttan ..	8,685	4,480	4,205	1,370	1,256	114	7,315	3,224	4,091	96	94	2
Others ..	15,478	7,906	7,572	3,621	2,981	640	11,857	4,925	6,932	278	261	17
CHRISTIAN ..	**262,809**	**129,874**	**132,935**	**133,947**	**79,606**	**54,341**	**128,862**	**50,268**	**78,594**	**13,031**	**9,040**	**3,991**
Anglo-Indian ..	1,384	648	736	1,003	512	491	381	136	245	517	231	286
European ..	104	55	49	100	51	46	4	1	3	96	50	46
Indian-Christian ..	261,321	129,171	132,150	132,844	79,040	53,804	128,477	50,131	78,346	12,418	8,759	3,659
JAIN ..	**171**	**98**	**73**	**86**	**73**	**13**	**85**	**25**	**60**	**5**	**5**	..
JEW ..	**1,190**	**577**	**613**	**561**	**353**	**208**	**629**	**224**	**405**	**107**	**65**	**42**
BUDDHIST ..	**78**	**39**	**39**	**63**	**36**	**27**	**15**	**3**	**12**	**34**	**25**	**9**
ZOROASTRIAN ..	**3**	**1**	**2**	**3**	**1**	**2**	..	..	..	**2**	**1**	**1**

TABLE XV.

PART I.—LANGUAGE.

IMPERIAL TABLE XV.

PART I.—LANGUAGE.

LANGUAGE	Persons	Males	Females
1	2	3	4
COCHIN STATE	**1,205,016**	**589,813**	**615,203**
A. Vernaculars of India	**1,203,731**	**589,200**	**614,531**
VERNACULAR OF THE STATE.			
Malayalam	1,088,081	530,737	557,344
VERNACULARS FOREIGN TO THE STATE.	115,650	58,463	57,187
Bengali	3	3	..
Goanese	12	11	1
Gujarati	1,253	689	564
Hindi	2,486	1,295	1,191
Kachchhi	714	386	328
Kanarese	4,493	2,387	2,106
Konkani	22,338	11,311	11,027
Marathi	5,210	2,612	2,598
Marwari	1	1	..
Parsi	8	4	4
Pashto	3	3	..
Tamil	66,164	33,247	32,917
Telugu	12,142	6,016	6,126
Tulu	731	442	289
Urudu	79	45	34
Indian unspecified	13	11	2
B. Vernaculars of Asiatic Countries beyond India	**515**	**273**	**242**
Arabic	236	129	107
Chinese	1	1	..
Hebrew	266	136	130
Japanese	1	1	..
Persian	1	1	..
Singhalese	7	2	5
Syriac	3	3	..
C. European Languages	**770**	**340**	**430**
Basque	4	4	..
English	630	263	367
Flemish	2	..	2
French	1	..	1
Gaelic	1	1	..
German	2	..	2
Italian	9	..	9
Portuguese	114	65	49
Spanish	6	6	..
Welsh	1	1	..

TABLE XV.

PART II —BI-LINGUALISM.

Note.—Figures in certain cases are duplicated on account of tri- or poli-lingualism: for those who use more than one subsidiary language are shown under each head. The Statement attached to this table as a supplement exhibits in detail the figures for tri- and poli-lingualism.

IMPERIAL TABLE XV.

PART II.—BI-LINGUALISM.

MOTHER TONGUE	Number of persons speaking mother tongue		Number of persons speaking subsidiary language							
			Malayalam		Tamil		Konkani		English	
	Males	Females	Males	Females	Males	Females	Males	Females	Males	Females
1	2	3	4	5	6	7	8	9	10	11
COCHIN STATE	589,813	615,203	47,708	45,543	6,693	5,600	32	30	28,153	8,048
A. Vernaculars of India										
1. VERNACULAR OF THE STATE										
Malayalam ..	530,737	557,344	..	..	3,388	1,023	20	8	21,783	7,559
2. VERNACULARS FOREIGN TO THE STATE										
Bengali ..	3	..	..	..	..	..	..	..	2	..
Goanese ..	11	1	9	..	1	..	..	..	7	..
Gujarati ..	689	564	405	265	1	3	..	..	93	1
Hindi ..	1,295	1,191	1,239	930	445	549	..	..	182	4
Kachchhi ..	386	328	307	273	4	1	..	..	56	2
Kanarese ..	2,387	2,106	2,025	1,712	1,080	989	5	4	74	6
Konkani ..	11,311	11,027	9,769	9,092	84	31	..	..	958	72
Marathi ..	2,612	2,598	2,248	2,142	36	21	2	2	254	21
Marwari ..	1	..	..	..	..	..	..	..	..	..
Parsi ..	4	4	1	2	..	..	..	..	..	..
Pashto ..	3	..	3	..	..	..	..	..	..	..
Tamil ..	33,247	32,917	25,798	24,528	..	..	1	1	4,476	320
Telugu ..	6,016	6,126	5,064	5,815	1,593	3,153	..	..	167	21
Tulu ..	442	289	371	209	18	2	..	..	28	..
Urdu ..	45	34	41	29	2	1	2	..	7	2
Indian unspecified ..	11	2	10	2	..	..	..	..	1	..
B. Vernaculars of Asiatic Countries beyond India.										
Arabic ..	125	107	113	99	3	..	..	..	3	..
Chinese ..	1	..	..	..	1	..	..	..	..	..
Hebrew ..	136	130	112	117	..	..	..	..	13	5
Japanese ..	1	..	..	..	..	..	..	..	1	..
Persian ..	1	..	..	..	1	..	..	..	1	..
Singhalese ..	2	5	2	3	..	1	..	..	1	..
Syriac ..	3	..	2	..	..	..	..	..	3	..
C. European Languages										
Basque ..	4	..	1	..	..	..	..	..	4	..
English ..	263	367	188	280	30	23	1	14	..	..
Flemish ..	..	2	..	..	..	..	..	..	..	1
French ..	..	1	..	..	..	..	..	..	..	..
Gaelic ..	1	..	..	..	..	..	..	..	1	..
German ..	..	2	..	1	..	1	..	..	..	2
Italian ..	..	9	..	..	..	..	..	..	..	9
Portuguese ..	65	40	55	43	6	2	1	1	41	23
Spanish ..	6	..	5	..	..	..	..	..	5	..
Welsh ..	1	..	1	..	..	..	..	..	1	..

SUPPLEMENT TO TABLE XV.

PART II—BI-LINGUALISM.

MOTHER TONGUE	Number of persons speaking more than one subsidiary language																	
	Malayalam and Tamil		Malayalam and Konkani		Malayalam and English		Tamil and Konkani		Tamil and English		Konkani and English		Malayalam, Tamil and Konkani		Malayalam, Tamil and English		Malayalam, Konkani and English	
	Males	Females	Males	Females	Males	Females	Males	Females	Males	Females	Males	Females	Males	Females	Males	Females	Males	Females
1	2	3	4	5	6	7	8	9	10	11	12	13	14	15	16	17	18	19
A. Vernaculars of India.																		
1. VERNACULAR OF THE STATE.																		
Malayalam ..	..	..	..	..	..	..	..	..	817	154	3	1	..	..	..	..	..	..
2. VERNACULARS FOREIGN TO THE STATE.																		
Goanese ..	..	..	..	..	..	..	..	..	..	..	..	..	..	..	1	..	..	..
Gujarati ..	..	3	..	..	69	1	..	..	..	..	..	..	..	..	1	..	..	..
Hindi ..	337	117	..	..	131	2	..	..	3	..	..	..	..	..	26	2	..	..
Kachchhi ..	2	1	..	..	52	2	..	..	1	..	..	..	..	..	..	..	..	..
Kanarese ..	953	888	2	2	27	3	..	..	2	..	..	..	1	..	41	2	1	1
Konkani ..	47	22	..	..	621	65	..	..	..	..	..	..	..	..	27	2	..	..
Marathi ..	16	11	2	2	222	20	..	..	1	..	..	..	..	..	15	..	..	..
Tamil ..	..	..	1	1	4,403	314	..	..	..	..	..	..	..	..	..	..	..	..
Telugu ..	1,251	2,607	..	..	49	6	..	..	10	2	..	..	..	..	106	13	..	..
Tulu ..	16	2	..	..	26	..	..	..	..	..	..	..	..	..	2	..	..	..
Urdu ..	2	1	2	..	6	2	..	..	..	..	..	..	..	..	..	..	..	..
Indian unspecified ..	..	..	..	..	1	..	..	..	..	..	..	..	..	..	..	..	..	..
B. Vernaculars of Asiatic Countries beyond India.																		
Arabic ..	1	..	..	..	1	..	..	..	..	..	..	..	..	..	2	..	..	..
Hebrew ..	..	..	..	..	11	5	..	..	..	..	..	..	..	..	..	..	..	..
Persian ..	..	..	..	..	..	..	..	..	1	..	..	..	..	..	..	..	..	..
Singhalese ..	..	..	..	..	1	..	..	..	..	..	..	..	..	..	..	..	..	..
Syriac ..	..	..	..	..	2	..	..	..	..	..	..	..	..	..	..	..	..	..
European Languages																		
Basque ..	..	..	..	..	1	..	..	..	..	..	..	..	..	..	..	..	..	..
English ..	19	10	1	..	..	..	..	..	..	..	..	..	..	..	..	..	..	..
German ..	..	..	..	..	..	..	..	..	..	..	..	..	..	..	..	1	..	..
Portuguese ..	..	1	..	..	28	20	..	..	..	..	1	1	..	..	6	1	..	..
Spanish ..	..	..	..	..	4	..	..	..	..	..	..	..	..	..	..	..	..	..
Welsh ..	..	..	..	..	1	..	..	..	..	..	..	..	..	..	..	..	..	..

TABLE XVI.

RELIGION.

Note.—Animists are not shown separately in this Table. The Primitive Tribes given in Table XVIII returned themselves as Hindus and they have, therefore, been classed as Hindus according to instructions.

Distribution of Christian population by Sect and Race.

Race	Total			Roman Catholics		Romo-Syrians		Other Syrians		Others	
	Persons	Males	Females	Males	Females	Males	Females	Males	Females	Males	Females
1	2	3	4	5	6	7	8	9	10	11	12
COCHIN STATE.	334,870	166,195	168,675	54,080	54,523	90,789	92,843	17,769	18,399	2,657	2,910
European and allied Races ..	112	58	51	17	13	2	5	2	..	30	34
Anglo-Indians ..	1,717	920	[illegible]	766	752	50	117	..	..	24	28
Indian Christians..	333,041	165,317	167,724	54,257	53,756	90,697	92,721	17,766	18,399	2,597	2,848

TABLE XVI.

RELIGION.

TALUKS.	POPULATION			HINDU			MUSLIM			CHRISTIAN			JAIN			JEW			BUDDHIST			ZOROASTRIAN		
	Persons	Males	Females	Persons	Males	Females	Persons	Males	Females	Persons	Males	Females	Persons	Males	Females	Persons	Males	Females	Persons	Males	Females	Persons	Males	Females
1	2	3	4	5	6	7	8	9	10	11	12	13	14	15	16	17	18	19	20	21	22	23	24	25
Cochin State ..	**1,205,016**	**589,813**	**615,203**	**780,484**	**377,933**	**402,551**	**87,902**	**44,794**	**43,108**	**334,870**	**166,195**	**168,675**	**210**	**118**	**92**	**1,451**	**721**	**730**	**96**	**51**	**45**	**3**	**1**	**2**
Cochin-Kanayannur ..	**350,268**	177,242	173,026	184,437	93,143	91,294	23,313	12,279	10,034	141,092	71,053	70,039	209	117	92	1,294	638	656	20	11	9	3	1	2
Cranganur ..	**42,531**	21,099	21,432	28,839	14,170	14,669	11,155	5,605	5,550	2,537	1,324	1,213	..	..	.	..	..	..	..	..	..	..	..	..
Mukundapuram ..	**263,722**	127,738	135,984	165,561	79,175	86,386	13,228	6,722	6,506	84,745	41,743	43,002	..	..	..	156	82	74	32	16	16	..	..	..
Trichur ..	**239,257**	115,523	123,734	162,013	77,493	84,520	7,885	4,014	3,841	69,315	33,962	35,353	..	..	..	1	1	..	43	23	20	..	..	..
Talapilli ..	**202,424**	96,173	106,251	147,791	69,401	78,390	23,919	11,875	12,044	30,713	14,896	15,817	1	1	..	..	..	..	..	..	..	..	..	..
Chittur ..	**106,814**	52,038	54,776	91,843	44,551	47,292	8,502	4,269	4,233	6,468	3,217	3,251	..	..	..	..	..	..	1	1	..	..	..	..

TABLE XVII.

RACE, TRIBE OR CASTE.

Note.—Non-indigenous castes, which are numerically of minor importance, are lumped together in the tables as "minor castes".

IMPERIAL TABLE XVII.

RACE, TRIBE OR CASTE.

Caste and Religion	Persons	Males	Females
1	2	3	4
COCHIN STATE.	1,205,016	589,813	615,203
HINDU	780,484	377,933	402,551
Agamudaiyan	264	123	141
Ambalavasi	9,211	4,538	4,673
Adikal	25	14	11
Chakkiyar	50	20	30
Chakkiyar Nambiyar	76	50	26
Chengazhi Nambiyar	185	94	91
Kallattu Kurup	370	163	207
Marar	2,016	997	1,019
Nambiyassan	769	380	389
Pisharodi	1,459	722	737
Pushpakan Nambiyar	389	189	200
Putuvai	471	216	255
Tiyyattunni	11	6	5
Unni	169	89	80
Variyar	3,221	1,598	1,623
Ambattan	1,570	776	794
Arayan	6,574	3,457	3,117
Baniya	153	75	78
Boya	231	127	104
Brahman	41,324	21,013	20,311
Embran	1,571	953	618
Gauda	627	370	257
Gujarati	206	114	92
Konkani	9,661	4,828	4,833
Marathi	193	104	89
Malayali — Elayad	941	508	433
Malayali — Muttad	304	151	153
Malayali — Nambudiri	5,918	3,004	2,914
Tamil	21,754	10,884	10,870
Telugu	54	30	24
Others	95	67	28
Chakkan	2,162	1,065	1,097
Chakkiliyan	839	437	402
Chaliyan — Chaliyan	397	205	192
Chaliyan — Pattariyan	1,921	927	994
Chavalan	992	497	495
Chetti	5,339	2,544	2,795
Chunnambottan	115	55	60
Dasi	395	146	249
Devangan	3,055	1,533	1,522
Eluthassan	18,536	9,026	9,510

IMPERIAL TABLE XVII—(*cont.*)

RACE, TRIBE OR CASTE.

Caste and Religion	Persons	Males	Females
1	2	3	4
HINDU—(*cont*).			
Eravalan	541	271	270
Idaiyan	385	200	185
Iluvan	276,649	132,875	143,774
Irulan	240	137	103
Kadan	267	148	119
Kaikolan	3,714	1,820	1,894
Kakkalan	732	370	362
Kallan	1,096	530	566
Kammalan	45,546	22,085	23,461
Kallasari	3,852	1,880	1,972
Kollan	9,276	4,530	4,746
Marasari	23,430	11,263	12,167
Moosari	1,460	727	733
Tattan	5,956	2,942	3,014
Tolkollan	1,572	743	829
Kanakkan	13,192	6,567	6,625
Kaniyan	3,841	1,950	1,891
Kavara	790	416	374
Kavundan	3,680	1,868	1,812
Kootan	228	107	121
Kshatriya	2,128	1,015	1,113
Gujarati	275	142	133
Karnataka	167	97	70
Marathi	107	27	80
Malayali	1,467	673	794
Rajput	46	22	24
Others	66	54	12
Kudumi Chetti	16,104	8,216	7,888
Kurukkal	319	158	161
Kusavan	3,295	1,690	1,605
Malayan	3,185	1,645	1,540
Nambidi	410	176	234
Nanjanattu Pillai	330	204	126
Nayadi	152	76	76
Nayar	142,637	66,225	76,412
Odan	1,514	766	748
Otta-naikan (Odde)	2,765	1,422	1,343
Panan	3,603	1,771	1,832
Pandaran	4,860	2,384	2,476
Panditattan	2,964	1,549	1,415
Pulayan	82,043	39,982	42,061
Pulluvan	170	84	86

IMPERIAL TABLE XVII.—(*cont.*)

RACE, TRIBE OR CASTE.

Caste and Religion	Persons	Males	Females
1	2	3	4
HINDU—(*cont*).			
Samantan	571	277	294
Sambavan (Parayan)	11,562	5,734	5,828
Sambavan (Parayan) Tamil	352	175	177
Tarakan	929	433	496
Tottiyan	196	88	108
Ullatan	778	375	403
Vadukan	1,313	605	708
Vaisyan	685	369	316
Valan	11,684	5,979	5,705
Valluvan	212	105	107
Vaniyan	856	431	425
Vannan	443	243	200
Velakkattalavan	3,699	1,815	1,884
Velan	10,895	5,205	5,690
Vellalan	5,299	2,629	2,670
Veluttedan	3,922	1,816	2,106
Vettuvan	11,797	5,943	5,854
Vilkurup	1,779	842	937
Minor Castes	1,404	736	668
Caste unspecified	1,635	869	766
No caste	15	13	2
MUSLIM	87,902	44,794	43,108
Bora	74	48	26
Hanavi	54	27	27
Jonakan	57,371	29,150	28,221
Kachchhi	684	357	327
Pathan	2,275	1,134	1,141
Ravuttan	10,927	5,633	5,294
Shabi	287	154	133
Saiyad	43	28	15
Sheik	202	110	92
Others	15,985	8,153	7,832
CHRISTIAN	334,870	166,195	168,675
Anglo-Indian	1,717	820	897
European (British Subjects)	72	38	34
European others	40	20	20
Indian Christian	333,041	165,317	167,724
JAIN	210	118	92
JEW	1,451	721	730
Black Jew	1,307	659	648
White Jew	144	62	82
BUDDHIST	96	51	45
ZOROASTRIAN	3	1	2

TABLE XVIII.

VARIATION OF POPULATION OF SELECTED TRIBES.

Note:—1. Separate figures for 1881 are not available.

2. The previous Censuses do not show any returns for the "Irulan" tribe.

TABLE XVIII.

VARIATION OF POPULATION OF SELECTED TRIBES.

RELIGION AND TRIBE	Persons					Variation (Increase + Decrease —)				Net variation 1891 to 1931 Increase + Decrease —	Males					Females				
	1931	1921	1911	1901	1891	1921 to 1931	1911 to 1921	1901 to 1911	1891 to 1911		1931	1921	1911	1901	1891	1931	1921	1911	1901	1891
1	2	3	4	5	6	7	8	9	10	11	12	13	14	15	16	17	18	19	20	21
Cochin State ..	5,163	1,400	4,168	3,887	3,877	+3,763	−2,768	+281	+10	+ 1,286	2,682	847	2,120	1,967	1,906	2,511	553	2,048	1,920	1,971
HINDU.																				
Eravalan ..	541	..	503	292	..	+ 541	− 503	+ 211	+292	+ 541	271	..	245	149	..	270	..	258	143	..
Irulan ..	240	..	..	..	..	+ 240	..	..	..	+ 240	137	..	..	..	..	103	..	..	..	..
Kadan ..	267	274	447	310	231	− 7	− 173	+ 137	+ 89	+ 46	148	148	210	161	94	119	126	237	149	137
Malayan ..	3,185	594	2,461	2,631	3,094	+ 2,591	− 1,867	− 170	−463	+ 91	1,645	441	1,280	1,330	1,513	1,540	153	1,181	1,301	1,551
Nayadi ..	152	119	220	215	123	+ 33	− 101	+ 5	+ 92	+ 29	76	47	124	116	61	76	72	96	99	62
Ullatan ..	778	413	537	439	439	+ 365	− 124	+ 98	..	+ 339	375	211	261	211	208	403	202	276	228	231

TABLE XIX.

EUROPEAN AND ALLIED RACES AND ANGLO-INDIANS BY RACE AND AGE.

IMPERIAL TABLE XIX.

European and Allied Races and Anglo-Indians by Race and Age.

TABLE XIX.

EUROPEAN AND ALLIED RACES AND ANGLO-INDIANS BY RACE AND AGE.

A—EUROPEAN AND ALLIED RACES (INCLUDING ARMENIANS)

PROVINCE, STATE OR AGENCY	TOTAL			(a) British subjects																
				All ages			0—13		14—16		17—23		24—33		34—43		44—53		54 and over	
	Persons	Males	Females	Persons	Males	Females	Males	Females	Males	Females	Males	Females	Males	Females	Males	Females	Males	Females	Males	Females
1	2	3	4	5	6	7	8	9	10	11	12	13	14	15	16	17	18	19	20	21
Cochin State ..	1,829	878	951	72	38	34	5	8	..	1	4	5	12	5	9	0	5	3	3	3

PROVINCE, STATE OR AGENCY	(b) Others																
	All ages			0—13		14—16		17—23		24—33		34—43		44—53		54 and over	
	Persons	Males	Females	Males	Females	Males	Females	Males	Females	Males	Females	Males	Females	Males	Females	Males	Females
1	22	23	24	25	26	27	28	29	30	31	32	33	34	35	36	37	38
Cochin State ..	40	20	20	2	..	..	1	2	3	5	7	2	7	4	1	5	1

B—ANGLO-INDIANS.

PROVINCE, STATE OR AGENCY	All ages			0—3		4—6		7—13		14—16		17—19		20—29		30—39		40—49		50—59		60—69		70 and over	
	Persons	Males	Females	Males	Females	Males	Females	Males	Females	Males	Females	Males	Females	Males	Females	Males	Females	Males	Females	Males	Females	Males	Females	Males	Females
	39	40	41	42	43	44	45	46	47	48	49	50	51	52	53	54	55	56	57	58	59	60	61	62	63
Cochin State ..	1,717	820	897	90	88	82	74	157	154	68	68	48	57	99	154	80	102	70	93	61	58	38	32	27	17

TABLE XX.

SUMMARY FIGURES FOR TALUKS.

IMPERIAL TABLE XX.

Summary figures for Taluks.

TABLE XX.

SUMMARY FIGURES FOR TALUKS.

TALUK	Area in square miles	Population 1931			Population 1921	Percentage of variation		No. of persons per square mile in		Distribution by Religion													
										Hindu		Muslim		Christian		Jain		Jew		Buddhist		Zoroastrian	
		Persons	Males	Females		1921—1931	1911—1921	1931	1921	Males	Females	Males	Females	Males	Females	Males	Females	Males	Females	Males	Females	Males	Females
1	2	3	4	5	6	7	8	9	10	11	12	13	14	15	16	17	18	19	20	21	22	23	24
Cochin State ..	**1,480·28**	**1,205,016**	**589,813**	**615,203**	**979,080**	**+23·1**	**+6·6**	**814**	**662**	**377,833**	**402,551**	**44,794**	**43,106**	**168,195**	**168,675**	**118**	**92**	**721**	**730**	**51**	**45**	**1**	**2**
Cochin-Kanayannur ..	158·52	350,268	177,242	173,026	279,384	+25·4	+5·5	2,210	1,768	93,143	91,294	12,279	10,934	71,053	70,039	117	92	638	656	11	9	1	2
Cranganur ..	17·51	42,531	21,099	21,432	34,808	+22·2	+4·9	2,429	2,248	14,170	14,669	5,605	5,550	1,324	1,213	..	..	..	..	..	..	..	..
Mukundapuram ..	510·00	263,722	127,738	135,984	208,713	+26·4	+7·6	517	409	79,175	86,386	6,722	6,506	41,743	43,002	..	..	82	74	16	16	..	..
Trichur ..	245·50	239,257	115,523	123,734	198,813	+25·4	+12·4	975	779	77,493	84,520	4,044	3,841	33,062	35,353	..	..	1	..	23	20	..	..
Talapilli ..	256·00	202,424	96,173	106,251	170,154	+19·0	+3·1	791	665	69,401	78,390	11,875	12,044	14,896	15,817	1	..	..	..	..	..	..	..
Chittur ..	292·75	106,814	52,038	54,776	95,208	+12·2	+4·3	365	325	44,551	47,292	4,269	4,233	3,217	3,251	..	..	..	..	1	..	..	..

PART II

B.— STATE TABLES

STATE TABLE I.

AREA AND POPULATION OF TALUKS.

STATE TABLE I.

AREA AND POPULATION OF TALUKS.

TALUKS	Area in square miles	Number of		Number of occupied houses	POPULATION				PERCENTAGE OF VARIATION		Number of persons per square mile in 1931
		Towns	Villages		1931			1921 (both sexes)	1921 to 1931	1911 to 1921	
					Persons	Males	Females				
1	2	3	4	5	6	7	8	9	10	11	12
Cochin State ..	1,480·28	12	272	207,563	1,205,016	589,813	615,203	979,080	+23·1	+6·6	814
Cochin-Kanayannur ..	158·52	4	36	89,954	350,268	177,242	173,026	279,384	+25·4	+5·5	2,210
Cranganur ..	17·51	1	5	7,553	42,531	21,099	21,432	34,808	+22·2	+4·9	2,429
Mukundapuram ..	510·00	2	60	44,879	263,722	127,738	135,984	208,713	+26·4	+7·6	517
Trichur ..	245·50	1	72	39,261	239,257	115,523	123,734	190,813	+25·4	+12·4	975
Talapilli ..	256·00	2	74	35,314	202,424	96,173	106,251	170,154	+19·0	+3·1	791
Chittur ..	292·75	2	25	20,602	106,814	52,038	54,776	95,208	+12·2	+4·3	365

STATE TABLE II.

POPULATION OF TALUKS BY RELIGION AND LITERACY.

STATE TABLE II.

POPULATION OF TALUKS BY RELIGION AND LITERACY.

TALUK	HINDUS											
	Brahmans				Other Hindus				Depressed Classes			
	Number of Persons		Number Literate		Number of Persons		Number Literate		Number of Persons		Number Literate	
	Males	Females	Males	Females	Males	Females	Males	Females	Males	Females	Males	Females
1	2	3	4	5	6	7	8	9	10	11	12	13
Cochin State ..	**21,013**	**20,311**	**13,866**	**6,718**	**294,634**	**317,874**	**116,727**	**49,822**	**62,286**	**64,366**	**4,496**	**913**
Cochin-Kanayannur ..	8,170	7,467	5,105	1,779	71,097	69,694	33,381	14,127	13,876	14,133	2,435	425
Cranganur ..	750	705	492	183	11,942	12,565	4,884	2,343	1,478	1,399	137	44
Mukundapuram ..	2,767	2,792	1,768	974	60,074	66,826	22,387	8,467	16,374	16,768	748	176
Trichur ..	3,943	3,580	2,850	1,633	62,070	69,329	27,813	12,794	11,480	11,611	676	179
Talapilli ..	3,216	3,442	2,178	1,340	53,896	61,260	19,590	8,935	12,189	13,688	363	73
Chittur ..	2,167	2,325	1,473	806	35,555	38,200	8,672	3,156	6,829	6,767	137	16

STATE TABLE II.—(cont.)

POPULATION OF TALUKS BY RELIGION AND LITERACY.

TALUK	MUSLIMS				CHRISTIANS				JAINS				JEWS			
	Number of Persons		Number Literate		Number of Persons		Number Literate		Number of Persons		Number Literate		Number of Persons		Number Literate	
	Males	Females	Males	Females	Males	Females	Males	Females	Males	Females	Males	Females	Males	Females	Males	Females
	14	15	16	17	18	19	20	21	22	23	24	25	26	27	28	29
Cochin State ..	**44,794**	**43,108**	**10,304**	**1,783**	**166,195**	**168,675**	**79,809**	**84,826**	**118**	**92**	**73**	**18**	**721**	**730**	**356**	**211**
Cochin-Kanayannur ..	12,279	10,931	3,464	414	71,053	70,039	34,959	21,565	117	92	73	15	638	656	315	197
Cranganur ..	5,605	5,550	1,435	296	1,324	1,213	645	368	..	..	..	..	..	..	..	..
Mukundapuram ..	6,722	6,506	1,643	305	41,743	43,002	17,799	12,354	..	..	..	..	82	74	41	14
Trichur ..	4,044	3,841	1,194	246	33,962	35,353	17,851	13,706	..	..	..	..	1	..	..	..
Talapilli ..	11,875	12,044	1,760	399	14,896	15,817	7,830	6,147	1	..	..	..	..	..	..	..
Chittur ..	4,269	4,233	868	63	3,217	3,251	725	186	..	..	..	..	..	..	..	..

STATE TABLE II.—(*cont.*)

POPULATION OF TALUKS BY RELIGION AND LITERACY.

TALUK	BUDDHISTS				ZOROASTRIANS				NUMBER LITERATE						Literate in English	
	Number of Persons		Number Literate		Number of Persons		Number Literate		Aged 0—15		Aged 15—20		Aged 20 and over			
	Males	Females	Males	Females	Males	Females	Males	Females	Males	Females	Males	Females	Males	Females	Males	Females
	30	31	32	33	34	35	36	37	38	39	40	41	42	43	44	45
Cochin State ..	**51**	**45**	**37**	**27**	**1**	**2**	**1**	**2**	**53,985**	**37,131**	**32 166**	**19,872**	**130,518**	**56,981**	**28,537**	**8,442**
Cochin-Kanayannur ..	11	9	10	5	1	2	1	2	18,276	12,954	11,474	6,682	57,033	18,923	11,738	3,329
Cranganur ..	..	..	..	..	..	..	..	..	1,687	1,079	1,073	568	4,833	1,587	767	327
Mukundapuram ..	16	16	8	6	..	..	..	..	11,459	7,413	6,395	3,986	26,540	10,897	3,317	1,085
Trichur ..	23	20	18	16	..	..	..	..	12,732	9,285	7,485	5,075	30,185	14,214	7,225	2,441
Talapilli ..	..	..	..	..	..	..	..	..	7,312	5,136	4,350	2,875	20,159	9,083	3,187	879
Chittur ..	1	..	1	..	..	..	..	..	2,559	1,264	1,489	686	7,768	2,277	2,303	381

STATE TABLE III.

INFIRMITIES BY SELECTED CASTES, TRIBES OR RACES.

Note.—The following statement exhibits combination of infirmities by Race, Caste, Sex and Age.

Race and Caste	Sex	Age	Infirmities
Hindu.			
Kudumi Chetti ..	Male	30	Insane and Blind
Kammalan ..	Female	25	Deaf-Mute and Leper
Malayali Kshatriya ..	Male	44	Insane and Leper
Muslim.			
Jonakan ..	Male	50	Blind and Leper
Christian.			
Indian-Christian ...	Female	60	Blind and Leper
Do ...	do	48	Insane and Deaf-Mute

Persons suffering from more infirmities than one are included under each head.

STATE TABLE III.

INFIRMITIES BY SELECTED CASTES, TRIBES OR RACES.

Caste, Tribe or Race	Population dealt with			Insane			Deaf-mutes			Blind			Lepers		
	Persons	Males	Females	Persons	Males	Females	Persons	Males	Females	Persons	Males	Females	Persons	Males	Females
1	2	3	4	5	6	7	8	9	10	11	12	13	14	15	16
COCHIN STATE	1,205,016	589,813	615,203	637	358	279	488	283	205	1,595	758	837	745	553	192
HINDU	780,484	377,933	402,551	391	227	164	300	169	131	1,188	534	654	484	348	136
Ambalavasi ..	9,211	4,538	4,673	9	8	1	5	4	1	28	10	18	3	2	1
Amlattan ..	1,570	776	794	..	..	..	2	2	..	1	1	..	1	1	..
Arayan ..	6,574	3,457	3,117	2	2	..	2	1	1	5	4	1	3	3	..
Brahman ..	41,324	21,013	20,311	41	31	10	10	6	4	55	26	29	16	14	2
Konkani ..	9,661	4,828	4,831	7	5	2	..	..	..	2	2	..	1	1	..
Malayali ..	7,163	3,663	3,500	7	6	1	2	1	1	11	5	6	3	3	..
Tamil ..	21,754	10,884	10,870	17	11	6	6	4	2	31	15	16	7	5	2
Others ..	2,746	1,638	1,108	10	9	1	2	1	1	11	4	7	5	5	..
Chaliyan ..	2,318	1,132	1,186	..	..	..	..	..	..	4	3	1	4	2	2
Chakkan ..	2,162	1,065	1,097	3	1	2	..	..	..	1	..	1	..	..	..
Chetti ..	5,339	2,544	2,795	7	4	3	4	3	1	..	..	..	1	1	..
Devangan ..	3,055	1,533	1,522	..	..	..	2	2	..	3	3	..	1	1	..
Eluthasan ..	18,536	9,026	9,510	5	2	3	5	2	3	59	35	24	14	12	2
Iluvan ..	276,649	132,875	143,774	127	68	59	111	65	46	369	166	203	168	118	50
Kalkolan ..	3,714	1,820	1,894	4	4	..	..	..	..	1	..	1	..	..	..
Kammalan ..	45,546	22,085	23,461	23	13	10	26	14	12	68	34	34	48	38	10
Kanakkan ..	13,192	6,567	6,625	15	10	5	5	4	1	19	2	17	12	5	7
Kaniyan ..	3,841	1,950	1,891	2	1	1	2	1	1	1	..	1	..	..	..
Kavundan ..	3,680	1,868	1,812	1	..	1	..	..	..	6	2	4	..	..	..
Kshatriya ..	2,128	1,015	1,113	1	1	..	1	1	..	5	1	4	3	2	1
Malayali ..	1,467	673	794	1	1	..	1	1	..	4	1	3	3	2	1

Others ..	661	342	319	..	..	..	..	..	..	1	..	1	..	..	..
Kudumi Chetti ..	16,104	8,216	7,888	8	4	4	6	3	3	15	9	6	9	9	..
Kusavan ..	3,298	1,690	1,605	..	..	..	3	1	2	4	4	..	..	..	..
Malayan ..	3,185	1,645	1,540	2	1	1	1	1	..	9	7	2	4	9	2
Nayar ..	142,637	66,225	76,412	74	33	41	47	23	24	288	104	184	81	59	22
Nambidi ..	410	176	234	1	1	..	..	..	..	1	1	..	..	..	..
Ottanaikan (Odde) ..	2,768	1,422	1,343	2	1	1	2	1	1	5	4	1	3	1	2
Panan ..	3,603	1,771	1,832	2	1	1	1	..	1	8	5	3	4	3	1
Pandaran ..	4,860	2,384	2,476	2	2	..	5	5	..	5	3	2	3	3	..
Panditattan ..	2,964	1,549	1,415	2	1	1	2	..	2	..	..	..	1	..	1
Sambavan (Parayan) ..	11,562	5,734	5,828	4	2	2	7	4	3	17	8	9	10	6	4
Pulayan ..	82,043	39,982	42,061	16	6	10	19	10	9	117	59	58	69	44	25
Vaisyan ..	685	369	316	1	..	1	..	..	..	..	..	..	..	..	..
Valan ..	11,684	5,979	5,705	2	2	..	5	4	1	12	5	7	3	3	..
Velakkattalavan ..	3,099	1,815	1,884	2	1	1	1	1	..	6	3	3	..	..	..
Velan ..	10,895	5,205	5,693	4	4	..	4	1	3	12	7	5	5	4	1
Vellalan ..	5,299	2,629	2,670	5	5	..	3	3	..	5	3	2	1	1	..
Veluttedan ..	3,922	1,816	2,106	2	2	..	1	..	1	5	3	2	2	2	..
Vettuvan ..	11,797	5,943	5,854	..	..	..	5	3	2	23	9	14	4	3	1
Others ..	20,236	10,119	10,117	22	16	6	13	4	9	31	13	18	11	9	22
MUSLIM	87,902	44,794	43,108	56	29	27	45	30	15	83	50	33	50	39	11
Jonakan ..	57,371	29,150	28,221	30	11	19	33	21	12	62	37	25	39	31	8
Ravuttan ..	10,927	5,633	5,294	4	2	2	4	2	2	8	3	5	3	2	1
Others ..	19,604	10,011	9,593	22	16	6	8	7	1	13	10	3	8	6	2
CHRISTIAN	334,870	166,195	168,675	188	100	88	142	83	59	323	173	150	211	166	45
Anglo-Indian ..	1,717	820	897	2	2	..	..	..	..	..	..	..	..	..	..
Indian Christian ..	333,041	165,317	167,724	186	98	88	142	83	59	323	173	150	211	166	45
JEW	1,451	721	730	2	2	..	1	1	..	1	1	..	..	..	..
Black Jew ..	1,307	659	648	2	2	..	1	1	..	1	1	..	..	..	..

STATE TABLE IV.

SUBSIDIARY OCCUPATIONS OF AGRICULTURISTS.

Principal Occupations only.

PART—I. NON-CULTIVATING OWNERS AND OTHER RENT RECEIVERS.
II. CULTIVATING OWNERS.
III. CULTIVATING TENANTS.
IV. FARM SERVANTS AND FIELD LABOURERS.

Note.—1. Non-cultivating owners and other rent receivers include non-cultivating proprietors taking rent in money or kind and non-cultivating tenants (groups 1 and 6 (b): and farm servants and field labourers include groups 2, 3, 4 and 7.

2. Number who returned Agricultural subsidiary occupations as given in columns 4 and 5 of this Table includes the figures for all the sub-orders of order 1.

STATE TABLE IV.

SUBSIDIARY OCCUPATIONS OF AGRICULTURISTS—PRINCIPAL OCCUPATIONS ONLY.

I. NON CULTIVATING OWNERS AND OTHER RENT RECEIVERS. II. CULTIVATING OWNERS. III. CULTIVATING TENANTS. IV. FARM SERVANTS AND FIELD LABOURERS.

OCCUPATION	Total number of I. Non-cultivating owners and other rent receivers, II. Cultivating owners, III. Cultivating tenants IV. Farm servants and Field labourers, as the case may be, as principal occupation		Number who returned subsidiary occupations				Details of Subsidiary occupations returned									
			Agricultural		Non-Agricultural		Non-cultivating proprietors taking rent in money or kind		Estate Agents and Managers of owners		Estate Agents and Managers of Government		Rent collectors, clerks, &c.		Cultivating owners	
	Males	Females	Males	Females	Males	Females	Males	Females	Males	Females	Males	Females	Males	Females	Males	Females
1	2	3	4	5	6	7	8	9	10	11	12	13	14	15	16	17
I. Non-cultivating owners and other rent receivers ..	4,070	3,220	466	157	1,137	1,154	..	..	29	1	10	..	21	..	157	22
II. Cultivating owners ..	18,454	4,617	3,837	422	2,878	1,713	166	30	39	..	16	1	29	..	..	..
III. Cultivating tenants ..	39,133	8,905	6,705	612	5,118	2,851	55	6	36	2	..	..	33	5	703	67
IV. Farm servants and other field labourers ..	61,450	65,993	2,463	431	4,293	23,613	23	3	..	..	..	..	..	..	75	83
Total I, II, III & IV	**123,407**	**82,735**	**13,471**	**1,622**	**13,426**	**29,331**	**244**	**39**	**104**	**3**	**26**	**1**	**83**	**5**	**935**	**172**

STATE TABLE IV.—(*cont.*)

SUBSIDIARY OCCUPATIONS OF AGRICULTURISTS—PRINCIPAL OCCUPATIONS ONLY.

I. NON-CULTIVATING OWNERS AND OTHER RENT RECEIVERS. II. CULTIVATING OWNERS. III. CULTIVATING TENANTS. IV. FARM SERVANTS AND FIELD LABOURERS.

OCCUPATION	Details of Subsidiary Occupations returned															
	Tenant Cultivators		Agricultural labourers		Coconut cultivation		Cultivation of pan-vine		Rubber plantation		Tea plantation		Market gardeners, flower and fruit growers		Forest officers, Rangers, Guards, etc.	
	Males	Females	Males	Females	Males	Females	Males	Females	Males	Females	Males	Females	Males	Females	Males	Females
	18	19	20	21	22	23	24	25	26	27	28	29	30	31	32	33
I. Non-cultivating owners and other rent receivers ..	43	9	8	8	89	66	35	13	..	..	..	..	68	36	2	..
II. Cultivating owners ..	1,261	126	146	39	872	109	404	38	1	..	1	..	863	63	2	..
III. Cultivating tenants ..	..	..	1,183	264	913	50	681	28	9	..	..	..	2,837	182	5	..
IV. Farm servants and other field labourers ..	338	57	..	..	644	61	272	29	..	..	..	..	450	65	1	..
Total I, II, III and IV ..	1,642	192	1,337	311	2,518	286	1,392	108	10	..	1	..	4,218	346	10	..

STATE TABLE IV.—(*cont.*)

SUBSIDIARY OCCUPATIONS OF AGRICULTURISTS—PRINCIPAL OCCUPATIONS ONLY.

I. NON-CULTIVATING OWNERS AND OTHER RENT RECEIVERS. II. CULTIVATING OWNERS. III. CULTIVATING TENANTS. IV. FARM SERVANTS AND FIELD LABOURERS.

OCCUPATION	Details of Subsidiary Occupations returned															
	Wood cutters and charcoal burners		Collectors of forest produce		Cattle and buffalo breeders and keepers		Herdsmen, Shepherds and breeders of other animals		Fishing and pearling		Hunting		Exploitation of building materials (including stone, materials for cement manufacture and clay)		Cotton ginning, cleaning and pressing	
	Males	Females	Males	Females	Males	Females	Males	Females	Males	Females	Males	Females	Males	Females	Males	Females
	34	35	36	37	38	39	40	41	42	43	44	45	46	47	48	49
I. Non-cultivating owners and other rent receivers ..	1	..	2	..	1	2	..	..	1	..	..	..	..	..	3	..
II. Cultivating owners ..	3	..	1	1	25	15	8	..	65	1	..	..	1	..	..	..
III. Cultivating tenants ..	105	1	5	4	95	3	45	..	115	..	..	..	3	..	..	..
IV. Farm servants and other field labourers ..	309	36	55	80	188	8	108	9	327	87	35	..	40	..	..	..
Total I, II, III and IV ..	418	37	63	85	309	28	161	9	508	88	35	..	44	..	3	..

STATE TABLE IV—(*cont*).

SUBSIDIARY OCCUPATIONS OF AGRICULTURISTS—PRINCIPAL OCCUPATIONS ONLY.

I. NON-CULTIVATING OWNERS AND OTHER RENT RECEIVERS. II. CULTIVATING OWNERS. III. CULTIVATING TENANTS. IV. FARM SERVANTS AND FIELD LABOURERS.

OCCUPATION	Details of Subsidiary Occupations returned															
	Cotton spinning, sizing and weaving		Manufacture of rope, twine, string and other fibres		Working in leather		Bone, ivory, horn, shell, &c., workers (except buttons)		Sawyers		Carpenters, turners and joiners, &c		Basket makers and other industries of woody materials including leaves and thatchers and builders working with bamboo, reeds or similar materials		Smelting, forging and rolling of iron and other metals	
	Males	Females	Males	Females	Males	Females	Males	Females	Males	Females	Males	Females	Males	Females	Males	Females
	50	51	52	53	54	55	56	57	58	59	60	61	62	63	64	65
I. Non-cultivating owners and other rent receivers ..	6	4	1	1	..	..	1	..	..	..	2	..	..	1	1	..
II. Cultivating owners ..	18	8	53	24	2	..	..	..	23	..	8	..	3	5	1	..
III. Cultivating tenants ..	23	..	68	13	..	..	..	..	135	..	57	..	40	26	..	..
IV. Farm servants and other field labourers ..	21	9	362	404	..	..	..	..	68	..	10	..	671	1,370	1	..
Total I, II, III & IV ..	68	21	484	442	2	..	1	..	226	..	77	..	714	1,402	3	..

STATE TABLE IV—(*cont.*)

SUBSIDIARY OCCUPATIONS OF AGRICULTURISTS—PRINCIPAL OCCUPATIONS ONLY.

I. NON-CULTIVATING OWNERS AND OTHER RENT RECEIVERS. II. CULTIVATING OWNERS. III. CULTIVATING TENANTS. IV. FARM SERVANTS AND FIELD LABOURERS.

OCCUPATION	Details of Subsidiary Occupations returned															
	Blacksmiths, other workers in iron, makers of implements, etc.		Workers in brass, copper and bell-metal		Potters and makers of earthen-ware		Brick and tile makers		Manufacture of matches, fire works and other explosives		Manufacture and refining of vegetable oils		Rice pounders and huskers and flour grinders		Butchers	
	Males	Females	Males	Females	Males	Females	Males	Females	Males	Females	Males	Females	Males	Females	Males	Females
	66	67	68	69	70	71	72	73	74	75	76	77	78	79	80	81
I. Non-cultivating owners and other rent receivers ..	..	..	..	..	..	..	1	..	2	..	3	..	..	1	..	..
II. Cultivating owners ..	14	1	..	..	2	1	1	..	2	..	51	1	7	11	..	..
III. Cultivating tenants ..	2	..	6	..	13	3	6	..	3	..	106	1	..	16	1	..
IV. Farm servants and other field labourers ..	1	1	4	1	5	..	3	..	..	..	37	10	5	152	..	..
Total I, II, III and IV ..	**17**	**2**	**10**	**1**	**20**	**4**	**11**	..	**7**	..	**187**	**12**	**12**	**180**	**1**	..

STATE TABLE IV—(cont.)

SUBSIDIARY OCCUPATIONS OF AGRICULTURISTS—PRINCIPAL OCCUPATIONS ONLY.

I. NON-CULTIVATING OWNERS AND OTHER RENT RECEIVERS. II. CULTIVATING OWNERS. III. CULTIVATING TENANTS. IV. FARM SERVANTS AND FIELD LABOURERS.

OCCUPATION	Details of Subsidiary Occupations returned															
	Sweetmeat and condiment makers		Toddy drawers		Manufacturers of tobacco		Tailors, milliners, dress-makers and darners		Embroiderers, hat-makers and makers of other articles of wear		Washing and cleaning		Barbers, hair-dressers and wig-makers		Other industries connected with the toilet	
	Males	Females	Males	Females	Males	Females	Males	Females	Males	Females	Males	Females	Males	Females	Males	Females
	82	83	84	85	86	87	88	89	90	91	92	93	94	95	96	97
I. Non-cultivating owners and other rent receivers ..	..	..	4	..	..	..	2	3	..	..	3	..	9	1	..	..
II. Cultivating owners ..	9	..	180	..	..	..	7	9	..	..	21	6	18	1	..	3
III. Cultivating tenants ..	20	9	773	1	2	..	20	1	1	..	38	1	99	..	..	..
IV. Farm servants and other field labourers ..	7	7	266	..	..	..	21	..	..	..	18	21	14	10	..	..
Total I, II, III and IV ..	36	16	1,228	1	2	..	50	12	1	..	80	28	140	12	..	3

STATE TABLE IV—(*cont.*)

SUBSIDIARY OCCUPATIONS OF AGRICULTURISTS—PRINCIPAL OCCUPATIONS ONLY.

I. NON-CULTIVATING OWNERS AND OTHER RENT RECEIVERS. II. CULTIVATING OWNERS. III. CULTIVATING TENANTS.
IV. FARM SERVANTS AND FIELD LABOURERS.

OCCUPATION	Details of Subsidiary Occupations returned ..															
	Lime burners, cement workers, excavators & well sinkers; stone cutters & dressers; brick layers & masons; builders (other than buildings made of bamboo or similar materials), painters, decorators of houses, tilers, plumbers, &c.		Carriage, cart, palki, &c., makers and wheelwrights		Printers, engravers, book binders, &c.		Makers of musical instruments		Makers of Jewellery and ornaments		Other miscellaneous and undefined industries (toy making, taxidermy, &c.)		Scavenging		Ship owners, boat owners and their employees, officers, mariners, &c., Ships' brokers, boatmen and towmen	
	Males	Females	Males	Females	Males	Females	Males	Females	Males	Females	Males	Females	Males	Females	Males	Females
	98	9	100	101	102	103	104	105	106	107	108	109	110	111	112	113
I. Non-cultivating owners and other rent receivers ..	6	..	..	..	3	..	..	..	2	..	..	..	..	1	2	..
II. Cultivating owners ..	32	..	2	..	7	..	1	..	7	1	5	..	..	4	15	..
III. Cultivating tenants ..	190	10	7	..	5	..	..	..	6	..	1	1	..	..	22	..
IV. Farm servants and other field labourers ..	192	32	2	..	9	..	..	..	1	..	..	3	..	1	80	..
Total I, II, III and IV	420	42	11	..	24	..	1	..	16	1	6	4	..	6	119	..

STATE TABLE IV—(*cont.*)

SUBSIDIARY OCCUPATIONS OF AGRICULTURISTS—PRINCIPAL OCCUPATIONS ONLY.

I. NON-CULTIVATING OWNERS AND OTHER RENT RECEIVERS. II. CULTIVATING OWNERS. III. CULTIVATING TENANTS. IV. FARM SERVANTS AND FIELD LABOURERS.

OCCUPATION	Details of Subsidiary Occupations returned															
	Persons (other than labourers) employed in harbours, docks, rivers and canals including pilots		Labourers employed on harbours, docks, rivers and canals		Persons (other than labourers) employed on the construction and maintenance of roads and bridges		Labourers employed on roads and bridges		Owners, Managers and employees (excluding personal servants) connected with mechanically driven vehicles (including trams)		Owners, Managers and employees (excluding personal servants) connected with other vehicles		Palki, etc., bearers and owners		Pack elephant, camel, mule, ass and bullock owners and drivers	
	Males	Females	Males	Females	Males	Females	Males	Females	Males	Females	Males	Females	Males	Females	Males	Females
	114	115	116	117	118	119	120	121	122	123	124	125	126	127	128	129
I. Non-cultivating owners and other rent receivers ..	..	..	..	..	2	..	..	..	7	..	3	..	..	..	1	..
II. Cultivating owners ..	1	..	..	..	7	..	1	..	17	..	65	..	1	..	7	..
III. Cultivating tenants ..	3	..	5	..	8	..	27	4	28	..	490	..	1	..	3	..
IV. Farm servants and other field labourers ..	15	..	6	..	12	..	70	7	5	..	93	1	26	2	2	..
Total I, II, III and IV ..	19	..	11	..	23	..	98	11	57	..	651	1	28	2	13	..

STATE TABLE IV—(*cont.*)

SUBSIDIARY OCCUPATIONS OF AGRICULTURISTS—PRINCIPAL OCCUPATIONS ONLY.

I. NON-CULTIVATING OWNERS AND OTHER RENT RECEIVERS. II. CULTIVATING OWNERS. III. CULTIVATING TENANTS. IV. FARM SERVANTS AND FIELD LABOURERS.

OCCUPATION	Details of Subsidiary Occupations returned															
	Porters and messengers		Railway employees of all kinds other than coolies		Labourers employed on railway construction and maintenance and coolies and porters employed on railway premises		Post Office, telegraph and telephone services		Bank Managers, money-lenders, exchange and insurance agents, money changers and brokers and their employees		Brokers, commission agents, commercial travellers, warehouse owners and employees		Trade in piece goods, wool, cotton, silk, hair and other textiles		Trade in skins, leather, furs, feathers, horn, etc., and the articles made from these	
	Males	Females	Males	Females	Males	Females	Males	Females	Males	Females	Males	Females	Males	Females	Males	Females
	130	131	132	133	134	135	136	137	138	139	140	141	142	143	144	145
I. Non-cultivating owners and other rent receivers ..	..	..	..	..	..	..	8	..	176	64	3	..	22	..	..	..
II. Cultivating owners ..	2	..	1	..	..	..	8	..	234	19	7	..	87	..	..	..
III. Cultivating tenants ..	12	1	..	..	10	..	1	..	92	9	16	..	36	..	..	..
IV. Farm servants and other field labourers ...	67	2	..	..	..	..	..	..	9	7	29	..	29	12	1	..
Total I, II, III and IV ..	81	3	1	..	10	..	17	..	511	99	55	..	174	12	1	..

STATE TABLE IV—(*cont.*)

SUBSIDIARY OCCUPATIONS OF AGRICULTURISTS—PRINCIPAL OCCUPATIONS ONLY.

I. NON-CULTIVATING OWNERS AND OTHER RENT RECEIVERS. II. CULTIVATING OWNERS. III. CULTIVATING TENANTS. IV. FARM SERVANTS AND FIELD LABOURERS.

OCCUPATION	Details of Subsidiary Occupations returned															
	Trade in wood (not fire-wood)		Trade in barks		Trade in bamboos and canes		Trade in thatches and other forest produce		Trade in metals, machinery, knives, tools, etc.		Trade in pottery, bricks and tiles		Trade in Drugs, dyes, paints, petroleum, explosives, etc.		Venders of wine, liquors, aerated waters and ice	
	Males	Females	Males	Females	Males	Females	Males	Females	Males	Females	Males	Females	Males	Females	Males	Females
	146	147	148	149	150	151	152	153	154	155	156	157	158	159	160	161
I. Non-cultivating owners and other rent receivers ..	6	..	..	..	1	..	..	..	..	..	..	1	..	..	2	..
II. Cultivating owners ..	28	..	..	..	4	..	..	..	8	..	..	..	1	..	39	..
III. Cultivating tenants ..	24	..	..	1	2	..	2	..	5	..	10	..	7	1	44	7
IV. Farm servants and other field labourers ..	3	5	..	..	10	1	3	..	2	..	..	2	6	..	17	3
Total I, II, III and IV ..	61	5	..	1	17	1	5	..	15	..	10	3	14	1	102	10

STATE TABLE IV—(*cont.*)

SUBSIDIARY OCCUPATIONS OF AGRICULTURISTS—PRINCIPAL OCCUPATIONS ONLY.

I. NON-CULTIVATING OWNERS AND OTHER RENT RECEIVERS. II. CULTIVATING OWNERS. III. CULTIVATING TENANTS. IV. FARM SERVANTS AND FIELD LABOURERS.

OCCUPATION	Details of Subsidiary Occupations returned															
	Owners and managers of hotels, cook-shops, sarais, etc. (and employees)		Hawkers of drink and food stuffs		Grain and pulse dealers		Dealers in sweet-meats, sugar and spices		Dealers in dairy products, eggs, and poultry		Dealers in animals for food		Dealers in fodder for animals		Dealers in other food stuffs	
	Males	Females	Males	Females	Males	Females	Males	Females	Males	Females	Males	Females	Males	Females	Males	Females
	162	163	164	165	166	167	168	169	170	171	172	173	174	175	176	177
I. Non-cultivating owners and other rent receivers ..	11	1	..	..	30	1	2	2	5	7	..	..	..	..	7	..
II. Cultivating owners ..	31	..	..	..	273	5	32	2	20	14	14	..	..	..	181	..
III. Cultivating tenants ..	42	..	..	..	205	4	91	9	58	18	7	..	2	4	432	4
IV. Farm servants and other field-labourers ..	15	2	2	..	29	22	22	46	4	5	62	8	7	33	89	20
Total I, II, III & IV ..	99	3	2	..	537	32	147	59	87	44	83	8	9	37	709	24

STATE TABLE IV—(*cont.*)

SUBSIDIARY OCCUPATIONS OF AGRICULTURISTS—PRINCIPAL OCCUPATIONS ONLY.

I. NON-CULTIVATING OWNERS AND OTHER RENT RECEIVERS. II. CULTIVATING OWNERS. III. CULTIVATING TENANTS. IV. FARM SERVANTS AND FIELD LABOURERS.

OCCUPATION	Details of Subsidiary Occupations returned															
	Dealers in tobacco		Dealers in opium		Dealers in Ganja		Trade in ready made clothing and other articles of dress and the toilet (hats, umbrellas, socks, ready-made shoes, perfumes, etc.)		Trade in furniture, carpets, curtains and bedding		Hardware, cooking utensils, porcelain, crockery, glassware, bottles, articles for gardening, etc.		Dealers and hirers in mechanical transport motors, cycles, etc.		Dealers and hirers in other carriages, carts, boats, etc	
	Males	Females	Males	Females	Males	Females	Males	Females	Males	Females	Males	Females	Males	Females	Males	Females
	178	179	180	181	182	183	184	185	186	187	188	189	190	191	192	193
I. Non-cultivating owners and other rent receivers ..	3	..	1	..	..	..	1	..	..	..	..	..	..	..	..	..
II. Cultivating owners ..	15	..	..	..	1	..	1	..	1	..	..	..	8	..	1	1
III. Cultivating tenants ..	14	..	..	..	..	..	14	..	15	..	4	..	..	..	124	2
IV. Farm servants and other field labourers ..	1	..	..	..	..	..	..	..	2	31	10	..	2	..	31	..
Total I, II, III & IV	33	..	1	..	1	..	16	..	18	31	14	..	10	..	156	3

STATE TABLE IV—(*cont.*)

SUBSIDIARY OCCUPATIONS OF AGRICULTURISTS—PRINCIPAL OCCUPATIONS ONLY.

I. NON-CULTIVATING OWNERS AND OTHER RENT RECEIVERS. II. CULTIVATING OWNERS. III. CULTIVATING TENANTS. IV. FARM SERVANTS AND FIELD LABOURERS.

OCCUPATION	Details of Subsidiary Occupations returned															
	Dealers and hirers of elephants, camels, horses, cattle, asses, mules, etc.		Dealers in fire-wood, charcoal, coal, cow-dung, etc.		Dealers in precious stones, jewellery (real and imitation) clocks, optical instruments, etc.		Dealers in rags, stable refuse, etc.		General store-keepers and shop-keepers otherwise unspecified		Itinerant traders, pedlars and hawkers (other than food, etc.)		Other trades (including farmers of pounds, tolls and markets)		Employed in the Police	
	Males	Females	Males	Females	Males	Females	Males	Females	Males	Females	Males	Females	Males	Females	Males	Females
	194	195	196	197	198	199	200	201	202	203	204	205	206	207	208	209
I. Non-cultivating owners and other rent receivers ..	..	..	2	..	5	..	..	..	49	1	..	..	1	2	4	..
II. Cultivating owners ..	5	..	11	..	1	..	..	..	242	..	..	..	25	..	8	..
III. Cultivating tenants ..	37	..	27	4	..	..	..	..	364	4	1	..	35	2	2	..
IV. Farm servants and other field labourers ..	13	..	40	96	3	..	..	4	90	5	5	..	8	2	..	..
Total I, II, III and IV ..	58	..	80	100	9	..	..	4	748	10	6	..	69	6	14	..

STATE TABLE IV—(*cont.*)

SUBSIDIARY OCCUPATIONS OF AGRICULTURISTS—PRINCIPAL OCCUPATIONS ONLY.

I. NON-CULTIVATING OWNERS AND OTHER RENT RECEIVERS. II. CULTIVATING OWNERS. III. CULTIVATING TENANTS. IV. FARM SERVANTS AND FIELD LABOURERS.

OCCUPATION	Details of Subsidiary Occupations returned															
	Service of the State		Service of Indian and Foreign States		Municipal and other local (not village) service		Village officials and servants other than watchmen		Priests, ministers, etc.		Monks, nuns, religious mendicants, etc.		Other religious workers		Servants in religious edifices, burial and burning grounds, pilgrim conductors, circumcisers, etc.	
	Males	Females	Males	Females	Males	Females	Males	Females	Males	Females	Males	Females	Males	Females	Males	Females
	210	211	212	213	214	215	216	217	218	219	220	221	222	223	224	225
I. Non-cultivating owners and other rent receivers ..	22	1	2	..	22	..	17	..	85	..	2	..	14	2	56	12
II. Cultivating owners ..	35	..	1	..	17	..	24	..	40	..	5	..	20	2	33	3
III. Cultivating tenants ..	11	..	1	..	8	..	19	..	24	..	1	..	14	..	28	..
IV. Farm servants and other field labourers ..	2	..	..	..	..	..	..	..	16	1	..	..	11	1	12	..
Total I, II, III and IV ..	70	1	4	..	47	..	60	..	165	1	8	..	59	5	129	15

STATE TABLE IV—(*cont.*)

SUBSIDIARY OCCUPATIONS OF AGRICULTURISTS—PRINCIPAL OCCUPATIONS ONLY.

I. NON-CULTIVATING OWNERS AND OTHER RENT RECEIVERS. II. CULTIVATING OWNERS. III. CULTIVATING TENANTS. IV. FARM SERVANTS AND FIELD LABOURERS.

OCCUPATION	Details of Subsidiary Occupations returned															
	Lawyers of all kinds including quasis, Law agents and mukhtiars		Lawyers' clerks, petition writers, etc.		Registered medical practitioners including occulists		Other persons practising the healing arts without being registered		Midwives, vaccinators, compounders, nurses, masseurs, etc.		Professors and teachers of all kinds		Clerks and servants connected with education		Public scribes, stenographers, etc.	
	Males	Females	Males	Females	Males	Females	Males	Females	Males	Females	Males	Females	Males	Females	Males	Females
	226	227	228	229	230	231	232	233	234	235	236	237	238	239	240	241
I. Non-cultivating owners and other rent receivers ..	8	..	7	..	3	1	21	2	..	..	90	15	1	..	5	..
II. Cultivating owners ..	23	..	21	..	11	..	97	1	1	..	100	3	7	..	1	..
III. Cultivating tenants ..	4	..	5	..	17	..	54	1	..	..	35	..	4	..	11	..
IV. Farm servants and other field labourers ..	2	..	..	..	2	..	26	1	..	1	3	..	..	..	2	..
Total I, II, III and IV ..	37	..	33	..	33	1	198	5	1	1	228	18	12	.	19	..

STATE TABLE IV—(*cont.*)

SUBSIDIARY OCCUPATIONS OF AGRICULTURISTS—PRINCIPAL OCCUPATIONS ONLY.

I. NON-CULTIVATING OWNERS AND OTHER RENT RECEIVERS. II. CULTIVATING OWNERS. III. CULTIVATING TENANTS. IV. FARM SERVANTS AND FIELD LABOURERS.

OCCUPATION	Details of Subsidiary Occupations returned															
	Authors, editors, journalists and photographers		Artists, sculptors and image makers		Scientists, (Astronomers, Botanists, etc.)		Horoscope casters, astrologers, fortune tellers, wizards, witches and mediums		Musicians (composers and performers other than military), actors, dancers, etc.		Managers and employees of places of public entertainments, race courses, societies and clubs		Proprietors (other than agricultural lands) fund and Scholarships holders and pensioners		Private Motor drivers and cleaners	
	Males	Females	Males	Females	Males	Females	Males	Females	Males	Females	Males	Females	Males	Females	Males	Females
	242	243	244	245	246	247	248	249	250	251	252	253	254	255	256	257
I. Non-cultivating owners and other rent receivers ..	1	..	..	..	..	..	14	..	10	2	4	..	258	103	1	..
II. Cultivating owners ..	..	..	4	..	1	..	18	1	38	1	3	..	224	48	1	..
III. Cultivating tenants ..	3	..	..	..	..	..	26	1	65	..	..	..	114	8	..	..
IV. Farm servants and other field labourers ..	..	..	..	..	..	..	21	..	39	..	..	..	14	2	..	..
Total I, II, III and IV ..	3	..	4	..	1	..	82	2	142	3	7	..	610	161	2	..

STATE TABLE IV—(*cont.*)

SUBSIDIARY OCCUPATIONS OF AGRICULTURISTS—PRINCIPAL OCCUPATIONS ONLY.

I. NON-CULTIVATING OWNERS AND OTHER RENT RECEIVERS. II. CULTIVATING OWNERS. III. CULTIVATING TENANTS.
IV. FARM SERVANTS AND FIELD LABOURERS.

OCCUPATION	Details of Subsidiary Occupations returned											
	Other domestic service		Manufacturers, businessmen and contractors otherwise unspecified		Cashiers, accountants, book-keepers, clerks, and other employees in unspecified offices and ware houses and shops		Mechanics otherwise unspecified		Labourers and workmen otherwise unspecified		Beggars and Vagrants	
	Males	Females	Males	Females	Males	Females	Males	Females	Males	Females	Males	Females
	258	259	260	261	262	263	264	265	266	267	268	269
I. Non-cultivating owners and other rent receivers ..	40	917	7	..	37	8	..	..	7	..	..	..
II. Cultivating owners ..	53	1,533	31	..	51	1	1	..	72	4	5	..
III. Cultivating tenants ..	96	2,641	20	..	35	..	5	..	464	44	10	..
IV. Farm servants and other field labourers ..	212	21,012	3	..	4	..	1	..	874	165	16	6
Total I, II, III and IV ..	**401**	**26,102**	**61**	..	**11**	**9**	**7**	..	**1,417**	**213**	**31**	**6**

STATE TABLE V.

ORGANISED INDUSTRY.

STATE TABLE V.

ORGANISED INDUSTRY

Industry	Total population engaged			Directional, Supervising and Clerical staff							Welfare Doctors, Compounders, Schoolmasters, etc.		Operatives			
				Managers		Supervising and Technical		Clerical					Adult		Immature	
									Other							
	Persons	Males	Females	Indian	Other	Indian	Other	Indian	Males	Females	Indian	Other	Males	Females	Males	Females
1	2	3	4	5	6	7	8	9	10	11	12	13	14	15	16	17
COCHIN STATE.	13,014	10,454	2,560	114	3	1,604	11	372	..	..	39	..	7,018	1,919	1,322	618
Pasture and Agriculture																
Dairy Farms ..	154	127	27	1	..	12	..	5	..	..	3	..	81	20	25	7
Stock raising Farms ..	1	1	..	1	..	..	..	..	..	..	..	..	..	..	..	..
Production of Manure ..	4	..	4	..	..	..	..	..	..	..	..	..	..	4	..	..
Cultivation of Special Crops																
Coffee Plantations ..	370	203	167	..	..	6	..	6	..	..	..	..	191	167	..	..
Rubber Plantations ..	2,166	1,746	420	8	1	51	11	33	..	..	3	..	1,336	276	301	144
Tea Plantations ..	1,498	959	539	..	..	6	..	13	..	..	3	..	817	420	120	119
Others ..	14	1	13	..	..	..	..	..	..	..	..	..	1	10	..	3
Fishing and Hunting																
Fish Curing Works ..	2	2	..	..	..	..	..	..	..	..	..	..	1	..	1	..
Mines																
Petroleum Wells ..	17	17	..	1	..	..	..	..	..	..	..	..	16	..	..	..
Textiles																
Cotton Spinning Mills ..	67	63	4	..	..	56	..	..	..	..	..	..	7	3	1	..
Cotton Weaving Mills ..	1,180	872	308	6	..	251	..	56	..	..	2	..	394	214	180	77
Cotton Presses ..	1	1	..	..	..	..	..	..	..	..	..	..	1	..	..	..

STATE TABLE V—(*cont.*)

ORGANISED INDUSTRY.

Industry	Total population engaged			Directional, Supervising and Clerical staff							Welfare Doctors, Compounders, Schoolmasters, etc.		Operatives			
				Managers		Supervising and Technical		Clerical					Adult		Immature	
									Other							
	Persons	Males	Females	Indian	Other	Indian	Other	Indian	Males	Females	Indian	Other	Males	Females	Males	Females
1	2	3	4	5	6	7	8	9	10	11	12	13	14	15	16	17
Coir Factories ..	1,612	1,348	264	..	..	5	..	30	..	..	..	..	1,157	239	156	25
Woollen Mills ..	1	1	..	..	..	..	..	1	..	..	..	..	..	..	..	..
Silk Factories ..	3	..	3	..	..	2	..	..	..	..	1	..	..	..	..	..
Hides, Skins, and Hard Materials from the Animal Kingdom																
Tanneries ..	1	1	..	..	..	..	..	1	..	..	..	..	..	..	..	..
Leather and Leather dying Works ..	6	6	..	..	..	5	..	..	..	..	..	..	1	..	..	..
Wood																
Extraction of Timber and Timber yards ..	30	30	..	..	..	1	..	3	..	..	..	..	26	..	..	..
Saw Mills ..	77	77	..		..	28	..	10	..	..	4	..	33	..	..	..
Willow Works ..	8	4	4	..	..	..	..	..	..	..	..	..	..	..	4	4
Cane and Basket Factories ..	27	21	6	..	..	..	..	..	..	..	..	..	21	5	..	1
Metals																
Iron and Steel Works ..	46	46	..	1	..	8	..	..	..	..	..	..	34	..	3	..
Iron piping, Machinery and Engineering Workshops ..	70	70	..	1	..	7	..	1	..	..	..	..	60	..	1	..
Steel trunk Factories ..	1	1	..	1	..	..	..	..	..	..	..	..	..	..	..	..
Cutlery Works ..	3	3	..	..	..	1	..	..	..	..	..	..	2	..	..	..
Type Foundries ..	3	2	..	1	..	..	..	1	..	..	..	..	..	..	..	..
Brass Copper, Bronze and Tin Foundries ..	287	235	52	..	..	47	..	1	..	..	..	..	151	38	36	14

STATE TABLE V—(*cont.*)

ORGANISED INDUSTRY.

Industry	Total Population engaged			Directional, Supervising and Clerical staff							Welfare Doctors, Compounders, Schoolmasters, etc.		Operatives			
				Managers		Supervising and Technical		Clerical					Adult		Immature	
									Other							
	Persons	Males	Females	Indian	Other	Indian	Other	Indian	Males	Females	Indian	Other	Males	Females	Males	Females
	2	3	4	5	6	7	8	9	10	11	12	13	14	15	16	17
Ceramics																
Brick works ..	419	355	64	9	..	135	..	20	..	..	..	..	119	35	74	27
Tile works ..	1,089	886	203	20	..	20	..	12	..	..	1	..	676	147	157	56
Pottery works ..	30	30	..	..	..	2	..	1	..	..	..	..	23	..	4	..
Chemical Products, properly so called and Analogous																
Match Factories ..	339	246	93	1	..	60	..	8	..	..	5	..	68	68	104	25
Fireworks and Explosives Factories ..	8	8	..	..	..	..	..	1	..	..	..	..	6	..	1	..
Soda water Factories ..	10	10	..	2	..	3	..	1	..	..	..	..	3	..	1	..
Ice Factories ..	3	3	..	..	..	2	..	..	..	..	..	..	1	..	..	..
Oil Mills ..	904	894	10	7	1	153	..	55	..	..	5	..	651	10	22	..
Manufacture and refining of Mineral oils ..	194	194	..	1	..	89	..	17	..	..	..	..	83	..	4	..
Candle Factories ..	1	1	..	..	..	..	..	..	..	..	..	..	1	..	..	..
Soap Factories ..	48	48	..	2	..	6	..	1	..	..	..	..	34	..	5	..
Chemicals, Drugs, Anticeptics and Pharmaceutical works generally ..	11	11	..	..	..	2	..	5	..	..	4	..	..	..	..	..
Factories of Leather and Metal Polishes ..	11	10	1	..	1	1	..	2	..	..	..	..	5	1	1	..
Food Industries																
Rice Mills ..	802	482	320	19	..	135	..	35	..	..	..	..	256	236	38	83
Pulse Mills ..	1	1	..	..	..	..	..	..	..	..	..	..	..	..	1	..

STATE TABLE V—(cont.).

ORGANISED INDUSTRY.

Industry	Total population engaged			Directional, Supervising and Clerical Staff							Welfare Doctors, Compounders, Schoolmasters, etc.		Operatives			
				Managers		Supervising and Technical		Clerical					Adult		Immature	
	Persons	Males	Females	Indian	Other	Indian	Other	Indian	Other Males	Other Females	Indian	Other	Males	Females	Males	Females
1	2	3	4	5	6	7	8	9	10	11	12	13	14	15	16	17
Flour Mills ..	1	1	..	..	..	..	..	..	..	..	..	..	1	..	..	..
Biscuit Factories ..	1	1	..	..	..	..	..	..	..	..	..	..	..	..	1	..
Bakeries ..	28	28	..	3	..	6	..	6	..	..	..	..	10	..	3	..
Fruit canning etc., Factories ..	21	5	16	..	..	1	..	..	..	..	..	..	2	6	2	13
Sugar Factories and Refineries ..	9	8	1	1	..	5	..	..	..	..	..	..	3	..	..	..
Ginger-bleaching works ..	9	9	..	..	..	..	..	..	..	..	..	..	9	..	..	..
Distilleries ..	2	2	..	..	..	2	..	..	..	..	..	..	..	..	..	..
Tobacco, Snuff, Bidi and Cigarette Factories ..	1	1	..	..	..	..	..	1	..	..	..	..	..	..	..	..
Water works ..	7	7	..	..	..	3	..	1	..	..	..	..	3	..	..	..
Industries of dress and the toilet																
Tailoring works ..	1	..	1	..	..	..	..	..	..	..	..	..	..	1	..	..
Furniture Industries																
Furniture Factories ..	36	36	..	..	..	1	..	..	..	..	..	..	33	..	2	..
Building Industries																
Stone and Marble works ..	5	5	..	..	..	5	..	..	..	..	..	..	..	..	..	..
Construction of means of transport																
Bicycle works ..	1	1	..	..	..	1	..	..	..	..	..	..	..	..	..	..
Motor car works ..	63	63	..	1	..	54	..	3	..	..	..	..	5	..	..	..

STATE TABLE V—(*cont*).

ORGANISED INDUSTRY.

Industry	Total population engaged			Directional Supervising and Clerical staff							Welfare Doctors, Compounders, Schoolmasters etc.		Operatives			
				Managers		Supervising and Technical		Clerical					Adult		Immature	
									Other							
	Persons	Males	Females	Indian	Other	Indian	Other	Indian	Males	Females	Indian	Other	Males	Females	Males	Females
1	2	3	4	5	6	7	8	9	10	11	12	13	14	15	16	17
Coach-building works ..	2	2	..	..	..	..	..	..	..	..	..	..	2	..	..	..
Railway works ..	354	321	33	1	..	47	..	11	..	..	..	..	248	15	14	18
Ship-building yards ..	391	390	1	6	..	136	..	10	..	..	5	..	231	..	3	..
Production and transmission of physical force (Heat, Light, Electricity, Motive power, etc.) Gas works and Electric Light and power																
Hydro-Electric works ..	3	3	..	..	..	1	..	1	..	..	..	..	1	..	..	..
Other Electric works ..	8	8	..	1	..	7	..	..	..	..	..	..	..	..	..	..
Telephone works ..	1	1	..	..	..	1	..	..	..	..	..	..	..	..	..	..
Miscellaneous and undefined Industries																
Printing Presses ..	361	357	4	15	..	145	..	12	..	..	1	..	140	2	44	2
Photo works ..	7	7	..	..	..	1	..	..	..	..	..	..	6	..	..	..
Electro-plating works ..	4	4	..	..	..	1	..	..	..	..	..	..	1	..	2	..
Factories of Jewellery and Ornaments of Gold and Silver ..	31	31	..	..	..	11	..	..	..	..	..	..	10	..	10	..
Cinema Films Production ..	4	4	..	..	..	2	..	1	..	..	..	..	1	..	..	..
Transport by road (Mechanically driven vehicle)																
Motor Transport ..	50	50	..	1	..	39	..	3	..	..	2	..	6	..	..	..
Tramways ..	32	32	..	..	..	..	..	..	..	..	..	..	31	..	1	..
Transport by Water																
Motor and Steam Boats ..	63	61	2	1	..	39	..	5	..	..	..	..	16	2	..	..